I0084238

Vital Records

of the Towns of

Eastham and Orleans

An authorized facsimile reproduction of
records published serially 1901-1935 in
The Mayflower Descendant.
With an added index of persons.

COL. LEONARD H. SMITH JR.
&
NORMA H. SMITH

Copyright 1976, 1980
Leonard H. Smith Jr.

Reprinted for
Clearfield Company, Inc. by
Genealogical Publishing Co., Inc.
Baltimore, Maryland
1993

Contents

PREFACE

In 1901 the Society of Mayflower Descendants in Massachusetts began printing in its quarterly, *The Mayflower Descendant*, the vital records of Eastham (including Orleans), Mass., as they had been literally transcribed from the original records by George Robert Bowman. The printing continued, irregularly, until the demise of the publication in 1937. Unfortunately the printing of the transcript was not completed. (*The Mayflower Descendant* was revived in 1985.)

This volume is a facsimile reproduction of the Eastham town records which were published, with the addition of a name index. The index was first published, separately, in 1976. The publication of the combined works in a single volume is a result of the gracious consent of the Society of Mayflower Descendants in Massachusetts, for which our thanks are extended.

Our thanks are also extended to the State Street Trust Company of Boston, Mass., for this permission to use its illustrations of the town seals of Eastham and Orleans.

1862 Apr 4   Bounds between Orleans and Harwich established.

1862 Apr 14 Bounds between Orleans and Chatham established.

1867 Mar 23 Bounds between Orleans and Eastham established and part of each town annexed to the other town.

1935 Jun 20 Bounds between Orleans and Brewster re-established.

*Old Style, or according to the Julian calendar. The present calendar, the Gregorian or New Style, was adopted by an Act of Parliament of Great Britain. It was ordered that September 3, 1752, should become September 14 and that the legal year should commence with the first of January, instead of March 25, beginning January 1, 1752. To change Old Style to New Style add 10 days to a 17th century date and 11 to an 18th century date.

(From "Historical Data Relating to Counties, Cities and Towns in Massachusetts", by Kevin H. White.)

Eastham

1651 Jun 7* "That the Towne of Nawsett[1] be henceforth called and knowne by the name of Eastham ..." (Ply. Col. Rec., Vol XI, p. 59)

1678 Mar 5* Eastham and purchasers on both sides to settle the bounds.

1763 Jun 16 Part established as the district of Wellfleet.

1772 Jul 14 Part of Harwich annexed.
1797 Mar 3   Part established as Orleans.
1839 Mar 9   Part annexed to Orleans.
1847 Apr 26 Part annexed to Wellfleet.
1867 Mar 23 Bounds between Eastham and Orleans established and part of each town annexed to the other town.

1887 May 6   Bounds between tidewaters of Eastham and Wellfleet established.

[1]NAWSETT:
1643 - -   Mentioned in a list of towns having freemen able to bear arms. (Ply. Col. Rec., Vol VIII, p. 177)

1645 Mar 3* "... those that goe to dwell at Nossett ..." granted land. (Ply. Col. Rec., Vol II, p. 81)

1646 Jun 2* Established as a town. (Ply. Col. Rec., Vol II, p. 102)

1651 Jun 7* The name of the town of Nawsett changed to Eastham.

Orleans

1797 Mar 3   Incorporated as a town, from part of Eastham.

1839 Mar 9   Part of Eastham annexed.
1861 Feb 20 Bounds between Orleans and Brewster established.

5

THE MAYFLOWER DESCENDANT

A Quarterly Magazine

OF

Pilgrim Genealogy and History

1901

———

VOLUME III

———

BOSTON

PUBLISHED BY THE

MASSACHUSETTS SOCIETY OF MAYFLOWER DESCENDANTS

1901

EASTHAM, MASS., VITAL RECORDS.

Literally transcribed from the Original Records,

BY GEORGE ERNEST BOWMAN.

In 1797 the town of Eastham was divided and one part was incorporated as the town of Orleans. The original records of the town of Eastham are in the possession of the town of Orleans. The first volume is in a very dilapidated condition and should be preserved by the Emery Process. The earliest vital records are found in the second part of the first volume.

[Vol. I, Pt. II, p. 4]

Anna Bills the Wife of Thomas Bills died the first day of September in the yeare 1675

Thomas Bills and Joanna Twining wear maried the second day of may in the year 1676

Joseph doane and Mary godfrey wear Maried the : 8th day of Jenuary in the year : 1690

Mary doane the daughter of Joseph doane was borne the fiftenth day of November in the year. 1691

*Compare age stated in the will.

Joseph doane the son of Joseph doane was borne the fiftenth day of November in the year : 1693

Rebecca doane the daughter of Joseph and Mary Doane was borne at Eastham : the fourth day : of September : 1698

Hannah Doane the Daughter of Joseph and Mary Doane was born at Eastham the Seventeenth Day of November in the year 1700

Daniel Doane the Son of Joseph & mary Doan was born at Eastham the eighth day of Januarie : 1702/3

Phebe Doane the Daughter of Joseph and Mary Doane was Born at Eastham the twenty ninth day of october 1704

Elisha Doane the Son of Joseph and Mary Doane was Born at Eastham the third day of febuary Anno Dom 1705/6

Joshua Doane the Son of Joseph and Mary Doane was Born at Eastham yᵉ fourth day of December Anno dom 1709

Lidya Doane : the daughter of Joseph and Mary Doane was Born at Eastham on the ninth day of febuary anno Domini 1714/15

Elisabeth Doane the daughter of Joseph and Mary Doane was Born at Eastham on the twentieth day of may anno Domini : 1717 :

Sarah Doane the Daughter of Joseph and Mary Doane was Born at Eastham on the Eleventh day of September anno dom : 1719

Mis Mary Doane the wife of Joseph Doan esqr dyed on the 22ᵈ day of July anno domini : 1725

Joseph Doane Esqr & Mrs Desire Berry were maried by Mr samuel Osbon the 29 day of february 1727/8

Desire the daughter of Josep Doane born the (worn) December 1728

[p. 5] Thomas Bills a daughter Named Anna Borne the 28th day of June in the yeare 1673

Thomas Bills a daughter Named Elizabeth borne the twentie third day of august in the yeare 1675

Thomas Bills a sonn Named Nathaneel borne the : 25th : day of June in the year 1677

Mercy Bills the daughter of Thomas Bills was borne the fourtenth day of april : 1679

Mehitabel Bills the daughter of Tho : Bills was borne the 26th day of March : 1681

Thomas Bills the son of Tho. bills was borne the 22ⁿᵈ day of March 1684

gershom bills the son of Tho : Bills was borne the fifth day of June in the year : 1686

Joanna Bills the daughter of Tho : bills was borne the second day of december in the year 1688

Ruth Higgins the daughter of Joseph and Ruth Higgins was borne the eleventh day of September 1700

Eliezer Atwood Dyed on the twenty ninth day of March anno Domini 1729

Elisha young and Elisabeth mirrick were married by Jonathan Sparrow esqur on the tenth day of febrary 1703/4

Elisha young the son of Elisha young was Born at Eastham the 27th day of october anno domini 1704

James Maker and mercy Smith were married by Jonathan Sparrow Esqur on the fifteenth day of febuary 1703/4

Joseph Covel of monomoy and Hannah Bassett were married by Jona-than Sparrow Esqur on the first day of march 1703/4

Edward Smale of monomoy and Sarah Nickerson were married by Jonathan Sparrow Esqur on the third day of april 1704

James Brown Junr and Ruth Snow were married by Jonathan Sparrow Esqur on the thirteenth day of april 1704

Joseph Brown the Son of James and Ruth Brown was Born at Eastham the fifth day of febuary 1704/5

Jesse Brown the son of James and Ruth Brown was Born at eastham January ye 21th 1706/7

Zilpah Brown the daughter of James and Ruth Brown was Born at Eastham october ye 18th 1708

Ruth Brown the Daughter of James and Ruth Brown was born at East-ham the Sixth day of october Anno Dom: 1710

Jane Brown the Daughter of James and Ruth Brown was Born in East-ham on the nineteenth day of June anno Domini 1713

James Brown the son of James and Ruth Brown was Born at Eastham on the fourth day of June anno Domini: 1715

George Brown the son of James and Ruth Brown was born at Eastham on ye thirtieth day of December anno domini: 1716.

Rebecca Brown the daughter of James and Ruth Brown was Born at Eastham april ye 23: anno domini: 1718

Beniamin Brown the son of James & Ruth Brown was Born at eastha the twentyfourth day of June anno domini 1720

James Maker Jur and Mary Taylor were married by mr Samuel Treat April ye 17th 1706

(To be continued.)

Rebecca young the daughter of Elisha and Elisabeth young was born at Eastham the fifth day of october anno Domini 1706

Elisabeth Young the Daughter of Elish and Elisabeth young was born at Eastham the 24th day of may 1711

Joseph Doane Esqr Dide July the 27 = 1757

[p. 6] George Crispe and Hephzibah Cole Weare Maried the : 24th : of: May : 1677 :

Mary Crispe the daughter of George Crispe was borne the ninth day of december : 1678

Mercie Crisp the daughter of george Crisp was borne the : 15th of october: 1681

George Crisp died the : 28th of July: 1682

Nicholas Snow and lydia shaw wear married the 4th day of aprill : 1689

Nicholas Snow a son borne the . 30th . day of Jenuary in the year : 1691 92 : Named Jonnathan

Hannah Harding the Daughter of Maziah and Hannah Harding was Born at Eastham febuary the 15th 1694

Thomas Harding the Son of Maziah and Hannah Harding was Born at Eastham november the 13th 1699

James Harding the Son : of Maziah and Hannah Harding was Born at Eastham november the 2nd 1702

Mary Harding the Daughter of Maziah Harding was Born at Eastham the Second day of april Anno Dom 1706

Elisabeth Harding the Daughter of Maziah and Hannah Harding was Born at Eastham in Aprill : 1708

phebe Harding the Daughter : of Maziah and Hannah Harding was Born at Eastham in April Anno : 1710

Nathan Harding the son of Maziah and Hannah Harding was Born at Eastham october ye 29th Anno Dom : 1711

Cornelius Harding the son of Maaziah and Hannah Harding was born at Eastham on the thirty first day of march anno domini 1716/17,

Mrs Mercy Cole Died the 25 of september 1735 in the 63 year of her age

Daniel Cole Died the 15th of June 1736 in the 70th year of his age

[pp. 7 – 10 are missing]

[p. 11] John ffreeman and Sarah Merrick weare Maried the Eightenth of december: 1672 :

John ffreeman the sonn of John ffreeman was borne the third day of september : 1674 : and died

Sarah ffreeman the daughter of John ffreeman was borne in September: 1676

John ffreeman an other son Named John borne in July: 1678

Rebecca ffreeman the daughter of John ffreeman was borne the 28th day of Jenuarie. 1680

Nathaniel ffreeman the son of John ffreeman was borne the . 17th of march : 1683

benjamine ffreeman the son of John ffreeman was borne in July: 1685

Marcy ffreeman the daughter of John ffreeman was borne the third of Agust in the year: 1687

EASTHAM AND ORLEANS, MASS., VITAL RECORDS.

(Continued from page 181.)

[Vol. I, Pt. II, p. 12] John Mulford the son of Thomas Mulford was borne in July in the year : 1670

Patience Mulford the daughter of Thomas Mulford Was borne the : 17th day of agust : 1674

Anna Mulford the daughter of Thomas Mulford Was borne the : 23d : day of March in the year : 1676 : alias : 77

Hannah Mulford the widdow of Thomas Mulford dyed february ye 10th 1717/18

Georg Shaw and Constant doane Wear Maried the : 8th. day of Jenuary in the year : 1690 : & George shaw died the second day of May 1720

George Shaw a sonn Named Elkanan : borne the 7th day of october in the year : 1691

Rebeca Shaw the daughter of George and Constant Shaw was Born the 10th day of March Anno dom 1693

George Shaw the Son of George and Constant Shaw was Born ye twenty-ninth day of December anno dom 1695

Hannah Shaw the Daughter of George and Constant Shaw was Born the twentieth day of June anno dom 1698

John heard the son of John heard was born the : seventeenth day of Jenuary in the year : 1688 :

grace heard the daughter of John heard was borne the eleventh day of Jenuary in the year : 1692 :

Jacob : Hord : the Son of John and Deborah Hord was borne the : twelvth day of april in the year on thousand Six hundred ninety and five–1695

John Binny of Hull and Hannah Paine were married by Jonathan Sparrow Esqur on the thirty first day of may 1704

John Seers of yarmouth and Priscilla ffreeman were marryed by Jonathan Sparrow Esqur on the first day of June 1704

John Shaw the Son of George and Constant Shaw was Born the Sixth day of october anno dom 1700

Jonathan Shaw the Son of George and Constant Shaw was Born the Seventeenth day of febuarie anno dom 1703/2

Samuell Mayo and abigaile Sparrow were Married by Mr Samuell Treat on the Sixth day of august anno domini : 1713

James Robins and Thankfull Higgins were married by Mr Samuell Treat on the fifteenth day of april anno domini : 1714

[p. 13] Joseph Collens and Ruth Knowles were Maried the twentieth day of March in the year 1671 ales 1672

Joseph Collens a daughter borne named Saraie the second day of Jeneuarie in the yeare 1672

Joseph Collens sonne borne Named John the 18th day of december in the year : 1674

9

Joseph Collens a daughter borne named lidia July : 1676

Joseph Collens a son borne named Joseph : June : 1678 :

Joseph Collens a daughter borne named Hannah ; the latter end of feburarie 1680

Jonathan Collens the son of Joseph Collens was born the twentieth day of agust in the year of our lord . 1682

Jane Collens the daughter of Joseph Collens was born the third day of march in the year of our lord : 168$\frac{3}{4}$

Benjamin Collens the son of Joseph Collens was born the sixth day of feburary one thousand six hundred eighty and seven

James Collens the son of Joseph Collens was born the tenth day of march in the year . 1689 and died the last day of march : 1689

Martha Brown the daughter of James and deborah Brown was Born at Eastham the last week in march 1694

James Brown the Son of James and Deborah Brown was Born at Eastham June 14th 1696

Deborah Brown the daughter of James and deborah Brown was Born at Eastham in the mounth of April : 1699

Liddiah Brown the daughter of James and deborah Brown was Born in may 1701

Thomas Brown the Son of James and Deborah Brown was born at Eastham March the 4th 1702/3

Jane Brown the Daughter of *

Joshua Merrick and Lidia Mayo were married by Mr Samuell Treat on the fourth day of June anno Domini 1714 '

[p. 14] Joseph Snow the sonne of Joseph Snow was borne the : 24th : of November : 1671

Benjamine Snow the sonne of Joseph Snow was borne the : 9th day of June : 1673

Mary Snow the daughter of Joseph Snow was borne the : 17th day of october : 1674 :

Sarie Snow the daughter of Joseph Snow was borne the : 30th of aprill : 1677

Ruth Snow the daughter of Joseph Snow was borne the : 14th : of october : 1679

Steven Snow the sonne of Joseph Snow was borne the 24th of feburarie : 1681

lidia Snow the daughter of Joseph Snow was borne the : 20th : of July : 1684

Rebeckah Snow the daughter of Joseph Snow was borne the : 4th : of december : 1686

James Snow the son of Joseph Snow was borne the 31th day of March in the year : 1689

Jane Snow the daughter of Joseph was borne the 27th day of March i. the : 1692

Josiah Snow the Son of Joseph Snow was borne the twenty seventh day of November : In the year one thousand six hundred ninety an : foure

* Left unfinished.

Lieut Joseph Snow dyed on the third day of January anno dom 1722/3 *

Samuell Harding and Elisabeth Eldred were Married the 28th day of august anno dom 1707 by mr Samll Treat

Nicholas Harding the son of Samuell and Elisabeth Harding was Born at Eastham on the twenty fourth day of June Anno Dom : 1708

Samuell Harding the son of Samuell and Elisabeth Harding was Born at Eastham the twenty first day of december Anno Dom : 1709

John Harding the son of Samuell and Elisabeth Harding was Born at Eastham the fourth day of November Anno Dom : 1711

John Harding the son of Samuel and Elisabeth Harding (the secund of ys name) was Born at Eastham the seventh day of July anno domini : 1713

Zephaniah Harding the son of Samuel and Elisabeth Harding was Born at Eastham the 11th day of may anno : 1715

Elisabeth Harding the Daughter of Samuel and Elisabeth Harding was Born at Eastham : may ye 9th 1717

Joseph Harding the son of Samuel and Elisabeth Harding was Born at Eastham ye 19th day of may anno dom : 1719

(*To be continued.*)

THE MAYFLOWER DESCENDANT

A Quarterly Magazine

OF

Pilgrim Genealogy and History

1902

———
VOLUME IV
———

BOSTON

PUBLISHED BY THE

MASSACHUSETTS SOCIETY OF MAYFLOWER DESCENDANTS

1902

EASTHAM AND ORLEANS, MASS., VITAL RECORDS.

(Continued from Vol. III, p. 231.)

[Vol. I, Pt. II, p. 15] Jonnathan Bangs and Mary Mayo weare maried the 16th Day of July in the yeare 1664

Eadward Bangs the sonne of Jonnathan Bangs was borne the last Day of september in the yeare 1665

Rebeckah Bangs the Daughter of Jonnathan Bangs was borne the first Day of feburarie in the yeare 1667

Jonnathan bangs the sonne of Jonnathan Bangs was borne the last Day of aprill in the yeare 1670

Jonnathan Bangs the sonne of Jonnathan Bangs Deasessed the 11enth Day of May 1670

Mary Bangs the Daughter of Jonnathan Bangs was borne the 14th of Aprill 1671

Jonathan Bangs the sonn of Jonathan Bangs Was borne the 4th day of May 1673

Hannah Bangs the daughter of Jonathan Bangs was borne the four-tenth of March 1676

Thamoson Banges the daughter of Jonathan Banges was borne in May in the yeare: 1678:

Samuel Banges the sonne of Jonathan Banges was borne the: 12th: of July in the yeare: 1680

Mercie Banges the daughter of Jonathan Banges was borne the: 7th: of Jennuarie in the yeare: 1682

Elizabeth Bangs the daughter of Jonathan Bangs was borne the 15 day of May in the year 1685

Sarah Banges the daughter of Jonnathan Banges was born in Agust in the year. 1689:

lydia Banges the daughter of Jonnathan Banges was born the Second day of october in the year. 1689:

(worn) Ridley and Mary Strout were Married by (Mr) Samuell Treat the third day of august Anno dom 1708

(D)aniel Hamilton and Sarah Snow were married by (Mr) Samuell Treat on the fifth day of august anno dom 1708

[p. 16] Georg godfraie the son of george godfraie was borne the 2d of Jenuarie in the yeare: 1662

Samuel godfraie the son of george godfraie was borne the 27th of Jenuarie 1664

Moses godfraie the son of george godfraie was borne the 27th of Jenuar(y) 1667

Hannah godfraie the daughte of george godfraie: was borne the 25th of aprill. 1669:

Mary godfraie the daughter of george godfraie was borne the 2nd of June in the year. 1672

Ruth godfraie the daughte of george godfraie was borne the first day of Jenuarie: 1675

Richard godfraie the son of george godfraie was borne the 11th of June: 1677

Jonnathan godfray the son of george godfray was borne the 24th of June: 1682

Elizabeth godfrie the daughter of george godfrie was borne the tenth day of September: 1688

Sarah Mayo the daughter of James and Sarah mayo was Born at Eastham the fourteent(h) day of Januarie 1702/3

Henry Mayo the son of James and Sarah ma(yo) was Born at Eastham the 3d day of may 1705

John Mayo the son of James and Sarah Mayo (was) Born at Eastham the fourteenth day of october 1707

[p. 17] Thomas Crosby the sonne of Mr Thomas Crosby was borne the seventh day of April in the year. 1663

Simon Crosbe the sonne of Mr Thomas Crosbe was borne the 5th Day of July in the yeare 1665

Sarah Crosbe the Daughter of Mr Thomas Crosbe was borne the 24th of March in the yeare 1667

Joseph Crosbe the sonne of Mr Thomas Crosbe was borne the 27th of Jennuarie in the yeare 1668

Mr Thomas Crosbe two sonns borne at a bearth named John borne the 4th Day of December in the yeare 1670

John Crosbe the sonne of Mr Thomas Crosbe Deseased which was one of the children borne at a beirth : buried the 11enth Day of feburarie 1670

William Crosby the sonne of Mr Thomas Crosby was borne in march in the year. 1673

Ebenezer Crosby the sonne of Mr Thomas Crosby was borne the twenty eight day of March in the year. 1675 :

anne and mercy Crosby the daughters of Mr Thomas Crosby and a sonne that died named Increase all three at a bearth borne aprill the fourteenth an fifteenth in the year. 1678:

Eliezer Crosby the sonne of Mr Thomas Crosby was borne the one and thirtieth of March in the year: 1680:

Samuell Baker and Patience Berrie were married by Nathaniel freeman Esqur the Eleventh day of Januarie 1709/10

Ebenezer Severence and (*) Tomlin were married by Nathanll freeman Esqur febuary ye 14th 1709/10

Samuell Robins and Desire chase were married by Joseph Doane Esqur on ye 18th day of June anno Dom 1713

[p. 18] Thomas paine junior and hannah shaw wear maried the: 5: of august: 1678

hannah paine the daughter of Thomas paine was borne the: 6: of aprill: 1679

hugh paine the sonn of Tho: paine: jun: was borne the: 5th: day of July: 1680

hannah paine the daughter of Tho: paine jun: died the: 17th: of November: 1681

hugh paine the sonne of Tho: paine jun: died the: 29th: of November: 1681

Thomas paine the sonne of Tho: paine jun: was borne the: 28th: day of feburarie in the yeare: 1681/2

Thomas paine junior another daughter Named Hannah: borne the: 12th: day of May: 1684

Jonathan Paine the Sone of Thomas and Hannah Paine Jun was borne the first Day of febuary: 1685: 86

Abygaile Paine the Daughter of Thomas and Hannah Paine was borne the fourth day of march: 1687: 88 ad Shee dyed the twenty fist day of January: 1688: 9

Thomas Paine had another daughter named Abygaile borne: the tenth day of november: 1689

Phebee Paine the daughter of Tho: and Hannah Paine was borne the fourteenth day of march: 1690: 91

Elkenah Paine the son of Thomas and Hannah Paine was borne: the first Day of febuary: 1692: 93

* The given name was omitted.

Moses Paine the Son of Thomas and Hannah Paine was Borne the twenty eighth day of September In the yeare 1695

Phebe Paine the Daughter of Thomas and Hannah Paine Dyed the 21 day of January: 1698/9

Joshua Paine the Son of Thomas and Hannah Paine was Borne the twenty eighth day of august: in the year: 1697

Thomas and Hannah Paine had another daughter named Phebe borne: the eleaventh day of (*) in the year: 1698/9

Lidia Paine the Daughter of Thomas and Hannah Paine was borne at Eastham the fourth day of december in the year 1700

Barnabas Paine the son of Thomas and Hannah Paine was Born ye 13th day of November anno 1705

[p. 19] Joshua Bangs and Hannah skuder weare Maried the first Day of December in the yeare 1669

The Children of Jabez snow recorded

Jabez snow a son Named Jabez: borne the: 6th day of september in the yeare 1670

Jabez snow a son Named Edward borne the: 26th: of March: 1672:

Jabez Snow a daughter Named Sarah borne the: 26th: of feburarie: 1673

Jabez Snow a daughter Named grace borne the first day of feburarie: 1675

Thomas Snow the son of Jabiz Snow dyed the secund day of april in the year 1697

Liut: Jabiz Snow dyed the seaven and twentieth day of december: in the year 1690:

Samuell Treat Jur and Joanna Vickery were married by mr Samll Treat the twenty-seventh day of october Ann(o) Dom 1708

Richard Stevens and Abigaile Treat were married mr Samuel Treat the twenty-seventh day of october Anno dom 1708

William Dyer and Hannah Strout were Married by mr Samll Treat the fifteenth day of aprill Anno dom 1709

Thomas Smith Junr and Joanna Mayo were married by mr Samll Treat November ye 3d Anno dom 1709

[p. 20] Nathaniel Mayo and Elizabeth Wixam wear married the 28th of Jenuarie 1678

Nathaniel mayo the son of nathaniel mayo was borne the 7th of July: 1681:

Bathsuah mayo the daughter of Nathanell mayo was borne the 23th of September: 1683

Nathanel Mayo a daughter borne named alis the, 29: day of aprill in the year 1686

Nathanel Mayo a sonne borne Named Ebenezer the: 13th: of July in the year: 1689

* This appears to be "february" altered to January, but may be the reverse.

Nathanael Mayo a daughter Named Hannah borne the sixteenth day of June in the year 1692

Elisha mayo the son of Nathanel and Elizebeth mayo was Borne the twenty eight day of april In the year 1695

Robert Mayo the Son of Nathanael and Elizebeth Mayo was borne the three and twentieth day of march: 1697

Nathanael Mayo Senr and Mercy young were Married by Nathanal freeman Esqur the tenth day of June anno dom 1708

Elisabeth Mayo the wife of Nathanael Mayo dyed in december 1799*

Bathshebe Mayo the wife of Thomas freeman and Daughter of Nathanael Mayo dyed the ninth day of January 1706

Robert Young and Joanna Hix were Marryed the twenty secund day of march In the year 1693:4

Robert Young the son of Robert Young was borne the Eleventh day of april in the year 1695 and dyed the 23rd day of June following

Robert and Joanna Young had another Son named Robert borne the eleventh day of December in the yeare 1696

Lidia Young the Daughter of Robert and Joanna Young was Borne at Eastham the nine and twentyeth day of May: 1699:

Joannah Young the daughter of Robert and Joannah Young was Born at Eastham the first day of June in the year 1703

Jennet Young the daughter of Robert and Joannah Young was Born at Eastham the twenty secund Day of may 1708

Robert Mayo the son of Nathanael Mayo dyed on the 26th day of July 1707

Ebenezer Mayo the son of Nathanael Mayo dyed on ye ninth day of November 1709

Nathanael Mayo Senr dyed on ye 30th day of November: 1709

[p. 21] John Smith and Hannah Williams weare Maried the 24th of May in the yeare 1667

Elizabeth Smith the Daughter of John Smith was Borne the 24th of feburarie in the yeare 1668

John Smith a daughter borne named Sarah the 27th day of March in the yeare 1671 ales 1672

William Nicherson and Mary Snow wear Maried the 22th of Jenuary: 1690

William Nicherson a daughter borne March the 17th: 1694 Named Mercy

Nicholas Nicherson the son of William Nicherson was born the Nintenth day of March in the year: 1694:

Thankfull Paine the daughter of Nicholas and Hannah Paine was borne at Eastham : the fourteenth day of march in (the) year one thousand six hundred ninety n(ine) alias seven hundred : 1699/700

Prisilla Paine the daughter of Nicholas and Hannah Pain(e) was born the sixteenth day of october Anno 1701

* This is plainly a mistake for 1699.

Phillip Paine the son of Nicholas and Hannah Paine was born at
   Eastham on yᵉ eighteenth day of November: 1704

Lois Paine the daughter of Nicholas and Hannah Paine was Born at
   Eastham the twentyninth day of September Anno Dom 1705

Abigaile Paine the Daughter of Nicholas and Hannah Paine was
   Born at Eastham august yᵉ 3ᵈ 1707

Hannah Paine the Daughter of Nicholas and Hannah Paine was
   Born at Eastham the twenty fourth day of September Anno
   1709

Philip Paine the son of Nicholas and Hannah Paine dyed on the
   tenth day of april anno dom 1725

Mrˢ Hannah Paine wife of Mr Nicholas Paine Died the 24 day of
   January 1731/2

[p. 22] Steven Twinning and Abigael younge weare Maried the: 3ᵈ:
   day of Jenuarie in the yeare of our lord: 1683:

Steven Twining a sonne Named Steven borne the: 30ᵗʰ: of december in the year 1684

Eliazer Twining the sonne of Steven Twinning was borne the: 26 of
   November 1686

Nathanel Twining the sonne of Steven Twinning was borne the 27ᵗʰ
   day of March 1689

Steven Twining a daughter Named Mercy borne the eight day of
   September in the year: 1690

John Twining the sonne of Steven Twinning was borne the fifth day
   of March: 169⅔

Sarah Rich the daughter of Richard and Anne Rich was born in
   Eastham January the 22ᵈ 1695/6

Richard Rich the Son of Richard and Anne Rich was Born in Eastham febuary the 28ᵗʰ 1698/9

Rebeckah Rich the daughter of Richard and Anne Rich was Born at
   Eastham June the 15ᵗʰ 1701

Zaccheus Rich the son of Richard and Ann Rich was Born at Eastham the 2ⁿᵈ day of april Anno domini 1704

Obadia Rich the son of Richard and Anne Rich was Born at Eastham the fifteenth day of July: 1707

Prissilla Rich the Daughter of Richard and Anne Rich was Born at
   Eastham febuary yᵉ 5ᵗʰ 1709/10

Huldah Rich the Daughter of Richard and anne Rich was Born
   at Eastham in the month of July anno Domini: 1712

Joseph Rich the son of Richard and Anne Rich was Born at Eastham on the fifth day of october anno domini: 1715:

Prissilla Rich the Daughter of Richard and Anne Rich Dyed in the
   beginning of July anno domini 1716

Silvanus Rich the son of Richard and anna Rich was Born at Eastham on yᵉ fourth day of september ano dom 1720

(*To be continued.*)

EASTHAM AND ORLEANS, MASS., VITAL RECORDS

(Continued from page 34.)

[p. 23] steven Merick and Mercy Bangs weare Maried the 28th of December in the yeare 1670

Steven Merick the sonn of Steven merick was borne the 26th day of March 1673

Richard Webber and Sarrah Strout were Married by mr Samll Treat march ye 4th 1707/8

Nathanll Mayo Jur and Ruth Doane were married by Mr Samll Treat July ye 13th 1710

Elisabeth Mayo the Daughter of Nathanael and Ruth Mayo was born at Eastham on the twenty ninth day of September Anno Domini 1712

Nathanael Mayo the son of Nathanael and Ruth Mayo was Born at Eastham on the twenty fourth day of august anno 1714

abigaile mayo the daughter of Nathanael and Ruth Mayo was Born at Eastham on ye twenty fourth day of September anno domini 1716

Ruth mayo the daughter of Nathanael and Ruth Mayo was Born at Eastham on the Seventeenth Day of November anno domini 1719

Abigail mayo the daughter of Nathanael and Ruth Mayo dyed March ye 8th 172¾

Jeremiah Smith and Hannah atwood was maried the 3d of Januarie in the year: 1677

Mercy Smith the daughter of Jeremiah Smith was borne the: 17d of feburarie: 1678

Abigaell Smith the daughter of Jeremiah Smith was borne the first day of June: 1681

Jeremiah Smith the sonne of Jeremiah Smith was borne the 18th of Agust 1685

Hannah Smith the daughter of Jeremiah and Hannah Smith was Borne at Eastham : about the middle of September in the year Sixteen hundred ninety and one :

Jeremiah Smith Senior dyed on the 29th day of April Anno Dom 1706

Hanah Smith Widdow of Jeremiah Smith Deceased dyed on the twenty ninth day of March Anno domini 1729

George luis the Son of Thomas and Jone lewis was Born at Eastham anno Dom 1691 on the sixth day of may

Nathanael lewis the son of Thomas and Jone lewis was Born at Eastham on the 31th day of march anno Dom : 1696

Rebecca Lewis the daughter of Thomas and Jone lewis was Born at Eastham on the 17th day of march anno Dom : 169⅞

Beniamin Lewis the son of Thomas and Jone lewis was at Eastham on the 8th day of october anno Domini 1700

Sarah Lewis the daughter of Thomas and Jone lewis was Born at Eastham on the 2nd day of June anno : dom : 1702

Sophia Lewis the Daughter of Thomas and Jone lewis was Born at Eastham on the 9th day of may anno dom 1704

[p. 23a] Eldad attwood and anna Snow weare Maried the : 14th : of feburarie 1683

Marie attwood the daughter of Eldad attwood was borne the latter end of November in the yeare ; 1684

John Atwood the Son of Eldad and Anne Atwood was born the tenth day of August 1686

Anne Atwood the Daughter of Eldad and Anne Atwood was Born in January 1687/8

Deborah atwood the Daughter of Eldad and Anne Atwood was born in March 1690

Sarah Atwood the Daughter of Eldad and Anne Atwood was Born in April 1792 *

Eldad Atwood the Son of Eldad and Anne Atwood was Born July the ninth 1695

Ebenezer Atwood the Son of Eldad and Anne Atwood was born in march 1697/8

Beniamen Atwood the Son of Eldad and Anne Atwood was born in June 1701

Ralph Smith the Son of Thomas and Mary Smith was Born at Eastham the twenty third day of october annodom 1682

Rebecca Smith the Daughter of Thomas and mary Smith was Born at Eastham the last day of march Anno dom 1685

Thomas Smith the Son of Thomas Smith was Born at Eastham the twenty ninth day of Januarie anno dom 1687/8

David Smith the Son of Thomas and mary Smith was Born at Eastham the latter end of march Anno dom 1691

* This is evidently an error for " 1692."

THE MAYFLOWER DESCENDANT

An Illustrated Quarterly Magazine

or

Pilgrim Genealogy, History and Biography

1903

————

VOLUME V

————

BOSTON

PUBLISHED BY THE

MASSACHUSETTS SOCIETY OF MAYFLOWER DESCENDANTS

1903

142   *Eastham and Orleans, Mass., Vital Records.*

Jonathan Smith the Son of Thomas and mary Smith was Born at Eastham the fifth day of July Anno dom 1693

Isaac Smith the son of Thomas and mary Smith was Born at Eastham the 3d day of June 1695

Jesse Smith the Son of Thomas and mary Smith was Born at Eastham the 31st day of January Anno dom 1703/4

Isaac Smith the Son of Thomas and mary Smith dyed the 26th day of april Anno : 1704

Mary Smith Widdow and relict of Thomas Smith Dyed on the 22d day of March anno domini 1726/7

John Higgins and Hannah Mayo were married by Mr Samuell Treat on the fifth day of august anno Domini : 1713

John Taylor and abigaile Hopkins were married by Mr Samuel Treat on the third day of September anno Domini : 1713*

Abiah Harding and Rebecca young were married by Mr Samuel Treat on the twenty fourth day of September anno Domini 1713

[p. 24] John Knowles and Apphiah Bangs weare Maried the 28th of December in the yeare 1670

Eadward knowles the sonn of John knowles was borne the 7th day of November in the yeare 1671

John knowles the sonn of John knowles was borne the 10th day of July in the yeare 1673

John knowles a daughter named Rebecah borne the second day of March in the yeare 1674 ales 75

William Twining Junior and Ruth Cole wear Maried the 21th of March : 1688/89

William Twining Junior a daughter borne Named Elizabeth agust 25th 1690

Thankfull Twining the daughter of William and Ruth Twining was Borne the eleventh : day : of January in the year : 1696 : 7

Ruth : Twining the daugter of William and Ruth Twining was Borne at Eastham : the Seaven and twentieth day of august in the year 1699

Hannah the daughter of William and Ruth Twining was born the 1st day of April 1702

William Twining the Son of William and Ruth Twining was Born at Eastham the Secund day of September in the year 1704

Barnabas Twining the Son of William and Ruth Twining was Borne at Eastham the twenty ninth day of September in the year of our Lord 1705

Mercy Twining the Daughter of William and Ruth Twining was born at Eastham the 20th day of febuary anno 1707/8

(*To be continued.*)

* This entry has been crossed out.

[p. 14] Marke Sno and An Cook maryed 18 January 16[worn] *
William Walker and Sara Sno maryed 25 January [worn]†
Jonathan Sparo and Rebeca bangs maryed october 28 : 1654
Richard Higinse his Children
a daughter named Mary borne septembr 27 1652
a sonn named elyakim borne october 20 1654
a sonn named Jonathan borne in the towne of new Plimworth in July 1637
a sonn there born allso named Beniamin born in June in the yeere 1640
Joh ‡ Yats the sonn of John Yats borne in the town of Duxborough in augost in the yeere 1650
Robert Wixom a daughter named Jemimah born 30 aughost 1655
Jonathan Sparo a sonn named John was borne 2 novembr 1656
Mark Sno a daughter Named Anna borne 7 July 1656
Richard Knowlse a daughter named mehittabell borne 20 may 1653
an other daughter borne to him 28 september 1656 named barbara
Anna Sno the wife of mark Sno buryed 25 July 1656
William Twining Junear a daughter named Suzanna borne 25 Jenuary 1654

The Children of William Merick
a sonn named William borne 15 september 1643
allso a sonn named Steeven borne 12 may in the yer 1646
allso a daughter named Rebecca borne 28 July 1648
allsoe a daughter named Mary borne 4 novembr 1650
allso a daughter named Ruth borne 15 may 1652
allso a daughter named Sara born 1 aughost 1654
allso a sonn named John borne 15 January 1656
Henry Adkinse a sonn named Isake born 14 Jun 1657
Daniell Cole his Children
a sonn named John born 15 July 1644
allsoe a sonn named Tymothy borne 15 septembr 1646
allsoe a daughter named hephzibah borne 15 april 1649
allsoe a daughter named Ruth borne 15 april 1651
allsoe a sonn named Israell borne 8 June 1653
allsoe a sonn name James borne 30 nomber 1655
William Walker a sonn named John born 3 December 16 [worn] §

(To be continued.)

* "1654" in Plym. Col. Births, Marriages & Burials, p. 16.
† "25 February, 1654." Ibid., p. 16.
‡ "John "born "15th" of August. Ibid., p. 32.
§ "24 November 1655." Ibid., p. 16.

EASTHAM AND ORLEANS, MASS., VITAL RECORDS.

(Continued from Vol. IV, p. 142.)

[Since the copying of these records was begun the books have been repaired by the Emery process and the one formerly called Volume I has been marked "Land Grants, 1659-1710; Births, Marriages, Deaths, 1649-1760." Another volume contains a few records of earlier date, consequently all the vital records in that volume are here given.]

[Volume Marked "Meetings, 1650–1705; Ear Marks, Miscellaneous, 1648–1770."]
[p. 11] The Children of Jabez Snow recorded *
Jabez Snow one sonn Named Jabez borne the 6th september 1670
Jabez Snow one sonn Named Edward borne the 26th of March 167?
Jabez Snow a daughter Named sarah borne the 16th * of feburar[y]
1673
Jabez Snow a daughter Named grace borne the fift day of feburarie
1675

[p. 13] Raph Smith a daughter named Deborough born 8 march 1654
William Twining Junear a daughter named Joanna borne 30 may 1657

* Compare record in Mayflower Descendant, IV : 32.

17

EASTHAM AND ORLEANS, MASS., VITAL RECORDS.

(*Continued from page 23.*)

[p. 25] Israel Cole and Mary Rogers was Maried the : 24 : of aprill : 1679

Hannah Cole the daughter of Israel Cole was borne the : 28th : of June : 1681

Israel Cole a Sonne borne Named Israel : the : 28th of June in the year : 1685 :

Jonathan Godfrey and Mercy Mayo were married by Joseph Doan Esqr on ye 30th day : of october Anno Dom 1707

Joseph merrick Juner and Mary young were marryed by mr Samuell Treat febuary ye 5th : 1712/13

Simon Crosby and Mary Nicherson was Maried the : 27th day of agust : 1691

Simon Crosby a son borne the : 11enth day of July : 1692 : Named Samuel

Elizabeth Crosby the daughter of Simon Crosby was born the : 15th day of September in the year . 1693

Samuell Horton and Hannah atwood were married by mr Samuell Treat on the twentyeighth day of January anno domini 171¾

John horton Son of Samuel & hannah horton was born april 24 . 1715

hannah horton Daughter of Samuel & hannah horton was born february 25 : 1717/18

nathaniel horton Son of Samuel & hannah horton was born february 24 : 1720/21

Susanah horton Daughter of Samuel & hannah horton was born December 24 : 1723

Abigel horton Daughter of Samuel & hannah horton was born December 26 : 1725

Elizabeth horton Daughter of Samuel & hannah horton was born October 2 : 1727

Samuel horton Son of Samuel & hannah horton was born October 16 : 1729

James horton Son of Samuel & hannah horton was born march 1 : 1730/31

[p. 26] James Rogers and Marie paine weare maried the 11enth of Jenuarie in the yeare 1670

Samuel Rogers (otherwise baptised James and soe to be Called april 1680)* the sonne of James Rogers was borne the 30th day of october 1673

*The words enclosed in parentheses were interlined by the same hand, in different ink.

Mary Rogers the daughter of James Rogers was borne the ninth day of November 1675

abigael rogers the daughter of James Rogers was borne the : 2nd of march : 1677/8

Theophilas Crosby the sonne of Joseph Crosby was borne the one and thirtieth day of december in the year . 1693 :

Israel Young and Katharine frost were Married by Mr Samuell Treat the 3d day of June annodom 1708

Note Mary, widw of Jas Rogers above Married Israel Cole *

[p. 27] Isaace peper and apphia ffreman wear Married the : 7th : of october in the year : 1685

Apphiah pepper the daughter of Isaace pepp was born the 24th day of feburary in the year of our lord : 1687

Mary pepper the daughter of Isaace pepper was born the 7th day of Agust in the year of our lord 1690

Isaace pepper the son of Isaace pepper was born the . 29th day of July . in the year of our lord . 1693

Robert Pepper the Son of Isaac and Apphia Pepper was borne the fifteenth day of febuary : In the year 1695 : 6

Elizebeth Pepper : the daughter of Isaac and apphia Pepper was borne at Eastham the eleaventh day of July : in the year : 1698

Joseph Pepper the son of Isaac and Apphia Pepper was borne at Eastham the first day of november : 1700

Joseph Pepper dyed the first day of may 1703

Solomon Pepper the Son of Isaac and apphia Pepper was Born at Eastham ye 15th day of Januarie 1703

Joseph Pepper the Son of Isaac and Apphia Pepper was Born at Eastham the 24th day of febuarie 1704/5

John Cole Senior Dyed the Sixth Day of January anno Domini 17 5/4

[p. 28] John Cole and Ruth Snow weare maried the 12eth Day of December in the yeare 1666

John Cole a Daughter named Ruth was borne the 11nth Day of march in the yeare 1667 ales 1668

John Cole a sonne named John was borne the 6th Day of march in the yeare 1669 ales 1670

Hephzebah Cole the daughter of John Cole was borne about the Midle of June 1672

Hannah Cole the daughter of John Cole was borne the : 27th of March in the yeare : 1675

Joseph Cole the son of John Cole was borne the : 11th : of June in the year : 1677 :

May Cole the daughter of John Cole was borne the 22th day of october : 1679

Sarah Cole the daughter of John Cole was borne the 10th day of June : 1682

* This entry is in a modern hand.

Ruth Cole the wife of John Cole Senior dyed January ye 27th 1716/17

Daniel Cole Jur and Sarah Hubbard were married by Joseph Doane Esqur on the 10th day of June annodom 1708

Daniel * Cole the Son of Daniel and Sarah Cole was Born at Eastham the eighth day of July 1709

Eliner Cole the Daughter of Daniel and Sarah Cole was Born at Eastham ye Sixteenth day of april : 1711

Daniel Cole the Son of Timothy Cole dyed the nineteenth day of august Anno Dom : 1711

James Smith and Hannah Rogers were married by Mr Samuell Treat febuary ye 19th 1712/13

Levi Smith the Son of James and Hannah Smith was Born at Eastham on the fifteenth day of march anno Domini : 1713/14

Solomon Smith the Son of James and Hannah Smith was Born at Eastham on the eigth day of march anno domini : 17 15/16 †

James Smith the Son of James and Hannah Smith was born at Eastham on ye eighth day of april annodom : 1718

Joshua Smith the Son of James and Hannah Smith was born at Eastham on ye nineteenth day of July annodomini 1720

Grace Smith the daughter of James and Hannah Smith was Born at Eastham on ye Seventeenth day of December Anno 1722

Benjamin Smith the Son of James and Hannah Smith was born at Eastham on ye third day of october annodomini 1724

Phinias Smith Son of James & hannah Smith was born the 7th day of march 1728/9

[p. 29] Samuel Browne and Martha harding weare maried : the : 19th of feburarie : in the year : 1682

Samuel browne a daughter borne named bethiah the : 22nd : of Jenuarie : in the year : 1683 and died in June the 27 : in the year : 1685

Samuel browne another daughter borne named bethia the ninth day of September in the year : 1685

Martha Browne the daughter of Samuel browne was borne June the : 24th in the year of our lord god : 1688 :

Samuel ‡ browne the son of Samuel Browne was borne the 7th day of November in the year of our lord . 1690

Martha Browne the daughter of Samuel Browne : died on the 4th day of November in the year . 1691

Samuel Browne senior died on the third day of december in the year : 1691 being aged about thirty one years

John Walker and Mercy Brown were Married by Joseph Doane Esqur on the 18th Day of october Anno Dom : 1711

* "Hubbert" was crossed out and "Daniel" interlined.

† "15/16" over "16/17."

‡ "Joseph" crossed out and "Samuel" interlined in same hand as original entries.

THE MAYFLOWER DESCENDANT

An Illustrated Quarterly Magazine

OF

Pilgrim Genealogy, History and Biography

1904

———

VOLUME VI

———

BOSTON
PUBLISHED BY THE
MASSACHUSETTS SOCIETY OF MAYFLOWER DESCENDANTS
1904

Samuell Walker the Son of John and Mercy Walker was Born at Eastham on the 3ᵈ day of May anno domini : 1713

Mercy Walker the Daughter of John and Mercy Walker was Born at Eastham on the fourth day of march anno domini : 1717/18

John Waker the son of John and Mercy Walker was Born in Eastham on the seventh day of april anno domini : 1720

Joshua Walker the son of John and Mercy walker was born at Eastham on ye fourth day of march anno domini 1721/2

Sarah Walker the Daughter of John and Mercy Walker was Born at Eastham on the 25ᵗʰ day of January anno domini 1723/4

Mehitabel Waker the Daughter of John and Mercy Walker was Born at Eastham on ye fourth day of april anno domini 1728

John Walker Died January the 28 Day 1760

[p. 30] William Merrick and Abigaell Hopkins weare Maried the three and twentieth Day of May in the yeare 1667

William Merick a Daughter named Rebecca borne the 28ᵗʰ Day of November 1668

(To be continued.)

EASTHAM AND ORLEANS, MASS., VITAL RECORDS.

(*Continued from Vol. V, p. 198.*)

William merick a sonn named William borne the first Day of august in the yeare 1670

William Merick the sonn of William Merick junior Died the twentieth Day of March 1670 ales 1671

Martha Harding the Daughter of Josiah and Hannah Harding was Born the twenty third day of December anno dom 1693

Elisabeth Harding ye daughter of Josiah and Hannah Harding was Born the third day of January anno 1696/5

Joshua Harding the son of Josiah and Hannah Harding was Born at Eastham the 27th day of october anno 1698

Bethia Harding the Daughter of Josiah and Hannah Harding was Born at Eastham the ninth day of aprill 1701

Josiah Harding the son of Josiah and Hannah Harding was Born at Eastham the seventh day of march anno dom 1704/3

Mary Harding the Daughter of Josiah and Hannah Harding was born at Eastham ye fifteenth day of September anno dom : 1707

Jesse Harding the son of Josiah and Hannah Harding was Born at Eastham the 26th day of march anno dom 1709

Ebenezer Harding the son of Josiah and Hannah Harding was Born at Eastham on the twentieth day of July anno domini : 1712

Bethya Harding the daughter of Josiah and Hannah Harding was Born at Eastham on ye twelf day of may anno domini 1716

[p. 31] Samuel paine and patience freeman wear maried the : 31th of Jenuarie : 1682

Samul paine the son of Samuel paine was borne the : 30th of october : 1683

Samuel paine a daughter named Mercy : borne the fifth day of Agust in the year : 1686

Samuel paine a son borne Named Nathanel the : 9th : of July : 1689

Ebenezer Paine the son of Samuel and Patience Paine was borne the seaventeenth : day of June : in the year 1692

Elizebeth Paine the daughter of Samuel and Patience Paine was borne the eleventh day of June : in the year : 1694

Joshua Paine the son of Samuel and Patience Paine was borne the twentyeth day of may in the year . 1696

Isaac Paine the son of Samuel and Patience Paine was borne at Eastham the third day of January : In the year 1698/9

Mary Paine the daughter of Samuel and Patience Paine was Born at Eastham the twenty fourth day of febuary Anno dominie 1703/4

Nathanael Paine the son of Samuel Paine dyed the 14th day of march anno 1704

Seth Paine the son of Samuell and Patiene Paine was Born at Eastham the fifth day of october Anno dom 1706

Samuell Paine the son of Samuell and Patienc Paine dyed the fifth day of october . 1706

Samuell Paine sener Dyed on the thirteenth day of october anno Domini : 1712

Seth Paine the son of Samuel & Patience Paine dyed on the 23d day of march anno domini : 1722/3

[p. 32] Ephraim Doane and Mary Knowles was Maried the : 5th of feburarie : 1667

Ephraim Doane a Daughter borne named patience the 28th of Jenuarie 1668 and died in the year : 1675

Ephraim Doane a Daughter borne named apphrah : the 18th of July 1670

Ezekiah doane the sonne of Ephraim doane was borne the last weke in august : 1672

Thomas doane the son of Ephraim doane was borne the fourth day of September 1674

Ebenezer doane the son of Ephraim doane was borne in the month of april in the yeare : 1676

Nehemiah doane the son of Ephraim doane was borne in the month of august in the year : 1670* and died in feburarie in the year : 1674*

patience doane the daughter of Ephraim doane was born the last week in aprill : 1682

Ruhama doane the daughter of Ephraim doane was borne the last day of aprill : 1685

Ebenezer ffreeman and Abigaile young were married by Mr Samuell Treat the 12th day of october : 1710

Bennet ffreeman the Daughter of Ebenezer and Abigaile freeman was born at Eastham the seventeenth day of december Anno domini 1711

Thankfull ffreeman the Daughter of Ebenezer and abigail ffreeman was Born at Eastham on the fifteenth day of febuary anno Domini : 1714/15

Anne ffreeman the daughter of Ebenezer and abigail freeman was Born at Eastham the six day of June anno domini 1716

Ebenezer ffreeman the son of Ebenezer and abigail ffreeman was Born at Eastham on the thirtieth day of November anno dom : 1719

[p. 33] Steven Snow and Susanna Rogers was marryed the 13th of December 1665

Samuel Smith Junior and Bershuah lothrop wear Married May : 26th 1690

Samuel Smith Junior a son Named Samuel † borne : the : 13th day of feburary : 1691

*Sic. †"James" was crossed out and "Samuel" interlined in the same hand.

Joseph Smith the Son of Samuel Smith Junior was Borne the Ninth day of october in the year : 1692

Stephen Snow and Mary Bigford ware married the ninth day of april : 1701

Mary Melvile the daughter of david and Mary Melvile was Borne at Eastham the 31rst day of July : 1699

Beniamin Cooke and Mercy Paine were married by Mr Samuell Treat november ye 23d 1710

Shuball Cooke the son of Beniamin and Mercy Coke was Born at Eastham on the day of april anno domini : 1711 :

Joseph Cooke the son of Beniamin and Mercy Cooke was Born at Eastham on the twelf day of May anno domini : 1710 *

Nathanael Cooke the son of Beniamin and mercy Cooke was Born at Eastham on the sixth day of July anno dom : 1717

Richard Cooke the son of Beniamin and Mercy Cooke was Born at Eastham on the twenty third day of November anno domini : 1718

[p. 34] Thomas Rogers was marryed with Elizabeth Snow the 13th of December. 1665.

Elizabeth Rogers the daughter of Thomas Rogers was borne the 8th of october. 1666

Joseph Rogers the sonne of Thomas Rogers was borne the first day of February 1667

Hannah Rogers the daughter of Thomas Rogers was borne the twen-tyeth of March 1669

Thomas Rogers the sonne of Thomas Rogers was borne the 6th Day of March 1670 ales 71

Thomas Rogers the sonne of Thomas Rogers Died the 15th of March 1670 ales 71

Thomas Rogers another Sonn Borne named Thomas borne the 6th day of May 1672

Eliazer Rogers the sonn of Thomas Rogers Was Borne the 3d day of November 1673

Nathaniel Roggers the son of Thomas Roggers was borne the 18th of Jenuarie 1675

Elizabeth Rodgers the Wife of Thomas Rodgers died the : 16th day of June : 1678

[p. 35] John doane Junior and Mehitabel Scuder weare Maried the last day of June in the year : 1686

John Doane the son of John and Mehetabel Doane was borne

Solomon Doane the son of John and Hannah Doane was Borne may : 12th : 1698

Icchabod Higgins dyed June ye 1st 1728

John Higgens the sonne of Ichabod Higgens was borne the eight day of June in the year of our lord . 1692

* Sic.

Nathaniel Higgens the son of Ichabod Higgens was borne the first day of June in the yeare of our Lord one thousand six hundred and ninety foure

Thankfull Higens the Daughter of Ichabod and Meletiah Higens was born at Eastham the four and twentyeth day of august : 1696

Liddia Higens the Daughter of Ichabod and Melatiah Higens was borne at Eastham the thirteenth day of april in the year : 1698

Ebenezer Higgins the son of Icchabod and Melatiah Higgins was born in Eastham Aprill the 15th 1701

Martha Cooke the Daughter Joshua and Pacienc Cooke was Born at Eastham the twenty sixth day of aprill Anno domi 1706

Josiah Cooke the son of Joshua and Patience Cooke was Born at Eastham the 30th day of august 1707

Joshua Cooke the son of Joshua and Patience Cooke was Born at Eastham the 23d day of march : 1708/9

Mercy Cooke the Daughter of Joshua and Patience Cooke was Born at Eastham the secund day of september Anno Domini 1712

Ebenezer Cooke the son of Joshua and Patience Cooke was Born at Eastham November the 25th 1711

Ephraim Cooke the son of Joshua and Patience Cook was Born at Eastham on the sixteenth day of september anno dom . 1712

Ruhama Cooke the daughter of Joshua and Patience Cooke was Born at Eastham on the 18th day of febuary anno domini 1713/14

Simeon Cooke the son of Joshua and Patience Cooke was Born at Eastham on the twenty fourth day of august anno dom : 1715

Moses Cooke the son of Joshua and Patience Cooke was Born at Eastham on the eleventh day of may anno domini : 1717

[p. 36] Jonathan Higgens was marryed with Elizabeth Rogers in January 1660.

Beriah Higgens the sonne of Jonathan Higgens was borne the 29th of September 1661

Jonathan Higgens the sonne of Jonathan Higgens was borne the latter end of August 1664

Jonnathan Higens a sonne named Joseph was borne the 14th Day of feburarie in the yeare 1666

Elizabeth Higgens the daughter of Jonnathan Higgens was born the . 11th . day of feburary : 1680

Mary Higgens the daughter of Jonnathan Higgens was born the . 22th . day of January : 1682

Rebecca Higgens the daughter of Jonnathan Higgens was born the last day of November in the year . 1686

James Higgens the son of Jonnathan Higgens was born the . 22th . . day of July : 1688

Sarah Higgens the daughter of Jonnathan Higgens was born the . 18th . of october . 1690

Joshua Cooke and Patience Doan were married by mr Samll Treat the seventh day of febuary Anno Dom 1705/6

[p. 37] Elisha paine and Rebecca doane was Maried the twentieth
day of Jenuarie : 1685
abigael paine the daughter of Elisha paine was borne the fifth day of
January : 1686
Elisha paine the sonne of Elisha paine was borne the 29ᵗʰ of december : 1693.

(*To be continued.*)

EASTHAM AND ORLEANS, MASS., VITAL RECORDS.

(*Continued from page 16.*)

Joseph Snow juʳ and Sarah Smith wear Maried in december the
fiftenth : 1690
Thankfull Snow the daughter of Joseph Snow Jun : was borne the
fiftenth day of december in the year of our lord . 1692.
Joseph Snow Junʳ died on the twentyfirst day of Januarie anno 1705/6
Mary Paine the Daughter of Elisha and Rebecca Paine was borne
the first day of february one thousand six hundred ninety and
five : six :
Solomon Paine the son of Elisha and Rebecca Paine was borne the
16ᵗʰ: day of may : 1698
Dorcas Paine the Daughter of Elisha and Rebecca Paine was borne
at Eastham the four and twentyeth day of february In the year :
1699 : alias 1700.

[p. 38] Sammuell Freeman was marryd with Mercy Southerne the
12ᵗʰ of May . 1658.
Samuell Freeman hath a Daughter borne the . 11 december 1651 *
named Abthya.
Samuell Freeman . hath . a sonne named Sammuell borne the the
26 . of march . 1662
Samuel . ffreeman a Daughter named apphiah borne the first of
jennuarie 1666
Samuel freeman a sonn named Constant borne the last of march .
1669
Elizabeth ffreeman the Daughter of Samuel ffreeman Was born : the
26ᵗʰ Day of June 1671
Marcy
Hannah Smith the Daughter of John and Sarrah Smith was Born at
Eastham the eighteenth day of march anno dom : 1695/6
Joseph Smith the son of John and Sarah Smith was Born at Eastham
the 28ᵗʰ day of december anno Dom : 1697
Sarah Smith the Daughter of John and Sarah Smith was born at
Eastham the sixth day of November Anno Dom : 1699
Williams Smith the son of John and Sarah Smith was Born at Eastham
the sixth day of September Anno Dom : 1702
Lidia Smith the Daughter of John and Sarah Smith was Born at
Eastham Aprill yᵉ 24ᵗʰ 1704
Seth Smith the son of John and Sarah Smith was Born at Eastham
the twenty eighth day of Januarie Anno : dom : 1705/6

* Sic.

Richard Sparow : deceased the : eaight of Jenuary in the : yeare one thousand Six hundred & Sixti

Apthiah ffreeman the Daughtr of Samuell ffreeman : Deceased the : ninetenth of ffebuary in the yeare one thousand Six hundred & Sixti

Nathanyell Mayo deceased the

Elizabeth . Atkins the wife of Henry Atkins deceased the seventeenth of March in the yeare one thousand Six hundred Sixty one alias sixty two

Josiah Cooke senior deseased the sevententh of october in the yeare one thousand six hundred seventie three

Nicholas Snow senior decesed the fiftenth day of November* in the year one thousand six hundred sevetie six

Mary Crispe the wife of george Crispe died the one and twentieth day of feburarie one thousand 600 seventie six :

Constant Snow which was the Wife of Nicholas Snow died about the Midle of october in the year : 1677

James Rogers died the : 13mth : of aprill . 1678

Ann Twining which was the Wife of William Twining senior died the twentieseventh day of feburari[e] In the year of our lord one thousand six hundred and eightie

John Younge senior died the : 28th : of Jenuary in the yeare : 1690/91

Abigael younge the wife of John younge sen. died the 7nth : day of April in the year : 1692

Steven atwood senior died the latter end of feburay in the year 1694/5 :

Lieut Joshua Banges dyed the fourteenth day of Jan[uar]ly anno dom 1709/10

[p. 41] John Sparrow and apphiah Trase weare maried the fifth of December : 1683

Rebeckah Sparrow the the daughter of John Sparrow was borne the : 23rd . of December : 1684

John Sparrow the sonne of John Sparrow was borne the 24th : of agust : 1687;

John Sparrow a daughter named Elizabeth borne the : 19th : of January : 1689 :

Steven Sparrow the Sun of John Sparrow was borne the sixth day of September in the year of our lord one thousand six hundred ninety and four

apphiah Sparrow Died the 15 day of December 1739

Samuell freeman Junr and mary Paine were Married by Mr Samuell Treat the ninth day of october Anno dom : 1712

Elisabeth ffreeman the Daughter of Samuell and Mary freeman was Born at Eastham on the fourth day of march anno Domini 1714/15

*"November" was written first. This was crossed out and "october" was written above, but was crossed out and "November" interlined. Both changes are in the same hand as the original entry.

Elisabeth Smith the daughter of John and Sarah Smith was Born at Eastham in march 1707/8

Rebecca Smith the Daughter of John and Sarah Smith was Born at Eastham in march Anno dom : 1709/10

John Smith the son of John and Sarah Smith was born at Eastham on the thirteenth day of march anno Domini : 1712/13

[p. 39] Samuell ffreeman and Elizabeth Sparrow weare maried the fifth of feburarie : 1684

Samuell ffreeman a daughter named prissila borne the 27th of october. 1686

Samuel ffreeman the sonne of Samuel ffreeman Borne the first day of September in the year 1688

Elizebeth ffreeman the daughter of Samuel and Bashua ffreeman was borne the nineteenth day of april in ye year 1694

Barnabas ffreeman the son of Samuel and Bashua ffreeman was borne the last day of January in the year : 1695 : 6

Nathaniel : ffreeman the son of Samuel and Bashua ffreeman was borne at Eastham : the seaventh day of may : 1698 in the year one thousand six hundred ninety and eight :

David ffreeman the Son of Saml and Bashua ffreeman was Borne at Eastham : the Eight and twentyeth day of January : in the year 1699/700

Elisha ffreeman the Son of Samuel and Bathshuah ffreeman was born at Eastham the ninth day of December 1701

James ffreeman the Son of Samuel and Bathshuah ffreeman was Born at Eastham on the fourth day of august 1704

Enoch ffreeman the son of Samuel and Bathshua ffreeman was Born at Eastham the nineteenth day of May anno dom 1706

Simeon ffreeman the Son of Samuell and Bathshua ffreeman was Born at Eastham on the twentythird day of febuary anno dom 1707/8

John ffreeman the son of Samuel and Bathshua ffreeman was Born at Eastham the fifth day of January Anno dom 1709/10

Abigaile ffreeman the Daughter of Samuell and Bathshua ffreeman was Born at Eastham on the tenth day of July 1713

The D Abigaile ffreeman dyed on ye 16th day of July anno domini 1714

Capta Samuell ffreeman had another Daughter named abigaile Born on the fifth day of may anno domini : 1715

Capt Samuel ffreeman Died January 30th 1742/3

[p. 40] William Twineing Senior Decesed the fiftenth :* Day of Apreill in the year : of or Lord one thousand six hundred fifty nine

Joseph : Rogers : Juner Decesed the twentiseventh Day of December in the year one thousand Six hunderd & Sixty :

*"Sevententh" was crossed out, and "fiftenth" interlined in the same hand.

Samuel ffreeman the son of Samuel and mary ffreema was Born at Eastham on the twentysecund day of November anno domini : 1716

James ffreeman the Son of Samuel and Mary ffreeman was Born at Eastham on the sixteenth day of September anno domini : 1718 and Died July 22 : 1754

Alice and Rebecca ffreeman the Daughters of Samuel and Mary ffreeman were born at Eastham on the twentyseventh day of february anno domini : 1719/20

Prissilla ffreeman the daughter of Samuel and Mary ffreeman was Born at Eastham on the sixteenth day of December anno domini 1725

Hannah ffreeman the Daughter of Samuel and Mary ffreeman was Born at Eastham on the fourteenth day of march anno domini 1726/7

Marcy ffreeman Daughter of Samuel & Mary ffreeman was born at Eastham the 21 day of March 1729/30 Died the 5th november 1736

abigel ffreeman Daughter of Samuel & Mary ffreeman was born July 9th 1731

Barnabas ffreeman son of Samuel & mary freeman was born September 12 1733 Died the 8 of October 1736

Barnabas ffreeman son of Samuel ffreeman & Mary ffreeman was born at Eastham was born the 23 of february 1736/7

Deacon Samuel freeman Died at Eastham may 30 : 1751

Mary freeman the Dafter of Samuel and mary freeman was Born in Eastham febuary 24 : 1722 and Died octobar 18 : 1754

[p. 42] James Cole the Sonne of Danyel Cole was borne in december in the yeare . 1655

Daniell Coole hath a Daughtr named Mary was borne the 10th of March : in the year one thousand Six hunderd fifty eaight

William Cole the Sonne of Danyel Cole was borne the 15 Septemb in the yeare . 1663

Ruth Cole the wife of Daniel Cole dyed the fifteenth day of december : in the year 1694 : in the sixty seaventh year of her age

Daniel Cole dyed the one and twentyeth day of december in the year 1694 in the Eigtyeth year of his age

Mary hopkins wife of Joshua hopkins died the first day of March 1733/4

Rebecca Cole the widdow of Job Cole dyed the 29th of december : 1693 being about 88 year old

Ruth Collins the wife of Joseph Collins Senior dyed on the twenty-eighth day of august anno domini : 1714

[p. 43] Samuel Knowles and Mercy ffreeman wear maried december in the year 1679

James Knowles the sonne of Samuel Knowles was borne the : 13th day of agust : 1680 :

Mercy Knowles the daughter of Samuel Knowles was borne the : 13th day of September : 1681

Samuel Knowles the sonne of Samuel Knowles was borne the : 15th of Jenuarie : 1682

Nathanel Knowles the sonne of Samuel Knowles was borne the : 15th of may : 1686

Richard Knowles the son of Samuel Knowles was borne the latter end of July in the year 1688

Rebeckah Knowles the daughter of Samuel Knowles was borne about the midle of March in the year . 1690

John Knowles the son of Samuel Knowles was borne about the midle of aprill in the year : 1692

Ruth Knowles the daughter of Samuel and Mercy Knowles was born at Eastham in November in the year 1694

Cornelius Knowles the son of Samuel and Mercy Knowles was born at Eastham in october in the year of our Lord 1695

Amos Knowles the son of Samuel and Mercy Knowles was born at Eastham Annoque dominie 1702

John Nickerson of monomoy and mary his wife were married by Capta Sparrow July the 11th 1706

William Eldred of monomoy and Sarah Conant were married by Capta Sparrow Januarie the 30th 1706/7

James young and Mary Higgins were marryed by capta Sparrow febuary the 12th 1704

[p. 44] John Mayo and Hannah Lecraft ware Mareid the first Day of Jenuary in the year one thousand Six hundered fifty one.

John Mayo hath a Son named John was borne the the fiftenth of December in one thousand Six hundered fifty two :

also a Son named William borne the : Seventh of ocktober in the yeare one thousand Six hundered fifty four

Also a Son named James borne the third day of ocktober in the yeare one thousand Six hundered fifty six

Also a Son named Samuel borne the Second day of Apreill in the year one thousand Six hundered fifty eaight.

Also a Sonne named Elisha borne the fourth day of November in the yeare one thousand Six hundred Sixty one

Also a Sonne named Danyell borne the five and twentyeth of June in the yeare one thousand Six hunderd Sixty foure

John Mayo a sonn named Nathaniel borne the 2nd of aprell in the yeare 1667

John mayo a sonn named Thomas borne the 24th June in the yeare 1670 and died the 11enth day of August 1670

John Mayo another Sonn Borne named Thomas the 15enth of July 1672

[p. 45] Joseph Young and Sarah davis wear maried the 23 day of october : 1679

Samuel Younge the sonne of Joseph Younge was borne the 23 of September : 1680

Joseph and Isaace twins : the sonns of Joseph Younge wear borne the : 19 . day of december in the year . 1682

James Younge the sonne of Joseph Younge was borne the : 4 . day of april . 1685

Thomas Paine Junr and Thankfull Cob were married on the seventeenth day of may 1705

Thankfull Paine the Daughter of Thomas and Thankfull Paine was Born at Eastham the ninth day of July anno dom 1707

Samuel Smith and Abigail freeman were married by mr Samuell Treat on the ninth day of october anno Dom : 1712

Mary Smith the daughter of Samuel and Abigaile Smith was Born at Eastham on the twentythird day of June anno domini : 1713

Zoath Smith the Son of Samuel and Abigaile Smith was born at Eastham on the eleventh day of December anno Domini : 1716

Abigaile Smith the Daughter of Samuel and Abigaile Smith was Born at Eastham on the Seventeenth day of December anno domini : 1718

Martha Smith the Daughter of Samuel and Abigaile Smith was Born at Eastham on the twentythird day of august anno domini : 1721 :

Bathshua Smith the Daughter of Samuel and Abigaile Smith was Born at Eastham on the ninth day of May anno domini : 1723

Grace Smith Daughter of Samuel and Abigle Smith was Born at Eastham on the fiftenth day of June 1725

Susana Smith Daughter of Samuel and abigle Smith was Born at Eastham on the twenty fifth day august 1727

Samuel Smith Son of Samuel and abigle Smith was Born at Eastham on the twenty first of february 1729/30

Joseph Smith Son of Samuel and Sarah Smith was born at Eastham the ninth day of September 1741

[Pages 46–49 are missing.]

[p. 50] William Walker & Sarah Snow ware Mareid at Eastham the twenty fift of Jenuary in the yeare 1654

William Walker a son named John Borne at Eastham the 24 day of november in the yeare one thousand Six hundred fifty five :

William Walker a Sone named William borne at Eastham the 12 of ocktober in the yeare one thousand Six hundred fifty Seven :

William Walker a Son named William borne the Second of Aughust in the yeare on thousand Six hunderd fifty nine.

William Walker a daughter named Sarah borne the thirtyeth of July in the yeare on thousand Six hundred Sixty two.

William Walker a daughter named Elizabeth borne the 28 of September in the yeare one thousand Six hundred Sixty foure

Jabesh Walker the sonne of William Walker was borne the 8th of July one thousand Six hundred Sixty Eight

Caleb Lumbard of monomoy and Elisabeth Smale were maried on the first day of September Anno dom 1705

Jeremiah Bigford and Hannah young were Maried on the twenty-sixth day of october anno dom 1705

Debora Bigford the daughter of Jeremiah and Hannah Bigford was Born at Eastham the Secund day of febuary anno 1705/6

Hannah Bigford the daughter of Jeremiah and Hannah Bigford was Born at Eastham in the begining of may anno 1708

(*To be continued.*)

THE MAYFLOWER DESCENDANT

An Illustrated Quarterly Magazine

OF

Pilgrim Genealogy, History and Biography

1905

———

VOLUME VII

———

BOSTON

PUBLISHED BY THE

MASSACHUSETTS SOCIETY OF MAYFLOWER DESCENDANTS

1905

Isaac Mayo the Son of Theophilus and Rebecca Mayo was Born at Eastham the sixteenth day of June anno domini 1708

Rebecca Mayo the daughter of Theophilus and Rebecca Mayo was Born at Eastham on the secund day, of december anno dom : 1710

Ebenezer Mayo the son of Theophilus and Rebecca mayo was Born at Eastham on the first day of march anno domini : 1712/13

Experience Mayo the daughter of Theophilus and Rebecca Mayo was Born at Eastham on the third day of april anno domini 1716

Theophilus Mayo the son of Theophilus and Rebecca Mayo was Born at Eastham the seventeenth day of September [ann]o domini 1718

[torn]h Mayo the daughter of Theophilus and Rebecca [Mayo] was Born at Eastham July ye 30th 1721

[torn] Mayo was Born September ye 22 : 1724 and dyed october ye 13th following
look in the new book

[Pages 52-63 are missing.]

[p. 64] Joseph Harding and Bethiah Cook ware maried the fourth Day of Apreill in the yeare on thousand Six hundered & Sixty

Martha Harding the daughter of Joseph Harding was borne the thirteenth day of december on thousand Six hundred and Sixty two.

Mary Harding the daughter of Joseph Harding was borne the 19th of August 1665

Joseph Harding the sonne of Joseph Harding was borne the eight of July 1667

Josiah Harding the sonne of Joseph Harding was borne the 15 of August 1669

Maziah harding the sonne of Joseph harding was borne the first day of November in the yeare 1671*

John harding the sonne of Joseph harding Was borne the 9th day of october in the yeare 1673

Joshua Harding the son of Joseph Harding was borne the 15th day of feburarie in the year : 1675

Nathannel Harding the sonn of Joseph Harding was borne the 25th day of december in the yeare : 1674†

Abiah Harding the son of Joseph Harding was borne the : 26th : of Jenua[rie] 1679

Samuel Harding the sonne of Joseph harding was borne the first day of September : 1683

John Harding the son of Joseph Harding Dyed the fourteenth Day of June in the year 1697

Moses Hatch and m^{rs} Hannah Banges were married by Mr Samuell Treat the twenty-third day of June anno don : 1712

*The "1" was written over "3."   † Sic.

EASTHAM AND ORLEANS, MASS., VITAL RECORDS

(Continued from Vol. VI, p. 207)

[p. 51] [*] was maried the first day of May in the year 1684 Joseph Meyrick Died June 15 1737

Elizabeth Merrick the daughter of Joseph merrick was borne the first day of Jenuarie in the yeare : 1685 :

Mary Merick the daughter of Joseph Merick was borne the . 7th. day of May 1687

Joseph Merick a son borne Named Joseph March the 8th : 1689/90

William : Meyrick the Son of Joseph : and Elizebeth Meyrick was borne at Eastham : the twenty sixth : day of January : in the year 1692 : 93

Isaac Meyrick the Son of Joseph and Elizebeth Meyrick was borne at Eastham : the twelfth day of august in the year one thousand six hundred ninety and nine 1699

Thomas ffreeman Junr of Harwich and Mary Smith of Eastha were maryed on the seventeenth day of october 1707 by Joseph Doan Esqu^r

William Baker and Bennet Smith were marryed by Capta Sparrow august ye 2 : 1705

John Ellis and Martha Severence were married by Capta Sparrow June ye 21st : 1706

Thomas ffreeman and Bathsheba Mayo were married by Capta Sparrow august ye 22nd : 1706

Theophilus Mayo and Rebecca Smith were married by Capta Sparrow august ye 16th 1705

Asa Mayo the Son of Theophilus and Rebcca mayo was Born at Eastham July ye 29th 1706

*The top of this leaf has been cut off.

Eliezer Rogers and Martha young were married by Mr Samuell Treat ye twenty secund day of august Anno Dom : 1712

[p. 65] Marke Snow and Anna Cooke was Marryed the 18th of January 1654

Anna Snow the daughter of Marke Snow was borne the 7th of July 1656

Anna Sow * the wife of Marke Snow Desessed the 25th of July 1656

Elizabeth Snow the daughter of marke Snow died the 18th of Jenuarie 1675

Mark Snow the sonne of Nicholas Snow was borne the : 9th ; of May : 1628 :

Jane prence the daughter of Mr Thomas prence was borne the first day of November in the yeare : 1637

Jabez Snow the Son of Jabez and Elisabeth Snow was Born at Eastham July ye 22th 1696

Joshua Snow the Son of Jabez and Elisabeth Snow was Born at Eastham March ye 12th 1700

Elisabeth Snow the Daughter of Jabez and Elisabeth Snow was Born at Eastham october ye 8th 170[†]

Silvanus Snow the Son of Jabez and Elisabeth Snow was born at Eastham febuary : ye 16th : Anno : 170¾

Tabitha Snow the Daughter of Jabez and Elisabeth Snow was Born at Eastham march ye 21th Anno dom : 170⅞

Samuell Snow the Son of Jabez and Elisabeth Snow was Born at Eastham on the 22nd day of January Anno dom : 170⅚

Edward Snow the Son of Jabez and Elisabeth Snow was born at Eastham may ye 18th Anno 1711

Mr Jabez Snow Ser Died October : ye : 14 : 1750

Mrs Elisabath Snow Died March : ye : 3 : 1755

[p. 65a] Marke Snow : & Jane Prence ware mareied the ninth of January one thousand Six hundred & Sixti

Marke Snow had a daughter named Mary was borne the last day of November 1661 in the yeare one Thousand Six hundred Sixty one

Nicholas Snow the sonne of Marke Snow was borne the Six of December 1663

Elizabeth Snow the daughter of Marke Snow was borne the 9th of May 1666

Thomas Snow the sonne of Marke Snow was borne the 6th of August 1668

Sarah Snow the daughter of Marke Snow was borne the 10th of May 1671

Mark Snow a sonn Named prence borne the twenty second day of May in the yeare 1674

* Sic.

† The last figure is doubtful, but probably is a "2" written over some other figure.

Mark Snow an other daughter Named Elizabeth borne the two and twentieth of June : 1676 and died the 22th of march in the year : 1677 : 78

Hannah Snow the daughter of Mark Snow was borne the : 16th : of September : 1679

Benjamin Higens and Sarah freeman ware Married the two and twentieth day of may 1701

Priscilla Higgins the daughter of Beniamin and Sarah Higgins was Born at Eastham the seventeenth day of November 1702

Thomas Higgins the son of Beniamen and Sarah Higgins was Born at Eastham June the 24th 1704

Sarah Higgins the daughter of Beniamin and Sarah Higgins was Born at Eastham July ye 13th 1706

Paul Higgins the son of Benjamin and Sarah Higgins was Born at Eastham the 25th day of June Anno Dom 1708

Reliance Higgins the daughter of Benjamin and Sarah Higgins was Born the thirteenth day of may anno dom 1710

Elisabeth Higgins the daughter of Beniamin and Sarah Higgins was Born at Eastham the first day of april 1712

Experience Higgins the Daughter of Beniamin and Sarah Higgins was Born at Eastha the 31th of January anno dom : 1713/114

Beniamin Higgins the son of Beniamin and Sarah Higgins was Born at Eastham on the first day of march anno Domini : 1715/16

Thankfull Higgins the Daughter of Beniamin and Sarah Higgins was Born at Eastham on ye 28th day of october anno domini : 1717

look in the new Book for ye rest

[p. 65b] Joshua Hopkins and Mary Cole wear maried the : 26th : day of May : 1681

John Hopkins the sonne of Joshua Hopkins was borne the : 16 of april . 168¾ :

abigael Hopkins the daughter of Joshua was borne the : 9th day of March : 168⅚

Joshua Hopkins a sonne borne Named Elisha the 17th of december : 1688 :

Liddiah the daughter of Joshuah and Mary Hopkins was born at Eastham April the 1st 1692

Mary the Daughter of Joshuah and Mary Hopkins was born at Eastham the 20th of Januarie : 1694/5

Joshuah Hopkins the Son of Joshuah & Mary Hopkins was born at Eastham the 20th of febuarie : 1697/8

Hannah the Daughter of Joshuah and Mary Hopkins was born the 25th of march 1700

John Hopkins dyed the 24th of June 1700

Phebe the daughter of Joshuah and Mary Hopkins was born the 11th of march 1702

Sarah Snow the daughter of Stephen and Margeret Snow was Born at Eastham on ye 13th of february ano Domini 1712

Stephen Snow Junr and Margeret Elkens were married at Eastham by mr Samuel Treat the 12th day of July 1705

Margeret Snow the Daughter of Stephen & margeret Snow was Born at Eastham the 14th day of may anno Dom 1706

Stephen Snow the Son of Stephen and Margeret Snow was Born at Eastham on ye twenty first day of march Anno dom 1708

Lidiah Snow the daughter of Stephen and Margeret Snow was Born at Eastham march ye 26th 1710

Elkins Snow the Son of Stephen and Margeret Snow was Born at Eastham march ye 24th 1713/14

Jane Snow the Daughter of Stephen and Margeret Snow was Born at Eastham april ye 22th 1716

Robert Snow the Son of Stephen and Margeret Snow was Born at Eastham february ye 22th 1717/18

John Snow the Son of Stephen and Margeret Snow was Born at Eastham march ye 30th 1720

Mercy Snow was Born at Eastham on the twenty fourth day of february anno dom : 1721/2

Ruth Snow the Daughter of Stephen and Margeret Snow was Born at Eastham on ye Eleventh day of December anno domini 1725

[p. 66] Johnathan Higens & Elizebeth Rogers ware marreid the ninth of January one thousand Six hunderd & Sixti
Steven Hopkins and Mary Merrek weare maried the three and twentieth Day of May in the yeare 1667 :

Elizabeth hopkins the Daughter of Steven Hopkins was borne the last weeke in June in the yeare . 1668

Steaven Hopkins a sonn borne named Steaven about the midle of July in the yeare 1670

Judah Hopkins the sonne of Steven Hopkins was borne about the midle of January . 1677

Ruth Hopkins the daughter of Steven Hopkins was borne about the begining of November in the year . 1674

Samuel Hopkins the sonne of Steven Hopkins was borne the midle of march . 1682

Nathanel Hopkins the sonne of Steven Hopkins was borne about the midle of march in the year . 1684

Joseph Hopkins the sonne of Steven Hopkins was borne in the year . 1688

Benjamin Hopkins the sonne of Steven Hopkins was borne the midle of feburary : 1690

Mary Hopkins the daughter of Steven Hopkins was borne the . 15th. day of aprill 1692

Stephen Hopkins and Bethya Atkins ware married the Seaventh day of april : 1701

Simon Newcome and Hannah Carter were Married at Eastham by mr Treat the 15th day of august 1705

[p. 67] John Snow and Mary Smale weare Maried the : 19th of September : 1667

Hannah Snow the daughter of John Snow was borne the 26th of agust in the yeare : 1670 :

Mary Snow the daughter of John Snow was borne the 10th of march : 1672

abigaell Snow the daughter of John Snow was borne the 14th of october in the yeare 1673

Isaace Snow the the sonne of John Snow was borne the : 10th of agust : 1683

Lydia Snow the daughter of John Snow was borne the 29th day of September in the year; 1685

Elisha Snow the Sonne of John Snow was borne the tenth day of January in the year 1684/5

pheby Snow the daughter of John Snow was borne the 27th day of June in the year 1689

David Doane and Doritha Horton ware Married the 30th day of September : 1701

Jonathan Doan the son of David and Doritha Doan was Born at Eastham the seventh day of July 1702

Hannah Doan the Daughter of David and Doritha Doan was Born at Eastham march the 5th 1703/4

Keziah Doane the Daughter of David and Doritha Doane was Born at Eastham may ye 26th 1706

John Doane the son of David and Doritha Doane was Born at Eastham may ye 3d : 1708

Nathan Doane the son of David and Doritha Doane was Born at Eastham June ye 17th 1710

[p. 67a] John Banges & Hannah Smaly ware mareid the twenty third of Jenuary one thousand Six hunderd & Sixti

Rebeckah Snow the daughter of John Snow was borne the 23 day of July in the yeare : 1676

John Snow the sonne of John Snow was borne the 3rd of may in the yeare : 1678

John Collins and Hannah Doane ware Married : the 12th Day of february : 1704/5

Solomon Collins the son of John and Hannah Collins was Born at Eastham January ye 26th 1707/8

John Collins the son of John and Hannah Collins was Born at Eastham the sixth day of febuary anno Domini 1703/4

Samuell Collins the son of John and Hannah Collins was Born at Eastham November ye 26th : 1705

Martha Collins the daughter of John and Hannah Collins was Born at Eastham January ye 26th 1707/8

John Collins the son of John and Hannah Collins was Born at Eastham the secund day of November Anno : Domini : 1709

Hannah Collins the daughter of John and Hannah Collins was Born at Eastham November ye 2nd : 1711

Joseph Collins the son of John and Hannah Collins was Born at Eastham august ye 14th 1713

David Collins the son of John and Hannah Collins was Born at Eastham about the 20th day of april anno domini 1715

Joshua Harding and Sarah Smith were maried at Eastham June 26 1702

Theodore Harding the Son of Joshuah and Sarah Harding was born at Eastham the twentyfifth day of may 1705

Seth Harding the Son of Joshua and Sarah Harding was Born on the Secund day of January anno 1707/8

Gideon Harding the Son of Joshua and Sarah Harding was born at Eastham : July ye 14th 1711

Seth Harding the Son of Joshua and Sarah Harding dyed the third day of April anno domini : 1721

[p. 68] Daniel Smith and Mary Younge was Maried the 3rd day of March . 1676

daniel Smith the son of daniel Smith was borne the 8th day of Jenuarie . 1678 :

Content Smith the daughter of daniel Smith was borne the 8th day of June : 1680 :

abigael Smith the daughter of daniel Smith was borne the the last day of april in the year : 1683 :

James Smith the son of daniel Smith was borne the last week in april in the year : 1685 :

Nathanel Smith the son of daniel Smith was borne the last week of october in the year : 1687 :

Mary Smith the daughter of danll Smith dyed febuary ye 16th 1705/6

Mary Smith the daughter of daniel and mary Smith was borne at Eastham : the Eighth day of January : 1693

Elisha Higgins and Jane Collens were maried at Eastham September the 30th 1701

Elisha Higgins the son of Elisha and Jane Higgins was Born at Eastham the third day of January anno dom 1701/2

Martha Higgins the daughter of Elisha and Jane Higgins was Born at Eastham ye fifth day of January anno Dom 1703/4

Beriah Higgins the son of Elisha and Jane Higgins was Born at Eastham the fifteenth day of January anno Dom : 1705/6

Alice Higgins the Daughter of Elisha and Jane Higgins was Born at Eastham the 2?th day of November Anno Dom 1707

Apphya Higgins the daughter of Elisha and Jane Higgins was Born at Eastham on the twenty secund day of November Anno : Dom 1709

Jonathan Higgins the son of Elisha and Jane Higgins was Born at Eastham october ye 8th : anno Dom : 1711

Elisebeth Higgins the Daughter of Elisha and Jane Higgins was Born at Eastham 1713
the rest in ye new Book

Thomas Howse of yarmouth and Content Smith were maried at Eastham december 11th 1701

Samuell Cash and Patience Pike were marryed by mr Samuell Treat febuary ye 5th : 1712/13

Mary Sparrow the Daughter of Richard and mercy was Born at Eastham on the tenth day of march anno domini : 1718/19

Prissilla Sparrow the daughter of Richard and Mercy Sparrow was Born at Eastham on the eighth day of July anno domini : 1722

[p. 68a] Joseph Cole and Elisabeth Cob were maried at Eastham febuarie the 4th 1701 : 2

Gershom Cole the son of Joseph and Elisabeth Cole was Born at Eastham the first day of march in the year 1702/3

Ruth Cole the Daughter of Joseph and Elisabeth Cole was Born at Eastham the Eleventh day of march Anno dom 1704/5

Patience Cole the Daughter of Joseph and Elisabeth Cole was Born at Eastham the eighth day of december anno dom 1706

Elisabeth Cole the daughter of Joseph and Elisabeth Cole was born at Eastham ye tenth day of febuary anno dom 1708/9

Sarah Cole the daughter of Joseph and Elisabeth Cole was Born at Eastham on the eigth day of march Anno Dom : 1710/11

Reliance Cole the daughter of Joseph and Elisabeth Cole was Born at Eastham august ye 2th 1713

Elisabeth Cole the wife of Joseph Cole dyed on the sixteenth day of may anno : 1714

Reliance Cole dyed august ye 2nd 1724

William Mereck hath a Son named Isacca was borne Sixth of Jenuary : one thousand Six hunderd & Sixti

Joseph Merricke the Sonne of William merricke was borne the first of June one thousand Six hundred Sixty two

Beniamin Merricke the Sonne of William Merricke was borne the first of february in the yeare one thousand Six hundred Sixty foure

Richard Sparrow and Mercy Cob were maried at Eastham febuarie the 4th 1701 : 2

Richard Sparrow the Son of Richard and Mercy Sparrow was born at Eastham the tenth day of november Anno 1702

Rebecca Sparrow the daughter of Richard and Mercy Sparrow was Born at Eastham the twelfth day of october Anno dom 1704

Mercy Sparrow the Daughter of Richard and Mercy Sparrow was born at Eastham december ye 6th 1706

Sarah Sparrow the daughter of Richard and Mercy Sparrow was born at Eastham on the twentyeth day of July Anno Dom : 1708

Hannah Sparrow Sparrow the Daughter of Richard and Mercy Sparrow was Born at Eastham the twelvth day of october Anno Dom : 1711

Elisebeth Sparrow the daughter of Richard and Mercy Sparrow was Born at Eastham the eighteenth day of april : anno domini : 1717 :

ook in ye new Book for the rest

20

Richard Godfrey and Lidiah ffreeman were maried at Eastham febuarie the 4th 1701/2
Shuball Hinckley & lidiah Banges were Maried by Nathaniel ffreeman Esquer april ye 17th 1712
William ffreeman and Mercy Pepper were married by Nathaniel ffreeman Esquer october ye 16th 1711
Nathanael Eldred and Sarah Conant were Married by Nathanael ffreeman Esquer September ye 4th : 1712 :
John Mayo Juner and Susanna ffreeman were Married by Nathanael ffreeman Esquer october ye 22 : 1712

(To be continued)

EASTHAM AND ORLEANS, MASS., VITAL RECORDS

(Continued from page 20)

[p. 69] Joseph Paine and Patience Sparrow weare Maried the : 27th : of May : 1691
Joseph Paine a sonne named Ebenezer borne the eight day of aprill in the year : 1692

Hannah Paine the daughter of Joseph and Patience Paine was born the fifth day of July in the year : 1694 ;

Joseph Paine Sener dyed on ye first day of october anno : 1712 *

Joseph Paine the Son of Joseph and Patience Paine was borne the twenty ninth day of march : in the year of our lord one thousand six hundred ninty and Seaven :

Richard Paine the Son of Joseph and Patience Paine was borne in Eastham Eastham ye five and twentieth day of march : 1699

Judah Hopkins and Hannah Mayo were maryed at Eastham April the 14th 1702

Thomas Rich and Mercy Knowles were married at Eastham July 23 : 1702

Thomas Rich the Son of Thomas and mercy Rich was Born at Eastham the twenty Secund day of december Annodom : 1702

Mercy Rich the Daughter of Thomas and mercy Rich was Born att Eastham the eighth day of august Anno Dom : 1704

James Rich the Son of Thomas and Mercy Rich was born at Eastham January ye 10th 1705/6

Joseph Rich the son of Thomas and Mercy Rich was Born at Eastham the first day of January annodom 1707⅞

David Rich the Son of Thomas and Mercy Rich was Born at Eastham the seventeenth day of march Annodom 1710

Sarah Rich the daughter of Thomas and mercy Rich was Born at Eastham September ye 1st : 1712

John Rich the son of Thomas and Mercy Rich was Born at Eastham on ye fourteenth day of September annodomini 1714

Thankfull Rich the daughter of Thomas and mercy Rich was Born at Eastham on the fourteenth day of october 1716

Samuel Rich the Son of Thomas and Mercy Rich was Born at Eastham on the fourteenth day of may annodom : 171[worn]

[p. 69a] Mary Hopkins the daughter of Giles Hopkins was borne in November in the yeare 1640

Steven Hopkins the Sonne of Giles Hopkins was borne in September in the yeare . 1642

John Hopkins the Sonne of Giles Hopkins was borne in the yeare 1643 and died being 3 months old

Abigail Hopkins the daughter of Giles Hopkins was borne in october in the year . 1644.

Deborah Hopkins the daughter of Giles Hopkins was borne in June in the yeare 1648

Caleb Hopkins the Sonne of Giles Hopkins was borne in January in the yeare 1650

Ruth Hopkins the daughter of Giles Hopkins was borne in June in the yeare 1653

Joshua Hopkins the Sonne of Giles Hopkins was borne in June in the yeare . 1657

* This entry was interlined in a different hand.

Giles Hopkins hath a Son named William was borne the 9th of January one thousand Six hunderd & Sixti

Elizabeth Hopkins the daughter of Giles Hopkins was borne In November in the yeare 1664 and died being a moneth old

Jeremiah Smith and Abigaile Smith were married by mr Samuell Treat August ye 9th 1711

Simeon Smith the Son of Jeremiah and Abigaile Smith was Born at Eastham on ye tenth day of may anno Domini : 1712

Jeremiah Smith the Son of Jeremiah and Abigaile Smith was Born at Eastham on the twenty Secund day of febuary anno domini 1713/14.

Nathanael Smith the Son of Jeremiah and abigaile Smith was Born at Eastham on the Secund day of april : annodomini : 1718 1718

Jonathan Smith the Son of Jeremiah Smith & abigel Smith was born the 19th day of July 1725

[p. 70] David Younge and Ann Doane weare Maried the twentieth day of January in the year : 1687 :

david Young a daughter borne Named abigael borne in the year : 1688 the 28 of december

Rebecka younge the daughter of david younge was borne the 14 day of october in the year 1689

anna younge younge the daughter of david younge was borne the 5th day of october in the year : 1691

Hannah Young the daughter of david and ann young was borne the Sixth day of September In the year : 1693

John young the Son of David and Ann young was borne the twentyeth day of march In the year : 1694:5 :

Prisscilla young the daughter of david and ann young was borne the twentysixth day of June : In the year : 1697

Dorcas young the Daughter of David and Anne young was borne at Eastham : the Sixteenth 16 day of December In the year 1699

David young the son of David and Anne young was born at Eastham the twentiefift of September 1701

Lois young the Daughter of David and Ann young was Born at Eastham the second Day of November Annodom 1704

Easther young the Daughter of David and Anne young was Born at Eastham the sixteenth day of November * Anno Dom : 1706

Henry young the son of David and Anne young was Born at Eastham the twenty third day of march Anno Dom 1710/11

[p. 70a] Bennaiah Dunham and Elizabeth Tillsson was marryed the 25th of october 1660

Beniah Donnham hath a Son named Edman was borne the 25 of July in the yeare one thousand Six hundered & Sixti one

John Dunham the Sonne of Bennaiah Dunham was borne the 22th of August and dyed the 6 of September 1663

* "october 17" was written and crossed out and the entry completed as printed.

Elizabeth Dunham the daughter of Bennaiah Dunha[m] was borne the 20th of November 1664

Hannah Dunham the daughter of Bennaiah Dunham was borne the 4th June 1666

Beniamin Dunham the Sonne of Bennaiah Dunham was borne the 28th of october 1667

Hannah Dunham the daughter of Bennaiah Dunham dyed the 23d of december 1667

Elizabeth Dunham daughter of Bennaiah Dunham dyed the last day of December 1667

Jonathan Collens and Elisabeth vickerie were married at Eastham by mr Sam'll Treat the 27th day of Januarie 1704/5

Timothy Cole Jun' and Apphia Pepper were married by Joseph Doan Esqu' on ye second day of November anno 1709

Doritha Cole the daughter of Timothy and apphya Cole was Born at Eastham the 22nd day of September Anno Dom 1710

Doritha Cole the daughter of Timothy Cole above sd dyed the eighth day of febuary Anno 1710/11

Doritha Cole the Daughter of Timothy and apphia Cole was Born at Eastham may ye 15th 1712

Isaac Cole the son of Timothy and apphia Cole was Born at Eastham on the thirtieth day of may anno Dom : 1714

Susanna Cole the daughter of Timothy and apphia Cole was Born at Eastham on the fifteenth day of July annodomini : 1716 :

Apphia Cole the Daughter of Timothy and apphia Cole was Born on ye 20th day of march annodomini : 1718/18* : and dyed on ye 27th day of June annodom : 1718

Apphia Cole the wife of Timothy Cole above sd dyed on the Sixth day of april annodom : 1718

[p. 70b] John adkins the son of Henerie adkins deceased †

Desire Cooke the daughter of Josia Cooke was borne the fourteenth day of June 1694

Deborah Cooke the Daughter of Josiah and Mary Cooke was borne at Eastham the tweft Day of april : in the year 1696 :

John Cooke the Son of Josiah and Mary Cooke was borne at Eastham the ninth day of april in the year : 1698

Mary Cooke the Daughter of Josiah and Mary Cooke was borne at Eastham the Eighth Day of february : in the year 1700

Isaac Peirce and Jane young were married by Joseph Doane Esqu' the ninth day of march 1709/10

[p. 71] Henry Atkins hath a Sonne named Samuell was borne the last of february in the yeare one thousand Six hundred fifty one

Also another Sonne named Isaac was borne the fifteene day of June in the yeare one thousand six hundred fifty seven

* Sic.

† This entry is directly opposite the birth of John on the next page.

Henry Atkins was marryed to Bethya Lennett the 25th of March in the yeare of our lord 1664

Henry Atkins hath a daughter named Desire borne the 7th may 1665

Henry Atkins hath a Sonne named John was borne the fifteene day of December in the yeare one thousand Six hundred Sixty Six

Joseph Atkins the Sonne of Henery adkins was borne the 4th Day of march in the yeare 1669

Nathanel adkins the son of Henerie adkins was borne the 25th of december : 1667

Thomas adkins the son of Henerie adkins was borne the 19th of June : 1671

John adkins the son of Henerie adkins was borne the first of August : 1674

Mercy adkins the daughter of Henerie adkins was borne the : 24th of November : 1676

Samuel atkins the son of Henry atkins was Born ye 25th day of June annodom 1679

Samuell Knowles Junior and Bethia Brown were married by Joseph Doane Esqu' the seventh day of November Annodom 1709

Enos Knowles ye Son of Samuel and Bethia Knowles was Born at Eastham on the 30th day of april anno Dom : 1712

Azuba Knowles the Daughter of Samuel and Bethia Knowles was Born at Eastham on the 6th day of february annodomini : 1713/14

Samuel Knowles the Son of Samuel and Bethia Knowles was Born at Eastham on the 6th day of october anno Domini : 1715

Nathanael Knowles the Son of Samuel and Bethia Knowles was Born at Eastham on the 6th day of october annodom : 1717

Jerusha Knowles the daughter of Samuel and Bethia Knowles was Born at Eastham the ninth day of march annodomini 1719/20

Seth Knowles the son of Samuel and Bethia Knowles was Born at Eastham January ye 20th annodomini : 1721/22

(*To be continued*)

THE MAYFLOWER DESCENDANT

An Illustrated Quarterly Magazine

OF

Pilgrim Genealogy, History and Biography

1906

———

VOLUME VIII

———

BOSTON

PUBLISHED BY THE

MASSACHUSETTS SOCIETY OF MAYFLOWER DESCENDANTS

1906

EASTHAM AND ORLEANS, MASS., VITAL RECORDS

(*Continued from Vol. VII, p. 239*)

[p. 71a] George Ward and Rebecca Newcome were married by Nathan[ll] ffreeman Esqu[r] the 26 day of march 1711

Rebeckah Higgens the daughter of Benjamine Higgens died in march in the year : 1675 :

John Higens the sone of Benjamin Higens died the 13th of June in the year : 1689

Jonathan young and Deborah Newcome were married by Nathan[ll] ffreeman Esqu[r] the seventh day of march Anno dom 1710/11

[p. 72] Beniamin Higgens was marryed with Lidya Banges the 24 day of December 1661*

Ichabod Higgens the Sonne of Beniamin Higgens was borne the 14th of November . 1662.

Richard Higgens the Sonne of Beniamin Higgens was borne, the 15th day of october 1664

John Higgens the Sonne of Beniamin Higgens was borne the 20th of November 1666

Joshua Higgens the sonn of Beniamine Higgens was borne the first Day of october in the yeare 1668

Lidia Higgens the Daughter of Beniamine Higgens was borne the latter end of May in the yeare 1670

Isace Higens the sonn of Beniamine Higens was Borne the last day of august 1672

Rebeckah Higgens the daughter of Benjamin Higgens was borne the 14th day of June 1674

Samuel Higgens the sonn of Beniamine Higgens was borne the seventh day of March : 1676:77

Beniamine Higgens the sonne of Beniamine Higgens was borne the 15th of September in the yeare : 1681

Banges Atwood the son of Joseph and Bethya atwood was Born at Easham on the twenty first day of June Anno Dom 1711

*The "1" was made over a "2."

Nathanael atwood the son of Joseph and Bethya Atwood was Born at Eastham april y[e] 18th 1713

Bethiah atwood the Daughter of Joseph and Bethya atwood was Born at Eastham on the 26th day of march anno domini : 1715

Hannah atwood the daughter of Joseph and Bethia atwood was Born at Eastham on the 14th day of December anno Domini 1716

Mary atwood the Daughter of Joseph and Bethia atwood was Born at Eastham on the fifteenth day of November anno domini : 1718

Joseph Atwood the son of Joseph and Bethia atwood was Born at Eastham the nineteenth day of february anno domini : 1720/21

Joshua atwood the son of Joseph and Bethia atwood was Born at Eastham october y[e] 27th 1722

John atwood the son of Joseph and Bethia atwood was Born at Eastham on y[e] seventh day of february annodom 1726/7

Elisha Atwood was Born in Eastham Aprel 25 : 1725

[p. 73] Thomas Snow and hannah Sears wear Maried the eight day of feburary in the year : 1692

Elizabeth Snow the daughter of Thomas Snow was borne the 25th day of october . 1693 :

Samuell Brown Sen[r] and Ruth young were married by Joseph Doane Esqu[r] the twentyfirst day of october Anno dom 1708

Abigail Brown the daughter of Samuel and Ruth Brown was Born at Eastham on the twenty Eighth day of July annodomini 1709

Samuel Brown the son of Samuel and Ruth Brown was Born at Eastham on the twenty seventh day of april annodomini 1711 : and dyed on y[e] the the thirtyfirst day of Janary annodomini : 1713

Samuel Brown the son of Samuel and Ruth Brown was Born at Eastham on the twentyfifth day of January annodomini 1713/14

Mehetabel Brown the Daughter of Samuel and Ruth Brown was Born at Eastham on the first day of December annodomini : 1714.

Ruth Brown the daughter of Samuel and Ruth Brown was Born at Eastham on the twenty fifth day of December annodomini : 1716.

Hannah Sears the daughtor of Silas Sears was borne in december in the year : 1672 :*

Eliezer Atwood and Joanna Strout were married by Joseph Doane Esqu[r] June y[e] 14th 1709

[p. 73a] Richard Higgens and Mary Yates was marryed the† october 1651

Mary Higgens the daughter of Richard Higgens was borne the 27th of September 1652

*This entry is in the same hand as the marriage of Thomas Snow on this page.

† The day of the month was omitted.

Eliakim the Sonne of Richard Higgens was borne the 20th of october 1654

Jadiah the Sonne of Richard Higgens was borne in march 1656 alias 1657

Zera Higgens the Sonne of Richard Higgens was borne June . 1658.

Thomas Higgens the Sonne of Richard Higgens was borne January 1661

Lidia Higgens the Daughter of Richard Higgens was borne July 1664

Jonathan Paine and Sarah mayo were married by Joseph Doane Esqr the twenty seventh day of october anndom 1709

Nathan young and Rebecca Shaw were married by Joseph Doane Esqr the eighth day of June anno 1710

Elkenah young the Son of Nathan and Rebecca young was born at Eastham the 17th day of June Anno Domini 1711

Nathan young the Son of Nathan and Rebecca Young was Born at Eastham the twenty Second day of January anno Dom: 1713/14

Rebecca young the Daughter of Nathan and Mary* young was Born at Eastham on ye 24th day of march annodomini : 1717/18

Mary young the Daughter of Nathan and Mary young was Born at Eastham on ye fourth day of may anno : 1719

Joshua young the Son of Nathan and Mary young was Born at Eastham on ye first day of april annodom 1721

Martha young the Daughter of Nathan & Mary young was Born at Eastham on ye tenth day of february anno : 1723/4

Seth Young the Son of Nathan and Mary young was Born at Eastham on the Second day of may annodomini 1725

Martha young Daughter of Nathan & Mary younfg was born the first day of october 1726

Seth young Son of Nathan & Mary young was born the third day of May 1731

[73b] John Paine the Sonne of John Paine was borne the eighteenth day of September in the year of our lord . 1690

Mary Paine the daughter of John Paine was borne the twenty eight day of January in the year of our lord . 1693

William : Paine the son of John and Bennet Paine was borne the sixth day of June : 1695

Benjamin Paine the Son of John and Bennet Paine was Borne the twenty Second day of febuary in the year 1696:7

Sarah Paine the Daughter of John and Bennet Paine was borne the fourteenth day of april in the year 1699

Elisabeth Paine the daughter of John and Bennet Paine was Borne the second day of June in the year 1702

Theophilus Pain the Son of John and Bennet Paine was born at Eastham the seventh day of febuarie in the year 1703/4

* "Rebecca" was crossed out and "Mary" interlined in the same hand.

Josiah Paine the Son of John and Bennet Paine was Born at Eastham the the eighth day of march Anno dom 1705:6

Nathaniel Paine the Son of John & Bennet Paine was Born at Eastham the eighteenth day of November Anno 1707

Rebecca Paine the Daughter of John and Bennet Paine was Born at Eastham the thirtieth* day of october Anno dom 1709

Mercy Paine the Daughter of John and Bennet Paine was Born at Eastham the third day of April Anno Dom 1712

Benjamin Paine the Son of John and Bennet Paine was Born at Eastham on the eighteenth day of may anno Domini 1714

Benjamin Paine the son of John and Bennet Paine Died on the fifteenth day of December anno : Dom : 1713

Bennet Paine the wife of John Paine dyed on the thirtieth day of May anno Domini : 1716

Benjamin Paine the son of John and Bennet Paine (being the Secund of that name) dyed on the fourteenth day of January anno Domini 1716/17

See the rest recorded in the new Booke in page 29

Josiah Paine the Son of John and Bennet Paine dyed on the Seventh day of may anno Domini 1728

Nathanael Paine the Son of John and Bennet Paine dyed on the fourth day of November anno Domini 1728

[p. 74] Steven Snow and Susanna Rogers was marryed the 28th of october 1663.

Jehshua Snow the daughter of Steven Snow was borne the 25th of July 1664

Hannah Snow the Daughter of Steaven Snow was borne the second Day of Jenuarie 1666

Micajah Snow the Sonn of Steven Snow was borne the 22th of December 1669

Bethiah Snow the daughter of Steven Snow was borne the first day of July 1672

Steven Snow and mary Bigford ware married the 9th day of april 1701

Stephen Snow died on munday the Seventeenth day of December 1705

Ralph Smith and Mary Mayo were married by mr Samuell Treat on the 23d day of october : 1712 :

1 Isaac Smith Son of Ralph & Mary Smith was born November the 17 : 1716

2 Phebe Smith Daughter of Ralph & Mary Smith was born May 16 : 1720

3 Thomas Smith Son of Ralph & Mary Smith was born June 14 : 1723

4 Enoch Smith Son of Ralph & mary Smith was born November the 10 : 1725

* "twentyninth" was crossed out and "thirtieth" interlined in the same hand and ink.

5 Mary Smith Daughter of Ralph & Mary Smith was born November 7th 1728

6 Jonathan Smith Son of Ralph & Mary Smith was born December 30th 1730

7 Ezra Smith Son of Ralph & Mary Smith was born December 10th 1732

[p. 74a] Sarah Roggers the daughter of Joseph Roggers was borne the twentieth day of November in the year 1691 :

Elizabeth Roggers the daughter of Joseph Roggers was borne the two and twentieth day of September in the year : 1693 :

[p. 75] John young the sonne of John young was borne the 16th of november 1649

Joseph young the sonne of John young was borne the 12th of November 1651 and died being 13 weekes old

Joseph young the sonne of John young was borne the last weeke in December 1654

Nathanyell young the sonne of John young was borne the first week in April 1656

Mary young the daughter of John young was borne the 28th of Aprill 1658

Abigail young the daughter of John young was borne in the third weeke in october 1660

David young the sonne of John yong was borne the 17th day of April 1662

Lidia young the daughter of John young was borne the [*] 1664

Robert Younge the sonn of John Younge was borne the third weeke in April 1667

Henerie Younge the son of John Younge was borne the 2nd weeke of april 1670

Henerie Younge the son of John Younge was borne the 17th day of march 1672

[p. 75a] Steven Hopkins Jun : and Sarah howes was maried the nintenth day of may 1692

Jonnathan Hopkins the Son of Steven Hopkins Jun ; was borne the twentieth day of Agust in the year . 1693

Nehemiah Doane the son of Hezekiah and Hannah Doane was borne the seventeenth day of December In the year 1692

Mary Doane the Daughter of Hezeekiah and Hannah Doane was borne the last day of august : In the year : 1694 :

Ephraim Doane the son of Hezekiah and Hannah Doane was borne the first day of april in the year 1696 :

[p. 76] william Sutton and Damaris Bishop was marryed the 11 of July 1666

* Space was left for the month and day.

William Sutton hath a daughter named Alce was borne the thirteene of May 1668

Thomas Sutton the Sonne of William Sutton was borne the eleventh day of November 1669

Marah Sutton the Daughter of William Sutton was borne the fourth Day of october 1671

Remick Cole the Son of Thomas and Lidia Cole was borne at Eastham the thirteenth day of february : In the year 170$\frac{1}{0}$

Robert Cole the Son of Thomas and Liddiah Cole was born at Eastham the twenty seventh day of febuarie 1702/3

Abner Cole the Son of Thomas and Lydia Cole was born at Eastham the twentythird day of June 1706

Hazael Cole the Son of Thomas and Lidia Cole was Born at Eastham June y^e 27th 1708

Jerusha Cole the Daughter of Thomas and Lidia Cole was Born at Eastham April ye 23 : 1711

Abiel Cole the Daughter of Thomas and Lidia Cole was Born at Eastham on the twenty seventh day of april anno dom : 1713

Charity Cole the daughter of Thomas and Lidia Cole was Born at Eastham on the eighteenth day of may anno Domini 1717

George Strout and Bridget Cooley were Married by Joseph Doane Esqr on the Secund day of august 1708

Joseph Merrick and Elisabeth Remick were married by mr Samuell Treat on ye seventh day of July : anno Dom : 1712

Rebecca merrick the daughter of Joseph and Elisabeth merrick was Born at Eastham on the Seventeenth day of September 1713

[p. 76a] Grace Smith the daughter of Samuel Smith : died the first day of december in the year : 1691

Samuel Smith the sonne of Samuel Smith deseased the : 22nd day of September 1692 : aged about : 24 : years

Joseph Smith the son of Samuel Smith deseased the : 22nd day of September : 1692 : aged about 21 : years

Samuel Doan the Son of Samuel and Martha Doan was born at Eastham the thirtieth day of october 1697

Sarah Doan the daughter of Samuel and martha Doan was born at Eastham the fifteenth day of may in the year of our Lord 1699

Dinah Doan the daughter of Samuel and Martha Doan was born at Eastham the thirtieth day of december Anno dom 1700

Dorcas Doane the daughter of Samuel and Martha Doan was born at Eastham the fifteenth day of June Anno dom 1703

Solomon Doan the son of Samuel and Martha Doan was Born at Eastham the Eighth day of November Anno 1705

Simeon Doane the Son of Samuel and Martha Doane was Born at Eastham the first day of December Anno Domini 1708

[p. 77] Samuell Smith and Mary Hopkins ware marryed the 3 day of January 1665

Samuel Smith a Sonne borne : and died : in march : 1667

Samuell Smith the sonne of Samuell Smith was borne the 26th day of May 1668

Mary Smith the Daughter of Samuel Smith was borne the third Day of Jenuary : 1669 :

Joseph Smith the sonn of Samuel Smith was borne the tenth Day of aprill 1671

John Smith the sonn of Samuel Smith was borne the 26th day of May in the yeare 1673

Grace Smith the daughter of Samuel Smith was borne the fift day of September 1676

Rebeckah Smith the daughter of Samuel Smith was borne the : 10th of december : 1678

Mr Samuel Smith dyed the two and twentieth day of march in the year 1696:7 : in the 55 yea[r] of his age

Elisabeth Cooke the daughter of Caleb & Deliverance Cooke was Born at Eastham the Secund day of august anno Dom : 1711 :

Abigail Cooke the Daughter of Caleb and Deliverance Cooke was Born at Eastham the twenty Secund day of december anno Dom : 1712

(To be continued)

EASTHAM AND ORLEANS, MASS., VITAL RECORDS

(Continued from page 18)

[p. 77a] Elizabeth Cooke the Daughter of Josiah Cooke Died the 2cnd weeke in april 1670

Josiah Cook of Eastham Died the 31 day of January 1731/2

David Linnel the Son of Jonathan and Elizebeth Linnel was Borne the 28th day of January In the year 1693⅜

Elizebeth and Hannah Linnel the daughters of Jonathan and Elizebth Linnel ware borne the seventeenth day of april In the yeare 1696

Abigail Linnel the daughter of Jonathan and Elizebeth Linnel was borne at Eastham the first day of July : in the year : 1699

Jonathan Linnel the Son of Jonathan and Elizebeth Linnel was born at Eastham the fourth day of august : 1701

Thomas Linnel the son of Jonathan and Elisabeth Linnel was Born at Eastham october the 12th 1703

Elisha Linnel the son of Jonathan and Elisabeth Linnel was Born at Eastham the fiftenth day of febuary annodom 1705⅞

Elisabeth Linnell the Daughter of Jonathan Linnell dyed on the 17 of may anno Dom 1714

Elisabeth Linnell the wife of Jonathan Linnel died on the twenty Seventh day of July annodomini 1725 :

[p. 78] Josiah . Cooke and Deborah Hopkins was marryed the 27 day* . of July . 1668

Josiah Cooke hath a daughter was borne the twelfth day of october named Elizabeth in the yeare 1669

Josiah Cooke hath a sonn named Josiah Borne the twelvth Day of november† in the yeare 1670

Josiah Cooke a sonn borne named richard the first day of september in the yeare 1672

Josiah Cooke another daughter Named Elizabeth borne about the Midle of June : 1674

Caleb Cooke the sonn of Josiah Cooke was borne the : 15th of November : 1676

deborah Cook the daughter of Josiah Cook was borne the : 15th of feburarie : 1678

Joshua Cooke the sonne of Josiah Cooke was borne the 4th day of feburarie : 1682

Benjamin Cooke the son of Josiah was borne in feburarie the 28 1686

* "last weeke" was crossed out and "27 day" written in the margin.

† "latter end of october" was crossed out and "twelvth Day of november" interlined in the same hand and ink.

Joshuah Knowles the son of John and Mary Knowles was born at Eastham the sixth day of July 1696

John Knowles the son of John and Mary Knowles was Born at Eastham the son of John and Mary Knowles was Born at Eastham the twentie eighth day of June 1698

Seth Knowles the son of John & Mary Knowles was born at Eastham the seventh day of august 1700

Paul Knowles the son of John and mary Knowle[s] was born at Eastham august the 8th 1702

James Knowles the son of John and Mary Knowles was Born at Eastham on the fourth day of November : 1704

Jesse Knowles the son of John and Mary Knowles was Born at Eastham on the first day of april : 1707

Mary Knowles the Daughter of John and mary Knowles was Born at Eastham october ye [*] 1709

[p. 78a] John doane and Rebecca Pette weare Maried the : 14th of Jenuarie : 1684

John Doan Senior dyed the fifteenth day of March : 1707/8

Christian Remich : the Son of Abraham and Elizebeth Remich : was borne the Sixtenth day : of december in the year 1694

Abraham : Remich the Son of abraham and Elizebeth Remich was borne at Eastham the twentyeth day of may : in the year 1696

Marcy : Remich the daughter of Abraham and Elizebeth Remich : was borne at Eastham the twentyninth day of July : in the year : 1698

Elizebeth Remich the daughter of Abraham and Elizebeth Remich was borne at Eastham the twefth day of September In the : 1700

[p. 79] John Doane and Hannah Banges was marryed the last of Aprell 1662

John Doane was borne the Sonne of John Doane was borne the 20th day of March 1662 alias 63 And dyed the 15 May 1663

A Second Sonne was borne named John Doane . the 29th of May 1664

Ann Doane the daughter of John Doane was borne the 25 of July in the yeare 1666

Rebecka the daughter of John Doane was borne the 12 of May 1668

John Doane : a sonne named Isaace was borne the second Day of June : in the yeare 1670

John Doane a sonne Named Samuel borne the second day of March in the yeare 1673

Nathaniel Mayo and Mary Brown were marryed by Capta Jonathan Sparrow the twenty eighth day of october 1703 †

Rebecca Mayo the Daughter of Nathaniel and Mary Mayo was Born att Eastham in the month of April in the year of our Lord 1697

* The day was not filled in.

† Sic.

William Mayo the Son of Nathaniel and Mary Mayo was Born at Eastham in the month of august 1699

Robert Mayo the Son of Nathaniel and Mary Mayo was Born at Eastham in the month of June Anno Dom 1701

Mary Mayo the Daughter of Nathaniel and Mary Mayo was Born at Eastham in the month of october Anno Dom 1704

Mehitable Mayo Daughter of Nathaniel Mayo & Mary Mayo was born the 3 day of april 1705

Nathaniel Mayo son of Nathaniel & Mary Mayo was born in Eastham born the last day* of June 1711

Phebee Mayo Daughter of Nathaniel & Mary Mayo born June 1709

ann Mayo Daughter of Nathaniel & Mary may born November 1707

pricila Daughter of Nathaniel & Mary may born in march 1708

[p. 80] Barnabas Wixam the Son of barnabas Wixam was born the fifteenth day of September . 1693 and dyed in the month of april following

Joshua wixam the Son of Barnabas and Sarah wixam was Borne the fourteenth day of march In the year : 1695

Lidia Wixam the Daughter of Barnabas and Sarah Wixam was borne the twelvth day of June : In the yeare : 1697 ;

Robert Wixam the Son of Barnabas and Sarah Wixam was Borne at Eastham the nine and twentyeth Day of may 1698

Prence Wixam the Son of Barnabas and Sarah Wixam was borne : at Eastham : decembr : 2nd : 1700

Beriah Smith and Susannah Savage were marryed by Capta Jonathan Sparrow the Sixteenth day of June 1703

Mary Smith the Daughter of Beriah and Susanna Smith was Born the one and twentieth day of may Anno Dom 1704

Samuell Smith the Son of Beriah and Susannah Smith was Born the third day of September 1706

[p. 81] John Rogers antd Elizabeth Twining was marryed the 19th day of August 1669

John Rogers a sonn borne named Samuel the first day of November in the yeare 1671 and died the third day of december 1671

John Rogers the sonn of John Rogers was borne the fourth day of November 1672

Judah Rogers the sonne of John Rogers was born[e] the : 23 : of November : 1677

Joseph Rogers the sonne of John Rogers was borne the : 22 : of feburarie 1679

Elizabeth Rogers the Daughter of John Rogers was borne the : 23 : of october : 1682

Eliazer Rogers the sonne of John Rogers was borne the : 19 : of May : 1685

* "third day" was crossed out and "last day" interlined in the same hand.

Mehitabel Rogers the daughter of John Rogers was borne the : 13th of March . in the year : 1686/7

Hannah Rogers the daughter of John Rogers was borne the : 5th day of Agust : 1689

Nathanel Roggers the son of John Roggers was born the third day of october in the year . 1693

Joseph Rogers and Mercy Crisp were Married by capta Jonathan Sparrow the thirteenth Day of october 1703

Crisp Rogers the son of Joseph and Mercy Rogers was Born att Eastham the seventeenth day of febuary Anno Dom : 1704/5

Elkenah Rogers the son of Joseph and Mercy Rogers was Born at Eastham the thirteenth day of febuary 1704

Martha Rogers the daughter of Joseph and Mercy Rogers was Born at Eastham the 26th day of febuary : 1708/9

Elisabeth Rogers Widdow relict of John Rogers Senior dyed on the 10th day of march annodomini : 1724/5

[p. 81a] Abigael ffreeman the daughter of Nathaneel ffreeman was born the twenty second day of feburary in the year . 1693

Nathaneel ffreeman the son of Nathaneel ffreeman was born the eleventh day of feburary in the year . 1694 ;

John ffreeman the son of Nathaniel and Mary ffreeman was born the fifteenth day of June in the year . 1696

Mary ffreeman the daughter of Nathanel and Mary ffreeman was borne at Eastham the third day of october in the year 1698

Eliezer : ffreeman the son of Nathaniel and Mary freeman was borne at Eastham the 23rd of april 1701

Liddiah ffreeman the Daughter of Nathanll and Mary ffreeman was Born att Eastham the 14th day of october Anno dom 1703

Mrs Mary ffreeman wife of Nathaniel freeman Esqr Died the 29 day of January 1742/3

[p. 81b] John Smith and Mary Eldrigd was married the last day of November in the yeare 1668 *

John Smith the sonne of John Smith was borne the 18th day of october in the yeare 1669 *

Jeremiah Smith the sonn of John Smith was borne the 27th Day of December in the yeare 1670 *

William Smith the sonn of John Smith was Borne the second day of august 1672 *

Bennitt Smith the daughter of John Smith was borne the tenth day of feburarie 1674 * †

Mary Smith the daughter of John Smith was borne the : 30th of November : 1676 *

* The entries on page 81b are given as they appear in the original. The first six were made at one. time, all in the same hand. The seventh is in the same hand, but made with different pen and ink. The last six are in a different hand and ink, but were made all at one time.

† The "4" of "1674" was written over "3," in the same ink.

[p. 82] Thomas ffreeman and Rebackah Sparrow Weare Maried the last day of december in the yeare 1673

Marcy ffreeman the daughter of Thomas ffreeman was borne the last week in october in the year: 1674:

Thomas ffreeman the son of Thomas ffreeman was borne the Eleventh day of october in the year: 1676:

Jonathan ffreeman the son of Thomas ffreeman was borne the: 11th of November: 1678

Simound ffreeman the son of Thomas ffreeman was borne the: 11enth of october: 1680

Joseph ffreeman the son of Thomas ffreeman was borne the 11enth of feburarie: 1682*

Joshua ffreeman the son of Thomas ffreeman was borne the 7enth day of March: 1683*

Hannah ffreeman the daughter of Thomas ffreeman was borne the 28th day of September. 1687

Prence ffreeman the sonne of Thomas ffreeman was borne the third day of January. 1689

Mrsuld ffreeman the sonne of Thomas ffreeman was borne the 27th day of march: 1691

Mary Melvile the daughter of David and Mary Melvil was Borne at Eastham the last day of July: 1699

Thomas Melvel the son of David and Mary melvel was Born att Boston † the twentyfifth day of July Anno domini 1697

Abigail and Elisabeth Melvel the Daughters of David and Mary Melvel were Born att Eastham the 28th day of may Anno Dom. 1702

David Melvel the Son of David and Mary Melvel was Born at Eastham the seventeenth day of october Anno Dom 1704

[p. 83] Thomas Mulford Jun and Mary Basset was Maried the 28 day of october: 1690

Anna Mulford the daughter of Thomas Mulford Jun: was born the 28th day of July in year. 1691:

Dorcas mulford the daughter of Thomas mulford Jun: was born the sixth day of march. 1693

Mary Molford the daughter of Thomas and Mary mulford was borne the twenty Sixth day of June: In the yeare: 1695

Hannah Mulford the daughter of Thomas and Mary Mulford was born at Eastham: the fift day of September: 1698

Elisabeth Mulford the daughter of Thomas and mary Mulford was born at Eastham the last day of June in the year 1701

Thomas Mulfford the Son of Thomas and Mary Mulfford was Born at Eastham October the 20th 1703

Jemima Mullford the daughter of Thomas and Mary Mulfford was. Born october ye 13th 1706

* "1683" was crossed out and "1682" written after it, in the same hand.
† "Eastham" was crossed out and "Boston" interlined in the same hand.

Mehitabel Smith the daughter of John Smith was borne the first day of May in the year: 1691*

Marcy Smith the daughter of John and Mary Smith was borne at Eastham ye seventeenth day of September in the year 1676*

Beriah: Smith the Son of Mary and John Smith was borne at Eastham the secund day of march in ye year 1679/ alias 1680*

Bethya Smith the Daughter of John and Mary Smith was borne at Eastham the Sixteenth day of January in the year 1681/2*

Ebenezer Smith the Son of John and Mary Smith was borne at Eastham the sixteenth day of January: 1679/ alias 1680*

Mary Smith the daughter of John and Mary Smith was borne at Eastham the fifteenth day of January: 1677 alias 1678*

Mary Smith the daughter of John and Mary Smith dyed in ye begining of march in the year: 1671/2*

[p. 81c] Ebenezer Savage and Joannah Newcome were married by Capta Jonathan Sparrow the thirtieth day of march 1703

Stephen Cole and Elisabeth Berry were marryed by Joseph Doane Esqr the sixth day of march Anno Domini 1711/12

Prence ffreeman and Mary Doane were married by Joseph Doane Esqr the 20th day of march 1711/12

Hatsel freeman son of Prince ffreemanan was born the seventh day of march 1716/17

Hannah freeman Daughter of Prince ffreeman was born 31 day of may: 1719

Mary Daughter of Prince ffreeman was born in may 1721

Susanah Daughter of Prince ffreeman was born in may 1723

Barnabas son of Prince ffreeman was born In february 20 day 1724-5

Kezia Daughter of Prince ffreeman was born about the middle of october 1726

Moses ffreeman son of Prince & mary freeman was born the eleventh day of november 1730

bennonie gray the son of Edward gray was borne in the mounth of March: 1681

Thomas Newcomb and Elizebeth Cooke were Married the first week of october in the year 1693

Edward Newcomb: the Son of Thomas and Elizebeth Newcomb: was borne at Eastham the third day august 1695

Thomas Newcomb: the Son of Thomas and Elizebeth Newcomb was borne at Eastham ye thirteenth day of august in the year 169[worn]

Simon Newcomb the Son of Thomas and Elizebeth newcomb was borne at Eastham the last day of November 1699

* The entries on page 81b are given as they appear in the original. The first six were made at one time; all in the same hand. The seventh is in the same hand. The last six are in a different hand, but made with different pen and ink. The last six were made all at one time.

Isaac Baker and Sarah Rich were married at Eastham by mr Samuel Treat the 25 day of febuary 1702/3

Simeon Baker the son of Isaac and Sarah Baker was Born the twentyfourth Day of July 1702

Samuel Baker the son of Isaac and Sarah Baker was Born at Eastham the first day of September 1704

Isaac Baker the son of Isaac and Sarah Baker was Born in Eastham September ye Anodom 1709

Joseph Baker the son of Isaac and Sarah Baker was Born at Eastham January ye 6th Anno dom 1707/8

Richard Baker the son of Isaac and Sarah Baker was Born at Eastham march ye 31th 1712

Sarah Baker the. daughter of Isaac and Sarah Baker was Born at Eastham the 19th day of July annodom : 1717

[p. 83a] Thomas Mayo and barberie Knowles Weare Maried the : 13th : day of June in the yeare 1677

Thomas Mayo a sonne Borne Named Thomas : the third day of Aprill : 1678

Thomas Mayo a sonne borne Named Theophilas the last day of october : 1680

Thomas Mayo hath a daughter borne Named Mary the 6th of agust : 1683

Mercie Mayo the daughter of Tho : Mayo was borne the : 19th of Jenuarie : 1685

Thomas Mayo a daughter borne Named Ruth : the : 20th day of Januarie : 1688

Thomas Mayo a sonne borne the 25 day of September 1691 Named Judah :

Thomas Mayo a daughter Named lydia borne the twelfth day of June in the year . 1694

Richard Mayo the Son of Thomas and Barbary Mayo : was Borne the thirteenth day of January in the year one thousand Six hundread ninety and Six:Seaven

Thomas Mayo had a son borne the first day of august 1699 and dyed the eighteenth of the Same month

Thomas Mayo dyed on ye 23d day of april annodomini 1729

Israel Mayo : the Son of Thomas and Barbary mayo : was borne at Eastham the twelfth day of august : 1700

Barbara Mayo the wife of Thomas Mayo Dyed febuary ye 23 : 1714/15

Samuel Higgins and Hannah Cole were married at Eastham by mr Samuel Treat the fourth day of November 1703.

Israel Higgins the son of Saml & Hannah Higgins was Born at Eastham the twentysixth day of Aprill Anno Dom 1706

Theodor Higgins the son of Saml & Hannah Higgins was Born at Eastham the twenty sixth day of october Anno Dom 1707

Ichabod Higgins the son of Saml and Hannah Higgins was Born at Eastham near the latter end of June Anno Dom 1709

Samuell Higgins the son of Samuell and Hannah Higgins was Born at Eastham on the 19th day of July anno dom : 1713

Hannah Higgins the wife of Samuel Higgins dyed on the 25th day of february annodomini 1716/17

Samuell Higgins Dyed on the 10 day of December 1761

(To be continued)

EASTHAM AND ORLEANS, MASS., VITAL RECORDS

(Continued from page 95)

[p. 84] John Smith and Bethyah Snow ware maryed the fourteenth day of may : 1694

James Smith the son of John and Bethyah Smith was Borne the thirteenth day of febuary : 1694:5 and dyed the tweny seaventh day of may In the year 1696

Samuel Smith the Son of John and Bethya Smith was borne the twenty fift day of may in the year : 1696

George : Williamson of Marshfeild and Mary Chrisp of this Town ware married the fift day of december : 1700

Thomas gold of Topsfeild and marcy yeats of Harwich ware married by mr Sam¹ Treat of this Town : decemb 2ⁿᵈ : 1700

William : Brown and Susannah Harding ware ware married the seaven and twentyeth day of october : 1699 :

Susannah Brown the Daughter of William and Susannah Brown was Born at Eastham october the 30ᵗʰ 1700

Liddiah Brown the Daughter of William and Susannah Brown was Born at Eastham April the 30ᵗʰ 1702

[p. 85] Mʳ Samuel Treat and Elizabeth Mayo Weare Maried the sixtenth of March 1674

Jane Treat the daughter of Mʳ Samuel Treat was borne the sixth of december 1675 *

Elizabeth Treat the daughter of Mʳ Samuel Treat was borne the 24ᵗʰ of July : 1676 : *

Sarai Treat the daughter of Mʳ Samuel Treat was born the : 20ᵗʰ of June 1678

Samuel Treat the sonn of Mʳ Samuel Treat was born July : 1680

Mary Treat the daughter of Mʳ Samuel Treat was born the : 16ᵗʰ : of March : 168²₁

Robert Treat the sonn of Mʳ Samuel Treat was born feburay the twenty fourth in the year of our lord : 1683 :

Abigail Treat the daughter of Mʳ Samuel Treat was born the thir- tenth day of June in the year of our lord : 1686

* Sic.

Daniel Doane the Son of Israel and Ruth Doane was Born at Eastham on the ninth day of august anno Domini: 1714
Edmond Doane the son of Israel and Ruth Doane was Born at Eastham on the 20th day of april anno dom 1718
Ruth Doane the Wife of Israel Doane dyed on the seventh day of June anno Domini 1728

[p. 87] Hannah Smalley the Daughter of Benjamin and Rebecca Smalley was Borne at Eastham the twentyfifth day of november In the year of our lord 1695
Rebecca Smalley the daughter of Benjamin and Rebecca Smally was Borne at Eastham the seaven and twentyeth day of april: 1697
Benjamin Smalley the son of Benjamin and Rebecca Smally was borne the three and twentyeth day of January in the year 1700/1
Joseph Atkins the son of Joseph and Martha Atkins was born at Eastham December* ye 9th 1701
Martha Atkins the Daughter of Joseph and Martha Atkins was Born at Eastham November ye 9th 1711
Anne Atkins the Daughter of Joseph and Martha Atkins was Born at Eastham December ye 12th 1713
Paul Atkins the son of Joseph and Martha Akins was Born at Eastham august ye 11th 1716
James Atkins the son of Joseph and Martha Atkins was Born at Eastham December ye 25th 1718
John Atkins the son of Joseph and Martha Atkins was Born at Eastham January ye 18th annodom: 1720/21
Uriah Atkins the son of Joseph and Martha atkins was Born at Eastham on ye 7 day of September: 1722
Hannah Atkins the Daughter of Joseph & Martha Harding† was Born at Eastham o[n] ye fourth day of april annodomini: 1726
John Molford and Jemima Higens ware Married the first day of November: 1699

[p. 88] Richard Walker the son of Jabez and Elizebeth Walker was Borne the first day of June: in the yeare of our lord: 1695
Rejoyce Walker the Daughter of Jabiz and Elizebeth Walker Borne the thirteenth day of may in the yeare: 1697
Mary Walker the daughter of Jabez and Elisabeth Walker was born at Eastham September the 14th 1699
Jeremiah Walker the son of Jabez and Elisabeth Walker was Born at Eastham May the 17th 1702

* "November" was crossed out and "December" interlined in the same hand.

† This is plainly an error of the town clerk, who began the entry "Hannah Harding" but blotted out the word "Harding," and then completed the entry as transcribed.

Joseph Treat the sonn of Mr Samuel Treat was born the nintenth day of November in the year of our lord: 1690
Joshua Treat the sonn of Mr Samuel Treat was born the sevententh day of March in the year of our lord: 1692
John Treat the sonn of Mr Samuel Treat was born the sevententh day of May in the year of our lord 1693
Nathaniel Treat the Son of Mr Samull and Elizebeth Treat was borne the fifteenth day of april in the year: 1694
Mrs Elizebeth Treat the wife of Mr Saml Treat dyed the fourth day of december in the year 1696: in the 44 year of her age
Mr Saml Treat and Mrs Abigaile Easterbrooke ware married the 29th day of august in the year 1700
Eunice Treat the Daughter of mr Samuel and mrs abigaile * Treat was Born at Eastham the twenty seventh day of September 1704
Robert Treat the Son of mr Samuell and Mrs Abigaile * Treat was born at Eastham the twentyfirst day of January 1706/7

[p. 86] Constant freeman and Jane Treat ware Marryed the Eleventh day of october In the year one thousand Six ninety and four
Robert ffreeman the Son of Constant and Jane ffreeman was borne the twelvth day of august: In the year: 1696
Jane ffreeman the Daughter of Constant and Jane ffreeman was Borne the twentyeth day of september In the year 1697 and Shee dyed the nineteenth day of february following:
Constant and Jane ffreeman had anoter Daughter named Jane born the fift day of march: In the year 1698:9:
Constant ffreeman the Son of Constant and Jane ffreeman was borne the five and twentyeth day of march: 1700:
Mercy ffreeman the Daughter of Constant and Jane ffreeman was Born the thirty first day of august Anno Dom 1702
Hannah ffreeman the Daughter of Constant and Jane ffreeman was Born the third day of May anno Dom 1704
Eunice ffreeman the Daughter of Constant and Jane ffreeman was Born at Eastham the twenty fifth † Day of November Anno Dom 1705
Elisabeth ffreeman the Daughter of Constant and Jane freeman was Born at Pamet the fourth day of febuary anno: 1707/8
Israel Doan the son of Israel and Ruth Doan was Born at Eastham the secund day of November 1701
Prenc Doan the son of Israel and Ruth Doan was Born at Eastham the 20th Day of march Anno Dom 1703/4
Elnathan Doane the son of Israel and Ruth Doane was Born at Eastham the ninth day of April Anno dom 1709
Abigaile Doane the Daughter of Israel and Ruth Doane was Born at Eastham ye 29th day of December Anno Dom 1706

* "Elisabeth" was crossed out and "Abigaile" interlined in the same hand.

† "Seventh" was crossed out and "fifth" written in the margin in the same hand.

Benjamin Snow and Thankfull Boorman ware Married : by Capt
   Sparrow June * 6 : 1700
Benjamin Snow the Son of Benjamin and Thankfull Snow was borne
   at Eastham the fifth day of february : 1700/1
Elisabeth the daughter of Beniamine and Thankfull Snow was Born
   at Eastham october the 10th † 1702
Stephen Attwood Junr and Martha Pike ware married : by Capt
   Sparrow the twenty sixth day of June : 1700

   (To be continued)

Mercy Walker the Daughter of Jabez and Elisabeth Walker was Born
   at Eastham the seventh day of November Anno Dominie 1704
Benjamin Young and Sarah Snow ware Married the fifteenth day
   of february : 1699/700
Thankfull young the Daughter of Benjamin and Sarah young was
   Borne at Eastham the twentyeth day of december in the year
   1700
John young the Son of Beniamin and Sarah young was Born at
   Eastham the 19th day of April Anno 1702
Daniel young the Son of Beniamin and Sarah young was Born at
   Eastham April the 4th 1704

[p. 89] James Cole and Hannah Childs were married the tenth day
   of January : In the years 168¾
Mary Cole the Daughter of James and Hannah Cole was borne the
   fourteenth day of September In the year one thousand six
   hundred eighty and four
Ruth Cole the Daugter of James and Hannah Cole was borne the
   thirteenth day of November In the year : one thousand six
   hundred eighty & six
James Cole the Son of James and Hannah Cole was borne the
   twenty fift day of november In the year one thousand six
   hundred ninety : and three :
Edward Knowls and Ann Ridley ware married the seaven and
   twentyeth day of february : 1699/700
Elisabeth Knowles the daughter of Edward and Anne Knowles was
   Born at Eastham the sixt day of october 1700
Thomas Knowles the son of Edward and Ann Knowles was Born
   at Eastham the first day of April 1702
Mercy Knowles the daughter of Edward and Ann Knowles was Born
   at Eastham the 16th day of November Anno dom 1704
Ann Knowles the Dafter of Edward and Ann Knowles was born in
   Eastham aprel 19 : 1707
Edward Knowles and the Widdow Sarah Mayo were married by
   Nathanael freeman Esqur febuary ye 27th 1711/12
Edward Knowles the son of Edward and Sarah Knowles was Born
   at Eastham on the third day of february Annodomini : 1713/14
Hannah Knowles the Daughter of Edward and Sarah Knowles was
   Born at Eastham on the twenty third day of June annodomini :
   1717.
Deacon Edward Knowles Died November 16th 1740
Sarah Knowles the wife of Deacon Edward Knowles Died the Last
   of february : 1753

[p. 90] Grace Hammilton : the Daughter of Daniel and Mary Hammilton was borne the third day of august In the year 1694 and
   dyed the twentyeth day of the same month
Thomas Hammilton the Son of Daniel and Mary Hammilton was
   Borne the first day of September In the year 1695

THE MAYFLOWER DESCENDANT

An Illustrated Quarterly Magazine

OF

Pilgrim Genealogy, History and Biography

1907

———

VOLUME IX

———

BOSTON

PUBLISHED BY THE

MASSACHUSETTS SOCIETY OF MAYFLOWER DESCENDANTS

1907

EASTHAM AND ORLEANS, MASS., VITAL RECORDS

(Continued from Vol. VIII, p. 247)

[p. 91] Jonathan : Cole the son of John and Mary Cole was borne the fourth day of october in the yeare one thousand Six hundred ninety and foure

John Cole the Son of John and Mary Cole was born the fourteenth day of october In the year one thousand Six hundred ninety and Six

Mary Cole the daughter of John and Mary Cole was borne the five and twentyet day of august in the year 1698

James Cole the son of John and Mary Cole was born the twentie third day of october 1700

Nathan Cole the son of John and Mary Cole was born the twentie-first day of Januarie 1702/3

Joshua Cole the son of John and Mary Cole was Born att Eastham the 20th day of march Annodom 1704/5

Moses Cole the son of John and Mary Cole was Born at Eastham the 22nd day of July annodom 1707

Phebe Cole the Daughter of John and and mary Cole was Born at Eastham the 29th day of october anno Dom 1709/10

Thankfull Cole the Daughter of John and Mary Cole was Born at Eastham october ye 20th 1712

Joseph Cole the son of John and Mary Cole was Born at Eastham the thirteenth day of october anno Domini : 1714

Thankfull Cole the Daughter of John and Mary Cole was Born at Eastham on the nineteenth day of october annodom 1716

february 17th 1731/2 then Mrs Mary Cole wife of Liutt John Cole Died.

Lift John Cole Died on the 13th day December 1746

Machiel Attwood and Prudence Rogers ware Married the 25th day of october : 1700

[p. 92] Nathaniel Atkins the Son of Nathaniel and Winnie Atkins was borne the twentyfirst day of november In the year 1694

Henry Atkins the son of Nathaniel and Winnie Atkins was Borne at Eastham the secund day of august in the year 1696

Bethiah Atkins the Daughter of Nathaniel and Winnie Atkins was borne at Eastham the fourth day of may : 1698

Joshua Atkins the son of Nathaniel and Winefred atkins was Born at Eastham in April anno 1702

Isaiah Atkins the son of Nathan'll and Winnefred atkins was Born at Eastham the twenty fourth day of febuary 1703/4

Elisabeth Atkins the Daughter of Nathan'll and Winnefred Atkins was Born at Eastham on the fourth day of January Anno dom 1708/9

John Snow and Elizebeth Ridley ware married the 25th day of february : 1700/1

Joshua Snow the Son of John and Elisabeth Snow was Born * the 22nd day of September Anno Dom 1701

Anne Snow the Daughter of John and Elisabeth Snow was Born the 17th day of July Anno Dom 1703

Elisabeth Snow the Daughter of John and Elisabeth Snow was born the 27th day of March Anno Dom 1705

John Snow the son of John and Elisabeth Snow was Born the 27th day of December Anno 1706

Zaccheus Higgins the son of Richard Higgins dyed the 22nd day of august anno Dom 1715

[p. 93] Joshua Higens the Son of Richard and Sarah Higens was Borne the third day of december In the year 1695 :

Eleezer Higens the Son of Richard and Sarah Higens was Borne the ninth day of febuary in the year 1696:7 :

Theophilas Higens the Son of Richard and Sarah Higens was born the sixth day of may in the year one thousand six hundred ninety and Eight 1698

Jediah Higens the Son of Richard and Sarah Higens was borne at Eastham the Eighth day of february in the year 1699/700

Zacheus Higgins the son of Richard and Sarah Higgins was born at Eashan Januarie the eleventh 1701/2

Esther Higgins the Daughter of Richard and Sarah Higgins was Born at Eastham febuary the 23d 1703

David Higgins the son of Richard and Sarah Higgins was Born at Eastham April ye 5th 1706

Ruben Higgins the son of Richard and Sarah Higgins was Born at Eastham January ye 6th 1708/9

Moses Higgins the son of Richard and Sarah Higgins was Born at Eastham march ye 24th 1710/11

abigaile Higgins the daughter of Richard and Sarah Higgins was Born ye 8th day of august : 1715

Thomas Doane and Patience Mulford ware marryed the 28th day of february : 1700/1

Thomas Doan the son of Thomas and Patience Doan was Born at Eastham the tenth day of Januarie 1701/2

*"at Eastham" was written after "Born," but was crossed out in the same ink.

Elisabeth Doan the Daughter of Thomas and Patience Doan was Born at Eastham the fifth day of febuary Anno Dom : 1703/4

Abigaile Doane the Daughter of Thomas and Patience Doane was Born at Eastham the twentyeigth day of March 1708

Ruben Doane the son of Thomas and Patience Doane was Born the twenty first day of march Annodom 1705/6

Benjamen Doane the son of Thomas and Patience Doane was Born at Eastham the twenty sixth day of December Anno Dom 1710

[p. 94] Martha Young the daughter of of Henry and Sarah Young was borne the twenty eighth : day of July 1695 :

Elizebeth Young the Daughter of Henry and Sarah Young was borne the eighteenth day of January : 1687:8 :

Reliance Young the Daughter of Henry and Sarah Young was borne at Eastham the third day of march in the year : 1699/700

Moses Young the son of Henry and Sarah young was Born at Eastham the fifteenth Day of november 1702

Thomas Young the son of Henry and Sarah young was Born at Eastham the twenty fourth day of october in the year 1705

Henry young dyed the 26th day of April in the year of our Lord 1706

Nathaniel Harding and Hannah Collins ware married march : 20th : 1700/1

Thankfull Harding the daughter of Nathaniel and Hannah Harding was Born at Eastham April 3d : 1703

[p. 95] William Cole and Hannah Snow ware Marryed the secund day of december in the year 1686

Elisha Cole the son of William and Hannah Cole was borne the twenty sixth day of January in the yeare one thousand six hundred eighty eight nine

David Cole the son of William and Hannah Cole was the fourth of october 1691

Hannah Cole the Daughter of William and Hannah Cole was born the fifteenth of december : 1693

Jane Cole the Daughter of William and Hannah Cole was borne the fourth day of January : in the year : 1695:6 :

Hannah Cole the wife of William Cole Died the 23rd day of June 1737

Steven Hopkins and Bethyah Atkins ware marryed the ninth day of april 1701

Thomas Mayo and Elizebeth Higens ware married the 3rd day of april 1701

Elisabeth Mayo the Daughter of Thomas and Elisabeth mayo was born the first day of may 1702

Thankfull Mayo the daughter of Thomas and Elisabeth mayo was born at Eastham the tenth day of Januarie 1703/4

Bathsheba Mayo the Daughter of Thomas and Elisabeth mayo was Born at Eastham the twenty seventh day of April Annodom 1705

Eliakim Mayo the son of Thomas and Elisabeth Mayo was Born at Eastham the first day of april : 1707

Sarah Mayo the daughter of Thomas and Elisabeth Mayo was Born at Eastham the twelvth day of June Anno Dom 1710

Sarah mayo above sd dyed July ye 27th 1711

Joshua Mayo the son of Thomas & Elisabeth Mayo was born at Eastham the twentyeighth day of may annodom 1712

Mercy mayo the daughter of Thomas and Elisabeth mayo was Born at Eastham on the 27th day of februarie annodom 1718/19

Hannah Mayo the daughter of Thomas and Elisabeth Mayo was born at Eastham on the eighth day of November annodom : 1724

Elisabeth mayo the wife of Thomas Mayo Junr dyed on the fourth day of November annodom 1721

[p. 96] John Rogers and Prisscillah Hamblin : ware Married the twenty third day of april : 1696

Timothy Dimock and Abigail Doan were Married by captain Jonathan Sparrow the seventeenth Day of march 1702/3

William Nickerson of Monomoy and Liddiah Maker were married by capt Jonathan Sparrow on the fourth Day of November 1703

Joseph Collens & Rebecca Sparrow were marryed by Capt Jonathan Sparrow the twenty fifth day of march 1703

Lois Collens the Daughter of Joseph and Rebecca Collens was Born at Eastham the twenty fourth day of November Anno 1704

Nathaniel Covel and Judeth Nickerson of Monanoy ware marryed the fivft day of march : 1696:7

Isaac Doane and Margaret wood ware Married the Secund day of december 1700

Isaac Doane the son of Isaac and Margaret Doane was Born at Eastham on the 25 day of July anno : 1701

Hannah Doan the daughter of Isaac and Margeret Doane was Born at Eastham on the 26th day of februarie anno domini : 1702/3

Jerusha Doane the Daughter of Isaac and Margeret Doane was Born at Eastham January ye 23d : 1704/5

Hulda Doane the Daughter of Isaac and Margered Doane was Born at Eastham on the 15th day of January : 1706/7

Isaiah Doane the son of Isaac and Margeret Doane was Born at Eastham on the third day of November annodomini : 1708

Margeret Doane the Daughter of Isaac and Margeret Doane was Born at Eastham on ye 6th day of march : 1710/11

Anne Doane the Daughter of Isaac and Margeret Doane was Born at Eastham on the 17th day of october annodomini : 1715

[p. 97] Micaiah Snow and Marcy Young wear marryed the Twenty fift day of November : 1697

John Snow the Son of Micaiah and mercy Snow was borne at Eastham the six and twentieth day of may : In the year 1700

Stephen Snow the Son of Micaiah and Mercy Snow was Born at Eastham the 19th day of may Anno 1702

Jonathan Snow the Son of Micaiah & Mercy Snow was Born at Eastham the sixteenth day of January Anno 1703/4

Phebe Snow the daughter of Micajah and Mercy Snow was Born at Eastham the seventeenth day of July 1707

Jesse Snow the Son of Micajah and mercy Snow was Born at Eastham the 27th day of october anno Dom 1709

David Snow the Son of Micaiah and Mercy Snow was Born at Eastham on the 30th day of october anno Dom : 1711 :

Mercy Snow the Daughter of Micaiah & mercy Snow was Born at Eastham on the twenty Sixth day of September anno Dom : 1713

Miciah Snow the Son of micaiah and Mercy Snow was Born at Eastham on ye 15th day of December annodomini : 1716

Ruth Snow the Daughter of Micaiah and Mercy Snow was Born at Eastham on ye 14th day of march annodomini 1717/18

James Rogers and Susannah Treasey wear marryed the seventeenth day of february : 1697:8 :

Mary Rogers the daughter of James and Susannah Rogers was borne at Eastham the tweth day of november in the year one thousand six hundred ninety and eight

Isaac Rogers the son of James and Susanannah Rogers was Born at Eastham december the 8th 1701

Susannah Rogers the daughter of James and Susannah Rogers was Born at Eastham the nineteenth day of January 1703/4

James Rogers the son of James and Susannah Rogers was Born at Eastham the secund day of may Anno Dom 1706

Abigaile Rogers the daughter of James and Susanna Rogers was Born at Eastham the third day of august anno Dom 1708

Thomas Rogers the son of James and Susannah Rogers was Born at Eastham october ye 21th 1710

Mr James Rogers Died Septembar 8 : 1751

[p. 98] Samuel Hedg and Grace Snow were Married the eighth day of december : 1698

Thankfull Hedg the Daugter of Samuel and Grace Hedg was borne at Eastham the nine and twentyeth day of august: 1699

Mary Hedg the Daughter of Samuel and Grace Hedge was Born at Eastham November the twentieth day 1701

Lamuel Hedg the son of Samuel and Grace Hedg was Born at Eastham the tenth day of January 1703/4

Elisha Hedg the son of Samuel and Grace Hedg was Born at Eastham the fourth day of febuary 1705/6

Elisabeth Hedg the daughter of Samuel and Grace Hedg Was Born at Eastham the fourteenth day of april Annodom : 1708

Lamuell Hedg the son of Samell and Grace Hedg was Born at Eastham the fourth day of march Anodomini 1709/10

Jabez Hedg the son of Samuell and Grace Hedg was Born at Eastham the thirteenth day of april anno Domini : 1712

Thankfull Hedg the Daughter of Samuel and Grace Hedge was Born at Eastham on the seventeenth day of april anno Dom : 1714

Samuell Hedg dyed on the nineteenth day of may anno : 1714

Mary Hedg dyed on the 17th day of may anno : 1714

Ebenezer Snow and Hope Hortton were married the two and twentyeth day of december in the year 1698

Susanna : Snow the Daughter of Ebenezer and Hope Snow was borne at Eastham : the Sixth day of february In the year : 1699/700

Thomas Snow the son of Ebenezer and Hope Snow was Born at Eastham the first day of febuarie Anno 1701/2

Ebenezer Snow the Son of Ebenezer and Hope Snow was born at Eastham the Sixteenth day of febuary 1703/4

Nathaniel Snow the Son of Ebenezer and Hope Snow was Born at Eastham the Seventh day of febuary anno 1705/6

Henry Snow the Son of Ebenezer and Hope Snow was Born at Eastham the Sixth day of January : 1707/8

Thankfull Snow the daughter of Ebenezer and Hope Snow was Born at Eastham on the twenty third day of July annodomini : 1714

Elisha Snow the Son of Ebenezer and Hope Snow was Born at Eastham on the ninth day of october anno Domini : 1716

Hope Snow the daughter of Ebenezer and hope Snow was Born at Eastham on the eighteenth day of November anno Domini : 1718
the rest of Ebenezer Snows children are recorded in the new Booke

[p. 99] John Yeats and Abigail Rogers were marryed the eleaventh day of January : 1698

Mercy Higgins the daughter of Isaac and Liddiah Higgins was Born the twentieth day of march 1697

Sarah Higgins the daughter of Isaac and Liddiah Higgins was Born the third day of august 1699

Benjamine Higgins the son of Isaac and Liddiah Higgins was Born at Eastham the nineteenth day of April 1701

Elkenah Higgins the Son of Isaac and Liddiah Higgins was Born at Eastham the tenth day of November 1703

Rebecca Higgins the daughter of Isaac and Lidia Higgins was Born at Eastham on the 10th day of october annodomini : 1705

Isaac Higgins the son of Isaac and Lidia Higgins was born at Eastham on the third day of July annodom : 1708

Hannah Higgins the daughter of Isaac and Lidia Higgins was Born at Eastham on ye eleventh day of September annodomini : 1712

Lidia Higgins the daughter of Isaac and Lidia Higgins was Born at Eastham on the third day of July annodomini : 1718

Rebekah Smith the Daughter of William and Hiphzibah Smith was borne at Eastham the thirteenth Day of february one thousand six hundred ninetie & eight alias nine

Liddiah Smith the daughter of William and Hiphzibah Smith was born at Eastham october the 13th 1702

Bethia Smith the Daughter of William and Hiphzibah Smith was Born at Eastham the tenth day of November 1708

Samuel Snow the Son of Ebenezer and Hope Snow was Born at Eastham on the fourtenth day of februarie annodomini : 1705/6

Aaron Snow the Son of Ebenezer and Hope Snow was Born at Eastham on the twentythird day of march annodomini : 1705

[p. 100] Thomas Cooke the Son of Richard and Hannah Cooke was Borne at Eastham ye Seaven and twentyeth day of april : 1697

Hannah Cooke the daughter of Richard and Hannah Cooke was Borne at Eastham January : 25th : 1699/700

Caleb Cook the Son of Richard and Hannah Cooke was born at Eastham September the 11th : 1702

Elisabeth Cooke the daughter of Richard and Hannah Cooke was Born at Eastham the thirtieth day of November Anno 1704

Sarah Cooke the daughter of Richard and Hannah Cooke was Born at Eastham annodom : 1707 on the 27th day of November

Deborah Cooke the Daughter of Richard and Hannah Cooke was born at Eastham on ye 22nd day of august annodom : 1710

Anne Cooke the Daughter of Richard and Hannah Cooke was Born at Eastham on ye 15th day of September anno Dom : 1712

Abigaile Cooke the Daughter of Richard and Hannah Cooke was Born at Eastham on ye 8th day of June : annodom : 1715

Thankful Cooke the Daughter of Richard and Hannah Cooke was Born at Eastham on ye 12th day of June anno : 1717

Mr Richard Cooke died Aprel 25 : 1754

Sarah Brown the daughter of John Brown was Born at Eastham in November Anno : 1690

John Brown the Son of John Brown was Born at Eastham the Seventh day of July Anno Dom : 1692

Hannah Brown the Daughter of John Brown was Born at Easham the first day of may Anno dom : 1694

Zebulon Brown the Son of John Brown was Born at Eastham the Seventeenth day of march Anno Domini 1696

David Brown the Son of John Brown was Born att Eastham the first day of may Anno dom 1699

Mary Brown the Daughter of John Brown was Born at Eastham in may Annodom 1704

[p. 101] Thomas Rogers and Sarah Treat ware married the 10th day of december 1700

Sarah Rogers the Daughter of Thomas and Sarah Rogers was Born at Eastham the twenty Seventh day of october Anno Dom 1701

febe Rogers the Daughter of Thomas and Sarah Rogers was Born at Eastham the first day of November Anno Domini 1703

Mary Rich the wife of John Rich dyed on the fourth day of January annodomini : 1722/3

John Rich and Mary Treat ware married the tenth day of december : In the year 1700

THE MAYFLOWER DESCENDANT

An Illustrated Quarterly Magazine

OF

Pilgrim Genealogy, History and Biography

1913

VOLUME XV

BOSTON

PUBLISHED BY THE

MASSACHUSETTS SOCIETY OF MAYFLOWER DESCENDANTS

1913

14

Mary Rich the Daughter of John and Mary Rich was Born at Eastham the fourtenth day of febuary Anno 1701/2

Robert Rich the Son of John and Mary Rich was Born at Eastham the twenty third day of october Anno 1703

John Rich the Son of John and Mary Rich was Born at Eastham the twenty third day of January anno 1705/6

Ruben Rich the son of John and Marry Rich was born at Eastham the sixth day of febuary anno 1707/8

Joshua Rich the son of John and Mary Rich was Born at Eastham the thirty first day of march Anno : 1710

Moses Rich the son of John and Mary Rich was born at Eastham July yᵉ 8ᵗʰ 1712

Roben Rich the son of John Rich above sd dyed in febuar in yᵉ year 171¾

and Moses Rich above sd dyed in february : 1713/14

Ruben and Thankfull Rich the son and daughter of John and mary Rich were born at Eastham on the thirteenth day of april anno domini : 1715

(To be continued)

51

Phebee Smith Daughter of John Smith junr & phebee his wife was born January 7th 1737/8

Ruth Smith Daughter of John Smith junr was born the 11th of July 1739

John Smith Son of John Smith junr was born the 17th day of november 1740

Betty Smith Daughter of John and phebe Smith was born june ye 23d 1743

Silvenos Smith Son of John and phebe Smith was born april ye 27th 1745

Heman Smith Son of John and phebe Smith was born December ye: 21th 174[worn]

Samuell Airie & Mary Mayo were married by Joseph Doane Esqur on the tenth day of march anno domini: 1714/15

oliver airie the Son of Samuel and Mary airie was Born at Eastham on the fifteenth day of September anno domini: 1717

Thomas airie the Son of Samuel and Mary airie was Born at Eastham on on Seventh day of may annodomini: 1719:

Joseph Airie the Son of Samuel and Mary Arey was Born at Easth[am] the 24th day of may annodomini: 1715

Ruth and Mary Arey were born in Eastham on the thirtieth day June annodomini: 1721: both the daughters of Samuel and mary Arey

Joshua ary Son of Samuel ary & mary ary was born 8th march 1722

Zelotas Ary Son of Samuel & Mary ary was born 31 May 1724

Paul ary Son of Samuel & Mary ary was born april 22: 1726

Elizabeth Collens Daughter of Prince collens was born the 24 of September 1737

Dorathy Collens Daughter of Prince Collens was born the 19 of September 1739

Abiel Collens Daughter of Prince Collens was born the second of october 1741

Mr Samuel Mayo and mrs Mary Sweat were married by Nathanael ffreeman Esqur on the 31 day of august annodomini 1727/8

Sarah Daughter of Nathaniel Rogers born the 17 october 1735

[p. 2] John Hallett and Mehitabel Brown were married by Joseph Doane esqur on the fourteenth day of march anno Domini: 1714/15

Joseph Smaley of Truro and Prissilla young of Eastham were married by Joseph Doane Esqur on the twenty fourth day of april anno Domini: 1718

Benjamin Mayo the Son of Theophilus and Rebecca Mayo was Born at Eastham on the twenty first day of July annodomini 1726

Theophilus mayo departed this Life october the 6 day 1763

Stephen King and and Abigaile atwood were married by Joseph Doane Esqur on the thirteenth day of october annodomini: 1715

Thomas Luis Senior dyed on the 19th day of march annodom: 1717/18

Thomas Mayo Senr dyed on the twenty Secund day of april anno domini 1729

EASTHAM AND ORLEANS, MASS., VITAL RECORDS

TRANSCRIBED BY GEORGE ERNEST BOWMAN

(Continued from Vol. IX, p. 14)

[Book marked " Births 1701 . 1781 " etc.]

[On 1st. index page] [worn] hannah born July 30 1729

Jonathan rogers son to James hanah rogers Born August 3 : 1750

Rebecca Linnel bo[rn] october 21 1763

Danel Coles Daughter Martha born april 24 : 1735

[p. 1] Joseph atkins the son of Joseph and Martha atkins was Born at Eastham on the ninth day of december anno Domini : 1701

Martha atkins the Daughter of Joseph and Martha atkins was born at Eastham November ye 9th 1711

Anne atkins the daughter of Joseph and Martha atkins was Born at Eastham on ye 12th day of december anno Domini : 1714

Thomas Snow the Son of Beniamin and Thankfull Snow was Born at Eastham on the Sixth day of febuary annodomini 1706/7

Susanna Snow the daughter of Beniamin and Thankfull Snow was Born at Eastham on the twelf day of November annodomini 1708

Rebecca Snow the daughter of Beniamin and Thankfull Snow was Born at Eastham on the twentysixth day of September annodom : 1710

Thankfull Snow the daughter of Beniamin and Thankfull Snow was Born at Eastham on the eighteenth day of Januarie annodomini : 1712/13

Jane Snow the daughter of Beniamin and Thankfull Snow was Born at Eastham on the fourth day of march anodomini : 1714/15

november 27 : 1755 then James Atkens and mary Cole boath of Eastham ware marraid by samuel smith Esq

James Linkhornew and Lidia Snow were married by mr Samuell Treat on the tenth day of febuary anno Domini : 1714/15

James Linckeloo son of James & Lidea Linkeloo was born 25 of may 1716

Lidea Linkeloo Daughter of James & Lidea linkeloo was born July 4 : 1718

Lydia linkernue the wife of James linkernue died march 18 : 1738

mr Israel Doane and mrs Mercy Sparrow were married by Joseph Doane Esqr on the 17th day of april anno Domini 1729

march 22 : 1756 then garsham Ryder of proventtown and Elesabath peirse of Eastham ware marid by samuel smith Esqr

[p. 5] Joseph Smith and Mary hopkins were married by Mr Samuel Treat on the twentyfourth day of June annodomini 1715

Aprel 1 : 1755 then simeon nucomb of Eastham and Expearnce Ary of Truro ware marraid by samuel smith Esqr

Jacob Hurd and Rebecca Higgins were married at Eastham by mr Samu[el] Treat on the eleventh day of august 1715

Barnabas harding was Born Desember 20 : 1726

Thomas Paine Jun and Alice Gross Both of Eastham were married by mr Isaiah Lewis minster february 22 day 1759 Entred by me Edward Knowles Town Clerk

[p. 6] Joshua Doane and Mary ffreeman were maried at Eastham by mr Samuell Treat on ye thirteenth day of october annodom : 1715

Ebenezer Baker and Hannah Higgins were married on the twenty ninth day of September annodomini : 1715 by Joseph Doane Esqr

Bartholomew ffish of Sandwich and Hannah Harding of Eastham were married by Joseph Doane Esqr on the ninth day of october annodomini 1716

Ebenezer Steward of Chatham and Ruth Higgins of Eastham were married by Joseph Doane Esqr on the eleventh day of october annodomini 1716

Joseph Sweat the Son of Benjamin and Sarah Sweat was Born at Eastham on the ninth day of february annodomini 1728

Benimin sweat the sun of benimin and sarah sweat was Born at Eastham Aprel : ye : 4 : 1739

Samuel Crosbie and Ruth Cole were married by Nathanael ffreeman Esq on the 21th day of November 1717 : *

Ebenezer Baker and Hannah Higgins were married by Joseph Doane Esqr on the twenty ninth day of September 1715 †

William Mitchell of chatham and Sarah Higgins of Eastham were married by Joseph Doane Esqr on the tenth day of april anno Domini : 1717

Joseph Burge of yarmouth and Thankfull Snow of Eastham were married by mr Samuel ozburn aprill ye 11th 1723

Joseph Collins Senior Dyed the 18th 1723/4 ‡

[p. 3] John Higgins and Hannah Mayo were married by mr Samuel Treat on the fifth day of august anno Domini : 1713

Hannah Higgins the Daughter of John and Hannah Higgins was Born at Eastham on the Sixth day of march annodomini : 1714/15

Bathsheba Higins the Daughter of John and Hannah Higgins was Born at Eastham on the 13th day of June annodomini 1718 §

Abigail Higgins the Daughter of John and Hannah Higgins was born at Eastham on the 25th day of october annodomini : 1720

John Higgins the Son of John and Hannah Higgins was Born at Eastham on the twentyfifth day of November annodomini : 1722

Robert Higgins the Son of John and Hannah Higgins was born at Eastham on the twentyfourth day of August Annodomini 1724

Ichabud higgins Son of John & hannah higgins was born in Eastham the 26 day of april 1729 entred ♀ Joseph Doane Town clerk

Jonathan Cole and Hope young were Married on the fifteenth day of febuary annodomini 1715/16 by Joseph Doane Esqr in Eastham

Elisabeth Cole the Daughter of Jonathan and hope Cole was born at Eastham on the twentyfifth day of December annodom : 1716

Jonathan Cole the Son of Jonathan and Hope Cole was Born at Eastham on the eleventh day of may annodomini : 1718

Hope Cole the daughter of Jonathan and Hope Cole was Born at Eastham on ye 10th day of January annodomini : 1720/21

Ruth Cole the daughter of Jonathan and Hope Cole was Born at Eastham on the 10th day of July annodomini : 1722

Dorcas Cole the Daughter of Jonathan and Hope Cole was Born at Eastham on ye 30th day of June annodomini 1724

Mercy Cole the Daughter of Jonathan and Hope Cole was Born at Eastham on the thirtieth day of may annodomini 1726

Nathanael Cole the Son of Jonathan and Hope Cole was born at Eastham on twenty eighth day of December annodomini 1727

Jesse Cole Son of Jonathan and Hope Cole was born in Eastham august 28 day 1732

[p. 4] Mary Snow the daughter of Benjamin and Thankfull Snow was Born at Eastham the eighteenth day of febuary annodomini 1705

* This entry has been crossed out.   See original page 14.
† This entry has been crossed out.   See original page 6.
‡ The month was omitted in the original.
§ "Thankfull Hig Hashaba" was crossed out, and then the entry was made as printed.

Seth Harding Son of Theoder & Sarah Harding was born the 17th day of april 1734

hanah sweat the Dafter of Beninin and sarah sweat was born at East-ham June : ye : 5 : 1743*

noah sweat the sun of Beninin and sarah sweat was born at Eastham march : ye : 31 : 1746*

[p. 7] William Meyrick and Elisabeth Harding were married in East-ham by mr Samuell Treat on the twentieth day of october anno-dom : 1715

William Merrick the Son of William and Elisabeth Merrick was born on the fifteenth day of January annodomini 1715/16

William Merrick the Son of William and Elisabeth Merrick was Born at Eastham on the fifth day of april annodomini : 1718

Betty Merrick the daughter of William and Elisabeth Merrick was Born at Eastham on ye 6th day of June annodomini 1720

Joseph Mayo and & apphia atwood were married at Eastham by mr Samuell Treat on the fifth day of april : annodomini : 1716

James Mayo the Son of Joseph and Apphia Mayo was Born at East-ham on the twelf day of august annodomini : 1716

Hannah Mayo the daughter of Joseph and apphia Mayo was Born at Eastham on ye 28th day of february annodomini : 1719/20

[p. 8] James Robins and Thankfull Higgins were married by mr Samuel Treat on the fifteenth day of april annodomini 1714

Joseph Robins the Son of James and Thankfull Robins was Born at Eastham on the first day of May annodomini 1714

Jonathan Sparrow the Son of Richard and Mercy Sparrow was Born at Eastham on the 17th day of December annodomini 1724

Richard Sparrow Senr dyed on the thirteenth day of april annodomini 1728

Andru walker and sarah Doane Both of Eastham ware married in Eastham By Mr Isaiah Lues Clar novembar 14 : 1754

Anna walker the Dafter of Andru and sarah walker was born in East-ham march 23 : 1756

nathaniel walker the sun of Andru walk and sarah walker was Born in Eastham november 25 : 1757

Joshua walker son of Andrew and Sarah walker was born in Eastham in July 11 day 1759

Sarah walker wife of Andrew walker Died may the 30 Day 1761

Sarah walker Daughter of Andrew and Sarah walker was Born in Eastham the 24 Day of may 1761 and Died the 14 Day of June 1761

Sarah walker Daughter of Andrew and Dorcas wases Born in East-ham october the 20 Day 1763

peter walker Son of Andrew and Dorces was born in Eastham the 28 Day of December 1764

andrew walker Son of andrew and Dorces was Born in Eastham october 5 1769 :

*The "4" was written over a "3", in both of these entries.

marcy walker Daughter of andrew and Dorces walker was born in Eastham January the 3 day 1771

John walker Son of andrew and Dorces walker was Born in Eastham 16 Day octobr 1775

Samuel Phinney of Barnstable and Bethya Smith of Eastham were married by Nathanael ffreeman Esqur on the 30th day of april annodom : 1713

Thomas Hambleton of chatham and Rebecca Mayo of Eastham were married by Nathanael ffreeman Esqur on the third day of may 1716

George Luis and Grace Hedg were married by Nathanael ffreeman Esqur on the 21th day of July annodomini : 1716

Joseph gorge and Easter Cloyes Boath of Eastham were marrid in Eastham By Mr Isaiah Lues Clar January 30 : 1755

[p. 9] Elisha Mayo and Hannah Linnell were marryed by Joseph Doane Esqu the twentieth day of febuary anno Domini : 1716/17

Benjamin Green and Anne Nucome were Marryed by Mr Benjamin We[bb] on ye 29th day of august 1727

Moses wile Jr and Ruth young Boath of Eastham ware married in Eastham By Mr Isaiah Lues Clar January 15 : 1755

Samuell Brown Son of Samuel

martha Brown Daughter of Samuell and Mather Brown was Born in Eastham the 9 day of may 1744

Bethiah Brown Daughter of Samuell and Martha Brown was Born in Eastham January the 12 Day 1746

Jonathan Collins and Susanna walker were Married by mr Samuel Treat on the twenty Seventh day of June annodomini : 1716

Beniamin Hamlin and anne Mayo were married by John Doa[ne] Esqr on ye 25th day of october annodomini : 1716

Dorkes Cole the Dafter of Benimin and Desier Cole was Born in Eastham July : ye : 5 : 1753

Stephen young and Abigail freeman Boath of Eastham ware marrid in Eastham by Mr Isaiah Lues Clar febuary 20 : 1755

[p. 10] Mercy Cole the daughter of Joseph and Mercy Cole was Born at Eastham on the twentyfourth day of September annodomini : 1716

Joseph Cole the Son of Joseph and Mercy Cole was Born at Eastham on ye eighteenth day of may annodom : 1718

Mary Cole the daughter of Joseph and Mercy Cole was Born at East-ham on the 30th day of april annodomini : 1721

william higgens and Abigail mayo Both of Eastham ware marid in Eastham By Mr Joseph Crocker Clark on Aprel 1 : 1756

Nathanael Smith and abigaile gross were married by mr Samuel Treat on the fifth day of october annodomini : 1716*

Mary Smith the daughter of Nathanael and Abigail Smith was Born at Eastham on ye on ye twentysixth day of april Annodom 1725

* See original page 58.

EASTHAM AND ORLEANS, MASS., VITAL RECORDS

(Continued from page 58)

[p. 11] Joseph Merrick Jun[r] and Elisabeth Twining were married by M[r] Samuel Treat on the twentyfifth day of october 1716

Ruben merrick the son of Joseph and Elisabeth Merrick was Born at Eastham on the 23[d] day of July 1713

Mary Merrick the Daughter of Joseph and Elisabeth Merrick was Born at Eastham on the last day of July annodomini 1717

Joseph Merrick Jun[r] dyed on y[e] 25th day of June annodomini : 1721

William Luis and Elisabeth Sweat were married by John Doane Esqu[r] on y[e] 13th day of october annodomini : 1719

Joseph higgens Jr and sarah Burgas Boath of Eastham ware marid in Eastham By M[r] Joseph Crocker Clark on march 18 : 1756

Joseph Higgins Son of Joseph and Sarah Higgins was Born at Eastham June 27 : 1757

Absulom Higgins Son of Joseph and Sarah Higgins was Born at Eastham August 22 : 1759 and Dide March y[e] 16 : 1760

Marcy Higgins Daugh of Joseph and and Sarah Higgins was Born at Eastham Febuary y[e] 15 : 1761

Absulom Higgins Son of Joseph and Sarah Higgins was Born at Eastham July the 20 : 1763

Sarah Higgins Daughter of Joseph and Sarah Higgins was Born at Eastham July y[e] 20 : 1766 Dide Jenuary 31 : 1767

Sarah Higgins Daughter of Joseph and Sarah Higgins was Born at Eastham March y[e] 14 : 1768

Joseph Higgins Died august y[e] 12 : 1768

William Brown and anne palmer were married by M[r] Samuel Treat on the Seventeenth day of December annodomini : 1716.

Israel Higgins and Ruth Brown were married by m[r] Benjamin Webb on y[e] Secund day of November annodomini 1727

Israel higgins Son of Israel & Ruth higgins was born the third day of october 1728 entred ℣ Joseph Doane Town clark

Jese higgins Son of Israel & Ruth higgins was born 26 June 1731 entred ℣ Joseph Doane Town clark

abigel Smith Daughter of Nathaniel & abigel Smith was born in Eastham the 15 day of november 1728 entred ℣ Joseph Doane Town clerk

mary Swet the Dafter of John and Ziba Swet was Born in Eastham march y[e] : 5 : 1755

Joseph Swet Sun of John and Ziba Swet was Born September the Third 1757

Barnabas Sweat and anna Sweat Son and Baughter * of John and Zibe Sweat was born in Eastham april 10 day 1760

(To be continued)

Ruth higgins Daughter of Israel & Ruth higgins was born the 5th : day of June 1733

June 8 : 1735 then Silvenis higgins Son of Israel higgins born

october 9 1737 then Lidea higgins Daughter of Samuel higgins wa[s] born

[p. 12] Isaac Pepper Junr and Elisabeth ffreeman were married by Joseph Doane Esqr on the twentyfirst day of february annodomini : 1716/17

Eunas snow the Dafter of Robart snow and marcy* snow was Born in Eastham January 15 : 1744

Bethiah snow the Dafter of robart and mary* snow was Born in Eastham november 27 : 1748

Marcy* Snow wife of Robert Snow Departed this Life the 4 day of october † 1771

Jonathan higgens ye 3 : and Sarah Combs Boath of Eastham ware marrid in Eastham By mr Isaiah Lues minester novambar 22 : 1753

John Treat and abigaile young were married by Nathanael ffreeman Esqr on the sixth day of December annodom : 1716

anna Sparrow daughter of Stephen and apphia Sparrow was born at Eastham on the 26th day of october 1747

Robart young and Joanna Covei Boath of Eastham were marrid in Eastham By Mr Isaiah Lues clar January 31 : 1754

willam Covel Died January ye 18th 1760 In the 88 yeare of His age

Recorded by me Jabez Snow Towne Clerck

[p. 13] Nathan young and Mary Merrick were married by Nathanael ffreeman Esqr on ye twelf day of august annodon : 1717

Enock higgens Jr and mary Atkens Boath of Eastham ware marrid in Eastham By Mr Isaiah Lues Clar febuary 21 : 1754

William Walker Junr and anne young were married by Nathanael ffreeman Esqr on ye 24th day of october : annodom : 1717

Susanna Walker the daughter of William and anne Walker was Born at Eastham on the fifth day of october annodom 1718

Prissilla Walker the daughter of William and anne Walker was Born at Eastham on the sixth day of march annodomini : 1719/20

Nathanael Walker the Son of William and Anne Walker was Born at Eastham on the seventeenth day of January annodomini : 1721/2

Hannah Walker the daughter of William and anne Walker was Born at Eastham on ye 25th day of September annodomini 1724

Anne Walker the Daughter of William and anne Walker was born at Eastham on ye 18th day of December annodomini 1726

Andrew Walker the son of William and Anne Walker was Born at Eastham on the twentyninth day of June anno Domini 1728

william walker son of william walker & Anne was born the fifteenth day of September 1730

* Sic.

† "Sepr" was crossed out and "october" interlined.

David Walker Son of william & Anne walker was born the thirty day of September 1732 entred ₱ me Joseph Doane Town Clark

Eleazor walker Son of william walker & Anne walker was born the 22d day of march 1734/5

[p. 14] Samuel Crosbie and Ruth Cole were married by Nathanael ffreeman Esqr on the twentyfirst day of November annodom : 1717

mr Josiah Oaks and mrs Margeret Haugh were married on the tenth day of November annodomini 1724 : by mr Nathanael Stone

Hannah Oaks the daughter of mr Josiah and Mrs Margaret Oaks was born was Born at Eastham on the nineteenth day of may annodomini 1725 : and dyed on ye twentieth day of June following

Joshua Doane Oakes the Son of mr Josiah and Mrs Margeret Ooakes was Born at Eastham on the Secund day of June anno domini 1726

urian Oaks the Son of mr Josiah and mrs Margeret Oaks was born at Eastham on ye 20th day of November annodomini 1728

Samuel Oakes Son of Mr Josiah Oakes & Mrs Margret Oakes was born at Eastham the 24th day of January anno Domini 1730/31 entred ₱ Joseph Doane Town clerk

Edward Tayler-Jarvis Son of John Jarvis and Ann Jarvis was Born in Eastham September the 9 1755

Thomas Cob of Hingham and Mercy ffreeman of Eastham were married by Joseph Doane Esqr on the fourteenth day of october 1717

Edward Hall of Harwich and Sarah Cole of Eastham were married by Joseph Doane Esqr on the 27th day of November annodom : 1717

John Smith of Chatham and Elisabeth Brown of Eastham were marryed by mr Benjamin Webb on ye 21th day of September annodom 1727

Jonathan Rogers and Elisabeth Cooke were Marryed by Mr Benjamin Webb on ye 18th day of January annodomini 1727/8

[p. 15] Stephen Sparrow and anne Mulford were married by Joseph Doane on the Seventh day of November anno Domini 1717

John Sparrow the Son of Stephen and anne Sparrow was Born at Eastham on the Sixth day of July annodom : 1719

Thomas Sparrow the Son of Stephen and Anne Sparrow was Born at Eastha[m] on the fifth day of february annodomini : 1720/21

Stephen and Elisabeth Sparrow the children of Stephen and An[ne] Sparrow were born in Eastham on the eighteenth day of march anno : I[worn]

Nathanael Sparrow the Son of Stephen and Anne Sparrow was Born at Eastham on the fourth day of march annodomini 1724/5

Richard Sparrow the Son of Stephen and Anne Sparrow was born at Eastham on the Sixteenth day of July annodomini 1727

Joshua Sparrow Son of Stephen Sparrow & anne Sparrow was born the 28th day of may 1730 entred ₱ Joseph Doane Town clark

Apphia Sparrow Daughter of Stephen & anna Sparrow was born the 18 day of July 1731 entred ℗ Joseph Doane Town clark

James Sparrow Son of Stephen & Anna Sparrow was born the 22 day of october 1735

William Dennis of Marblehead and Rebecca luis of Eastham were married by mr Samuel ozburn on the first day of November anno domini : 1718

Seth Clark of Harwich and Huldah Doane of Eastham wer[e] Married by mr Benjamin Webb on ye 14th day of february anno 17[worn]

Isaac Bacon of Province Town and Keziah Doane of Eastham we[re] Married by mr Benjamin Webb on ye 19th day of May anno domini 1728

Thankful Smith Daughter of Barnabas and Reth Smith was born 16 Day of October 1755

martha Smith Daughter of Barnabas and Ruth Smith was born July 6 : 1758

[p. 16] [Sarah Rogers the daughter of Nathanael and Elisabeth Rogers was Born at Eastham on the fourth day of April annodomini : 1717*]

Joseph Doane the Son of Joseph and Debora Doane was Born at Eastham on the first day of May annodomini 1727

Nathaniel Doane Son of Joseph Doane junr & Debro Doane was born the 23 day of march 1730/31 entred ℗ Joseph Doane Town clark

Samuale pierce and Ruth paine Both of Eastham ware marid in Eastham By Mr Joseph Crocker Clark on febuary 8 : 1757 [Nathan young and mary merrick were Married at Eastham by Nathanael ffreeman Esqur on the †]

Eldad atwood and Mary ‡ Snow were Marryed by Mr Benjamin Webb on ye 15th day of february Annodomini 1727/8 sarah Atwood the Dafter of Eldad and marget Atwood was Born Eastham may 8 : 1729

Benimin Atwood the sun of Eldad and marget Atwood was Born in Eastham febuary 21 : 1731

marget Atwood the Dafter of Eldad and marget atwood was Born in Eastham febuary 25 : 1733

Lydia Atwood the Dafter of Eldad and marget Atwood was Born in Eastham Aprel 5 : 1735

Deborah Atwood the Dafter of Eldad and marget Atwood was Born in Eastham June 6 : 1737

Jamimah Atwood the Dafter of Eldad and marget Atwood was Born in Eastham July 29 : 1739

*This entry has been crossed out. See original page 25.

†This entry has been crossed out. See original page 13.

‡This is plainly an error. The intention, on original page 214, gives the name as "Margeret".

[p. 17] Joshua Knowles and Sarah Paine were married by Nathanael ffreeman Esqur on the thirteenth day of march annodomini : 1717/18

Jesse Knowles the Son of Joshua and Sarah Knowles was Born at Eastham on ye thirteenth day of april annodomini : 1723

Rebecca Knowles the Daughter of Joshua and Sarah Knowles was born at Eastham on the twentythird day of may annodomini : 1726

Sarah Knowles the Daughter of Joshua and Sarah Knowles was born at Eastham march ye 10th 1727/8

Joshua Knowles Son of Joshua Knowls & mary * Knowls was born in Eastham the 27 day of april 1730 entred ℗ me Joseph Doane Town clerk

Simeon Knowles Son of Joshua and Sarah Knowels was Born in Eastham august 11 day 1737

Sarah Knowles Daughter of Joshua and Sarah Knowles was Born in Eastham June 3 Day 1732:

Josiah Knowles Son of Joshua and Sarah Knowles was Born in Eastham may 24 Day 1735

Susanah Knowles Daughter of Joshua Knowles and Sarah Knowles was Born in Easteham march the 21th 1740 Entred ℗ Jabes Snow Town Clarck

Sarah Knowles wife of Joshua Knowles Died July 12 : 1772

Mr Joshua Knowles Died may 27 : 1786

William Twining Junr and Apphya Luis were married by mr Benjamin Webb on ye 21th day of february annodomini 1727,8

December 28 : 1730 then Abigel Twining Daughter of william Twining junr & apphia was born

Thomas Twining Son of william Twining & apphia Twining was born the 5th of July 17[worn]

December 30 : 1736 then Ruth Twining Daughter of william Twining was born

William Twining Son of william Twining was born the 16th day of March 1737/8

November 4th 1741 then Elijah Twining Son of william Twining was born

Eliezer Twining Son of William Twining was born the 18th day of march 1743/4

William Twining Died the 17th of November 1769

[p. 18] Robert Young Junr and and Elisabeth Pepper were married in Eastham by mr Nathanael Stone on the third day of october anno domini : 1717 entred aprile ye 17th 17[worn]

Samuel Young the Son of Robert and Elisabeth Young was Born at Eastha on the twentieth day of December annodomini 1726

Robert Young the Son of Robert and Elisabeth Young was Born at Eastham on ye Seventeenth day of august annodomini 1728

Abigel Young Daughter of Robart and Elisabeth Young was born at Eastham December ye 3d 1730

*Sic.

Hannah Treat Daughter of John Treat was born the fourth of march 1719

Abigel Treat Daughter of John Treat was born 14 day of March 1721

Elizabeth Treat was born the 10th of May 1723 the Daughter of John Treat

Rachel Treat Daughter of John Treat was born first day of november 1725

Mercy Treat Daughter of John Treat was born the 13 day of march 1728

Serah Treat Daughter of John Treat was born the 23 day of october 1730

Martha Treat Daughter of John Treat was born the 17 day of March 1733

Phebee Treat Daughter of John Treat was born the 17 day of november 1737

Ebenezer Selew Son of Asa and Marcy Selew was born in Eastham on the 9th day of august 1745

John Selew Son of Asa and mercy Selew was born in Eastham on the 23d day of november 1746

Asa Selew Son of philip Selew died in Eastham on the 29th day of July 1747

[p. 20] Abigail Crowell the Daughter of John and Alice Crowell was Born on the third day of June Annodomini 1715

Jabez Crowell the Son of John and Alice Crowell was Born on the fourth day of June annodomini : 1717

Elkenah Higgins and Rebecca Allen were married by Joseph Doane Esqr on the twenty Secund day of february annodomini 1727/8

Treat mores Son of John mores and Susannah mores was Born in Eastham the fifth Day of December 1775

Phebe mores Daughter of Susannah mores was Born in Eastham February 5 Day 1778

Abia Harding and Rebecca young were married by mr Samuel Treat on the twentyfourth day of September annodomini : 1713

Isaac Harding the Son of Abia and Rebecca Harding was Born at Eastha on ye twenty Sixth day of September annodom : 1716

Ezekiel Harding the Son of Abia and Rebecca Harding was Born at Eastham on the twentythird day of June annodom : 1719

Josiah Harding the Son of Abia and Rebecca Harding was Born at Eastham on ye third day of march annodomini : 1723

Abia Harding the Son of Abia and Rebecca Harding was Born at Eastham on ye Sixth day of march annodomini : 1725

David Harding the Son of Abiah & Rebecca harding was born at Eastham the 28th day of July 1729 entred ⅌ Joseph Doane Town Clark

David harding Son of abiah & Rebeckah harding was born the first day of January 1731/2 entred ⅌ me Joseph Doane Town clark

[p. 21] Jonathan Snow and Thankfull ffreeman both of Eastham were married by Joseph Doane Esqr on the 16th day of october : 1718

Elisabeth young daughter of Robart and Elisebeth Young was born at Esthan on ye 26th day of August 1733

Silvenus Young Son of Robart and Elisebeth Young was born at Eastham on the 23d day of april 1735

Sineon Young Son of Robart and Elisebeth Young was born at Eastham on the 23d day of november 1738

Samuel Higgins and Thankfull Mayo were married by Nathanael freeman Esqr the 20th day of march annodomini 17/18

William Higgins the Son of Samuel and Thankfull Higgins was Born at Eastham the Sixteenth day of august annodomini : 1719

John Higgins the Son of Samuel and Thankfull Higgins was Born at Eastham the Sixteenth day of December annodomini 1720

Sineon Higgins the Son of Samuel and Thankfull Higgins was born at Eastham on ye Sixteenth day of January annodomini : 1722/3

Lidea Doane Daughter of Joseph Doane junr was born 25 of May 1741

Dorkis Doane Daughter of Joseph Doane was born the Second of November 1742

Salvenas Ary was Born in Eastham febuary : ye : 27 : 1726

James Stubbs & Sarah Cehoon Both of Eastham were married by mr Isaiah Lewis november 2 Day 1758 entred by me Edward Knowles Town Clerk

[p. 19] Christarn Remick and Hannah ffreeman were marryed in Eastham by mr Nathanael Stone on the tenth day of october Anno Domini : 1717 : entred april ye 17th 1718

Mercy Remick the Daughter of Christarn and Hannah Remick was Born at Eastham on ye 30th day of November annodomini 1718

Hannah Remick the daughter of Christran and Hannah Remick was born at Eastham on the twentyfirst day of march annodomini : 1720/21

Elisabeth Remick the Daughter of Christarn and Hannah Remick was Born at Eastham the Secund day of January annodomini : 1722/3

Christarn Remick the son of Christarn and Hannah Remick was Born at Eastham on ye 18th day of April anno Domini 1726

Daniel Remick the son of Christarn and Hannah Remick was born at Eastham on the Eleventh day of July anno Domini 1729

Isaac Remick Son of Christian & Hannah Remick was born at Eastham the ninth day of february 1732/3 entred ⅌ me Joseph Doane Town clark

Joseph Remick Son of Christian Remick was born the 21 day of march 1738/9

Sarah Remick daughter of Cristian and Hannah Ramick was born ye 9th of april 1742

Joseph Remick Son of Cristian and Hannah Rameck was born ye 8th day of June 1744

Experience Treat Daughter of John Treat & Abigel Treat was born the 25th of march 1717*

* "4" was changed to "25" and "1719" to "1717", both in the same hand.

Isaac Snow the Son of Jonathan and Thankfull Snow was Born at Eastham on the fourth day of february annodomini 1719/20

Experience Snow the daughter of Jonathan and Thankfull Snow was born at Eastham on the 31th day of may annodomini : 1721

Lidia Snow the daughter of Jonathan and Thankfull Snow was Born at Eastham on ye 22th day of october annodomini 1722

Elisabeth Walker the daughter of Richard and Joanna Walker was Born at Eastham on the twentieth day of September annodomini 1722

Nathanael Walker the Son of Richard and Joanna Walker was born at Eastham on ye eighth day of march annodomini : 1724/5

Matthew Walker the Son of Richard and Joanna Walker was Born at Eastham on ye twelf day of September annodomini 1727

[James Atwood the sun of James Atwood was born in Eastham August the 31 : 1715*]

thankful Atwood the Dafter of James and mercy Atwood was born in Eastham April 16 : 1741

marcy Atwood the Dafter of James and marcy Atwood was born in Eastham July 16 : 1744

James Atwood the sun of James and marcy Atwood was born in Eastham August : 31 : 1746

Jesse Atwood the sun of James and marcy Atwood was born in Eastham may : 1 : 1749

mehetable Atwood the Dafter of James and marcy Atwood was born in Eastham may 21 : 1751 and Died octobar 17 : 1752

mehetable Atwood the Dafter of James and marcy Atwood was borne in Eastham octobar 18 : 1753

[p. 22] John Taylor and Abigaile Hopkins were married by mr Samuel Treat on the third day of September anno Domini : 1713

Mary Taylor the Daughter of John and Abigaile Taylor was Born at Eastham on the first day of November annodom : 1714

John Taylor the Son of John and Abigaile Taylor was Born at Eastham on the 17th day of april annodomini : 1717:

Anne Taylor the daughter of John and abigaile Taylor was Born at Eastham on the twentyfifth day of march annodom : 1719

Abigail Taylor the daughter of John and Abigail Taylor was Born at Eastham on the fourteenth day of June annodom : 1721

Edward Taylor the Son of John and Abigail Taylor was Born at Eastham on the 24th day of april annodomini 1723

Abigail Taylor the Daughter of John and Abigail Taylor was born at Eastham on the Sixth day of october anno Domini 1726

nathan smith and mary freeman Boath of Eastham ware marride in Eastham By Mr Joseph Crocker Clark on march 28 : 1755 Entred pr Thomas Knowles Town Clar

July ye 8 : 1756 Jerusha Smith Daughter of nathan and mary Smith was Born at Eastham

October ye 3 : 1758 Phebe Smith Daughter of nathan and mary Smith was Born at Eastham

June ye 5 : 1760 Tamzon Smith Daughter of nathan and mary Smith was Born at Eastham

August ye 3 : 1762 Ruth Smith Daughter of nathan and Mary Smith was Born at Eastham

March ye 15 : 1763 Zoeth Smith Son of Nathan and mary Smith was Born at Eastham

May ye 15 : 1765 Gideon Smith Son of Nathan and Mary Smith was Born at Eastham

January ye 7 : 1767 Isaac Smith Son of Nathan and Mary Smith was Born at Eastham

George ward the Son of George and Rebecca Ward was Born at Eastham on the Secund day of November 1712

Mary Ward the daughter of George and Rebecca Ward was Born at Eastham on the thirtieth day of July annodomini : 1715 annodomini

Prissilla Ward the daughter of George and Rebecca Ward was Born at Eastham on the twentyeighth day of December annodom : 1717

Joseph ward Son of Georg and Rebecca ward was born at Eastham on the 8th day of october 1725

Elisabeth ward daughter of Georg and Rebecca ward was born att Eastham on the 4th day of march 1729/03*

Elisabeth wilcut born at Eastham on the 4th day of february 1725

[p. 23] Joseph Higgins Junr and Mercy Remick were married by mr Samuel ozburn on ye Eighteenth day of february annodomini : 1718/19

Jane snow the Dafter of James and hanah snow was Born in Eastham octobar 28 : 1743

Ruth snow the Dafter of James and hanah snow was Born in Eastham Septembar 23 : 1746

William snow the sun of James and hanah snow was born in Eastham novembar 18 : 1748

James snow the sun of James and hanah snow was Born in Eastham July 27 : 1751

hanah snow the Dafter of James and hanah snow was Born in Eastham July 21 : 1755

Seth Snow Son of James and Hannah Snow was Born in Eastham october 11 Day 1758

Zeviah Snow Daughter of James and Hannah Snow was Born in Eastham April 13 Day 1761

Susanah Snow Daughter of James and Hannah Snow was Born in Eastham march 6 Day — 1765

Hannah Snow wife of James Snow Died in July 12 Day 1766

William Norket and Ruth Mayo were married by mr Samuel ozburn on the fifth day of march annodomini : 1718/9

William Norket the Son of William and Ruth Norket was Born at Eastham on the twentyeighth day of December annodomini : 1719

Ruth Norket the wife of William Norket dyed on the fourteenth day of January annodomini : 1719/20

*Sic.

*This entry has been crossed out in the original.

hannah Norkut Daughter of william norkut was born the 20th day of June 1733

September the first 1735 then Experience Norcot Daughter of William Norkot was born

Abner Norkut Son of william norkut was born the 25th day of March 1738

Prissila norcot Daughter of william norcut was born the 14 day of January 1739/40

(To be continued)

EASTHAM AND ORLEANS, MASS., VITAL RECORDS

(Continued from page 76)

[p. 24] Jonathan Mayo and Thankfull Twining were Married by mr Samuel ozburn on the ninth day of april annodomini : 1719

Ruth Mayo the daughter of Jonathan and Thankfull mayo was born at Eastham on the Sixteenth day of march annodomini 1720/21

Hannah Mayo the daughter of Jonathan and Thankfull Mayo was born at Eastham on ye Sixth day of December annodomini 1721

Elisabeth Mayo the daughter of Jonathan and Thankfull Mayo was born at Eastham on the first day of September annodomini 1723

Rebecca Mayo the Daughter of Jonathan and Thankfull mayo was born at Eastham on the thirtyfirst day of may annodomini 1725

Theophilus Mayo the Son of Jonathan and Thankfull mayo was born at Eastham on ye Secund day of april Annodomini 1727

Jonathan Mayo the Son of Jonathan and Thankfull Mayo was Born at Eastham on ye Seventeenth day of March * annodomini 1728/9

february 4th 1731/2 then Thankfull mayo Daughter of Jonathan & Thankfull mayo was born entred ℗ me Joseph Doane Town Clark

April 13 : 1733 then Mary Mayo Daughter of Jonathan & Thankfull Mayo was born

[April 7th 1733 then Rebecka mayo Daughter of Jonathan & Thankfull Mayo was born †]

Ebenezor May Son of Jonathan Mayo was born the 9th day of ffebruary 1734/5

Constant Mayo Daughter of Jonathan Mayo was born 8th day of Aprill 1737

Jerusha Mayo was Daughter of Jonathan Mayo born 25 day of august 1739

Look Below for Deaths

Thomas Twining and Alice mayo Boath of Eastham ware married in Eastham By Mr Joseph Crocker Clark in in January 16 : 1755 Entred pr Thomas Knowles Town Clar

Hannah Mayo Daughter of Jonathan and Thakful Mayo Died may ye 16th 1767

Jonathan Mayo Died may ye 17th 1768

Thankful mayo Wife of Jonathan mayo Died 28 of august 1779

[p. 25] Elisabeth Rogers the daughter of Nathanael and Elisabeth Rogers was Born at Eastham on the tenth day of January annodom : 1718/19

Sarah Rogers the daughter of Nathanael and Elisabeth Rogers was Born at Eastham on ye fourth day of april annodomini: 1717

* "April" was crossed out and "March" interlined, in the same hand.
† This entry was crossed out.

Nehemiah Rogers the Son of Nathanael and Silence Rogers was Born at Eastham on the 31th day of october annodomini 1723:

Ruth Rogers the Daughter of Nathanael and Silence Rogers was born at Eastham on ye 31th day of July annodomini 1725

Jabiz Rogers Son of Nathaniel & Silence Rogers was born June 30th 1727

Temperance Daughter of nathaniel & Silence Rogers was born December 3 : 1729

Mehitable Daughter of nathaniel & Silence Rogers was born December 9th 1731 entred ℗ Joseph Doane Town clark

Sarah Rogers Daughter of Nathaniel & Silence Rogers was born the 17th day of october 1735

nathaniel Rogers Son of Nathaniel & Silence Rogers was born the 29th day of aprill 1738

Prince Knowls Son of Samuel Knowls the third was born the 30th day of October 1736

[p. 26] Joshua Cole the Son of Elisha and anne Cole was Born at Eastham on the ninth day of october anno domini : 1715

unice cole the daughter of Elisha and anne Cole was Born at Eastham on the twentyfourth day of November annodomini: 1717

Joseph Hatch Abigael Brown Jun both of Eastham were married by mr Isaiah Lewis march the 1 Day 1759 Entred by me Edward Knowles Town Crerk

Mary Crocker Daughter of Job and Mercy Crocker was born at Eastham on the 3d day of November 1748 and Died may ye 31 : 1755

Apphia Crocker Dafter of Job and marcy Crocker was Born in Eastham on the 22 Day of August 1750

marcy Crocker the Dafter of Jobe and marcy Crocker was Born in Eastham octobar: ye: 3: 1752

mary Croker the Dafter of Job and marcy was Born in Eastham Septembar 31: 1756

nathaniel Croker the sun of Job and marcy Croker was Born in Eastham June 30: 1758

Relianc Crocker Daughter of Job and Marcy Crocker was Born in Eastham June ye 9th 1760

[p. 27] Charles Luis the Son of Thomas and [*] Luis was Born on the nineteenth day of october annodomini: 1716

Thomas Luis the Son of Thomas and [*] Luis was Born on the ninth day of June annodomini: 1718

may 29: 1755 then David harding and sarah Brown Boath of Eastham ware marid in Eastham By Mr Edward Chever Clark

Daniel Eldridg of Eastham and Elisabeth Atkins of Chatham were married by Nathanael ffreeman Esqur on ye 31 day of January annodom 1727/8

Daniel Eldrig Son of Daniel and Elisabeth Elisasebeth Eldrig was born at Eastham on the 7th day of march 1729/03†

* Spaces were left for the given name of the mother.
† Sic.

Thankfull Doane the Dafter of Capt Elisha and hope Doane was Born in Eastham febuary 21 : 1745 and Died August 16 : 1747

Elisha Doane the sun of Elisha and hope Doane was borne in Eastham April 2 : 1747 and Died septembr 2 : 1747

hanah Doane the Dafter of Elisha and hope Doane was Born in Eastham febuary the 5 : 1749

Isaiah Doane the sun of Elisha and hope Doane was Born in Eastham octobar 27 : 1753

hope Doane the Dafter of Elisha and hope Doane was Born in Eastham march 24 : 1756

Elisha Doane Son of Elisha an hope Doane was Born in Eastham the*

[p. 28] Hannah Higgins the Daughter of Samuel and Mehittabell Higgins was Born on the twelf day of July : 1719

Ebenezer Higgins the Son of Samuel and Mehitabell Higgins was Born at Eastham on the twentyfirst day of July annodom : 1721

Martha Higgins the daughter of Samuel and Mehitabel Higgins was Born at Eastham on the Secund day of october annodom : 1723

Susanna Higgins the Daughter of Samuel and Mehittabell Higgins was born at Eastham on the third day of february annodomini 1725/6

Jonathan Higgins the Son of Samuel and Mehetabel Higgins was born at Eastham on the third day of april annodomini 1728

Samuel Higgins Son of Samuel Higins & Mehitable higgins was born in Eastham the Sixth day of august 1730 entred P Joseph Doane Town clerk

Eliakim Higgins Son of Samuel & Mehitable higgins was born the 21 day of January 1732/3 entred P Joseph Doane Town clark

may 22 : 1755 then Jabez Snow Jr and Elisabath Doane Boath of Eastham ware marid in Eastham By Mr Edward Chever Clark

Josiah Snow Son of Jabez and Elisabeth Snow was Born otober 17th 1755

Hannah Snow Daughter of Jabez and Elisabeth Snow was Born September the 10th 1757

Silvanus Higgins Son of Samuel and Mehetible Higgins was born 12 day of october 1736

Prince Higgins the Son of Samuel Higgins and Mehetible was born April 28 1741

Barshaba Dafter of Samuel and marget freeman was Born in harwich may 30 : 1738

Immanuel white of Barnstable and Martha Cole were maried in Eastham by Joseph Doane Esqur on the nineteenth day of august annodom : 1719

Elkenah Paine of Truro and Reliance Young of Eastham were married by mr Samuel Ozburn on the tenth day of march annodomini 1719/20

*This entry was left unfinished.

[John Crowell of yarmouth and experience Higgins of Eastham were married by Nathanael freeman Esqur february ye 25th 1719/20*]

[p. 29] Zacheus Higgins the Son of Benjamin and Sarah Higgins was Born at Eastham on the fifteenth day of august annodomini : 1719

Solomon Higgins the Son of Benjamin and Sarah Higgins was Born at Eastham the eighth day of September annodomini : 1721

Lois Higgins the Daughter of Benjamin and Sarah Higgins was Born at Eastham the Sixth Day of august annodom : 1723

Isaac Higgins the son of Benjamin and Sarah Higgins was Born at Eastham on the twelf day of July annodomini 1725

Freeman Higgins the Son of Benjamin and Sarah Higgins was Born at Eastham on ye twenty eighth day of July annodomini 1727

John Paine Senr and Alice Mayo were married by mr Samuel Ozburn on the third day of march annodomini : 1719/20

Hannah Paine the Daughter of John and Alice Paine was Born at Eastham on wednesday the eleventh day of January annodomini : 1720/21

James Paine the Son of John and Alice Paine was Born at Eastham on the Seventeenth day of December anno domini 1723/4 †
being tuesday

Hannah Paine the daughter of John and Alice Paine dyed on ye 28th day of January anno Domini: 1723/4

James Paine the Son of John and Alice Paine Dyed on the twentythird day of february annodomini : 1723/4

Thomas Paine the Son of John and Alice Paine was Born at Eastham on the Sixth day of april annodomini 1725

Alice and Hannah Paine the daughters of John and Alice Paine were born at Eastham on ye fourth day of December anno Domini 1728

Mr John Paine Dyed on the 18th day of October anno Domini 1731 entred P Joseph Doane Town clark

[p. 30] Joshua Higgins Junr and Ruth Twwining were married by mr Samuel osborn on ye 15th day of october annodomini: 1719

Sarah Higgins the daughter of Joshua and Ruth Higgins was born at Eastham the twentyeighth day of march annodomini : 1721

Zacceus Higgins the Son of Joshua and Ruth Higgins was Born at Eastham on the thirteenth day of December annodomini 1722 and Died the Sixth day of april 1726

Ruth Higgins the daughter of Joshua and Ruth Higgins was Born at Eastham on the fifteenth day of august anno Domini 1725

Zacceus Higgins the Son of Joshua and Ruth Higgins was Born at Eastha on ye eighth day of october annodomini 1727

Hannah Higgins Daughter of Joshua & Ruth Higgins was born at Eastham the eight ‡ day of March 1729/30

*This entry has been crossed out. See original page 30.

† Sic.

‡ "Sixth" was crossed out and "eight" interlined.

Joshua higgins Son of Joshua & Ruth higgins was born the third day of July 1732 entred ℘ Joseph Doane Town clark

William Higgins Son of Joshua & Ruth Higgins was born the fifth day of September 1734

Rachel higgins Daughter of Joshua higgins was born the 23 day of august 1737

Easther Higgins Daughter of Joshua Higgins was born the 7th day of february 1739/40

Levie Higgins Son of Joshua Higgins was born the 27 day of June 1742*

Prissila Higgins Daughter of Joshua higgins junr was born the first day of may 1743*

february David walker Son of Thankfull Brown and Grand Son to william walker was Born in Eastham february the 6 day 1759

Ebenezer Rogers of Harwich and Hannah Cooke of Eastham were married by mr Samuel Ozburn on the 24th day of march : 1719/20

John Crowell of yarmouth and experience Higgins of Eastham were married by Nathanael ffreeman Esqur on the third day of march annodomini : 1719/20

[p. 31] John ffreeman the Son of John and Thomison ffreeman was Born at Eastham on the 30th day of Janary annodomini: 1719/20

Mary ffreeman the Daughter of John and Thomison ffreeman was Born at Eastham the 27th day of march annodomini : 1721

Mercy ffreeman the daughter of John and Thomison ffreeman was Born at Eastham on the on the eighth day of may annodomini: 1722

Abigail ffreeman the Daughter of John and Thomison ffreeman was born at Eastham on the Sixth day of June annodomini : 1723

Joseph ffreeman the Son of John and Thomison ffreeman was born at Eastham on ye twentysixth day of January annodom : 1724/5

Gideon ffreeman the Son of John and Thomison ffreeman was Born at Eastham on the third day of may annodomini 1726

Hannah freeman Daughter of John & Thomison ffreeman was born in Eastham the 12 day of July 1728

Joshua ffreeman Son & Eunis ffreeman Daughter of John & Thomison freeman ware born in Eastham the first day of May 1730

Joshua ffreeman Son of John ffreeman and Thomison ffreeman was born in Eastham november 29th 1731

Tamsen ffreeman Daughter of John ffreeman and Tamsen ffreeman was Born at Eastham July the 3th 1734

Moses Bacor Son of Samuel and Deborah bacor was born in Eastham the 14th day of october 1727

Samuel Baker Son of Samuel and Deborah baker was born in Eastham December the 8th 1729

Isaac Baker Son of Samuel and Deborah Baker was born in Eastham Aprel ye 20th 1733

Deborah Baker Daughter of Samuel and Deborah Baker was born in Eastham august ye 8th 1735

*Sic.

Ebenezer and Thankful Baker Son and Daughter of Samuel and Deborah Baker was born at Eastham September ye 18th 1737

Sarah Baker Daughter of Samuel and Deborah Baker was Born at Eastham Desember ye 13th 1740

(To be continued)

EASTHAM AND ORLEANS, MASS., VITAL RECORDS

(Continued from page 164)

[p. 32] Medad atwood the Son of Stephen atwood Was Born at Eastham January y[e] 16th 1658/9

Mercy Atwood the Daughter of Medad and Esther atwood was Born at Eastham June y[e] 26th 1686

Abigaile Abigaile atwood the daughter of Medad & Esther atwood was Born at Eastham June y[e] 15th : 1689

David atwood the Son of Medad & Esther atwood was Born at Eastham on the 20th day of october annodom : 1691

Samuel atwood the Son of Medad and esther atwood was Born at Eastham on y[e] 20th day of march annodom : 1795 *

Esther atwood the Daughter of Medad and Esther atwood was Born at Eastham on y[e] 15th day of march annodom : 1699

Phebe atwood the daughter of Medad and Esther atwood was Born at Eastham on y[e] 9th day of June annodom : 1702

Nathan atwood the Son of Medad and Esther atwood was Born at Eastham on y[e] 27th day of June annodom : 1705

Williams Smith and Debora Walker were Married by m[r] Benjamin Webb on y[e] 3[d] day of october annodomini 1728

Ephraim Dean and widow martha young Both of Eastham were married by m[r] Isaiah Lewis on y[e] 31 day of January 1760 Entred by me Edward Knowles Town Clerk

[p. 33] Jesse Eldridg the Son of Elisha & Dorcas Eldridg was Born at Eastham on the ninth day of august annodom : 1715 †

Elisha Eldridg the Son of Elisha and dorcas Eldridg was Born at Eastham on the Seventeenth day of march annodomini : 1717/18

Mary and Dorcas Eldrid; the daughters of Elisha and Dorcas Eldridg were born at Eastham on the fifteenth day of march annodom : 1720/21

Phebe harding the Dafter of Carnelas and priseler harding was Born in Eastham Desembar 8 : 1742

* Evidently an error for "1695."

† The "5" was made over "4."

Joseph hardin the sun of Carnelas and prisile harding was Born in Eastham novembar 1 : 1744

presila harding the Dafter of Carnelas and prisila harding was Born in Eastham march 3 : 1747

Lucia harding the Dafter of Carnelas and prisila harding was Born in Eastham february 27 : 1750

nathan harding the sun of Carnelas and prisila harding was Born in Eastham April 8 : 1752

Carnelas harding the sun of Carnelas and prisila harding was Born in Eastham march 17 : 1754

seth harding the sun of Carnelas and prisila harding was Born in Eastham August 4 : 1756

Seth Smith and Anne Knowles were married by mr Benjamin Webb on ye 3d day of october annodomini 1728

David Higgins the Son of Isaiah & Anna Higgins was Born in Eastham August 13 1759

Richard Higgins the Son of Isaiah & Anna Higgins was born in Eastham April : 5 : 1762

[p. 34] John Hopkins the Son of Elisha and Experience Hopkins was Born at Eastham on the twentyniuth day of april annodomini : 1719 :

mary Cob the Dafter of nathan and Bethiah Cob was Born at Barnstable June 24 : 1737

nathan freeman the sun of John freeman Jr and bethiah freeman was born in Eastham Desembar 5 : 1744

marcy freeman the Dafter of John and bethiah freeman was born in Eastham July : 16 : 1745

betty freeman the Dafter of John and bethiah freeman was born in Eastham June : 1 : 1747 and Died Desmbr 7 : 1748

nathaniel freeman the sun of John and bethiah freeman was Born in Eastham January 7 : 1749

bety freeman the Dafter of John and bethiah freeman was born in Eastham septembar 23 : 1750

David meeker and phebe Couel Both of Eastham ware marrid in Eastham by Mr Isaiah Lues Septembar 10 : 1753

Grace Witheril the Daughter of John and Mercy witheril was Born at Eastham on ye first day of November annodomini : 1716

Theophilus Witheril the Son of John and Mercy Witheril was Born at Eastham on ye 30th day of January annodomini : 1719/20

William Witheril the Son of John and mercy Witheril was Born at Eastham in the month of march annodomini 1721/2

Lusana Witheril the Daughter of John and Mercy Witheril was born at Eastham on ye 20th day of august annodomini : 1725

Seth Smith Juner and Thankful Baker Both of Eastham were married by mr Isaih Lewis minster January 18 Day 1759 Entred by me Edward Knowles Town Clerk

Barnabas Smith the Son of Seth & Thankful Smith was born in Eastham Frebuary 27 : 1762

William Smith Son of Seth and thakfull Smith was Born in Eastham July 1 day 1764

Sarah Smith Daughter of Seth and thankfull Smith was Born in Eastham the 10 Day January 1767

Jesse Smith Son of Seth and Thankfull Smith was Born in Eastham 28 Day June 1769

Seth and Ebenezer Smith Sons of Seth and Thankfull Smith was Born in Eastham the 12 Day may 1772

Samuel Smith Son of Seth and thankfull Smith was Born in Eastham the 15 Day January 1775

[p. 35] Joshua Paine of Truro and Rebecca Sparrow of Eastham were married by mr Samuel ozburn on the twentieth day of october : 1720

Jonathan Smith and Thankfull Paine both of Eastham were married by mr Samuel ozburn on the twentieth day of october annodom : 1720

Expears Linel the Dafter of Jonathan and mary Linel was born in Eastham novembar 18 : 1748

Thomas Linel the Sun of Jonathan and mary Linel was Born in Eastham august ye 8 : 1750

Ruth Linel was Born in Eastham may ye 16 : 1752

Zeruiah linel was Born in Eastham aprel 26 : 1754

uriah linel was Born in Eastham febury 16 : 1756

Marcy Linell wife of Jonathan Linell Dide march ye 25 : 1760

Samuell Linell Son of Jonathan and Rachal* Linell was Born at Harwich march the 18 : 1764

Marcy Linell Daughter of Jonathan and Rachal Linell was Born at harwich apely ye 18 : 1766

Lettice Linell Daughter of Jonathan and Rachal Linell was Born at harwich may the 20 : 1768

John Snow the Son of John and Hannah Snow was Born at Eastham on the ninth day of february annodomini : 1723/4

Solomon Coomes and Content Mayo were married by Nathanael freeman Esqur on ye Secund day of february anno Domini 1725/6

Samuel Cooms Son of Sollomon Cooms & Content Cooms was born in Eastham the 18th day of December 1726

Sarah Cooms Daughter of Sollomon Cooms & Content cooms was born in eastham the fourth day of April 1729 entred ℙ Joseph Doane Town clarke

Elisha Bigfut and mary mayo Both of Eastham ware marrid in Eastham By Mr Isaiar lues July 10 : 1753

Dennis Collings Son of Michael & Rebecca Collings was born November the 30 — 1757

Fraces Collings Daughter of Michael and Rebecca Collings was born November the 19 — 1759

* "Marcy" was erased and "Rachal" written above.

Rebecca Collings Daughter of Michael & Rebecca Collings was born in Eastham march 12 1771

[p. 36] Samuel King and Abigaile Linnell Both of Eastham were Married by mr Samuel ozburn on the Sixteenth day of october annodomini 1720

Elisabeth King the daughter of Samuel and abigail King was born at Eastham on ye twentyseventh day of November annodomini 1725

July 23 : 1756 then asa mayo of Eastham and hannah Couel of harwich was married By John freeman Justis pease Recorded pr Thomas Knowles Town Clar

Jabez Snow Junr and Elisabeth Paine both of Eastham were Married by mr Samuel Ozburn on ye 27th day of october annodom 1720

unice Snow the Daughter of Jabez and Elisabeth Snow was Born at Eastham on the 30th day of November annodomini 1722

Elizabeth Snow Daughter of Jabiz Snow & Elisabeth Snow was born at Eastham the 12th day of January 1730/1

Jabiz Snow the Son of Jabiz Snow junr & eliabeth Snow was born June 19 : 1733

Joshua Snow Son of Jabiz Snow junr was born September 29 : 1735

Edwardard Snow Son of Jabiz Snow junr was born January 26 : 1737

Hannah Snow Daughter of Jabiz Snow junr was born July 28 : 1740

Deacon Jabez Snow Died the Six Day of Sepember 1760

Deacon Snow wife Died the Sixth Day of July 1772

Thomas godfree of Chatham and mary Couel of Eastham ware marrid in Eastham by Mr Iaiah Lues march 8 : 1753

Solomon Higgins and margaret holbrook Jun both of Eastham were married by mr Isaiah Lewis minster January 24 Day 1760 Entred pr me Edward Knowles Town Clerk

[p. 37] Nathanael ffreeman Junr and Hannah Merrick were married by mr Samuel ozburn on the Sixth day of april annodomini : 1721

Nathanael freeman the Son of Nathanael and Hannah ffreeman was Born at Eastham the ninth day of march annodomini : 1722/3

Elisabeth freeman the daughter of Nathanael and Hannah ffreeman was Born at Eastham on the twelf day of april annodomini 1725

Ruth freeman the daughter of Nathanael and Hannah ffreeman was born at Eastham on the thirtieth day of September annodomini 1727

martha ffreeman Daughter of Nathaniel and Hannah ffreeman was born at Eastham on the 28th day of february anno domini 1737

Susana ffreeman daughter of Nathanll and Hannah ffreeman was born at Eastham on the forth day november annodomini 1739

mary ffreeman daughter of Nathanll and Hannah ffreeman was born at Easham on the forth day of january anno domini 1742/3

Hannah ffreeman daughter of Nathaniel and Hannah ffreeman was born at Eastham on the Savententh day of December anno Domini : 1746

Barnabas young Jr and Anna mayo Boath of Eastham ware married in Eastham by Mr Isaiah Lues febuary 15 : 1753

Ebenezer Dyer of Truro and Sarah Doane of Eastham were married by mr Webb on the on the ninth day of June Annodomini : 1720

John Allen of Marblehead and Rebecca Doane of Eastham were married by Joseph Doane Esqr on ye 3d day of october annodomini : 1723

Eunis allen Daughter of John Allen & Rebecka allen was born in Marblehed the thirtyfirst of July annodomini 1725 entred pr Joseph Doane Town clerk

[p. 38] Hannah Snow the daughter of Ebenezer and Hope Snow was Born at Eastham on the fifteenth day of December annodomini : 1720

Bathshua Snow the Daughter of Ebenezer and Hope Snow was Born at Eastham on the fourth Day of october annodomini 1723

Ebenezer Snow dyed on the ninth day of april annodomini : 1725 *

Samuel Snow the Son of Ebenezer Snow Dyed on the tenth day of June anno Domini 1728

Nathanael Higgins and Elisabeth † atwood were married by Nathanael freeman Esqr on ye 26 day of february annodom : 1717/18

Nathanael Higgins the Son of Nathanael and Elisabeth Higgins was Born at Eastham on ye 12th day of february annod domini : 1719/20

Daniel Higgins the Son of Nathanael and Elisabeth Higgins was born at Eastham on ye 30th day of march annodomini : 1722

Enock higgins Son of Nathaniel & Elizabeth higgins was born the 5th day of September 1724

Thomas higgins Son of nathaniel & Sarah higgins was born the 13th day of april 1730

Nathan higgins Son of Nathaniel & Sarah higgins was born the 15th day of March 1730/1

Elifelet nickerson of harwich and mary higgens of Eastham ware marid in Eastham By Mr Joseph Crocker Clark on march 4 : 1756 Entred ꝑr Thomas Knowles Town Clar

Elisha Smith and Jennett higgens Both of Eastham ware married in Eastham By Mr Joseph Croker Clark in march 18 : 1756 Entred pr Thomas Knowles Town Clar

Josiah Smith Son of Elisha and Jennett Smith was Born in Eastham April 13 1758 ‡

Moses Smith Son of Elisha and Jennett was Born in Eastham march 31 Day 1760 and Died January 30 : 1761

the above named Josiah Smith Died in august 18 : 1762

Moses Smith Son of Elisha and Jennet Smith was born in Eastham January the 21 . 1762

Josiah Smith Son of Elisha and Jennet Smith was born in Eastham April the 30th 1764

* "1725" written over "1724."

† "Deborah" was crossed out and "Elisabeth" interlined in the same hand.

‡ "1758" was written over "1762."

Eunice Smith Daughter of Elisha Smith and Jennet Smith was Born in Eastham May 27 - 1766

Elisha Smith the 5 Son of Elisha and Jennet Smith was Born in Eastham the 5 Day of august 1772

[p. 39] John atwood and Thankfull Williamson were married by Joseph Doane Esqur on the twentyeighth day of September annodom : 1721

William Atwood the Son of John and Thankfull atwood was Born in Eastham on the fourteenth day of april annodomini 1719

John Atwood the Son of John and Thankfull atwood was Born in Eastham on ye 25th day of September annodomini : 1725

Mary atwood the Daughter of John & Thankfull atwood was born the 15 day of february 1723

Thankfull atwood Daughter of John & Thankfull atwood was born the 28 day of May 1727

Ephraim Atwood Son of John and Thankfull atwood was born Marct the 9th 1728

Timothy Atwood Son of John & Thankfull atwood was born July the 5th 1731

Simeon Atwood Son of John & Thankfull atwood was born november the third 1733

Ebenezer Higgins and Abigail Cole were married by Joseph Doane Esqur on ye 5th day of october annodom : 1721

Cornelius Higgins the Son of Ebenezer and abigaile Higgins was born at Eastham July ye 21th 1722

Experience Higgins the daughter of Ebenezer and abigaile Higgins was born at Eastham on the 23 day of march annodomini 1723 4

Asenath Higgins the daughter of Ebenezer and Abigail Higgins was born at Eastham on ye Sixth day of July annodom : 1726

Isaiah higgins Son of Ebenezor higgins & abigel higgins was born in Eastham the 5 of april 1727

Elkenah higgins Son of Ebenezor & abigel higgins was born in Eastham the 12 of november 1729 entred ℣ me Joseph Doane Town clerk

Ebenezor higgins Son of Ebenezor & abigel higgins was born the 26 day of June 1731 entred ℣ Joseph Doane Town clark

[p. 40] Thomas Gross and Jane Cole both of Eastham were married by Joseph Doane Esqur on the 7th day of December annodomini 1721:

Thomas Gross Son of Thomas Gross was born the 9th of october 1718 entred pr Joseph Doane Town clerk

Elnathan snow and pheebe sparrow Boath of Eastham ware married in Eastham By Mr Joseph Crocker Clark Desembar 4 : 1755 Entred pr Thomas Knowles Town Clar

Ebenezer Higgins 3d and Elisabeth myrick Both of Eastham were married by mr Cheever Clerk anno domi february 22 : 1755 Entred pr Edward Knowles town Clerk

Zobeth higgins Son of Ebenezer and Elisabeth higgins was Born in Eastham april the 8 Day 1756

Icabord higgins Son of Ebenezer and Elisabeth higgins was Born in Eastham august the 27 Day 1759

Joseph higgins Son of Ebenezer and Elisabeth higgins was Born in Eastham January the 9 Day 1762

tamesin higgins Daughter of Ebenezer and Elisabeth higgins was born in Eastham June the 12 . 1760

Cornelius higgins Son of Ebenezer and Elisabeth higgins was born in Eastham may the 30 . 1766

Ephraim higgins Son of Ebenezer and Elisabeth higgins was born in Eastham July 25 . 1771

lucy higgins daughter of Ebenezer & Elisabeth higgins was born in Eastham July 30 1768

Timothy Cole and Elisabeth Sparrow were married by mr ozburn on the fourth day of may annodomini : 1721

Timothy Cole the Son of Timothy and Elisabeth Cole was born at Eastham on ye twentyseventh day of august annodom 1722

Elisabeth Cole the wife of Timothy Cole dyed on the thirtifirst day of august annodom : 1722

Timothy Cole the Son of Timothy and Elisabeth Cole dyed may ye 4th 1722

Timothy Cole and Martha Almony were Married by mr Samuel Ozburn on the fourth day of September annodomini 1723

Apphya Cole the Daughter of Timothy and Martha Cole was Born at Eastham on the fifth day of october annodomini : 1724

Timothy Cole the Son of Timothy and apphia * Cole was Born att Eastham on ye twentythird day of may annodomini 1728 and Died in novembr 1752

Martha Cole the daughter of Timothy and Martha Cole dyed april the 25 : 1728 :

Martha Cole Daughter of Timothy & Martha Cole was born the ninth day of march 1729/30

Elizabeth Cole Daughter of Timothy & Martha cole was born ye 12 of July 1732 entred ℣ Joseph Doane Town clark

Jesse Cole Son of Timothy Cole & martha Cole was born 11 day of august 1735 and Died in Desembar ye 10 : 1753

[p. 41] Nathanael Mayo and Mehitabell Rogers were married by mr ozburn on the fifteenth day of march annodomini : 1721/2

John Mayo the Son of Nathanael and Mehitabell Mayo dyed on the 15th day of march Annodomini 1724/5

John Mayo the Son of Nathanael and Mehitabell Mayo was born at Eastham on the fourth day of october annodomini 1725

Abigail Mayo the daughter of Nathanael and Mehetabell Mayo was born at Eastham on ye eighteenth day of June annodomini 1728 and Died the 7th of october 1731

Mehitable Mayo Daughter of Nathaniel Mayo was born the 9th day of may 1732

Ruth Mayo Daughter of Nathaniel Mayo was born the 31 July 1734

* Sic.

THE
MAYFLOWER DESCENDANT

1620   1920

A QUARTERLY MAGAZINE OF
PILGRIM GENEALOGY AND HISTORY

VOLUME XVI

1914

PUBLISHED BY THE

MASSACHUSETTS SOCIETY OF
MAYFLOWER DESCENDANTS

BOSTON

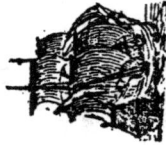

234

Look on this Side for two of Ebenezer Higgins Children
Abraham Higgins Son of Ebenezer and Elisabeth higgins was Born
  in Eastham February 3ᵈ 1773
David Higgins Son of Ebenezer and Elisabeth Higgins was Born in
  Eastham December 3ᵈ 1776
Samuel Doane the Son of Samuel and Thankfull Doane was born at
  Eastham on yᵉ Seventh day of June annodomini 1722
Samuel Doane and Thankfull Robins were married by mʳ Webb on
  the Seventh day of June annodomini : 1720
Priscilla Doane the Daughter of Samuel and Thankfull Doane was
  Born at Eastham on the 23ᵈ day of December annodomini 1723
Thankfull Doane the daughter of Samuel and Thankfull Doane was
  Born at Eastham on yᵉ 12ᵗʰ day of march annodomini 1726
Lidea Doane Daughter of Samuel Doane & Thankfull Doane was
  born in eastham the Seventh day of December 1729 entred ℔
  Joseph Doane Town clerk
Timothy Doane Son oſ Samuel & Thankfull Doane was born Seventh
  day of July 1732 Entred ℔ me Joseph Doane Town clark
Martha Doane Daughter of Samuel Doane was born the 18ᵗʰ day of
  august 1735
Mʳ Timothy Cole Died april the 24 Day 1760

(*To be continued*)

EASTHAM AND ORLEANS, MASS., VITAL RECORDS

Transcribed by George Ernest Bowman

(Continued from Vol. XV, p. 234)

[p. 42] Josiah Snow and & Elisabeth Snow were married by Mr Webb on the 20th day of october annodomini : 1719

Elisabeth Snow the Daughter of Josiah and elisabeth Snow was born at Eastham on the eighteenth day of July annodomini 1721

Josiah Snow the Son of Josiah and Elisabeth Snow was born at Eastham on the 18th day of September annodomini 1723

Mary Snow the Daughter of Josiah and Elisabeth Snow was born at Eastham on the twentyfirst day of November annodomini : 1725

Aprel : 1755 then samuel horten Jr and mary Cushing Boath of Eastham ware marid in Eastham By Mr Edward Chever Clark

abigaiel Horten Daughter of Samuel and mary horten was Born in Eastham July 31 : 1755

Cushing Horten Son of Samuel and mary horten was Born in Eastham September 5 : 1757

Susanna Horten Daughter of Samuel and mary was Born in Eastham february 24 : 1760

Lurane Horten Daughter of Samuel and mary Horten was Born in Eastham march 15 : 1762

Mary Horten wife of Samuel Horten Died July 1767

Thomas Cooke and Dinah Doane were married by mr Webb on ye twentysecund day of october annodomini 1722

Ebenezer young Son of Elisha Jur and bethiah young was born at Eastham on the 16th day of december 1732

Joshua young Son of Elisha young Was born on the 6th day of march 1735

Elisha young Son of Elisha young was born on the 4th day of february 1737

Eliezer young Son of Elisha young was born on the 2d day october 1739

Jams Young Son of Elisha young was born november ye 30th 1741

Heman young Son of Elisha young was born may ye 24th 1744

Edmond young Son of Elisha young was born July ye 2d 1746

[p. 43] [Thomas Hulker and Debora Brown were married by mr Webb on the 14th day of September annodomini : 1721*]

febuary 13 : 1755 then scarlet gills and mary snow Both of Eastham ware marid in Eastham by Mr Edward Chever Clark

tabethy Gills the Dafter of scarlet and mary gills was Born in Eastham fubuary 29 : 1756

Elisha Higgins Junr and Sarah Luis were married by mr Webb on the nineteenth day of october annodomini : 1721

Jane Higgins the daughter of Elisha & Sarah Higgins was Born at Eastham on ye eighteenth Day of february annodomini 1722/3

Sarah† Higgins the daughter of Elisha and Sarah Higgins was Born at Eastham on ye first day of May annodomini 1725

Elisha higgins Son of Elisha higgins jur & Sarah higgins was born the first day of november 1727

Edward Higgins Son of Elisha higgins junr was born the 15th day of october 1733 entred ℙ Joseph Doane Town clark

Joseph higgins Son of Elisha higgins jun was born the 9th day of february 1734/5

Abigel higgins Daughter of Elisha higgins junr was born the 29th day of July 1737

Abiel higgins Daughter of Elisha higgins was born the 29 of December 1740

febry 20 : 1755 then Ebnezar higgens Jr and Elisabath myrik Boath of Eastham ware marid in Eastham by mr Edward Chever

[p. 44] Simon Nucome and Lidia Brown were married by mr Webb on the fifth day of april annodomini : 1722

[Elisabeth smith the Dafter of maier Zoath and smith was Born in Eastham febuary ye : 6 : 1755 ‡]

Jonathan Grew & Abigel Cole Married the 12th day of October 1721 by Nathaniel ffreeman Justice Peace

Susanah Grew the daughter of Jonathan and Abigail Grew was born at Eastham the 17th day of December annodomini : 1722

Daniel Grew the Son of Jonathan and Abigail Grew was Born at Eastham on the nineteenth day of August annodomini 1725

Jonathan Grew the Son of Jonathan and Abigail Grew was born at Eastham on ye twentyfirst day of april annodom : 1728

James Grew son of Jonathan & abigail Grew was born the 25 day of July 1731 entred ℙ Joseph Doane Town Clark

* This entry was crossed out. See original page 47.
† "Mary" was crossed out and "Sarah" interlined.
‡ This entry was crossed out. See original page 143.

Abigel Grew Daughter of Jonathan & Abigel Grew, was born the 9th day of August 1733

[p. 45] Nathanael Bacon the Son of Thomas and Mary Bacon was Born on thursday the Secund day of august annodommini : 1722 :

Ruth Bacon the Daughter of Thomas and Mary Bacon was Born at Eastham on ye Seventh day of february annodomini : 1724/5

Sarah Bacon the daughter of Thomas and Mary Bacon was born at Eastham on ye twentyninth day of april annodomini 1727

Thomas Bacon the Son of Thomas and Mary Bacon was Born at Eastham on ye eighth day of November anno Domini 1728

Nathan Bacon Son of Thomas & Mary Beacon was born in Eastham the 18th day of march 1730/31 Entred ℣ ne Joseph Doane Town clerk & sd nathan Died 30 September 1736

Jonathan Beacon son of Thomas & Mary Beacon born the 5th of october 1734

Nathan Beacon Son of Thomas Beacon was born the 14th day of april 1737

Samuel Atwood and Hannah Doane were married by mr Benjamin Webb on ye 17th day of october annodomini : 1722

David atwood the Son of Samuel and Hannah Atwood was Born at Eastham on the nineteenth day of September annodomini : 1723/4

phebe walker the Dafter of John walker Jr and hanah walker was born in Eastham August : ye : 3 : 1745

william myrick Jr and phebe Smith was married by the Revrd mr Edward Cheever in Eastham on the 25 Day of march 1756

John myrick Son of william and Phebe myrick was Born in Eastham the first Day of april 1757

Samuell myrick Son of william and phebe myrick was Born in Eastham the 12 Day of may 1759

Joseph myrick Son of william and phebe myrick was Born in Eastham the 28 Day of June 1761

Elisabeth myrick Daughter of william and phebe myrick was Born in Eastham april 1 Day 1763

Phebe myrick Daughter of william and Phebe myrick was Born in Eastham february 7 Day 1766

Phebe myrick wife of william myrick Departed this Life the 15 Day of february 1766

[p. 46] Ebenezer Paine and Hannah Hopkins Both of Eastham were married by Joseph Doane Esqur on the 13th day of December annodom 1722

Ebenezer Paine the Son of Ebenezer and Hannah Paine was Born at Eastham on ye 26th day of November anno Domini : 1722

Elisabeth Paine the daughter of Ebenezer and Hannah Paine was born at Eastham on ye Seventh day of July anno Domini 1724

Nathanael Paine the Son of Ebenezer and Hannah Paine was born at Eastham on the 15th day of august annodomini 1727

Abigaile Paine the daughter of Ebenezer and Hannah Paine was born at Eastham on ye 29th day of June annodomini 1729

John taler and susanah higgens Both of Eastham ware marid in Eastham By Mr Joseph Crocker Clark on April 22 : 1756

his Children Recorded in the new Book

Joseph Smith Juner and Elisabeth Knowles Both of Eastham were married by mr Benjamin Webb october ye 18th 1722

moses Smith Son of Joseph and Elisebeth Smith was born at Eastham December ye 15th 1723

Sarah Smith Daughter of Joseph and Elisabeth Smith was born at Eastham August ye 25 : 1725

Elisha Smith Son of Joseph and Elisabeth Smith was born at Eastham December ye 10th 1727

Lidya Smith Daughter of Joseph and Elisabeth Smith was born at Eastham Aprel ye 29th 1729

Joseph Smith Son of Joseph and Elisebeth Smith was born at Eastham march ye 23 : 1731/2

Nathan Smith Son of Joseph and Elisebeth Smith was born at Eastham December ye 25th 1732

Eunice Smith daughter of Joseph and Elisebeth Smith was born at Eastham december ye 23d : 1738

Isaac Smith Son of Joseph and Elisabeth Smith was born at Eastham January ye 10th 1740

Joshua Smith Son of Joseph and Elisabeth Smith was born at Eastham September ye 16th 1743

Joseph Smith Departed this Life March ye 9 Day 1763

Elisabeth Smith his wife Died march ye 6 Day 1761

[p. 47] Thomas Hulker and Debora Brown were married by mr Benjamin Webb on ye fourteenth day of September annodom 1721

Thomas Hulker the Son of Thomas and debora Hulker was Born at Eastham on ye third day of December annodomini : 1722

Robert Mayo and Debora Strout both of Eastham were married by mr Benjamin Webb on ye 30th day of January annodomini : 1722/3

Elifelet morse of falmoth in Casco Bay and martha mayo of Eastham ware marid in Eastham By Mr Joseph Crocker Clark on June 27 : 1757 Entred pr Thomas Knowles Town Clar

Thankful Harding Daugter of Samuel and content Hardin was born at Eastham on ye 25th day of June 1741

Elisabath Harding dauhter of Samuel and Content Harding was born at Eastham on the 8th day of august 1743

Lusia Harding Daughter of Samuel and content Harding was born at Eastham on ye 7th day of may 1746

Rebaca harding the Dafter of samuel and Content harding was born in Eastham novembar ye 29 : 1748

samuel harding the sun of samuel and Content harding was born in Eastham August : ye : 16 : 1751

Barnabas harding the sun of samuel and Content harding was Born in Eastham may 13 : 1755

Theodore harding and martha sears Both of Eastham ware marid in Eastham By Mr Joseph Crocker Clark on may 13 : 1756

Sarah harding Daughter of theoder and martha harding was born in Eastham Desmber 22 : 175[worn]

chloe harding Daughter of theoder and martha harding was born in Eastham augst 3 : 1758

Josiah harding Son of theoder and matha harding was born in Eastham october 15 : 1760

[p. 48] Lidia Mayo the daughter of Judah and Mary Mayo was Born at Eastham on the twentythird day of January annodomini: 1722/3

Timethy higgens the sun of freeman and martha higgens was Born in Eastham march 28 : 1749

Apphiah higgens the Dafter of freeman and martha higgens was Born in Eastham octobar 1 : 1752

Williams Smith & Dorcas Doane Both of Eastham were married by mr Benjamin Webb on ye 31th day of January annodomini: 1722/3

Dorcas Smith the wife of Williams Smith Dyed on the 12th day of march annodomini : 1726/7

Dorcas Smith the Daughter of Williams and Dorcas Smith was born at Eastham on ye twentyseventh day of march anno Domini : 1723/4

Experience Smith the Daughter of Williams and Dorcas Smith was born at Eastham on ye 20th day of May anno Domini : 1725

Samuel Smith the Son of Williams and Dorcas Smith was born at Eastham on ye twentieth day of february annodomini 1726/7

Anne Smith Daughter of Williams Smith was born 27 day of September 1733

Ebnezar yound* and Elisabeth myrick Both of Eastham ware marriade in Eastham By Mr Joseph Crocker Clark on novembar 28 : 1754   Entred pr Thomas Knowles Town Clar

[p. 49] Dorcas Sparrow the daughter of Jonathan and Dorcas Sparrow was Born at Eastham on ye 4th day of october annodomini : 1722

Jonathan Sparrow the Son of Jonathan and dorcas Sparrow was born at Eastham on the Second day of february annodomini 1725/6

Benjamin Sparrow the Son of Jonathan and Dorcas Sparrow was Born at Eastham on the Seventh day of october annodomini 1727

Isaac Sparrow the Son of Jonathan & Dorkis Sparrow was born in Eastham the 26 day of november 1730 entred ℙ Joseph Doane Town clerk.

Joshua Sparrow Son of Jonathan Sparrow junr was born September 4th 1735

Phebee Sparrow Daughter of Jonathan Sparrow junr was born the 3rd day of January 1737/8

Sollomon Sparrow Son of Jonathan Sparrow was born the 14 day of february 1739/40

Thomas Lamkin and Debora Nucome were married by John Doane Esqur on ye 28th day of January : 1719

Lydia linkernue the Dafter of James and Rebaca linkernue was Born in Eastham novambar 7 : 1740

*Young. See Intentions, original page 190.

Rebaca linkernue the Dafter of James and Rebaca linkernue was Born in Eastham July 26 : 1743

Joseph linkernue the sun of James and Rebaca linkernue was Born in Eastham Septembar 21 : 1745

James linkernue the sun of James and Rebaca linkernue was Born in Eastham August 26 : 1748

Josiah linkernue the sun of James and Rebaca linkernu[e] was Born in Eastham July : 16 : 1750

Ruth linkernue the Dafter of James and Rebaca linkernue was Born in Eastham Desembr 22 : 1752

suzanah linkernue the Dafter of James and Rebaca linkernu[e] was Born in Eastham July 26 : 1755

[p. 50] Richard Rich and and Hannah Doane were married by John Doane Esqur on the twentyeighth day of July annodomini : 1720

June 2 : 1757 then James Cohoon Jr and thankfull wiley Both of Eastham ware marrid in Eastham By Mr Isaiah Lues minester Recorded pr Thomas Knowles Town Clar

Thomas Thatcher and Sarah Rich were married in Eastham by John Doane Justice Peace November ye 11th 1720 Recorded ℙ John Paine Town clerk

william Chipman and martha treet Boath of Eastham ware marrid in Eastham by mr Isaiah Lues minastar in January 25 : 1753 Recorded pr Thomas Knowles Town Clark

marcy Cipman the Dafter of william and martha Cipman was Born in Eastham march 30 : 1754

mary Cipman the Dafter of william and marther Cipman was Born in Eastham septembar 1 : 1756

[p. 51] Luke Stubbs and mary Nucome were married by John Doane Esqur on the eleventh day of april annodomini 1723

June 2 : 1757 then fulk Dyer of Truro and Elisabath Atkens of Eastham ware married in Eastham by mr Isaiah Lues minestor Recorded pr Thomas Knowles Town Clar

Benjamin Snow and Martha Eldridg were married by mr Benjamin Webb august ye 7th 1723

Elizabeth Linel Daughter of Jonathan Linel was born the 22 day of July 1728

Thomas Linel Son of Jonathan Linel was born the Second day of June 1730

Serah Linel Daughter of Jonathan Linel was born 28d of april 1733

Heman Linel Son of Jonathan Linel was born the third day of September 1735

Elisha Linel Son of Jonathan Linel was born march the 8 : 1738

Abigel Linel Daughter of Jonathan Linel was born the 9th of june 1741

hannah Linel the Dafter of Jonathan linel was Born in Eastham febuary 14 : 1744

[p. 52] Elijah Hamlin the Son of Elisha and Elisabeth Hamlin was born at Eastham on the twentysecund day of march annodomini : 1722/3

[Richard Atwood the sun of Elezar Atwood was born in Eastham march 31 : 1718*]

marcy atwood the Dafter of Richard and mary Atwood was born in Eastham August : 16 : 1749

Luse Atwood the Dafter of Richard and mary Atwood was born in Eastham August : 7 : 1751

Jonathan Doane and Martha Higgins were married by mr Benjamin Webb august ye 8th 1723

Elisha Doane the sun of Jonathan and martha Doane was born in Eastham novembar ye : 25 : 1724

hanah Doane the Dafter of Jonathan and martha Doane was born in Eastham August 25 : 1726

James Doane the sun of Jonathan and martha Doane was borne in Eastham march : ye : 11 : 1728

Dorthey Doane the Darfter of Jonathan and martha Doane was born in Eastham octobar : ye : 8 : 1731

Elisabath Doane the Dufter of Jonathan and martha Doane was borne in Eastham march : ye : 7 : 1733

Jesse Doane the sun of Jonathan and martha Doane was born in Eastham febuary : ye : 2 : 1735

Seth Doane the sun of Jonathan and martha Doane was born in Eastham march : ye : 2 : 1737

Silvanus Doane the sun of Jonathan and martha Doane was born in Eastham July : ye : 4 : 1740

nathan Doane the sun of Jonathan and martha Doane was born in Eastham January : 31 : 1742/3

[p. 53] Eliezer Hamlin the Son of Eliezer and Sarah Hamlin was Born on the twentyfourth day of may annodom : 1723

Joanah† Atwood the Dafter of Elezar and Rebaca Atwood was born in Eastham Desembar 14●1736

Elezar Atwood the sun of Elezer and Rebaca Atwood was born in Eastham Aprel 18 : 1739

Joshua Atwood the sun of Elezar and Rebaca Atwood was born in Eastham may 21 : 1742

barnabas Atwood the sun of Elezar and Rebaca Atwood was born in Eastham octobar 18 : 1744

Rebaca Atwood the Dafter of Elezar and Rebaca Atwood was born in Eastham July 21 : 1747

nathaniel Atwood the sun of Elezar and Rebaca Atwood was born in Eastham septembar 16 : 1749

stephen Atwood the sun of Elezar and Rebaca Atwood was born in Eastham Desembar 3 : 1751

Deliveranc Atwood the Dafter of Elezar and Rebaca Atwood was Born in Eastham Aprel 19 : 1755

William Mayo and Hannah Snow were married by mr Benjamin Webb on ye 15th day of august annodomini : 1723

*This entry has been crossed out.

† "James" was crossed out and "Joanah" interlined in the same hand.

Elisha Mayo the Son of William and Hannah Mayo was born at Eastham on ye eighth day of September anno Domini 1724

hanah mayo the Dafter of william and hanah mayo was born in Eastham on the : 1 : of January 1731

mary mayo Dafter of william and hannah mayo was born in Eastham on the : 24 : may 1738

william mayo Departed this in april 1775

[p. 54] Richard Sparrow Junr and Hannah Shaw were married by Joseph Doane Esqur on ye 26th day of September annodom : 1723

Isaac Sparrow the Son of Richard and Hannah Sparrow was born at Eastham on ye fourth day of april annodomini 1725

Rebecca Sparrow the Daughter of Richard and hannah Sparrow was Born at Eastham on ye twenty Seventh day of January annodomini 1726/7

Hannah Sparrow Daughter of Richard Sparrow & hannah Sparrow was born the 5th day of March 1730/31 sd hannah Sparrow Died the 26 day of august 1736 entred P Joseph Doane Town clark

Hannah Sparrow Daughter of Richard Sparrow was born the Seventh day of august 1737

Mercy Sparrow Daughter of Richard Sparrow was born the 27th day of June 1739

gorge sesocks negro and hester hunt bouth of Eastham ware marrid in Eastham by mr Isaiah Lues minestar in febuary 7 : 1752 Recorded pr Thomas Knowles Town Clar

Seth Knowles and Martha Remick were married by mr Benjamin Webb on the 3d day of october annodomini : 1723

william wethrel and mary Brown boath of Eastham ware marrid in Eastham by mr Isaiah Lues minestar in novembr 16 : 1752 Recorded pr Thomas Knowles Town Clar

John wethrel sun of william and mary wethrel was Born in Eastham octobar 25 : 1753

hanah wethrel the Dafter of william and mary wethrel was Born in Eastham Aprel 2 : 1756

william withrel Son of william withrel and mary was Born in Eastham october 25 Day 1758

Theophilus withrel Son of william and mary withrel was Born in Eastham march* 16 Day 1761

Joseph Rich Son of Joseph Rich Born of mercy Brown in Eastham September 21 Day 1739

peter Nucomb Son of Simon and mercy Nucomb was Born in Eastham July 17 Day 1748

[p. 55] Joshua Brown and Rebecca Rich were married by Nathanael freeman Esqur on ye 18th day of april annodomini : 1723

Joshua Brown the Son of Joshua and Rebecca Brown was Born at Eastham on the twelf day of may annodomini : 1723

Knowles Brown the Son of Joshua and Rebecca Brown was Born at Eastham on the twelf day of December Annodomini : 1724

* "September" was crossed out and "March" interlined in the same hand.

Thankfull Brown daughter of Joshua and Rebecka Brown was born Eastham on the 10th day of march 1736/7

Cornelius Knowles and Elisabeth Remick were married by mr Benjamin Webb on the 31rt day of october annodomini : 1723

samuel coombs and Thankful Atkens boath of Eastham ware marrid in Eastham by mr Isaiah Lues in January 29 : 1752 Recorded pr Thomas Knowles Town Clar

Nathaniel Covell Son of Ruben and Hannah maker was Born in Eastham December 24 Day 1755 *

Ruben Covell Son of Ruben and hannah Covell was Born in Eastham the 23 Day of february 1761 *

[p. 56] John Cutler and Sarah Smith were married on the tenth day of april 1723 by Nathanael ffreeman Esqur

Sarah Cutler the wife of John Cutler dyed on the 17th day of July 1725

Joseph Higgins the Son of Elisha and Jane Higgins was Born at Eastham on ye [†] day of [†] annodomini : 1717

Ruth Higgins the daughter of Elisha and Jane Higgins was Born at Eastham on ye [†] day of [†] annodomini : 1719

Barnabas Higgins the Son of Elisha & Jane Higgins was Born at Eastham on the [†] day of [†] annodomini : 1722

Phillip Higgins the Son of Elisha and Jane Higgins was Born at Eastham on ye fourth day of march annodomini : 1724/5

January 23 : 1755 then Edward snow and martha Brown Boath of Eastham ware marid in Eastham By mr Edward Chever Clar

Thankful Snow Daughter of Edward and marther Snow was Born in Eastham october 14 1757

Elezabeth Snow Daughter of Edward and marther Snow was Born in Eastham January 3 day 1766

John Mulford and Mercy Harris were married by Mr Benjamin Webb on the 25th day of December annodomini : 1723

Jemima Mulford the daughter of John and Mercy Mulford was Born at Eastham on ye Sixth day of December Annodomini : 1724

Mercy Mulford the daughter of John and Mercy Mulford was Born at Eastham on ye third day of febuary annodomini 1725/6

John Mulford Son of John & Marcy Mulford was born at Eastham the 28th day of april 1728

John Mulford Died the 21 day of april 1730 entred ℙ Joseph Doane Town clerk

febuary 13 : 1755 then John Atwood and abigail freeman Boath of Eastham ware maried in Eastham By mr Edward Chever Clar

mary atwod Daughter of John and Abagel atwood was Born in Eastham September the 26 : 1756

John atwood son of John and abagal Atwod was Born in Eastham august 21rt 1758 and Died the 28 of of august 1759 Recorded by Jabez Snow Town Clerck

(To be continued)

* These entries have been crossed out.   See original page 65.

† Spaces were left for the month and day.

EASTHAM AND ORLEANS, MASS., VITAL RECORDS

(Continued from page 34)

[p. 57] Barnabas young and Rebecca † were married by Nathanael ffreeman Esqr on ye 27 day of august annodomini : 1713

Nathanael young the son of Barnabas and Rebecca young was Born at Eastham on the tenth day of april annodom : 1714

Rebecca young the daughter of Barnabas & Rebecca young was Born at Eastham on the twentythird day of September annodomini 1715

Barnabas young the son of Barnabas & Rebecca young was Born at Eastham on the eighteenth day of September annodomini : 1717:

Mercy young the Daughter of Barnabas and Rebecca young was Born at Eastham on the fifth day of September annodomini : 1719

Jane young the Daughter of Barnabas and Rebecc young was Born at Eastham on the 26th day of July annodomini : 1723 :

Judah rogars of harwich and Elisabath nickerson of Chatham ware marrid by Joseph Done Esqr August 29 : 1751

* Seamstress.

† The surname of the bride was omitted.

Thomas Atwood and Phebe Mayo were married by mr Benjamin Webb on the 23d day of april annodomini : 1724

Joshua pompmore and Darkes quanset boath of harwich ware marrid by Joseph Doane Esqr January 16 : 1752

octobr 22 : 1754 Then John merign and Rebaca peper Boath of Eastham ware marid in Eastham by Mr Edward Chever Clark Recorded pr Thomas Knowles Town Clar

[p. 58] Benjamin Webb the son of mr Benjamin & mrs Mehitabel Webb was on the twenty secund day of November annodomini :

1721
Mary Webb the Daughter of mr Benjamin Webb was Born at Eastham on the twentieth day of June annodomini 1724

Thomas Webb the Son of mr Benjamin and mrs mehitabel Webb was Born at Eastham on the twenty secund day of august annodomini 1726

Joseph swet and Ann freeman boath of Eastham ware marid in Eastham by mr Isaiah Lues minestar in January : 9 : 1752 Recorded pr Thomas Knowles Town Clar

Zilah Young the Daughter of David and lydia young was Born at Eastham may ye 10th 1766

Sarah Young Daughter of David and Lydia young was Born at Eastham March ye 28th 1768

Elisebath young Daughter of David and Lydia young was Born at Eastham July the 11 : 1770

[Nathanael Smith and Abigail Gross were married on the fifth day of october annodomini : 1716   See pag 10*]

Mary Smith the daughter of Nathanael and Abigail Smith was Born at Eastham on ye 26th day of april annodomini 1725*]

Hanah Cooke the wife of Caleb Cooke dyed on ye 17th day of march annodomini 1726/7

David young and Lydia smith Boath of Eastham ware marriade in Eastham By Mr Joseph Crocker Clark in octobar 3 : 1754 Recorded pr Thomas Knowles clar

Samuell Young Son of David and Lydia young was Born in Eastham march the 19 : 1756

Ann young Daughter of David & Lydia young was born in Eastham the 4 day of may 1757

David young son of David & Lydia young was born in Eastham the 31 Day of march 1759

Elezer young son of David and Lydia young was born in Eastham april 20 Day 1760

Moses young the Son of David and Lydia young was born in Eastham January the 10d 1762

Lydia Young the Daughter of David & Lydia young was born in Eastham May 30d : 1764

Look a Bove for the Rest of the Children

*These two entries were crossed out, and reference made to original page 10, were the entries are duplicated.   See ante, Vol. 15, p. 57.

[p. 59] Phebe Higgins the Daughter of Jonathan and Rebecca Higgins was Born at Eastham on the ninth day of february annodom 1722/3

Lamuel nucomb of Truro and phebe Atkens of Eastham was mared in Eastham by Mr Isaiah Lues minestar in novembar 28 : 1751 Recorded pr Thomas Knowles Town Clar

Martha Brown the Daughter of Samuel and Lidia Brown was Born at Eastham on the eighth day of July annodom : 1720

Samuel Brown the Son of Samuel and Lidia Brown was Born at Eastham on the eighteenth Day of July annodomini : 1722

Elisabeth Brown the Daughter of Samuel and Lidia Brown was born at Eastham on the first day of april annodomini : 1724

Lidea Brown Daughter of Samuel & Lidea Brown was born in april 1726

Bethiah Brown Daughter of Samuel & Lidea Brown in may 1728

Mary Brown Daughter of Samuel & Lidea brown born in march 1734

Jeminah Daughter of Samuel & Lidea Brown born march 1732

nathaniel Lues Jr of truro and Abigail Doane of Eastham ware married in Eastham By Mr Joseph Crocker Clark in novembar 7 : 1751 Entred pr Thomas Knowles Town Clar

Mr John paine and Mrs mary treet Boath of Eastham ware married in Eastham By Mr Joseph Crocker Clark in novembar 28 : 1751 Entred pr Thomas Knowles Town Clar

[p. 60] Roger Thomas and Susanna Snow were Married by Mr Samuel ozburn on ye fourtenth day of may annodomini 1724

Evan Thomas the Son of Roger and Susanna Thomas was Born at Eastham on ye Seventh day of march annodomini 1724/5

Anne Thomas the Daughter of Roger and Susanna Thomas was born at Eastham on ye first day of april annodomini 1726

Ebenezer Thomas the Son of Roger and Susanna Thomas was Born at Eastham on ye twelf day of october 1727

Prince Thomas Son of Roger & Suseana Thomas waas born the 13 day of May * 1729

Susana Thomas Daughter of Roger & Susana Thomas was born the fift day of December 1730

mary Cole and Sarah Cole Daughters of Joseph and Sarah Cole was born at Eastham on ye 9th day of September 1738

Ruben Cole Son of Joseph and Sarah cole was born at Eastham on ye 19th day of January 1742/3

abiall Cole Son of Joseph and Sarah Cole was born at Eastham on the 24th day December 1745

Henry Cole the Son of Joseph and Sarah Cole was born at Eastham on the ninth day of July 1748

Elisha Cob of Barnstable and Mary Harding of Eastham were married by mr Benjamin Webb on ye 25th day of february annodomini: 1724/5

Elisha Cob Son of Elisha Cob mary cob was born at Eastham the 6th day of June 1736.

* "april" was crossed out and "May" interlined, in the same ink.

Mary cobb Daughter of Elisha Cob & mary Cob was born at Eastham the first day of June 1726

Eunis Cob Daughter of Elisha Cob & mary Cob was born at Eastham the 5th day of october 1728

Phebee Cob Daughter of Elisha Cob & Mary Cob was born at Eastham the 31 day of January 1732/3

Joshua Cob Son of Elisha Cob & Mary Cob was born at Eastham the 20th day of april 1734

Elisha Cob Son of Elisha Cob & Mary Cob was born at Eastham the 6th day of June 1736

[p. 61] Thomas Knowles and Elisabeth Snow were married by Mr Benjamin Webb on ye sixth day of August annodomini 1724

Henry Knowls Son of Thomas Knowls was born the 30th day of August 1729

Anne Knowls Daughter of Thomas Knowls was born the 25th of august 1731

Abigel Knowls Daughter of Thomas Knowls was born the 8th day of march 1735

Bety Knowls Daughter of Thomas Knowls was born the 13th day of September 1738

Abigel Knowles Dafter to thomas Knowles was Born the 21 : day of Septembar 1727 and Died the 26 : of septembar 1727

Thomas Knowles sun of thomas Knowles was Born the 10 day of may 1733 and Died the : 13 : Day of June 1734

Thomas Knowles sun of thomas Knowles was Born the 13 of septembar 1738 and Died the 14 of novembar 1739

Deacon Thomas Knowles Died the 2th Day of march 1759 by the mesels and feafer

Elisabeth Knoles wife of Deacn thomas Knowles Died the The . 2th of September 1759

Jesse Smith and Sarah Higgins were married by mr Samuel ozburn in ye month of September 1724

Ruth Smith the daughter of Jesse and Sarah Smith was Born at Eastham on the eighteenth day of July annodomini 1725

David Smith the Son of Jesse and Sarah Smith was Born at Eastham on the twenty eighth day of January anno Domini 1726/7

Prisila Smith Daughter of Jesse & Sarah Smith born the 20th of July 1729

Sarah Smith Daughter of Jesse & Sarah Smith born 19 of July 1731

Eunis Smith Daughter of Jesse & Sarah Smith born 23 of february 172/3*

Jerusa Smith Daughter of Jesse Smith born first day of march 1734/5

Jesse Smith son of Jesse Smith born the first day of february 1736/7

[p. 62] Peter Severence and Elisabeth Cole were married by Mr Samuel Ozburn in September 1724

Theophilus Higgins and Joanna young were Married by Mr Samuel Ozburn on ye twentyfifth day of April annodomini 1724

* Sic.

Richard Higgins the Son of Theophilus and Joanna Higgins was Born at Eastham on ye 29th day of march annodomini 1725

Jennet Higgins the Daughter of Theophilus and Joanna Higgins was born at Eastham on the twentieth day of January annodomini 1726/7

Unice Higgins the Daughter of Theophilus and Joanna Higgins was born at Eastham on the twenty seventh day of march annodomini 1729

September 12 : 1731 Mary higgins Daughter of Theophilas & Joanah higgins born entred ℙ me Joseph Doane Town clark

December 28 : 1733 then Josiah higgins Son of Theophilas & Joanah higgins was born entred pr me Joseph Doane Town clark

Nathan Higgins Son of Theophilas Higgins was born the Second day of august 1736

Eliazer higgins Son of Theophilas higgins & Joanah higgins was born in October the 18th 1738

Levi Higgins Son of Theophilus and Joanna Higgens was born at Eastham on the 27th day of June 1743

Richard Higgins Son of Theophilus and Joanna Higgins died on the 11th day of august 1747

Josiah higgens the son of Theophilus and Joanna higgens Died Septembar 3 : 1757

Sarah Atwood Daughter of Ephraim and Bethiah Atwood was born in Eastham october the 7 Day 1756

Simeon Atwood Son of Ephraim & Bethiah Atwood was born at Eastham August ye 14th 1758

Bethiah Atwood Daughter of Ephraim & Bethiah Atwood was born in Eastham march the 16 : 1761

Ephraim Atwood juner Son of Ephraim and Bethiah Atwood was born in Eastham November the 2 : 1762

Joanna wife of Theophilus Higgins Died the 22 Day of march 1767

[p. 63] Joshua Hopkins Junr and prissilla Curtis were married by Mr Samuel ozburn on ye first day of october annodomini 1724

Joshua Hopkins the Son of Joshua and Prissilla Hopkins was Born at Eastham on the eighteenth day of July annodomini 1725

Prissilla Hopkins the Daughter of Joshua and Prissilla Hopkins was born at Eastham on ye Seventh day of June annodomini 1728

July 30 : 1729 then Hannah Hopkins Daughter of Joshuhua jur & Pricillia hopkins was born in Eastham.

Solomon Pepper and Phebe Paine were married by mr Samuel ozburn on ye fifteenth day of October annodomini 1724

Apphia Pepper the daughter of Solomon and Phebe Pepper was Born at Eastham on the tenth day of November annodomini : 1725

Phebee Pepper Daughter of Sollonon & Phebee Pepper was born In Eastham the 24th day of June 1728

abigrel Pepper Daughter of Sollomon Pepper was born the 27 day of october 1738

Sollomon Pepper Son of Sollomon Pepper was born the 8th day of april 1740

Beniamin pepper Son of Solomon and Phebe Pepper was born at Eastham april ye 29th 1744

[p. 64] Thomas Higgins and Sarah Vickery were married by mr Samuel Ozburn on ye twenty eighth day of January annodomini 1724/5

Elisabeth Higgins the Daughter of Thomas and Sarah Higgins was born at Eastham on the 20th day of february annodomini 1726/7

Seth higgins Son of Thomas & Sarah higgins was born at Eastham 22 of october 1729 entred ℙ Joseph Doane Town clerk

Moses Bixbe and Phebe Hopkins were Married by mr Samuel ozburn on ye eighteenth day of march annodomini 1724/5

Joseph Bixbe the Son of Moses and Phebe Bixbe was Born at Eastham on ye first day of January annodomini : 1725/6

march 23 : 1729/10 * then Joseph Bixbee Son of Moses Bixbee was born

December 3 : 1731 then Elizabeth Bixbee Daughter of moses Bixbee was born

December 21 : 1734 then Phebee Bixbee Daughter of moses Bixbe was born

March 2 : 1736/7 then John Bixbee Son of moses Bixbee was born

[p. 65] Ruth Mayo the Daughter of Israel and mercy Mayo was born at Eastham on the twentyfifth day of april annodom, 1725

Mercy Mayo the daughter of Israel and Mercy Mayo was Born at Eastham on the twelf day of april anno Domini 1728

Thomas Mayo Son of Israel & Mercy Mayo was born In Eastham the 20th day of may 1730 entred ℙ Joseph Doane Town clark

Prissilla mayo Daughter of Israel & marcy mayo was born the Sixth day of october 1732

Ellis mayo Daughter of Israel & marcy mayo born the Sixth day of march 1734/5

Phebee mayo Daughter of Israel mayo was born the 31 day of July 1728

Faster mayo Daughter of Irael mayo was born the the 12 day of november 1740

Daniel Eldrig and sarah holbrooks boath of Eastham ware marid in Eastham by Mr Isaiah Lues minestar in novembr 7 : 1751 Recorded pr Thomas Knowles Town Clar

Stephen Cole and Rebecca Mayo were married by mr Samu osborn on the 20th day of may annodomini : 1725

July 25 : 1754 then Ruben Covel and hanah maker Boath of Eastham was marid in Eastham By Samuel Smith Esqr Recorded pr Thomas Knowles Town Clar

Nathniel Covell Son of Ruben and hannah Covell was Born in Eastham the 24 Day of December 1755

* Sic.

Ruben Covell Son of Ruben and hannah Covell was Born in Eastham the 23 Day of february 1761

[p. 66] Edmond ffreeman and Lois Paine were married by mr Samuel osborn on the 22 day of april annodomini 1725

Loes ffreeman Daughter of Edmond ffreeman was born the third of September 1726

Edmond ffreeman and Sarah Sparrow were married by Joseph Doane Esqr on ye 25th day of September anno Domini 1729

Jonathan ffreeman Son of Edmond ffreeman was born the 22 day of ffebruary 1729/30

Edmond ffreeman Son of Edmond ffreemaman was born the 13 of ffebruary 1731

Elisha Freeman and Lidia Freeman were married by mr Samuel Osburn on the Seventh day of May annodomini 1725

Simeon bacer and mary Rich boath of Eastham ware marrid in Eastham by Isaiah Lues minestar in octobar 17 : 1751 Recorded pr Thomas Knowles Town Clar

Bethiah Cook Daughter of Richard and Rebecca Cook was Born in Eastham December 17 : 174 : *

Sarah Cook Daughter of Richard and Rebacce Cook was Born in Eastham october 31 Day 1742

Phebe Cook Daughter of Richard and Rebacca Cook was Born in Eastham march 27 Day 1745

Joanna Cook Daughter of Richard and Rebacca Cook was Born in Eastham march 25 Day 1747

Elisha Cook Son of Richard and Rebacca Cook was Born in Eastham July 4 Day 1750

Nathan Cook Son of Richard and Rebacca Cook was Born in Eastham october 26 Day 1751

Rebacca Cook Daughter of Richard and Rebacca Cook was Born in Eastham november 13 1753

Hannah Cook Daughter of Richard and Rebacca Cook was Born in Eastham December 22 Day 1756

Richard Cook Son of Richard and Rebacca Cook was Born in Eastham march 14 : 1759 and Died october 17 : 1759 :

Abigail Cook Daughter of Richard and Rebacca Cook was Born in Eastham november 22 Day 1760

Lydia Daughter of Richard and Rebacca Cook was Born in Eastham march 21 Day 1763 :

Apphiah Cook Daughter of Richard and Rebacca Cook was Born in Eastham September 16 Day 1765

[p. 67] Thomas Rich Jur and Thankfull Mayo were married by Mr Samuel Osborn on ye 7th day of october annodomini 1725

Amos Rich the Son of Thomas and Thankfull Rich was born at Eastham on ye fourth day of october annodomini 1726

Elisabeth Rich the daughter of Thomas and Thankfull Rich was born at Eastham on ye fifth day of July annodomini 1728

* A duplicate record on original page 91 gives this date as 1740. It also gives another child, Zenas, born 18 July, 1769.

Marcy Rich Daughter of Thomas & Thankfull Rich was born the first day of June 1731

Bethiah Daughter of Thomas & Thankfull Rich was born the 22 July 1733

Peeter Rich Son of Thomas & Thankfull Rich was born the 23 day of September 1735

Thomas hinkely of harwich and sarah Couel of Eastham ware married in Eastham By Mr Isaiah lues minestar novembar 1 : 1753

Isaac Merrick & Phebe Doane were Married by Joseph Doane Esqur on ye 30th day of September annodomini 1725

Isaac Merrick Dyed on the 5th day of march annodomini 1726/7

Isaac Meyrick Son of Isaac Meyrick & Phebee meyrick was born in Eastham the first day of June 1727 entred ₽ Joseph Doane Town clerk

Joseph Doane Son of Joseph & Debro Doane was born May the first 1727

Nathaniel Doane Son of Joseph & Debro Doane was born the 23 day of march 1730/31 entred ₽ Joseph Doane Town clark

[p. 68] Prence Doane and Elisabeth Godfree * were married by Joseph Doane Esqr on the third day of february annodomini 1725/6

Prince Doane Son of Prince & Elizabeth Doane was born November 12th 1726

Ruth Doane daughter of Prince & Elizabeth Doane was born September 20th 1728

Phebee Daughter of Prince & Elizabeth Doane was born December 10th 1730

Abigel Daughter of Prince & Elizabeth Doane was born June 17th 1732

Mary Daughter of Prince & Elizabeth Doane was born May the third 1734

gideon mayo and sarah Linel Both of Eastham ware marride in Eastham By Mr Joseph Crocker Clark on febuary 10 : 1757

Eles mayo Daughter of Gidion and : Sarah mayo was Borne in Eastham Dcsember 18th 1757 :

Mehetabel mayo Daughter of gidion may was Born in Eastham September : 1th 1759

Joseph Sparrow and Hannah Doane were married by Joseph Doane Esqur on the tenth day of march Annodomini 1725/6

Mary Sparrow Daughter of Joseph Sparrow & hannah Sparrow was born april 23 : 1726

Abigel Sparrow Daughter of Joseph Sparrow & hannah Sparrow was born august 9th 1729 entred ₽ Joseph Doane Town clerk

Lidea Sparrow Daughter of Joseph & hannah Sparrow was born 26 day of november 1731

Hannah Sparrow Daughter of Joseph & hannah Sparrow was born the 30 day of october 1734

* "Doane" was crossed out and "Godfree" interlined in the same hand.

EASTHAM AND ORLEANS, MASS., VITAL RECORDS

(Continued from page 76)

[p. 69] Zebulon Young and Mercy Sparrow were married by Joseph Doane Esqur on the twentysecund day of february annodomini 1725/6*

Thankful Young the daughter of Zebulon and Mercy young was Born on the eighth day of January annodomini 1725/6*

Nathanael young the Son of Zebulon and Mercy Young was born at Eastham on the fourteenth day of october annodomini 1728

Thankful young Daughter of Zebulon & Marcy young was born the 18th day of September 1731 entred ℗ Joseph Doane Town clark

September 30th 1733 then Zebulon young Son of Zebulon & Marcy young was born

Isaac young Son of Zebulon young was born 23 day of September 1735

Mercy young Daughter of Zebulon young was born 14 day of September 1737

Mercy young Wife of Zebulon young Died the fourteenth day of february 1739/40 Recorded by me Jabez Snow Town Clarck

Samuel Baker and Debora Eldridg were maryed by Joseph Doane Esqur on the twentyfourth day of february annodom : 1725/6

[Barnabas Cole the sun of salvenas was Born in Eastham march : ye : 28 : 1751 †]

Rachel Cole the Dafter of Joshua Cole and sarah Cole was born in Eastham Aprel : ye : 6 : 1752

Sarah Cole wife of Joshua Cole Died fabuery the 1 Day in the yeare 1759

Elezabeth Cole Daughter of Joshua and Sarah Cole Died January 13 : 1760

Ruth Cole Daughter of Joshua and Sary Cole Died august the 24 : 1760

Sarah Cole Daughter of Joshua and Sarah Cole was Born at Eastham November the 29th 1740

Nathan Cole Son of Joshua and Sarah Cole Died July 22 Day 1772

Rachel Cole Daughter of Joshua and Sarah Cole Died february 25 : 1772

[p. 70] Benjamin Bean and Mehitabell mayo were married by mr Benjamin Webb on the fifth day of august 1725

Sarah Been Daughter of Benjamin & Mehitable Been born 14 may 1727

Benjamin Been Son of Benjamin & Mehitable Been born May 9th 1729

*Sic.

† This entry has been crossed out. See original page 141.

76

Joseph Sparrow Son of Joseph Sparrow was born the 15 day of October 1736

Hannah Sparrow Daughter of Joseph Sparrow was born the 6th day of ffebruary 1738/9

Rebecka Sparrow Daughter of Joseph Sparrow was born the 7th day of april 1741

freeman higgens and thankfull paine Both of Eastham ware marid in Eastham By Mr Joseph Crocker Clark on July 14 : 1757

Martha & Thankfull Daughters of Freeman Higgins & Thankfull his Wife was born april 9th 1758

Zedekiah Son of Freeman Higgins & Thankfull his wife was born in Eastham april 11th 1760

Priscilla Daughter of Freeman Higgins & Thankfull his wife was born March 1th 1762

Marcy Daughter of Freeman Higgins & Thankfull was born august 9th 1764

Elisha Son of Freeman Higgins & Thankfull his wife was born Novemr 9th 1766 all in Eastham

(To be continued)

Ezekel holbrooks and martha mayo boath of Eastham ware marrid in Eastham by Mr Isaiah Lues minestar in octobar 10 : 1751 Recorded pr Thomas Knowles Town Clar

sarah holbrooks the Dafter of Ezekel and martha holbroks was Born in Eastham Aprel 5 : 1752

marcy holbrook Daughter of Ezekiel and martha holbrook was born in Eastham october the 1 Day 1753

martha holbrook Daughter of Ezekiel & martha holbrook was born in Eastham apriel 20 Day 1757

Samuel holbrook Son of Ezekiel & martha holbrook was Born february 24 Dar 1759

Joseph Snow and Mercy Knowles were married by mr Benjamin Webb on ye twentythird day of September annodomini 1725*

Nathaniel Snow Son of Joseph & Marcy Snow was born the 27th day of april 1725*

Edward Snow Son of Joseph & Mercy Snow was born the 23 day of December 1729

Joseph Snow Son of Joseph & Marcy Snow was born the first day of april 1735

Mercy Snow Daughter of Joseph Snow was born the 11th day of November 1737

Joseph Snow Son of Joseph Snow was born the 9th day of May 1742

february ye 17th 1743/4 Thankfull Snow Daughter of Joseph and marcy Snow was born

Samuell Higgins Son of Simeon and martha higgins was born in Eastham the 22 Day of november 1748

Seth higgens Son of Simeon and martha higgins was born in Eastham the 22 Day of november 1750

Nathan Higgins Son of Simeon and martha higgins was born in Eastham november 1 : 1752

Ruth higgins Daughter of Simeon & martha higgins was born in Eastham January 1755 and Died December 1759

thankfull higgins Daughter of Simeon and martha higgins was born in Eastham January 1 : 1757

John higgins Son of Simeon higgins and martha higgins was born in Eastham may 23 : 1759

Ruth Higgins Daughter of Simeon and martha higgins was Born in Eastham august 20 Day 1761

theodor Higgins Son of Simeon and marther higgins was Born in Eastham July 11 : 1765

[p. 71] Joseph Pepper and Rebecca Higgins were married by mr Benjamin Webb on ye 30th day of September annodomini 1725

Ruth Pepper Daughter of Joseph & Rebecka Pepper was born the 15th day of ffebruary 1726/7

Daniel Pepper son of Joseph & Rebecka Pepper was born the 10th day of September 1729 entred ℔ Joseph Doane Town clerk

Rebekah Pepper Daughter of Joseph & Rebeckah Pepper was born 31 day of august 1731

* Sic.

Samuell pepper was born in Eastham Son of Joseph and Rebecca pepper april 28 : 1734

Elisabeth pepper Daughter of Joseph and Rebacca pepper was Born in Eastham april 22 Day 1736

Lydia pepper Daughter of Joseph and Rebacca Pepper was Born in Eastham august 8 Day 1737

Hannah Pepper Daughter of Joseph and Rebacca Pepper was Born in Eastham february 22 Day 1740

Joseph Pepper Son of Joseph and Rebacca Pepper was born in Eastham July 1 Day 1744

Sarah Pepper Daughter of Joseph and Rebacca Pepper was Born in Eastham may 17 Day 1746

Rebacca pepper wife of Joseph pepper Departed this Life 15 Day January 1776

David Cole and Jerusha Doane were married by mr Benjamin Webb on the Seventh day of october annodomini 1725

Vashty Cole the daughter of David and Jerusha Cole was Born at Eastham on ye thirtieth day of June annodomini 1727

September 19th : 1729 William Cole Son of David & Jerusha Cole was born at Eastham

September 7th 1731 Jerusha Cole Daughter of David & Jerusha cole was born at Eastham

September 28th 1733 David Cole Son of David & Jerusha Cole was born at Eastham

Hannah Cole Daughter of David Cole was born the 28th day of march 1734

solomon harding the sun of Joseph and Eunas harding was Born in 1734

Eastham may 31 : 1752

simon harding the sun of Joseph and Eunas harding was Born in Eastham July 17 : 1754

John harding the sun of Joseph and Eunas harding was Born in Eastham october 26 : 1756

[p. 72] Seth Rider and Debora atwood were married by mr Benjamin Webb on ye Sixth day of January anno Domini 1725/6

Debro Rider Daughter of Seth Rider was born the 6 day of august 1727

Marcy Daughter of Seth Rider was born the 6th of august 1735

January 13 : 1758 then solomon higgens and Bethiah Chase both of Eastham ware marriade in Eastham by John freeman Esqr Recorded pr Thomas Knowles Town Clar

Solomon Higgins Son of Solomon and Bethiah Higgins was Born at Eastham July ye 4 : 1758

Obediah Higgins Son of Solomon and Bethiah Higgins was Born at Eastham March ye 21 : 1761

Henery Higgins Son of Solomon and Bethiah Higgins was Born at Eastham Decembr ye 15 : 1762

Mary Higgins Daughter of Solomon and Bethiah Higgins was Born at Eastham Decembr ye 10 : 1765

Ephriem snow the sun of Jease and Lowes snow was Born in Eastham may 3 : 1754

Lowes snow the Dafter of Jease and Lowes snow was Born in Eastham septembar 12 : 1757

Micaiaah Snow Son of Jesse and Lois Snow was Born November ye 14th 1759

Thankful Snow Daughter of Jesse and Lois Snow was Born at Eastham febuary 24th 1761

Paine Snow Son of Jesse and Lois Snow was Born at Eastham aprel ye 6th 1763

Tamson Snow Daughter of Jesse and Lois Snow was Born at Eastham March ye 9th 1765

Freeman Snow Son of Jesse and Lois Snow was Born at Eastham may ye 30th 1768

[p. 74] James Knowles and Anne Doane were married by Joseph Doane Esqur on the thirtyfirst day of march annodomini 1726

James Knowles the Son of James and Anne Knowles was Born at Eastham on the tenth day of October Annodomini 1727

Mary Knowles was born the 29th day of December 1730 the Daughter of James & Anne Knowles entred ℣ me Joseph Doane Town clark

Benimin smalley and Ann Cash boath of Eastham ware marrid in Eastham by Isaiah Lues minestar in march 20 : 1750/1 Recorded pr Thomas Knowles Town Clar

David newcomb of Truro & Elizabeth Gross of Eastham were married by mr Isaaih Lewis minster July 10 Day 1759 Entred Edward Knowles Town Clerk

William Norket and Prissilla Paine were married by Joseph Doane Esqur on the fourth day of august annodomini 1726

Ruth Norket the daughter of William and Prissilla Norket was Born at Eastham on ye fifteenth day of June annodomini 1728

Josiah Norcut Son of william & Prissilla norcut was born 25th day of January 1730/31

Freeman Knowls Son of Seth and Ruth Knowls was born at Easham on the 24th day of november 1745

nathaniel Knowles the sun of Seth and Ruth Knowles was Born in Eastham march 14 : 1750

Seth Knowles the sun of Seth and Ruth Knowles was Born in Eastham Aprel 20 : 1752

Ruth Knowles the Dafter of Seth and Ruth Knowls was Born in Eastham August 3 : 1754

[p. 75] Hope Rich the Daughter of John and Hope Rich was Born at Eastham on ye Seventh day of may annodomini : 1725

solomon snow and Lydia ryder boath of Eastham ware marrid in Eastham by Mr Isaiah Lues minestar in octobar 3 : 1751 Recorded pr Thomas Knowles Town Clar

suzanah snow the Dafter of soloman and lydia snow was Born in Eastham febuary 20 : 1752

Henery Higgins Son of Solomon and Bathiah Higgins Died Januery ye 4 : 1768

Bethiah Higgens Daughter of Solomon & Bethiah Higgens was Born april : 15 : 1769

Rebekah Higgens Daughter of Solomon and Bethiah Higgens was Born January 26 : 1771

Zaccheus Higgens Son of Solomon and Bethiah Higgens was born at Eastham Novenbar : 28 : 1772

Dean Higgens Son of Solomon Higgen and Bethiah Higgens was born Sept : 11 : 1774

Relians Higgen Daughter of Solomon Higgens was born Septembr : 12 : 1777

Abijah Higgens Son of Solomon Higgens was born may : 12 : 1779

Nathanael Harding of Truro and Hannah Young of Eastham were married by mr Samuel Osborn on the 30th day of November annodomini 1725

Pecock Grigg and Thankfull Brown were married by mr Samuel Osburn on ye Seventh day of December annodom 1725

Ebenezer Luis the Son of Thomas and Judith Luis was Born at Eastham on the eighth day of may anno Domini 1723

Debora Luis the Daughter of Thomas and Judith Luis was Born at Eastham on the Sixth day of June anno Domini 1725

march 2 : 1758 then Joseph Cuffe and marcy Tom Both of harwich ware married in harwich by John freeman Esqr Recorded ℣ Thomas Knowles Town Clar

[p. 73] Eliezer freeman and Rebecca Young were married by Mr Samuel Osborn on ye thirtyfirst day of march annodomini 1726

Rebecca freem the daughter of Eliezer & Rebecca ffreeman was Born at Eastham on ye twenty seventh day of december annodomini 1726

Eliezer freeman the Son of Eliezer and Rebecca ffreeman was Born at Eastham on ye Sixteenth day of June annodomini 1728

Phebee freeman Daughter of Eleazor & Rebecka ffreeman was born in Eastham the 24 day of march 1729/30

first Rebeka ffreeman Daughter of Eleazor ffreeman [was born]* the 4th day of november 1730 [and Died the]*

4 chid Rebecka was born march 21 & Died aprill 1733

5 child Seth was born the 19 of January 1733/4 & Died august 1734

Mary ffreeman Daughter of Eleazor & Rebecka ffreeman was born the 27 July 1735

Ebenezar Atwood and Hiphzibah Williamson were Married by Nathanael ffreeman Esqur on ye third day of february annodon 1725/6

Ruth Daughter of Ebenezor & Hipsiba Atwood was born april 18 : 1728

Ebenezor Son of Ebenezor & Hipsiba atwood was born november 3 : 1729 entred ℣ Joseph Doane Town clerk

*The words in brackets were crossed out in the same ink as the rest of the entry.

thankfull snow the Dafter of soloman and lydia snow was Born in Eastham January 3 : 1756

Joseph snow the sun of solomon and Lydia snow was Born in Eastham January 3 : 1758

hanah snow Daughter of Solomon & lydia Snow was Born in Eastham December 6 Day 1759

Lydia Snow Daughter of Solomon and Lydia Snow was Born in Eastham December 1761

James Higgins and Sarah Bixbe were married by mr Samuel osborn december ye 12th 1726

Richard Stepheus and Ruhamah Doane were married by mr Benjamin Webb on ye 22nd day of September annodomini 1726

John Cole Junr and Mercy Mayo were married by mr Samuel osborn on ye eighth day of february annodomini 1726/7

John Cole Son of John Cole junr & marcy his wife was born the first day of february 1728/9 entred ⅌ me Joseph Doane Town clerk

Theophilas Cole Son of John cole junr & Mercy cole was born in Eastham the 30 day of october 1730 entred pr me Joseph Doane Town clerk

april 7th 1733 then Rebecka Cole Daughter of John & Marcy Cole was born

August 11th 1735 then Mercy Cole Daughter of John Cole junr was born

David Crowell of Chatham and Thankfull Atwood of Eastham were married by mr Isaaih Lewis December 6 Day 1759 Entred Edward Knowles Town Clerk

[p. 76] James Cole and Mary Cole were married by mr Samuel osborn on the ninth day of february annodomini 1726/7 unice Cole the daughter of James and Mary Cole was Born at Eastham on the tenth day of June annodomini 1728

March 30 : 1730 then Sollomon Cole Son of James & mary Cole was born in Eastham entred ⅌ Joseph Doane Town clerk

December 10th 1731 then Lois Cole Daughter of James & Mary Cole was born in Eastham entred pr me Joseph Doane Town Clark

March the third 1733/4 then Mary Cole Daughter of James & mary cole was born

salvenas Ary and sarah snow boath of Eastham ware marrid in Eastham by Isaiah Lues minestar in febuary 21 : 1750/1 Recorded pr Thomas Knowles Town Clar'

salvenas Ary the sun of salvenas and hanah* Ary was Born in Eastham July 5 : 1754

Lydia Ary Daughter of Silvenus and Sarah ary was born in Eastham april the 24 Day 1757

Nathaniel ary Son of Silvenus and Sarah ary was born in Eastham october the 26 Day 1759

Thankfull ary Daughter of Silvenus and Sarah ary was born in Eastham December the 25 Day 1761

* Sic.

Caleb Cooke and Hannah Brown were married by mr Benjamin Webb on ye 7th day of april annodomini 1726

Elisha Hunter and Sarah atwood was Married by mr Benjamin Webb on ye 17th day of may annodomini 1726

Judah Rogers Junr of Harwich and Patience Cole of Eastham were married by Joseph Doane Esqur on ye 12th day of december annodom 1728

Simeon Smith of Province town and Susannah Stubs of Eastham was mared by mr Isaaih Lewis on the 29 Day of December* 1757 Entred Edward Knowles Town Clerk

[p. 77] Lidia Airie the wife of Richard Airie Dyed on the Secund day of march annodomini 1726/7

Silvanas Airie the Son of Richard and Lidia Airie was born at Eastham on the twenty sixth day of february annodom : 1726/7

Margeret and Ebenezer Airie the children of Richard and Lidia Airie were born at Eastham on the twenty seventh day of february annodomini 1726/7

Joshua young and Drusilla Cole Both of Eastham were married by mr Isaaih Lewis minester august 3 Day 1758 Entred Edward Knowles Town Clerk

Ruth Mayo the daughter of Jeremiah and Elisabeth Mayo was Born F: on the twenty eighth day of July annodomini 1725

Jeminah Mayo Daughter of Jeremiah Mayo was born the 18th of february 1730/1

Thomas Mayo Son of Jeremiah Mayo was born the 20th of april 1732

Joshua Mayo Son of Jeremiah Mayo was born the first day of January 1735/6

Jeremiah Mayo Son of Jeremiah Mayo was born the 10th day october 1739

Joseph Mayo & Benjamin Mayo Sons of Jeremiah Mayo ware born the 21 day of november 1742

Ebenezer newcomb and Experince Brown both of Eastham were married by mr Isaaih Lewis minster february 6 : 1758 Edward Knowles Town Clerk

[p. 78] Benjamin Higgins and Sarah Mayo were married by mr Benjamin Webb on the 8th day of September annodomini 1726

Phebee Daughter of Benjam Higgins & Sarah higgins was born the 24 day of September 1727

Sarah Daughter of Benjamin & Sarah higgins was born the 28 of april 1730

Hannah Daughter of Benjamin & Sarah higgins was born the 29 day of april 1732

Rebaca higgens the Dafter of Benimin and Sarah higgins was Born in Eastham may : ye : 11 : 1734

Elkeny higgens the sun of Benimin and sarah higgens was Born in Eastham novembr 10 : 1737

*"tenth Day of July" was crossed out and "29 Day of December" inter-lined in the same hand.

148

Benimin higgens the sun of Benimin and sarah higgens was Born in Easthm Desembr 11 : 1739
Lydia higgens the Dafter of Benimin and sarah higgens was Born in Eastham march 11 : 1741/2
marcy higgens the Dafter of Benimin and sary higgens was Born in Eastham novembr 10 : 1745
Isaac young and martha Atwood boath of Eastham ware marrid in Eastham by Isaiah Lues minestar in febuary 14 : 1750/1
Recorded pr Thomas Knowles Town Clar
Shadreck Seger & mary Hamlin were Married by Mr Benjamin Webb
Edmond Higgens Son of Beniamin and Hannah Higgens was Born at Eastham on ye 21th day of December 1740
Beniamin Higgens Son of Beniamin and Hanna Higgens was Born at Eastham on ye 29th day of November 1743
Lot Higgens Son of Beniamin and Hannah Higgins was born at Eastham on ye 21 day of ffebruary 1745/6

(To be continued)

EASTHAM AND ORLEANS, MASS., VITAL RECORDS

(Continued from page 148)

[p. 79] Richard Paine and Phebe Merrick were Married by mr Benjamin Webb on ye 20th day of october annodomini 1726
Hannah Paine Daughter of Richard Paine was born the 15th day of December 1738
John young Junr and Mary Airie were married by mr Benjamin Webb on ye 26th day of Januarie annodomini : 1726/7

william nucomb and vashty Cole boath of Eastham ware marrid in Eastham by Isaiah Lues minestar novembr 1 : 1750 Recorded pr Thomas Knowles Town Clar

prins nickerson of Chatham lydia Chohoon of Eastham ware marrid in Eastham by Isaiah Lues minestar in febuary 7 : 1750 Recorded pr Thomas Knowles Town Clar

[p. 80] Solomon Doane and Alice Higgins were married by mr bɛ.. jamin Webb on ye 3d day of august anno Domini 1727

January 5 : 1730 then Sollomon Doane Son of Sollomon Doane was born

July 4 : 1732 then Noah Doane Son of Sollomon Doane was born

January 23 : 1733 then Serah Doane Daughter of Sollomon Doane was born

September 16 then 1735 then Dorkis Doane Daughter of Sollomon Doane was born

March 13 : 1737 then Nehemiah Doane Son of Sollomon Doane born

april 21th 1739 then Joseph Doane Son of Sollomon Doane was born
March 27th 1741 then Isaac Doane Son of Sollomon Doane was born
ffebruary 7th 1742 then Bettee Doane Daughter of Sollomon Doane was born

Joshua Doane Son of Solonon and Alce Doane was born at Eastham on the ye 6 day of January 1744/5

John Rich Junr and Thankfull Seers were Married by mr John Avery on ye 13th day of april annodomini 1727

Thankfull higgens the Dafter of Thomas and Abigaiel * higgens was Born in Eastham Aprel : 9 : 1738

sarah higgens the Dafter of Thomas and Abigaiel * higgens was Born in Eastham July 17 : 1740

Solomon higgens the sun of Thomas and Abigaiel * higgens was Born in Eastham July 15 : 1743

[p. 81] David Higgins and Mercy Twining were married by mr Samuel Osborn on the fifth day of october annodomini 1727

Lamuel Higgins Son of David & Marcy Higgins was born in Eastham the 28 of January 1728/9 entred ꝑ Joseph Doane Town clerk

Dorathy Daughter of David & Marcy higgins was born the 16th day of March 1730/31

Jedediah Higgins Son of David Higgins was born the 16 april 1733

ReAnna Higgins Daughter of David higgins was born the 6 day June 1735

Elkenah higgins Son of David higgins was born the 13th day of October 1737

Nehemiah Higgins Son o

may 17 : 1757 then John wormely resident at Truro and Mrs Rachel Doane of Eastham ware married in Eastham by mr Isaiah lues minestar Recorded pr Thomas Knowles Town Clar

* "Thankfull" was crossed out and "Abigaiel" interlined.   See next page.

Thomas Higgins Junr & Abigail Paine were married by mr Samuel Osborn on ye twelf day of october annodomini 1727

Philip higgins Son of Thomas higgins junr & abigel higgins was born the 28th of January 1727/8

Thomas higgins Son of Thomas higgins junr born the first day of January 1729/03 *

Benjamin higgins Son of Thomas higgins junr born the 8th day of february 1731/2

Jonathan higgins Son of Thomas higgins junr & abigail higgins was born april the 10th 1734

Jease higgens the sun of Thomas and Abigail higgens was Born in Eastham febuary 21 : 1736

look in page 80 for the rest .

oliver Ary and Elissabath gould ware marrid in harwich by Joseph Doane Esqr 1738

oliver Ary sun of oliver and Elssabath Ary was born in Eastham novembar : 6 : 1742

Abigal Ary Dafter of oliver and Elisabath Ary was born in Eastham march 20 : 1745

Elisabath Ary the Dafter of oliver and Elisabath Ary was born in Eastham febuary 16 : 1747

Thomas Ary sun of oliver and Elisabath Ary was born in Eastham octobar 10 : 1751

Eunice Daughter of Oliver Arey and Elizabeth his wife was born at Eastham April 20th 1753

[p. 82] Elkenah Shaw the Son of George and Mercy Shaw was Born at Eastham on ye twentyfirst day of November annodomini 1724

John Shaw the Son of George and Mercy Shaw was born at Eastham on the Sixteenth day of September annodomini 1727

James Shaw son George & Marcy Shaw was born In Eastham the 12th day of october 1728

Mary Shaw Daughter of George & Marcy Shaw was born in Eastham the 7th day of June 1731 entred ꝑ Joseph Doane Town clark

Jediah Lumbart of Truro and marcy treet of Eastham ware marrid in Eastham by Isaiah Lues minestar in may 11 : 1750 Recorded pr Thomas Knowles Town Clar

John Lumbard Jr of Truro and sarah Cole of Eastham was marrid in Eastham by Isaiah Lues minestar in septembar 13 : 1750 Recorded pr Thomas Knowles Town Clar

Abner Snow the Son of Nathanael and Hannah Snow was Born at Eastham on ye twentieth day of January annodomini 1715

Joseph Snow the Son of Nathanael and Hannah Snow was Born at Eastham on the eleventh day of october annodomini 1718

Hannah Snow the daughter of Nathanael and Hannah Snow was born at Eastham on the third day of may annodomini 1720

Solomon Snow the Son of Nathanael and Hannah Snow was born at Eastham on the nineteenth day of July annodomini 1725

* Sic.

Sarah Snow the Daughter of Nathanael and Hannah Snow was born at Eastham on ye 30th day of may annodomini 1729

naler hatch of falmoth in Casco bay and martha Atkens of Eastham ware married in Eastham by mr Isaiah Lues minestar octobar 18 : 1756

Isaac freeman and Thankfull higgens Boath of Eastham ware married in Eastham by mr Isaiah Lues minestar novembar 25 : 1756

[p. 83] Ebenezer Harding the Son of James and Mary Harding was Born at Eastham on the Secund day of January annodomini 1727/8

James Harding Son of James and mary Harding was born at Eastham on the Saventeenth day of march anno domini 1731

Richard Ary the sun of Richard and [*] Ary was Born in Eastham octobar : ye : 5 : 1747

Timethy Ary the sun of Richard and [*] Ary was Born in Eastham march : 10 : 1752

Stephen Griffith Junr of Harwich and Phebe Merrick of Eastham were married by Joseph Doane Esqur on the eighth day of Juiy annodomini 1728

Abraham Son of Stephen Griffeth & Phebee his wife was born in Eastham the 20th day of September 1729 entred ℣ Joseph Doane Town clerk

april 17 : 1732 then Stephen Son of Stephen & Phebee Griffeth was born entred ℣ Joseph Doane Town clark

July 26 : 1734 then Phebee Daughter of Stephen & Phebee Griffeth was born

[p. 84] David ffreeman and Ruth ffreeman were married by mr Samuel Osborn on the fifteenth day of february anno Domini 1727/8

David ffreeman the Son of David and Ruth ffreeman was born att Eastham on the twentythird day of December annodomini 1728

David ffreeman Junr dyed on the 2nd day of august annodomini 1729 in susanah higgens the Dafter of Ebnezar and martha higgens was Born in Eastham may 27 : 1755

Samuel Attwood the Son of Christopher and Susannah Attwood was born at Eastham on the 24 day of July 1752

Joseph Attwood the Son of Christopher and Susannah Attwood was born at Eastham July ye 24 1752

Christopher Attwood the Son of Christopher and Susannah Attwood was born at Eastham may ye 6 day 1754

Hannah attwood the daugter of Christopher & Susannah Attwood was born Eastham march ye 2 1756

Gideon attwood the Son of Christopher & Susannah attwood was born Eastham Octer 27 1758

Thankful attwood the daugter of Christopher & Susannah attwood was born Eastham November 25 1760

Susannah attwood the daughter of Christopher & Susannah attwood was born Eastham October 1 1761

* Space was left for the wife's name.

Joseph Doane Esqur and Mrs Desire Berry were married by mr Samuel osborn on ye twentyninth day of february annodomini 1727/8

Desire Doane the daughter of Joseph and desire Doane was born at Eastham on ye fourth day of december anno Domini 1728

Elnathan Horting Son of Nathanael and unis Horting was born at Eastham on ye 11th day of June 1743

Nathanael Horting Son of Nathanael and unis Horting was born at Eastham on ye 2d day of february 1745

willam Horting Son of Natheal ad Eunice Horting was Born in Eastham the 11th of aprele 1750

Elisabeth Horting Daughter of Nathanel and Eunice horting was Borne in Eastham march the 1th 1753

James horting Son of Nathanel ad Eunice Horting was Born in Eastham november the 8th 1755

Eunice Horting Daughter of Nathanel and Eunice horting was Born in Eastham fabuery the 24th 1757

Jabez Horting Son of Nathanel and Eunice Horting was Borne in Eastham June the 7th 1759 and Died the 19 Day of July 1759

Nathaniel Horten Son of nathaniel & Eunice horten was born in Eastham february ye 2 Day 1746

obediah horten Son of nathaniel and eunice horten was born in Eastham octo 30 day 1747

hanah horten Daughter of nathel & eunice horten was born in Eastham april the 28 Day 1761

anne Horten Daughter of Nathanil and Eunice horten was Born in Eastham 28 Day December 1763

[p. 85] Robert Nickerson and Mercy Cole were married by mr Samuel Osborn on the Seventeenth day of September annodomini 1728

mary harding the Dafter of John Elisabeth harding was Born in Eastham septembr 13 : 1732

John harding Jr the sun of John and Elisabath harding was born in Eastham novembr 7 : 1734

hanah harding the Dafter of John and Elisabath harding was Born in Eastham novembar 8 : 1736

Arcelas harding the sun of John and Elisabath harding was Born in Eastham may 31 : 1740

Joshua harding the sun of John and Elisabath harding was Born in Eastham Aprel 23 : 1743

nathaniel harding the sun of John and Elisabath harding was Born in Eastham febuary : 5 : 1746

Ebnezar harding the sun of John and Elisabath harding was Born in Eastham June 17 : 1749

hanah harding the Dafter of John and Elisabath harding was Born in Eastham Aprel : 9 : 1752

Abigaile Brown the daughter of Zebulon and [*] Brown was Born at Eastham on ye 22 day of July annodomini 1727

* Space was left for the name of the wife.

Jane higgins Daughter of Briah and Jemima higgins was Born in Eastham march 28 Day 1748:

Rachel higgins Daughter of Briah and Jemima higgins was Born in Eastham July ye 5 Day 1750:

Jemima wife of Briah higgins Died September 7 : 1754

Epherim higgins Son of Briah and Abigail higgins was Born in Eastham february 5 Day 1757 and Died November 15 : 1759

Briah higgins Son of Briah and abigail higgins was Born in Eastham February the 3 Day 1759

June 1 : 1730 then Beriah higgins & Jemima Witherel ware maried by Mr Benjamin Webb

Briah higgins Son of Briah and Jemima higgins was Born in Eastham December 5 : 1731 :

marcy higgins Daughter of Briah and Jemima higgins was Born in Eastham may 31 Day 1733

Jemima higgins Daughter of Briah and Jemima higgins was Born in Eastham may 30 Day 1735 and Died may 23 : 1736 :

Joseph higgins Son of Briah and Jemima higgins was Born in Eastham march 1 Day 1737 :

Jemima higgins Daughter of Briah and Jemima higgins was Born in Eastham July 7 Day 1738 :

anna higgins Daughter of Briah and Jemima higgins was Born in Eastham april 17 Day 1740 :

John higgins Son of Briah and Jemima higgins was Born in Eastham may 27 Day 1742

Lot higgins Son of Briah and Jemima higgins was Born in Eastham Jun[e] the 20 : 1745 and Died December 10 : 1746 :

Lot higgins Son of Briah and Jemima higgins was Born in Eastham February 17 Day 1746 and Died may the 3 Day 1765

Look above for the Rest

[p. 86] Sarah Paine the daughter of William and Sarah Paine was born at Barnstable on ye Seventeenth day of September annodom 1728

Ruth Paine Daughter of William & Sarah Paine was Born at Eastham the 23 day of of March 1729/30

Josiah Paine Son of William & Sarah Paine was born in Eastham the 20th day of June 1732

Jedida Paine Daughter of William & Sarah Paine was born the 13 day of May 1734

Mrs Sarah Paine wife of William Paine Esqr Died the 16th day of January 1743/4

Sarah Higgins the Daughter of Eliakim & Bathsheba Higgins was born in Eastham November the : 18 : 1757

mary Higgins the Daughter of Eliakim and Bathshebe Higgins was born in Eastham September the : 25 : 1760

Eliakim Higgins Son of Eliakim and Basheba Higgins was Born in Eastham June 14 1764

Ruben Higgins Son of Eliakim and Basheba Higgins was Born in Eastham 31 Day of may 1773

freeman Son of Eliakim and Barshaba higgins was Born at Eastham may 21 — 1771

Joanna higgins Dafter of Samuel and Elisabath higgins was Born at Eastham 17 of august 1773

thomas higgins Son of Samuel and Elisabath higgins was Born at Eastham the 25 of July 1775 Recored by me Samuel higgins town Clerk

John Wing of Harwich and Mary Knowles were married by mr Benjamin Webb on ye twenty first day of february annodomini 1728/9

Mary Higgins the Daughter of Samuel and Elisabeth Higgins was born in Eastham April the 30 1760

Phebe Higgins the Daughter of Samuel and Elisabeth Higgins was born in Eastham February the 11 · 1762

Lydia Higgins Daughter of Samuel and Elisabeth Higgins was Born at Eastham Febuary ye 24 · 1767*

Rachel Higgins Daughter of Samuel and Elisebeth Higgins was Born at Eastham August ye 18 · 1767*

Daniel Higgins Son of Samuel and Elisebeth Higgins was Born at Eastham October ye 2 · 1769†

the next Carried to the midle of the Leaf By Samuel higgins town Clerk

[p. 87] Elkenah Linnell the Son of Thomas and Thankfull Linnell was born at Eastham on the twentyfourth day of June annodomini 1727

Jonathan Linnell the Son of Thomas and Thankfull Linnell was born at Eastham on the twentythird day of april annodomini 1729

Zephenia King the son of Stephen King was born the 8th day of March 1740/41

Stephen King Son of Stephen King was born the 29th day of april 1743

march the 22 · 1744 then Hatsall Nickerson & Hannah myrick were married

Bethiah nickerson daughter of Hatsall and hannah nickerson was born in Eastham April the : 11 · 1746

Hannah nickerson Daughter of Hatsall and Hannah nickerson was Born in Eastham December 27 1748

Sabara nickerson the Daughter of Hatsall and Hannah nickerson was born in Eastham April ye 18 1752

Heman Nickerson the Son of Hatsall and hannah nickerson was born in Eastham april the 3 1754

Nehemiah nickerson the Son of Hatsall and hannah Nickerson was born in Eastham May the 9 1756

Tabitha Nickerson the Daughter of Hatsall and Hannah nickerson was born in Eastham December the 4 1751

* Sic.

† "1769" was written over "1770".

Eunice Nickerson the Daughter of Hatsall and Hannah nickerson was born in Eastham may the 14 1760

Hatsall nickerson the son of Hatsall and hannah nickerson was born in Eastham June the 15 1761

[p. 88] James Atwood the Son of Israel and Hannah Atwood was born at Eastham on the twentyninth day of october annodomini 1728

Debro Atwood Daughter of Israel & hannah atwood was born January 11th 1729/30

Joseph Atwood Son of Israel & hannah Atwood was born march 11 : 1732/3

Hannah atwood Daughter of Isrel atwood was born the 12 day of march 1735/6 *

Experience atwood Daughter Israel atwood was born the 20th day of march 1739/10 †

Susana Atwood Daughter of Israel atwood was born the 16th day of october 1741

Daniel atwood Son of Isariel and Hannah atwood was Born in East ham September the 5 Day 1744

January 27 : 1757 then Robart rich Jr and mary sweet Boath of Eastham ware marriade in Eastham by Mr Isaiah Lues minestor
Recorded pr Thomas Knowles Clar

John Doane Junr and Mary Brown were married by mr Benjamin Webb on ye thirtieth day of January annodomini 1728/9

Elkanah Doane Son of John and mary Doane was born in Eastham August 7D 17[‡]

Ezekiel Doane Son of John and Mary Doane was born in Eastham June the first 1732 and died September the 25 1743

Rachel Doane the Daughter of John and Mary Doane was born in Eastham october the 18D 1734

Mary Doane Daughter of John and mary Doane was Born in Eastham June the 27 Day 1737

David Doane the Son of John and mary Doane was born in Eastham December 11d 1740

Ann Doane the Daughter John and mary Doane was born in Eastham January 5D 1744

Jesse higgens and Expearenc hinkely Boath of Eastham ware married in Eastham by mr Isaiah Lues minestar on the 28 of Aprel 1757
Recorded pr Thomas Knowles Town Clar

[p. 89] Caleb Cooke and Lidia Walker were Married by mr Benjamin Webb on ye twentieth day of february annodomini 1728/9

Samuell Cook Son of Calab and Lydia Cook was born in Eastham on the 31 Day of January 1732

Lydia Cook Daughter of Caleb and Lydia Cook was Born in Eastham april the 2 Day 1736

Caleb Cook Juner Son of Caleb and Lydia Cook was Born in Eastham on the 2 Day of June 1742

Susanah Cook Daughter of Caleb and Lydia Cook was Born in Eastham on the 5 Day of august 1744

John frasur and Anna Atkens Boath of Eastham ware marriade in Eastham by mr Isaiah Lues Clark on the 25 of novembar 1756
Recorded pr Thomas Knowles Town Clar

Daniel frasur the sun of John and Anna frasur was Born in Eastham novembar 21 : 1757

January : ye 26 : 1757 then Bethuel wiley and thankfull hinkley Boath of Eastham ware married in Eastham by mr Isaiah Lues minestar
Recorded pr Thomas Knowles Town Clar

Stephen Smith of Chatham and Bathsua Brown of Eastham were married before mr Benjamin Webb on ye ninth day of april annodomini 1729

[p. 90] Johua Peirce and Elisabeth Nucome were married by mr Benjamin Webb on ye twentyfourth day of July annodomini 1729

Nathaniel Bacon Son of Nathaniel and Aphia Bacon was Born in Eastham November the 10 Day 1757

Thomas Bacon Son of Nathaniel and Aphia Bacon was Born in Eastham September the 4 Day 1759

Nathan Bacon Son of Nathaniel and aphia Bacon was Born in Eastham the 8 Day of June 1761

Jesse Brown and Elisabeth Waker were married by mr Benjamin Webb on y fourteenth day of august annodomini 1729

Ruth Daughter of Jesse & Elizabeth Brown was born the 30 day of may 1730

Hannah Daughter of Jesse & Elisabeth Brown was born 24 day of may 1731

Elizabeth Brown daughter of Jesse Brown was born the 20th april 1733

Mehitable Brown Daughter of Jesse Brown was born the 28th of June 1737

Edmond ffreeman & Sarah Sparrow ware married by Joseph Doane Esqr September 25 : 1729 entred ℘ Joseph Doane Town clerk

[p. 91] Richard mayo & Rebecka Sparrow ware married by mr Samuel Osborn the 26 December 1728 entred ℘ Joseph Doane Town clerk

Richard mayo the Son of Richard & Rebecca mayo was born at Eastham on ye twenty secund day of october annodomini 1729

Eunis Mayo Daughter of Richard mayo was born the 22 day of october 1731

Rebecka Mayo Daughter of Richard mayo was born the 18 day of february 1733/4

Serah Mayo Daughter of Richard mayo was born the 19 day of June 1736

Ruth mayo Daughter of Richard mayo was born the eight day of July 1739

* See "Atwood" note, on page 256.   † The last two figures of the year have been erased.

† Sic.

Josph Hall of Medford and Abigail Brown of Eastham were married by Joseph Doane Esqur on the first day of January annodomini 1729/30

March 5th 1729/30 then Daniel young & Lide Paine of Eastham ware married by Joseph Doane Justice Peace entred ℘ Joseph Doane Town clark

moses young Son of Daniel & Lidea young was born the 27th day of april 1730

hanah young Daughter of Daniel & Lidea young was born the 18 day of December 1731

Bethah Cook Daughter of Richard and Rebacca Cook was Born in Eastham December 17 : 1740 *

Sarah Cook Daughter of Richard and Rebacca Cook was Born in Eastham october 31 Day 1742

Phebe Cook Daughter of Richard and Rebacca Cook was Born in Eastham march 27 Day 1745

Joanna Cook Daughter of Richard and Rebacca Cook was Born in Eastham march 25 Day 1747

Elisha Cook Son of Richard and Rebacca was Born in Eastham July 4 Day 175 †

Nathan Cook Son of Richard and Rebacca Cook was Born in Eastham october 26 Day 1751

Rebacca Cook Daughter of Richard and Rebacca Cook was Born in Eastham november 13 Day 1753

hannah Cook Daughter of Richard and Rebacca Cook was Born in Eastham october 22 Day 1756

Richard Cook Son of Richard and Rebacca Cook was born in Eastham march 14 : 1759 and Died october 17 : 1759

abigail Cook Daughter of Richard and Rebacca Cook was Born in Eastham November 22 Day 176 †

Lydia Cook Daughter of Richard and Rebacca Cook was Born in Eastham march 21 : 1763

apphia Cook Daughter of Richard and Rebacca Cook was Born in Eastham September 16 Day 1765

Zenas Cook Son of Richard and Rebacca Cook was Born in Eastham July 18 : 1769

[p. 92] lot Clark & mary Harding ware married by Mr Samuel osborn november 7th 1728 entred ℘ Joseph Doane Town clerk

[Richard Mayo & Rebeck Sparrow ware married by Mr Samuel osborn December 26th 1728 ‡]

namiah Rich The sun of Robart and lidia Rich was Born in Eastham march : ye : 3 : 1750

Ruben Rich the sund of Robart and lydia Rich was Born in Eastham August 12 : 1752

* See also original page 66.
† Sic.
‡ This entry was crossed out.   See original page 91.

Jedidiah Higgins & Phebee ffreeman ware married by mr Samuel osborn January 9th 1728/9 entred ℘ Joseph Doane Town clerk
Thomas Gray & Rachel ffreeman ware married by mr Samuel Osborn october 2nd 1729 entred ℘ Joseph Doane Town clerk
Thankfull Brown *

(*To be continued*)

THE
MAYFLOWER DESCENDANT

1620   1920

A QUARTERLY MAGAZINE OF
PILGRIM GENEALOGY AND HISTORY

VOLUME XVII

1915

PUBLISHED BY THE
MASSACHUSETTS SOCIETY OF
MAYFLOWER DESCENDANTS
BOSTON

EASTHAM AND ORLEANS, MASS, VITAL RECORDS

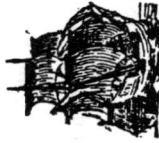

TRANSCRIBED BY THE EDITOR

(*Continued from Vol. XVI, p. 205*)

[p. 93] Joshua Paine & Phebe Snow were married by Mr Osborn March 19th 1729/30 entred ℗ Joseph Doane Town clerk

Samuel paine Son of Joshua and Phebe Paine was Born in Eastham January 28 Day 1730/31

Isaac paine Son of Joshua and Phebe paine was Born in Eastham Febuary the 13 Day 1737/38

Seth Paine Son of Joshua Paine and Phebe paine was Born in Eastham the 12 Day of June 1740

Joshua Paine Son of Joshua and Phebe Paine was Born in Eastham the tenth Day of may 1743

John Nucom & Hannah Bullard ware married by mr Benjamin Webb october 16 : 1729 entred ℗ Joseph Doane Town clerk

October 9th 1729 Joseph netis & Bette Job ware married by Mr Benjamin Webb entred ℗ Joseph Doane Town clerk

March 30 : 1728/9 John Bee & Martha nickason ware married by Nathaniel ffreeman Esqr entred ℗ Joseph Doane Town clerk

august 7th 1729 Nathaniel higgins and Sarah walker was maried by nathaniel ffreeman Esqr entred pr Joseph Doane Town clerk

*These two dates seem to conflict, but are printed as found on the record.

[p. 94] James Rogers junr & Hannah Godfrey ware married in chatham the 21 day of May 1730 by Joseph Doane Justice Peace entred ℗ Joseph Doane Town clerk

Lidea Rogers Daughter of James & Hannah Rogers was born the 9th day of april 1731 entred ℗ Joseph Doane Town clerk

James Rogers Son of James and hannah Rogers was born the 21 day of December 1732 entred ℗ me Joseph Doane Town clark

May 14th 1736 then Silvenis Rogers Son of James Rogers junr was born

[*Sarah Rogers Daughter of James Rogers junr was born the 26th day of march 1738*]

June 29th 1738 then Prince Rogers Son of James Rogers junr was born

August 7th 1704 † then Samuel Rogers Son of James Rogers was born Silvanas Rogers Son of Jams and Hannah Rogers was born ye 22 day of desember 1742

John Brown Died the 19th day of May 1730

Edward Bangs junr of Harwich & Rebecka Higgins of Eastham ware married in Eastham the ninth day of June 1730 by Joseph Doane Justice Peace Entred ℗ Joseph Doane Town clerk

Elkanah Brown and sarah Brown the sun and Dafter of James and Elisabath Brown was Born in Eastham July 18 : 1734

James Brown Jr the sun of James and Elisabath Brown was Born in Eastham July 12 : 1737

Jane Brown the Dafter of James and Elisabath Brown was Born in Eastham June 4 : 1740

Elisabeth Brown Daughter of James and anna Brown was Born in Eastham September 22 Day 1762

Jeremiah Ned & easter Simom ware married the 11 day of June 1730 by Joseph Doane Justice Peace entred ℗ Joseph Doane Town clerk

John Cookson & abagail Caveler Both of Eastham ware married the fourth Day of June 1761 by Samuell Smith Justice peace Entred pr Edward Knowles Town Clerk

august 6th 1730 then Moses Cusen & Experience abamon ware married in Eastham by Joseph Doane Justice Peace

august 6th 1730 then Richard abamon junr & Bettee myric was married in Eastham by Joseph Doane Justice peace entred ℗ Joseph Doane Town clerke

[p. 95] October 7th 1730 Joseph Rogers Son of chrisp & Mary Rogers was born in Eastham

Hannah Rogers Daughter of Jams and Hannah Rogers was born ye 11th day of fabruary 1744/5

Susanna Rogers Daughter of James and Hannah Rogers was born att Eastham on the 19th october 1748

*This entry was crossed out.

†Sic. Probably should have been entered "1740."

Jonathan Rogers the sun of James and hanah Rogers was Born in ᵖastham August 3 1750

november 10th 1730 then Relience Daughter of Garsham & Mary Cole was born in eastham entred ℗ me Joseph Doane Town clerk

Patience cole Daughter of Garsham & Mary Cole was born the 30th day of January 1732/3

Hannah Daughter of Garsham & mary Cole was born the 10th day of May 1735

July 16 : 1737 then Reliance Cole Daughter of Garsham cole was born

november 11th 1739 then Patience Cole Daughter of Garsham Cole was born

Moses Cole Son of Garsham Cole was born the 8th day of December 1741

Kezia Cole Dafter of Garsham Cole was born the 26th day of December 1743

azuba Cole Daughter of Gersham and Mary Cole was born on ye 26d of July 1746

January 14th 1730/31 Then Nehemiah harding of chatham & Pricilla collens ware married by Joseph Doane Justice Peace entred ℗ Joseph Doane Town clerk

february 11th 1730/31 then Josiah Cook junr & hannah Sparrow ware married In eastham by me Joseph Doane Justice entred ℗ Joseph Doane Town clerk

January 26 : 1731/2 then Elijah cook Son of Josiah & Hannah Cook was born entred ℗ me Joseph Doane Town clark

Elizabeth Cook Daughter of Josiah Cook was born the 24 of february 1733/4

Josiah Cook Son of Josiah cook was born the the third day of December 1735

Elijah Cook Son of Josiah Cook was born the eight day of June 1737

Joshua Cook Son of Josiah Cook was born the 12th day of april 1740

[p. 96] July 9th 1730 then Ephraim Covell & Mercy* Brown ware Married by Mr Benjamin Webb

Ami Covell Daughter of Ephraim & Marcy* Covell was born the 23 day of June 1731 entred pr Joseph Doane Town clark

may 30 : 1734 then Phebee Daughter of ephraim covell was born

December 10 : 1736 then Zerviah Daughter of ephraim Covel was born

Ephraim covell Son of Ephraim covell was born august 25 : 1739

amay Couel Dafter of of Ephram Couel and mary* Couel was Born in Eastham septembr the : 13 : 1743

solomon couel sun of Ephram and mary* couel was born in Eastham octobar 7 : 1745

Daniel Couel sun of Ephram and mary* Couel was born in eastham may the 27 : 1748

*Sic.

Mary Couel Dafter of Ephram and mary* Couel was born in Eastham July 10 : 1750

marcy Couel the Dafter of Ephram and mercy* couel was Born in Eastham July 21 : 1754

September 10 : 1730 then Samuel Doyley & Mary Brown junr ware married by Mr Benjamin Webb

November 27 : 1760 Then Isaac Hopkins Elisabeth ary both of Eastham ware married by John freeman Jestice Peace Entred by me Edwrd Knowles Town Cl

October 1rst 1730 then Simeon Doane & apphia higgins ware married by Mr Benjamin Webb

october 7th 1730 then Stephen Atwood & Sarah Collens ware married by Mr Benjamin Webb

[p. 97] October 8 : 1730 then Stephen Snow junr & Rebecka Snow ware married by mr Benjamin Webb

Ruben Snow Son of Stephen and Rebecca Snow was born at Eastham on the 14th day January 1733/4

Lidia Snow Daughter of Stephen and Rebecca Snow was born in Eastham on ye 24th day of march 1736

Rebecca Snow Daughter of Stephen and Rebecca Snow was born at Eastham on ye 7th day of august 1738

Phebe Snow Daughter of Stephen and Rebecca Snow was born at Eastham on the 8 Day of november 1740

Betty Snow daughter of Stephen and Rebecca Snow was born in Eastham on the 17 day of December 1743

October 8 : 1730 then Joshua cook jur & Zilpah Brown ware married by mr Benjamin Webb

Timothy Harding a Son of Barnabas harding and Elesabath Snow was Born in Eastham Second Day of may 1768

ffebruary 11 : 1730/31 then Thomas Rogers & Rebecka Collens ware married by Mr Benjamin Webb

September 2 : 1731 then Lazerus Griffeth and Lidea Doane ware married by Joseph Doane Justice Peace entred ℔ Joseph Doane Town clark

June 10 : 1733 then Mary Griffeth Daughter of Lazerus & Lidea Griffeth was born entred ℔ me Joseph Doane Town clark

[*Isaac Rogers Son of Thomas and Rebecka Rogers was born at Eastham on the 8th day of July 1745 †*]

[p. 98] September 23 : 1730 then Thomas Snow & Sarah young ware married by mr Isaiah Lues Minester entred ℔ Joseph Doane Town clark

May 21 : 1731 then Nathaniel Snow & Mary Doane ware married by Joseph Doane Justice Peace entred ℔ Joseph Doane Town clarke

June 6th 1733 then Samuel Snow Son of Nathaniel & Mary Snow was born in Eastham

*Sic.

† This entry was crossed out. See original page 117.

July 28 : 1736 then James Snow Son of Nathaniel Snow was born

february 9th 1739/40 then Doane Snow Son of nathaniel Snow was born

april the 19 1743 then nathaniel Snow Son of nathaniel Snow was born

June 11 : 1731 Then Barnabas Twining & Hannah Swet was married by Joseph Doane Justice Peace

Jonathan Twining Son of Barnabas & hannah Twining was born ye 26th day of march 1731/2

Barnabas Twining Son of Barnabas Twining was born the 20th day of January 1734/5

Barnabas Twining Son of Barnabas Twining was born July 7th 1737

John Twining Son of Barnabas Twining was born December 9th 1739

Stephen Twining Son of Barnabas and Hannah Twining was born at Eastham on the 19th day of march 1741/2

prince Twining Son of Barnabas and Hannah Twining was born at Eastham on the 23d day of July 1744

Barnabas Twining Departed this Life on the fifth Day of march 1766

June 1 : 1731 Then David Young junr & hannah Twining ware married by Joseph Doane Justice Peace

David young Son of David & hannah young was born the 19 day of october 1733

Ezra young Son of David young junr was born 28 day of november 1735

Eleazor young Son of David young junr was born the eight of february in the year 1737/8

nehemiah young Son of David young junr was born the 19th day of September 1739

[p. 99] June 3 : 1731 Then Ebenezor Mott & Deborah atwood ware married by Mr Benjamin Webb Entred ℔ Joseph Doane Town clark

September 2 : 1731 Then Thomas Savig & Martha Doane ware married by Mr Benjamin Webb married by Mr Benjamin Webb entred ℔ Joseph Doane Town clark

September 30th 1731 Then Lazerus Griffeth & Lidea Doane ware married in Eastham by Joseph Doane Justice Peace entred ℔ Joseph Doane Town clark

October 5th 1731 Then Jonathan Shaw & Sarah Rich was married in Eastham by Joseph Doane Justice Peace entred ℔ Joseph Doane Town clark

august 6 : 1730 then Thomas freeman & Dorathy Cole ware married by mr Samuel orsbon

february 16 : 1730 then Roulan fish & elizabeth harding ware married by mr Samuel orsbon

December 10 : 1730 then Daniel Cole & Martha Rogers ware married by Mr Samuel orsbon

february 18 : 1730 then Jacob Cook & marcy young ware married by mr Samuel Orsbon

September 23 : 1731 then John harding & elizabeth young ware married by mr Samll orsbon

September 30 : 1731 then David nickason & elizabeth Mayo ware married by mr Samuel orsborn all entred ℘ me Joseph Doane Town clark

Joshua Cole Son of Daniel & martha cole was born in Eastham the 9th day of ffebruary 1731/2 entred ℘ Joseph Doane Town clark:

martha Coale the Dafter of Daniel Coale and martha Cole was born in Eastham Aprel 24 : 1735

Daniel Cole the sun of Daniel and martha Cole was born in Eastham may 11 : 1739

heman Cole the sun of Daniel and martha Cole was Born in Eastham July 26 : 1749

Joshua Cole the Son of Daniel and matha Cole Died May the 31 Day 1754

James Cook Son of Joshua Cook junr & Zilpha cook was born June the 7th 1731 entred ℘ Joseph Doane Town clark

Marcy Cook Daughter of Joshua Cook junr & Zilpha Cook was born the 30 day of June 1733

Isayah Cook Son of Joshua cook junr & Zilpha cook was born the third day of June 1735

Isaiah Cook Son of Joshua Cook junr was born the 31 day of July 1737

[p. 100] January 27 : 1731/2 then Thomas Snow & abigail Doane ware married by Joseph Doane Justice Peace entred ℘ Joseph Doane Town clark

Elnathan Snow Son of Thomas Snow was born May the Second 1734

Abigel Snow Daughter of Thomas Snow was born March the 9th 1736/7

Susanna Snow Daughter of Thomas Snow was born the 31 day of march 1743

Ruth snow the Dafter of Thomas and abigail snow was Born in Eastham Aprel ye : 11 : 1749

february 3d 1731/2 then Ebenezer Cole & Elizabeth Cole ware married in Eastham by Joseph Doane Justice Peace entred ℘ Joseph Doane Town clark

Markis Cole Son of Ebenezor & Elizabeth Cole was born the 25th day of January 1732/3 entred ℘ me Joseph Doane Town clark

Markus Cole Son of Ebenezor & Elizabeth cole was born the eight day of april 1734

Ebenezor Cole Son of Ebenezor Cole was born the 12 day of february 1739/40

Elizabet! Cole Daughter of Ebenezor Cole was born the 25 day of february 1740/41

Jerusha cole Daughter of Ebenezer and Elisabeth cole was born at Eastham on the 18th day of april 1743

february 10th 1731/2 then Joshua Seers of yarmouth & Rebecka mayo of Eastham ware married in Eastham by Joseph Doane Justice Peace entred ℘ Joseph Doane Town clark

March 8th 1731/2 Then Henry young & Elizabeth higgins ware married In Eastham by Joseph Doane Justice Peace

april the 6th 1734 then Seth young Son of Henry & elizabeth young was born

Sollomon young Son of henry young was born the 14 of october 1735

sollomon Son of henry young born 18 day of may 1737

May 14th 1739 then Josiah young Son of hery young was born

anne young Daughter of Henry young was born the 4th day of December 1740

March 9th 1731/2 then Nathaniel Crosby & Hesther young ware married by Joseph Doane Justice Peace

Eunes young daughter of Henry and Elesibeth young was born at Eastham the 15th day of January 1742/3

Sarah Young daughter of Henry and Elesibeth young was born at Eastham the 6th day of february 1744/5

[p. 101] february 15th 1731/2 then Joseph hambleton & Martha Atkins ware married by Nathaniel Freeman Justice Peace entred pr Joseph Doane Town clark

John Hambleton the Son of Joseph and matha hambleton was Born at Eastham November ye 5 : 1747

Theoder harding Son of Theoder harding & Serah harding was born the 11th day of June 1730

Joshua harding Son of Theoder & Sarah harding was born the 22 day of march 1731/2

august 12 : 1732 then Seth higgins Son of Ichabud & Jane higgins was born entred pr me Joseph Doane Town clark

Margret Snow Daughter of Elkins Snow was born the Secnd day of august 1738

Suseanna Snow Daughter of Elkins Snow was born august 26 day of august 1741

Prissilla Snow Daughter of Elkins Snow was born 9 day of December 1743

Elkens snow sun of Elkens snow Disseased and susanah snow was born in Eastham Desembar : ye : 28 : 1745

[p. 102] april 27th 1732 then Richard Higgins Died

october 30 : 1732 then James Harding Died

october 15 : 1732 then Robert Pepper Son of Robert & Mary Pepper was born

marcy pepper the Dafter of Robart and mary pepper was Born in Eastham July 7 : 1737

Isaac pepper the sun of Robart and mary pepper was Born in Eastham Desembar ye : 7 : 1739

Mary pepper the Dafter of Robart and mary pepper was Born in Eastham August ye 1 : 1742

february the first 1732/3 then Jonathan Paine & Marcy Doane ware maried by Joseph Doane Justice Peace entred ℘ Joseph Doane

April 10th 1734 then Pheebee Paine Daughter of Jonathan & Marcy Paine was born

March 22 : 1732/3 then Ruben Meyrick and abigail higgins ware married by Mr Samuel Osborn entred ℣ Joseph Doane Town clark

Elizabeth Meyrick Daughter of Ruben myrick was born 22 november 1734

abigel merick Daughter of Ruben meyrick was born the 30th of august 1736

Joseph Meyrick Son of Ruben Meyrick was born July the 16 : 1738

Ruben meyrick Son of Ruben and abigel meyrick was born ye 12th of June 1742

Nathanll meyrick Son of Ruben and abigel Meyrick was born September ye 23d : 1744

April 12 : 1733 then Enos Knowls & Sarah Sparrow ware married by Mr Samuel Osborn entred ℣ Joseph Doane Town Clark

Bethia Knowls Daughter of Enos & Sarah Knowls born the 12 day of January 1734/5

[p. 105] Samuel Betee & Mary Harding ware married the first day of febuary 1732/3 in Eastham by Nathaniel freeman Justice Peace entred ℣ me Joseph Doane Town clark

Samuel Betee Son of Samuel Betee was born the 10th of april 1733

Thomas Betee son of Samuel Betee was born the 4th of September 1735

Gideon Betee Son of Samuel Betee was born the 7th of march 1738

Nathaniel Betee Son of Samuel Betee was born the 12th of January 1740

mary Batee dafter of Samuel Batee was born the 6th of July 1744

June 14 : 1733 then Jacob Davis of harwich & Mary Rogers of Eastham ware married In Eastham by Joseph Doane Justic Peace entred ℣ me Joseph Doane Town clark

Joseph Lewen of Plymouth & Rejoyce walker of Eastham ware married in Eastham the 9th day of november 1732 by Nathaniel freeman Justice Peace entred ℣ me Joseph Doane Town clark

September 23 : 1731 then Theoder higgins & Jane Brown ware married by Mr Benjamin Webb

april 9th 1734 then Thankfull higgins Daughter of Theoder higgins was born

September 28 : 1737 then Eunis higgins Daughter of Theoder higgins was born

october 7th 1731 then John mayo & Tabitha Snow ware married by Mr Benjamin Webb

april 19 : 1733 then John mayo Son of John mayo was born

September 25 : 1737 Bettee Mayo Daughter of John mayo was born

June 11 : 1739 then Susanna mayo Daughter of John mayo was born

June 1741 then Lemuel mayo Son of John Tabitha mayo was born

may 1743 then Sarah mayo Daughter of John may was born

march 1745 Simeon mayo Son of John mayo was born

may 1748 Abijah mayo Son of John mayo was born and Died march 1760

July 1751 then Elekiel mayo Son of John and Tabitha mayo was Born in Eastham

(To be continued)

July 2 : 1736 then Marcy Paine Daughter of Jonathan Paine & mercy Paine was born

October 20th 1738 then Experience Paine Daughter of Jonathan Paine and Mercy Paine was born

May 14th 1741 then Jonathan Paine Son of Jonathan & Mercy Paine was born

Mercy Paine Daughter of Jonathan & mercy Paine was born october 2 : 1743

[p. 103] July 12th 1732/3 then abigel Daughter of Easse* & Experience Mayo was born entred ℣ Joseph Doane Town clark

Lidea Mayo Daughter of Esse* mayo was born the 9th of may 1734

Sarah Mayo Daughter of Esse* mayo was born October 13th 1736

Debora Mayo Daughter of Esse* mayo was born the 17th day of. august 1738

Expearanc mayo the Dafter of asa and Expearinc mayo was born in Eastham Aprel : ye : 27 : 1741

Asa mayo the sun of Asa mayo and Expearnce mayo was born in Eastham August : ye : 18 : 1743

March the 8th 1732/3 Then Daniel Doane & Ruth Cole ware married by Joseph Doane Justice Peace entred ℣ Joseph Doane Town clark

Mary Doane Daughter of Daniel & Ruth Doane was born the 4th day of December 1733

Daniel Doane Son of Daniel Doane was born the first day of June 1736

Nathaniel Doane Son of Daniel Doane was born the 8th day of february 1738/9

Joseph Doane Son of Daniel Doane was born the 8th day of october 1741

Ruth Doane Daughter of Daniel Doane was born the first day of november 1744

Then † Timothy Doane and Sarah Higgins ware Married by Mr Cheever Entred pr Edward Knowles Town Clerk

May the 6 : 1759 then Timothy Doane Died

[p. 104] September the 15 : 173 ‡ Then George Shaw Son of John & Martha Shaw was born entred ℣ me Joseph Doane Town clark

April 1st 1733 then Martha Shaw Daughter of John & Martha Shaw was born entred ℣ Joseph Doane Town clark

June 18 : 1735 then John Shaw Son of John & martha Shaw was born entred ℣ Joseph Doane Town clark

November 15 : 1732 then Liutt John Cole & Mrs Sarah higgins ware married by Mr Samuel Osborn entred ℣ Joseph Doane Town clark

*Asa.   See fifth child.

† The date was not recorded.

‡ Sic.

EASTHAM AND ORLEANS, MASS., VITAL RECORDS

(Continued from page 37)

[p. 106] october 14 : 1731 then John Bee & Mercy Mulford ware married by Mr Benjamin Webb

Rebaca Bee the Dafter of John and marcy bee was Born at Eastham July : ye : 3 : 1732

marcy Bee the Dafter of John and marcy Bee was Born in Eastham Desembar : ye : 1 : 1733

martha Bee the Dafter of John and marcy Bee was Born in Eastham August 15 : 1739

December 3 . 1731 then Ichabud higgins & Jane Snow ware married by Mr Benjamin Webb

february 24 : 1732 John Mott & Lidea Snow ware married by Mr Benjamin Webb

January 27 : 1732 Eleazor Doane & hannah mayo ware married by Mr Benjamin Webb

June 5 . 1732 Cornelis Tower & hannah higgins ware Married by Mr Benjamin Webb

Jonas Dean and Sarah higgins both of Eastham were married by mr Isaaih Lewis april 13 Day 1758 Entred by me Edward Knowles Town Cler

march 23 : 1772 Silvenus Snow Died

[p. 107] July 26 : 1732 Robert Pepper & Mary Snow ware married by mr Benjamin Webb

october 12 . 1732 Samuel Snow & Elisabath * ffreeman ware married by Mr Benjamin Webb

samuel snow sun of samuel and Elisabath snow was born in Eastham 1735 . 12 in octobar

Abagil snow the Dafter of samuel and Elisabath snow was born in Eastham January 21 : 1733/4

marcy snow the Dafter of samuel and Elisabath snow was born in Eastham may 8 : 1737

treat snow the sun of samuel and Elisabath snow snow was born in Eastham may 27 : 1739

betty snow the Dafter of samuel and Elisabath snow was born in Eastham march 18 : 1741

mary snow was born november 27 : 1743

Joseph snow was born January 9 : 1745

sparrow snow was born July 16 : 1746 and Died in the year 1748

sparro snow was born Aprel 12 : 1748

pheby snow was born march : 6 : 1750

October 20 : 1732 John clark & Mercy wetherel ware married by Mr Benjamin Webb

* "Mary" was crossed out and "Elisabath" interlined in the same hand.

January 3 : 1733 Nathaniel Smith & Mercy walker ware married by Mr Benjamin Webb

february 1 . 1733 Silvenis Snow & hannah Cole ware married by Mr Benjamin Webb

September 29 : 1734 then Edward Snow Son of Silveni Snow & hannah his wife was born

March 29 : 1741 then Silvenis Snow Son of Silvenus Sno was born

may 9 : 1743 mary Snow Daughter of Silvanus and hannah Snow was born in Eastham

June 25 : 1745 Edward Snow Son of Silvanus and hannah Snow was born in Eastham

march 6 : 1748 tabathy Snow Daughter of Sil and hannah Snow was born in Eastham

in mrs hanah snow the wife of mr salvenas snow Died August : 3 : 1750 in 38 year age

May 10 : 1733 Willard Knowls & Bethiah Atwood ware married by Mr Benjamin Webb

willard Knowls son of willard Knowls was born october 26 : 1737

David Knowls Son of willard Knowls was born the 21 September 1739

July 22 : 1750 Collier Snow Son of Silvanus and mehitable snow was born in Eastham

June 22 : 1756 Silvanus Snow Son of Silvanus and mehitable Snow was born in Eastham

march 22 : 1759 then hannah Snow Daughter of Silvanus and mehitable Snow was born in Eastham mehitable Snow wife of Sil Snow Died

July 5 . 1733 Isaac higgins junr & Abigel freeman ware married by Mr Benjamin Webb

mary higgins Daughter of Isaac and abigail higgins was born in Eastham february 24 : 1735

Eunis higgins Daughter of Isaac & abigial higgins was Born in Eastham october 21 : 1736

Abraham higgins Son of Isaac and abigial higgins was Born in Eastham october 10 : 1738

Luce higgins Daughter of Isaac and abigiel higgins was Born in Eastham november 10 : 1740

Abigiel higgins Daughter of Isaac and abigiel higgins was Born in Eastham may 21 : 1743

Isaac higgins Son of Isaac and abigiel higgins was Born in Eastham June 15 : 1745

Jacob higgins Son of Isaac higgins and abigiel was Born in Eastham September 6 : 1747

Joseph higgins Son of Isaac higgins and abigiel higgins was Born in Eastham november 8 : 1749

Epheram higgins Son of Isaac higgins and abigiel was Born in Eastham november 13 : 1750

Abraham Son of Isaac Died December 15 : 1763
abraham higgins Son of Isaac and abigiel Died Decbe 15 1763

[p. 108] Elizabeth vickery Daughter of David & Martha vickery was born the 28th day of July 1733

hudson vickery sun of David and martha vickry was born in Eastham July 27 : 1736

Ruth Mereen Daughter of John and Rebacca mereen was Born in Eastham april 13 Day 1756

Hannah mereen Daughter of John and Rebacca mereen was Born in Eastham october 9 day 1758 and Died in april 11 day 1765

Daniel mereen Son of John and Rebacca mereen was Born in Eastham october the 5 Day 1760

Rebacca mereen Daughter of John and Rebacca mereen was Born in Eastham September the 13 Day 1762

Hannah mereen Daughter of John and Rebacca mereen was Born in wellfleet march the 20 Day 1766

Hanna Lues Daughter of Mr Isaiah Lues & Mrs Abigel Lues was born September 25 : 1731

Winslow Lewes born at Marshfield the Son of Mr Isaih and Abigel Lewes the third day of July 1741

January 31 : 1733/4 then Joshua Cole & Sarah Cole of Eastham ware married In Eastham by Joseph Doane Justice Peace

January 8th 1734/5 then Nathan Cole Son of Joshua & Sarah Cole was born

april 4th 1736 then Elizabeth cole daughter of Joshua cole was born

June 23 : 1737 then Ruth Cole Daughter of Joshua Cole was born

[*September 19 : 1737 then James cole Son of Joshua cole was born**]

march 9 : 1738/9 then Patience Cole Daughter of Joshua Cole was born and died may 23 : 1755

november the 20th 1742 then Joshua Cole Son of Joshua cole was born

may the 4th 1743 then Joshua Cole Son of Joshua cole Died.

february the 7th 1743/4 then Lidea cole Daughter of Joshua Cole was born

Joshua cole ye Son of Joshua and Sarah Cole was born at Eastham on the 5th day of march 1745/6

marcus Cole sun of Joshua and sarah Cole was born in Eastham march ye 29 : 1750

[p. 109] february 20th 1733/4 then David ned & Bethia nopie ware married by Joseph Doane Justice Peac[e]

September 23 : 1730† then Thomas Snow & Sarah young of eastham ware marrie by mr Isaiah Lues

Rachal Snow Daughter of Thomas and Sarah snow was born in Eastham may the 18 Day 1741†

october 14 : 1731 then Daniel crosby & of harwich & Ruth cole ware married by mr Isaiah Lues

turn to pd 69

*This entry was crossed out.

†Sic.

November 1 : 1732 then John ffry & Rachell witherel ware married
 by mr Isayah Lues

May 31 : 1732 then Thomas nucomb junr & Marcy Tilton ware married by mr Isaiah Lues

June 21 : 1733 then Thomas Adi and Thankfull atwood ware married
 by mr Isaiah Lues

July 17 : 1733 then Thomas Dill & Mehitable Brown ware married
 by mr Isaiah Lues

December 6th 1733 then James Stetson & Mrs Margeret Oats ware
 married by mr Isaiah Lues

January 24th 1733/4 then Elisha higgins junr & hannah atwood ware
 married by Mr Isaiah Lues

January 2 : 1734/5 then Mr Samuel Mayo & Mrs Ruth higgins ware
 married by Joseph Doane Justice Peace

february 12 : 1734/5 then Ephraim Cook & Mary Myrick ware Married by Joseph Doane Justice Peace

July 24 : 1735 then Nathaniel Mayo 3rd & mercy cole ware married
 by Joseph Doane Justice Peace

august 21 : 1735 then Joseph young & Rebecka nucomb ware married
 by Joseph Doane Justice Peace

October 8 . 1735 then Elisha Snow & abigel Doane ware married by
 Joseph Doane Justice Peace

December the 8th 1735 then Nathaniel Snow Son of Elisha & abigel
 Snow was born

october 29th 1737 then Ebenezer * Snow Son of Elisha and abigel
 born

Osborn Snow the Son of Elisha and abigel Snow was born august
 ye 30th 1741

Elisha Snow the Son of Elisha and abigel Snow was born November
 ye 4th 1745

(To be continued)

September the 9th 1744 then Elisha Doane Son of Elisha Doane was born

Sarah Doane Daughter of Elisha Doane was Born January ye 15th 1747

January 15 : 1733/4 then Stephen Totmon & Easther higgins ware married by Mr Samuel Osborn

January 23 : 1733/4 then william Meyrick & Elizabeth Osborn ware maried by Mr Benjamin Webb

william Meyrick Son of william & Elizabeth Meyrick was born october 26 . 1734

Stephen Totmon Son of Stephen Totmon was born the 4 day of april 1737

March 14 : 1733/4 then Warren Green & Mary Paine ware married by Mr Samuel osborn

Desire Green Daughter of Warren & Mary Green was born the 14th day of January 1734/5

Ruben Cook Son of Ephraim cook was born 20 day of august 1741

Isaac pene and Rebeca stephens Boath of Eastham ware married in Eastham by Mr Isaiah Lues Clar may 23 : 1755

[p. 111] Isaac : Mayo Son of Isaac & Patience Mayo was born february 23 : 1732/3 Died march 4th 1732/3

Isaac Mayo Son of Isaac & Patience Mayo was born June 6th 1734

John sweet and Zibiah young Both of Eastham ware marriade in Eastham By Mr Isaiah Lues Clar may 1 : 1754

John Doane Son of John Doane Esqr & Mrs Jane his wife was born the 17th of March 1733/4

Elisha pike Deborah Brown Boath of Eastham ware marrid in Eastham By Mr Isaiah Lues Clar June 14 : 1754

Jonathan Brown Son of Samuel & Lidea brown was born october 1 : 1734

Jonathan hiller and mary payne Boath of Eastham ware married in Eastham by Mr Isaiah Lues Clar may 22 : 1755

Sarah Hiller Daughter of Jonathan and mary hiller was Born in Eastham august the 31 Day 1756

Elizebeth hiller Daughter of Jonathan and mary hiller was Born in Eastham September the 8 Day 1758

Jonathan hiller Son of Jonathan and mary hiller was Born in Eastham may the 24 Day 1760

Tobias-Paine hiller Son of Jonathan and mary hiller was Born in Eastham apriel the 26 Day 1762

[p. 112] William Twining Died January 23 : 1734/5

mr John Sparrow Died the ffebruary 23 : 1734/5

october 25 : 1733 Ebenezor Brown & Rebecka Smith ware married by Mr Benjamin Webb

March 11 : 1734 John Dunkin & Keziah Bakon* ware married by mr Benjamin Webb

* "Doane" was crossed out and "Bakon" interlined, in the same hand.

EASTHAM AND ORLEANS, MASS., VITAL RECORDS

(Continued from page 82)

[p. 110] March 14th 1733/4 then Elisha Doane & Elizabeth Sparrow ware married by Joseph Doane Justice Peace

June* 26 : 1734† Then the Revd Mr John Avery & Mrs Ruth Knowls ware married by Mr Samuel Osborn

february 21 : 1735/6 then Rebecka Doane Daughter of Elisha Doane junr was born

april the 31 day 1738 then Mercy Doane Daughter of Elisha Doane was born and Dyed In february 1739/40

January 20 : 1739/40 then Silvenis Doane Son of Elisha Doane was born

Marcy Doane Daughter of Elisha Doane was born the 27 day of January 1741/2

* "January" was crossed out and "June" interlined, in the same hand.
† The "4" was written over "3".

march 14 : 1734 Lamuel Rich & Elizabeth harding ware married by Mr Benjamin webb

may 16 : 1734 James Brown junr & Elizabeth Smith ware married by Mr Benjamin webb

May 29 : 1734 Edward Knowls junr & ann Knowls ware Married by Mr Benjamin webb

march 7th 1734/5 then Sarah Daughter of Edward Knowls junr & ann Knowls was born

february 19 : 1736/7 then Benjamin Knowls Son of Edward Knowls junr was born

Hannah Knowls Daughter of Edward Knowls junr was born the 16 day of april 1739

Thomas Knowls Son of Edward Knowls & Ann Knowls was born the 30th day of January 1743/4

august 22th 1741 then Edward Knowles Son of Edward Knowls & ann Knowls was Born

february 6 : 1747/8 Elijah Knowles Son of Edward Knowles & ann Knowles was born

Sarah Knowles Daughter of Edwrd and Ann Died in December at Falmouth 1775.

august 22 : 1734 Prince collens & abiel Doane ware married by Mr Benjamin webb

Rebecka Collens Daughter of Prence collens was born the 20th of September 1735

September 19 : 1734 Nathaniel Mayo jur & hannah horton ware married by Mr Benja webb

Phebe Mayo Daughter of Nathaniel and hannah mayo was born in Eastham march the 12 1740

December 6 : 1734 David Rich & hannah Brown were married by Mr Benja webb

Elisabeth Rich Daughter of David and hannah Rich was born in Eastham march 15 1743

January 16 : 1735/6 James mayo & Elizabeth higgins married by Mr Benjamin webb

Joshua Mayo Son of James mayo was born the 25 day of July 1735

James mayo Son of James and Elizebeth mayo was born in Eastham october 12 : 1745

february 20 : 1735/6 Joseph Brown & Susana Cole Married by Mr Benja Webb

Jerusha Brown Daughter of Joseph Brown was born the 29 day of May 1738

Joseph Brown Son of Joseph and susanah Brown was Born at Eastham June ye 2d 1745

[p. 113] Sarah Cole Daughter of Daniel & Thankfull Cole was born november 11th 1729

Thankfull Cole Daughter of Daniel & Thankfull Cole was born march 30th 1731

Mary Cole Daughter of Daniel & Thankfull Cole was born march 16th 1733

Elizabeth Meyrick Daughter of Ruben meyrick was born the 22 day of november 1734

abigel Myrick Daughter of Ruben myrick was born the 30th day of august 1736

July 24 : 1735 then Nathaniel Mayo tertio & Mercy Cole both of Eastham ware married in Eastham ꝑ Joseph Doane Justice Peace

august 14th 1735 then Joseph Young & Rebecka Nucomb both of Eastham ware married in Eastham by Joseph Doane Justice Peace

[p. 114] october 16th 1735 then Samuel Knowls Son of capt Samuel Knowls & Hannah ffreeman ware married by Joseph Doane Justice Peace

May 16 : 1734 then Joseph Smale of Truroe & Jane Grose of Eastham ware married by Mr Isaiah Lues

June 27 : 1734 then william covel junr & Joanah atwood ware married by Mr Isaiah Lues

august 8 : 1734 then Jeremiah hawes of chatham & Phebee young of Eastham ware married by Mr Isaiah Lues

November 7th 1734 then Jesse Eldrege & Abigel Smith ware married by Mr Isaiah Lues

[p. 115] January 2 : 1734/5 then Thomas Holbrooks & Margret Doane were married by mr Isayah Lues

December 1st 1735 then Margret Holbrooks Daughter of Thomas holbrooks was born

Jeruse Done the Dafter of Thomas holbrooks was born in Eastham January 18 : 1737

Thomas holbroks was born in Eastham January 30 : 1739/40

Isaiah holbroks the sun of Thomas holbroks was born in Eastham may 23 : 1742

Abial holbroks the Dafter of Thomas holbroks was born in Eastham may 10 : 1745

John holbroks the sun of Thomas holbroks was born in Eastham octobar 18 : 1748

Isaac Doane holbroks the sun of Thomas holbroks was born in Eastham febuary 18 : 1741*

January 9th 1734/5 then Sam Sion & Mery wiknot ware married by Mr Isaiah Lues

June 26 : 1735 then John Harding junr & Thankfull Rich ware married by Mr Isaiah Lues

July 3 : 1735 then Moses higgins & Elizabeth Arey ware married by mr Isaiah Lues

Gideon Higgins Son of moses higgins was born the 22 day of July 1738

Elnathan higgins Son of Moses higgins was born the 31 day of may 1740

Jesse higgins Son of moses Higgins was born the 29th day of July 1743

*Sic.

Azubah Higgens Daughter of moses and Elizabeth Higgens was born
at Eastham January ye 22d 1744/5
David Higgins Son of moses and Elisabeth Higgens was born ye 1th
day of August : 1746
phebe higgens Dafter of moses and Elisabath higgens was born in
Eastham June 14 : 1749
May 30th 1734 then Seth Rider & Reliance Smith ware married by
mr Samuel Osborn
Seth Rider Son of Seth Rider was born the 6th day of December
1737
January* 30 : 1734 then Stephen Snow & Mary Cole ware married
by Mr Samuel Osborn
ffebruary 17 : 1736/7 then Moses Snow Son of Stephen Snow was
born
June the 30th 1738 then Heman Snow Son of Stephen Snow was born
[p. 116] July 2 : 1735 then archelus Lues & mary Tailler ware married
by Mr Samuel Osborn
Solomon Lewes Son of Archelus Lues was born the 20th December
1743/4
John Lues Son of Archelus Lues was born the 17 day of march
1742/3
July 17 : 1735 then Elisha Linel & Rebecka Paine ware married by
Mr Samuel Osborn
april 14 : 1736 then Hannah Linel Daughter of Elisha & Rebecka
Linel was born
Rebeca Linel the wife of Elisha Linel Died the 18th day of february
1743/4
October 9th 1735 then Ebenezor cook & Marcy Paine ware married
by Mr Samuel Osborn
Ruth Cook Daughter of Ebenezer Cook was born the 23 day of
January 1736/7
ffebruary 11th 1735/6 then Simeon Merifield & Thankfull Rider ware
married by Mr Samuel osborn
Daniel higgens the sun of Enoch and sarah higgens was Born in
Eastham octobar 24 : 1757
Sarah higgins Daughter of Enoch and Sarah higgins was Born in
Eastham april 24 1759
Elisabeth higgins Daughter of Enoch and Sarah higgins was Born in
Eastham march 15 Day 1761
Enoch higgins Son of Enoch and Sarah higgins was Born in Eastham
may 7 Day 1763
Abigail Higgins Daughter of Enoch and Sarah Higgins was Born in
Eastham January the 3 Day 1768
[p. 117] Mrs Mary Hopkins wife of Mr Joshua Hopkins Died the
first day of march 1733/4

* "June" was crossed out and "January" interlined, in the same hand.

September 30th 1736 then Henry Snow & Rebecka Berry both of
Eastham ware married by Joseph Doane Justice Peace
Azubah Sears Daughter of Josiah and Azubah Sears was born in
Eastham November the 5th 1747
Bethiah Sears Daughter of Josiah & Azubah Sears was born in
Eastham July 15 1750
David Sears the Son of Josiah and Azubah Sears was born in East-
ham April 14 1753
Samuel Sears Son of Josiah and Azubah Sears was born in Eastham
April 18 1755
Azubah the wife of Josiah Sears Died march 1762
Josiah Sears Departed this Life in January 1772
September 30th 1736 then Josiah Seers of chatham & Azubah Knowls
ware married by Joseph Doane Justice Peace
august 23 : 1737 then Marcy Daughter of Josiah Seers was born
february 25th 1742/3 then Jerusha Seers Daughter of Josiah Seers
was born
february the first 1744/5 then Josiah Seers Son of Josiah Seers was
born
October 7th 1736 then Elijah Doane & Suseana Lues ware married
by Joseph Doane Justice Peace
mercy Rogers Daughter of Thomas and Rebecca Rogers was Born
in Eastham on the 18 Day of april 1756
mary Rogers Daughter of Thomas and Rebecca Rogers was Born
in Eastham on the first Day of october 1758
December 2nd 1736 then Thomas Rogers & Rebeka higgins ware
married by Joseph Doane Justice Peace
Serah Rogers Daughter of Thomas Rogers was born the 26th day of
march 1738
Ruth Rogers Daughter of Thomas Rogers was born the 8th day of
october 1739
Thomas Rogers Son of Thomas Rogers was born the 25th day of
february 1742/3
Isaac Rogers Son of Thomas and Rebecka Rogers was born at East-
ham on the 8th day July 1745
Stephen Rogers Son of Thomas and Rebecca Rogers was born at
Eastham on the 24th day of January 1747
Solomon Rogers Son of Thomas and Rebecca Rogers was Born in
Eastham april the 28 Day 1750
Look a Bove for the Rest
[p. 118] Nathaniel Paine Son of Theophilas Paine was born the 7th
day of September 1736
Ruth Paine Daughter of Theophilas Paine was born the 3rd day of
february 1737/8
John Paine Son of Theophilas Paine was born the 20th day of July
1739
Ruth Doane Daughter of Simeon Doane born the 5th day of march
1733/4

abigel Doane Daughter of Simeon Doane born the 6th day of august 1735

Rebecka Cook Daughter of Thomas Cook born 3 of october 1720

Gideon Cook Son of Thomas Cook born July 23 : 1722

Sarah Cook Daughter of Thomas Cook born July 23 : 1724 esenath Daughter of Thomas Cook born may 3 : 1726

Dinah Cook Daughter of Thomas Cook born 22* february 2*: 1732/3

[p. 119] Barnabas Smith Son of Seth Smith was born the 31 day of may 1731

Rebecka Smith Daughter of Seth Smith was born the 22 day of March 1734/5

Seth Smith Son of Seth and ann Smith was born the 19th Day of July 1737

Edward Smith Son of Seth and ann Smith was born the 2d day of august 1739

ann Smith daughter of Seth and ann Smith was born the 1th day of march 1742/3

Elisabath smith Dafter of seth and ann smith was born in Eastham octobar 10 : 1745

ffebruary 25th 1736/7 then Elnathan Doane & Martha Paddock both of Eastham ware married In Eastham by Joseph Doane Justice Peace

Debro Doane Daughter of Elnathan was born the 26 day of may 1739

Daniel Doane Son of Elnathan Doane was born the 14 day of april 1741

August 12 : 1736 then aron Snow & Sarah Gross ware married In Eastham by mr Samuel osborn

ffebruary 25 : 1736/7 then Jesse nickason & Thankfull Cook ware maried by mr osborn

[p. 120] October 28 : 1736 then Elkenah young & Mercy mayo ware maried by Mr Samuel Osborn

Mr Job Avry of Truro and Mrs Jane Thacher of Eastham in the County of Barnstable in the provenc of the masetuset Bay in nue England ware married in Eastham by the Revrrd mr Benimin webb paster of the north church in the south presint in Eastham on the 30 Day of Desembr 1742 Recorded pr Thomas Knowles Town Clark of Eastham

January 13 : 1736/7 then Daniel Seers & Mercy Snow ware maried by mr Samuel Osborn

Ruth Doane the Dafter of samuel and Darcas Doane was Born in Eastham June the 3 : 1752 and Died January 5 : 1752

Joel Doane the sun of samuel and Dorcas Doane was Born in Eastham febuary 17 : 1754

Shubal Cook Son of Ephraim Cook was born the 6th day of June 1736.

Ruben Cook Son of Epraim Cook was born 20th of august 1741

Isaac Smith Son of Samuel and mary Smith was born november ye 13th 1743

*Sic.

Rebeca Smith daughter of Samuel and mary Smith was born august ye 31th 1747

[p. 121] Anna Doane daughter of Isaac Doane Jur was born 28 day of June 1736

John Brown and sarah Cook Boath of Eastham ware marrid in Eastham By Mr Isaiah Lues Clar febuary 19 : 1756

Survia Brown Daughter of John Brown and Sarah was Born in Eastham november the 21 Day 1756

Joshua Brown Son of John and Sarah Brown was Born in Eastham the 28 Day of January 1759

Elkenah Rogers Son of Elkenah Rogers was born the 9th day of July 1734

february 23 : 1738/9 then nathaniel Rogers Son of Elkenah Rogers was born

September the 6 . 1741 then Josiah Rogers Son of Elkenah Rogers was born

Elkenah Rogers Died September ye 10 : 1759

Elkenah Rogers Jur Died Novenber ye 18 : 1758

Isaac Bacor and hanah Cole Boath of Eastham ware marrid in Eastham By Mr Isaiah Lues Clar march 25 : 1756

Joshua Rogers Son of Elkenh and Mercy Rogers Born october 24 : 1755

Matha Rogers Daughter of Elkenah and Marcy Rogers Born was B october 24 day 1757

Elkenah Rogers Son of Elkenah and Mercy Rogers was Born at Eastham January the 1 Day 1760

June 19th 1737 then Mr Samuel Knowles Died

June 24th 1737 then Mathias Burges of yarmouth & Dorkis Cole of Eastham ware Married by Joseph Doane Justice Peace

Hannah Knowls Daughter of Willard Knowls born the 26 day of october 1733

Joseph Knowls Son of Willard Knowls born 22 day of october 1735

willard Knowls Son of willard Knowls was born october 26 : 1737

David Knowls Son of willard Knowls was born September 21 : 1739

Bethiah Knowls was born the 13th of January 1741/2

John Knowles the sun of willard and bethiah Knowles was Born in Eastham June 9 : 1744

mary Knowles the Dafter of willard and bethiah Knowles was Born in Eastham octobar 20 : 1746

tamparnce Knowles the Dafter of willard and bethiah Knowles was Born in Eastham march 4 : 1749

Rebacah Knowles the Dafter of willard and bethiah Knowles was Born in Eastham Aprel 12 : 1751

seth Knowles the sun of willard and bethiah Knowles was Born in Eastham may 16 : 1753

william Knowles Son of willard and bethiah Knowles born in Eastham may 14 : 1755

[p. 122] September the first 1737 then Joshua Doane & Mary freeman both of Eastham ware married in Eastham by Joseph Doane Justice Peace

Tamson Doane Daughter of Joshua Doane & Mary Doane was born in Eastham the 16th day of September 1738

Joshua Doane Son of Joshua Doane & mary Doane was born the third day of January 1739/40

Keziah Doane Daughter of Joshua Doane was born the 11th day of april 1742

Heman Doane Son of Joshua Doane was born the 11 day of January 1743/4

Eunice Doane Daughter of Joshua Doane was born apriel ye 12 : 1746

Seth Doane Son of Joshua Doane was Born april ye 12 : 1748

Joseph Doane Son of Joshua Doane was Born June ye 27 — 1750

Mary Doane Daughter of Joshua Doane was Born Jun ye 25 — 1752

Azariah Doane Son of Joshua Doane was Born June ye 16 — 1754

august 20 : 1732 then Joannah Covell Daughter of willm Covell junr was born

Zepheniah harding Son of John harding was born the 30 day of august 1736

nickolus harding sun of John harding Jr and ann harding was Born in Eastham octobar : ye : 6 : 1738

John harding sun of John and ann harding was born at Eastham July ye : 12 : 1745

thankful harding Dafter of John and ann harding was Born at Eastham march : ye : 12 : 1748

ann harding Dafter of John and ann harding was born at Eastham January 26 : 1749

Septemr 22 : 1737 then Jonathan halls negro man Siprus by his masters order was married to Martha Cupy by Joseph Doane Justice Peace

[p. 123] July 6 : 1737 then John King & Rachel nickason both of harwich ware married In Eastham by nathaniel ffreeman Justice Peace

March 14 : 1724/5 then Eunis atwood Daughter of Thomas atwood was born

September 26 : 1726 then Jonathan Atwood Son of Thomas atwood was born

July the 7th 1729 then nathaniel Atwood Son of Thomas atwood was born

August the 5th 1731 then Thomas Atwood Son of Thomas Atwood was born

March 1 : 1733/4 then Bangs Atwood Son of Thomas Atwood was born

August 19 : 1736 then Ruben atwood Son of Thomas Atwood was born

December 6th 1737 then Sollomon Swet & Serah Beaker was maried In Eastham by Joseph Doane Justice Peace

March 9th 1737/8 then Isaac Smith & Mary Sparrow ware married In Eastham by Joseph Doane Justice Peace

march 28th 1738 then Thomas Tobias & Elizabeth Job both of chatham ware married in Eastham by me Joseph Doane Justice Peace

[p. 124] april 4th 1737 then Stephen Totman Son of Stephen Totman was born

Joshua wile and suzanah hause Boath of Eastham ware marid in Eastham by mr Isaiah Lues Clar June 12 : 1755

Amos Knowls Son of Amos Knowls was born the 18 day of December 1730

Lidea Knowls Daughter of Amos Knowls was born the first day of august 1733

Rebecka Knowls Daughter of Amos Knowls was born the 20th day of april 1736

Ruth knowls daughter of Amos Knowls was born ye 10th of Desember : 1738

Isaac Knowls Son of Amos Knowls was born ye 3d day of June 1741

Rachel Knowls daughter of Amos Knowls was born ye 15th of January 1743/4

Richard Knowls Son of amos Knowls was born at Eastham on the 22d day of September 1746

March 28 : 1738 then Thomas Tobias & Elizabeth Job both of chatham ware married In Eastham by Joseph Doane Justice Peace

Joseph Paine Son of Richard * Paine was born the 10 day of april 1741

william Paine Son of Richard Paine was born September the 30th 1743

Hannah paine Daughter of Richard and phebe paine was born at Eastham on the 15th day of December 1738

Thomas paine Son of Richard and phebe paine was born at Eastham on the 19th of December 1745

Nathan Meyrick Son of Joseph Meyrick was born the 22 of August 1744

[p. 125] february 25 : 1736/7 Jesse nickason & thankfull cook ware married by mr Samuel osborn

ffebruary 2 : 1737/8 Zacheas higgins & Rebecka young both of Eastham ware married by mr Samuel osborn

samuel Basset of Truro and phebe young of Eastham ware marid in Eastham By Mr Isaiah Lues Clar January 12 : 1756

May 4th 1738 Ebed negro & Serah acholoo ware married by Mr Samuel osborn

*"Joseph" was crossed out and "Richard" interlined, in the same hand.

150

august 3rd 1738 then Stephen Cole junr of harwich & Rebecka Beaker
of Eastham were married in Eastham by Joseph Doane Justice
Peace

may 20* : 1736 Ebenezor atwood & Rebeckah young ware married
by Mr Isaiah Lewes

february 11 : 1736/7 Joseph Bogue & Lidea moses ware married by
Mr Isaiah Lewes

november 24 : 1737 Silas Peirce & Eunis Cole ware married by Mr
Isaiah Lewes

(To be continued)

THE

MAYFLOWER DESCENDANT

1620   1920

A QUARTERLY MAGAZINE OF
PILGRIM GENEALOGY AND HISTORY

VOLUME XIX

1917

PUBLISHED BY THE
MASSACHUSETTS SOCIETY OF
MAYFLOWER DESCENDANTS
BOSTON

January 16 : 1738/9 then capt Edward Bangs of Harwich & Ruth mayo of Eastham ware married in Eastham by Joseph Doane Justice Peace

December 8 : 1738 Samuel Cole & Dorkis young both of Eastham ware married by Joseph Doane Justice Peace

Dorkis Cole Daughter of Samuel Cole was born the 25 of october 1740

Hannah cole Daughter of Samuel cole was born the 13 day of January 1742/3

April 13 : 1739 then Joseph Rogers & Sarah harding ware married in Eastham by Joseph Doane Justice Peace

[p. 130] Tamson Doane Daughter of Joshua Doane & Mary Doane was born in Eastham the 16 day of September 1738

Margret Cole Daughter of Isaac Cole was born November 10th 1738

Anne Cole Daughter of Isaac Cole was born 3 of Desembar : 1740

Apphia Cole Daughter of Isaac cole was born the 16th day of february 1742/3

Susana Cole Daughter of Isaac and anne Cole was born ye 5th day of march 1744/5

Hannah cole daughter of Isaac and anne Cole was born at Eastham on the 21th day of June 1747

Isaac Cole the sun of Isaac Cole and anne Cole was Born at Eastham on the 21 of november 1749 and Died January 1750

Jesse Brown Son of Jesse Brown was born the first day of November 1738

Elisabath Cole Dafter of Isaac and Anne Cole was Born in Eastham march 15 : 1751

Timothy Cole the sun of Isaac and Anne Cole was Born in Eastham August : 6 : 1753 and Died novembar 10 Day 1755

martha Cole Daughter of Isaac and Anne Cole was Born in Eastham october the 1 Day 1757

April 19 : 1738 Jabiz Sparrow & mary young ware married In Eastham by Nathaniel Freeman Justice Peace.

Sarah Sparrow Daughter of Jabes and mary Sparrow was born at Eastham September ye 14th 1740

mary Sparrow Daughter of Jabez and mary Sparrow was born at Eastham march ye 13th 1743

Tohomas Sparrow Son of Jabez and mary Sparrow was born at Eastham December ye 3d 1745

Elizabeth Gross Daughter of Hinks Gross born the 28 of october 1735

EASTHAM AND ORLEANS, MASS., VITAL RECORDS

TRANSCRIBED BY THE EDITOR

(Continued from Vol. XVII, p. 150)

[p. 129*] December 29 : 1737 Capt Samuel Smith of Eastham & Mrs Sarah Payne of Boston ware married by Mr Isaiah Lewes

february 16 : 1737/8 william Covell junr & Elizabeth weber both of Eastham ware married by Mr Isaiah Lewes

David Covil Son of william and Elisabeth Covil was born at Eastham on the 11th day of September 1738

february 23 : 1737/8 Mr Zoheth Smith & Mrs Hannah Seers both of Eastham ware married by Mr Isaiah Lewes

June 15 : 1738 then Ebenezor Newcomb & Thankfull Freeman both of Eastham ware married by Mr Isaiah Lewes

*Pages 126, 127 and 128 were omitted in the numbering.

Elis Gross Daughter of Hinks Gross born the 28 day of november 1737

John ward Son of Joseph and mary ward was born in Eastham march 18 : 1750

william word Son of Joseph and mary ward was born in Eastham January 16 . 1752

David ward Son of Joseph and mary ward was born in Eastham June 1 day 1754

Elisha ward Son of Joseph and mary ward was born in Eastham october 29 : 1756

Ezekiel ward Son of Joseph and mary ward was born in Eastham June 22 day 1759

Daniel ward Son of Joseph and mary ward was born in Eastham Sept 21 : 1761

[p. 131] June 28th 1739 then Mr Thomas Atkins of chatham & Mrs Hope Snow of Eastham ware married In Eastham by Joseph Doane Justice Peace*

January 21 : 1733/4 then Abigel Snow Daughter of Samuel Snow was born

October 12 : 1735 then Samuel Snow Son of Samuel Snow was born

May the 8th 1737 then Mercy Snow Daughter of Samuel Snow was born

May 19 : 1739 then Treat Snow Son of Samuel Snow was born

march 5 Day 1761 then John Davis and hannah Twinin both of harwich ware married by John freeman Jestice peace Entred by me Edwd Knowles Town Cr

the marriages below not given into the clark last april by Reason thay ware brough in since

September 7th 1738 William Graham of Boston & ann hamlen of Eastham ware Married in Eastham by Mr Isaiah Leues Clark†

September 14th 1738 Benjamin Bullard & hannah nucomb both of Eastham ware married in Eastham by mr Isaiah Leues Clark†

September 28 : 1738 Ruben Rich & Martha Smith both of Eastham ware Married in Eastham by Mr Isayah Leues Clark†

August : ye 5 : 1739 then thankful rich Dafter of ruben rich and marther was borne

June : ye 5 : 1742 then mather rich the Dafter of ruben rich was borne

mary rich the Daufter of ruben rich was born nombr 29 : 1743

Abagill rich Dafter of ruben rich born Aprel 23 : 1745

*See duplicate record on original page 132.

† A clergyman was, at that time, called "clerk", pronounced "clark".

ruben rich sun of ruben rich born August 23 : 1748

Ruth Rich Dafter of ruben and ruth rich was Born in Eastham novem 11 : 1750

Elisha rich the sun of ruben and ruth rich was Born in Eastham January 27 : 1753

Isaac rich the sum of ruben and ruth rich was Born in Eastham Aprel 17 : 1755

[p. 132] March 1 . 1738/9 Daniel Mayo junr & Martha Holbrook both of Eastham ware Married in Eastham by Mr Isaiah Leues clark*

March 16th 1738/9 Joseph Newcomb of Eastham & Mary Eldrege of Truro or rather of Eastham ware married in Eastham mr by Isaiah Leues clark*

april 12th 1739 Joseph. Doane, third, & Dorcas Eldrege both of Eastham ware married in Eastham by Mr Isaiah Lues clark*

June 28th 1739 Abiezor Holebrook & Hannah Treat both of Eastham ware Married in Eastham by Isaiah Mr Leues clark*

June 28 : 1739 then Mr Thomas atkins of chatham & Hope Snow ware married in Eastham by Joseph Doane Justice Peace†

[p. 133] November 29th 1739 then Mr Joseph Paddock of yarmouth & Mrs Elizabeth Mayo of Eastham ware Married in Eastham by Joseph Doane Justice Peace

february the 11th 1739/40 then Joshua Doane junr & Rettee Meyrick both of Eastham ware Married in Eastham by Nathaniel Freeman Justice Peace.

September 20th 1739 then John Whitney of Harwich & Jerusha Knowls of Eastham ware married in Eastham by Mr Joseph crocker an ordained Minester in Eastham

November 20 : 1760 then David Ralph and Jedidah Cowet Both of harwich ware married by John freeman Justice peace Entred by me Edward Knowles Town Cler

January 9th 1739/40 then Daniel Freeman of Harwich & Mercy Freeman of Eastham ware Married In Eastham by Mr Joseph Crocker an ordained Minester in Eastham

January 10th 1739/40 then Nathaniel Knowls & Mercy freeman ware married in Eastham by Joseph Doane Justice Peace

December 17 : 1740 then Nathaniel Knowls Son of Nathaniel Knowls & Mercy Knowls was born in Eastham

January 11th 1739/40 then James Mitchel & Hannah Higgins both of Eastham ware married In Eastham by Mr Joseph Crocker an ordained Minester In Eastham.

*A clergyman was, at that time, called "clerk", pronounced "clark".

† See duplicate record on original page 131.

february 7th 1739/40 then Benjamin junr Higgins & Hannah Higgins both of Eastham ware married In Eastham by Mr Joseph Crocker an ordained minester in Eastham

[p. 134] february 21 : 1739/40 then Solomon Smith & Susannah Snow both of Eastham ware both married In Eastham by Mr Joseph Crocker an ordained minester in Eastham

Sollomon Smith Son of Solomon Smith was born in Eastham the third day of november 1741

The above marriages all above Copyed for the County clark

October 22 : 1732 then Nathan Snow Son of Benjamin Snow junr & martha Snow was born

Ruth Snow Daughter of Benjamin Snow junr was born 25th day of may 1724

Martha Snow Daughter of Benjamin Snow junr was born the 19th day of may 1726

Keziah Snow Daughter of Benjamin Snow junr was born about the midle of may 1724*

the above acount taken from their mother the 19th of may 1740

Joseph Cole Jr and mary younge was marriade in Eastham by mr Samuel osban Desembar 2 : 1736

James cole Son of Joseph Cole junr was born the 19 day of September 1737

Mary Cole Daughter of Joseph Cole Junr† was born the 12th day of February 1739/40

Phebee cole Daughter of Joseph Cole junr was born the 14th of november 1741

Kezia Cole Daughter of Joseph Jur and Mary Cole was born at Eastham on the 24th of march 1747

thankful Cole the Dafter of Joseph Cole Jr and mary Cole was Born in Eastham January : ye : 10 : 1750

Rebaca Cole the Dafter of Joseph and mary Cole was Born in Eastham July 30 : 1754

[p. 135] Elizabeth Thatcher Daughter of Thomas & Serah Thatcher was born at Billinsget in Eastham in the County of Barnstable In the Province of the Masachusetts Bay In New-england May the 24th 1725 Recorded in Eastham Town Book of Records of Marriages & births by me Joseph Doane Town clerk

November 13th 1740 then John Sparrow junr & Anne Atwood both of Eastham ware married in Eastham by Joseph Doane Justice Peace

*Sic.
†"the third" was first written, but was crossed out, and "junr" interlined in the same hand.

Thankfull Sparrow Daughter of John Sparrow junr was born January 2nd 1743/4

Lamuel Smith Son of Samuel Smith junr was born the 28 of September 1737

Sarah Smith Daughter of Samuel Smith junr was born the 23 day of october 1740

Lamuel Smith Son of Samuel Smith junr was born the 7th day of october 1742

Stephen Smith Son of Samuel Smith junr was born the 28th of September 1744

Ruben Smith Son of Samuel and Sarah Smith was born at Eastham on the 9th day of march 1746/7

april the 17th 1716 then Bathshua Smith Daughter of Joseph Smith & mary Smith was born and She sd Bashshua Died april 19 1722

October the fourth 1718 Mary Smith Daughter of Joseph & mary Smith was born

august 8th 1724 Bathshua Smith Daughter of Joseph & mary Smith was born

December the 21 : 1729 Samuel Smith Son of Joseph & Mary Smith was born

July 28 : 1732 then Huldah Smith Daughter of Joseph & Mary Smith was born

July 23 : 1739 then Rebecka Smith Daughter of Joseph Smith was born

Joseph Smith Son of Joseph and Rebecka Smith was born at Eastham the 17th day of october 1743

April the 17th 1741 then Mr Isaack Beaker & Lidea Hopkins bothe of Eastham ware married in Eastham by Joseph Doane Justice Peace.

September 27th 1739 then Stephen Cash of Truro & Anne Brown of Eastham ware married by Mr Isaiah Lewes Minester in Eastham

December 13th 1739 : then Elisha Cole junr & Prissila Smally both of Eastham ware married in Eastham by mr Isaiah Lewes Minester

april 22 : 1740 then Joseph harding & Eunice newcomb both of Eastham ware married in Eastham by mr Isaiah Lewes Minester look in pd 136

June 13th 1740 then John young & Jerusha Cole both of Eastham ware married in Eastham by Mr Isaiah Lewes minester

(To be continued)

EASTHAM AND ORLEANS, MASS., VITAL RECORDS

(Continued from page 105)

[p. 136] november 23 : 1738 then Isaac harding & experience Swet both of Eastham ware married in Eastham by Mr Isaiah Lewes minester

September 4th 1740 then James atwood & mercy young both of Eastham ware married in Eastham by mr Isaiah Lewes minester

January 22 : 1740/1 then Stephen King & hannah Peirce both of Eastham ware married in Eastham by Mr Isaiah Lewes minester

april 30th 1741 then Joshua hamlen & Mary Lewes both of Eastham ware married in Eastham by mr Isaiah Lewes minester

July the third 1740 then Capt Peleg Ford of marshfield & Mrs Phebee higgins of Eastham ware married In Eastham by Mr Joseph Crocker Minester

March the 5th 1740/1 then mr Isaac Hopkins of Harwich & mrs Thankfull Smith of Eastham ware married In Eastham by Mr Joseph crocker minester

Jonathan Hopkins Son of Isaac and Thankful Hopkin was born at Eastham on the 11th day of June 1747

Joseph hopkens sun of Isaac and thankful hopkens was born in eastham march 10 : 1750

Mary Tower Daughter of John Tower was born the tenth day of may 1736

Mercy Tower Daughter of John Tower was born the middle of august 1738

THE

MAYFLOWER DESCENDANT

1620   1920

A QUARTERLY MAGAZINE OF
PILGRIM GENEALOGY AND HISTORY

VOLUME XX

1918

PUBLISHED BY THE
MASSACHUSETTS SOCIETY OF
MAYFLOWER DESCENDANTS
BOSTON

FLORIDA STATE LIBRARY

186   *Eastham and Orleans, Mass., Vital Records*

Isaac hopkens sun of Isaac hopkens and thankful hopkins was born in Eastham octobar : yᵉ : 25 : 1752

May the 14ᵗʰ 1741 then Thomas Atkins junʳ of chatham & Thankfull Snow of Eastham ware married in Eastham by me Joseph Doane Justice Peace

June 4th 1741 then Judah Rogers & Susannah Rogers both of Eastham ware married in Eastham by Joseph Doane Justice Peace

The above & before Recorded marriage are carried in to the County clerk.

Susanna Rogers Daughter of Judah Rogers & susanna Rogers was born in Eastham the Sixth day of october 1742

novembr 13 : 1741 then : Jase harding sun of Joseph and eunes harding was born in Eastham

febuary : 11 : 1744 then hanah harding Dafter to Joseph and Eunas harding was born in Eastham

august : 18 : 1745 then samuel harding sun of Joseph and Eunas harding was born in Eastham

octobar 28 : 1747 then Joseph harding sun of Joseph and Eunas harding was born in Eastham

march : 23 : 1750 then Joshua harding sun of Joseph and Eunas harding was born in Eastham

look in pd 71 for the rest of the Children

[p. 137] Josiah Crocker the Son of the Revᵈ Mʳ Joseph and Reliance Crocker was born In Eastham the 15ᵗʰ day of March 1740/41 entred by me Joseph Doane Town clerk

Lucia crocker Daughter of mʳ Joseph and Reliance Crocker was born at Eastham yᵉ 28ᵗʰ day of may 1744 .

The Revᵈ mʳ Joseph Crocker Paster of the South Church of Christ in Eastham Departed this Life the Second Day of march 1772 Bangs Atwood Son of Nathaniel Atwood was born the 11ᵗʰ day of January 1736/7

Nathaniel atwood Son of Nathaniel Atwood was born the 4ᵗʰ day of October 1738.

Richard Atwood Son of Nathaniel Atwood was born the 7ᵗʰ day of June 1741

September 17 : 1741 then Joseph Snow junʳ & Thankfull Cole both of Eastham ware married in Eastham by Joseph Doane Justice Peace Entred & Recorded by me Joseph Doane Town clerk

Joseph Snow Son of Joseph Snow junʳ & Thankfull Snow was born at Eastham the 13ᵗʰ day of May 1743 entred by me Joseph Doane Town clerk

(To be continued)

EASTHAM AND ORLEANS, MASS., VITAL RECORDS

Transcribed by the Editor

(*Continued from Vol. XIX, p. 186*)

[p. 138] February 24 : 1741/2 then Ebenezar Snow & Lidea Smith both of Eastham ware married in Eastham by Joseph Doane Justice Peace

March the 5th 1741/2 then Constant Shaw Died
Nathaniel Freeman Son of Barnabas Freeman was born the 14 day of april 1741

July 30th 1741 then Thephilas Mayo junr & Thankfull higgins both of Eastham ware married in Eastham by mr Joseph Crocker minester

Theophilus son of Theophilus Mayo & Thankfull his wife was born December 30th 1752*

November 12 : 1741 then Isaac Larrance of Sandwich & Ruth Freeman widow of Eastham ware married in Eastham by mr Joseph Crocker minester

march 11 : 1741/2 then Joseph Ary & Hannah Rogers both of Eastham ware married in Eastham by mr Joseph Crocker minester

april 1 : 1742 then John Tayller junr & Phebee Higgins both of Eastham ware married in Eastham by mr Joseph Crocker minester the Children Recorded in the new Book

May the 6th 1742 then Thomas Nickason junr of chatham & Dorkis Sparrow of Eastham ware married in Eastham by Mr Joseph Crocker minester

May† 27th 1742 then Mecaiah Snow junr & Elizabeth freeman both of Eastham ware married in Eastham by mr Joseph Crocker minester

all the above carried to the county clerk

[p. 139] October the 8th 1742 then Ebenezor Higgins junr & Martha Burg both of Eastham was maried In Eastham by Joseph Doane Justice Peace

Elizabeth higgins Daughter of Ebenezor higgins was born the 24th day of January 1742/3

seth higgens the sun of Ebnezar and martha higgens was Born in Eastham may 17 : 1744

* "1742" appears to have been altered to "1752".
† "April" was first written, but was crossed out and "May" interlined, in the same hand.

hanah higgens the Dafter of Ebnezar and martha higgens was Born in Eastham July 8 : 1747

Ebnezar higgens the sun of Ebnezar and martha higgens was born in Eastham August 23 . 1749

Jonathan higgens the sun of Ebnezar higgens was born in Eastham August 4 : 1751

abisha higgens sun of Ebenezar and martha higgens was Born in Eastham jun 12 : 1753 Look in paig 84

October 18 : 1742 then Elkenah Nickason of chatham & Bathsheba Snow of Eastham ware Married in Eastham by Joseph Doane Justice Peace

Loock in the new Book for Rest of the children page 23*

november 25th 1742 then James Knowls of chatham & Sarah Doane of Eastham ware married In Eastham by me Joseph Doane Justice Peace

all the above 3 marriages are carried to the county clerk

Easther Higgins Daughter of Moses higgins was born the 7th of February 1739/40

Aron Higgins Son of Moses higgins was born the 14th of march 1741/2

Samuel Knowls Son of Samuel Knowls junr was born the 14th of September 1738

azubah Knowls Daughter of Samuel Knowls jun was born the 11th of november 1740

Hatsel Knowls Son of Samuel Knowls junr was born the 5th of november 1742

[p. 140] John Whitnee Son of Doctor John Whitnee was born the Second day of September 1740

Josiah Whitnee Son of Doctor John Whitnee was born the 7th of november 1741

Seth Whitnee Son of Doctor John Whitnee was born the 5th day of February 1742/3

Aron Dill Son of Thomas Dill was born July 30 : 1739

James Dill Son of Thomas Dill was born october 15 : 1741

Josiah harding Son of Isaac harding was born the 29 day of December 1741

David Higgins Son of Isaiah and Ann Higgins was Born in Eastham august 12 : 1759

Richard Higgins Son of Isaiah and ann Higgins was Born in Eastham april 5 : 1762

*This entry refers to children of Ebenezer Higgins, by wife Martha, and by a second wife, Hannah Yates, of Harwich, whom he married, at Harwich, 27 October, 1763.

EASTHAM AND ORLEANS, MASS., VITAL RECORDS

(Continued from page 96)

[p. 141] William Walker Died January 1743/4

Mrs Sarah Paine the wife of William Paine Esqr Died the 16th day of January 1743/4

Rebecka Linel the wife of Elisha Linel Died the 18th day of february 1743/4

Mrs Sarah Higins wife of Mr Benjamin Higgins Died the 21 day of January 1743/4

Mr† Melatia Higgins widow of Mr Ichabud higgins Died march 28 : 1744

Jedidah Smith Daughter of Gidien Smith was born the 12th day of October 1743

Loes Smith Daughter of Gidien Smith was born the 18th day of January 1744/5

Sollomon Cole Son of Silvenis Cole was born the 8th day of July 1743

Silvenos Cole Son of Silvenos Cole was born ye 13 day of march 1744/5

Nathanael Cole Son of Silvenos Cole was born at Eastham ye 8 day of august 1747

barnabas Cole the sun of salvenas Cole was Born in Eastham 'march 27 : 1751

hanah cole the Dafter of Salvenas Cole was Born in Eastham may : 26 : 1753

*The day of the month was omitted.

†Sic.

96

Benaiah Higgins Son of Isaiah and ann Higgins was Born in Eastham may 31 Day 1765

June the 16 : 1743 then Will Toby & Sarah Davis both of harwich ware married In Eastham by me Joseph Doane Justice Peace

Nathaniel Brown Son of Ebenezor Brown was born october 27 : 1734

Ebenezor Brown Son of Ebenezor Brown was born August 21 : 1736

Rebecka Brown Daughter of Ebenezor brown was born october 16 : 1738

Elizabeth Brown Daughter of Ebenezor brown was born February 18 : 1741

Damorus Brown Daughter of Ebenezor brown was born november the 2nd 1743

Hannah Brown daughter of Ebenezer and Rebecka Brown was born at Eastham on ye 3d day of november 1745

(To be continued)

Andru Cole the sun of salvenas and prisillah Cole was Born in Eastham Aprel 14 : 1755

moses Cahoone & Sarah Lewes both of Eastham ware married august the 6th 1741 by mr Isaiah Lewes minester

John cookson of Boston & mary Beaker of Eastham ware married December 31 : 1741 by mr Isaiah Lewes minester

william atwood & Bathsheba Smith both of Eastham ware married may 13 : 1744* by Mr Isaiah Lewes minester

Jedediah Lumberd of Truro & widow abigail hall ware married May 20th 1742 by Mr Isaiah Lewes minester

Daniel Cusens junr & Lidea Bogue alis moger indians ware married the January 21 : 1742

William cole of Eastham & Lidea Brown of Truro ware married august 4 : 1743

John wilcut of Hingham and Lidea Hawes of Eastham ware married august 30 : 1743
   by Isaiah Lewes minester

Elisha Doane third and Hope Rich both of Eastham ware married the 22 January 1743/4

David Brown junr and Hannah Doane ware† Daughter of Deacon Elisha Doane ware† married febr 23 : 1743/4 by Isaih Lewes minester

nathaniel Knowls of Eastham & mary maker of harwich ware married may the 8 : 1744 by Isaiah lewes minester

[p. 142] Elisha holebrook and Annah Mayo both of Eastham ware married May the 13 1742 by Mr Isaiah Lewes minester

May 27th 1742 then Micaijah Snow Junr & Elizabeth Freeman ware married both of Eastham by Joseph Crocker minester

January 7th 1742/3 Gideon Smith and abigail higgins was married both of Eastham by Joseph Crocker minester

February 3d 1742/3 Nathaniel Gould Junr of harwich & Jane Ary of Eastham ware married by Joseph.Crocker minester

June 30th 1743 Thomas Smith & Ruth mayo both of Eastham ware married by Joseph Crocker Minester

October 27th 1743 Daniel higgins & Ruth Rich both of Eastham ware married by Mr Joseph Crocker minester

November 24th 1743 Judah Rogers‡ & Loes young both of East- ham ware married by Mr Joseph Crocker minester

December 8th 1743 Mr John Paine & Mrs Thankfull Linel both of Eastham ware married by mr Joseph Crocker minester

*Sic.   †The first "ware" should have been crossed out.
‡"young" was first written, but was crossed out and the entry completed as printed.

february 14th 1743/4 Judah young & Mary Andros both of East- ham ware married by Mr Joseph Crocker minester

march 8th 1743/4 Benjamin Cole & Desire Smith both of Eastham ware married by Mr Joseph Crocker

march 30th 1744 Reuben Nickorson of harwich & Ruth Arey of Eastham ware married by Mr Joseph Crocker

Hannah Snow daughter of micaga and Elesibeth Snow was born ye 19th day of february 1742/3

Nathanel Snow Son of mycaga and Elesibeth Snow was born ye 12th day of december 1744

prence Snow Son of micaga and Elisabeth Snow was born ye 16th day of march 1746/7

Nathaniel Cooke Son of Nathaniel Cook was born the 25th of Jan- uary 1741/2

Shubal Cook Son of Nathaniel Cook was born the 23 day of Janu- ary 1743/4

pheby harding Dafter of Ezekel harding and mary harding was born the : 22 : Day of march 1747/8

[p. 143] Zoheth Smith Son of Zoheth Smith was born november the 20th 1738

Richard Smith Son of Zoheth Smith was born the 18th day of march 1741

hanah smith Dafter of Cptt Zoheth Smith and Ruth Smith was Born in Eastham Aprel 21th 1751

Elisabath Smith the Dafter of maier Zoheth Smith and Ruth Smith was Born in Eastham february 6 : 1755

Abigel Atwood Daughter of William Atwood was born 12th day of april 1743

Debro atwood Daughter of William Atwood was born the 5th day of July 1744

Simeon Smith Son of Simeon and abigel Smith was born in Sep- tember the 26th day 1739

Thomas Smith Son of Simeon and abigel Smith was born ye 6th day of february 1741/2

Jesse Smith Son of Simon* and abigel Smith was born the last day of february 1744/5

George Smith Son of Simeon and Abigail Smith was born in East- ham august the 16 Day 1746 :

Nehemiah Smith Son of Simeon and Abigail Smith was Born in Eastham December 14 Day 1751

Jeremiah Smith Son of Simeon and Abigail Smith was Born in Eastham april the 8 Day 1758

*Sic.

THE

MAYFLOWER DESCENDANT

1620   2020

A QUARTERLY MAGAZINE OF
PILGRIM GENEALOGY AND HISTORY

VOLUME XXIV

1922

PUBLISHED BY THE
MASSACHUSETTS SOCIETY OF
MAYFLOWER DESCENDANTS
BOSTON

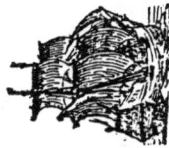

158   *Eastham and Orleans, Mass., Vital Records*

Richard Smith Son of Simeon and Abigail Smith was Born in Eastham Decbr 14 : 1760

Hannah Higgens daughter of Jams and Sarah Higgens was born in East[ham] June ye 6th day 1744

hezaaciah higgens sun of James higens Jr and Sarah higgens was Born in Eastham febuary : ye : 26 : 1750

[p. 144] Israel Cole the Son of Israel Cole jur was born at Eastham on the 12 day of January 1737/8

Thomas Cole the Son of Israel Cole jur was born at Eastham on the 17th day of march 1735/6

Unis Cole Daughter of Israel Cole Jur was born at Eastham on the 27th day april 1742

Phillip Cole Son of Israel cole Jur was born at Eastham on the 5th day of august 1744

Desier Cole Daughter of Beniamine and Desier Cole was born on the 23d day december 1744*

Rebaca Cole the Dafter of Benimine and Desier Coale was born in Eastham octobar ye : 6 : 1749

Benimin Cole the sun of benimine and Desier Cole was Borne in Eastham septembar : 15 : 1751

mehitable Cole the Dafter of Benimin and Desier Cole was Born in Eastham may 10 : 1745*

halet Cole the sun of Benimin and Desier Cole was Born in Eastham novembr 25 : 1747

January ye 15th 1744/5 mr wiliam paine Esqur mrs Elesabeth meyrick both of Eastham were maried by mr Jos[eph] Crocker minester

January ye 24th 1744/5 Thomas Sturges Jur of Barnstable and Sarah paine of East[ham] were maried by mr Joseph Crocker minester

February ye 21th 1744/5 Seth Knowls and Ruth Freeman were maried by mr Josep[h] Crocker minester

march ye 14th 1744/5 Elisha Linel and Martha Higgens both of Eastham were maried by mr Joseph Crocker minester the Children Recorded in the new Book

april ye 25th 1745 Nathnll Snow the 3d and mary Harding both of Eastham were maried by mr Joseph Crocker minester

ye 5 mariages above have ben Sent in to the County Clerk

(To be continued)

*Sic.

EASTHAM AND ORLEANS, MASS., VITAL RECORDS

TRANSCRIBED BY THE EDITOR

(Continued from Vol. XX, p. 158)

[p. 145] John mark and Rebkah Lent indians both of Eastham were married october ye 26th: 1744 by mr Isaiah Leuis minister

October ye 31st 1744 Eldad Nickerson Chatham and Mary Cahoon of Eastham were married by Mr Isaiah Lues minster

november ye 8th 1744 Ezekiel Harding and mary young both of Eastham were married by Mr Isaiah Leuis minester

february ye 18th 1744/5 Isace peirce of Eastham and Esther Couell Harwich were married by mr Isaiah Leuis minester

february ye 28th 1744/5 Thomas mayo of Harwich and Hannah Atkins of Eastham were married by mr Isaiah Luis minister

Simeon Nucomb and Jemimah Treat both of Eastham were married march ye 1th 1744/5 by mr Isaiah Lewis minester

Richard Ary and thankfull Atwod both of Eastham were married may 30th 1745 by mr Isaiah Lewis minester

Simon Newcomb ye 3d and marcy Brown Both of Eastham were married September ye 5th 1745 by mr Isaiah Lewis minester

Anthony Baker of yarmouth and Thankfull young of Eastham were married november ye 13th 1745 by mr Isaiah Lewes

Cornelias Jenney of Dartmouth and Eleaner young of Eastham were married December ye 3d 1745 by mr Isaiah Lewis minest[er]

the above list of marriages has ben Sent in to the county clerk

December ye 10th 1746 then Capt Zoheth Smith and mrs Ruth Mayo both of Eastham ware married by Joseph Doane Justis peace

October ye 31th 1745 then Nathaniel Bacon and apphia cole both of Eastham were married by mr Joseph Crocker Clerk

November ye 30th 1745 then Beniamin Smith and Ruth Snow both of Eastham were married by mr Joseph Crocker Clerk

January ye 2d 1745 then alexander martin and thankfull Rich were married by mr Joseph Crocker Clerk

february the 20th 1745 then Samuel Ary of Truro and Ruth Snow of Eastham were maried by mr Joseph Crocker Clerk

[p. 146] Isiaiah higgens and ann* mayo boath of Eastham ware marryed by Mr Isaiah Lewis minester in aprel 17 : 1748 Entred pr Thomas Knowles Town Clark

Joanah Higgens Daughter of Isaah And Joanna higgins was Borne the 24 Day of march 1749

Apphiah Higgens Daughter of Isaiah and Joannah Higgens was Born in Eastham September the 15 . 1751

aron Higgens Son of Isaiah and Joanna higgens was Born In Eastham march the 25 1754

Isaiah higgens Son of Isaiah and Joannah Higgens was Born march the 11 : 1757

Cornelus hamblin and Jane young boath of Eastham ware married by Mr Isaiah Lewes minester in June 23 : 1748 Entred pr Thomas Knowles Town Clark

Look for the Rest of Isaiah Higgins Childrens in page 140

philip higgens and mary wiley boath of Eastham ware marryed by Mr Isaiah Lues minestar in July 27 : 1748 Entred pr Thomas Knowles Town Clark

Jonathan harding of Truro and Abigil treat of Eastham ware married by Mr Isaiah Lewes minestar in octobar 13 : 1748 Entred by me Thomas Knowles Town Clark

richard Atwood and mary Atwood boath of Eastham ware marryed by Mr Isaiah Lues minestar in octobar 27 : 1748 Entred pr Thomas Knowles Town clark

Elisha bickfoord and Lucia holbrook boath of Eastham ware married by Mr Isaiah Lewes minester in november 10 : 1748 Entred pr Thomas Knowles Town Clark

[p. 147] Joshua Cook of provenc town and Content Coombs of Eastham ware marryed by Mr Isaiah Lewes minestar in novembar 17 : 1748 Entred pr Thomas Knowles town clark

Barnabas harding and ruth Atwood boath of Eastham ware marreyd by Mr Isaiah Lewes minestar in febuary 23 : 1748/9 Entred pr Thomas Knowles Town Clark

Jonathan young Jur and rebaca harding boath of Eastham ware marreyed by Mr Isaiah Lewes minestar in Aprel 12 : 1749 Entred pr Thomas Knowles Town Clark

Cristopher Atwood and susanah smith boath of Eastham ware marreyed by Mr Isaiah Lues minestar in Aprel 27 : 1749 Entred pr Thomas Knowles Town clark

* "Joanna" was first written, but the first two letters and the last were crossed out, in the same ink.

David Brown and Expearenc higgens boath of Eastham ware married by Mr Isaiah Lewes minestar in may 11 : 1749 Entred pr Thomas Knowles Town.Clark

[p. 148] James Atwood Jr and asenath higgens boath of Eastham ware marreyed by Mr Isaiah Lewes minestar in may 11 : 1749 Entred pr Thomas Knowles Town Clark

Barnabas Atwood the sun of James and asenath Atwood was Born in Eastham febuary 19 : 1750

John homer of yarmuth and Abigail osban of nantucket ware married in Eastham by Joseph Done Justes peas in septembr 28 : 1749 Entred pr Thomas Knowles Town Clark

Edman Done and the widdo Elisabath pain boath of Eastham ware marrid in Eastham by Joseph Done Esqr in novembr : ye : 10 : 1749 Entred pr Thomas Knowles Town Clark

Jonathan Sparrow Jur and Elisabath heard boath of Eastham ware marrid in Eastham by Joseph Done Esqr in november ye : 9 : 1749 Entred pr Thomas Knowles Town Clark

Joshua Sparrow the sun of Jonathan and Elisabath sparrow was Born in Eastham July : 12 : 1750

Elisabath sparrow the Dafter of Jonathan and Elisabath sparro[w] was Born in Eastham January 19 : 1752

Jabez sparrow the sun of Jonathan and Elisabath sparrow was Born in Eastham may 26 : 1754

stephen sparrow the sun of Jonathan and Elisabath sparrow was Born in Eastham march 3 : 1756 : Carried Below

Enock Done the sun of Enock Done Disseast and hanah Done was Born the furst of november 1738

bethier Done the Dafter of Enock Done Disseast and hanah Done was Born the 28 Day of Desembar 1740

Isack Son of Jonathan and Elisabath Sparrow was Born in Eastham march 27 : 1762

[p. 149] Enock higgens and Sarah Dmes* boath of Eastham ware marrid in Eastham by solomon Lumbart Esqr in febuary in the evning betwen the fourth and fifth day 1749 Entred pr Thomas Knowles Town Clark

Rhoda higgens the Dafter of Enock and sarah higgens was born in Eastham may the : 5 : 1751

nathaniel higgens the sun of Enock and sarah higgens was Born in Eastham may : 18 : 1753

Thomas higgens the sun of Eanock and sarah higgens was Born in Eastham Aprel 24 : 1755

look in page 116 for the rest of the Children

Jonathan Cole and suzanah horten both of Eastham ware marred by mr benimin webb minester in Eastham in Aprel : 2 : 1741 Recorded pr Thomas Knowles Town Clark

* Sic. The "Intention", on page 197 of the original, reads "Deanes".

David Cole sun of Jonathan Cole and suzanah Cole was born in Eastham July : ye : 2 : 1741

Elisabath Cole Dafter of Jonathan and suzanah Cole was born in Eastham may : ye : 11 : 1744

Jonathan Cole ju the sun of Jonathan and suzanah Cole was born in Eastham January : 2 : 1746/7

Hannah Cole Daughter of Jonethen Cole Borne in Eastham may the 6th 1750

Susanah Cole Daughter of Jonothen Cole Born In Eastham fabuary the 14th 1753

Abigal Cole Daughter of Jonathan Cole was Born in Eastham aprel the 24th 1756

Asa Cole Son of Jonathan Cole was Borne in Eastham febuary the 19th 1759

Carred to paige 162

marcy freeman Dafter of gidan freeman and hanah freeman was Born at Eastham in January 22 : 1748/9*

Mehetable walker the Dafter of samuel and Rebaca walker was Born in Eastham march 18 : 1754

Sarah walker the Dafter of Samuel and Rebaca walker was Born in Eastham september 11 : 1756

John walker Son of Samuell and Rebecca walker was Born in Eastham December 23 Day 1759

Rebacca walker wife of Samuell walker Dyed January 26 Day 1764

[p. 150] samuel walker the sun of samuel walker and Rebaca walker was born novembar : ye : 22 : 1743 and Disseast may : 1 : 1744

marcy walker the Dafter of samuel and Rebaca walker was Born octobar 22 : 1744

susannah walker Dafter of samuel and Rebaca walker was Born Aprel : ye : 4 : 1747

Liddia walker Dafter of samuel and Rebaca walker was Born August ye : 28 : 1749

Rebaca walker Dafter of samuel and Rebaca walker was born in Easth[am] septembar : ye : 15 : 1751

look in paig 149 for the rest

John Cole Jr and martha young boath of Eastham ware marrid in Eastham by Joseph Done Esqr in march : ye : 1 : 1749 Entred pr Thomas Knowles Town Clark

theoapulas Coale sun of John Coale Jr and marther Cole was borne in Eastham Aprel the 9 : 1751

Elkeny Cole the sun of John and martha Cole was Born in Eastham Aprel 19 : 1753

John Cole the sun of John and martha Cole was Born in Eastham febuary 28 : 1755

Look in the new Book in page 42 for the Rest of the Children

* Apparently an attempt was made to cross this entry out.

Ebenezer Atwood Son of Ebenezer and Rachal was born in Eastham april 23 1753

Nathan atwood Son of the above named was Born in Eastham Jan-uary : 8 : 1758

Ruth atwood Daughter of Ebenezer and Rachal was born in East-ham January 22 : 1760 :

Benjamin atwood Son of Ebenezer atwood was born in Eastham february 13 : 1762

[p. 152] Joseph Atkens of trurow and Jemima mayo of Eastham ware marrid in Eastham by Isaiah lues minestar in Desembar ye : 14 : 1749

Joshua Rich and hanah Bacor boath of Eastham ware marrid in Eastham by Isaiah Lues minestar in January : ye : 18 : 1749/50

Mrs Rebeca mayo wife to Mr Theopeulus mayo Died Desembar : ye : 22 : 1748

nathaniel freeman sun of Joseph freeman and pheba freeman was Born at Eastham novembar : ye : 18 : 1749

Joshua hopkens Jr and Rebaca sparrow boath of Eastham ware mar-rid by Joseph Crocker Clark in may : ye : 14 : 1747

freeman higgens and marther Cole boath of Eastham ware marrid in Eastham by Joseph Crocker Clark in novembar : 13 : 1747

(To be continued)

Thomas Knowles Son of henry and mary Knowles was Born in Eastham November 1771

Nathaniel Knowles Son of Henery Knowles and Mary Knowles was born in Eastham april 26 Day 1765

Thomas Knowles son of henry and mary Knowles was Born in Eastham on the 9 Day of march 1763

mary Knowles Daughter of henry & mary Knowles was Born in Eastham april 9 : 1761

August : 30 : 1749 then henry Knowles and mary Knowles boath of Eastham ware married in Eastham by mr Joseph Croker minestar Entred pr Thomas Knowles Town clark

frances Knowles Dafter of henry and mary Knowles was Born in Eastham January : 8th : 1749/5*

cared to pag 167

phebe Knowles the Dafter of henry and mary Knowles was Born in Eastham octobar 26 : 1751

Henry Knowles the sun of henry and mary Knowles was Born in Eastham febuary : 26 1753 and Died march : 7 : 1753

Henry Knowles the sun of henry and mary Knowles was Born in Eastham septembr : 3 : 1754

nathaniel Knowles the syn of henry and mary Knowles was Born in Eastham march 12 : 1757 and Died fabuary the 21 1759

azubah Knowles Daughter of Henry and mary Knowles was Born in Eastham april 1767

Look above

August 17 : 1749 then Elkanah Doane and Jeruase Cole boath of Eastham ware marrid in Eastham by Mr Isaiah Lues minester of Eastham Entred pr Thomas Knowles Town Clark

[p. 151] Jonathan webber of yarmath and hannah snow of Eastham ware marrid in Eastham August 31 : 1749 by Mr Isaiah Lues minestar Entred pr Thomas Knowles Town Clark

Joseph word and mary Treat boath of Eastham ware marrid by Isaiah Lues clark in Eastham octobar : 16 : 1749 Entred pr Thomas Knowles Town Clrk

nathaniel Cole and phebe higgens boath of Eastham ware marrid in Eastham by Isaiah Lues minestar in november : ye : 16 : 1749

Ebnezar Atwood iur and Rachal harding boath of Eastham ware marrid in Eastham by Isaiah lues minestar in novembar : ye : 30 : 1749

Daniel Atwood Son of Ebenezer and Rachal atwood was born in Eastham october 18 : 1750 and Died may 29 : 1751

hephzibah atwood Daughter of Ebenezer and Rachal atwood was born in Eastham march 30 : 1752 Died octr 27 : 1752

Eldad atwood Son of Ebenezer and Rachal atwood was born in Eastham December 15 : 1755

*Sic.

EASTHAM AND ORLEANS, MASS., VITAL RECORDS

(Continued from page 91)

[p. 153] novembar ye 13 : 1747 Elezar rogers Jur of harwigh and Rebaca higgens of Eastham waare mared by Joseph Croker Clark

febuary 25 : 1747 gidean freeman and hanah freeman boath of Eastham ware mared by Mr Joseph Croker Clark

marcy Dafter of gidan freeman and hanah freeman was born in Eastham January 22 : 1748/9

Rebaca freeman Dafter of gidan and hanah freeman was Born in Eastham novembr 8 : 1750

Betty Freeman Daughter of gidean Freeman and Hannah Freeman was Born at at Eastham September 24th 1753

mary freeman daughter of gidean freeman was Born at Eastham march ye 28 : 1757

Sarah freeman Daughter of gidean and hannah freeman was Born at Eastham May ye 31th 1760 and Dide December the 25 : 1760

Sarah freeman Daughter of gidean and Hannah freeman was Born at Eastham November ye 30th 1761

Hannah freeman Daughter of gidean freeman and Hannah freeman was Born at Eastham June ye 9th 1765

Look in page 73 for the Rest of the Children

novembar 10 : 1748 then Jesse snow and loes freeman boath of Eastham ware marred in Eastham by Joseph Croker Clark

philip young the sun of Loes freeman was Born in Eastham march 5 : 1744

sarah snow the Dafter of Jease and Loes snow was Born in Eastham septembar 15 : 1750

Edman snow the sun of Jease and Loes snow was Born in Eastham January 6 : 1752

febuary 16 : 1748 then Joseph freeman and febe paine boath of Eastham ware marrid in Eastham by Joseph Croker Clark

febuary 23 : 1748 then Zebulon young and abigel rogers boath of Eastham ware marrid in Eastham by Joseph croker Clark

[p. 154] Aprel 15 : 1749 then Isaac higgens Jr and Rebaca mayo boath of Eastham ware marrid in Eastham by Joseph Croker Clark

Relianc higgens the Dafter of Isaac and Rebaca higgens was Born in Eastham may 3 : 1750

Rebaca higgens the Dafter of Isaac and Rebaca higgens was Born in Eastham august 30 : 1753

Isaac higgens the sun of Isaac and Rebaca higgens was Born in Eastham octobar 16 : 1755

June 8 : 1749 then James Knowles and Abigel Atwood boath of Eastham ware marrid in Eastham by Joseph croker Clark

Thomisen Knowles Daughter of James and abigail Knowles was Born in Eastham march 1749

Lucretia Knowles Daughter of James and Abigail Knowles was born in Eastham in December 1751

Siruiah Knowles Daughter of James and Abiga[il] Knowles was Born in Eastham october 1753 :

James Knowles Son of James and Abigail Knowles was Born in Eastham January 1756 :

Paul Knowles Son of James and Abigail Knowles was born in Eastham January 9 : 1758

July 20 : 1749 then James Knowles of Chatham and Ruth mayo of Eastham ware marred in Eastham by Joseph Croker Cla[rk]

septembar 7 : 1749 then mathu williams of hebron and grase smith of Eastham ware marrid in Eastham by Joseph Croker Cla[rk]

novembar 23 : 1749 then John mulford and mary mirick boath of Eastham ware marrid in Eastham by Joseph Croker Clark

January 18 : 1749 then samuel pears and mary smith boat[h] of Eastham ware marrid in Eastham by Joseph Croker Clark

John mulford Jr the sun of John and mary mulford was Born in Eastham August 14 : 1750

[p. 155] febuary 6 : 1749 then Joseph Rodgers of harwich and Abigail twining of Eastham ware marrid in Eastham by Joseph Croker Clark

hulda mayo Dafter of Benimine and Sarah mayo was born in Eastham febuary the 7th 1748*

prisila harding Dafter of Isaac harding and Expearenc harding was Born in Eastham June ye : 9 : 1740 and Died in septembar 10 : 1741

Josiah Jr harding Jur sun of Isaac harding and Expearnc harding was Born in Eastham Desembar the 29 : 1741

prisila harding Dafter of Isaac and Expearnc harding was Born in Eastham febuary the : 9 : 1743

Isaac harding Jur sun of Isaac and Expearnc harding was born in Eastham septembar 23 : 1745 and Died octobar 17 : 1745

Abagil harding Dafter of Isaac and Expearnc harding was Born in Eastham febuary : 1 : 1747

Rebaca harding Dafter of Isaac and Expearnc harding was Born in Eastham novembar 23 : 1750

January ye : 10 : 1744 then samuel Doane the 3 and Darkes Coale ware marrid in Eastham by Mr Benimin webb minister Endrd pr Thomas Knowls Town Clark

Martha Doane the Dafter of samuel Doane the 3 and Darkes Doane was Born in Eastham January 12 : 1746

marcy Doane the Dafter of samuel and Darkes Doane was Born in Eastham novembar : ye : 12 : 1749

look in pd 120 for the rest of the Children

*The "8" was written over a "9" in different ink.

Desembar : yᵉ : 28 : 1751 then Thomas higgens : yᵉ : 3 and anna treet boath of Eastham ware marrid by Samuel Smith Esqr in Eastham

[p. 156] march : yᵉ : 11 : 1752 then samuel hopkens and sarah wile boath of Eastham ware marrid in Eastham by samuel smith Esqr

thankfull higgens Dafter of John and marsy higgens was Born in Eastham november : yᵉ : 29 : 1747

Abiezer holbrooks sun of Abiezer and hanah holbroks was Born in Eastham August 20 : 1741

Jesse hollbrooks the sun of Abizer and hanah holbrooks was born in Eastham July 24 : 1743

Jonathan holbrooks the sun of Abizer and hanah holbrooks was Born in Eastham July : yᵉ : 21 : 1745

Elisabath holebrooks the Dafter of Abizer and hanah hollbrooks was Born in Eastham octobar 14 : 1748

Luse holbrooks the Dafter of Abizer and hanah holbroo[ks] was born in Eastham Desembar 4 : 1750

marcy myrick the Dafter of Joseph and Lydia myrick w[as] Born in Eastham septembar 22 : 1744

Barbry myrick the Dafter of Joseph and lydia myrick was Born in Eastham July 21 : 1746

fear myrick the Dafter of Joseph and Lydia myrick was Born in Eastham Aprel 23 : 1749

Joseph myrick Jr the sun of Joseph and Lydia myrick was Born in Eastham June : 2 : 1751

[p. 157] Sarah Atkens the Dafter of Joseph and thankfull Atkens was Born in Eastham July : yᵉ : 21 : 1727

Phebe Atkens the Dafter of Joseph and thankful Atkens was Born in Eastham march 17 : 1729

Thankful Atkens the Dafter of Joseph and thankfl Atkins was Born in Eastham January : yᵉ : 24 : 1731

martha Atkens the Dafter of Joseph and thankful Atkens was Born in Eastham march 28 : 1733

mary Atkens the Dafter of Joseph and thankful Atkens was Born in Eastham febuary : yᵉ : 9 1735

anna Atkens the Dafter of Joseph and thankful Atkens was Born in Eastham January : yᵉ : 4 : 1736

Elisabath Atkens the Dafter of Joseph and thankful Atkens was Born in Eastham octobar 25 : 1738

Joseph Atkens the sun of Joseph and thankful Atkens was Born in Eastham June : yᵉ : 3 : 1741

hanah Atkens the Dafter of Joseph and thankful Atkens was Born in Eastham June 13 : 1743

Jamima Atkens the Dafter of Joseph and thankful Atkens was Born in Eastham septembar 15 : 1745

Juriah* Atkens the sun* of Joseph and thankful Atkens was Born in Eastham Aprel 13 : 1751

Elezear smith the sun of Levie and Jane smith was Born in Eastham January 4 : 1739

hanah Smith the Dafter of Levie and Jane smith was Born in East-ham Aprel : yᵉ : 9 : 1741

Elezabath Smith the Dafter of Levie and Jane Smith was Born in Eastham Aprel : yᵉ : 23 : 1743

[worn]Jean† Smith the Dafter of Levie and Jane Smith was Born in Eastham July : yᵉ : 1 : 1745

Ruth Smith the Dafter of Levie and Jane smith was Born in Eastham may : yᵉ : 6 : 1748

prissilla Smith the Dafter of Levie and Jane Smith was Born in Eastham march : yᵉ : 9 : 1752

Grace smith the Dafter of Levie and Jane Smith was Born in East-ham march : yᵉ : 15 : 1754

(To be continued)

EASTHAM AND ORLEANS, MASS., VITAL RECORDS

(Continued from page 141)

[p. 160*] Aprel 20 : 1753 then nathaniel paine and thankful young Boath of Eastham ware marrid in Eastham By m^r Joseph Croker Clar

John Paine Son of Nathaniel and Thankful paine was Born at Eastham August 31 : 1756

Bathsheba Paine Daughter of Nathaniel and Thankful Paine was Born at Eastham feburary 5 : 1758

Betty Paine Daughter of Nathaniel and thankful Paine was Born at Eastham Apriel 15 : 1760

Sarah Paine Daughter of Nathaniel and thankful Paine was Born at Eastham may : 8 : 1765 :

Nathaniel Paine Son of Nathaniel and thankful Paine was Born at Eastham July the 4 : 1768

may 23 1753 then william Croker of Barnstable and Lydia Knowles of Eastham was marrid in Eastham by Mr Joseph Croker Clar the above List of mariges has Ben sent to the County Clark

Solomon Linnell Son of Jonathan and Priscilla Linnell was Born at Eastham July ye 16 : 1764

Jonathan Linnell Son of Jonathan and Priscilla Linnell was Born at Eastham may ye 29 : 1766

Goold Linnell Son of Jonathan and Priscilla Linell was Born at Eastham January ye 3 : 1768

Benjamin Linell Son of Jonathan and Priscinlla Linell was Born at Eastham June ye 12 : 1770

January 10 : 1750 then Dct nathaniel Breed and Ann Knowles Boath of Eastham ware marrid in Eastham by Edward Chever Clar

nathaniel† Breed the sun of Dct nathaniel and Ann Breed was Born Recorded pr Thomas Knowles Town Clar in Eastham June : y^e : 4 : 1753

Delivearnc Breed the Dafter of nathaniel and ann Breead was Born in Eastham may : y^e : 6 : 1755

Abigail Breed the Dafter of nathaniel and Ann Breed was Born in Eastham may y^e : 30 : 1756

John Breed the sun of nathaniel and Ann Breed was Born in Eastham octobar y^e : 14 : 1757

Ebenezer Harding the Son of John Harding & Margaret Harding was born in Eastham February the 14 1758

Hannah Harding the Daug^tr of John & margaret Harding was born in Eastham april the 20 1760

*Pages 158 and 159 follow page 161.

†"Josiah" was crossed out and "nathaniel" interlined, both above and below, in the same hand and ink.

Lattis Harding the Daug^tr of John & margaret Harding was born in Eastham January the 17 : 1763

Apphiah Harding the Daughter of John & Margaret Harding was born in Eastham June the 29 1765

[p. 161] Isaac Sparrow and Rebaca Knowles boath of Eastham ware marrid in Eastham January 15 : 1746/7* by Mr Joseph Crocker Clar

Richard sparrow the sun of Isaac and Rebaca sparrow was Born in Eastham Desembar 5 : 1747

Sarah Sparrow the Dafter of Isaac and Rebaca Sparrow was Born in Eastham septembr 13 : 1749

Isaac sparrow Jur the sun of Isaac and Rebaca sparrow was born in Eastham June 7 : 1752

mercy sparrow was Born the Dafter of Isaac Sparrow and Rebaca sparrow in Eastham Aprel the 25 : 1754

Rebeca Sparrow Daughter of Isaac and Rebecca Sparrow was Born in Eastham october the 2 Day 1756

Josiah Sparrow Son of Isaac and Rebekah Sparrow was Born in Eastham February the 10 Day 1759

Hannah Sparrow Daughter of Isaac Sparrow and Rebekah Sparrow was Born in Eastham December the 8 Day 1761

Elisebeth Sparrow Daughter of Isaac Sparrow and Rebekah Sparrow as born at Eastham the twelfth Day of august 1764

Elkeny smith the sun of Jaremiah and Lydia smith was Born in Eastham Desembar 8 : 1738

David smith the sun of Jaremiah and Lydiah smith was Born in Eastham June 30 : 1741

Heman smith the sun of Jaremiah and Lydiah smith was Born in Eastham march 8 : 1744

philip smith the sun of Jaremiah and Lydiah smith was Born in Eastham January 25 : 1746†

Lydiah smith the Dafter of Jaremiah and Lydiah smith was Born in Eastham Desembar : 1749‡

marcy smith the Dafter of Jaremiah and Lydiah smith was Born in Eastham march 5 : 1753

Jaremiah smith Died Aprel 2 : 1754

John gills the sun of scarlet and tabathy gills was Born in Eastham June : 15 : 1748

abiga gills the sun of scarlet gills and tabathy gills was Born in Chatham septembar : y^e : 25 : 1750

tabatha gills the wife of scarlet gills Died in Eastham January : y^e : 9 : 1753

* "1747/8" was altered to "1746/7" in the same ink.

† "6" was written over "8" in different ink.

‡ "9" was written over "7" in the same ink as in the preceding correction.

Abijah gills Son of Scarlet and tabatha Gills Died march the 11 Day 1772

[p. 158*] mary Brown the Dafter of gorge and Ales Brown was Born in Eastham July : y^e : 21 : 1741

hephzibah Brown the Dafter of gorge and Ales Brown was Born in Eastham January : y^e : 6 : 1744/5

Zilpha Brown the Dafter of gorge and Ales Brown was Born in Eastham febuary : y^e : 10 : 1747/8

samuel Brown the sun of gorge and Ales Brown was Born in Eastham June : y^e : 3 : 1751

gorge brown the sun of gorge and Alce Brown was Born in Eastham march 22 : 1753

phebee brown the Dafter of gorge and Alce brown was Born in Eastham may : y^e : 20 : 1755

Prisillah Brown Daughter George and Alce Brown was Born in Eastham march 14 Day 1759

Theoder Brown Son of George and Alice Brown was Born in Eastham april 26 Day 1761

octobar y^e : 18 : 1750 then Rufus Cole and Elisabath hambelton boath of Eastham ware marrid in Eastham by Mr Joseph Croker Clar

August 29 : 1751 then Elisha Atwood and abigel freeman boath of Eastham ware marrid in Eastham by Mr Joseph Crocker Clar

David Atwood the sun of Elisha and abigail atwood† was Born in Eastham may 31 : 1752

Elisha atwood Son of Elisha and abigail atwood was born July 25 : 1754

Bangs atwod Son of Elisha and abigail atwood was born augut 25 : 1756

freeman atwood son of Elisha & abigail atwood was born June 10 : 1759

Gedion Atwood Son of Elisha and abigial atwood was Born at Eastham the 10 Day of September 1761

Abigail atwood Daughter of Elisha and abigail atwood was Born at Eastham Sep^t ye 4 : 1766

[p. 159*] octobar 3 : 1751 then Isaac taler of penbrook and Dorces higgens of Eastham ware marrid in Eastham by Mr Joseph Croker Clar

January : y^e : 9 : 1752 then Jonathan Linel : y^e : 3 of Eastham and priscilla gould of harwich was marrid in Eastham by Mr Joseph Croker Clar

Thomas Linnell the Son of Jonathan and Priscilla Linell was Born at Eastham October ye 18 : 1752

Josiah Linnell Son of Jonathan and Priscilla Linell was Born at Eastham December the 19 : 1755

* See footnote on page 189.

† "freeman" was first entered, but it was crossed out and "Atwood" interlined, in the same hand and ink.

THE
MAYFLOWER DESCENDANT

1620   2020

A QUARTERLY MAGAZINE OF
PILGRIM GENEALOGY AND HISTORY

VOLUME XXV

1923

PUBLISHED BY THE
MASSACHUSETTS SOCIETY OF
MAYFLOWER DESCENDANTS
BOSTON

192

Thankful Linnell Daughter of Jonathan and Priscilla Linnell was
   Born at Eastham february yᵉ 17ᵗ : 1757
Molly Linnell Daughter of Jonathan and Priscilla Linnell was Born
   at Eastham febuary the 28 : 1759
Faba Linnell Daughter of Jonathan and Priscilla Linnell was Born
   at Eastham may yᵉ 15 : 1762
Look to the next page for the Rest of the Children
January 23 : 1752 then Ichabid higgens and Bethiah Knowles Boath
   of Eastham ware marrid in Eastham By mʳ Joseph Croker Clar
Hannah freeman Daughter of Jonathan and thankful freeman ware
   Born at Eastham march yᵉ 6 : 1764
Thankful freeman Daughter of Jonathan and thankful freeman ware
   Born at Eastham may the 1 Day 1766
Mʳ Jonathan Freeman Died July the 2 — 1768
Loes freeman Daughter of Jonathan and thankful freeman was Born
   at Eastham July yᵉ 7 1768
march : 12 : 1752 then Jonathan freeman and thankful Linel boath
   of Eastham ware marrid in Eastham By mʳ Joseph Croker Clar
Edman freeman the sun of Jonathan and thankful freeman was Born
   in Eastham Desembr 15 : 1752
Abner freeman the sun of Jonathan and thankful freeman was Born
   in Eastham June 12 : 1755
Rebakah Freeman Daughter of Jonathan and thankful Freeman was
   Born at Eastham march yᵉ 26 — 1757
Sarah Freeman daughter of Jonathan and thankful freeman was
   Born at Eastham June yᵉ 6 : 1759
John Freeman Son of Jonathan and thankful freeman was Born at
   Eastham November yᵉ 10 — 1761
Look a Bove for the Rest of the Children

(To be continued)

EASTHAM AND ORLEANS, MASS., VITAL RECORDS

TRANSCRIBED BY THE EDITOR

(Continued from Vol. XXIV, p. 192)

[p. 162] hanah Renick the Dafter of Mr Cristan Jr and Sarah Remick was Born at harwich July 14 : 1753

Freeman Remick Son of Christan and Sarah Remick was Born in Eastham april 17 Day 1755

Elkenah Remick Son of Christan and Sarah Remick was Born in Eastham august the 11 Day 1757

Aprel 29 : 1753* then Benimin grean and hannah Connant Boath of Trurow ware marid by samuel smith justes of peas· Recorded pr Thomas Knowles Town Clar

septembr 6 : 1753 Then Timathy Jervis resident in Eastha[m] and ann taler of Eastham ware marid by Mr Joseph Croker minestar Recorded pr Thomas Knowles Clar

febuary 28 : 1754 Then Jonathan Twining and Tabytha Higgens Boath of Eastham ware marid in Eastham by Mr Joseph Croker minestar Recorded pr Thomas Knowles Clar

Nathan Twining Son of Jonathan & Tabitha Twining was born in Eastham march [†] : 1755

Lidya Twining Daur of Jonathan & Tabitha Twining was born in Eastham octo 7 : 1756

John Twining Son of Jonathan & Tabitha Twining was born in Eastham october 11 : 1758

Abigail Twining Daut of Jonathan & Tabitha Twining was Born in Eastham march 20 : 1760

Elisabeth Twining Daughter of Jonathan & Tabitha twining was born in Eastham Decbr 14 : 1761

Tabitha twining Daughter of Jonathan & tabitha twining was born in Eastham September 21 Day 1763

Mercy Twining Daughter of Jonathan & tabitha Twining was Born att Eastham apel 18 1765

Barnabas Twining Son of Jonathan and tabatha Twining was Born at Eastham may 14 1767

march 21 : 1754 Then Joshua Cole Jr and hannah Cole Boath of Eastham ware marid in Eastham by Mr Joseph Croker minestar Recorded pr Thomas Knowles Clar

[p. 163] September ye 23 : 1754 Joshua maker and Zeruiah Covel Boath of Eastham ware marid by samuel smith Justes peas Recorded pr Thomas Knowles Town Clar

*The "3" was written over a "4" in the same hand and ink.

†The day is either 3 or 5.

septembr 21 : 1750 then Thomas harding and sarah smith Boath of Eastham ware marid in Eastham by Mr Edward Chever

Ebenezer harding Son of thomas and Sarah harding was Born in Eastham october 28 : Day 1750

Thomas harding Son of Thomas and Sarah harding was Born in Eastham march the 14 Day 1752

January 3 : 1750 Then Joseph mayo Jr and hanah higgens Boath of Eastham ware marid in Eastham by Mr Edward Cher*

Abigail mayo Daughter of Joseph and Hannah Mayo† was Born in Eastham December‡ 1750

Rebacca mayo Daughter of Joseph and hannah mayo was born in Eastham July 5 Day 1755

Mary Mayo Daughter of Joseph and hannah Mayo was born in Eastham January first Day 1760

Theophilus Mayo born December 30 day 1752

[p. 164] Aprel 4 : 1751 then mr samuel mayo of harwich was marid to mrs marcy snow of Eastham by Mr Edward Chever Clar

April 1751 Then salvenas snow and mahetable walker Boath of Eastham ware marid in Eastham by Mr Edward Chever

Aprel 1751 then gorge ward and Bersilla Doane Boath of Eastham ware marid in Eastham by Mr Edward Chever Clar

Joseph word Son of Georg and Barzillah word was Born in Eastham octobr the 23 Day 1753

Benjamin word Son of george and Barzillah ward was born in Eastham April the 3 Day 1755

George ward Son of George and Barzillah ward was Born in Eastham June the 18 Day 1756

Lydia ward Daughter of George word and Berzillah was Born in Eastham march 21 Day 1760

Elisha Smith Son of phinehas and Ruth Smith was Born in Eastham may 7 Day 1764

Isaiah Smith Son of phinehas and Ruth Smith was Born in Eastham may 21 Day 1766

August 22 : 1751 then Isaac hopkens of Truro and Elisabath higgens of Eastham ware marid in Eastham by Mr Edward Chever Clar pr Thomas Knowles Town Clar

January 9 : 1752 then phenies smith and Ruth Doane Boath of Eastham ware marid in Eastham By Mr Edward Chever Clark Recorded pr Thomas Knowles Town Clar

Ebenezer Smith Son of phinehas and Ruth Smith was born in Eastham november 30 Day 1752

mary Smith Daughter of phinchas and Ruth Smith was born in Eastham December 1 Day 1754

*Cheever.

†"Higgins" was crossed out and "Mayo" interlined in the same hand and ink.

‡"January" was first written; but was crossed out, and the entry completed as here given.

THE

MAYFLOWER DESCENDANT

1620 2020

A QUARTERLY MAGAZINE OF
PILGRIM GENEALOGY AND HISTORY

VOLUME XXVII

1925

PUBLISHED BY THE

MASSACHUSETTS SOCIETY OF
MAYFLOWER DESCENDANTS
BOSTON

42

James Smith Son of phinehas and Ruth Smith was Born in Eastham may the 22 : Day 1756

Levi Smith Son of phinehas and Ruth Smith was Born in Eastham april the 25 Day 1758

Phebe Smith Daughter of phinehas and Ruth Smith was Born in Eastham December the 27 Day 1760

henry Smith Son of phinehas Smith was born in Eastham Decbr 23 : 1763

Look a Bove

[p. 165] Aprel 23 : 1752 then Thomas Dean of Barnstable and Abigail horten of Eastham ware marid in Eastham By Mr Edward Chever Clark Recorded pr Thomas Knowls Town Cl

Desmbr 8 : 1752 then Thomas Bee of Chatham and Elisabath vickers of Eastham ware marid in Eastham By Mr Edward Chever Recorded pr Thomas Knowles Town Clar

January 30 : 1752 then Jease Knowles and Sarah walker Boath of Eastham ware marid in Eastham by Mr Edward Chever Clark Recorded pr Thomas Knowles Town Clar

febuary 3 : 1753 John Knowles Son of Jesse and Sarah Knowles was Born

april 2 : 1755 marcy Knowles Daughter of Jesse and Sarah Knowles was Born

febuary 8 : 1757 hannah Knowles Daughter of Jesse & Sarah Knowles was Born

november 25 : 1758 Sarah Knowles Daughter of Jesse & Sarah Knowles was Born

Joshua Knowles Son of Jesse and Sarah Knowles was Born in Eastham April 6 Day 1763

mehetable Knowles Daughter of Jesse and Sarah Knowles was Born in Eastham January 6 Day 1765

January 12 : 1753 then Elkeny Brown and Expearnc smith Boath of Eastham ware marid in Eastham By Mr Edward Chever Clark Recorded pr Thomas Knowles Town Clar

Aprel 17 : 1753 then samuel Cook and Deborah atwood Boath of Eastham ware marid in Eastham By Mr Edward Chever Recorded pr Thomas Knowles Town Clar

(To be continued)

EASTHAM AND ORLEANS, MASS., VITAL RECORDS

Transcribed by George Ernest Bowman

(Continued from Vol. XXV, p. 42)

[p. 166] August 1: 1754 then Jonathan Colings of Truro and suzanah snow of Eastham ware marid in Eastham By Mr Edward Chever clark pr Thomas Knowles Town Clar

Augst : 9 : 1754 then Ruben snow and Elisabath Cortengel Boath of Eastham ware marid in Eastham By Mr Edward Chever Recorded pr Thomas Knowles Town Clar

Elisabath snow the Dafter of Ruben and Elisabath Snow was Born in Eastham febuary 3 : 1755

Ryail snow the Dafter of Ruben and Elisabath Snow was Borne in Eastham Desember ye 11 : 1756

John Snow the Son of Ruben and Elisabeth Snow was Born in Eastham November the 1 Day 1761

Octobr 16 : 1754 then Jease Cole and mary higgens, Boath of Eastham ware marid in Eastham By Mr Edward Chever Clar Recorded pr Thomas Knowles Town Clar

Ruth Cole Daudhter of Jesse and mary Cole was born in Eastham march 29 : 1756:

mary Cole Daughter of Jesse and mary Cole was Born in Eastham November 7 Day 1758

Jesse Cole Son of Jesse and mary Cole was born in Eastham may 4 : 1761

Marcy Cole Daughter of Jesse and mary Cole was Born in Eastham in may 1764

Dorces Cole Daughter of Jesse and mary Cole was Born in Eastham in april 1767

Bethiah Cole Daughter of Jesse and mary Cole was Born in Eastham 27 Day october 1769

mary Cole wife of Jesse Died november 1769

Octobr 18 : 1754 then Josiah myrick and Rachel Doane Boath of Eastham ware marid in Eastham By Mr Edward Chever Clark Recorded pr Thomas Knowls Town Clar

william Myrick Son of Josiah and Rachal myrick was Born in Eastham September 22 Day 1755

Heman Myrick Son of Josiah and Rachal myrick was Born in Eastham march 16 : 1757 and Died march 14 : 1759

Heman Myrick another Son of Josiah and Rachal Myrick was Born in Eastham april 28 Day 1760

Joshua Myrick Son of Josiah and Rachal Myrick was Born in Eastham may 18 : 1763 and Died may 31 : 1763

Josiah Myrick Son of Josiah and Rachel myrick was born in Eastham September the 20 1769

Joseph myrick Son of Josiah and Rachel myrick was born in Eastham april 26 . 1771

[p. 167] william walker Junr and Hanah Hinckly ware married at trurow by Sqr Barnabes Paine November The 17th 1757 Recorded by me Jabes Snow

Preselah walker Daughter of willam walker Jur and Hanah walker was Born at Eastham fabuer the 19th 1759 Recorded by me Jabes Snow

Hannah walker Daughter of william and hanner walker was Born in Eastham September the 9 Day 1762

David walker Son of william and Hannah walker was born in Eastham april the 19 Day 1765

phebe walker Daughter of william and Hannah walker was Born in Eastham april 21 Day 1773

Henery Knowles Son of Henery and mary Knowles Died at Sea in 20 october 1774

Mary Knowles wife of Henery Died the first Day of September 1772

Azubah Knowles Daughter of Henry and Mary Knowles was Born in Eastham November 5 Day 1767

Sarah Knowles Daughter of Henrey Knowles and mary Knowles was Born in Eastham august the 2th 1759 Recorded by me Jabez Snow Clark

Joseph Snow son of Nathaniel & Mary Snow was born February the 9 Day 1747

Bethiah Snow Daughter of Nathaniel & Mary Snow was born may the 2 Day 1749

Priscilla Snow Daughter of Nathaniel & Mary Snow was born August the 9 Day 1751

Nathanil Snow Son of Nathaniel Snow & nary Snow was born September the 14 Day 1753

Harding Snow Son of Nathaniel & Mary Sonow was born December ber the 8 Day 1755

Heman Snow Son of Nathaniel & Mary Snow was born December the 19 Day 1757

Edward Snow Son of Nathaniel & Mary Snow was born March the 23 Day 1760

Mary Snow Daughter of Nathaniel & mary Snow was born July the 3 day 1762

[p. 168] January the 24 : 1758 Then Mr Thomas paine and ms Phebe freeman ware marred by mr Joseph Crocker minester in Eastham

James paine Son of Thomas and Phebe Paine was Born in Eastham February the 16th 1759 Recorded pr me Jabez snow Town Clark

Josiah Paine the the Second Son of Thomas & Phebe Paine was born at Eastham the eighth Day of April A.D. 1760 Recorded per me Jabez Snow Town Clerk

Seth Paine Son of Thomas and Phebe Paine was Born in Eastham february the 11 Day 1762

Enoch Paine Son of Thomas and Phebe Paine was Born in Eastham January the 29 Day 1764

Seth Paine Died January 29 : 1765

Seth Paine Son of Thomas and Phebe Paine was Born in Eastham June 27 AD 1766

David Paine Son of thomas and Phebe Paine was Born in Eastham March the 19th 1768

Clement Paine the 7th Son of Thomas and Phebe Pane was Born at Eastham August the 11th 1769

Phebe Paine Daughter of Thomas Paine and Phebe Paine was Born in Eastham the 23 Day of march 1771 Being the Eighth Child and the first Daughter

marcy Snow Daghter of David Snow and Preselah Snow Borne merch the 6 : 1748 in Eastham

Jonathan Snow Son of Daved Snow an Preselah Snow was Born in Eastham September the . 13. 1749

Eunice Snow Daughter of David Snow and Preselah Snow was Born in Easthem fabuery the 8 : 1751

Stephen Snow Son of David Snow and Presilah Snow was Borne In Eastham November the 9 : 1752

Pheby snow Daughter of David Snow and Presilah Snow was Born in Eastham August the 28 : 1754

Prisellah Snow Daughter of David Snow and Priscilla Snow was Born in Easthem may the 19 : 1756

mary Snow Daughter of David Snow and Prisilla Snow was Born in Eastham August the 28 : 1758 Recorded by me Jabez Snow Town Clarck

David Snow Son of David and presilah Snow was Born at Eastham July 28th 1760

Moses Snow Son of David and Preselah Snow was Born at Eastham Febuary ye 17th : 1763

David Snow Died February 23 : 1776

[p. 169] August the 4th 1757 then Thomas Linel and Sarah Swete Both of Eastham were narred by mr Joseph Crocker in Eastham

Anna Linel Daughter of thomas and Sarah Linel was Born at Eastham August the 20 Day : 1758

Elisha Linel the Son of thomas and Sarah Linel was Born at Eastham Jenur : 22 Day : 1766

Heman Linel Son of thomas and Sarah Linel was Born at Eastham September 22 Day : 1767

Stephen Linnel Son of Thomas and Sarah Linnel was Born in Eastham the first Day of April : 1771

abigal Linnel Daughter of Thomas and Sarah Linnel was born February 10 : 1781

october the 27th 1757 Then Thomas mayo of Harvich and Sarah Higgens of Eastham ware married by mr Joseph Crocker in Eastham

November the 17th 1757 Then Nathanal Paine and Phebe mayo Both of Eastham ware married by mr Joseph Crocker in Eastham

January the 26th 1758 then Zebulon young Jur and Elisabeth Higgens Both of Eastham ware married by mr Joseph Crocker in Eastham

marcy young Daughter of Zebulon young Jur and Elisabeth young was Born in Eastham November the 19th 1758

Zebulon young the Son Zebelon young Jur and Elisabath young was Born in Eastham September the 2th 1760

[p. 170] fabuary the 10th 1758 Then Joseph Smith 3d and Ruth Knowles Both of Eastham were married by mr Joseph Crocker in Eastham

march The 24th 1757 Then John Harding Jur and margaret Cole Both of Eastham were married by mr Joseph Crocker in Eastham

Auggust ye 24th 1758 then Joseph Hambelton Jur and Hannah Cole Both of Eastham were married by mr Joseph Crocker in Eastham

Fabuery the 22th 1759 then Yats Nickerson and mary mayo Both of Eastham ware married by mr Joseph Crocker in Eastham

Eli Nickerson Son of yates and mary nickerson was Born in Eastham march 16 Day 1761:

Jonathan Nickerson Son of yates and mary Nickerson was Born in Eastham December 3 Day 1762:

Mayo Nickerson Son of yates and mary Nickerson was Born in Eastham october 5 Day 1764:

moly nickerson Daughter of yates and mary Nickerson was Born in Eastham December 19 : 1766

yates Nickerson Son of yates and Mary Nickerson Born at Eastham august 13–1772

Hannah Nickerson Dafter of yates Nickerson and Mary Nickerson Born at Eastham December 29 : 1775

Hannah Nickerson Dafter of yates and mary Nickerson Dyed may 9 1777

Eli Nickerson died in France of the Small = Pox in August 25 : 1794

[p. 171] aprel the 3th 1759 abiah Crosby and Sarah Higgens Both of Eastham were married by mr Joseph Crocker in Eastham

october the 2 : 1759 then Nathanel Brown of middeltown in Connetticut and Dorcas paine of Eastham were married by mr Joseph Crocker in Eastham

october 25 : 1759 then James Roggers and Elisabeth Linel Both of Eastham ware married by mr Joseph Crocker in Easthem

Ruth Rogers Daughter of James and Elisebath Rogers was born in Eastham the 9 Day of august 1760

Elisha Rogers Son of James and Elishabeth Rogers was born in Eastham June 29 : 1764

Elisha Rogers Son of Jeams and Elisebeth Rogers Died December 22 : 1766

Elisha Rogers Son of James and Elisebeth Rogers was Born at Eastham May ye 30 : 1767

aprel the 18 : 1760 then Gideon Higgens and Ruth Bangs* Both of Eastham were married by mr Joseph Crocker in Eastham

[p. 172] November the 20 1759 Then Thomas Stuts and Exsperenc Ryder Both of Eastham was married by Samuel Smith Justes of peace in Eastham

Fabuery the 21 : 1760 then Joseph Collings of Trurow and Tamson Newcomb of Eastham were married by Samuel Smith Justis of the peace

march the 13 : 1760 then Daniel Cole and Sarah Swet Both of Eastham was married by Samuel Smith Justic Peac

aprel the 3 : 1760 then Levi willey and Rebekah Stubs Both of Eastham ware married by Samuel Smith Justic peac

[p. 173] Susanah Cole the Wife of Jonathan Cole Departed this life the 21th of January 1760 Recorded by me Jabez Snow Towne Clarck

December 8 : 1760 then Entred the Intentions of marriage Betwen John Cookson and abigial Cavender Both of Eastham Edward Knowls town Clark

December 19 : 1760 then Entred the Intentions of marriage Betwen Edward Smith and hannah Smith Both of Eastham by me Edward Knowles Town Clark

January 30 : 1761 then Entred the Intentions of marriage Betwen Samuell Kenwrick of harwich and Esther mayo of Eastham Recorded pr me Edward Knowles town Clark

february 13 : 1761 then Entred the Intentions of marriage Betwen Thomas Brown and marcy mayo Both of Eastham

february 13 : 1761 then Entred the Intentions of marriage Betwen thomas holbrook and hannah harding Both of Eastham to marry

april 1 Day 1761 then Entred the Intentions of marriage Betwen hudson vickry and Sarah mayo Both of Eastham to marry together

april 4 : 1761 then Entred the Intentions of marriage Betwen Silvenus Doane and Phebe mayo Both of Eastham

april 9 : 1761 then Entred the Intentions of marriage Betwen Nathaniel atwood and prissilla freeman both of Eastham

april 7 : 1761 then Entred the Intentions of marriage Between Edward Smally of harwich and hannah Cole of Eastham

april 21 : 1761 then Entred the Intentions of marriage between Samuell perce and marcy Rider both of Eastham

June 11 : 1761 then Entred the Intentions of marriage between Shabner Sweat and Dorothy Collings Both of Eastham

June 27 : 1761 then entred the Intentions of marriage between John Doane and Betty Snow Both of Eastham

* So recorded. See intention on original page 175.

[J]July 7 : 1761 then entered the Intentions of marriage between Henery Rogers of harwich and Deborah nickerson of Eastham

July 4 : 1761 then Entred the Intentions of marriage between Elazer atwood juner and abigail higgins Both of Eastham

[J]July 4 : 1761 then Entred the Intentions of marriage between Josiah Knowles and Rebecca higgins Both of Eastham

then Entred the Intentions of marriage between william higgins and Elisabeth young both of Eastham

[p. 174] April the 4th 1760 then Entred the Intenshens of marriage Betwen John Holder Shaw and Sarah Cole Both of Eastham by me Jabez Snow Town Clark

aprel the 11th 1760 Then Entred the intenshens of marriage Between mr Zoheth Smith and ms Susanah Knowles Both of Eastham pr me Jabez Snow

June the 30th 1760 Then Entred the Intenshens of Marriage Betwe Gamaliel Hatch and Sarah Treate Both of Eastham by me Jabez Snow Town Clark

July the 2th 1760 Then Entred The Intenshens of mr Adam Ford of Pembruck and ms Rebekah Smith to proseed in marriage Jabez Snow Clark

August ye 5d : 1760 Then Entred ye Intenshens of Mr Christan Remick & Mrs Sarah Doane Both of Eastham to Proseed in marrig By order of Jabez Snow. Town Cl[ark]

August ye 5d : 1760 Then Entred ye Intenshens of Jonatha[n] Linil of Eastham & Rachel Smith of harwich to Proseed in marrig By order of Jabez Snow Town Clark

September* 27 : 1760. then Entred the Intentions of James Brown & Ann Snow Both of Eastham to proceed in marriage pr me Edward Knowls town Cl[ark]

october 4 : 1760 Then Entred the Intentions of Elezer walker and Sarah Snow Both of Eastham to proceed in marriage Edward Knowles Clark

October 10 : 1760 Then Entred the Intentions of James Young and Hanna[h] Burges Both of Eastham to proceed in marriage Edward Knowls town Clark

November 1 : 1760 then Entred the Intentions of Isaac Hopkins and Elisebeth ary Both of Eastham to proceed in marriage

November 1 : 1760 then Entred the Intentions of marriage between Simeon Rider now Resident in Eastham and mary young of Eastham Edward Knowles Town Clark

November 15 : 1760 then Entred the Intentions of Daniel hamilton and hanna[h] Sparrow Daughter of Richard Sparrow Both of Eastham to proceed in marriage Recorded by me Edward Knowles Town Clark

*"August" was crossed out and "September" interlined in the same hand and ink.

December 5 : 1760 then Entred the Intentions of marriage betwen Samuel Snow of Eastham and Sarah atkins of Chatham to proceed in marriage Recorded by Edward Knowles Town Clark

[p. 175] January The 10 : 1760 Entred the intenshens of marriage Betwen Epheram Dean and martha young Both of Eastham

January the 10th 1760 Then Entred the Intenshens of marriage Betwen Solomon Higgens and marget Holbrucks

January the 10th 1760 then Entred the Intenshens of marriage Betwen Levi willy and Rebeckah Stubs

January the 10th 1760 then Entred the Intenshens of marriage Betwen Daniall Cole and Sarah Swet

the above foure Cuppels was Entred by me Jabez Snow Town Clarck

Jannuery the 27th 1760 then Entred the intenshens of marriage Betwen Ebenezer mayo and marcy mayo Both of Eastham By Jabez Snow town Clarck

January the 28th 1760 then Entred the intenshens of marriage Betwen Eleazer Smith and martha Bee Both of Eastham pr me Jabez Snow Town Clarck

January the 28th 1760 Then Entred the Intenshens of marriag Betwen Gidien Higgens and Ruth Burges* Both of Eastham pr Jabez Snow Town Clarck

January The 30th 1760 then Entred the Intenshens of marriage Betwene Joseph Colens of Trurow and Tamsen Nucomb of Eastham by Jabez Snow Town Clarck

Fabuary The 2th 1760 Then Entred the intenshens of marriage Betwen Joseph Roggars of Harwich and Abigal Lewes of Eastham pr me Jabez snow Town Clarck

Fabuary the 2th 1760 then Entred the Intenshens of marriage Betwen Ezra young ad Constianc mayo Both of Eastham pr Jabez Snow Town Clarck

fabuary the 9th 1760 Then Entred The Intenshens of Beniamin Snow ad Barshaba Thomas Both of Eastham pr Jabez Snow Clarck

fabuary the 25 : 1760 Then Entred The Intenshens of marriage Betwen John mayo ad Lydia Cook† Both of Eastham by Jabez Snow Town Clarck

fabuery The 26 1760 then Entred the Intenshens of marriage Betwen Joseph Higgens and Hannah pepper Both of Eastham Jabez snow Town Clarck

march the 18 1760 then Entred the intenshens of marriage Betwen Moses Rich and Hannah Rich Both of Eastham by me Jabez Snow Town clarck

aprel the 4 : 1760 Then Entred the intenshens of marriage Betwen James Deane and Hannah atkens both of Eastham by me Jabez Snow Towne Clerck

(To be continued)

* So recorded. See original page 171.
† "Smith" was first written, but was crossed out, and "Cook" interlined, in the same hand and ink.

EASTHAM AND ORLEANS, MASS., VITAL RECORDS
(Continued from page 108)

[p. 176] Then Entred the Intentions of henery Rogers and Deborah Nickerson Both of Eastham to proceed in marriage†

then Entred the Intentions of marriage Between John freem[an] Esq and Elisabeth myrick Both of Eastham

then Entred the Intentiuos of marriage Between Silvanu[s] Snow and Deborah Cook Both of Eastham

Then entred the Intentions of marriage Between samuell Roge[rs] of Eastham and Deborah Basset of Chatham

then Entred the Intentions of marriage Between Joseph‡ [worn] and hannah Bigford both of Eastham

then Entred the Ententions of marriage Between Ebenezer [§] and mercy mayo Both of Eastham

then Entred the Intintions of marriage Between Edmund higgins and Easther higgins Both of Eastham

novembr 15 : 1761 then William Dean and mary Snow Both of Eastham Segnified their Intintions of marriage in order to be publis[hed]

* Leach.— Editor.
† No date was entered. A duplicate record, on original page 173, gives the date as 7 July, 1761.
‡ A modern hand has written "Ary" in pencil beneath the word "Joseph".
§ The surname, if entered, was worn off, and no date was recorded. See duplicate entry, on original page 175.

December 15 : 1761 Then Joseph paine of harwich and Sarah Smith of Eastham Segnified their Intintions of marriage in order to be publ[ished]

January 8 : 1762 Then Entred the Intentions of marriage Between Joshua higgins Juner and hannah Sparrow Both of Eastham

Decbr 22 : 1761 Then Entred the Intentions of Solomon Sweea[t] and Jemima Bigford Both of Eastham

January 16 : 1762 then Entred the Intentions of marriage Between Jam[es] Dill and abigail hickerman Both of Eastham

January 21 : 1762 then Entred the Intentions of marriage between Nathaniel Atwood Juner and Sarah Remick to be published

January 21 : 1762 then Entred the Intentions of marriage between barna[bas] Twining Juner and Abigail Nickerson of harwich to be published

february 20 : 1762 then Entred the Intentions of marriage between John perce and Sarah Baker both of Eastham

febr 23 : 1762 then Entred the Intentions of marriage Between Samu[el] Dill and Lydia higgins both of Eastham to be published

february 26 1762 then Entred the Intentions of marriage Between Josiah Rich of truro and Martha Rich of Eastham to be publi[shed]

march 1 : 1762 then Entred the Intentions of marriage Between Thomas Rogers of Eastham and hanah Crosbry of yarmouth to be publishe[d]

[p. 177] april 24 : 1762 Then Entred the Intention of marriage Betwen Isaac Foster of harwich and Eunice Freeman of Eastham to be published

[ap]ril 27 : 1762 Then Entred the Intention of marriage Between Reuben Cole and hannah Cole Both of Eastham to be published

may 1 : 1762 Then Entred the Intentions of marriage Between Elkanah Smith and Betty mayo Both of Eastham

[m]ay 27 : 1762 Benjamin Sweet Signified his purpose to marry with mercy Atwood Both of Eastham and was published by me Edward Knowles Town Clerk

[J]une 12 : 1762 Thomas Gould Signified his purpose to marrey with phebe Cole Both of Eastham and was published by Edward Knowles Clerk

Daniel Cole the 3d of Eastham Signified his purpose to marrey with mary* Cole of Harwich and was published by me Edward Knowles Town Clerk

August Then Entred the Intention of marriage Betwen willard Knowles and mercy Snow

october 1762 Then Entred the Intention of marriage Between Isaac paine Abigail Snow Both of Eastham

*"hannah" was crossed out and "mary" interlined, in the same hand and ink.

THE
MAYFLOWER DESCENDANT

1620 2020

A QUARTERLY MAGAZINE OF
PILGRIM GENEALOGY AND HISTORY

VOLUME XXVIII

1930

PUBLISHED BY THE
MASSACHUSETTS SOCIETY OF
MAYFLOWER DESCENDANTS
BOSTON

[o]ctober Then Entered the Intention of marriage Between Joshua
    mayo of Eastham and mehitable foster of harwich
[o]ctober Then Entred the Intention of marriage Between Samuell
    mayo and Abigail young Both of Eastham
october Then Entred the Intention of marriage Between Nehemiah
    young and Kezia Doane Both of Eastham
october Then Entred the Intention of marriage Between Henery
    young Abigail Rich Both of Eastham
Thomas Snow Jane Bee Both of Eastham have Been published by
    me Edward Knowles Town Clerk
october Then Entred the Intention of marriage between Lemuell
    Smith and mercy myrick Both of Eastham
David Rich and Thankfull Brown was Lawfully published by me
    Edward Knowles Town Clerk
[p. 178] october 16 Then Entered the Intention of marriage Between
    Richard Paine and Thankfull harding
Then Entred the Intention of marriage Between abel Eaten of
    Georgetown Sarah Brown of Eastham
Then Entred the Intention of marriage between Silas Snow of har-
    wich and Rebecca Snow of Eastham
Then Entred the Intention of marriage between Joshue mayo of
    Eastha[m] and mehitable forstor of harwich
Then Entred the intention of marriage Between Samuell mayo and
    Abigiel young Both of Eastham
Then Entred the Intention of marriage Between Samuel King of
    harwich and mary hickerman of Eastham
abiel Crosbry and Bennet paine Entred their Intention of marriage
Abiel Crosbry & Bennet Paine Entred thire intition
Novbr 20 then Entred the Intention of marriage Between Daniel
    Eldridge and Thankfull Combes Both of Eastham

(*To be continued*)

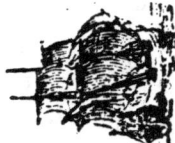

EASTHAM AND ORLEANS, MASS., VITAL RECORDS

TRANSCRIBED BY GEORGE ERNEST BOWMAN

(*Continued from Vol. XVVII, p. 188*)

20* Then Entred the Intention of marriage Between asa mayo and hannah Couell Both of Eastham

27 Then Entred the Intention of marriage Between Solomon Pepper juner and Abiel hopkins Both of Eastham

Then Entred the Intention of marriage Between Elnathan higgins and [†] Sparrow Both of Eastham

Decbr 18 = 1762 Then Entred the Intention of marriage Between Isaac young and Priscilla hopkins Both of Eastham

January 1 : 1763 then Entred the Intention of marriage Between Joseph young jr of Eastham and affier hopkins of Truro

January 1 : 1763 then Entred the Intention of marriage Between Lemuel mayo and mary mayo Both of Eastham

[p. 179] January 1 : 1763 then Entred the Intention of marriage Between Andrew Walker and Dorcas Paine Both of Eastham

22 Then Entred the Intention of marraige Between Benjⁿ Knowles and Mary Brown Both of Eastham

29 Then Entred the Intention of marriage Between Nathan Higgins and Jerusha mayo Both of Eastham and was published by me Edwᵈ Knowles Town Clerk

February 19 Then Entred the Intention of marriage Between Joshue maker and thankful Doane Both of Eastham and was published by me Edward Knowles Town Cr

March 18 then Entred the Intention of John Smith of Chatham and Lydia Snow of Eastham and was published by me Edward Knowles Town Cr

april 22 1763 Then Entred the Intention of Robert Stutson now Resedend in Eastham and Lydia Rich of truro and was published as the law Directs

april 22 1763 then Entred the Intention of marriage between Cypriant hinkely and mehetable Sweet Both of Eastham and was published

may 14 1763 Then Entred the Intention of Marriage Between Nehemiah Basset and Dorcas Cole Both of Eastham and was published

14 Then Entred the Intention of marriage Between Jabez Groas of Eastham and Dorothy alless of provincetown and was published

* This was 20 November, 1762.—*Editor.*

† Space was left for the given name.

‡ "Zephaniah" was crossed out and "Cyprian" interlined, in the same hand and ink.

Then Entred the Intention of marriage between Josiah Sears of Eastham and Mercy Hopkins of Harwich and was published

then Entred the Intention of marriage between Richard Rich juner of Truro and Betty Smith of Eastham and was published

Then Entred the intention of marriage between John Smith and Bathsheba hickerman both of Eastham and was published

augst 13 1763 then Entred the intention of marriage Between Solomon Lues and Elisabeth myrick Both of Eastham and was published

[p. 180] January 27 : 1759 then entred the intentions of Thomas paine Jr and Elles grose Boath of Eastham to proseed in marriage Recorded pr Thomas Knowles Town Clar

March the 7 : 1759 then Entred the intenshons of Nathanel Browne of mideltowne in Coniticut and Dorcas paine of Eastham to proseed in marig Recorded by me Jabez Snow Towne Clarck

march the 8 : 1759 then Entred the intenshons of Abiah Crsby* of Harwich and Sarah higgens to proseed in marriage Recorded by me Jabez Snow towne Clarck

March the 23 = 1759 Then Entread the Intentions of mr Samuel attwood of Eastham and mrs Expearenc Nickerson of Chatham to prosead in marriage By order of Jabez Snow Town Clark

march the 23 = 1759 Then Entred The intentions of Solomon young and Eunice Smith of Eastham to Proseed in marriage By order of Jabez Snow Town Clark

aprel the 7th : 1759 Then Entred the intenshens of william magner of Hingham ad Jemina mulford of Eastham to proseed In marriage pr Jabez snow Town Clarck

June the 14 : 1759 then Eetred the intenshons of marig Betwen David Newcomb of Trurow ad Elisabeth Groas of Eastham pr me Jabez Snow Town Clarck

August the 8 : 1759 then Entred the Entenshens of David Crooel of Chatham and Thanckfull Atwood of Eastham to proseed In maridg pr Jabeb snow Town Clarck

october the 2th 1759 Then Entred the intenshons of James Rogrs and Elisabeth Linnel Both of Eastham to proseed in marriage Recorded by me Jabez Snow Town Clarck

october the 24 : 1759 then Entred the Intenshons of Thomas Stutt and Exsperience Rider Both of Eastham to proseed in marriage Recorded pr me Jabez Snow Town Clarck

october the 27th 1759 then Entred the Intenshens of James atwood and Dehorah ary to prosead in marriage Recorded by me Jabez Snow Town Clarck

october the 27th 1759 Then Entred the Intenshens of marriage Betwen Benjamen Doane and Ruth Smith pr me Jabez Snow Town Clarck

[p. 181] may 20 : 1758 then David walker and thankful Brown Boath of Eastham Entred thare intentions to prosead in marriage Recorded pr Thomas Knowles Town Clar

*Crosby.

June 24 : 1758 then Entred the intentions of Joseph hanhelton Jr and hanah cole Boath of Eastham to prosead in marriage Recorded pr Thomas Knowles Town Clar

June 24 : 1758 then Entred the intentions of James stubs and Sarah Cohone Boath of Eastham to prosed in marriage Recorded pr Thomas Knowles Town Clar

August 12 : 1758 then Entred the intentions of yates nickerson and mary mayo Boath of Eastham to prosead in marriage Recorded pr Thomas Knowles Town Clar

August 12 : 1758 then Entred the intentions of Simeoun Knowles and Eunis mayo boath of Eastham to prosead in marriage Recorded pr Thomas Knowles Town Clar

August 30 : 1758 then Entred the intentions of Mr Simon nucomb and Mrs sarah higgens Boath of Eastham to prosead in marriage Recorded pr Thomas Knowles Town Clar

novembr 18 : 1758 then Entred the intentions of seth smith Jr and Thankful Bacor boath of Eastham to prosead in marriage Recorded pr Thomas Knowles Town Clar

Desembar 16 : 1758 then Entred the intentions of samuel higgens ye 3 of Eastham and Elisabeth Baset of Chatham to prosead in marriage Recorded pr Thomas Knowles Town Clar

Desembar 16 : 1758 then Entred the intentions of moses rich and thankful Atwood Boath of Eastham to prosead in marriage Recorded pr Thomas Knowles Town Clar

Desembar 16 : 1758 then Entred the intentions of Abiah harding of Eastham and Rebaca Lumbart of Truro to prosead in marriage Recorded pr Thomas Knowles Town Clar

January 3 : 1759 then Entred the intentions of Joseph Knowles and Elisabath pepper Boath of Eastham to prosead in marriage Recorded pr Thomas Knowles Town Clar

January 20 : 1759 then Entred the intentions of James Doane and Elisabath Rich boath of Eastham to prosead in marriage Recorded pr Thomas Knowles Town Clar

January 20 : 1759 then Entred the intentions of Joseph hatch and Abigail Brown Boath of Eastham to prosead in marriage Recorded pr Thomas Knowles Town Clar

[p. 182] septembar 17 : 1757 then Entred the intentions of Elkeny higgens and sarah Knowles Boath of Eastham to prosead in marriage Recorded pr Thomas Knowles Town Clar

octobar 15 : 1757 then Entred the intentions of william walker Jr of Eastham and harmah hinkely of Truro to prosead in marriage Recorded pr Thomas Knowles Town Clar

octobar 22 : 1757 then Entred the intentions of simeon smith of proventown and suzanah stubs of Eastham to prosead in marriage Recorded pr Thomas Knowles Town Clar

novembr 12 : 1757 then Entred the intentions of Joseph smith ye 3 : and Ruth Knowles Boath of Eastham to prosead in marriage Recorded pr Thomas Knowles Town Clar novembr 19 : 175? then Entred the intentions of Jonas Dean and sarah higgens Boath of Eastham to prosead in marriage Recorded pr Thomas Knowles Town Clar

Desembr 2 : 1757 then Entred the intentions of Isaac Brown and marcy higgens Boath of Eastham to prosead in marriage Recorded pr Thomas Knowles Town Clar

Desembar 17 : 1757 then Entred the intentions of Ebnezar nucomb of Truro and Expearnce Brown of Eastham to prosead in marriage Recorded pr Thomas Knowles Town Clar

Desembar 24 : 1757 Then Entred the intentions of Mr Thomas paine and Mrs phebe freeman Boath of Eastham to prosead in marriage Recorded pr Thomas Knowles Town Clar

Desembar 31 : 1757 then Entred the intentions of solomon higgens and Bethiah Chase Both of Eastham to prosead in marriage Recorded pr Thomas Knowles Town Clar

January 14 : 1758 then Entred the intentions of Joshua snow of Eastham and mary Doane of mansfield now resident in Eastham to prosead in marig Recorded pr Thomas Knowles Town Clar

January 28 : 1758 then Entred the intentions of Mr Thomas Dill and Mrs mary higgens Boath of Eastham to prosead in marriage Recorded pr Thomas Knowles Town Clar

february 10 : 1758 then Entred the intentions of samuel nucomb of Eastham and Deborah ridly of Truro to prosead in marriage Recorded pr Thomas Knowles Town Clar

April 15 : 1758 then Entred the intentions of Joshua young and Drusila Cole Both of Eastham to prosead in marriage Recorded pr Thomas Knowles Town Clar

April 22 : 1758 then Entred the intentions of Joshua mayo and Lydia pepper Boath of Eastham to prosead in marriage Recorded pr Thomas Knowles Town Clar

[p. 183] march 7 : 1757 then Entred the intentions of Jesse higgens and Expearance hinkely Boath of Eastham to prosead in marig Recorded pr Thomas Knowles Town Clar

march 12 : 1757 then Entred the intentions of James Cahoon and Thankfull wile Both of Eastham to prosead in marriage Recordd pr Thomas Knowles Town Clar

Aprel 20 : 1757 then Entered the intentions of John womley of Truro and Rachel Doane of Eastham to prosead in marig Recorded pr Thomas Knowles Town Clar

Apriel 20 : 1757 then Entred the intentions of fullk Dyer of Truro and Elisabath Atkens of Eastham to prosead in marriage Recorded pr Thomas Knowles Town Clar

may 2 : 1757 then Entred the intentions of Thomas Linel and sarah sweet Boath of Eastham to prosead in marriage Recorded pr Thomas Knowles Town Clar

may 27 : 1757 then Entred the intentions of Timothy Doane and sarah higgens Boath of Eastham to prosead in marriage Recorded pr Thomas Knowles Town Clar

June 17 : 1757 then Entred the intentions of Mr freeman higgens and Mrs Thankfull paine Both of Eastham to prosead in marrige Recorded pr Thomas Knowles Town Clar

July 2 : 1757 then Entred the intentions of Zebbulon young Jr and Elisabath higgens Boath of Eastham to prosead in marriage Recorded pr Thomas Knowles Town Clar

July 29 : 1757 then Entred the intentions of John griffut formerly of Almeny but now resident in Eastham and marcy Cooke of Eastham to prosead in marrig Recorded pr Thomas Knowles Town Cl

August 13 : 1757 then Entred the intentions of Mr Thomas mayo of harwich and Mrs sarah higgens of Eastham to prosead in marriage Recorded pr Thomas Knowles Town Clar

August 20 : 1757 then Entred the intentions of nathaniel paine Jr and phebe Jr mayo Both of Eastham to prosead in marriage Recorded pr Thomas Knowles Town Clar

septembr 3 : 1757 then Entred the intentions of Timothy Atwood of Eastham and susana harding of Chatham to prosead in marriage Recorded pr Thomas Knowles Town Clar

[p. 184] novembar 11 : 1756 then Entred the intentions of Benoni stebbens sefaring man and Rebaca Knowles of Eastham to prosead in marraig Recorded pr Thomas Knowles Town Clar

Desembr 11 : 1756 then Endred the intentions of solomon Doane Jr and mary Doane Boath of Eastham to prosead in marriage Recorded pr Thomas Knowles Town Clar

Desembar 24 : 1756 then Entred the intentions of gideon mayo and sarah Linel Boath of Eastham to prosead in marriage Recorded pr Thomas Knowles Town Clar

Desembar 24 : 1756 then Entred the intentions of lemuel pirss and Ruth paine Boath of Eastham to prosead in marig Recorded pr Thomas Knowles Town Clar

January 1 : 1757 then Entred the intentions of Bethuel wile and thankfull hinkly Boath of Eastham to prosead in marig Recorded pr Thomas Knowles Town Clar

January 1 : 1757 then Entred the intentions of smon* nucomb Jr of Eastham and grace harding of Chatham to prosead in marig Recorded pr Thomas Knowles Town Clar

January 22 : 1757 then Entred the intentions of Thomas paine Jr and marget holbrocks Boath of Eastham to prosead in marriage Recorded pr Thomas Knowles Town Clar

febuary 12 : 1757 then Entred the intentions of John harding Jr and marget Cole Boath of Eastham to prosead in marrig Recorded pr Thomas Knowles Town Clar

febuary 19 : 1757 then entred the intentions of Mr James Bangs of Eastham and Mrs Suzanah hallet of yarmht to prosead in marrig Recorded pr Thomas Knowles Town Clar

*Simon.
† Yarmouth.

febuary 26 : 1757 then Entred the intentions of James Brown Jr and ann higgens Boath of Eastham to prosead in marriage Recorded pr Thomas Knowles Town Clar

febuary 26 : 1757 then Entred the intentions of John hopkens of Truro and lydia snow of Eastham to prosead in marriage Recorded pr Thomas Knowles Town Clar

[p. 185] July 3 : 1756 then Entred the intentions of Mr samuel smith Jr and leydia myrick boath of Eastham to prosead in marraig Recorded pr Thomas Knowles Town Clar

July 3 : 1756 then Entred the intentions of Mr James Brown and Mrs hannah Doane Boath of Eastham to prosead in marraige Recorded pr Thomas Knowles Town Clar

July 3 : 1756 then Entred the intentions of John frasour and anna Atkens Boath of Eastham to prosead in marraig Recorded pr Thomas Knowles Town Clar

August 21 : 1756 then Entred the intentions of Elipelet mors of falmoth in Casco bay and martha mayo of Eastham to prosead in marriage Recorded pr Thomas Knowles Town Clar

octobar 2 : 1756 then Entred the intentions of naler hatch of falmoth in Casco bay and martha Atkens of Eastham to prosead in marraige Recorded pr Thomas Knowles Town Clar

octobar 23 : 1756 then Entred the intentions of Eliakim higgens of Eastham and Barshaba freeman of harwich to prosead in marraige Recorded pr Thomas Knowles Town Clar

octobar 23: 1756 then Entred the intentions of Robart rich Jr and mary swet Boath of Eastham to prosead in marraige Recorded pr Thomas Knowles Town Clar

octobar 23 : 1756 then Entred the intentions of Isaac freeman and thankfull higgens Boath of Eastham to prosead in marraige Recorded pr Thomas Knowles Town Clar

November 8 : 1756 then Entred the intentions of Theopulas mayo Jr of Eastham and martha* mayo of harwich to prosead in marraig Recorded pr Thomas Knowles Town Clar

novembar 8 : 1756 then Entred the intentions of Theopulas mayo Jr of Eastham and sarah mayo of harwich to prosead in marraige Recorded pr Thomas Knowles Town Clar

[p. 186] Desembar 13 : 1755 then Entred the intentions of John Lues of Eastham and hanah hopkens of truro to prosead in marig Recorded pr Thomas Knowles Town Clar

January 17 : 1756 then Entred the intentions of nathan snow and mary polle Boath of Eastham to prosead in marig Recorded pr Thomas Knowles Town Clar

January 24 : 1756 then Entred the intentions of John Brown and Sarah Cooke Boath of Eastham to prosead in marrig pr Thomas Knowles Town Clar

* So recorded. Apparently the town clerk neglected to cross out this entry after making the one following. Nine children of "Theophilus and Sarah Mayo", born 1757–1771, were recorded in the original records, 6: 39, 67.

January 31 : 1756 then Entred the intentions of Joseph higgens Jr and sarah Burgas Boath of Eastham to prosead in marriage Recorded pr Thomas Knowles Town Clar

febuary 7 : 1756 then Entred the intentions of thehoder harling and martha sears Boath of Eastham to prosead in mariage Recorded pr Thomas Knowles Town Clar

febuary 7 : 1756 Then Entred the intentions of gasham ryder Jr of provenc towne and Elisabath pirse of Eastham to prosead in marriag Recorded pr Thomas Knowles Town Clar

febuary 21 : 1756 Then Entred the intentions of samuel smith of provenc town and Ruth nucomb of Eastham to prosead in marig Recorded pr Thomas Knowles Town Clar

febuary 28 : 1756 Then Entred the intentions of william myrick Jr and phebee smith Boath of Eastham to prosead in marraige Recorded pr Thomas Knowles Town Clar

march 6 : 1756 Then Entred the intentions of Isaac sparrow Jr of Eastham and mary hopkens of harwich to prosead in marriage Recorded pr Thomas Knowles Town Clar

Aprel 6 : 1756 then Entred the intentions of John taler and susannah higgens Boath of Eastham to prosead in marriage Recorded pr Thomas Knowles Town Clar

may 1 : 1756 then Entred the intentions of the Revrnd Mr John Dennes of harwich and Mrs Ruth bacons of Eastham to prosead in marriage Recorded pr Thomas Knowles Town Clar

may 22 : 1756 then Entred the intentions of mr asa mayo of Eastham and Mrs hannah Covel of harwich to prosead in marraig Recorded pr Thomas Knowles Town Clar

June 14 : 1756 then Entred the intentions of David Cole and Joanah Atwood boath of Eastham to prosead in marraige Recorded pr Thomas Knowles Town clar

[p. 187] octobar 15 : 1755 then Entred the intentions of Mr Bryer higgens and Mrs Abigail higgens Boath of Eastham to prosead in marig Recorded pr Thomas Knowles Town Clar

octobar 18 : 1755 then Entred the intentions of Isaac Bacor and hanah Cole Boath of Eastham to prosead in marig Recorded pr Thomas Knowles Town Clar

octobar 24 : 1755 then Entred the intentions of Thomas mayo Jr of Eastham and Bethiah Atkens of Truro to prosead in marig Recorded pr Thomas Knowles Town Clar

octobar 24 : 1755 then Entred the intentions of Elnathan snow and phebe sparrow Boath of Eastham to prosead in marig Recorded pr Thomas Knowles Town Clar

octobar 25. 1755 then Entred the intentions of Ephraim Atwood of Eastham and Bethiah harding of Chatham to prosead in marig Recorded pr Thomas Knowles Town Clar

novembr 15 : 1755 then Entred the intentions of Elifalet nickerson of harwich and mary higgens of Eastham to prosead in marrig Recorded pr Thomas Knowles Town Clar novembar 15 : 1755 then Endred the intentions of Elezar ralph of harwich and hanah stephens of Eastham to prosead in marig Recorded pr Thomas Knowles Town Clar

novembar 22 : 1755 then Entred the intentions of william higgens and Abigail mayo Boath of Eastham to prosead in marig Re-corded pr Thomas Knowles Town Clar

novembr 29 : 1755 then Entred the intentions of Joshua Cooke of Eastham and hanah rogers of Truro to prosead in marig Re-corded pr Thomas Knowles Town Clar

Desembar 6 : 1745* then Entred the intentions of william Cole and Eunus higgens Boath of Eastham to prosead in marig Recorded pr Thomas Knowles Town Clar

Desembar 13 : 1755 then Entred the intentions of Israel Atwood and Elisabath mayo Boath of Eastham to prosead in marig Re-corded pr Thomas Knowles Town Clar

Desembar 13 : 1755 then Entred the intentions of samuel Baset of Truro and phebe young of Eastham: to prosead in marig Re-corded pr Thomas Knowles Town Clar

Desembar 27 : 1755 then Entred the intentions of hinks grose of Eastham and Bethiah rich of Truro to prosead in marig Recorded pr Thomas Knowles Town Clar

[p. 188] march 15 : 1755 then Entred the intentions of David harding and sarah Brown Boath of Eastham to prosead in marig Recorded pr Thomas Knowles Town Clar

march 22 : 1755 then Entred the intentions of samuel horten Jur and mary Cushing Boath of Eastham to prosead in marig Re-corded pr Thomas Knowles Town Clar

Aprel 26 : 1755 then Entred the intentions of Jabez Snow Jr and Elisabath Doane Boath of Eastham to prosead in in marig Recorded pr Thomas Knowles town clar

may 3 : 1755 then Endred the intentions of naiman holebroks of Eastham and mary conant of provenctown to prosead in marig Recorded pr Thomas Knowles Town Clar

may 3 : 1755 then Entred the intentions of Joshua wile and susanah hause Boath of Eastham to prosead in marig Recorded pr Thomas Knowles Town Clar

may 3 1755 then Entred the intentions of Jonathan hiller and mary paine Roath of Eastham to prosead in marig Recorded pr Thomas Knowles Town Clar

July 12 : 1755 Then Entred the intentions of Jease Doane and hanah Knowles Boath of Eastham to prosead in marig Recorded pr Thomas Knowles Town Clar

septembr 6 : 1755 then Entred the intentons of noah Doane of East-ham and Bethiah nickerson of yarmoth to prosead in marig Re-corded pr Thomas Knowles Town Clar

* Plainly an error for "1755"

septembr 13 : 1755 then Entred the intentions of lamuel* higgens of middletown in Connatict and hanah stephens of Eastham to prosd in marig Recorded pr Thomas Knowles Town Clar

septemb 20 : 1755 then Entred the intentions of michel Colings of Truro and Rebaca Bee of Eastham to prosead in marig Recorded pr Thomas Knowles town Clar

octobar 4 : 1755 then Entred the intentions of James Atkens and mary Cole Both of Eastham to proseal in marig Recorded pr Thomas Knowles Town Clar

Desembr 27 : 1755 then Entred the intentions of Elisha smith and Jennet higgens Boath of Eastham to prosead in marig Recorded pr Thomas Knowles Town Clar

[p. 189] octobar 26 : 1754 then Entred the intentions of Mr John pane and mrs marcy treet Both of Eastham to prosead in marig Recorded pr Thomas Knowles Town Clar

novembar 2 : 1754 then Entred the intentions of Thomas twining and alic mayo Boath of Eastham to prosead in marig Recorded pr Thomas Knowles Town Clar

novembar 9 : 1754 then Entred the intentions of Mr stephen young and Mrs Abigail freeman boath of Eastham to prosead in marig Recorded pr Thomas Knowles Town Clar

novembar 30 : 1754 then Entred the intentions of Ebnezar higgens Jr and Elisabath myrick boath of Eastham to prosead in marig Recorded pr Thomas Knowles Town Clar

novembar 30 : 1754 then Entred the intentions of scarlet gills and mary snow boath of Eastham to proseal in marig Recorded pr Thomas Knowles Town Clar

novembar 30 : 1754 then Entred the intentions of Edward snow and martha Brown Boath of Eastham to prosead in marig Recorded pr Thomas Knowles Town Clar

Desembar 7 : 1754 then Entred the intentions of Joseph gorge and Easter Cloyes Boath of Eastham to prosead in marig Recorded pr Thomas Knowles Town Clar

Desembar 28 : 1754 then Endred the intentions of moses wile Jr and Ruth young Boath of Eastham to prosead in marig Recorded pr Thomas Knowles Town Clar

January 25 : 1755 then Entred the intentions of nathan smith and mary freeman boath of Eastham to prosead in marig Recorded pr Thomas Knowles Town Clar

January 25 : 1755 Then Entred the intentions of Jathro higgins of Eastham and Ruth snow of harwich to prosead in marig Re-corded pr Thomas Knowles Town Clar

febuary 22 : 1755 then Entred the intentions of Isaac peney and Rebaca stephens Roath of Eastham to prosead in marig pr Thomas Knowles Town Cllar

* "Samuel" was changed to "lamuel", apparently in the same ink.

march : 1 : 1755 then Entred the intentions of simion nucomb and Experanc Ary Boath of Eastham to prosead in marig pr Thomas Knowles Town Clar

[p. 190] septembr 7 : 1754 Then Entred the intentions of Joshua maker and Zeviah Covel boath of Eastham to prosead in marig Recorded pr Thomas Knowles Town Clar

septembr 7 : 1754 Then Endred the intentions of Jease Cole and mary higgens Boath of Eastham to prosead in marig Recorded pr Thomas Knowles Town Clar

septembr 14 : 1754 then Entred the intentions of John merighn and Rebaca pepper Boath of Eastham to prosead in marig Recorded pr Thomas Knowles Town Clar

septembar 14 : 1754 then Entred the intentions of william Kent of Eastham and hannah Sears of yarmoth to prosead in marig Recorded pr Thomas Knowles Town Clar

septembr 21 : 1754 then Entred the intentions of Ebnezar young and Elisabath myrick boath of Eastham to prosead in marig Recorded pr Thomas Knowles Town Clar

septembar 21 : 1754 then Entred the intentions of nathaniel Lues of Trurow and Abigail Doane of Eastham to prosead in marig Recorded pr Thomas Knowles Town Clar

septembar 28 : 1754 then Entred the intentions of solomon hatch of falmoth and sarah Knowles of Eastham to prosead in marig Recorded pr Thomas Knowles Town Clar

octobar 19 : 1754 Then Entred the intentions of philip Covel of Eastham and Rebaca hopkens of Truro to prosead in marig Recorded pr Thomas Knowles Town Clar

octobar 19 : 1754 then Entred the intentions of Barnabas Smith and Ruth wile Both of Eastham to prosead in marig Recorded pr Thomas Knowles Town Clar

octobar 19 : 1754 then Entred the intentions of Andrew walker and sarah Doane Boath of Eastham to prosead in marig pr Thomas Knowls Town Clar

octobar 26 : 1754 then Entred the intentions of Mr Barnabas young of Eastham and Mrs ann pike of truro to prosead in marig Recorded pr Thomas Knowles Town Clar

[p. 191] febuary : ye : 23 : 1754 then Entred the intentions of Joshua Cole Jr and hannah Cole Both of Eastham to prosead in marig Recorded pr Thomas Knowles Town Clar

march ye : 30 : 1754 Then Entred the intentions of Joshua Knowles Jr of Eastham and mary harding of Trurow to prosead in marig Recorded pr Thomas Knowles Town Clar

Aprel 13 : 1754 then Entred the intentions of John swet and Zibatha young boath of Eastham to prosead in marig Recorded pr Thomas Knowles Town Clar

(To be continued)

EASTHAM AND ORLEANS, MASS., VITAL RECORDS
(Continued from page 16)

June ye : 1 : 1754 then Entred the intentions of Elisha pike and Deborah Brown Boath of Eastham to prosead in marig Recorded pr Thomas Knowles Town Clar

June ye : 22 : 1754 then Entred the intentions of Ruben Covel and hanah maker boath of Eastham to prosead in marig Recorded pr Thomas Knowles Town Clar

June 29 : 1754 then Entred the intentions of Mr Jonathan Colings Jr of Truro and Mrs suzannah snow of Eastham to prosead in marig Recorded pr Thomas Knowles Town Clar

July 13 : 1754 Then Entred the intentions of Ruben snow and Elisabath Cortengils Boath of Eastham to prosead in marig Recorded pr Thomas Knowles Town Clar

July 27 : 1754 then Entred the intentions of Mr James Brown and Mrs Ruth pepper Boath of Eastham to prosead in marig Recorded pr Thomas Knowles Town Clar

August 3 : 1754 then Entred the intentions of David young and Lydia smith boath of Eastham to prosead in marig Recorded pr Thomas Knowles Town Clar

August 23* 1754 then Entred the intentions of Josiah myrik and Rachel Doane Boath of Eastham to prosead in marig Recorded pr Thomas Knowles Town Clar

septembr 7 : 1754 Then Entred the intentions of John atwood and Abigil freeman boath of Eastham to prosead in marig Recorded pr Thomas Knowles Town Clar

[p. 192] August 17 : 1753 then Entred the intentions of Mr Timothy Jervis of norwalk and ann tailer of Eastham to prosead in marrig Recorded pr Thomas Knowles Town Clar

August 25 : 1753 then Entred the intentions of David David maaker and phebe Covel boath of Eastham to prosead in marrig Recorded pr Thomas Knowles Town Clar

septembr : 1 : 1753 then Entred the intentions of Thomas hinkely : ye : 3 of harwich and sarah Covel of Eastham to prosead in marig Recorded pr Thomas Knowles Town Clar

octobar 20 : 1753 then Entred the intentions of Jonathan higgens : ye : 3 and sarah coombs Boath of Eastham to prosead in marrig Recorded pr Thomas Knowles Town Clar

octobar 27 : 1753 then Entred the intentions of Joshua pers Jr and hepzibath nucomb boath of Eastham to prosead in marrig Recorded pr Thomas Knowles Town Clar

*The "3" was written over a "4".

Desembr 29 : 1753 then Entred the intentions of Abiah harding and Rebaca Lumbard Boath of Eastham to prosead in marig Recorded pr Thomas Knowles Town Clar and on January : 1 : 1754 the above sd Rebaca Lumbard came and forbid har intentions of marig with the above sd Abiah harding Recorded pr Thomas Knowles Town Clar

January 12 : 1754 then Entred the intentions of Robart young and Joanna Covel Boath of Eastham to prosead in marig Recorded pr Thomas Knowles Town Clar

January 12 : 1754 Then Entred the iitentions of Jonathan Twining and tabythy higgens Boath of Eastham to prosead in marig Recorded pr Thomas Knowles Town Clar

febuary 2 : 1754 then Entred the intentions of Enock higgens mary Atkens Boath of Eastham to prosead in marig Recorded pr Thomas Knowles Town Clar

[p. 193] June : ye : 28 : 1752 then Entred the intentions of Christan remick Jr of Eastham and sarah freeman of harwich to prosead in marrig Recorded pr Thomas Knowles Town Clark

Octobar : ye : 7 : 1752 then Entred the intentions of william wethrel and mary Brown boath of Eastham to prosead in marrig Recorded pr Thomas Knowles Town clar

novembar 11 : 1752 then Entred the intentions of Thomas Bee of Chatham and Elisabath vickery of Eastham to prosead in marrig Recorded pr Thomas Knowles Town clar

Desembar 2 : 1752 then entred the intentions of william chipman and martha treet boath of Eastham to prosead in marrig Recorded pr Thomas Knowles Town clar

Desembar 23 : 1752 then entred the intentions of Mr william Crocker of Barnstable and Mrs lydia Knowles of Eastham to prosead in marrig Recorded pr Thomas Knowles Town Clar

Desembar 30 : 1752 then Entred the intentions of Elkanah Brown and Expearanc smith boath of Eastham to prosead in marrig Recorded pr Thomas Knowles Town Clar

January 11 : 1753 then Entred the intentions of Barnabas young Jr and anna mayo boath of Eastham to prosead in marrig Recorded pr Thomas Knowles Town clar

January 27 : 1753 then entred the intentions of Mr Jonathan starr and Mrs mary higgens both of Eastham to prosead in marrig Recorded pr Thomas Knowles Town clar

febuary 3 : 1743* then Entred the intentions of Thomas godfry of Chatham and mary Covel of Eastham to prosead in marrig Recorded pr Thomas Knowles Town Clar

febuary 3 : 1753 then Entred the intentions of Samuel Cooke and Deborah Atwool boath of Eastham to prosead in marrig Recorded pr Thomas Knowles Town Clar

* This is plainly an error for "1753".

febuary 24 : 1753 then Entred the intentions of nathaniel paine and thankful young boath of Eastham to prosead in marig Recorded pr Thomas Knowles Town clar

march 12 : 1753 then Entred the intentions of Elisha Bigford and mary mayo boath of Eastham to prosead in marrig Recorded pr Thomas Knowles Town Clar

[p. 194] novembar 16 : 1751 then Entred the intentions of Jonathan Linel ye 3* of Eastham and priscilla gould of harwich to prosead marrig Recorded pr Thomas Knowles Town Clark

novembar 16 : 1751 then Entred the intentions of phenies smith and Ruth Doane boath of Eastham to prosead in marrig Recorded pr Thomas Knowles Town Clark

novembar 23 : 1751 then Entred the intentions of Thomas higgens : ye : 3 and Anna treat boath of Eastham to prosead in marrig Recorded pr Thomas Knowles Town Clark

Desembar 21 : 1751 Then Entred the intentions of Jase Knowles and sarah walker boath of Eastham to prosead in marrig Recorded pr Thomas Knowles Town Clark

January 10 : 1752 Then Entred the intentions of samuel Combs and thankful adkens boath of Eastham to prosead in marrig Recorded pr Thomas Knowles Town Clark

January 17 : 1752 Then Entred the intentions of Elkanah Linel and mary sparrow boath of Eastham to prosead in marrig Recorded pr Thomas Knowles Town Clark

January 17 : 1752 Then Entred the intentions of gorge sesaks negro man of Eastham and hestar toby inden of yarmath to prosead in marrig Recorded pr Thomas Knowles Town Clark†

January 19 : 1752 then Entred the intentions of gorge sesacks and hester toby boath of Eastham to prosead in marrig Recorded pr Thomas Knowles Town Clark

febuary 8 : 1752 then Entred the intentions of Jonathan freeman and Thankful Linel boath of Eastham to prosead in marrig Recorded pr Thomas Knowles Town Clark

febuary 15 : 1752 then Entred the intentions of samuel hopkens and sarah wile boath of Eastham to prosead in marrig Recorded pr Thomas Knowles Town Clark

march 2 : 1752 Then Entred the intentions of Thomas Dean Jr of barnstable and Abigail horten of Eastham to prosead in marrig Recorded pr Thomas Knowles Town Clark

may 16 : 1752 then Entred the intentions of Daniel Amos and martha brown of Eastham to prosead in [ma]rrig Recorded pr Thomas Knowles Town Clark

[p. 195] July : ye : 20 : 1751 then Entred the intention of Mr theopulas mayo and Mrs Rachel higgens boath of Eastham to prosead in marrig Recorded pr Thomas Knowles Town Clark

* "Jr" was crossed out and "ye 3" interlined, in the same hand and ink.
† This entry was crossed out.

July 20 : 1751 then Entred the intentions of Elisha Atwood and Abigail freeman boath of Eastham to prosead in marrig Recorded pr Thomas Knowles Town Clark

August 3 : 1751 then Entred the intentions of solomon snow and Lydia Ryder boath of Eastham to prosead in marrig Recorded pr Thomas Knowles Town Clark

septembr 2 : 1751 then Entred the intentions of Daniel Cusens of Eastham and Elisabath Dick of harwich to prosead in marrig Recorded pr Thomas Knowles Town Clark

septnbr 7 : 1751 then Entred the intentions of Mr Ezekiel holbroks and Mrs martha mayo boath of Eastham to prosead in marrage Recorded pr Thomas Knowles Town clark

septnbr 7 : 1751 then Entred the intentions of Mr simion Bacon and Mrs mary Rich boath of Eastham to prosead in marrig Recorded pr Thomas Knowles Town Clark

octobar 5 : 1751 Then Entred the intentions of Joseph sweet Jr and Ann freeman boath of Eastham to prosead in marrig Recorded pr Thomas Knowles Town Clark

octobar 26 : 1751 Then Entred the intentions of Isaac King of harwich and Lydia sparrow of Eastham to prosead in marrig Recorded pr Thomas Knowles Town Clark

novembar 2 : 1751 then Entred the intentions of Ichabod higgens and bethiah Knowls boath of Eastham to prosead in marrig pr Thomas Knowles Town Clark

novembar 6 : 1751 then Entred the intentions of Lamuel nucomb of truro and phebee Atkens of Eastham to to prosead in marrig pr Thomas Knowles Town Clark.

[p. 196] Novembar 17 : 1750 then Entred the intentions of Joseph mayo Jr and hanah higgens Jr boath of Eastham to prosead in marrig Recorded pr Thomas Knowles Town Clark

Desembar : ye 15 : 1750 then Entred the intentions of Dct nathanael Breed and ann Knowles boath of Eastham to prosead in marrig Recorded pr Thomas Knowles Town Clark

January : ye : 19 : 1750/50* then Entred the intentions of Ezekiel Andres of Eastham and thankful rogers of harwich to prosead in marrig Recorded pr Thomas Knowles Town Clark

febuary 2 : 1750/51 then Entred the intentions of salvenas Ary and sarah snow both of Eastham to prosead in marrig Recorded pr Thomas Knowles Town Clark

febuary : 2 : 1750/51 then Entred the intentions of beninin smalley and ann Cash of Eastham to prosead in marrig Recorded pr Thomas Knowles Town Clark

march 2 : 1750/51 then Entred the intentions of mr samuel mayo of harwich and Mrs marcy snow of Eastham to prosead in marrig Recorded pr Thomas Knowles Town Clark

* This is plainly an error for 1750/51.— Editor.

march 15 : 1750/50* then Entred the intentions of Isaac hopkens of truerow and Elisabath higgens Jr of Eastham to prosead in marrig Recorded pr Thomas Knowles Town Clark

march 23 : 1750/51 then Isaac taler of penbrok and Dorcas higgens of Eastham Entred thare intentions to prosead in marrig Recorded pr Thomas Knowles Town Clark

march 30 : 1751 then entred the intentions of gorge word and Zilliah Doand Both of Eastham to prosead in marrig Recorded pr Thomas Knowles Town Clark

Aprel : 10 : 1751 then Entred the intentions of salvenas snow and mehetable walker both of Eastham to prosead in marrig Recorded pr Thomas Knowles Town Clark

June 29 : 1751 then Entred the intentions of Daniel Eldrig and sarah holbroks boath of Eastham to prosead in marrig Recorded pr Thomas Knowles Town Clark

[p. 197] January : ye : 6 : 1749 then Entred the Intentions of Enock higgens and sarah Deanes both of Eastham to prosead in marrig Entred pr Thomas Knowles Town Clark

febuary : ye : 3 : 1749 then Entred the intentions of John Cole Jr and marther young both of Eastham to prosead in marrig Entred pr Thomas Knowles Town Clark

febuary 23 1749 then Entred the intentions of Mr Ichabod higgens and Mrs Elisabath hambelton boath of Eastham to prosead in marrig Entred pr Thomas Knowles Town Clark

febuary 26 : 1749 then the above sd Ichabod higgens came and forbid his being published

Aprel 28 : 1750 then Entred the intentions of Mr Jediah Lumhart of trurow and Mrs marcy treat of Eastham to prosead in marrig Entred pr Thomas Knowles Town Clark

May : ye : 5 : 1750 then Entred the intentions of John Lumhart Jr of trurow and sarah Cole of Eastham to prosead in marrig Entred pr Thomas Knowls town Clark

June : ye : 16 : 1750 then Entred the intentions of Mr Rufus Cole and Mrs Elisabath hambelton boath of Eastham to prosead in marrig Recorded pr Thomas Knowles Town Clark

July : ye : 7 : 1750 then Entred the intentions of Mr heziciah Doane of Eastham and Mrs Elisabath Croel of Chatham to prosead in marrig Recorded pr Thomas Knowles town clark

August.25 : 1750 then Entred the intentions of Mr Thomas harding and sarah smith boath of Eastham to prosead in marrig Recorded pr Thomas Knowles Town Clark

septembr 15 : 1750 then Entred the intentions of william nucomb and vashti Cole boath of Eastham to prosead in marrig Recorded pr Thomas Knowles Town Clark

octobar : 6 : 1750 then Entred the intentions of prins nickson of Chatham and lida Cohune of Eastham to prosead in marrig Recorded pr Thomas Knowles Town Clark

*This is plainly an error for 1750/51.— Editor.

novembar 17 : 1750 then Entred the intentions of Isaac young and martha Atwood boath of Eastham to prosead in marrig Recorded pr Thomas Knowles Town Clark

[p. 198] August : ye : 5 : 1749 Then Entred the intentions of samuel stubs of Eastham and Ann Rich of Truro to prosead in marrig Entred pr Thomas Knowles Town Clark

August 5 : 1749 Then Entred the intentions of Mr Jonathan webar of yarmath and hannah snow of Eastham to prosead in marrig Entred pr Thomas Knowles Town Clark

August 12 : 1749 Then Enterd the intentions of henery Knowles and mary Knowles Both of Eastham to prosead in marrig Entred pr Thomas Knowles Town Clark

september : ye : 16 : 1749 Then Enterd the intentions of Ebnezar Atwood Jr and Rachel harding both of Eastham to prosead in marrig Recorded pr Thomas Knowles Town Clark

August 19 : 1749 Then Entred the intentions of Mr Joseph Atkens of Truro and Mrs Jemimah mayo of Eastham to prosead in marrig Entred pr Thomas Knowles Town Clark

september 21 : 1749 Then Entred the intentions of Joseph word and mary treat Jr both of Eastham to prosead in marrig Recorded pr Thomas Knowles Town Clark

octobar : ye : 3 : 1749 Then Enterd the intentions of Mr Ednand Done and Mrs Elisabath paine boath of Eastham to prosead in marrig Endred pr Thomas Knowles Town Clark

novembar : ye : 4 : 1749 Then Entred the intentions of John mulford and mary mirick both of Eastham to prosead in marrig Entred pr Thomas Knowles Town Clark

Desembar : ye : 11 : 1749 Then Entred the intentions of samuel pers and mary smith both of Eastham to prosead in marrig Entred pr Thomas Knowles Town Clark

Desembar ye : 28 : 1749 then Entred the intentions of Joshua rich and hanah Bacor both of Eastham to prosead in marrig Entred pr Thomas Knowles Town Clark

Desembar : ye : 28 : 1749 then Entred the intentions of Joseph rogers jur of harrig* and Abigal twining of Eastham to prosead in marrig Entred pr Thomas Knowles Town Clark

[p. 199] Aprel ye : 19 : 1749 Then Entred the intentions of James Atwood jr and asenath higgens both of Eastham to prosead in marrig Entred by me Thomas Knowles Town clark

Aprel : ye : 22 : 1749 then Entred the intentions of Mr mathew williams of hebron and mrs grace smith of Eastham to prosead in marrig Entred pr me Thomas Knowles Town Clark

may : ye : 20 : 1749 Then Entred the intentions of James Knowles and Abigail Atwood both of Eastham to prosead in marrig Entred pr Thomas Knowles Town Clark

may : ye : 25 : 1749 Then Entered the intentions of Mr James Knowles of Catham† and Mrs ruth mayo of Eastham to prosead in marrig Entred pr Thomas Knowles Town Clark

*Harwich, Mass.
†Chatham, Mass.

may : ye : 29 : 1749 Then Entred the intentions of Mr Jonathan sparrow jur and Mrs Elisabath heard both of Eastham to prosead in marrig Entred pr Thomas Knowles Town Clark

June 2 : 1749 Then Enterd the intentions of Mr Benimine higgens of Eastham and Mrs marcy hopkens of Truero to prosead in marrig Entred pr Thomas Knowles Town Clark

June 10 : 1749 Then Entred the intentions of Zacchaus higgens of Eastham and mary Corsbary of harwich to prosead in marrig Entred pr Thomas Knowles Town Clark

June 10 : 1749 Then Entred the intentions of Elcany Done and Jerusa Cole boath of Eastham to prosead in marrig Entred pr Thomas Knowles Town Clark

June 24 : 1749 Then Entred the intentions of Mr giles hopkens of Eastham and Mrs bethiah homer of yarmath to prosead in marrig Entred pr Thomas Knowles Town Clark

July 29 : 1749 Then Entred the intentions of nathaniel Cole and pheaby higgens Both of Eastham to prosead in marrig Entred pr Thomanas Knowles Town Clark

[p. 200] September ye 13th 1748 then Entred the intentions of Jonathan Harding of Truro and Abigel Treat of Eastham to proceed in marriage

September ye ye 19th 1748 then entred the intentions of Elisha Bickford and Lusha Holbrok both of Eastham to proced in marriage

October ye 1th 1748 then Entred the intentions of Nathanael walker of Eastham mariam Hatch of Felmouth to proceed in marriage

October ye 7th 1748 then Entred the intentions of Jesse Snow and Lois Freeman both of Eastham to proceed in marriage

January ye 21th 1748 then Entred the intentions of Barnabas Harding and Ruth Atwod both of Eastham to proceed in marriage

January ye 21th 1748 then Entred the intentions of Joseph Freeman and phebe paine both of Eastham to proceed in marriage

January the 28th 1748 then Entred the intentions of John mayo Jur of Eastham and Ruth Nickerson of Harwich to proceed in marriage

february ye 2d 1748 then entred the intentions of Jonathan young Jur and Rebecca harding both of Eastham to proceed in marriage

february ye 4th 1748 then Entred the intentions of mr Zabulon young and Mrs Abigel Rogers botht of Eastham to proceed in marriage

february . ye 18th 1748/9 then entred the intentions of mr John Berey of yarmouth and mrs mary walker of Eastham to proceed in marriage

march ye 4th 1748/9 then entred the intentions of Isaac higgins 3 and Rebecca may both of Eastham to proceed in marriage

march : ye : 22 : 1748/9 then Entred the intentions of Cristopher Atwood and suzanah smith both of Eastham to prosead in marrige pr me thomas Knowls Town Clark

march : ye : 31 : 1749 then Entred the intentions of Mr David Brown and Mrs Experanc higgens Both of Eastham to prosead in marrig pr me Thomas Knowls Town Clark [p. 201] July ye 1[*] 1747 then entered the intentions of Ebenezer Hurd of Harwich and mary Chipman of Eastham to proceed in marriage

august ye 5th 1747 then entered the intentions of Joseph perce and Susanna nucomb both of Eastham to proceed in marriage

October : ye 1th 1747 then Richard Cob of truro Entred his intentions to marry with Elisabeth Treat of Eastham

October ye 3rd 1747 then Seth Hopkins entred his intentions to marry with Elisabeth Cohoon both of Eastham

October ye 31th 1747 then Mr Joseph Cole Entred his intentions to marry with mrs Rebecca Harding both of Eastham

November ye 25th 1747 then Mr Job Crocker of Eastham Entred his intentions to marry with mrs mercy Knowls of Harwich

January : ye 23 1747/8 Gedion Freeman Entred his intentions to marry with Hannah Freeman both of Eastham

february ye 13th 1747/8 then Thomas mulford of Truro Entred his intentions to mrry with Rachel Treat of Eastham

february ye 25th 1747/8 then Isaiah Higgens entred his intentions to marry with Joanna† mayo both of Eastham

march ye 4th 1747/8 then Beniamine Hamblin and Lidya young both of Eastham entred their intentions to marry each with other

march ye 10th 1747/8 then Beniamin young and Thankful Hinkly both of Eastham Entred their intentions to marry each with the other

march ye 22d 1747/8 then Richard atwod and mary atwod both of Eastham Entred their intentions to marry Each with the other

may ye 7th 1748 then Jabez walker of Eastham entred his intentions to marry with Sarah atwod of province Town

may ye 7th 1748 then Joshua Cook of province town and Content Coums of Eastham entred their intentions to marry each with other

June ye 25th 1748 then Entred the intentions of Elkanah Rogers of Eastham and mercy Burges of Harwich to marry Each with other

July ye 5th then entred the intentions philip Higgens and Mary wiley both of Eastham to proceed in marriage

[p. 202] Freeman Knowls Son of Seth and Ruth Knowles was born at Eastham on ye 24th day of november 1745‡

may ye 6th 1746 Coll John Knowls of Eastham and mrs Rebecca Chanly were married by Joseph Crocker Clerk

may ye 22d 1746 then moses Smith and Rebecca Sparrow both of Eastham were married by mr Joseph Crocker Clerk

October ye 2d 1746 then Joshua Hurd of harwich and Elisabeth paine of Eastham were married by mr Joseph Crocker Clerk

october ye 13th 1746 then Benjamin Brown and Betty Cook both of Eastham were married by mr Joseph Crocker Clerk

December ye 24th 1746 then Seth Harding and Elisabeth wilcot both of Eastham were married by Joseph Crocker Clerk

*The last figure has been marked over and is doubtful.

† See Mayflower Descendant, 24: 87 and 15: 228 and 20: 95, 96.—Editor.

‡ This entry was crossed out; see Mayflower Descendant, 16: 145.

December ye 25th 1746 then Stephen Sparrow jur and apphia pepper both of Eastham were married by mr Joseph Crocker Clerk

January ye 8th 1747 then Jonathan Linel jur and mercy mayo both of Eastham were married by mr Joseph Crocker Clerk

January ye 15th 1747* then Isaac Sparrow and Rebecca Knowls both of Eastham were married by mr Joseph Crocker Clerk

February ye 26th 1746 then Richard Rogers of Harwich and Sarah Higgens of Eastham were married by mr Joseph Crocker Clerk

march ye 5th 1747* then David Snow and priscilla Sparrow both of Eastham were married by mr Joseph Crocker Clerk

april ye 8th 1747 then John Higgens jur and marcy mulford both of Eastham were married by mr Joseph Crocker Clerk

the a bove List of marriages has been Sent to the County Clerk

Jedidiah lumbart and widow phebe Hawse both of Eastham ware married by Mr Isaiah Luis clerk Jauary ye 8th 1746/7

Barnabas Cook mercy walker both of Eastham were married march ye 4th 1746/7

Solomon Luis and Hannah Cahoon both of Eastham were married march ye 16th 1746/7

Reuben Rich and Ruth Brown both of Eastham were married July ye 2d 1747

Joseph peirce Susannah newcomb both of Eastham were married october ye 8th 1747

Mr Joseph Cole and the widow Rebecca Harding both of Eastham married novemr 25th 1747

Richard Cob of Truro Elisabeth Treat of Eastham were married november ye 26th 1747

Mr Job Crocker of Eastham and mrs mercy Knowls of Harwich were married January ye 14th 1747/8

Thomas Mulford of Truro and Rachel Treat of Eastham were married march ye 10th 1747/8

Benimin Hamblen and lydia young both of Eastham were married march ye 24th 1747/8

Seth Hopkins and Elisabeth cahoone both of Eastham were married april ye 14th 1748

beniamin young and the wido Thankful Hinkly both of Eastham were married april ye 14th 1748

all by mr Isaiah Luis Clerk

all above has been Sent to the County Clerk

[p. 203 is blank]

[p. 204] Eunice Smith born June 27 1777

[p. 205] May ye 25th 1716 Jonathan Collens gave notice of [worn] to have the banns of matrimony published betwixt him self and Su-san[na] Walker

(To be continued)

* The last "7" was written over a "6". See Mayflower Descendant, 24: 190.
— Editor.

EASTHAM AND ORLEANS, MASS., VITAL RECORDS

(Continued from page 83)

June ye 28th 1717 Nathan young gave notis of his desire to have the banns of matimoney published betwixt him self and mary Merrick

September ye 4th 1717 Thomas Cob of Hingham gave account of the intention of him self and Mercy Freeman of Eastham to contract marriage and desired it should be published

September ye 4th 1717 Stephen Sparrow gave account of the intention of him Self and Anne Mulford to contract marriage : in order to have it published

September the 14th : 1717 : Robert young Junr Gave account of the Intention of him self and Elisabeth Pepper to contract marriage :

September ye 14th Christian Remick gave account of the intentions of him self with Hannah Freeman to contract narriage

September ye 28th 1717 Edward Hall of Harwich aquainted me with his intention to Contract marriage with the widdow Sarah Cole of Eastham in order to be published

September ye 28th 1717 : Samuel crosbie gave account of his intention to contract marriage with Ruth Cole in order to have their in-tentions published

* The first Tuesday of February, 1771, was the fifth of that month. — *Editor.*

october ye 23d : 1717 : Samuel Brown Junr gave account of his intent to contract marriage with Lidya Fish of Sandwich in order to have it published

January ye 7th 1717/18 Charles Paine of Boston gave order to have his inten[t] to marry with Elisabeth Newcom : published

february ye 8th 1717/18 Joshua Knowls Signified his desire to have his intent to marry with Sarah Paine published

february ye 8th 1717/18 Samuel Higgins Senior Signified his desire to have his inten[t] to marry with Thankfull Mayo published

february ye 26th 1717/18 David Smith Signified his Intent to marry with Sarah Higgins in order to be published

march ye 6th 1717/18 Joseph Smale of Truro Signified his intent to marry with prissilla young of Eastham in order to have it published

April ye 18th 1718 John Atwood of Eastham Signified his intent to marry with Thankfull Gray of Harwich in order to have it published

[Ju]ne ye 5th 1718 Samuel Higgins Junr of Eastham Signified his intent to marrie wi[th] Meh[e]t[a]b[e]ll Finnie of Barnstable in order to be published

[p. 206] [Jul]y y[e 1]8 : 1718 William Badishall of Truro Signified his inten[tion] to marrie with mary atwood of Eastham in order to be published

July ye 19th 1718 Samuel Smith of Chatham Signified his intention to marry with Mercy Higgins Senior of Eastham in order to be published

August ye 23 1718 : Isaac Atwood Signified his intention to marry with mehetabell Gray of Harwich in order to be published.

September ye 2nd 1718 : Jonathan Dyer of Truro Signified his inten-tion to contract marriage with Susannah Brown of Eastham in order to be published.

September ye 4th 1718 Jonathan Snow Signified his intention to marrie with Thankful Freeman in order to be published

September ye 15th 1718 Eldad atwood Signified his intention to marry with Sarah Gray of Harwich in order to be published

September ye 30th* 1718 George Luis Signifyed to me the intention of William Dennis of Marblehead to marry with Rebecca Luis of Eastham in order to have it published

January ye 31th 1718/19 Joseph Higgins Junr Signified to me his in-tention to to contract marriage with Mercy Remick in order to have it published

January ye 31th 1718/19 Nathanael Higgins Signified his intention to contract marriage with Elisabeth atwood in order to have it pub-lished

January ye 31th 1718/19 Elisha Doane of Cape Cod Signified his in-tention to contract marriage with Hannah Cole Junr of Eastham

* "October ye 1st" was crossed out and "September ye 30th" interlined in the same hand and ink.

february ye 14th 1718/19 Jonathan Mayo Signified his intention to contract marriage with Thankfull Twining in order to have it published

february ye 14th 1718/9 John Freeman Jur of Eastham Signified his intention to Contract marriage with Thomison Seers of Harwich in order to be published

february ye 14th 1718/9 William Norket Signified his intention to Contract marriage with Ruth mayo both of Eastham in order to be published

august the 14th 1719 : William luis Signified his intention to marrie with Elisabeth Sweat : Both of Eastham

august ye 15th 1719 Josiah Snow Signified his Intention to contract marriage with Elisabeth Snow late of Harwich now of Eastham

September ye 12th 1719 Joshua* Higgins Junr Signified his intention to marrie with Ruth Twining Junr in order to be [p]ublished

[p. 207] September ye 19th 1719 Thomas Cook Signified his intention to marry with Dinah Doane

December ye 12th 1719 Thomas Lamkin Signified his intention to contract marriage with Debora Newcome in order to be published

January ye 23d 1719/20 Elkenah Paine of Truro Signified his intention to contract matrimonie with Reliance young of Eastham in order to be published

January ye 30th 1719/20 John Paine entred his purpouse to marry with Alice Mayo

february ye 6th 1719/20 John Crowell of yarmouth Signified his purpouse to marrie with Experience Higgins of Eastham

february ye 13th 1719/20 Richard Walker of Eastham Signified his purpuse to marry with Joanna Tomlin of needham

february ye 13th : 1719/20 Ebenezer Rogers of Harwich Signified his purpose to marrie with Hannah Cooke of Eastham

march ye 19th 1719/20 Joshua Treat Signified his purpose to marrie with Mercy Higgins

April ye 4th 1720 Ebenezer Dyer of Truro Signified his purpose to marrie with Sarah Doane of Eastham

april ye 29th 1720 David vickery of Truro Signified his purpouse to contract marriage with Martha mayo of Eastham

April ye 29th 1720 James Cohoon Signifyed his purpouse to Contract marriage with Mary Rich of Eastham

may ye 14th 1720 Samuel Doane Junr Signified his purpose to contract marriage with the widdow Thankfull Robins

June ye 6th 1720 the Reverdd mr Beniamin Webb of Eastham Signified his purpose to contract marriage with mrs Mehitabell Williams of Bridgwater in order to be published

June the 16th : 1720 Thomas Nucome Junr of Eastham Signified his purpose to contract marriage with Hephziba Wood of Sd Eastham in order to be published

* " Richard" was crossed out and "Joshua" interlined in the same hand and ink.

July ye 1st 1720 Richard Rich Junr Signified his purpose to contrac[t] marriage with Hannah Doane in order to be published

July ye 9th 1720 Nathanael Snow Signified his purpose to contract marriage with Elisabeth Eldridg of Harwich

July ye 23 : 1720 Capta Jonathan Banges of Harwich Signified his purpose to marrie with mrs Ruth young of Eastham in order to be published

[p. 208] august ye 13th 1720 Joshua Higgins Signified his purpose to contract marriage with Prissilla Bigsbee of Boxford in order to be published

September ye 16th 1720 Jabez Snow Junr Signified his purpouse to contract marriage with Elisabeth Paine in order to be published

September ye 16th 1720 Jonathan Smith Signified his purpose to contract marriage with Thankfull Paine in order to be published

September ye 23d : 1720 Thomas Thatcher of Eastham Signified his purpose to marrie with Sarah Rich of Eastham in order to be published

September ye 24 : 1720 Joshua Paine of Truro Signified his purpose to marrie with Rebecca* Sparrow of Eastham

September ye 24th 1720 Samuel King Signified his purpose to marrie with Abigail Linnell Both of Eastham

March ye 11th 1720 Nathanael Freeman Signified his purpose to marry with Hannah Merrick in order to be published

march ye 25th 1721 John Knowles Junr Signified his purpose to marry with mehittabell Walker

march ye 25th 1721 Timothy Cole Signified his purpose to marry with Elisabeth Sparrow

July ye 25th 1721 Thomas Holker Signified his purpose to marry with Deborah Brown in order to be published

July ye 29th 1721 Thomas Bacon of Eastham Signified his purpose marrie with mary Sciffe of chilmark in order to be published

august ye 12th 1721 John atwood of Eastham Signified his purpose to marrie with Thankfull williamson of the sam Town in order to be published

august ye 18th 1721 John Snow Signified his purpose to marry with Hannah Merrick of Harwich in order to be published

august ye 19th 1721 Jonathan Sparrow Junr Signified his purpose to marry with Dorcas Vickery now resident in Harwich in order to be published

September ye 1st 1721 Ebenezer Higgins Signified his purpose contract marriage with abigail Cole Junr in order to be published

September ye 16th 1721 Elisha Higgins Junr Signified his purpose to marrie with Sarah luis in order to be published

September ye 23d 1721 Jonathan Grew Signified his purpose to marry with abigail Cole in order to be published

*"Elisabeth," and "Junr," after "Sparrow", were crossed out, and "Rebecca" was interlined in the same hand and ink.

[p. 209] November ye 18th 1721 Thomas Gross of Eastham Signified his purpose to marry with Jane Cole of Sd Eastham in order to be published

January ye 5th 1721/2 Nathanael Rogers of Eastham Signified his purpose to marry with Silence Dimmock of Harwich in order to be published

January ye 25th 1721/2 Elisha Hamlin of Harwich Signified his purpose to marry with Elisabeth Mayo Senior of. Eastham in order to be published

January ye 27th 1721/2 Judah Mayo Signified his purpose to marry with Mary Hamilton of Chatham in order to be published

february ye 9th 1721/2 Thomas Luis of Eastham Signified his purpose to marrie with Judith Smith of Harwich

february ye 10th 1721/2 Jonathan Higgins Junr Signified his purpose to marry with Rebecca Hopkins of Harwich in order to be published

february ye 7th 1721/2 Nathanael May Signified his purpose to marry with Mehitabell Rogers both of Eastham

march ye 7th 1721/2 Simon Nucome Junr Signified his purpose to contract mariage with Lidia Brown, Both of Eastham in order to be published

March ye 10th 1721/2 John young Signified his purpose to marrie with Dinah Baker of Chatham in order to be published

august ye 23d 1722 Samuel atwood Signified his purpose to marrie with hannah Doane in order to be published

September ye 7th 1722 Joseph Smith Junr Signified his purpose to marry with Elisabeth Knowles in order to be published

September ye 8th 1722 Nathanael Freeman Junr of Eastha Signified his purpose to marry with mary Paine of Barnstable in order to be published

September ye 15th 1722 Jonathan Smith Signified his purpose to marry with Prissilla Higgins in order to be published

october ye 6th 1722 Thomas Mayo Junr Signified his purpose to marry with Elisabeth Roger in order to be published

January ye 12th 1722/3 Robert Mayo Signified his purpose to marry with Debora Strout, Both of Eastham in order to be published

January ye 12th 1722/3 Williams Smith Signified his purpose to marry with Dorcas Doane in order to be published

february y 1st 1722/3 Joshua Brown of Eastham Signified his purpose to marry with Rebecca Rich of truro in order to be published

february ye 16th 1722/3 Joseph Burge of yarmouth Signified his purpose to marrie with Thankfull Snow of Eastham in order to be published

[p. 210] march ye 16th 1722/3 Luke Stubbs Signified his purpose to contract marriage with Mary Nucome in order to be published

march ye 26th 1723 John Cutler Signified his purpose to marry with Sarah Smith in order to be published

april ye 25th 1723 Beniamin Snow Junr Signified his purpose to marrie with Martha Eldridge in order to be published

may ye 18th 1723 William Mayo Signified his purpose to marry with Hannah Snow in order to be published

June ye 1st 1723 Jonathan Doane Signified his purpose to marry with Martha Higgins

June ye 29 : 1723 John Allin of Marblehead Signified his purpose to marry with Rebecca Doane of Eastham in order to be published

June ye 29 : 1723 Richard Sparrow Junr Signified his purpose to marry with Hannah Shaw in order to be published

august ye 3d 1723 Timothy Cole Signified his purpose to marry with Martha Alemony in order to be published

august ye 2th 1723 John Rich of Eastham Signified his purpose to marry with Hope Seers of chatham

august ye 24th 1723 Seth Knowles Signified his purpose to marry with Martha Remick in order to be published

September ye 13th 1723 Israel Mayo Signified his purpose to marry with Mercy Rider of yarmouth in order to be published

September ye 23 : 1723 Cornelius Knowles Signified his purpose to marry with Elisabeth Remick in order to be published

November ye 9th 1723 mr John Mulford Signified his purpose to marry with Martha Harris in order to be published

March ye 7th 1723/4 Theophilus Higgins Signified his purpose to marrie with Joanna young in order to be publishel

april ye 4th 1724 Thomas atwood Signified his purpose to marry wth Phebe mayo in order to be published

April ye 11th 1724 Roger Thomas Signified his purpose to marry with Susannah Snow in order to be published

June ye 20th 1724 Thomas Knowles Signified his purpose to marry with Elisabeth Snow, in order to be published

July ye 4th 1724 Jesse Smith Signified his purpose to marry with Sarah Higgins in order to be published

July ye 11th 1724 Peter Severence of Harwich Signified his purpose to marry with Elisabeth Cole of Eastham in order to be published

July ye 15th 1724 Moses wilie Signified his purpose to marry with thankfull young in order to be published

[p. 211] July ye 17th 1724 Nathanael Covell Signified his purpose to marry with Easter Atwood in order to be published

July ye 29th 1724 mr Josiah oaks Signified his purpose to marry with mrs Margeret Haugh both of Eastham in order to be published

august ye 22 1724 George Shaw Signified his purpose to marry with mercy Rich in order to be published

September ye 5th 1724 Solomon Pepper gave account of his purpose to marry with Phebe Paine in order to be published

September ye 10th 1724 Joshua Hopkins Ju Signified his purpose to marry with prissilla Curtis in order to be published

September ye 12th 1724 Jeremiah Walker Signified his purpose to marrie with Easter Tomlin in order to be published

January ye 8th 1728 Isaac Doane Junr Signified his purpose to marry with anne Haugh, in order to be published

January yᵉ 9ᵗʰ 172⁴⁄₅ Thomas Higgins Signified his purpose to marrie with Sarah Vickery in order to be published

January yᵉ 25ᵗʰ 1724/5 Elisha Cob of Barnstable Signified his purpose to marrie with Mary Harding of Eastham in order to be published

february yᵉ 4ᵗʰ 1724/5 Edmond Freeman Signified his . purpose to marrie with Lois Paine in order to be published

february yᵉ 20ᵗʰ 1724/5 Moses Bigsbee Signified his purpose to marry with Phebe Hopkins in order to be published

March yᵉ 6ᵗʰ 1724/5 Moses young Signified his purpose to be published Thankfull Hawse of chatham in order to be published

April yᵉ 10ᵗʰ 1725 Elisha Freeman Signified his purpose to marrie with Lidia Freeman in order to be published

May yᵉ 1ˢᵗ 1725 Stephen Cole of Harwich Signified his purpose to marry with Rebecca Mayo of Eastham in order to be published

may yᵉ 21ᵗʰ 1725 Jeremiah Mayo Signified his purpose to narry wᵗʰ Elisabeth Mulford

July yᵉ 16ᵗʰ 1725 Benjamin Bean now resident at Billingsgate precinct in Eastham Signified his purpose to marry with Mehitabel Mayo of Eastham

August yᵉ 27ᵗʰ 1725 Jonathan Linnell Junʳ Signified his purpose to marry with Abigaile finny of Barnstable in order to be published

[p. 212] August yᵉ 28ᵗʰ 1725 Joseph Snow Signified his purpose to marry with Mercy Knowles in order to be published

August yᵉ 28ᵗʰ 1725 Joseph Pepper Signified his purpose to marry with Rebecca Higgins in order to be published

August yᵉ 28ᵗʰ 1725 Isaac Merrick Signified his purpose to marry with Phebe Doane in order to be published

September yᵉ 3ʳᵈ 1725 Richard Honiwell of Boston Signified his purpose to marrie with Content Mayo of Eastham in order to be published

September yᵉ 4ᵗʰ 1725 Joseph Doane of Eastham Signified his purpose to marrie with debora Paddock of Chatham in order to be published

September yᵉ 4ᵗʰ 1725 Thomas Rich Junʳ Signified his purpose to marrie with Thankfull mayo in order to be publishd

September yᵉ 17ᵗʰ 1725 David Cole Signified his purpose to marry with Jerusha Doane in order to be published

october yᵉ 1ˢᵗ 1725 Nathanael Harding of Truro Signified his purpose to marry with Hannah young* of Eastham in order to be published

october yᵉ 30ᵗʰ 1725 Pacock Grigg Signified his purpose to marry with Thankfull Brown in order to be published

January† yᵉ 8ᵗʰ 1725/6 Prenc Doan Signified his purpose to marry with Elisabeth Godfree in order to be published

Janary† yᵉ 8ᵗʰ 1725/6 Benjamin Sweat of Eastham Signified his purpose to marry with Sarah Eldridg of Truro in order to be published

Janary yᵉ 8ᵗʰ 1725/6 Samuel Baker Signified his purpose to marry with Debora Eldridg Both of Eastham in order to be published

Janary yᵉ 15ᵗʰ 1725/6 Ebenezer Atwood Signified his purpose to marry with Hiphziba Williamson in order to be published

*"Doane" was crossed out and "young" interlined in the same hand and ink.

†"December" was crossed out and "January" interlined in the same hand and ink.

January yᵉ 15ᵗʰ 1725/6 Solomon Cooms Signified his purpose to marry with Content mayo of Eastham in order to be published

february yᵉ 5ᵗʰ Caleb Cooke Signified his purpose to marry with Hannah Brown in order to be published

february yᵉ 19ᵗʰ 1725/6 Joseph Atkins Junʳ of Eastham Signified his purpose to Marry with Thankfull Paine of Truro in order to be published

february yᵉ 19ᵗʰ 1725/6 James Knowles Signified his purpose to marry with Anne Doane in order to be published

february yᵉ 19ᵗʰ 1725/6 Eliezer Freeman Signified his purpose to marry with Rebecca younŋ in order to be published

february yᵉ 19ᵗʰ 1725/6 Joseph Sparrow Signified his purpose to marry with Hannah Doane in order to be published

march yᵉ 5ᵗʰ 1725/6 Elisha Hunter Signified his purpose to marry with Sarah Atwood of Eastham in order to be published

July yᵉ 2ᵗʰ 1726 Thomas Linnell of Eastham Signified his purpose to marry with Thankfull Hopkins of Harwich in order to be published

[p. 213] July yᵉ 9ᵗʰ 1726 John young Junʳ Signified his purpose to marry with Mary Airie both of Eastham in order to be published

July 16ᵗʰ 1726 William Norket of Harwich Signified his purpose to marry with Prissilla Paine of Eastham in order to be published

august yᵉ 11ᵗʰ 1726 Richard Stephens of Truro Signified his purpose to marry with Ruhama Doane of Eastham in order to be published

august yᵉ 13ᵗʰ 1726 Benjamin Higgins Signified his purpose to marry wᵗʰ Sarah Mayo in order to be published

august yᵉ 19ᵗʰ 1726 Zebulon Brown Signified his purpose to marry with Tabitha Lewis of Barnstable in order to be published

august yᵉ 29ᵗʰ 1726 Shadreck Seger Signified his purpose to marry wᵗʰ mary Hamlin in order to be published

october yᵉ 1ˢᵗ 1726 Richard Paine Signified his purpose to marry with Phebe merrick in order to be published

october yᵉ 15ᵗʰ 1726 James Higgins Signified his purpose to marry with Sarah Bixbe in order to be published

January yᵉ 14 : 1726/7 John Cole Junʳ Signified his purpose to marry with Mercy Mayo in order to be published

January yᵉ 14ᵗʰ 1726/7 James Cole Signified his purpose to narry with Mary Cole in order to be published

march yᵉ 8ᵗʰ 1726/7 John Rich Junʳ Signified his purpose to marry with Thankfull Seers (both of Eastham)* in order to be published

April yᵉ 15ᵗʰ 1727 Israel Atwood Signified his purpose to marry with Hannah Studley of yarmouth in order to be published

May yᵉ 12ᵗʰ 1727 Richard Airie of Eastham Signified his purpose to marry with Hannah Burge resident in Eastham in order to be published

June yᵉ 24ᵗʰ 1727 Solomon Doane Signified his purpose to marry with Alice Higgins in order to be published

*The parentheses appear in the original.

July ye 15th 1727 Benjamin Green of Hull Signified his purpose to marry with Anne Nucome of Eastham in order to be published

July ye 15th 1727 mr Samuel Mayo Senior Signified his purpose to marry with mrs mary Sweat in order to be published

July ye 26th 1727 John Smith of Chatham Signified his purpose to marry with Elisabeth Brown of Eastham, in order to be published

august ye 12th 1727 David Higgins Signified his purpose to marry with mercy Twining in order to be published

august ye 26 1727 Israel Higgins Signified his purpose to marry with Ruth Brown in order to be published

September ye 2d 1727 William Paine of Eastham Signified his purpose to marry with Sarah Bacon of Barnstable in order to be published

[p. 214] September ye 7th 1727 Thomas* Higgins Junr Signified his purpose to marry with Abigaile Paine in order to be published

September ye 16th 1727 Seth Hinckly of Truro Signified his purpose to marry with Thankful atwood of Eastham

September ye 23 : 1727 Jonathan Rogers of Harwich Signified his purpose to marry with Elisabeth Cooke of Eastham

December ye 11th 1727 Daniel Eldridg of Eastham Signified his purpose to marry with Elisabeth Atkins of Chatham in order to be published

December ye 30th 1727 David Freeman Signified his purpose to marry with Ruth Freeman, in order to be published

January ye 20th 1727/8 William† Twining Signified his purpose to marry with Apphia Lewis in order to be published

Janary ye 20th 1727/8 Crisp Rogers of Eastham Signified his purpose to marry with Mary yeats of Harwich in order to be published

January ye 23 : 1727/8 Eldad Atwood Signified his purpose to marry with Margeret Snow in order to be published

January ye 25th 1727/8 Seth Clark of Harwich Signified his purpose to marry with Huldah Doane of Eastham in order to be published

february ye 1st 1727/8 Joseph Doane Esqur Signified his purpose to marry with Desire Berry in order to be published

february ye 3d 1727/8 Elkenah Higgins Signified his purpose to marry with Rebecca Allen in order to be published

April ye 25th 1728 mr Isaac Bacon of Province Town Signified his purpose to marry with Keziah Doane of Eastham in order to be published

June ye 15th 1728 Stephen Griffith Junr of Harwich Signified his purpose to marry with Phebe Merrick of Eastham in order to be published

August ye 10th 1728 John Wing of Harwich Signified his purpose to Marry with Mary Knowles of Eastham in order to be published

August ye 23d 1728 Robert Nickerson Signified his purpose to marry with Mercy Cole in order to be published

* "Benjamin" was crossed out and "Thomas" interlined in the same hand and ink.

† "Barnabas" was crossed out and "William" interlined in the same hand and ink.

August ye twentyfourth 1728 Daniel Cole of Eastham Signified his purpose to marry with Thankfull Burge of Harwich in order to be published

September ye 7th 1728 Seth Smith Signified his purpose to marry with Anne Knowles in order to be published

September ye 29th Williams Smith Signified his purpose to marry with Debora Walker in order to be published

october ye 12th 1728 Lot Clark of Harwich Signified his purpose to marry wth mary Harding of Eastham in order to be published

November ye 16th 1728 Richard Mayo Signified his purpose to marry with Rebecca Sparrow in order to be published

November ye 16th 1728 Judah Rogers of Harwich Signified his purpose to marry with Patience Cole of Eastham in order to be published

November ye 29th 1728 Jedediah Higgins Signified his purpose to marry with Phebe Freeman in order to be published

January ye 4th 1728/9 Theodore Harding Signified his purpose to marry with Sarah Hamilton in order to be published

(*To be continued*)

EASTHAM AND ORLEANS, MASS., VITAL RECORDS

(Continued from page 117)

[p. 215] January yᵉ 11ᵗʰ 1728/9 John Doane Junᵣ Signifyed his purpose to marry with Mary Brown in order to be published

January yᵉ 16ᵗʰ 1728/9 Matthew Collins of Boston Signifyed his purpose to marry with yᵉ Widdow Mary Mayo of Eastham in order to be published

february yᵉ 1ˢᵗ 1728/9 Caleb Cooke Signified his purpose to marry with Lidia Walker in order to be published

June yᵉ 17ᵗʰ 1729 Joshua Pierce Signified his purpose to marry with Elisabeth Nucome in order to be published

June 14ᵗʰ 1729 Thomas Boreman Signified his purpose to Marry with Martha George both Indians of Eastham

June yᵉ 28ᵗʰ 1729 John Nucome of Eastham Signified his purpose to marry with [*] Ballard of truro in order to be published

July yᵉ 5ᵗʰ 1729 Jesse Brown Signified his purpose to marry with Elisabeth Walker in order to be published

august yᵉ 16ᵗʰ 1729 Joseph Netas Signified his purpose to marry with Betty Job in order to be published

August yᵉ 30ᵗʰ 1729 Edmond Freeman Signified his purpose to marry with Sarah Sparrow in order to be published

September yᵉ 5ᵗʰ 1729 Thomas Gray of Harwich Signified his purpose to marry with Rachel Freeman of Eastham in order to be published

November yᵉ 1ˢᵗ 1729 Nathanael Higgins Signified his purpose to mary with Sarah Walker in order to be published

November yᵉ 4ᵗʰ 1729 Joseph Hall of Medford Signified his purpose to marry with Abigail Brown of Eastham in order to be published

November yᵉ 10ᵗʰ 1729 John Shaw of Eastham Signified his purpose to marry with Marth Knowles of Chatham in order to be published

December yᵉ 13ᵗʰ 1729 Amos Knowles of Eastham Signified his purpose to marry with Rebecca Dillingham of Harwich in order to be published

January yᵉ 3ᵈ 1729/30 Gershom Cole Signified his purpose to marry with Mary Rogers of Harwich in order to be published

January yᵉ 31ᵗʰ 1729/30 Joshua Paine Signified his purpose to marry with Phebe Snow in order to be published

January yᵉ 31ᵗʰ 1729/30 Paul Seers Signified his purpose to marry with Anne Atkins Both of Eastham in order to be published

february yᵉ 5ᵗʰ 1729/30 Robert Rich of Eastham Signified his purpose to marry with Lidia Collins of Truro in order to be published

* *Space was left for the given name.

December 5 : 1730 then entred the Intentions of Nathaniel Snow & Mary Doane to proseed in Marriage ℙ me Joseph Doane Town clerk

December 30th 1730 then entred the Intentions of Thomas Rogers of Truro & Rebecka Collens of Eastham to proseed in marriage ℙ me Joseph Doane Town Clerk

January 16th 173/31* then entred the Intentions of Rouland Fish of Falmouth & Elizabeth Harding of Eastham to proseed in mar-riage ℙ Joseph Doane Town clerk

January 16th 1730/31 then entred the Intentions of Josiah Cook junr & Hannah Sparrow to proseed in marriage ℙ me Joseph Doane Town clerk

January 23 : 1730/31 then entred the Intentions of Elkenah Rogers & Reliance Yates to proseed In marriage ℙ me Joseph Doane Town clerk.

February 3 : 1730/31 then entred the Intentions of Jacob Cook of Province Town & Marcy Young of Eastham to proseed in Mar-riage ℙ me Joseph Doane Town clerk

March 10th 1730/31 then entred the Intentions Ebenezor Mute of Hull & Debro Atwood of Eastham to proseed in marriage ℙ me Joseph Doane Town clark

[p. 217] May the first day 1731 then entred the Intentions of Barna-bas Twining & Hannah Swet both of Eastham to proseed in Marriage. ℙ me Joseph Doane Town clark

May 21 : 1731 then entred the Intentions of Henry Young & Elener Cole both of Eastham to proseed in marriage. ℙ me Joseph Doane Town clarke

June 12 : 1731 Then entred the Intentions of David young junr & Hannah Twining both of Eastham to proseed in marriage. ℙ me Joseph Doane Town clark

June 25 : 1731 Then entred the Intentions of Jonathan Shaw & Sarah† Rich both of Eastham to proseed in marriage. ℙ me Joseph Doane Town clark

July 23 : 1731 Then entred the Intentions of John Harding & Elisa-beth Young both of Eastham to Joyn In marriage ℙ me Joseph Doane Town clark

July 29th 1731 Then entred the Intentions of Thomas Savidg of Truroe & Martha Doane junr of Eastham to Joyn in marriage ℙ me Joseph Doane Town Clark

July 31 : 1731 Then entred the Intentions of Elisha Young of East-ham junr & Bethia Smith late of Chatham now of Eastham to Joyn in marriage. ℙ me Joseph Doane Town clark.

August 7th 1731 Then entred the Intentions of David Nickason of Chatham & Elisabeth Mayo of Eastham Daughter of Nathaniel Mayo to Joyn in marriage ℙ me Joseph Doane Town clark

*This is plainly an error for 1730/31.

† "Marcy", and "junr" after "Rich", were crossed out, and "Sarah" was interlined in the same hand and ink.

---

february ye 14th 1729/30 Daniel Young Signified his purpose to marry with Lidia Paine in order to be published

march 21 : 1729/03* James Rogers junr of Eastham Signified his Intention of marrige with Hannah Godfrey of chatham in order to be published entred ℙ Joseph Doane Town clark

april 25 : 1730 Then Thomas Mulford junr of Truroe & Mary Smith of Eastham their Intentions of Marrigage Signified & entred ℙ Joseph Doane Town Clark

May 23 : 1730 Then entred the Intentions of Edward Bangs junr of Harwich & Rebecka Higgins of Eastham to proseed in marriage entred ℙ Joseph Doane Town clerk

[p. 216] May 16th 1730 then was Signified the Intentions of Marriage between Beriah Higgins and Jemima Witherel both of Eastham entred ℙ Joseph Doane Town Clark

June 9th 1730 then entred the Intentions of marriage between Ephraim Covell & Marcy Brown both of Eastham Entred ℙ me Joseph Doane Town clerk

June the 19th 1730 Then Thomas Freeman of Harwich Signified his Intentions of Marriage with Dorothy Cole of Eastham Entred ℙ Joseph Doane Town clerk

July the eleventh 1730 then entred the Intensions of Samuel Dilee of Province Town and Mary Mayo junr of Eastlam to proseed in Marriage entred ℙ Joseph Doane Town clerk

July 30 : 1730 then Thomas Brown of Eastham Signified his Inten-tion to proseed In marriage with Abigel Ockillee entred ℙ Joseph Doane Town clerk

August 27th 1730 then entred the Intentions of Stephen Atwood of Province Town & Sarah Collens of Eastham to proseed in mar-riage entred ℙ me Joseph Doane Town Clerk

August 28th 1730 then entred the Intentions of Thomas Snow & Sarah Young both of Eastham to proseed in marriage. entred ℙ Joseph Doane Town clerk

September 12th 1730 then entred the Intentions of Simion Doane & Applia higgins to proseed in marriage entred pr me Joseph Doane Town clerk

September 19th 1730 then entred the Intentions of Stephen Snow Son of Stephen Snow & Rebecka Snow to proseed in marriage ℙ mee Joseph Doane Town clerk

September 19th 1730 then entred the Intentions of Joshua Cook & Zilpha Brown to proseed in marriage ℙ me Joseph Doane Town clerk

November 14th 1730 then entred the Intentions of Daniel Cole & Martha Rogers to proseed in marriage ℙ me Joseph Doane Town clerke

December 3 : 1730 then the Intentions of Nelemiah harding of Chatham & Priscilla Collens of Eastham to proseed in Marriage ware entred ℙ me Joseph Doane Town clerk

*This is plainly an error for 1729/30.

february 19th 1731/2 then entered the Intentions of Nathaniel Crosby of Harwich & Hester Young of Eastham to proseed in Marriage ℘ me Joseph Doane Town clark

March the first day 1731/2 then entered the Intentions of James Allen of Boston and Bashua Mayo of Eastham to proseed in marriage ℘ me Joseph Doane Town clark

April 22 : 1732 then entered the Intentions of Cornelas Tower of Hingham and Hannah Higgins of Eastham to proseed in marriage ℘ me Joseph Doane Town clark

May 6th 1732 then entred the Intentions of Isaac Mayo of Eastham & Patience Rogers of Harwich to proseed in Marriage ℘ Joseph Doane Town clark

June. 26 : 1732 then entred the Intentions of John Doane of Eastham Esqr and Mrs Jane Baxter of Hull to proseed in marriage ℘ Joseph Doane Town clark

July 11th 1732 Then entred the Intentions of Robert Pepper & Mary Snow to proseed in Marriage ℘ me Joseph Doane Town clark

July 21 : 1732 then entred the Intentions of John Brown of Eastham & Marcy Nucomb of Truroe to proseed in marriage ℘ me Joseph Doane Town clark

August 3rd : 1732 Entred the Intentions of Joseph Luen of Plymouth & Rejoyce Walker to proseed In marriage ℘ me Joseph Doane Town clark

August 25th 1732 then entred the Intentions of Samuel Snow & Elizabeth Freeman to proseed in marriage entred ℘ me Joseph Doane Town clark

[p. 219] August 26 : 1732 then entred the Intentions of John Clark of Rowley & Mercy Witherell to proseed in marriage Pr Joseph Doane Town clark

October 14th 1732 then entred the Intentions of Nathaniel Smith of harwich & Marcy Walker of Eastham to proseed in marriage ℘ me Joseph Doane Town clark

October 18th 1732 Then entred the Intentions of John Fry a Resident in Eastham & Rachell Witherel of Eastham to proseed in marriage ℘ me Joseph Doane Town clark

October 28 : 1732 then entred the Intentions of Liutt John Cole & Mrs Sarah Higgins to proseed In marriage ℘ me Joseph Doane Town clark

December 11th 1732 then entred the Intentions of Silvenis Snow & Hannah Cole to proseed in marriage ℘ me Joseph Doane Town clark

January 12th 1732/3 then entred the Intentions of Jonathan Paine & Marcy Doane both of Eastham to proseed in marriage ℘ me Joseph Doane Town clark

January 20th 1732/3 then entred the Intentions of Samuel Betee & Mary Harding both of Eastham to proseed in marriage ℘ me Joseph Doane Town clark

August 29th 1731 Then entred the Intentions of Daniel Crosby of Harwich & Ruth Cole of the north precinct of Eastham to Joyn in Marriage ℘ me Joseph Doane Town clark

September 3 : 1731 Then entred the Intentions of Lazarus Griffeth of Harwich & Lidea Doane of Eastham to Joyn in Marriage. ℘ me Joseph Doane Town clark

September 4th 1731 Then entred the Intentions of Theoder Higgins & Jane Brown both of Eastham to Joyn in Marriage. ℘ me Joseph Doane Town clark

September 4th 1731 Then entred the Intentions of Ese Mayo of Eastham & Exprience Yates of harwich to Joyn in marriage . ℘ me Joseph Doane Town clark

September 11th 1731 Then entred the Intentions of John Bee of Harwich & Marcy Mulford of Eastham to Joyn in marriage ℘ Joseph Doane Town clark

September 11th 1731 Then entred the Intentions of John Mayo & Tabitha Snow to proseed in marriage ℘ me Joseph Doane Town clark

November 7th 1731 then entred the Intentions of John Mott of Situate & Lidea Snow of Eastham to proseed in marriage ℘ me Joseph Doane Town clark

November 13 : 1731 then entred the Intentions of Eleazor Doane & Hannah Mayo both of Eastham to proseed in marriage ℘ me Joseph Doane Town clark

november 20 : 1731 then entred the Intentions of Ichabud Higgins & Jane Snow to proseed in marriage ℘ me Joseph Doane Town Clark

December 21 : 1731 Then entred the Intentions of Thomas Snow & Abigel Doane to proseed in marriage ℘ me Joseph Doane Town Clark

[p. 218] December 31 : 1731 then entred the Intentions of Joshua Seers of Yarmouth & Rebecka Mayo of Eastham Daughter of Theophilas Mayo to proseed in Marriage ℘ me Joseph Doane Town clark

January 8th 1731/2 then entred the Intentions of Ebenezor Cole & Ruth Cole to Joyn in marriage ℘ me Joseph Doane Town Clark

January 14th 1731/2 then entred the Intentions of Ruben Doane & Sarah Horf* to Joyn in marriage entred pr me Joseph Doane Town clark

January 22 : 1731/ 2 Then entred the Intentions of Joseph Hambleton of Chatham and Martha Atkins of Eastham to Joyn in Marriage by me Josepl Doane Town clark

february 5th 1731/2 then entred the Intentions of Henry Young & Elizabeth higgins to proseed in marriage ℘ me Joseph Doane Town clark

* Probably an error for " Whorf."—*Editor.*

January 17th 1732/3 then entered the Intentions of Daniel Doane & Ruth Cole to proseed in marriage ℔ me Joseph Doane Town Clark

March the 3rd 1732/3 then entred the Intentions of Ruben Meyrick & Abigel Higgins to proseed in marriage ℔ me Joseph Doane Town clark

March 24th 1732/3 then entred the Intentions of Enos Knowls & Sarah Sparrow both of Eastham to Joyn In marriage entred ℔ me Joseph Doane Town clark

april 13th 1733 then entred the Intentions of Willard Knowls & Bethiah Atwood to Joyn In Marriage ℔ me Joseph Doane Town Clark

April 21 : 1733 then entred the Intentions of Mr John Every & Mrs Ruth Knowls to Joyn in Marriage
Then also entred the Intentions of Thomas Nucomb junr & Marcy Tilton to Joyn in marriage

May 24th 1733 Then entred the Intentions of Jacob Davis of harwich and and Mary Rogers of Eastham to proseed in marriage

May 26 : 1733 Then entred the Intentions of Thomas Addis & Thankfull Atwood to proseed in marriage

June 2 : 1733 then entred the Intentions of Thomas Dill & Mehitable Brown of Eastham to proseed in marriage

[p. 220] June 16 : 1733 then entred the Intentions of Isaac higgins junr & Abigel Freeman to proseed in Marriage pr me Joseph Doane Town Clark

October 30th 1733 then entred the Intentions of Mr James Stutson of Hingham & Mrs Margret Oakes of Eastham to proseed in Marriage ℔ me Joseph Doane Town clark

November 10th 1733 then entred the Intentions of Theophilas Paine of Eastham & Hannah Beacon of Barnstable to proseed in marriage pr me Joseph Doane Town Clark

December 5th 1733 then entred the intentions of Stephen Totman of Truroe Junr and Hester Higgins to proseed in marriage ℔ me Joseph Doane Town clark

December 8 : 1733 then entred the Intentions of Joshua Cole & Sarah Cole both of Eastham to proseed In marriage ℔ me Joseph Doane Town Clark

December 22 : 1733 then entred the Intentions of Elisha Doane & Elizabeth Sparrow both of Eastham to proseed in marriage by me Joseph Doane Town clark

December 28 : 1733 then entred the Intentions of Mr William Meyrick of Harwich and Mrs Elizabeth Orsbon to proseed In marriage by me Joseph Doane Town clark

January 5th 1733/4 then entred the Intentions of Elisha Higgins junr & Hannah Atwood both of eastham to proseed in marriage entred ℔ Joseph Doane Town clark

January 18 : 1733/4 then entred the Intentions of Warren Green of Barnstable & Mary Paine of Eastham to proseed in marriage entred ℔ me Joseph Doane Town clark

February 2nd 1733/4 then entred the Intentions of David Ned & Rachell nopies to proseed in marriage

February 21 : 1733/4 then entred the Intentions of Lamuel Rich of Truero & Elizabeth Harding to proseed in marriage

March 2nd 1733/4 then entred the Intentions of Doctor John Dunkin and Mrs Keziah Doane to proseed in marriage

April 12 : 1734 then entred the Intentions of Seth Rider & Reliance Smith to proseed in marriage

April 12th 1734 then entred the Intentions of Joseph Smally of Trueroe & Jane Gross of Eastham to proseel in marriage

April 20 : 1734 then entred the Intentions of James Brown junr & Elizabeth Smith to proseed in Marriage

May 3 : 1734 Then entred the Intentions of Israel Comes & Experience Higgins to proseed In Marriage

May the 4th 1734 then entred the Intentions of Edward Knowls junr & Ann Knowls to proseed In marriage Shee having obtained License for the Same as the Law directs

May 18 : 1733* Then entred the Intentions of Prence Collens & Biell Doane both of Eastham to proseed in marriage

June 1 : 1734 then entred the Intentions of William Covell junr and Joanna Atwood to proseed in marriage

June 4th 1734 then entred the Intentions Hinks Gross of Eastham and abigel† Crowell of chatham to proseed in marriage

[p. 221] June 21 : 1734 then entred the Intentions of Ephraim Pratt & Bulah Williamson both of Eastham to proseed in marriage

July the 10th 1734 then entred the Intentions of Beriah Smith of Province Town & Elizabeth Knowls of Eastham to proseed in Marriage

July 19th : 1734 then entred the Intentions of Jeremiah Haws of Chatham & Phebee Young to proseed in marriage

July 27th 1734 then entred the Intentions of Thomas Kenwrick of Eastham and Ann Aatkins to proseel in marriage

August 5th 1734 then entred the Intentions of Jesse Eldrege & Abigel Smith to proseed in Marriage

august 17th 1734 then entred the Intentions of Nathaniel Mayo junr & Hannah Horton to proseed in marriage

august 24 : 1734 then entred the Intentions of Barnabas Freeman of Eastham and Mary Stone of Harwich to proseed in marriage

august 26 : 1734 then entred the Intentions of Benjamin Chadwell of Linn and Mary Dilee to proseed in marriage

September 8th 1734 then entred the Intentions of Jeremiah Nickason of Eastham and Debro Yates of Harwich to proseed in marriage

October 19th 1734 then entred the Intentions of Thomas Holbrooks & Margret Doane Daughter of Isaac Doane to proseed in marriage

October 26th 1734 then entred the Intentions of David Rich & Hannah Brown to proseed in marriage

*This is probably an error for 1734.— Editor.
†"Hannah" was crossed out and "abigel" writen in the margin in the same hand and ink.

December 7th 1734 then entered the Intentions of Samll Sihon & Mary wekenet Indians of Eastham to proseed in marriage

December 15 : 1734 then entered the Intentions of Mr Samuel Mayo & Mrs Ruth Higgins of Eastham to proseed in marriage

December 21 : 1734 then entered the Intentions of James Mayo & Elizabeth Higgins to proseed in marriage

December 27 : 1734 then entered the Intentions of Stephen Snow junr & Mary Cole to proseed in marriage

January 25 : 1734/5 then entred the Intentions of Ephraim Cook & Mary Meyrick to proseed in marriage

January 31 : 1734/5 then entred the Intentions of Elisha Linel & Recka* Paine to proseed in marriage

February the first 1734/5 then entred the Intentions of Joseph Brown & Susanah Cole to proseed in Marriage

February 15 : 1734/5 then entred the Intentions of Sam Jo Molato and Marcy Adam to Joyn in marriage

[p. 222] April 26th 1735 then entred the Intentions of Nathaniel Mayo the third of Eastham & Marcy Cole to proseed in marriage

May 14th 1735 then entred the Intentions of John Harding junr & Thankfull Rich to proseed in marriage

June 17 : 1735 then entred the Intentions of moses Higgins & Elizabeth Arey to proseed in marriage

June 19th 1735 then Archeles Lues of Plymouth & Mary Tailer of Eastham their Intentions to proseed in marriage was entred

June 28th 1735 then entred the Intentions of Jonathan Higgins jur & Rachel Doane to proseed in marriage

July 5th 1735 then entred the Intentions of Simmeon Smith & Abigel Cook both of Eastham to proseed in marriage

august 2nd 1735 then entred the Intentions of Samuel Knowls Tersio† of Eastham and Hannah Freeman of Harwich to proseed in marriage

September 6th 1735 then entred the Intentions of Barnabas Eldrege of Chatham and Mary Hurd of Eastham to proseed in marriage

September 11 : 1735 then entred the Intentions of William Williams of Sebrook & Elizabeth Gross of Eastham to proseed in marriage

September 12 : 1735 then entred the Intentions of Ebenezer Cook & Marcy Paine both of eastham to proseed in marriage

September 24 : 1735 then entred the Intentions of Elisha Snow & Abigel Doane both of Eastham to proseed in marriage

January 7th 1735/6 then entred the Intentions of Nathaniel Atwood and Abigel Stephens both of Eastham to proseed in marriage

January 15 : 1735/6 entred the Intentions of Simeon Merifeld of Provice Town and Thankfull Rider of Eastham to proseed in Marriage

February 24 : 1735/6 then entred the Intentions of Eleazor Atwood & Rebecka Young both of Eastham to proseed in Marriage

*This was probably an error for Rebecka.

† "Tersio" for "Third".

February 26 : 1735/6 then entered the Intentions of Benjamin Collens junr of Truro & Jerusha Stephens of Eastham to proseed in marriage

February 26 : 1735/6 then entered the Intentions of Mulford Eldrege of Eastham, and Biel Porenton of Truroe to proseed in marriage

April 10th 1736 then entered the Intentions of Richard Beaker & Elizabeth Witherel to proseed in Marriage

June the third 1736 then entred the Intentions of William Freeman junr of Harwich and Hannah Atwood of Eastham to proseed in Marriage

[p. 223] June 12 : 1736 then entred the Intentions of Josiah Seers of Chatham & Zuba Knowls of Eastham to proseed in Marriage

July 10 : 1736 then entred the Intentions of Aron Snow & Serah Gross to proseed in marriage

July 17 : 1736 then entred the Intentions of Elijah Doane & Susannah Lues to proseed In marriage

July 24 : 1736 then entred the Intentions of Israel Young junr & Phebee Fish to proseed in marriage

August 25th 1736 then entred the Intentions of Thomas Rogers & Rebecka Higgins both of Eastham to to seed* in marriage

August 28 : 1736 then entred the Intentions of Henry Snow & Rebecka Berry to proseed in marriage

August 30th 1736 then entred the Intentions of Enock Doane and Hannah Harding to proseed in marriage

September 11 : 1736 then entred the Intentions of John Smith junr & Phebee Snow to proseed in marriage

September 25 : 1736 then entred the Intentions of Samuel Smith & Serah Snow both of Eastham to proseed in marriage

October 2nd 1736 then entred the Intentions of Elkenah Young & Marcy Mayo to proseed in marriage

October 23 : 1736 then entred the Intentions of Joseph Cole junr & Mery* young junr to proseed in marriage

October 23 : 1736 then entred the Intentions of Josh Bogue molato & Jemima Ray† Indian to proseed in marriage

November 30th 1736 then entred the Intentions of Eleazeser unquit & Elis Japhet to proseed in marriage

November 13th 1736 then entred the Intentions of Daniel Seers of Yarmouth & marcy Snow of Eastham to proseed in marriage

December 11th 1736 then entred the intentions of Jesse Nickason of harwich & Thankfull Cook of Eastham to proseed in marriage

December 15 : 1736 Then entred the Intentions of Jonathan Dyer of Truro & Ketura Doane of Eastham to proseed in marriage

January 8 : 1736/7 then entred the Intentions of Israel Cole junr and Remembrance Burges to proseed in marriage

*Sic.

† "Ralph" was crossed out and "Ray" written in the margin in the same hand and ink.

January 8 : 1736/7 then entred the intentions of Nathan Harding and Anne Brown to proseed in marriage

January 22 : 1736/7 then entred the Intentions of Elnathan Doane & Martha* Padlock to proseed in marriage

[p. 224] January 22 : 1736/7 then entred the Intentions of Joseph Bogue & Lidea Moses to proseed in marriage

February 19th 1736/7 then entred the Intentions of Nathaniel Freeman of Harwich & Martha Brown of Eastham to proseed in marriage

May 20th 1737 then entred the Intentions of Matthias Burges of Yarmouth and Dorkas Cole of Eastham to proseed in marriage

May 21 : 1737 then entred the Intentions of Joshua Higgins & Jane Maker to proseed in Marriage

September 13 : 1737 then entred the Intentions of John Harding junr of Eastham and Anna Tour† of Hingham to proseed in marriage

September 24 : 1737 then entred the Intentions of Paule Higgins & Rebecka Mayo to proseed in marriage

September 24 : 1737 then entred the Intentions of Elkens Snow & Susanna Walker to proseed in marriage

September 24 : 1737 then entred the Intentions of Joshua Higgins & Mary Beaker to proseed in Marriage

September 24 : 1737 then entred the Intentions of James Hickman and Mary Smith both of eastham to proseed in marriage

October 1 : 1737 then entred the Intentions of Joseph Cole the third and Serah Nickason of harwich to proseed in marriage

October the 8th 1737 then entred the Intentions of Levie Smith & Jane Snow to proseed in marriage

October 29 : 1737 then entred the Intentions of Mr Samuel Smith of Eastham & Mrs Mary Paine to proseed in Marriage

Silas Pirce & Unis Cole entred their Intentions of marriage the 3 day of november 1737

november 3 : 1737 then entred the Intentions of Zacheus Higgins and Rebecka Young to proseed in marriage

November 18 : 1737 then entred the Intentions of Sollomon Swet & Serah Beaker both of Eastham to proseed in marriage

December 10 : 1737 then entred the Intentions of Pasheler Collens of Eastham & Jane Maker of Harwich to proseed in marriage

January 9th 1737/8 then entred the Intentions of Zoah Smith and Hannah Seers both of Eastham to proseed In marriage

January 14th 1737/8 then entred the Intentions of William Long of Eastham and Serah Cahoone of Harwich to proseed in marriage

[p. 225] January 19 : 1737/8 then entred the Intentions of William Covel & Elizabeth Weber to proseed in marriage

January 27 : 1737/8 then entred the Intentions of Lance Lot Clark of Chatam and Patience Brown of Eastham to proseed in marriage

*"Prissilah" was crossed out and "Martha" interlined in the same hand and ink.

†Tower.

January 28 : 1737 then entred the Intentions of Isaac Cole & Anne Doane to proseed in marriage.

January 28 : 1737 then entred the Intentions of Isaac Smith & Mary Sparrow to proseed in marriage

February 11th 1737 then entred the Intentions of Jerimiah Smith third & Lidea Lincolne* both of Eastham to proseed in marriage

february 18 : 1737/8 then entred the Intentions of Oliver Arey of Eastham and Elizabeth Gould of Harwich to proseed in marriage

March 14 : 1737/8 then entred the Intentions of Thomas negro man of Eastham Servant of Joshua Higgins & Elizabeth Job of Chatam Indian woman to proseed in marriage

april 1 : 1738 then entred the Intentions of Stephen Cole of Harwich & Rebecka Nickason now of Eastham to proseed in marriage

april 14 : 1738 then entred the Intentions of Ebenezor Nucom & Thankfull Freeman both of Eastham to proseed in marriage

april 14th 1738 then entred the Intentions of Ebit negro man Sarvant of Mr Jonathan Smith of Eastham & Serah Achooloo now of Eastham to proseed in marriage

July 8 . 1738 then entred the Intentions of Mr William Grayham of Boston & Mrs Anne Hamblen of Eastham to proseed in marriage

July 22nd 1738 then entred the Intentions of Mr Joseph Smith of Eastham and Mrs Rebecka Tatcher† of Barnstable to proseed in marriage

August 26 : 1738 then entred the Intentions of Benjamin Bullard & Hannah Nucomb both of Eastham to proseed in marriage

August 29 : 1738 then entred the Intentions of Nathan Young jur & Mary Atwood to proseed in marriage

September 2nd 1738 then entred the Intentions of James Lincolne junr & Rebecka Brown to proseed in marriage

September 9th 1738 then entred the Intentions of Ruben Rich & Martha Smith to proseed in marriage

September 23 : 1738 then entred the Intentions of Isaac Harding & Experience Treat to proseed in Marriage

September 23 : 1738 then entred the intentions of Abnor Snow & Elizabeth Cole to proseed in marriage

[p. 226] October 7th 1738 then entred the Intentions of Daniel Mayo junr & Martha Hollbrooke to proseed in marriage.

November 16th 1738 then entred the Intentions of Simeon Cook & Melatia Robens both of Eastham to proseed in Marriage.

November 17‡ : 1738 then entred the Intentions of Samuel Cole & Dorkis Young both of Eastham to proseed in Marriage.

December 8 : 1738 entred the Intentions of David Doane of Eastham & Sarah Tacther† of Truero to proseed in marriage.

*"Snow" was crossed out and "Lincolne" interlined in the same hand and ink.

†Thatcher.

‡"7" was written over "8" in the same ink.

THE
MAYFLOWER DESCENDANT

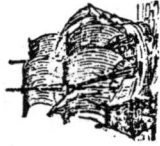

1620 2020

A QUARTERLY MAGAZINE OF
PILGRIM GENEALOGY AND HISTORY

VOLUME XXIX

1931

PUBLISHED BY THE
MASSACHUSETTS SOCIETY OF
MAYFLOWER DESCENDANTS
BOSTON

182

December 26 : 1738 entred the Intentions of Capt Edward Bangs of
Harwich & Mrs Ruth Mayo of Eastham to proseed in marriage

February 19th : 1738/9 entred the Intentions of Joseph Nucomb of
Eastham & Mary Eldrege to proseed in marriage

March 8 : 1738/9 then entred the Intentions of Joseph Doane Son of
Deacon Elisha Doane and Dorkis Eldrege to proseed in Marriage
both of Eastham

March 9th 1738/9 then entred the Intentions of Jabiz Sparrow & Mary
Young both of Eastham to proseed in marriage

March 27th 1739 then entred the Intentions of Mr Joseph Rogers &
Mrs Sarah Harding both of Eastham to proseed in marriage

April 21rst 1739 then entred the Intentions of Phillip Selue of Harwich & Phebee Atwood of Eastham to proseed in marriage

May 11th 1739 then entred the ententions of Garsham Hamlen of Barnstable and Hannah Olbeni of Eastham to proseed in marriage

June the first 1739 then entred the Intentions of Thomas Atkins of
Chatham and Hop* Snow to proseed in marriage.

June the first 1739 then entred the Intentions of Habijah Holbrooks
& Hannah Treat both of Eastham to proseed in Marriage.

June 4th 1739 entred the Intentions of Samuel Harding of Eastham
& Content† of the Township of Hingham to proseed in marriage

August 18th 1739 then entred the Intentions of John Gould of Harwich
& Ruth Godfrey of Eastham to proseed in marriage.

August 25 : 1739 then entred the Intentions of Mr John Whitner of
Harwich & Mrs Jerusha Knowls of Eastham to proseed in
Marriage.

August 25 : 1739 then entred the Intentions of James Michell & Hannah Higgins to proseed in marriage

august 29 : 1739 then entred the Intentions of Stephen Cash of Truero
& Anne Brown of Eastham to proseed in marriage.

September 4th 1739 then entred the Intentions of Elisha Cole junr &
Prissila Smalee both of Eastham to proseed in marriage.

(To be continued)

*Hope.

†The surname was omitted. She was Content James.—Editor.

EASTHAM AND ORLEANS, MASS., VITAL RECORDS

Transcribed by George Ernest Bowman

(*Continued from Vol. XXVIII, p. 182*)

[p. 227*] September 13th 1739 then entered the Intentions of the Revd Mr Joseph Crock[er] and Mrs Reliance Allen of Falmouth in the County of York† to proseed in marriage.

November the first day 1739 then entered the Intentions of Joseph Paddock of Yarmouth & Mrs Elizabeth Mayo of Eastham to proceed in marriage.

November 3rd 1739 then entered the Intentions of Mr Nathaniel Knowls of Eastham and Mrs Mercy Freeman of Harwich to proseed in marriage.

November 23 : 1739 then entered the Intentions of Elisha Higgins & Elizabeth Brown both of Eastham to proseed in marriage

November 24th 1739 then entered the intentions of Daniel Freeman of Harwich and Mercy Freeman of Eastham to proseed in marriage

January 11th 1739/40 then entered the Intentions of Joseph Harding & Eunis Nucomb both of Eastham to proseed in marriage

January 12 : 1739/40 then entered the Intentions of Benjamin Higgins Son of Benjamin Higgins & Hannah Higgins Daughter of James Higgins to proseed in marriage

February 2 : 1739/40 then entered the Intentions of Sollomon Smith & Suseanna Snow both of Eastham to proseed in marriage

March 8th 1739/40 then entered the Intentions of Samuel Paine of Eastham and Desire Green of Barnstable to proseed in marriage

March 12th 1739/40 then entered the Intentions of Samuel Higgins & Elizabeth Harding both of Eastham to proseed in marriage

april 11th 1740 then entered the Intentions of Samuel Higgins 3rd of Eastham and Mary Smith of Truro to proseed In marriage

May the 9th 1740 then entered the Intentions of John Young & Jerusha Cole‡ both of Eastham to proseed in marriage

May 26 : 1740 then entered the Intentions of Mr Pelegg Forge§ of Marshfield & Mr Phebee Higgins of Eastham to proseed in marriage

June 4th 1740 then entered the Intentions of Jeremiah Bigford & Abigel Holbrooks both of Eastham to proseed in marriage.

* Of original volume marked "Births 1701-1781", etc.
† Now in Maine.
‡ "Doane" was crossed out and "Cole" was interlined in the same hand and ink.
§ Evidently an error for "Ford".

June 21 : 1740 then entered the Intentions of James Atwood & Mercy Young both of Eastham to proseed in marriage.

July 12th 1740 then entered the Intentions of John Sparrow junr & Anne Atwood both of Eastham to proseed in marriage

august 23 : 1740 then entered the Intentions of Richard Cook junr & Rebecka Mayo to proseed in marriage.

September 27th 1740 then entered the Intentions of Isaac Hopkins of Harwich and Thankfull Smith of Eastham to proseed in marriage.

[p. 228] September 27 : 1740 then entered the Intentions of George Brown & Elies* Freeman to proseed in Marriage

September 27 : 1740 then entered the Intentions of Nathaniel Cook & Mercy Remick to proseed in marriage.

October 22 : 1740 then entered the Intentions of George Almony & Phebee Smith both of Eastham to proseed in marriage

November 21 : 1740 then entered the Intentions of Corneles Harding and Prissila Curtis both of Eastham to proseed in marriages.

December the 19th 1740 then entered the Intentions of Stephen King & Hannah Perce both of Eastham to proseed in marriage.

January 24th 1740/41 then entered the Intentions of Jonathan Cole & Suseannah Horton to proseed in marriage

March 14th 1740/41 then entered the Intentions of Isaac Beaker & Lide Hopkins to proseed in Marriage.

March 21 : 1740/41 then entered the Intentions of Joshua Hamlen & Mary Lewes both of Eastham to proseed in marriage

March 21 : 1740/41 then entered the Intentions of Zachariah Twining & Elizabeth Tour† both of Eastham to proseed in marriage

april 4 : 1741 then entered the Intentions of Joseph Snow junr & Thankfull Cole to proseed in marriage

april 4th 1741 then entered the Intentions of William Meyrick junr & Lidea Higgins to proseed in Marriage both of Eastham

april 11 : 1741 then entered the Intentions of Mr John Smith of Eastham and Mrs Bethia Haws of Chatham to proseed in Marriage

april 18th 1741 then entered the Intentions of Thomas Atkins junr & Thankfull Snow to proseed in Marriage.

april 25 : 1741 then entered the Intentions of Samuel Brown junr & Martha Harding both of Eastham to proseed in marriage.

april 25th 1741 then entered the Intentions of Theophilas Mayo junr and Thankfull Higgins both of Eastham to proseed in marriage

april 27 : 1741 then entered the Intentions of John Cookson of Boston & Mary Beaker of Eastham to proseed in marriage

May 8th 1741 then entered the Intentions of Judah Rogers & Susanna Rogers both of Eastham to proseed in marriage.

May 13 : 1741 then entered the Intentions of Moses Cahoon & Sarah Lewes both of Eastham to proseed in marriage.

* Alice.
† Tower.

May 30 : 1741 then entered the Intentions of Paul Atkins & Sarah Sawyer of Scarbee* Intend to proceed in Marriage.

[p. 229] June the 25th 1741 then entered the Intentions of Thomas Holker junr & Rebecka Knowls Daughter of Joshua Knowls both of Eastham to proceed in marriage & he the sd Thomas Holker then desired sd Intentions might be published as the Law directs entred by me Joseph Doane Town clerk and accordingly on the 25th day of June† 1741 the Banns of Matrimony to publish the Intentions of the above Named Thomas Holker junr & Rebecka Knowls was Setup to publish their sd intentions to proceed in marryage by me Joseph Doane Town clerk.

June the 29th day 1741 then Mr Joshua Knowls the Father of the above named Rebecka Knowls personally came & declered to me the Subscriber that he forbid the Banns of Matrimony betwixt his Daughter Rebecka Knowls & Thomas Holker junr & thereupon I took down the Banns of Matrimony that I had Set up to publish the Intentions of Marriage betwixt the above too persons Joseph Doane Town clerk

July the third then Joshua Knowls Sent a writing under his hand desiring me again to publish Thomas Holker junr & his Daughter Rebecka & there upon I again Setup their publishment in order for marriage . Joseph Doane Town clerk

July 29 : 1741 then entered the Intentions of Abner Snow & Rebecka Cook both of Eastham to proceed in marriage

august the first 1741 then entered the Intentions of Thomas Winslow junr of Harwich and Serah Higgins of Eastham Daughter of Elisha Higgins junr of Eastham to proceed in marriage

September 12 : 1741 then entered the Intentions of Silvenis Cole & Prissilla Walker both of Eastham to proceed in marriage

October 31 : 1741 then entered the Intentions of Mr Isaac Larrance of Sandwich & Mrs Ruth Freeman of Eastham to proceed in Marriage

December 5th 1741 then entered the Intentions of John Freeman junr & Bethia Cobb both of Eastham to proceed in marriage

December 5th 1741 then entered the Intentions of Robert Snow & Mercy‡ Smith both of Eastham to proceed in marriage

January the 7 : 1741/2 then entered the Intentions of Joshua Smith & Mercy Snow both of Eastham to proceed in marriage

January the 23rd 1741/2 then entered the Intentions of Samuel Walker and Rebecka Freeman both of Eastham to proceed in marriage.

January 23. 1741/2 then entered the Intentions of Ebenezor Snow and Lidea Smith both of Eastham to proceed in marriage

February 6th 1741/2 then entered the Intentions of Joseph Arey and Hannah Rogers both of Eastham to proceed in marriage

* Scarboro, Me.?
† "July" was crossed out and "June" interlined in the same hand and ink.
‡ "Mary" was crossed out and "Mercy" interlined in the same hand and ink.

February 6th 1741/2 then entered the intentions of John Tailler Junr & Phebee Higgins both of Eastham to proceed in Marriage

February the 6th 1741/2 then entered the Intentions of Samuel Paine of Eastham and Mary Gould of Harwich to proceed in marriage.

[p. 230] February 12th 1741/2 then entred the Intentions of Elisha Cobb of Eastham & Bethiah Bangs to proseed in marriage

February 13 : 1741/2 then entred the Intentions of Moses George* & Beck Ned Indians of Eastham to proseed in marriage

February 20th 1741/2 then entred the Intentions of Thomas Nickason junr of Chatham and Dorkis Sparrow of Eastham to proseed in marriage

March the 12 : 1741/2 then entred the Intentions of William Atwood & Basheba Smith both of Eastham to proseed in Marriage.

March 27th 1742 then entred the Intentions of Jedediah Lumbert of Truro and Abigel Hall of Eastham to proseed in marriage

March 27 : 1742 then entred the Intentions of Giddeon Smith & Abigel Higgins both of Eastham to proseed in marriage

April the first 1742 then Elisha Holbrook & Serah May both of Eastham entred their Intentions of marriage

April the third 1742 then entred the Intentions of James Higgins junr of Eastham and Serah Seers of Yarmouth to proseed in marriage

April the 10 : 1742 then entred the Intentions of Nathaniel Horton & Eunis Snow both of eastham to proseed in Marriage

April 14th 1742 then entred the Intentions of Joseph Atwood of Eastham and Debro Seers of Chatham to proseed in marriage.

April 24 : 1742 then entred the Intentions of Mecaiah Snow junr & Elisabeth Freeman both of Eastham to proseed in marriage

May the 14th 1742 then entred the Intentions of William Cole of Eastham & Lidea Bown of Truro to proseed in Marriage.

July 24 : 1742 then entred the Intentions of James Snow and Hannah Higgens both of Eastham to proseed in marriage.

September 22 : 1742 then entred the Intentions of Ebenezor Higgins and Martha Burges both of Eastham to proseed in marriage

October 2 : 1742 then entred the Intentions of Elkenah Nickason of Chatham and Bathsheba Snow of Eastham to proseed in marriage

October 9 : 1742 then entred the Intentions of James Knowls of Chatham and Sarah Doane of Eastham to proseed in Marriage.

October 22 : 1742 then entred the Intentions of Mr Joh Avery of Truro & Mrs Jane Thatcher of Eastham to proseed in Marriage.

December the 2nd 1742 then entred the Intentions of Daniel Cusens & Lidea Moger Indians both of Eastham to proseed in marriage

December 31 : 1742 then entred the Intentions of Nathaniel Gould of Harwich & Jane Ary of Eastham to proseed in Marriage

[p. 231] January 1 : 1742/3 then entred the Intentions of Mr Ebenezor Mayo of Eastham & Mrs Appiah Freeman of Harwich to proseed in marriage

*"Ned" was crossed out and "George" interlined, in the same hand and ink.

January 24 1742/3 then entered the Intentions of Benjamin Lumbert of Truro & Elizabeth Snow of Eastham to proseed in marriage

February 5 : 1742/3 then entered the Intentions of Joseph Meyrick of Eastham & Lidea Godfrey of Chatham to proseed in marriage

February 12 : 1742/3 then entered the Intentions of Barnabas Higgins of Eastham and Mary Smith of Truro to proseed in marriage

February the 19th 1742/3 then entered the Intentions of Cornelis Higgins & Sarah Haws both of Eastham to proseed in marriage

February 27 : 1742/3 then entered the Intentions of Thomas Smith & Ruth Mayo both of Eastham to proseed in marriage

March the 29th 1743 then entered the Intentions of John Willcut of Hingam alies Conehassett & Lidea Hamlen of Eastham to proseed in marriage.

april 16th 1743 then entred the Intentions of Will Toby & Serah Davis both of Eastham to proseed in marriage.

april the 30th 1743 then entered the Intentions of Ruben Nickason of Harwich & Ruth Ary of Eastham to proseed in marriage

September 17 : 1743 then entred the Intentions of Elisha Doane third & Hope Rich both of Eastham to proseed in Marriage.

October 1 : 1743 then entered the Intentions of Ruben Nickason of Harwich and Ruth Ary of Eastham to proseed in marriage.

October 1 : 1743 then entred the Intentions of Zackeus Rogers of Harwich and Elizabeth King to proseed in Marriage.

October 8 : 1743 then entred the Intentions of Daniel Higgins and Ruth Rich to proseed in marriage. both of Eastham

October 29 : 1743 then entred the Intentions of Mr John Paine and Mrs Thankfull Linel to proseed in marriage. both of Eastham

October 29 : 1743 then entered the Intentions of Judah Rogers and Lois Young both of Eastham to proseed in marriage

October 29 : 1743 then entered the Intentions of Zebulon young both* of Eastham to proseed in marriage

December 13 : 1743 then entred the Intentions of David Brown junr and Hannah Doane Daughter of Deacon Elisha Doane both of Eastham to proseed in Marriage.

December 13 : 1743 then entred the Intentions of Elisha Doan the third & Hope Rich to proseed in marriage

[p. 232] January 13 : 1743/4 then entered the Intentions of Seth Myrick of Harwich & Elizabeth Brown† of Eastham to proseed in Marriage

January 14th 1743/4 then entered the Intentions of Ebenezor Harding and Lidea Brown both of Eastham to proseed in marriage

January 30 1743/4 then entered the Intentions of Judah Young & Mary Andris to proseed in Marriage

*The lady's name was not entered.

†"Myrick junr" was crossed out and "Brown" interlined in the same hand and ink.

February 18 : 1743/4 then entered the Intentions of Sollomon Dyer of Truro and and Sarah Atkins of Eastham to proseed in marriage

February 18 : 1743/4 then entered the Intentions of Benjamin Cole and Desire Smith both of Eastham to proseed in marriage

March 2nd 1743/4 then entered the Intentions of Mr Thomas Brown & Mrs Bety Doane both of Eastham to proseed in marriage

March 2nd 1743/4 then entered the Intentions of Mr Hatsel Nickorson & Mrs Hannah Myrick both of Eastham to proseed in marriage

March 24 : 1743/4 then entred the Intentions of Hezekiah Doane of Chatham Esqr and Mrs Sarah Knowls to proseed in marriage

april 21 : 1744 then Entred the Intentions of Nathaniel Knowls of Eastham and Mary Maker of Harwich to proseed in marriage

June 12th 1744 then entred the Intentions of John Walker junr and Hannah Remick both of Eastham to proseed in marriage

July 21 : 1744 then entred the Intentions of Eldad Nickorson of Chatham and Mary Cahoone of the north Precinct in Eastham to proseed in marriage

July 21 1744 entred the Intentions of Zachariah Twining Indian man & Marcy Jo both of Eastham to proseed in marriage.

August 17 : 1744 then entered the Intentions of Ezekiel Harding & Mary Young both of Eastham to proseed in marriage.

August 18 : 1744 then entered the Intentions of David Doane junr & Lidea Brown junr both of Eastham to proseed in marriage

october 27 : 1744 then entred the Intentions of Nathaniel Smith junr & Mary Young junr both of Eastham to proseed in marriage

November 3 : 1744 then entred the Intentions of Nathan Kinney of Chatham & Lidea Young of Eastham to proseed in marriage.

November 28 : 1744 then entred the Intentions of Thomas Sturges junr & Sarah Paine to proseed in marriage.

November 16 : 1744 entred the Intentions of Joshua Ralph Indian Justice & experience cusens both Indians late of Eastham to proseed in marriage

January 26 : 1744/5 then entred the Intentions of Seth Knowls & Ruth Freeman both of Eastham to proseed in marriage

[p. 233] December 14 : 1744 then entred the Intentions of Samuel Doane the third and Dorkis Cole both of Eastham to proseed in marriage

December 22 : 1744 then entred the Intentions of Thomas Mayo of Harwich and Hannah Atkins of Eastham to proseed in marriage

December 29 : 1744 then entred the Intentions of Simeon Nucomb & Jemima Treat to proseed in marriage

December 29th 1744 then entred the Intentions of William Paine Esqr and Mrs Elizabeth Meyrick to proseed in marriage.

February 1 : 1744/5 then entred the Intentions of Isaac Pirce of Eastham and Hester Covell of Harwich to proseed in marriage

February 2nd 1744/5 then entred the Intentions of Isaac Smith of Eastham & Mary Freeman of harwich Intend to proseed in marriage

February 9th 1744/5 then entred the intentions of Elisha Linel &
Martha Higgins both of Eastham to proseed in marriage
march ye 16th 1744/5 then entred the intentions of Nathaniel Snow ye
3d and Mary Harding both of Eastham to prosead in marige
april ye 13th 1745 then entred the intentions of Richard Ary and
Thankful Atwod both of Eastham to prosead in mariage
may ye 11th 1745 then entred the intentions of Alexander Marten now
rezident in Eastham and Thankfull Rich of Eastham to prosead
in mariage
July the 19th 1745 Anthony Bakor of Yarmouth Signified his intentions to mary with Thankful Young of Eastham
August ye 13th 1745 then Entred the intentions of Simon Nucomb and
marcy brown boath of Eastham to proseed in mariage
august ye 23d : 1745 then entred the intentions of George Brown and
Rebecka Meyrick boath of Eastham to prosed in marriage
September ye 7th 1745 then entred the intentions of Nathanll Bacon
and Apphiah Cole boath of Eastham to prosead in marriage
October ye 9th 1745 then entred the intentions of Joshua Brown of
Eastham and Sarah Beel of Boston to proceed in marriage
October ye 19th 1745 then entred the intentions of Beniamine Smith
and Ruth Snow both of Eastham to proceed in marriage
october ye 26th 1745 then entred the intentions of Beniamine Hamblen
and Lusa Holbroks both of Eastham to proceed in marriage
[p. 234] December ye 28th 1745 then entred the intentions of Samuel
Ary of Truro and Ruth Snow of Eastham to proceed in marriage
February ye : 8th 1745/6 then entred the intentions of Moses Smith
and Rebeckah Sparrow both of Eastham to proceed in marriage
march ye 14th 1745/6 then entred the intentions of Isra* Jackson negro
of Truro and Marcy Jo of Eastham indian to proceed marriage
march ye 21th 1745/6 then entred the intentions of Elisha Higgens of
Eastham and Rachel Hopkens of Harwich to proceed in marriage
Aprill ye 19th 1746 then entred the intentions of Coll John Knowls of
Eastham and Rebeckah Chanle now resident in Eastham to pro-
ceed in marriage
may ye 3d 1746 then entred the intentions of Simeon Higgens and
Martha Snow boath of Eastham to proceed in marrig
June ye 11th 1746 then Entred the intentions of Beniamin Brown
and Betty Cook both of Eastham to proceed in marriage
July . ye . 5th 1746 then entred the intentions of Philip Higgens and
Johannah Mayo boath of Eastham to proceed in marriage
July ye 21th 1746 then entred the intentions of Barnabas Cook and
Mercy Walker boath of Eastham to proceed in marriage
august ye 16th 1746 then entred the intentions of Joshua Atwod of
Eastham and Mary Knowls of Truro to proceed in marriage
august ye 16th 1746 then entred the intentions of Joshua Hurd of Har-
wich and Elisebeth paine of Eastham to proceed in marriage

* Sic.

September ye 27th 1746 then entred the intentions of Isaac Sparrow
and Rebecca Knowls both of Eastham to proceed in marriage
Jediah Lumbart and Phebe Haus boath of Eastham Entred their intentions to marry each with other October ye 2d 1746
October ye 24th 1746 then Entred the intentions of John Snow of
Eastham and Phebe Hatch of Falmouth to proceed in marriage
november ye 1th 1746 then Entred the intentions of Stephen Sparrow
Jur and Apphia Pepper both of Eastham to proceed in marriage
november ye 1th 1746 then entred the intentions Jonathan Linel Jur
and mercy mayo both of Eastham to proceed in marriage
[p. 235] November ye 14th 1746 then entred the intentions of Zoheth
Smith and Ruth Mayo boath of Eastham to proceed in marriage
november ye 29th 1746 then entred the intentions of Beniamin Mayo of
Eastham and Sarah Snow of Harwich to proceed in marriage
november ye 29th 1746 then Entred the intentions of Seth Harding
and Elisabeth Willcut boath of Eastham to proceed in marriage
December ye 19th 1746 then entred the intentions of Richard Rogers
of Harwich and Sarah Higgens of Eastham to proceed in marriag
January ye 10th 1746/7 then entred the intentions of Joshua Hopkins
Jur and Rebaca Sparrow boath of Eastham to proceed in marriage
January ye 10th 1746/7 then entred the intentions of David Snow and
priscilla Sparrow boath of Eastham to proceed in marriage
January ye 28th 1746/7 then entred the intentions of Solomon Lewis
and Hanah Cohoon both of Eastham to proceed in marriage
February ye 14th 1746/7 then entred the intentions of Philip Higgens
of Eastham and Phebe Lewis of Truro to proceed in marriage
February ye 20th 1746/7 then entred the intentions of Freeman Higgens and Martha Cole both of Eastham to proceed in marriage
march ye 20th 1746/7 then entred the intentions of John Higgens Jur
and Mercy mulford both of Eastham to proceed in marriage
april ye 11th 1747 then entred the intentions of Moses Crosby of Harwich and Abigel Sparrow of Eastham to proceed in marriage
apri ye 24th 1747 then Entred the intentions of Scarlot Gails and
Tabitha Nickerson both of Eastham to proceed in marriage
May ye 29th 1747 then entred the intentions of Cornelius Rich and
Rhoda Fish both of Eastham to proceed in marriage
June ye 6th 1747 then Entred the intentions of Eliezer Rogers of Har-
wich and Ruth Higgens of Eastham to proceed in marriage
June ye 30th 1747 then Entred the intentions of Jesse atwod and Ruth
Young both of Eastham to proceed in marriage
June ye 30th 1747 then Entred the intentions of John Young Jur of
Eastham and Lidya Dier of Truro to proceed in marriage
July ye 10th 1747 then entrel the intentions of Cornelius Hamblen and
Jane young both of Eastham to proceed in marriage

[The Vital Records in the original book of Town Records marked
"Births 1701 . 1781", etc, end here.—Editor.]

(To be continued)

THE
MAYFLOWER DESCENDANT

1620 2020

A QUARTERLY MAGAZINE OF
PILGRIM GENEALOGY AND HISTORY

VOLUME XXXI

1933

PUBLISHED BY THE

MASSACHUSETTS SOCIETY OF
MAYFLOWER DESCENDANTS

BOSTON

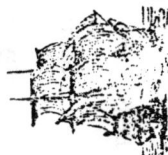

EASTHAM AND ORLEANS, MASS., VITAL RECORDS

TRANSCRIBED BY GEORGE ERNEST BOWMAN

(*Continued from Vol. XXIX, p. 17*)

[In this article we begin printing literal transcripts of the original entries of births, etc., in the Eastham, Mass, records, No. 6.]

No. 6. BIRTHS AND MARRIAGES.

[*On inside of first cover*]
William Andres was Born in Harwich the 20 Day of may 1752

[*On fifth page of index*]
John Hopkins grandson to Stephn Snow was Born in Truro 27 : april 1758

[p. 1] Ezra young and Constant mayo Both of Eastham were married by Revd Joseph Crocker on the Seventh Day of august 176, Entred Edward Knowles town Clerk

Jonathan young the Son of Ezra and Constant young was Born at Eastham august ye 26 May 1762

Jonathan young the Son of Ezra young and Constant young Dide august ye 14 = 1767

Jonathan young the Son of Ezra young and Constant young was Born at Eastham July the 23 Day = 1768

Jonathan young Son of Mr Ezra young Died novenber ye 23 = 176)

Jonathan young Son of hannah Burges Both of Eastham were married at Eastham by mr Joseph Crocker Clerk on the 27 day of November 1760 Entred by me Edward Knowles town Clerk

John Holder : Shaw and Sarah Cole Both of Eastham were married in Eastham by mr Joseph Crocker Cl on the 4 day of December 1760 Entred by me Edward Knowles town Clerk

[p. 2] December 25 : 1760 Daniel Hamilton and Hannah Sparrow Both of Eastham was married by mr Joseph Crocker Clr Entred by Edward Knowles Town Clerk

Paul Hamilton Son of Daniel and Hannah Hamilton was Born in Eastham february the 10 Day 1762

Content Hamilton Daughter of Daniel and Hannah hamilton was Born in Eastham february the 8 Day 1765

Benjamin Hamilton Son of Daniel and Hannah hamilton was Born in Eastham March the 26 Day 1767

February 26 : 1761 Doctr Samuell Kenwreck of Harwich and Esther mayo of Eastham were married by mr Joseph Crocker Clr Entred by me Edward Knowles town Clerk

[p. 3] August 6 : 1761 william Higgins and Elizebeth young Both of Eastham were married by mr Joseph Crocker Clerk Entred by me Edward Knowles Town Clerk

Expearne Higgins Daughter of William Higgins and Abigal Higgins was Born at Eastham January the 28th 1757

Abigal Higgins Daughter of William and abigal Higgins was Born at Eastham September the 20th 1758

Ruth Higgins Daughter of william and Elezebath Higgins was Born at Eastham September the 9th 1762

Hannah Higgins Daughter of William and Elezebeth Higgins was Born at Eastham November the 17th 1764

Roburt Higgins Son of William and Elezebath Higgins was Born at Eastham January the 12th 1767

august 7 : 1761 Henery Rogers of Harwich and Deborah Nickerson of Eastham were married by mr Joseph Crocker Clerk Entred by me Edward Knowles town Clerk

oct 22 : 1761 Solomon Freeman of Harwich and Desire Doane of Eastham were married by mr Joseph Crocker Clerk Entred by me Edward Knowles town Clerk

November 12: 1761 Samuell Rogers of Eastham and Deborah Bassett of Chatham were married by mr Joseph Crocker Clr Entred by me Edward Knowles town Clerk

Ledia Rogers daughter of Samuell and Deborah Rogers was Born at Eastham april ye 10th 1763

Deborah Rogers Dafter of Samuell and Deborah Rogers was Born at Eastham June ye 27th 1765

James Rogers Son of Samuell Rogers and Deborah Rogers was Born at Eastham June ye 24th 1767

[p. 4] Novbr 26 : 1761 Ebenezer Mayo and Mercy mayo Both of Eastham were married by mr Joseph Crocker Clerk Entred by me Edward Knowles town Clerk

December 17 : 1761 Edmond Higgins and Esther Higgins Both of Eastham were married by Mr Joseph Crocker Clerk Entred by me Edward Knowles town Clerk

Nathaniel Son of Elkenah and Betty Smith was Born in Eastham November 9 Day 1762:

Heman Son of Elkenah and Betty Smith was Born in Eastham october 7 Day 1764

Elkenah Son of Elkenah and Betty Smith was Born in Eastham may 7 Day 1766

Betty Daughter of Elkenah and Betty Smith was Born in Eastham april 18 : 1772

Ezekiel Son of Elkenah and Betty Smith was Born in Eastham November 27 : 1773

Ledda Daughter of Elkenah Smith and Betty february 29 : 1776

Rebecca Daughter of Elkenah and Betty Smith was Born in Eastham 29 Day of october 1779 [p. 5] Febr 5 : 1762 Joshua Higgins juner and Hannah Sparrow Both of Eastham were married by mr Joseph Crocker Clerk Entred by me Edward Knowles town Clerk

Hatsuld Higgins Son of Joshua and Hannah Higgins was Born at Eastham November ye 28 : 1762

Zenas Higgins Son of Joshua Higgins was Born at Eastham ye 11 = 1764 and Died ye 1 day of April 1765

Zenas Higgins Son of Joshua and Hannah Higgins was Born at Eastham Jun ye 19 = 1766 and Died october ye 2 = 1766

Prisila Higgins Daughter of Joshua and Hannah Higgins was Born at Eastham october ye 22 = 1767 and Died august ye 23 = 1768

Joshua Higgins Son of Joshua and Hannah Higgins was Born at Eastham July ye 27 = 1769

June 10 : 1762 Isaac Foster of Harwich and Eunice Freeman of Eastham were married by mr Joseph Crocker Clerk Entred by me Edward Knowles town Clerk

July 20 : 1762 Daniel Cole iuner of Eastham and mary Cole of Harwich were married by mr Joseph Crocker Clr Entred by me Edward Knowles town Clerk

Jabez Jackson son of Joseph Jackson & hannah his wife born Jan 15th 1793

[p. 6] November 4 : 1762 Nehemiah young and Keziah Doane Both of Eastham were married by mr Joseph Crocker Clr Entred by me Edward Knowles town Clerk

Keziah young wife of Nehemiah young Died July ye 25 = 1763

November 5 : 1763 Abiel Crosbey and Bennet Paine Both of Eastham were married by mr Joseph Crocker Clr Entred by me Edward Knowles town Clerk

Joseph Linkhornew Children recored

Joseph Linkhornew Son of Joseph and ann Linkhornew was Born in Eastham July 26 . 1770

James Linkhornew Son of Joseph and ann Linkhornew was Born in Eastham august 14 : 1772

Isaac and Hannah Cobbs Children Recorded that was Born in Harwich

Isaac Cobb Son of Isaac and hannah Cobb was Born in harwich September the 14 Day 1770

Freeman Cobb Son of Isaac* and Hannah Cobb was Born in harwich January the 19 Day 1772

April 7 : 1763 John Smith of Chatham and the widow Lydia Snow of Eastham were married by mr Joseph Crocker Clr Entred by me Edward Knowles town Clerk

Joseph Lewis of truro and Hannah Cole of Eastham was married in Eastham on the 22 Day of February 1770 by the Reverd mr Cheever Entred by me Edward Knowles Town Clerk

*"Elkenah" was crossed out and "Isaac" interlined in the same hand and ink.

[p. 7] November 11 : 1762 Thomas Gould and Phebe Cole Both of Eastham were married by mr Joseph Crocker Clr Entred by me Edward Knowles Town Clerk

Mary Gould Daughter of Thomas and Phebe gould was Born at Eastham November ye 6 = 1764

Thomas gould Son of Thomas and Phebe gould was Born at Eastham September ye = 11 = 1765

Ruth gould Daughter of Thomas and Phebe gould was Born at Eastham August ye 11 = 1767

Paine Gould Son of Thomas and Phebe gould was Born in Eastham Jun the 6 = 1770

December 9 : 1762 Isaac Paine and Abigail Snow Both of Eastham were married by mr Joseph Crocker Clr

Phebe Paine Daughter of Isaac and Abigail Paine was Born in Eastham September 1 Day 1763

Ebenezer Paine Son of Isaac and Abigail Paine was Born in Eastham September 5 Day 1765

Thomas Paine Son of Isaac and Abigail Paine was Born in Eastham November Second Day 1766

Abigial Paine Daughter of Isaac and Abigail Paine was Born in Eastham the 17 Day of September 1769

Joshua Paine Son of Isaac and Abigail Paine was Born in Eastham the 17 Day of July 1772

Isaac Paine Son of Isaac & Abigail Paine was Born in Eastham in may : 1775

marcy paine Daughter of Isaac & Abigail paine was Born in Eastham in october 1779

[p. 8] December 16 : 1762 Asa mayo Juner and Hannah Covell Both of Eastham were married by mr Joseph Crocker Clr Entred by me Edward Knowles town Clerk

Isaac mayo Son of asa juner and Hannah mayo was born in Eastham october the 27 Day 1763

Decbr . 16 1762 Solomon Pepper juner and Abiel Hopkins Both of Eastham were married by mr Joseph Crocker Clr Entred by me Edward Knowles town Clerk

Isaac Pepper Son of Solomon abiel Pepper was Born in Eastham march 18 Day : 1764

Apphiah Pepper Daughter of Solomon and Abial Pepper was Born in Eastham october 3 Day 1765

Robort Pepper Son of Solomon and abial pepper was Born at Eastham December ye 6 = 1768

Molle Pepper Daughter of Solomon Pepper and abiel Pepper was Born in Eastham the 11 Day of october 1769

Abiel Pepper wife of Solomon Pepper Departed this Life the 25 Day of September 1771

Knowles Pepper Son of Solomon & Phebe Pepper was Born in Eastham the 15 Day of June 1773

Phebe Pepper Daughter of Solomon & Phebe Pepper was Born in Eastham the 25 Day of April 1775

Elisha Pepper Son of Solomon & Phebe Pepper was Born in Eastham the 23 Day of April 1777

Anne Pepper Daughter of Solomon & Phebe Pepper was Born in Eastham the 31 Day of March 1779

Abial Pepper Daughter of Solomon and phebe Pepper was Born in Eastham october 12 — 1781

Solonon Pepper Son of Solomon and Phebe Pepper was Born in Eastham the 13 Day of 1783 october

[p. 9] December 23 : 1762 Elnathan Higgins and Mercy Sparrow Both of Eastham were married by mr Joseph Crocker Clr Entred by me Edward Knowles town Clerk

Jabez Higgins Son of Elnathan and marcy Higgins was Born at Eastham December the 11 Day 1763

mary Higgns Daughter of Elnathan Higgins and marcy Higgins was Born at Eastham may the 3 Day 1766

Moses Higgins Son of Elnathan and Marcy Higgins was Born at Eastham October 19 : 1770

Marcy Higgins Dafter of Elnathan and Marcy Higgins was Born at Eastham January 19 : 1775

January 20 : 1763 Isaac young and Priscilla Hopkins Both of Eastham were married by mr Joseph Crocker Clr Entred by me Edward Knowles town Clerk

Thankful young Daughter of Isaac young and Priscilla young was Born at Eastham august ye : 16th 1764

Rebaca young Daughter of Isaac and Priscilla young was Born at Eastham Jun ye 15th 1766

Marcy young Daughter of Isaac and Priscilla young was Born at Eastham August ye 7th 1768

[p. 10] February 17 : 1763 Nathan Higgins and Gerusha mayo Both of Eastham were married by mr Joseph Crocker Clr Entred by me Edward Knowles town Clerk

october 19 : 1762 Samuell mayo and Abigail young Both of Eastham were married by Samll Smith Jestess peace Entred by me Edward Knowles town Clerk

December 2 : 1762 Ruben Cole and Hannah Cole Both of Eastham were married by John Freeman Jestes peace

[p. 11] april 2 : 1761 Thomas Brown Juner and mercy mayo Both of Eastham was married by the Revrd Isaiah Lues Clr Entred by me Edward Knowles town Clerk

april 15 : 1761 Thomas Holbrook and Hannah Harding Both of Eastham was married by mr Isaiah Lues Clr Entred by me Edward Knowles town Clerk

September 24 : 1761 Edward Smalley of Harwich and Hannah Cole of Eastham was married by mr Isaiah Lues Clr Entred by me Edward Knowles town Clerk

october 1 : 1761 Hudson Vickery and Sarah mayo Both of Eastham was married by my Isaiah Lues Clr Entred by me Edward Knowles town Clerk

November 24 : 1761 Joseph Ary and Hannah Bickford Both of Eastham was married by mr Isaiah Lues Clr Entred by me Edward Knowles town Clerk

January 14 :.1762 Solonon Sweat and Jemima Bickford Both of Eastham was married by mr Isaiah Lues Cler Entred by me Edward Knowles town Clerk

march 25 : 1762 Josiah Rich of truro and matha Rich of Eastham was married by mr Isaiah Lues Clr Entred by me Edward Knowles town Clerk

September 8 : 1762 Benjamin Sweat and mercy Atwood Both of Eastham was married by mr Isaiah Lues Clr Entred by me Edward Knowles town Clerk

December 9 : 1762 Daniel Eldredge and widow Thankfull Combs Both of Eastham were married by mr Isaiah Lues Clr Entred by me Edward Knowles Clerk

[p. 12] January 27 : 1763 Henry young and abigail Rich Both of Eastham was married by mr Isaiah Lues Clr Entred by me Edward Knowles town Clerk

February 17 : 1763 Benjamin Knowles and mary Brown Both of Eastham was married by mr Isaiah Lues Clr Entred by me Edward Knowles town Clerk

obed Knowles Son of Benjamin and Mary Knowles was Born in Eastham august the 28 Day 1764

obed Knowles Son of Benjamin and mary Knowles Died april 7 : 1765

obed Knowles Son of Benjamin and mary Knowles was Born in Eastham July the 24 Day 1766

Gorge Knowls Son of Benjamen and Mary Knowls was Born at Eastham may ye 14th 1768

Alice Knowls Daughter of Benjamin and mary Knowls was Born at Eastham June ye 26 = 1770

alice Knowles Daughter of Benjamin and mary Knowles Died December the 30 Day 1771

Edward Knowls Son of Benjamin and mary Knowles was Born in Eastham September 15 Day 1772

Edward Knowles Son of Benjamin and mary Knowles Died

Benjamin Knowles Son of Benj. and mary Knowles was Born in Eastham the 19 Day of September 1774

Edward Knowles Son of Benj. and mary Knowles was Born in Eastham march 25 : 1776

Freeman Knowles Son of Benjn and mary Knowles was Born in Eastham Sept 20 : 1778

Mary Knowles Daughter of Benjamin and mary was Born in Eastham November 25 — 1780

Lydda Knowles Daughter of Benjamin and mary Knowles was Born in Eastham the 1 Day of may 1783

THE

MAYFLOWER DESCENDANT

1620 2020

A QUARTERLY MAGAZINE OF
PILGRIM GENEALOGY AND HISTORY

VOLUME XXXII

1934

PUBLISHED BY THE
MASSACHUSETTS SOCIETY OF
MAYFLOWER DESCENDANTS
BOSTON

FLORIDA STATE LIBRARY

178   *Eastham and Orleans, Mass., Vital Records*

Benjamin Dill Son of Samuell Dill and Lydia Dill was born in Eastham July the 5 Day 1763

Thomas Paine and Reliance Roggers Both of Eastham was married in Eastham February 20 : 1770 by the Revrd mr Cheever Entred by me Edward Knowles town Clerk

[p. 13] Eleazer Walker and Sarah Snow Both of Eastham was married by mr Edward Cheever Clr Entred by me Edward Knowles town Clr

Aaron walker Son of Eleazer and Sarah walker was born in Eastham September 14 Day 1761

Zibiah walker Daughter of Eleazer and Sarah walker was born in Eastham September 25 --- 1763

Aaron walker Son of Eleazer and Sarah Died Novbr 30 : 1764

Susannah and Rachal walker Daughters of Eleazer and Sarah walker was Born in Eastham august the 5 Day 1765

Aaron walker Son of Eleazer and Sarah walker was Born in Eastham october 12 Day 1767

Lucy walker Daughter of Elazer and Sarah walker was Born in Eastham october 6 Day 1769 and Died July 1772

Eleazer walker Son of Eleazer and Sarah walker was Born in Eastham the 15 Day of october 1771

Lucy walker Daughter of Eleazer and Sarah walker was Born in Eastham 20 Day october 1773

Benjamin walker Son of Eleazer and Sarah walker was Born in Eastham 2 Day november 1775

Jerusha walker Daughter of Eleazer and Sarah walker Born in Eastham 21 Day october 1778

January the 20 Day 1764 John Snow Died with the Smal pox in the fourty fourth year of his age

uriah Doane Son of Benjamin and Ruth Doane was Born in Eastham october the 7 Day 1761

William Doane Son of Benjamin and Ruth Doane was Born in Eastham april the 2 Day 1764 and Died June the 13 Day 1765

(*To be continued*)

EASTHAM AND ORLEANS, MASS., VITAL RECORDS

Transcribed by the Editor

(Continued from Vol. XXXI, p. 178)

[No. 6, p. 14] January 26 : 1764 Thomas Knowles of Eastham and Thankfull Crosby of Harwich was married at Harwich by mr Isaiah Dunster Clerk

Hannah Knowles Daughter of Thomas and Thankfull Knowles was Born in Eastham August the 22 Day 1765

Ezubah Knowles Daughter of Thomas and Thankfull Knowles was Born in Eastham april 9 Day 1767 and Died the 13 Day of June 1767

Knowles Daughter of thomas and thankfull Knowles was In Eastham

Edward Knowles Son of thomas and Thankfull Knowles was Born In Harwich

Thankfull Knowles wife of thomas Knowles Died In Harwich the Nineteenth Day of November 1770

Edward Knowles Son of Thomas and Thankfull Knowles Died In Eastham the 18 Day of february 1771

Elezebath Doane Daughter of James and Elezebath Doane was Born in Eastham march the 15 Day 176*

Timothy Doane Son of James and Elisebath Doane was born in Eastham may the 4 Day 1761

Joshua Doane Son of James and Elisabeth Doane was born in Eastham November 27 1762

[p. 15] Seth Doane Son of Silvenus and Phebe Doan was Born in Eastham November the 21 Day 1761

Elisabeth Doane Daughter of Silvenus and Phebe Doane was Born in Eastham may the 1 Day 1764

Elisha Doane Son of Silvenus and Phebe Doane was Born in Eastham July 25 Day 1766

Abijah mayo Son of John and Lydia mayo was Born in Eastham may the 24 Day 1761

Joshiah mayo Son of John and Lydia mayo was Born in Eastham February the 18 Day 1763

Abijah mayo Son of John mayo and Lydia mayo Died

Abijah mayo Son of John and Lydia mayo was Born in Eastham June 4† : 1765

Susannah mayo Daughter of John and Lydia may was Born in Eastham april 27 : 1768

* This entry has been crossed out.
† "24" was first written, but the "2" was crossed out.

John mayo Son of John and Lydia mayo was Born in Eastham the 23 Day of august 1771

[p. 16] David Doane and Hannah Knowles Both of Eastham ware married in Eastham by mr Edward Cheever Clr the 31 Day of august 1764 Recorded by me Edward Knowles town Clr

Nathaniel Doane Son of David and Hannah Doane was born in Eastham June the 20—1765

Edward Doane Son of David and Hannah Doane was Born in Eastham November the 30 Day 1766

Edward Doane Son of David and hannah Doane Died February 16 : 1767

Anne Doane Daughter of David and Hannah Doane was Born in Eastham march 22 Day 1766†

marcy Doane Daughter of David and Hannah Doane was Born in Eastham July the 3 Day 1770

mary Doane Daughter of David and Hannah Doane was Born in Eastham January 19 : 1773

Priscilla Doane Daughter of David and Hannah Doane was Born in Eastham June 25 1775

Hannah Doane Daughter of David and hannah Doane was Born in Eastham the 27 Day of may 1780

Noah Doane Son of Noah and Bethiah Doane was Born in Eastham January the 1 Day 1757

Zenos Doane Son of Noah and Bethiah Doane was Born in Eastham January the 19 Day 1761

Prissilla Doane Daughter of Noah and Bethiah Doane was Born in Eastham December the 7 Day 1762

Lot Doane Son of Noah and Bethiah Doane was Born in Eastham may the 22 Day 1755

Elkenah and Jerusha Cobb Children Recorded

Elkenah Cobb Born Born in Harwich January 19 Day 1781

Scotto Cobb Born in Eastham November 1 Day 1783

[p. 17] Hannah Knowles Daughter of Samuell Knowles and abigia[l] Knowles was born in Eastham october the 4 Day 1764

abigial Knowls Daughter of Samuell Knowls and abigial Kwls was Born in Eastham august the 2 Day 1767

Silvenus Rogers Son of Prence and Susanna Rogers was Born in Eastham october the twenty Ninth Day 1766

Edward Knowles Juner and Phebe walker Both of Eastham was marred in Eastham the Twenty Ninth Day of September 1767 by the Revrd Edward Cheever Clr

Hannah Knowles Daughter of Edward and Phebe Knowles was Bourn In Eastham September fourth Day 1769

Edward Knowles Juner Died at See the twenty first Day of february 1771 and in the 30 year of his age

Ezeriah Son of Jesse and Ann Smith was Born in Eastham the 5 Day of october 1765

Abigail Smith Daughter of Jesse and Ann Smith was Born in Eastham the 6 Day of october 1767

[p. 17a] Nehemiah Doane Son of Nehemiah and Lydia Doane was Born in Eastham 17 Day of July 1757

Elijah Doane Son of Nehemiah and Lydia Doane was Born in Eastham the 17 Day of may 1772

Samuel Dill Doane Son of Nehemiah and Lidia Doane was Born in Eastham the 27 Day of June 1774

mehetable Doane Daughter of nehemiah and Lydia Doane was Born in Eastham in November 1776

Elezer Smith and Martha Bee was married in Eastham the 20 Day of March 175* by mr Edward Cheever minster Recorded by me Edward Knowles Town Clerk

marcy Smith Daughter of Elezer and martha Smith was Born in Eastham november 20 Day 1761 : Died august 9 : 1762

Levi Smith Son of Elezer and Martha was Born in Eastham November ber 23 Day 1762:

Benjamin Son of Elezer and martha Smith was Born in Eastham November 18 : 1764

Joel Smith Son of Elezer and martha Smith was Born in Eastham october the 23 Day 1766

marcy Smith Daughter of Elezer and martha Smith was Born in Eastham august 12 : 1768

Eunice Smith Daughter of Elezer and martha Smith was Born in Eastham November the 5 Day 1770

Joshua Smith Son of Elezer and Martha Smith was Born in Eastham may 12 : 1772

Silvenus Snow and Deborah Cook Both of Eastham was married in Eastham on the 11 Day of november 1761 by mr Edward Cheever minster Recorded by me Edward Knowles Town Clerk

Shabner Sweat and Dorathy Collings Both of Eastham was married in Eastham on the 12 Day of november 1761 by mr Edward Cheever minster Recorded by me Edward Knowles Town Clerk

William Dean and mary Snow Both of Eastham was married in Eastham on the 14 Day of January 1762 by mr Edward Cheever minster Recorded by me Edward Knowles Town Clerk

[p. 17b] Joseph Paine of Harwich and Sarah Smith of Eastham was married in Eastham on the 18 Day of February 1762 by mr Edward Cheever minster Recorded by me Edward Knowles Town Clerk

Samuell Dill and Lydia Higgins Both of Eastham was married in Eastham on the Sixtenth Day of march 1762 by mr Edward Cheever minster Recorded by me Edward Knowles Town Clerk

James Dill and Abiagail Hickerman Both of Eastham was married in Eastham on the 18 Day of march 1762 by mr Edward Cheever minster Recorded by me Edward Knowles Town Clerk

Lamuell Smith and Marcy myrick Both of Eastham was married in Eastham in November 1762 by mr Edward Cheever minster Recorded by me Edward Knowles Town Clerk

*Sic.

Treat mores Son of John and Susanna mores was Born in Eastham 5 Day Decembr 1775

Richard Paine and Thankfull Harding Both of Eastham was married in Eastham november the 15 Day 1762 by me Edward Cheever minster Recorded by me Edward Knowles Town Clerk

Rachal Paine Daughter of Richard and Thankfull Paine was Born in Eastham 20 Day of January 1764

Josiah Paine Son of Richard Paine and Thankfull Paine was Born in Eastham 29 Day July 1767

Rebacca Paine Daughter of Richard and Thankfull was Born in Eastham 7 Day of august 1769

Samuell King of Harwich and mary Hickman of Eastham was married in Eastham on January the 6 Day 1763 by mr Edward Cheever minster Recorded by me Edward Knowles Town Clerk

Capt John Snow of Harwich and Elisabeth Smith of Eastham was married in Eastham on the 9 Day of august 1764 by mr Edward Cheever minster Recorded by me Edward Knowles Town Clerk

Benjamin Higgins and Hannah mayo Both of Eastham was married in Eastham on the 21 Day of august 1766 by mr Edward Knowles Town Clerk

[p. 17c] Samuell Cooks marriage is Recorded in the old Book of Records

Gideon Cook Son of Samuell Cook and Deborah Cook was Born in Easthani January 27 Day 1754

Joseph Cook Son of Samuell and Deborah was Born in Eastham July the 14 Day 1756

Dorcas Cook Daughter of Samuell and Deborah Cook was Born in Eastham april the 21 Day 1758

Samuell Cook Son of Samuell Cook and Deborah Cook was Born in Eastham the 16 Day of June 1760

Deborah Cook Daughter of Samuell and Deborah was Born in Eastham the 13 Day of october 1762

Hannah Cook Daughter Samuell and Deborah Cook was Born in Eastham July 17 Day 1765

John Cook Son of Samuell and Deborah Cook was Born in Eastham January the 4 Day 1768

Hannah Cook Daughter of Samuell and Deborah Cook was Born [in Eastham*] the 29† Day of may 1770 Died in July 1724‡

The wife of Samuel Cook Died the 11 Day of April 1772§

abigal Higgins Daughter of Elkanah and Sarah higgins was Born in Eastham the 28 Day of august 1758

Elkanah Higgins Son of Elkanah and Sarah higgins was Born in Eastham the 29 Day of august 1760

*The words in brackets were crossed out in the same ink.
†"30" was changed to "29" in a different ink.
‡"June 1773" was changed to "July 1772" in a different ink.
§"1773" was changed to "1772" in a different ink.

Lydia Higgins Daughter of Elkanah and Sarah Higgins was born in Eastham the 26 Day of July 1762

Benjamin Higgins Son of Elkanah and Sarah Higgins was Born in Eastham September 23 : 1767

Asenath Higgins Daughter of Elkanah and Sarah Higgins was Born in Eastham october 23 : 1769

Susanna Higgins Daughter of Elkanah and Sarah Higgins was Born in Eastham august 12 : 1771

Jedida Higgins Daughter of Elkanah and Sarah Higgins was Born in Eastham July 22 : 1764

Joshua Higgins Son of Elkanah Higgins and Sarah his wife was Born in Eastham October the 15 : 1775

Susanna Daughter of Elkanah Higgins & Sarah his wife was born August the 12 = 1771

Sarah Daughter of Elkanah Higgins & Sarah his wife was born in Eastham November the 3 = 1773

[p. 17d] Jonathan Cole and Rhode Snow was married in Eastham the Eight Day of october in the year 1761 by Edward Cheever minister

Josiah Cole Son of Jonathan and Rhoda Cole was Born in Eastham June the 21 Day 1763

Clooe Cole Daughter of Jonathan and Rhode Cole was Born in Eastham January 21 Day 1765

James Cole Son of Jonathan Cole and Rhode Cole was Born in Eastham February the 19 Day 1767

Edward Smith and Hannah Smith was married in Eastham January the fifteenth Day 1761 By mr Edward Cheever minster Recorded by me Edward Knowles Town Clerk

John Freeman Esqr and mrs Elizabeth myrick Both of Eastham was married in Eastham by mr Edward Cheever minster on the 26 Day of october 1761 Entred by me Edward Knowles Town Clerk

Josiah Knowles and Rebecca Higgins Both of Eastham was married in Eastham on the 29 Day of october 1761 by mr Edward Cheever minster Entred by me Edward Knowles Town Clerk

Elkenah Knowles Son of Josiah and Rebacca Knowles was Born in Eastham the 8 Day of December 1762

Josiah Knowles Son of Josiah and Rebacca Knowles was Born in Eastham the 23 Day of July 1766

alice Knowles Daughter of Josiah and Rebacca Knowles was Born in Eastham the 13 Day September 1769

Rebekah Knowles Daughter of Josiah and Rebekah Knowles was born in Eastham September 24 : 1774:

Elezer Atwood and Abigail Higgins was married in Eastham Both Belong to Eastham on the 5 Day of november 1761 by mr Edward Cheever menster Recorded by me Edward Knowles Town Clerk

[p. 18] Samuell Brown and Barbary myrick Both of Eastham was married in Eastham on the 22 Day of november 1764 by mr Edward Cheever minster Entred by me Edward Knowles Town Clerk

Benjamin Smith and Elizabeth Sparrow Both of Eastham was married in Eastham on the 8 Day of February 1770 by the Revrd mr Cheever Entred By me Edward Knowles town Clerk

Heman Crosby of Harwich and Tabathy Hopkins of Eastham was married on the 21 Day of march 1765 by mr Edward Cheever minster Entred by me Edward Knowles Town Clerk

Edmund Hawes of Barnstable and Hannah Snow of Eastham was married on June 19 Day 1766 by mr Edward Cheever minster Entred by me Edward Knowles Town Clerk

Gideon Baty and Rachal Knowles Both of Eastham was married in Eastham on the 18 Day of September 1766 by mr Edward Cheever minster Entred by me Edward Knowles Town Clerk

Sally Baty the Daughter of Gideon and Rachal Baty was Born at Eastham august ye 29 = 1768 and Died July ye 26 1769

Nathan Doane and Eunice Snow Both of Eastham was married in Eastham on october the 16 Day 1766 by mr Edward Cheever minster Entred by me Edward Knowles Town Clerk

Daniel Doane Son of Nathan and Eunice Doane was Born att Eastham September the 19 = 1768

Ruben Doane Son of Nathan and Eunice Doane was Born in Eastham 26 Day of June 1776

marcy Doane Daughter of Nathan and Eunice Doane was Born in Eastham 31 Day of may 1778

Ebenezer Dyer of Truro and Phebe Smith of Eastham was married in Eastham on the 6 Day of november 1766 by mr Edward Cheever minster Entred by me Edward Knowles Town Clerk

[p. 19] Simeon mayo and Sarah Cook Both of Eastham was married in Eastham on the 4 Day of December 1766 by mr Edward Cheever minster Recorded by me Edward Knowles Town Clerk

Phebe mayo Daughter of Simeon and Sarah mayo was Born in Eastham July 25 : 1767

Joseph mayo Son of Simeon and Sarah mayo was Born in Eastham June 5 Day 1769

Thomisen mayo Daughter of Simeon and Sarah mayo was Born in Eastham Decbr 24 : 1771

Sarah mayo Daughter of Simeon and Sarah mayo was Born in Eastham January 6 : 1774

Silvenus Brown and Fear myrick Both of Eastham was marriad in Eastham on the 17 Day of December 1766 by mr Edward Cheever minster Recorded by me Edward Knowles Town Clerk

Phebe the daughter of John and Rachel cook was born in Eastham September Seventeenth 1788

John Cook Jr the Son of John Cook and Rachel his wife was born in Eastham august 14th 1792

(To be continued)

EASTHAM AND ORLEANS, MASS., VITAL RECORDS

(Continued from page 44)

Jonathan Bascom and Temprence Knowles Both of Eastham was married in Eastham on the 23 Day of December 1766 by mr Edwd Cheever minster Recorded by me Edward Knowles Town Clerk

Timothy, Son of Jonathan Bascom & Temperance his wife, was born in Eastham, May 2d 1767.

Jonathan Bascom, Son of the above, was born in Eastham, June 19th 1769.

Abigail Bascom, Daughter of Do was born in Eastham, August 29th 1771.

Jonathan Bascom, Son of Do was born in Eastham, May 16th 1776.

Tempy Bascom Daughter of Do was born in Eastham, June 17th 1778.

William Bascom, Son of Do was born in Eastham, May 19th 1780.

Phebe Bascom, Daughter of Jona Bascom & Phebe his Wife, born May 22 : 1783

Charles, Son of Jona & Betty Bascom, born, Augt. 20 . 1787.

[p. 20] Philip Smith and Sarah mayo Both of Eastham was married in Eastham on the 22 Day of January 1767 by mr Edward Cheever minster Recorded by me Edward Knowles Town Clerk

James Snow and Ruth Higgins Both of Eastham was married in Eastham on the 17 Day of February 1767 by mr Edward Cheever minster Entred by me Edward Knowles Town Clerk

Seth Doane and Elisabeth Cole Both of Eastham was married in Eastham on the 19 Day of February 1767 by mr Edward Cheever minster Recorded by me Edward Knowles Town Clerk

David Smith and Phebe Snow Both of Eastham was married in Eastham on the 5 Day of march 1767 by mr Edward Cheever minster Recorded by me Edward Knowles Town Clerk

John Gills and Lidia Linkernu Both of Eastham was married in Eastham on the 12 Day of march 1767 by mr Edward Cheever minster Entred by me Edward Knowles Town Clerk

John Gills Son of John and Lidia Gills Born at Eastham Sept 20th 1767

William Gills Son of John and Lidia Gills Born at Eastham November 20th 1768

[p. 21] David Cole and Betty Doane Both of Eastham was married in Eastham on the 2 Day of april 1767 by mr Edward Cheever minster Recorded by me Edward Knowles Town Clerk

Aubah Cole Daughter of David and Betty Cole was Born in Eastham october 16 : 1769

David Cole Son of David and Betty Cole was Born in Eastham november 3 Day 1771

Ebenezer Cole Son of David and Bette Cole was Born in Eastham 4 day July 1773

Betty Cole Daughter of David and Betty Cole was Born in Eastham 17 Day July 1775

Simon Nuconb of wellfleet and Elisabeth Harding of Eastham was married on the 10 Day of april 1767 by mr Edward Cheever minster Recorded by me Edward Knowles Town Clerk

Daniel Atwood and Anne Doane Both of Eastham was married in Eastham on the 1 Day of october 1767 by mr Edward Cheever minster Recorded by me Edward Knowles Town Clerk

Samuell Harding of wellfleet and Martha Brown of Eastham was married in Eastham on the 6 Day of october 1767 by mr Edward Cheever minster Recorded by me Edward Knowles Town Clerk

[p. 22] Benjamin Penfield of wellfleet and Joanna Cook of Eastham was married in Eastham by mr Edward Cheever minster on the 24 Day of December 1767 Recorded by me Edward Knowles Town Clerk

Silvenus Smith and Hannah Nickerson* Both of Eastham was married in Eastham on the 11 Day of February 1768 by mr Edward Cheever minster Recorded by me Edward Knowles Town Clerk

Edward Snow and Betty myrick Both of Eastham was married in Eastham on the 18 Day of february 1768 by mr Edward Cheever minster Recorded by me Edward Knowles town Clerk

Henry mayo and Lucy Higgins Both of Eastham was married in Eastham on the 26 Day of february 1768 by mr Edward Cheever minster Recorded by me Edward Knowles Town Clerk

[p. 23] James mayo and Martha Doane Both of Eastham was marred in Eastham on the 1 Day of March 1768 by mr Edward Cheever minster Entred by me Edward Knowles Town Clerk

Ebenezer Higgins Jur of Eastham and Hanna Yats of harwich was married in harwich 27 Day of October 1763 by mr Joseph Crocker minster Recorded by me Joshua Doane Town Clerk

Heman Higgins Son of Ebnezer martha Higgins was Borne at Eastham apreal ye 18th 1757

Thankful Higgins Daughter of Ebnezer and Martha Higgins was Born at Eastham may the 16th 1759

Elkanah Higgins Son of Ebenezer and Hannah Higgins was Born at Eastham November the 18th 1764

Marther Higgins Daughter of Ebenezer and† Higgins was Born at Eastham febuary the 18th 1767

Oliver Aery and Mary Cole Both of Eastham was marrid in Eastham on the 3 Day of November 1763 by mr Joseph Crocker minster Recorded by me Joshua Doane Town Clerk

*"Martha Doane" was crossed out and "Hannah Nickerson" interlined in the same hand and ink.

† The wife's name was not entered.

[p. 24] Nehemiah Basset of wellfleet and Dorcas Cole of Eastham ware Marrid in Eastham the 3 Day of november 1763 by mr Joseph Crocker Minster Recorded by me Joshua Doane Town Clerk

Solomon Lewis and Elezabeth Myrick Both of Eastham ware marred in Eastham the 24 Day of November 1763 by mr Joseph Crocker Minster Recorded by me Joshua Doane town Clerk

Samuell Knowls and Abigal Linnell Both of Eastham ware marrid in Eastham by Mr Joseph Crocker minster December 29th 1763 Recorded by me Joshua Doane Town Clerk

Philip young and Azube Higgins Both of Eastham ware marrid in Eastham the 22 Day of march 1764 by Mr Joseph Crocker Minster Recorded by me Joshua Doane Town Clerk

Ruth young Dafter of Phillip and azube young was Born at Eastham November the 17 = 1765

Solomon Sparrow and Keziah Cole Both of Eastham ware marrid in Eastham november the 15th 1764 by mr Joseph Crocker Minster Recorded by me Joshua Doane Town Clerk

Joseph Son of Solomon Sparrow and Kezia his wife was born Novr 11th 1765

Joseph Son of Solomon Sparrow and Kezia his wife was born June 23 : 1766*

Seth Son of Solomon Sparrow and Kezia his wife was born Janry 10 1769

Vicry Son of Solomon Sparrow and Kezia his wife was born August 19 1770

Dorcas Daughter of Soln Sparrow and Kezia his wife was born Febr 6 1773

Kezia Daughter of Soln Sparrow and Kezia his wife born Janry 15 1775

Molly Daughter of Soln Sparrow and Kezia his wife was born July 20 1777

[p. 25] Thomas Twining and Anna Cole Both of Eastham ware marrid in Eastham the October 24th 1765 by mr Joseph Crocker Minster Recorded by me Joshua Doane Town Clerk

Stephen Twining the Son of Thomas and Anna Twining was Born at Eastham September ye 28 = 1767

William Twining the Son of Thomas and Anna Twining was Born at Eastham December ye 14 1769

Benjamin Pepper and Hanna Freeman Both of Eastham ware marrid in Eastham Octor the 28th 1765 by Mr Joseph Crocker Minster Recorded by Joshua Doane Town Clerk

Marcy Pepper Daughter of Benjamin and Hanna Pepper was Born at Eastham October the 1 Day 1766

Abigal Pepper Daughter of Benjamin and Hanna Pepper was Born at Eastham March the 20 Day : 1768

*Sic.

Tamson Pepper Daughter of Benjamin and Hannah Pepper was Born at Eastham February ye 5 : 1770

Simon peper Son of Benjamine and hannah peper was Born at East-ham may 10 — 1772

Sarah peper Dafter of Benjamine and hannah peper was Born at East-ham April 25 : 1775* and Dyed the 25 of July 1774*

freeman peper Son of Benjamin and hannah peper was Born at East-ham September 3 — 1776

Salla peper Dafter of Benjamin and hannah peper was Born at East-ham April 9 — 1779:

Benjamine peper Son of Benjamin and hannah peper was Born at Eastham September 16 — 1781

Hannah peper Dafter of hannah pepr Born at Eastham may : 13 : 1784

Haskel peper Son of Benjamin peper and hannah Born at Eastham febuary 6 : 1787

anson Kendrick and Azube Sears Both of Eastham ware Marrid in Eastham Octo : 29th 1765 by Mr Joseph Crocker Minster

[p. 26] Hetsell Knowls and marah Freeman Both of Eastham ware mar-red at Eastham Octo : 31 == 1765 by Mr Joseph Crocker Minster Entred by me Joshua Doane Town Clerk

Thomas Dexter and Hannah higgins both of Eastham war marrid In Eastham Octo : the 31th 1765 By mr Joseph Crocker Minster En-tred by me Joshua Doane Town Clerk

David Snow of harwich and mary Cole of Eastham ware marrid at Eastham December the 5th 1765 By mr Joseph Crocker Minster Entred by me Joshua Doane Town Clerk

December ye 30th 1765 Amos Knowls Jur and Abigil Pepper Both of Eastham ware marrid at Eastham by mr Joseph Crocker minster Entred By me Joshua Doane Town Clerke

James Knowls Son of Amos and Abigal Knowls was Born at Eastham november the 17 Day 1765

Richard Knowls Son of amos and abigal Knowls was Born at East-ham Sept the 13 Day 1767

Lydia Knowls Daughter of amos and abigal Knowls was Born at East-ham august the 4 = 1768

Amos Knowls the 3 Son of amos and abigal Knowls was Born at East-ham Sept the 19 = 1769

Solomon Knowls Son of Amos and abigal Knowls was Born at East-ham October ye 24 = 1770

Phebe Knowls Daughter of Amos Knowles and Abigail Knowles was Born in Eastham the 24 Day of July 1774

Edward Son of Amos Knowles and Abigail his wife was born in East-ham the 22d August 1778

George Brown Knowles Son of Amos Knowles & Mary his wife was born January 20th 1788

[p. 27] Janeuary 2 1766 Joshua Harding and Hanna Freeman Both of Eastham ware warried at Eastham by mr Joseph Crocker minster Entred by me Joshua Doane Town Clerke

* So recorded.

January 16 1766 Prince Higgins and Keziah Freeman Both of Eastham was marrid at Eastham by Mr Joseph Crocker minster Entred by me Joshua Doane Town Clerk

Prince Son of Prince and Keziah higgins was born 19 January : 1777 he Departed this Life the 1 of nomber 1777

Prince higgins Son of prince and Keziah higgins was born the 15 of December 1778

Naomi Dafter of prince and Keziah higgins was born 2 may 1781

Adah Dafter of prince and Keziah higgins was born 10 June 1783

Josiah Son of prince and Keziah higgins was born 16 June 1785

the other of their Children Loock in the 63 page of this Boock

January 22th 1766 John Foster of Harwich and hanna Goold of harwich was marrid by Mr Joseph Crocker Minster Entred by me Joshua Doane Town Clerk

January 23th 1766 John Gould and Apphia Cole Both of Eastham ware marrid By Mr Joseph Crocker Minster Entred By me Joshua Doane Town Clerk

Sarah Goold Daughter of John and aphiah Gould was Born at Eastham November ye 3th 1768

[p. 28] January 30th 1766 Simion Higgins Jur and Martha Knowle Both of Eastham ware marrid at Eastham by Mr Joseph Crocker minster Entred By me Joshua Doane Town Clerk

James Higgins Son of Simeon Higgins & Martha his wife was born February 7th 1781

April the 8 1766 Prince Rogers Susannah Snow Both of Eastham was marrid By Mr Joseph Crocker minster Entred By me Joshua Doane Town Clerk

Selvenus Rogers Son of Prinse and Susanna Rogers was Born at East-ham october ye 29th 1766

Prinse Rogers Son of Prinse Rogers and Susanna Rogers was Born at Eastham August ye 16th 1768

Rebekah Rogers Daughter of Prinse and Susanah Rogers was Born at Eastham November ye 1th 1769

Hannah Dafter of prince and Susanah Rogers Born at Eastham october 19: 1771

Ebenezer Son of prince and Susanah Rogers Born at Eastham Decem-ber 16 1773

Joshua Son of prince and Susanah Rogers Born at Eastham march 6: 1775

Susanah Dalter of prince and Susanah Rogers Born at Eastham feb 26* 1779

Israel Son of prince and Susanah Rogers Born at Eastham march 19: 1779

lucy Dafter of prince and Susanah Rogers Born at Eastham June 22: 1781

Octo ye 30 1766 the Revd mr willm Shaw of marshfield and mrs Lucia Crocker of Eastham ware marrid by Mr Joseph Crocker minster Recorded by me Joshua Doane Town Clerk

*The year was not recorded.

November ye 20 1766 Jonathan Hopkins of harwich and Tamsan Doane of Eastham ware marred by Mr Joseph Crocker minster Entred pr m Joshua Done Town Clerk

Mary Hopkins Daughter of Jonathan and Tamsan Hopkins was Born at Harwich november ye 25: 1768

[p. 29] December ye 18: 1766 Heman Snow and Jedida Smith Both of Eastham ware marrid at Eastham By Mr Joseph Crocker minster Entred by me Joshua Doane Town Clerk

Gideon Smith Snow Son of Heman and Jedida Snow was Born at Eastham October ye 28: 1767

Mary Snow Daughter of Heman and Jedida Snow was Born at Eastham November ye 5: 1769

Thankfull Snow Daughter of Heman and Jedida Snow was Born in Eastham august 16: 1771

Sarah Daughter of Heman Snow and Jedidah his wife was born June 7th 1773

Heman Snow Son of Heman Snow and Jedidah his wife was born Oct. 20 1775

Abiathar Son of Heman Snow and Jedidah his wife was born Dec 9th 1779

Nabby Daughter of Heman Snow and Jedidah his wife was born June 4th 1788

January 15: 1767: David Higgins and Lydia Hopkins Both of Eastham was marrid at Eastham By Mr Joseph Crocker minster Entred by me Joshua Doane Town Clerke

David and Richard Higgens Sons of David Higgens and Lydia was Born at Eastham September 27: 1767

Hannah Higgens Daughter of David Higgens and Lydia was Born at Eastham august 14: 1770

Sparrow Higgens Son of David Higgens and Lydia was Born at Eastham april: 30: 1772

Ruben Higgens Son of David Higgens and Lydia was Born at Eastham march: 20: 1774

Lydia Higgens Daughter of David Higgens was Born at Eastham Sept: 10: 1775

Look for the Rest in page 40

January 22: 1768* Nathaniel Snow and Thankful Hopkins Both of Eastham was marrid at Eastham By Mr Joseph Crocker minster Entred By me Joshua Doane Town Clerk

Samuell Snow the Son of Nathaniel and Thankful Snow was Born at Eastham Octor ye 30: 1767*

James Snow Son of nathaniel and Thankful Snow was Born at Eastham July ye 28: 1769

Nathaniel Snow Son of Nathaniel and Thankful Snow was Born in Eastham the 11 Day of July 1771

* So recorded.

Febuary 19 . 1767 Levi Higgins and Bathsheba Young Both of Eastham was marred at Eastham By Mr Joseph Crocker minester Entred by me Joshua Doane Town Clerk

Nehemah Higgins Son of Levi Higgins and Bathsheba Higgins was Born at Eastham December 25 . 1767

[p. 30] Febuary 26 . 1767 Nathaniel Snow Jur and Hanna Twining Both of Eastham was marrid at Eastham By Mr Joseph Crocker minster Entred by me Joshua Doane Town Clerk

April ye 7th 1767 William myrick and Hanna Peine Both of Eastham was marrid By Mr Joseph Crocker minster Entred by me Joshua Doane Town Clerk

Dorcas myrick Daughter of william and hannah myrick was Born in Eastham the 12 Day of September 1769

Hannah myrick Daughter of william and Hannah myrick was born in Eastham the 16 Day of July 1771

Gideon son of William Myrick & Hannah was born Dec 14th 1772

Rebekah & Ruth twin daughters of William & Hannah Myrick born 22 May 1775

William son of William Myrick & Hannah his wife was born Apr 25 1777

Lucy daughter of William Myrick & Hannah his wife was born July 10 1779

Gideon son of William Myrick & Hannah his wife was born Apr'l 29 1781

October 13: 1767 Joseph Doane and Susannah Cole Both of Eastham was Married at Eastham By Mr Joseph Crocker minster Entred By me Joshua Doane Town Clerk

Isaac Doane Son of Joseph and Susannah Doane was Bourn in Eastham August 6 Day 1768

Joseph Doane Son of Joseph and Susannah Doane was Born in Eastham the 4 Day of July 1771

october 15: 1767 John Lewis and mary Bate Both of Eastham was marrid at Eastham By Mr Joseph Crocker minster Entred By me Joshua Doane Town Clerk

[p. 31] November 12: 1767 Joseph Mayo and Ruth Snow Both of Eastham was marrid at Eastham by Mr Joseph Crocker minster Entred by me Joshua Doane Town Clerk

November 19: 1767 James Knowls of Chatham and Sarah Mayo of Eastham was married at Eastham By Mr Joseph Crocker minster Entred by me Joshua Doane Town Clerk

November 26: 1767 Israel Higgins and Mary Snow Both of Eastham was married at Eastham By Mr Joseph Crocker minster Entred By me Joshua Doane Town Clerk

December 31: 1767 Nathaniel Harding and Keziah Cole Both of Eastham was married at Eastham By Mr Joseph Crocker minster Entred by Joshua Doane Town Clerk

[p. 32] Febuary 25 . 1768 Prince Freeman and Martha Freeman Both of Eastham was married at Eastham By Joseph Crocker minster Entred By me Joshua Doane Town Clerk march ye 3 . 1768 Philip Young and anne Snow Both of Eastham was marrid att Eastham By Mr Joseph Crocker minster Entred By me Joshua Doane Town Clerk

azuba Young Daughter of Phillip and anna young was Born at Eastham September 21: 1769

anna Daughter of Philip and anna young was Born Sept 4: 1772

Jonathan freeman young Son of Phillip and anne young was borne at Eastham July 16: 1774

Look below for the Rest

March ye 17 1768 Thomas Doane Residnt in Chatham and Elizebeth Lewis of Eastham was married By Mr Joseph Crocker minster

December 5: 1766 William Paine of Eastham and Sarah Mayo of Harwich was married in harwich by John Freeman Justice peace Entred by me Edward Knowles town Clerk

Snow young Son of Philip and anne young was born at Eastham august 10: 1776

Mary Daughter of Philip young and anne young was born at Eastham January 19: 1779

Micajah Snow young Son of Philip and anne young was born at Eastham april: 13: 1781

Nathanel young Son of Philip and anne young was Born at Eastham July 31: 1784

Thankful young Daughter of Philip and anna young was Born at Eastham may 8: 1787

[p. 33] these are the Children of John Taylor which he had By his first wife Phebe

Rebekah Taylor Daughter of John and Phebe Taylor was born at Eastham febuary the 9th 1743:

Jonathn Taylor Son of John and phebe Taylor was Born at Eastham in the Begining of November: 1744 Liveed two years and Eighteen Days and Died

Abigal and Phebe Taylor Daughters of John and Phebe Taylor was Born at Eastham may the 6th 1746

Edward Taylor Son of John and Phebe Taylor was Born at Eastham thirteenth Day of July: 1749:

Benjamin Taylor Son of John and Phebe Taylor was Born at Eastham October 26th 1752

Lidya Taylor Daughter of John and Phebe Taylor was Born at Eastham June the 1th 1754 and in October the 14th 1757 She Died

Phebe Taylor the Wife of John Taylor Died the 30 Day of Jenuary 175: Children had by his Second wife

Mary Taylor Daughter of John Susannah Taylor was Born at Eastham May the 14th 1758

John Taylor Son of John and Susannah Taylor was was Born at Eastham July the 13th 1760

David Taylor Son of John and Susannah Taylor was Born at Eastham June the 10th 1763

Eunice Taylor Daughter of John and Susannah Taylor was Born at Eastham June the 11th 1767

Enoch Atwood and Azubah Cole ware married in Eastham february 8 Day 1770 by mr Cheever minister

Bangs atwood Son of Enoch and Azubah atwood was born in Eastham march 18th 1771

mary Atwood Daughter of Enoch and Azubah Atwood was Born in Eastham the 3(Day of July 1772

Seth Paine Son of Seath and Sarah Paine was Born in Eastham the 24 of February 1775

Seth Paine Died 29 Day of april 1775

David Rogers Son of David and ——— Rogers was born in Eastham February 6th 1782

[p. 34] Rebekah Linell Daughter of Elisha and Martha Linell was Born in Eastham November ye 17 Day 1745 OS

John Linell Son of Elisha and Martha Linell was Born at Eastham June ye 25th 1747 OS

Enoch Linell Son of Elisha and Martha Linell was Born at Eastham March ye 23th 1749 OS

Martha Linell Daughter of Elisha and Martha Linell was Born at Eastham January the 2th 1751 OS

Mehetable Linell daughter of Elisha and and Martha Linell was Born at Eastham September the 23th 1753 OS

Elice Linell Daughter of Elisha and Martha Linell was Born at Eastham September ye 2th 1755: NS

Bisier Linell Daughter of Elisha and Martha Linell was Born at Eastham September ye 6th 1757

Elisha Linell Son of Elisha and Martha Linell was Born at Eastham July ye 23th 1760

Samuell Linell Sone of Elisha and Martha Linell was Born at Eastham January the 12 Day 1763

Elezebath Linell Daughter of Elisha and and Martha Linell was Born at Eastham January 11th 1765

Hannah Linell Daughter of Elisha and Martha Linell was Born at Eastham June the 23th 1767

Mary Linell Daughter of Elisha and Martha Linell was Born at Eastham Jenuary ye 30: 1770

Thomas Snow Son of Elnathan and Phebe Snow was Born at Eastham September ye 16th 1756

Isaac Snow Son of Elnathan and Phebe Snow was Born at Eastham October ye 8th 1758

Phebe Snow daughter of Elnathan and Phebe Snow was Born at Eastham October ye 13th 1760

Aaron Snow Son of Elnathan and Phebe Snow was Born at Eastham July ye 12th 1763

Abigail Snow Daughter of Elnathan and Phebe Snow was Born at Eastham December ye 28th 1766

Dorkis vicory Snow Daughter of Elnarthan Snow and Pheby Snow was born at Eastham July: 15: 1772

Elnarthan Snow Son of Elnarthan Snow and Pheby Snow was Born at Eastham July 2: 1776

Mercy Snow Daughter of Elnathan and Phebe Snow was born at Eastham April 18: 1780

[p. 35] Lydia Hopkins Daughter of Joshua and and Rebacah Hopkins was Born at Eastham febuary the 7th 1747/8

Rebekah hopkins Daughter of Joshua and Rebecah hopkins was Born at Eastham Novcuber 9th 1749

Mary hopkins Daughter of Joshua and Rebecah hopkins was Born at Eastham June the 25th 1751

Joshua hopkins Son of Joshua hopkins and Rebecah hopkins was Born at Eastham September the 19th 1753

John hopkins Son of Joshua and Rebecah hopkins was Born at Eastham february the 9th 1756

Elkanah hopkins Son of Joshua and Rebecah hopkins was at Eastham may the 18th 1758

Marcy hopkins Daughter of Joshua and Rebecah hopkins was Born at Eastham November the 13th 1761

Abigail hopkins Daughter of Joshua aud Rebecah hopkins was at Eastham Desember the 19th 1764

Elisha hopkins Son of Joshua and Rebecah hopkins was at Eastham may the 20th 1767

Curtis hopkins Son of Joshua and Rebecah hopkins was born at Eastham octobar: 26: 1772

Watson young and Elisebeth Smith Both of Eastham ware marred at Eastham October ye 10: 1769 By John Freeman Justice Entred By me Joshua Doane town Clerk

John Young Son of Watson Young & Elizabeth his wife was born in Eastham in June 21th Day in the year 1784

[p. 36] Elknah Linell Son of Elknah Linell was Born at Eastham april the 21 Day 1753

Joseph Linell Son of Elknah and Mary Linell was Born at Eastham December the 3 Day 1754

Benjamin Linell Son of Elknah and mary Linell was Born at Eastham December ye 5 day 1756

Joshua Linell Son of Elknah and Mary Linell was Born at Eastham may ye 11 day 1759

Edmond Linell Son of Elknah and mary Linell was Born at Eastham July the 13 day 1761

Rebeca Linell Daughter of Elknah and Mary Linell was Born at Eastham October 21 Day 1763

Marah Linell Daughter of Elknah and mary Linell was Borne at Eastham apriel the 17th 1766

Henery Cole and Desire Basset Both of Eastham ware marrid August the 18th 1768 by John Freeman Justice peace Entred by me Joshua Doane Tow Clerk

Marcy Pepper wife of Joseph Juner Died February 5: 1776

(To be continued)

EASTHAM AND ORLEANS, MASS., VITAL RECORDS

(Continued from page 70)

[p. 37] Mr Barnabus Freeman and Bathiah Knowls ware Married at Eastham November the 3th 1763 By Edward Chevers Clerk

Samuell Freeman Son of Barnabus and Bethiah Freeman was Born at Eastham August ye 11: 1764

Mary Freeman Daughter of Barnabus and Bethiah Freeman was Borne at Eastham March ye 3th 1766

James Freeman Sone of Barnabus and Bethiah Freeman was Born at Eastham September ye 28: 1767

Thomas Sparrow & Ester Smith Both of Eastham ware marrid November ye 24th 1768 By John Freeman Justice Peace Entred by me Joshua Doane town Clerk

*Incorrectly printed "Mary" in Vit. Rcds. Scituate, 2:457.

†The footstone reads: "Mr Michael Turner"

‡Incorrectly printed "10" in Vit. Rcds. Scituate, 2:457.

[p. 38] Josiah Mayo the Son of Joshua and Sarah Mayo was Born at Eastham October ye 26th 1768

Martha Twining Daughter of Barnabus and Abegal Twining was Born at Eastham December ye 21: 1764

Hannah Twining Daughter of Barnabus and abegal Twining was Born at Eastham December ye 7: 1766

Molla Twining Daughter of Barnabus and Abegal Twining was Born at Eastham October ye 25: 1768

David Twining Son of Barnabas & Abigail Twining his wife was born at Eastham April 11 1774

Barnabas Twining and Abigail Knowles were Married by the Revd Mr Bascom November the 14th 1760

Tamsen daughter and Jonathan Son of Jonathan Twining Jur and Tamsen his wife was born in Orleans May 13th 1799

[p. 39] Rebekah Mayo Daughter of Benjamen and Sarah Mayo was Born at Eastham febuary ye 7th 1750

Elesebeth Mayo Daughter of Theophilus and Sarah Mayo was Born at Eastham October ye 22: 1757

Experence Mayo Daughter of Theophilus and Sarah Mayo was Born at Harwich aprel ye 20: 1759

Tryphene Mayo Daughter of Theophilus and Sary Mayo was Born at Harwich October ye 4: 1760

Benjamin Mayo Son of Theophilos and Sarah Mayo was Born at harwich June ye 19: 1762

Jonathen Mayo Son of Theophilos and Sarah Mayo was Born at Eastham July ye 12: 1764

Eebnezer Mayo Son of Theophilos & Sarah mayo was Born to Eastham august ye 25: 1765

Heman Mayo Son of Theophilos and Sarah mayo was Born at Eastham May ye 18: 1768

Sammual Mayo the Son of Theophilos and Sarah Mayo was Born October ye 10th 1769

Jesse Cole of Eastham and Sarah Lewis of truro was married in Eastham on the 29 Day of march 1770 by Revd Cheever Entred by me Edward Knowles town Clerk

Jesse Cole Son of Jesse and Sarah Cole was Born in Eastham 23 april 1772

Philip Higgins Leida Hopkins Both of Eastham was married in Eastham the 12 Day of July 1770 By the Revd mr Cheever Entred by me Edward Knowles Town Clerk

[p. 40] Joshua Paine and Mercy Higgins was married at Eastham april ye 26: 1768 By Edward Cheever Minster Entred pr me Joshua Doane town Clerk

Shaw Higgins Son of David and Lydia Higgens was Born at Eastham april 10: 1777

apphiah Higgens Daughter of David and Lydia Higgens was Born at Eastham april 9: 1779

oliver Higgens Son of David and Lydia Higgens was Born at Eastham april 3: 1781

Prisilla Higgens Daughter of David and Lydia Higgens was Born at Eastham may the 2: 1783

John Knowls and Susannah Walker Both of Eastham ware married By Edward Cheever Minster the 19 Day of June 1769 Entred pr me Joshua Doane town Clerk

Robert Knowles Son of John and Susannah Knowles was Born in Eastham may 19: 1770

John Knowles Son of John and Susannah Knowles was Born in Eastham December 29: 1771

Samuell Horten & Elezebeth Collins Both of Eastham was Married att Eastham March ye 24: 1768 By Edward Cheevers Minster Entred pr me Joshua Doane town Clerk

John Horten Son of Samuel and Elesebeth Horten was Born in Eastham January 16 Day 1770

Elnathan Horten Son of Samuel and Elesebath Horten was Born in Eastham march 1772

[p. 41] Isaac Myrick and Mercy Doane Both of Eastham ware married at Eastham february ye 9: 1769 By Edward Cheever Minster Entred By me Joshua Doane town Clerk

Barnabas Atwood and Abigail Mayo Both of Eastham ware Married at Eastham March ye 28: 1769 By Edward Cheever minster Entred pr me Joshua Doane town Clerk

Ebenezer Higgins and Content Harding was married in Eastham on the 25 Day of December* by the Revd mr Cheever Entred by me Edward Knowles town Clerk

Ruben Smith and Phebe Snow was married in Eastham on the 19 Day of march By the Revd mr Cheever 1771 Entred by me Edward Knowles town Clerk

[p. 42] Nathan Cole Son of John and Martha Cole was Born at Eastham July 23 Day 1760

Theofulos Cole Son of John and Martha Cole was Born at Eastham Sept 29 Day 1765

Mercy Cole Daughter of John and Martha Cole was Born at Eastham May ye 23 Day 1768

Catup Trowbridge Lat Resedent in Eastham and Elisebeth Young of of Eastham ware Marride in Eastham October ye 12: 1769 By John Freeman Justice peace Entred By me Joshua Doane town Clerk

Bryan Martin and Elisebeth Higgins Both of Eastham was marrid november the 11th 1768 By Joseph Crocker Clerk Entred By me Joshua Doane town Clerk

John Martin Son of Bryan and Elisebeth martin was Born at Eastham December ye 9 Day 1768

Elanor Marten the Daughter of Bryan and Elisebeth Martin was Born at Eastham June the 13: 1770

*The year was not recorded.

John Atwood and martha Cheever Both of Eastham was married in Eastham on the 14 Day of march 1771 By the Revd mr Cheever Entred by me Edward Knowles town Clerk

John Atwood Son of John and Martha Atwood was Born in Eastham January 10 Day 1773

[p. 43] Josiah Rogers and Abigail Arey Both of Eastham was marride January ye 12: 1769 By Joseph Crocker Clerk Entred By me Joshua Doane town Clerk

Josiah Rogers Son of Josiah and Abegal Rogers was Born at Eastham Sept ye 17th 1769

Zenas Son of Josiah Rogers and Abigail his wife was born at Eastham October the 28th 1771

Abigail Daughter of Josiah Rogers and Abigail his wife was born at Boston January 30th 1774

Seth Son of Josiah Rogers and Abigail his wife, was born at Eastham March the 25th 1776

Abiather Son of Josiah Rogers and Abigail his wife was born at Eastham March the 7th 1778

William Son of Josiah Rogers and Abigail his wife was born at Eastham September 19th 1780

Luthar Son of Josiah Rogers and Abigail his wife was born at Eastham Oct 19. 1782

Josiah Son of Josiah Rogers & Abigail his wife was born at Eastham June 26th 1789

Isaiah Doane and Rebeca Smith Smith* Both of Eastham was marride December the 15: 1768 By Joseph Crocker Cleark Entred By me Joshua Doane tow Clerk

Nathaniel Myrick and Elesabath Ary Both of Eastham ware marrid February ye 2: 1769 By Joseph Crocker Clerk Entred By me Joshua Doane town Clerk

[p. 44] Heman Smith and Sarah Myrick Both of Eastham was marride Febuary the 2: 1769 By Joseph Crocker Clerk Entred By me Joshua Doane town Clerk

Joshua Crosby and Thankful Cole Both of Eastham was Marrid February the 17: 1769 By Joseph Crocker Clerk Entred By me Joshua Doane town Clerk

Deborah Crosby Daughter of Joshua Crosby and Thankful Crosby was born at Eastham Decembar: 17: 1769

Joseph Crosby Son of Joshua Crosby and Thankful crosby was born at Eastham octobar 22: 1771

Rebecca Crosby Daughter of Joshua Crosby and Thankful Crosby was born at Eastham august 28: 1776

Joshua Crosby Son of Joshua and Thankful Crosby was born at Eastham January 6: 1779

Abiel Son of Joshua Crosby and Thankfull his wife was born July 25th 1782

*The second "Smith" probably was an error of the town clerk.—*Editor.*

'Abiel Cole and Hannah Linell Both of Eastham was marride March ye 2: 1769 By Joseph Crocker Clerk Entred By me Joshua Doane town Cerk

Abigail Daughter of Dn Abiel Cole & Abigail his wife was born July 12th 1795*

Sally Daughter of Dn Abiel Cole & Sarah his wife was born May 9th 1794

Hitty Daughter of Dn Abiel Cole & Sarah his wife was born November 3th 1797

Jonathan Son of Dn Abiel Cole & Sarah his wife was born August 18th 1799

[p. 45] Prince Snow and Relience Paine Both of Eastham was married March the 9: 1769 By Joseph Crocker Clerk Entred By me Joshua Doane town Clerk

Eliezer Freeman jur and Elisebeth Snow Both of Eastham was marride March the 9: 1769 By Joseph Crocker Clerk Entred By me Joshua Doane town Clerk

Elkanah young Rebeca Higgins Both of Eastham was married march the 16: 1769 By Joseph Crocker Clerk Entred By me Joshua Doane town Clerk

[p. 46] Jesse Kinney of Harwich and Mary Hopkins of Eastham was marride November the 2: 1769 By Joseph Crocker Clerk Entred By me Joshua Doane tow Clerk

Sarah Kinny Daughter of Jesse Kinny and mary his wife was Bor at Eastham September 3: 1770

Jesse Kinny Son of Jesse Kinny and mary his wife was Born at Eastham July: 15: 1772

Heman Kinny Son of Jesse Kinny and mary his wife was Born at Eastham July 7: 1776

Nathan Kinny Son of Jesse Kinny and mary his wife was Born September 1: 1778

John Kinney Son of Jesse and mary Kinny was Born febuary 13: 1774

thankfull Kinny Dafter of Jesse Kinney and mary was Born november-ber 29: 1775

allen Son of Jesse Kinny & may his wife was born Janr 7th 1789

Polly Daughter of Jesse Kenny and Mary his wife was born at Eastham July ye 18th 1792

Heman Kenny Son of Jesse Kenny & mary his wife was Born September 5th 1797 in orleans

Archilaus Harding and Mercy Sears Both of Eastham was marride November ye 23: 1769 By Joseph Crocker Clerk Entred By me Joshua Doane town Clerk

Marcy Rogers Daughter of Reuben Rogers & Sarah Kenny was born in Orleans March 22th 1798

Freeman Knowls Esther myrick Both of Eastham was Maride November ye 23: 1769 By Joseph Crocker Clerk Entred By me Joshua Doane tow Clerk

*The 1795 was partly erased.

(*To be continued*)

(To be continued)

EASTHAM AND ORLEANS, MASS., VITAL RECORDS

(Continued from page 115)

[p. 47] Joseph Hopkins and Mary Higgins Both of Eastham was married January ye 12: 1770 By Joseph Crocker Clerk Entred By me Joshua Doane town Clerk

Smith Hopkins Son of Joseph and mary Hopkins was Born at Eastham octobar ye 13: 1770

Thankful Hopkins Daughter of Joseph and mary Hopkins was Born at Eastham July: 28: 1772

Rebecah Hopkins Daughter of Joseph and mary was Born at Eastham octobar 25: 1774

Susanna Hopkins Daughter of Joseph and mary Hopkins was Born at Eastham Novembar 24: 1776

Mary Hopkins Daughter of Joseph & mary Hopkins was Born at Eastham april: 5th 1779

Giles Hopkins Son of Joseph and mary Hopkins was Born at Eastham march the 30: 1781

Look below for the Rest

Dr John Davis and mercy Crocker was marride at Eastham January ye 12: 1770 By Joseph Crocker Clerk Entred By me Joshua Doane town Clerk

Edward Smith and and Grace Gould Both of harwich was Marrid By John Freeman Esqr November ye 30: 1769 Entred pr me Joshua Doane town Clerk

Joseph Hopkins Son of Joseph Hopkns and mary his wife was Born at Eastham octobar ye 20: 1783

Prissilla Hopkins Daughter of Joseph and mary Hopkins was born at Eastham July ye 22: 1785

Sally Hopkins Daughter of Joseph and mary Hopkins was born at Eastham July ye 28: 1788

[p. 48] Myrick Paine the Sone of Joseph and Phebe paine was Born at Eastham July the 22th 1768

Joseph Paine Son of Joseph and Phebe pain was Born in Eastham the 6 Day of october 1771

Richard Paine and Phebe paine Son and Daughter of Joseph and Phebe paine was Born in Eastham the 24 Day of September 1773

Uriah Paine Son of Joseph and Phebe Paine was Born in Eastham November 27 Day 1775

Thomas Paine the Son of Joseph Paine and Phebe his wife was born march 2d 1778

Samuel Baty of Eastham and Rosanna Carr Resedent of Eastham was married December ye 18: 1770 By John Freeman Justice a peace Entred pr me Joshua Doane town Clerk

Isaac Young Sarah Higgins was marred June the 21: 1770 By John Freeman Justice peace Entred By me Joshua Doane town Clerk

Pricilla yound* Daughter of Isaac yound* and Sarah his wife was Born 15 Day of august: 1771

Isaac young Son of Isaac and Sarah young was Born at Eastham July: 17: 1773

[p. 49] William Twining the Son of Elijah and Lois twining was Born at Eastham November ye 13: 1763

Elezer Twining Son of Elijah and Lois Twining was Born at Eastham may the 29: 1765

Ruth Twining Daughter of Elijah and Lois Twining was Born at Eastham December ye 2: 1766

Joseph Twining Son of Elijah and Lois Twining was Born at East-ham Sept ye 28: 1768 and Died January the 24: 1769

Nehemiah young and Abigael Talor was marred at Eastham apriel ye 26: 1770 By Joseph Crocker Cle Entred pr me Joshua Doane town Clerk

Kezia young the Daughter of Nehemiah and Abigal young was Born at Eastham march the 14: 1771

Abigail Daughter of Nehemiah Young & Abigail his wife was born in Eastham December 29: 1772

Jonathan Son of Nehemiah Young & Abigail his wife was born in Eastham November the 3: 1774

Linda Daughter of Nehemiah Young & Abigail his wife was born in Eastham Sept the 18th 1776

Lucy Daughter of Nehemiah Young & Abigail his wife was born in Eastham November 22th 1777

Linda Daughter of Nehemiah Young & Abigail his wife was born in Eastham June 21: 1780

Apphiah Daughter of Nehemiah Young & Abigail his wife was born in Eastham June 25: 1782

Phebe Daughter of Nehemiah Young & Abigail his wife was born in Eastham September 24: 1784

The Revd Mr Simeon Williams of Wamouth and Mrs Anna Crocker of Eastham was married October: 25: 1770 by Joseph Crocker Clerk Entred By me Joshua Doane tow Clerk

Frances Son of Nehemiah Young & Abigail his wife was born in Eastham May 26th 1787

*So recorded.

[p. 50] Jesse Nickerson of Harwich and Eunice Snow of Eastham was married at Eastham December ye 20: 1770 By Joseph Crocker Clerk Entred By me Joshua Doane town Clerk

Prince Twining and Hannah Rogers Both of Eastham was marred January ye 3: 1771 By Joseph Crocker Clerk Entred By me Joshua Doane town Clerk

Thankful Daughter of Prince and hannah Twining was Born at East-ham the 31 Day of august: 1773

Jonathan Son of Prince and Hannah Twining was Born 25 of may: 1775

Hannah Daughter of Prince and Hannah Twining was Born 4 of June 1777

Lidy Daughter of Prince and Hannah Twining was Born 21 of april 1779

Cloe Daughter of prince and Hannah Twining was Born 18 of april 1781

Prince Son of prince and Hannah twinning was Born 30 of apriel 1783

Lucy Daughter of prince and Hannah twinning was Born 29 of apriel 1785

mary Doane Daughter of Joshua and Ruth Doane was Born in East-ham on the 18 Day of august 1769:

Sarah Doane Daughter of Joshua and Ruth Doane was Born in East-ham on the 15 Day of november 1770

Joshua Doane Jr Son of Joshua & Ruth Doane was born June 10th 1772

Solomon Doane Jur Son of Joshua & Ruth Doane was Born Janary 31th 1777

[p. 51] Doan Snow and Apphiah Crocker Boath of Eastham was mar-ried in Eastham by John Freeman, Esqr on the 31 Day of may 1771

Barnabas Cook and Phebe Cook was married in Eastham by mr Cheever Feb 1: 1770

marcy Cook Daughter of Barnabas and Phebe Cook was Born in Eastham the 12 Day of august 1770 Entred by me Edward Knowles town Clerk

Barnabas Cook was Drowned on the 24 Day of September 1771 Com-ing from the Banks a whaling

Willard Knowles and Marcy Snow was married in Eastham*

Treat Knowles Son of willard and marcy Knowles was Born in East-ham october 25: 1763 and Died may 29: 1765

Treat Knowles Son of willard and marcy Knowles was Born in East-ham october 29 Day 1768

mary Knowles Daughter of willard and marcy Knowles was Born in Eastham July 8 Day 1767 and Died September 29:

willard Knowles Son of willard Knowles jr and marcy Knowles was Born in Eastham march 25 Day 1769

Abigail and Marcy Knowles Daughters of willard and marcy Knowles was Born in Eastham may 29: 1771 and Died 5 y 9 months old

*The date was not entered.

Exparance Knowles Daughter of willard and marcy Knowles wa[s] Born in Eastham march 7: 1774

Nathaniel Atwood Knowles Son of Willard and marcy Knowles wa[s] Born in Eastham June 22: 1776

[p. 52] molly mayo Daughter of Lamuel and mary mayo was born in Eastham July the 19 . 1763

Dilly mayo Daughter of Lamuel and mary mayo was born in Eastham June the 20 . 1765

tabitha mayo Daughter of Lamuel and mary mayo was born in Eastham September 18 . 1767

Elisha mayo Son of Lamuel and mary mayo was born in Eastham September the 8 . 1770

thomas Cook Son of Caleb and Jane Cook was brn in Eastham march the 20 . 1766

David Cook Son of Caleb and Jane Cook was born in Eastham the 15 . 1768

Sarah Cook Daughter of Caleb & Jane Cook was born in Eastham october 7 . 1770

Jane Cook Daughter of Calab and Jane Cook was Born in Eastham 6 Day march 1773

Hannah Cook Daughter of Calab and Jane Cook was Born in Eastham 6 Day of December 1775

Nathan Cook Son of Calab and Jane Cook was Born in Eastham 7 Day of may 1778

William Cook Son of Calib and Jane Coock was Born in Eastham November 13th 1780

Susannah Coock Son* of Caleb & Jane was Born in Eastham June 29th 1783

Ruth Smith Coock Dafter of Caleb and Jane was Born in Eastham august 21: 1785

lydea Coock Dafter of Caleb Coock and Jane Coock was born Eastham January 28th 1788

December 26: 1771 Robert Snow and Eunice Horten Both of Eastham was married in Eastham by the Revd mr Cheever Entred by me Edward Knowles Town Clerk

[p. 53] Bartlett Paine Son of Seth and Sarah Paine was Born in Eastham September 13 Day 1769

Betty Paine Daughter of Seth Paine and Sarah Paine was Born in Eastham the 12 Day December 1771

Joshua Smith and Phebe Doane was Marriade in Eastham the 29 Day of october in the year 1765 by mr Cheever minster

Rachal Smith Daughter of Joshua and Phebe Smith was Born in Eastham September 15 Day 1767

Betty Smith Daughter of Joshua and Phebe Smith was Born in Eastham July 20 . 1768

Timothy Smith Son of Joshua and Phebe Smith was Born in Eastham the 5 Day of august 1770

* So recorded.

Ephraim Son of Joshua Smith & Phebe his Wife was born April 25th 1783

Timothy Son of Timothy Smith & Kezia his Wife was born the 2d of September 1800

June 4: 1772 Nathaniel Parker of Falmouth and Tabathe Gill of Eastham was married in Eastham by the Revd mr Cheever Entred by me Edward Knowles Town Clerk

april 30: 1771 Samuell Doane and Elisabeth Snow Both of Eastham was married in Eastham by the Revd mr Cheever Entred by me Edward Knowles town Clerk

November 7: 1771 Samuell Horten and Tabatha mayo Both of Eastham was married in Eastham by the Revd mr Cheever Entred by me Edward Knowles Town Clerk

November 14: 1771 Isaiah Holbrook of wellfleet and Tabatha Chipman of Eastham was married in Eastham by the Revd mr Cheever Entred by me Edward Knowles town Clerk

[p. 54] March 26: 1772 Stephen Snow Juner and Lidia Smith Both of Eastham was married in Eastham by the Revd mr Cheever Entred by me Edward Knowles Town Clerk

april 9 1772 William Snow and Dorcas Cook Both of Eastham was married in Eastham by the Revd mr Cheever Entred by me Edward Knowles Town Clerk

april 16 1772 Solomon Pepper Juner and Phebe Knowles Both of Eastham was married in Eastham by the Revd mr Cheever Entred by me Edward Knowles Town Clerk

april 30 1772 Moses Lewes of Truro and Rebacca Knowles of Eastham was married in Eastham by the Revd mr Cheever Entred by me Edward Knowles Town Clerk

November 19: 1772 John Doane and Priscilah atwood Both of Eastham was married in Eastham by the Revd mr Cheever Entred by me Edward Knowles Town Clerk

[p. 55] June 11 1772 Samuel Cook and Thankful Brown Both of Eastham was married in Eastham By the Revd mr Cheever Entred by me Edward Knowles Town Clerk

September 3: 1772 David Atwood and Sabery Nickerson Both of Eastham was married in Eastham by the Revd mr Cheever Entred by me Edward Knowles town Clerk

Decbr 31 1772 Aaron Higgins and Abigail Atwood Both of Eastham was married in Eastham by the Revd mr Cheever Entred by me Edward Knowles town Clerk

[p. 56-1] December 31: 1772 David Smith and Abigail Newcomb Both of Eastham was married in Eastham by the Revd mr Cheever Entred by me Edward Knowles Town Clerk

February 4: 1773 Samuel Brown of wellfleet and Susannah Cole of Eastham was married in Eastham by the Revd mr Cheever

February 18: 1773 Isaac Doane Holbrook of wellfleet and Lucy Doane of Eastham was married in Eastham by the Revd mr Cheever

Josiah Sparrow of Eastham and mercy Smith of Chatham was married January 10th 1782: by Joseph Doane Esqr Entred by Isaac Sparrow Town Clerk

Lydia Sparrow Daughter of Josiah Sparrow and mercy his wife was Borne at Eastham october: 19: 1782

Josiah Sparrow Son of Josiah and mercy Sparrow was Born at Eastham march 13: 1785

mercy Sparrow Daughter of Josiah and mercy Sparrow was Born at Eastham may 28: 1788

Zerviah Sparrow Daughter of Josiah Sparrow and mercy his Wife was Born at Eastham march 15: 1790

Samuel Sparrow Son of Josiah Sparrow & Mercy his wife was born Novr 3th 1792

Harry Sparrow Son of Josiah Sparrow & Marcy his wife was born Novr 14th 1795

Sarah Sparrow Daughter of Josiah & Marcy his wife was born March 21th 1798

James Linnel Sparrow Son of Josiah & Marcy his wife was born June 2d 1801

Hannah Snow Sparrow Dautr of Josiah & Marcy his wife was born Janu 1th 1805

[p. 56-2] Elijah Knowles and Rebacca Harding Both of Eastham was married in Eastham the Second Day of april 1774 By the Revend mr Cheever

Henry Knowles Son of Elijah and Rebacca Knowles was born in Eastham the 20 Day of July 1775

Ann Knowles Daughter of Elijah and Rebacca Knowles was Born in Eastham 26 Day of august 1777

Harding Knowles Son of Elijah and Rebacca Knowles was Born in Eastham 25 Day of October 1779

Elijah Son of Elijah and Rebacca Knowles was Born in Eastham first Day January 1782

Elisabeth Daughter of Elijah and Rebacca Knowles was Born in Eastham August 5 Day 1784

Lucy Knowles daughter of Elijah and Rebeca Knowles was born in Eastham april 5th 1786

Phebe Knowles daughter of Elijah and Rebeca Knowles was born in Eastham June 21st 1788

marcy Knowls Daughter of Henery and Phebe Knowles was Born in Eastham the 29 Day of June 1777

abigail Knowles Daughter of Henry and Phebe Knowles was Born in Eastham the 16 Day of Febr 1779

Henry Knowles Son of Henry and Phebe Knowles was Born in Eastham 5 Day September 1780

Eastham Births
[p. 57]
William Andres Son of William & mary Andres 23 march 1776

Stephen Snow Andres Son of William & mary Andres 22 Febr 1778

Betty Snow Andrus Daughter of william & mary andrus 27 July 1780

Thomas Son of Thomas and Rebekah ary born 30 may 1780

Hannah Daughter of Thomas ary and Rebecca 7 July 1782

Joseph Son of Thomas and Rebeckah ary was born 22 may 1785

Phebe Daughter of Thomas and Rebekah ary was born 27 June 1787

Rebekah Daughter of Thomas ary and Rebekah his wife 23 July 1789

Sukah Daughter of Thos Arey & Rebecca his wife 27 August 1791

Marcy Daughter of Thos Arey & Rebecca his wife 12 October 1795

Hannah Daughter of Thomas Arey Jr & Hitty his wife was born 18 January 1803

Nehemiah the Son of David Attwood and Sabery 3 Novembr 1772

Joseph Son of David attwood and Sabery was born at Harwich 11 march 1775

Tamzy Daughter of David attwood and Sebray his Wife was Born at Harwich 17 may 1779

Lucy Arey daughter of Oliver Arey & Marcy 18 March 1769

Oliver Arey Son of Oliver Arey & Marcy 15 March 1775

Ruth Arey daughter of Oliver Arey & Marcy 15 May 1778

Eastham Births
[p. 58-I]
Gideon Son of Gideon Baty & Rachel 4 December 1770

Sally Daughter of Gideon Baty & Rachel 29 August 1768

Rachel Daughter of Gideon Baty & Rachel 21 Septr 1773

Thomas Son of Nathaniel Baty & Elizabeth 6 Novr 1765

Prince Son of Nathaniel Baty & Elizabeth 12 July 1767

Rebecca Daughter of Nathaniel Baty & Elisabeth 5 Oct 1769

Nathaniel Son of Nathaniel Baty & Elisabeth 7 Febr 1772

Eunice Horten Daughter of Nathaniel & Eunice 24 June 1776

Nathaniel Brown Horten Son of nathni & Eunice 22 June 1778

James Horten Son of Nathaniel & Eunice 29 march 1780

(To be continued)

THE
MAYFLOWER DESCENDANT

1620 2020

A QUARTERLY MAGAZINE OF
PILGRIM GENEALOGY AND HISTORY

VOLUME XXXIII

1935

PUBLISHED BY THE
MASSACHUSETTS SOCIETY OF
MAYFLOWER DESCENDANTS

BOSTON

EASTHAM AND ORLEANS, MASS., VITAL RECORDS

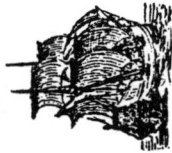

TRANSCRIBED BY THE EDITOR

(Continued from Vol. XXXII, p. 177)

[No. 6, on p. 58-1] Under "Eastham Births"

Abijah Son of Benoni Baker and Abigail 23 Februry 1784
Bennoni Son of Benoni Baker and Abigail [*] February 1786
Joshua Son of Benoni Baker and Abigail 10 June 1788
Abigail Daughter of Benoni Baker & Abigail 27 May 1790
Obadiah Son of Benoni Baker and Abigail 30 August 1792
Mary Daughter of Benoni Baker & Abigail 29 Novr 1794
Vicery Son of Benoni Baker and Abigail 22 July 1797
Dean Son of Benoni Baker and Abigail 2 July 1799
Phebe Daughter of Benoni Baker & Abigail 29 March 1801
Elsa Daughter of Benoni Baker & Abigail 29 Novem 1802
Thomas Baker Son of Benoni Baker & Abigail 14 June 1804
Mercy Sparrow Daughter of Benoni Baker & Abigail 6 January 1806
Henry Son of Benoni Baker & Abigail his wife 7 July 1808
Abiel Cole Son of Edward Cole & Phebe his wife was born in Frankfort
  County of Hancock† 18 August 1789
Dorcas Daughter of Benoni Baker & Abigail his wife was born 8
  October 1810

[p. 58-2]   Eastham Births

Temperence Daughter of William Crocker & Lydia 15 January 1763
Epheriam Son of Heman Cole and Mercy Cole 12 August 1777
Ellanor Daughter of Heman Cole and Mercy 21 Septembr 1779
Thankful Cheever Daughter of Samuel & Thankful Cheever 10 April
  1782
Samuel Cheever Son of Doc^t Samuel and Thankfull Cheever 6 Sept 1783
John Geyer Coffin son of Obadiah Coffin & Mary his wife was born
  23 April 1800
Isaiah Son of Nathan Cole & Anna his wife was born 1 July 1802
Nathan Son of Ebenezar Chase was born 17 June 1788
Lidia Cook Daughter of Joseph and Sarah Cook was borne at Eastham
  4 August 1780
Joseph Cook Son of Joseph and Sarah Cook 12 August 1782
Lettis Daughter of Abial Cole and Hannah Cole 6 Dcember 1770
Jonathan Son of Abial Cole and Hannah 24 Octobar 1774
Hannah Daughter of Abial Cole and Hannah 20 October 1777
Abial Son of Abiel Cole and Hannah Cole 23 febrery 1782
Sarah Cole Daughter of Joshua Cole and Susanna 23 August 1774

*"23" appears to have been altered to "13".—*Editor.*

†Hancock County, Maine.—*Editor.*

Nathan Cole Son of Joshua Cole and Susanna 18 June 1776
Joel Cole Son of Joshua Cole and Susanna 26 August 1779
Asa Cole Son of Joshua Cole and Susanna 15 Novembr 1781
Joshua Cole Son of Joshua and Susanah Cole was Born 26 Apriel 1784
Lidy Cole Daughter of Joshua Cole and Susannah 16 Octobr 1786
John Cole Son of Joshua Cole and Susannah 3 July 1790
Reuben Cole Son of Reuben Cole & Hannah 22 Octr 1774
Sarah Cole Daughter of Joshua Cole & Susanna 24 Novr 1793

[p. 59]
Eastham Births

Joshua Son of Joshua Doane Jr & Ruth 20 June 1772
Ruth Crocker Davis Daughter of Dr John Davis & Mercy 26 March 1770
Job Crocker Davis Son of Dr John Davis & Mercy 18 Novr 1771
Mercy Daughter of Dr John Davis & Mercy 31 Agust 1773
John Son of Dr John Davis & Mercy 29 Novr 1775
Robert Son of Doct John Davis & Mercy 4 Jany 1778
Dorcas Doane Daughter of Joel Mhetable Doane 12 Octobr 1778
Timothy Son of John & Bety Doane 13 May 1762
Heman Son of John Doane & Bety 15 March 1764
Abigal Daughter of John Doane Jr & Bety 21 March 1771
Sarah Daughter of John Doane Jr & Bety 18 Janur 1767
Bety Daughter of John Doane Jr & Bety 21 March 1769
John Son of John Doane Jr & Bety 19 April 1777
Simeon Son of John Doane Jr & Bety 31 July 1780
Hitty Davis Daughter of Dot John Davis and Mercy 13 October 1779
Beriah Son of Tymothi Doane and Jedidah 25 November 1782
Nathaniel Son of Dr John Davis and Mercy 8 Febr 1782
Keziah Doane Dafter of Azariah & Molly Doane Born at Eastham 2 Octor 1785
Joshua Doane Son of Azariah and Molly Doane was Born at Eastham 1 may 1787

[p. 60]
Heman Doane Son of Azariah and Molly Doane was Born 9 May 1789
Seth Doane Son of Azariah Doane & Molly 30 August 1791
Azariah Son of Azariah Doane and Molly 16 Octr 1794
Tamsen Daughter of Azariah Doane & Molly 27 Septr 1795
Polly daughter of Azariah Doane and Molly 27 Novr 1797
Eliza Daughter of Azariah Doane and Molly his wife 14 July 1801

Eastham Births

Joshua Emmes Son of Joshua Emmes & Hannah 18 July 1777
Freeman Knowels Son of Willaam Knowels & Rebecca Knowels was Born 27 Novem 1779
Olive Knowels dafter of Willaam Knowels & Rebaca Knowels was Born 5 Janu 1782
Tempe Knowels dafter of Willaam & Reback Knowels was Born 23 April 1784
Rebaca Knowels dafter of Willaam Knowels and Rebeca Knowels was Born 23 Octb 1786
Abigil Knowels dafter of Willaam Knowels and Rebeca Knowels was Born 9 March 1789

[p. 61]
Eastham Births

Joseph Son of Joseph Freeman & Phebe his 16 May 1751
John Son of Joseph Freeman & Phebe 3 March 1758
Josiah Son of Joseph Freeman & Phebe 24 July 1761
Nathaniel Son of Joseph Freeman & Phebe 7 April 1764
Thomas Son of Joseph Freeman & Phebe 7 Decr 1767
Mary Daughter of Joseph Freeman & Phebe 7 March 1770
James Son of Isaac Freeman & Hannah 10 April 1774
Ruth Daughter of Isaac Freeman and Hannah 6 July 1776
Dorcas Daughter of Isaac Freeman & Hannah 27 Octr 1778
Dorothy Freeman Daughter of Isaac and Hannah Freeman 20 Octbr 1780
Isaac Freeman Son of Isaac Freeman and Hannah 15 Novbr 1783
Hezekiah Freeman Son of Isaac and Hannah Freeman Born 8 March 1786
Isaac Freeman Son of William Freeman and Elezebeth Freeman was Born at Eastham 28 Febry 1789
Joseph Freeman Son of Josiah Freeman and Phebe 7 February 1787
Abigail Freeman Daughter of Josiah Freeman and Phebe 1 febry 1789
Josiah Freeman Son of Josiah Freeman and Phebe 6 June 1804
Hatsel Freeman Son of Elisha Freeman & Lydia 1805
Elisha Freeman Son of Elisha Freeman & Lydia 5 Novr 1790

[p. 62]
Eastham Births

Abigail Daughter of John Gould & Aphia 20 Oct 1770
Aphia Daughter of John Gould & Aphia 29 Oct 1772
Phebe Daughter of Joseph Gould & Hannah 15 March 1754
Thomas Son of James Gould & Rebecca His Wife Born 14 August 1793
James Son of James Gould & Rebecca His wife was Born 6 June 1795
Eliza Daughter of John Grayham & Betsey his wife was born 7 October 1808

[p. 63]
Eastham Births

Archelaus Son of John Harding & Elisabeth 31 May 1740
Nathaniel Son of John Harding & Elisabeth 5 February 1746
Joshua Son of John Harding & Elisabeth 23 April 1743
Ebenezer Son of Thomas Harding & Sarah 28 October 1750
Thomas Son of Thomas Harding & Sarah 14 March 1752
James Son of Thomas Harding & Sarah 1 Augt 1762
Gideon Son of Thomas Harding & Sarah 12 Augt 1765
Mercy Daughter of Archelaus Harding & Mercy 14 September 1770
Azubah Daughter of Archelaus Harding & Mercy 24 July 1772
Theodoar Son of Theodoar Hopkins & Hannah 1 November 1752
Mehetiable Daughter of Prince Higgins & Kezia 16 July 1768
Peggy Daughter of Prince Higgins & Kezia 25 July 1770
Kezia Daughter of Prince Higgins & Kezia 17 September 1772
Josiah Son of Joshua Harding & Hannah 12 June 1768
Joshua Son of Joshua Harding & Hannah 12 July 1770
Josiah Son of Edmund Higgins & Easther 18 Sept 1762
Darcos Daughter of Edmund Higgins & Esther 20 Sept 1765

Hannah Daughter of Edmund Higgins & Esther 15 Oct' 1767
Rachel Daughter of Edmund Higgins & Esther 15 Sep' 1770
Jonathan Son of Edmund Higgins & Esther 7 April 1773
Archelaus Son of Archelaus Harding & Mercy 17 Jan' 1774
Thomas Son of Elisha Higgins & Mary his Wife 10 No' 1773
Jerusha Daughter of Zacheus Higgins & Mercy his Wife 19 No' 1750
Mercy Daughter of Zacheus Higgins & Mercy his Wife 7 June 1752
Richard Son of Zacheus Higgins & Mercy his Wife 31 August 1754
Seth Son of Zacheus Higgins & Mercy his Wife 1 June 1756
Mary Daughter of Zacheus Higgins & Mercy his Wife 27 Feb' 1759
Zacheus Son of Zacheus Higgins & Mercy his Wife 1 April 1761
Tully Son of Zacheus Higgins & Mercy his Wife 31 August 1762
Knowles Son of Zacheus Higgins & Hannah his Wife 25 Sep' 1773
[p. 64]

                    Eastham Births

Seth Higgens Son of Nathan Higgens and Zuriah 31 July 1780
Elliot Son of Nathan Higgens and Zuriah 3 Septebr 1782
Rebekah Higgens Daughter of Nathan and Zuriah Higgens his wife was Born 4 Octobr 1785
Syrenus Son of Nathan Higgens and Zuriah his wife 10 Septembr 1787
Polly Daughter of Nathan Higgens & Zuriah 11 Novebr 1789
Mary Daughter of Abisha Higgens and Mary 27 Novembr 1778
Anna Daughter of Isack Hopkins and Elisabath born 2 July 1762
James Son of Isack Hopkins and Elisabath born 12 Nomber 1764
Warrin Son of Eliakim Higgins and Sarah Born 14 July 1786
Nathan Son of Zaccheus Higgins and Rebecca his wife 6 June 1756
Lydia Higgins Daughter of Elkenah and Elisabeth Higgins 18 Novbr 1787
Bethiah Daughter of John Higgins & Sarah his wife 15 June 1787
Hannah Mayo Daughter of John Higgins & Sarah his Wife 16 July 1789
Tabith Daughter of Solomon Higgeus and Abigail 2 Octobr 1777
Miriam Daughter of Solomon Higgens & Abigail 2 March 1782
Solomon Son of Solomon Higgens and Abigal 18 July 1784
Hiram Son of Solomon Higgens and Abigal 7 July 1786
Isaac Higgens Son of Beriah Higgens & Abigail 17 July 1784
Rachel Higgens Daughter of Beriah Higgens & Abigail 24 Septembr 1787
Jerusha Higgins Daughter of Simeon Higgins & Martha 12 Nov' 1777
Elisabeth Daughter of Richard Higgins & Rebeccah 29 July 1793
Lydia Daughter of Richard Higgins & Rebecca 21 July 1795
[p. 65]

                    Eastham Births

Freman Son of Seth Knowles & Ruth 24 November 1745
Nathaniel Son of Seth Knowles & Ruth 14 March 1750
Seth Son of Seth Knowles & Ruth 20 April 1752
Ruth Daughter of Seth Knowles & Ruth 3 August 1754
Samuel Son of Seth Knowles & Ruth 6 November 1756
Amasa Son of Seth Knowles & Ruth 15 April 1758
Abiathar Son of Seth Knowles & Ruth 5 Febuary 1760
Mary Daughter of Seth Knowles & Ruth 14 December 1762
Hannah Daughter of Seth Knowles & Ruth 4 October 1764

Cloe Daughter of Seth Knowles & Ruth 28 December 1766
Jerusha Daughter of Seth Knowles & Ruth 15 October 1768
Abner Son of Seth Knowles & Ruth 1 February 1770
John Son of Amos Knowles & Rebeckah 1 June 1749
Lydia Daughter of Amos & Abigail Knowles 22 August 1772
Exxa Daughter of Seth Knowles & Ruth 2 November 1773
Lucy Daughter of Jonathan Kenwrick & Hannah 6 Dec' 1772
William Son of David Knowles & Elisabeth 23 Jan' 1770
David Son of David Knowles & Elisabeth 10 March 1771
Margerey Daughter of David Knowles & Elisabeth 23 No' 1772
Benjamin Son of Benjamin Knowles & Mary 29 Sep' 1774
Joshua Son of John Knowles & Thankfull 29 Sept 1775
Joanna Daughter of John Knowles & Thankfull 3 Nov' 1777
Samuel Knowles Son of Sam' Knowles & Abigail 14 Jany 1774
Thomas Knowles Son of Seth and Hannah Knowles 9 August 1777
Mary Knowles Dafter of Seth Knowles and Hannah 29 November 1779
Bethiah Knowles Dafter of Seth and Hannah Born 9 august 1781
Seth Knowles Son of Seth and Hannah Born 3 January 1784
Hannah Knowles Dafter of Seth and Hannah Born 8 February 1786
Samuel Knowles Son of Abiatha Knowles and Hannah 9 April 1786
Sally Daughter of Abithar Knowles & hannah 9 March 1788
[p. 66]

                    Eastham Births

Benjamin Son of Jonathan Linnel & Precilla 3 May 1770
Heman Linnel Son of Heman Linnel and Sarah his wife 11 Sept 1775
James Linnel Son of Heman and Sarah Linne born 6 Decembr 1776
Joshua Linnel Son of Heman and Sarah Linnel born 9 Octobr 1778
Isaac Linnel Son of Heman and Sarah Linnel born 22 October 1780
Sally Linnel Daughter of Heman Linnel and Sarah was born 10 Sep' 1782
Anna Linnel Daughter of Eliasha Linnel & Phebe 24 July 1788
Phebe Daughter of Elisha Linnel & Phebe 25 Nov' 1790
Thankfull Daughter of Elisha Linnel & Phebe 1 July 1792
Polly Daughter of Elisha Linnel & Phebe 31 July 1795
Stephen Son of Elisha Linnel & Phebe born 6 July 1802
Josiah Son of Josiah Linnell & Ales Born at Eastham 14 Decm' 1780
Hitta Dafter of Josiah Linnell & Ales Born at Eastham 14 Decem' 1783
Jonathan Son of Josiah Linnell & Ales Born at Eastham 10 Novem' 1786
Sally Daughter of Elisha Linnel & Phebe in Orleans 11 May 1799
Solomon Son of Josiah Linnell & Ellice Born 22 July 1788
John Son of Josiah Linnell & Ellice Born 5 September 1790
John Lewis Son of Solomon Lewis & Elizabeth his wife 17 February 1765
Polly Linnel Daughter of Israel Linnel & Easther his wife 16 Decembr 1798
Zeruiah Linnel Daughter of Uriah Linnel and Thankful Linnel was Born at Eastham 15 Septembr 1786
Jonathan Linnel Son of Uriah Linnel was Born 16 february 1789
Uriah Linnel Son of Uriah & Thankfull Linnel 7 Janur 1791

Joshua Linnel Son of Uriah & Thankfull Linnel 8 Novr 1793
Sally Daughter of Uriah Linnel and Thankfull 19 Septemr 1795
Washington Son of Uriah Linnel & Thankfull 8 October 1797
Elijah Son of Uriah Linnell & Thankfull 30 October 1799
James Son of Uriah Linnel & Thankfull 18 August 1802
Sarah Linnell Daughter of Mary Chase was Born at Eastham 30 May 1772
Haskel son of Uriah Linnel & Thankful his wife 25 August 1805
Mercy Linnel Daughter of Edmond & Sarah 31 Octobr 1790
Rebecca Linnel Daughter of Edmond & Sarah Linnel 14 June 1792
Joseph Linnell Son of Edmond & Sarah Linnel 14 July 1794
Sarah Daughter of Edmond Linnel & Sarah Linnl 8 April 1796
Eles Daughter of Edmond Linnel & Sarah Linnel 16 November 1797
Edmond Son of Edmond Linnel & Sarah Linnel 6 August 1799
Isaac Young Son of Edmond Linnel & Sarah 26 april 1801
Mary Daughter of Edmond Linnel & Sarah 21 April 1803

[p. 67]

Eastham Births

Gideon Son of William Myrick & Hannah 14 Dec 1772
Sarah Daughter of Theophilus Mayo & Sarah 12 April 1771
Isaac Son of Sears Mayo and 6 April 1791
Eunic Daughter of Sears Mayo and 7 May 1793
Isaiah Son of Sears Mayo and 27 August 1795
Sears Son of Sears Mayo & Anna his wife was born 25 July 1797
Josiah Son of Sears Mayo & Anna his wife was born 30 June 1799
Samuel Mayo Son of Uriah Mayo & Mercy 29 August 1773
Carline Daughter of Sears Mayo 2 September 1802
Sarah Mayo Daughter of Uriah Mayo & Mercy 19 April 1776
Uriah Mayo Son of Uriah Mayo and Mercy 6 March 1779
Mercy Mayo Daughter of Uriah Mayo & Mercy 19 June 1780
Heman mayo Sone of Jonathan and Anna Mayo Born at Eastham 23 Decemb 1779
Hannah Mayo Dafter of Jonathan and Anna Mayo Born at Eastham 14 March 1781
Jonathan Mayo Son of Jonathan and Anna Mayo Born at Eastham 9 Sept 1782
Joseph Mayo Son of Jonathan and Anna Mayo Born at Eastham 1 Sept 1783
Benjamine Mayo Son of Jonathan and Anna Mayo Born at Eastham 11 May 1786
Euns and Polly Mayo Daughters of uriah and Mercy Mayo was Born at Eastham 22 June 1785
Benjamin Son of Jonathan Mayo & Anna 20 August 1789
Sarah Daughter of Jonathan Mayo and Anna 17 June 1793
Anna Daughter of Jonathan Mayo & Anna 24 May 1796
John Son of John Mulford & Ruth his wife was born 22 January 1801
Seth Son of Thomas Mayo & Mary his Wife was born 21 April 1776
Sparrow Mayo Son of Samuel & Anna Mayo was born 23 Septr 1793
Abner Son of Theoplius and Susanah Mayo was Born at Eastham 23 Novemb 1777

Simeon Son of Theoplius Mayo and Susanah was Born at Eastham 23 June 1781
Theoplius Son of Theoplius Mayo and Susanah was Born at Eastham 7 Septr 1784
Asaph Son of Theophilus Mayo & Marcy his wife was born 23 October 1790
Robert Son of Theophilus Mayo & Marcy his wife was born 17 November 1793
Susanna Daughter of Theophilus Mayo & Marcy his wife was born 29 June 1796
Samuel Son of Theophilus Mayo & Marcy his wife was born 18 March 1802

[p. 68]

Eastham Births

Nehemiah Smith Son of Nehemiah Smith and Jedida his Wife was born July 16th 1776
Anner Daughter of Nehemiah Smith & Jedida his wife was born Sepr 16 - 1778
Richard Son of Nehemiah Smith & Jedida his wife was born Sepr 19th 1780
Polly Daughter of Nehemiah Smith & Jedida his wife was born Sepr 11th 1783
Oliver Son of Nehemiah Smith & Jedida his wife was born August 16th 1789
Nabby Daughter of Nehemiah Smith & Jedida his wife was born Novemr 22th 1788
Davis Son of Nehemiah Smith & Jedida his wife was born April 16th 1791
Dean Son of Nehemiah Smith & Jedida his wife was born May 31th 1794
Simeon Son of Nehemiah Smith & Jedida his wife was born Novemr 6th 1796

[p. 69]

Eastham Births

Simeon Son of Benjamin Peper & Hannah 10 May 1772
Seth Doane Son of John Parker & Eunice 12 Oct 1771
Thomas* Knowles Son of Soloman Pepper Jur & Phebe 15 June 1773
Phebe Daughter of Soloman Pepper Jur & Phebe 25 April 1775
Elisha Son of Soloman Pepper Jur & Phebe 23 April 1777
Timothy Doane Paine Son of Joshua and Marcy Paine 22 Febr 1770
Sarah Paine Daughter of Joshua & Marcy Paine 25 May 1774
Joshua Paine Son of Joshua & Mercy Paine 27 July 1777
Samuel Paine Son of Joshua and Mercy Paine 11 June 1779
Susanna Paine Daughter of Ebenezer Paine & Sarah 26 Octobar 1789
Marcy Paine Daughter of Ebenr and Sarah Paine 7 August 1791

[p. 70]

Eastham Births

Enoch Son of Crisp Rogers & Bethiah 18 November 1759
Bethiah Daughter of Crisp Rogers & Deborah 8 August 1768
Mary Daughter of Crisp Rogers & Deborah 9 March 1770

* Apparently an attempt was made to cross out the name Thomas. — Editor.

Rebeca Daughter of Thomas Rogers Jr & Mercy 20 Nov 1773
James Son of James Rogers & Elisabeth 20 Oct 1773
Stephen Son of Thomas Rogers Jr & Mercy 24 Janr 1775
Joseph Son of Joseph & Sarah Remick 16 Augst 1779
Sarah Daughter of Joseph & Sarah Remick 25 [*] 1781
Rebekah Daughter of Thomas Rogers & Mercy 20 March 1781
Josiah Son of Jonathan Rogers & Hannah Born at Eastham 15 Febuary 1777
Jonathan Son of Jonathan Rogers & Hannah Born at Eastham 1 July 1781
Hannah Dafter of Jonathan Rogers & Hannah Born at Eastham 8 August 1783
Salley Dafter of Jonathan Rogers & Hannah Born at Eastham 14 Novb 1785

(To be continued)

*The day of the month was omitted.

†Elizabeth (Gray) Arnold was the third daughter of Edward Gray of Plymouth, by his first wife, Mary Winslow³ (*Mary² Chilton, James¹*). Edward Gray, the grantee in this deed, was a half brother of Elizabeth (Gray) Arnold. His mother was Dorothy Lettice. — *Editor.*

‡Little Compton was in Massachusetts until 1747.

Zedekiah Snow Son of Princ Snow and Reliance 10 Decem 1778
Joseph Crocker Son of Doane Snow & Aphiah 8 June 1772
Phebe Daughter of Edward Smith & Grace 25 Sept 1771
Samuel Son of Edward Smith & Grace 20 June 1772
Elizabeth Daughter of Edward Smith & Grace 20 Sept 1773
Lucy Daughter of Isaac Smith and Elizabeth 12 June 1769
Prince Son of Isaac Smith and Elisabeth 2 Janr 1773
James Knowles Snow Son of Sparrow and Lucy 13 Decbr 1776
Cloe Daughter of John and Bashaba Smith 12 Janur 1764
Hulda Baughter of John and Bashaba 30 Octobr 1765
Phebe Daughter John and Bashaba 11 Janur 1768
John Son of John and Bashaba 17 May 1770
Samuel King Son of John and Bashaba 1 August 1771
Zerviah Daughter of John and Bashaba 1 March 1774
Silvenus Son of John and Bashaba 12 Febr 1777
Bety Daughter of John and Bashaba 17 april 1779
Asa Smith Son of John Smith & Bashaba his wife was born 11 april 1785
Anne Daughter of Isaac Sparrow Ju & Mary 10 July 1774
Mary Daughter of Richard Sparrow and Elizebith 21 August 1772
Elisebith Daughter of Richard Sparrow and Elizebith 3 Sept 1774
Isaac Sparrow Son of Richard Sparrow and Elzebeth 27 Sept 1776
Rebekah Daughter of Richard Sparrow and Elezebith 25 April 1779
Tabitha Daughter of Richard Sparrow and Elezibeth 18 may 1787
John Sparrow Son of Thomas and Ester Sparrow Born 16 July 1769
Seth Sparrow Son of Thomas and Ester Sparrow Born 5 July 1771
Doan Son of Doane Snow & Aphiah Born at Eastham 16 January 1774
Charls Lee Son of Doane Snow & Aphiah Born at Eastham 26 march 1777
Apphia Dafter of Doane Snow & Aphiah Born at Eastham 7 January 1779
Simon Son of Doane Snow & Aphiah Born at Eastham 17 Septem 1780
Isaac Freeman Son of Doane Snow & Aphiah Born at Eastham Son of Doane Snow & Aphiah Born at Eastham 7 Decemr 1782
Sulliven Son of Doane Snow & Aphiah Born at Eastham 12 August 1785

[p. 72]
Eastham Births
Stephen Son of Thos Twining & Anna 28 Sept 1767
William Son of Thos Twining & Anna 14 Dec 1769
Alice Daughter of Thos Twining & Anna 6 Febr 1772
Lyda Daughter of John Tayler and Anna Born at Eastham 22 June 1785
Isaac Son of John Taylor & Anna Born at Eastham 11 febuary 1787
Davis Son of John Taylor and Anna Born at Eastham 6 October 1788
Anna Daughter of John Taylor and Anna was Born 23 August 1790

EASTHAM AND ORLEANS, MASS., VITAL RECORDS

(Continued from page 18)

[On page 70] Thomas Son of Prince and Susanah Rogers Born at Eastham 27 January 1784
Abiail Dafter of Prince and Susanah Rogers Born at Eastham 24 Decr 1785
Timothy Son of Jonathan Rogers and Hannah 27 february 1788
Marcy Daughter of Thomas Rogers & Sarah his Wife 4 August 1801
Lurana Daughter of Thomas Rogers & Sarah his wife was born in Orleans 4 July 1803
Susanna Daughter of Judah Rogers and Rebecca 24 July 1779
Tempe Daughter of Judah Rogers and Rebecca 13 April 1781
Joseph Lothrop Son of Judah Rogers & Rebecca 23 Febr 1783
Deborah Daughter of Judah Rogers and Rebecca 25 June 1785
Judah Son of Judah Rogers and Rebecca 12 August 1787
Adnah Son of Judah Rogers and Rebecca 19 April 1789
Josiah Son of Judah Rogers and Rebecca 16 July 1791
Alven Son of Judah Rogers and Rebecca 12 April 1793
Isaac Son of Judah Rogers and Rebecca 27 July 1796
Isaac Son of Thomas Rogers and Sarah his Wife 11 June 1806
Joseph & Benjamin Sons of Henry Rogers & Deborah his wife 2 Novm 1777
Thomas son of Thomas Rogers & Sarah his wife 18 May 1808
Nabby Daughter of Samuel Rogers & Deborah his 23 July 1780
Allen Rogers Son of Samuel Rogers & Anna his wife was born at Ellitors* 21 Fbry 1786
Sullivan Rogers Son of Daniel Rogers & Abigail his wife 20 Decm 1796

[p. 71]
Eastham Births
Mercy Daughter of Joseph Smith & Ruth 17 May 1759
Temperance Daughter of Joseph Smith & Ruth 1 June 1762
Ruth Daughter of Joseph Smith & Ruth 1 September 1764
Knowles Son of Joseph Smith & Ruth 11 April 1767
Dean Son of Joseph Smith and Ruth 20 January 1769
Lydia Daughter of Joseph Smith & Ruth 3 April 1771
Elisabeth Daughter of Isaac Sparrow & Rebecca 12 Augt 1764

* So recorded.— Editor.

Eunice Daughter of John Taylor and Anna 10 May 1792
John Taylor Son of John Taylor and Anna 4 July 1794
Sally Daughter of John Taylor and Anna his wife 29 August 1796
James Son of John Taylor and Anna was born in Orleans 19 August 1798
Joseph Son of John Taylor & Anna was born in Sepr 6 Septerbr 1800
Waters and Richard Sons of John Taylor & Anna was born in 30 May 1803
Phebe Daughter of Benjamin Taylor and Eunice 1 October 1777
Joseph Son of Benja Taylor and Eunice 29 July 1779
Ruth Daughter of Benja Taylor and Eunice 5 August 1781
Benjamin Son of Benja Taylor and Eunice 2 February 1784
Abigail Daughter of Benja Taylor and Eunice 14 June 1786
Jonathan Son of Benja Taylor and Eunice 27 July 1788
Edward Son of Benja Taylor and Eunice 8 October 1790
Simeon Son of Benja Taylor and Eunice 26 Septembr 1791
Zoheth Son of Benja Taylor and Eunice 12 March 1794
Richard Son of Benja Taylor & Eunice 14 Sept 1796
Abigail daughter of Benja Taylor & Eunice 25 Novr 1799
Benjamin Son of Benja Taylor & Eunice 2 June 1802
Mehitable Daughter of David Taylor and Hannah 17 August 1788
Joshua Son of David Taylor and Hannah 27 March 1790
Polly Daughter of David Taylor and Hannah 19 Octr 1793
Hannah Daughter of David Taylor and Hannah 12 Novr 1794
Amasa Son of David Taylor and Hannah his wife 23 Febr 1796
David Son of David Taylor & Hannah was born in Orleans 22 Jany 1798
Almena Daughter David Taylor and Hannah was born 9 Novr 1802
Banges Son of David Taylor and Hannah his wife 28 Novr 1804
[p. 73]
Eastham Births
Thomas Son of Benja Linnel and Deborah 27 July 1788
Benjamin Son of Benja Linnel & Deborah 14 May 1790
Deborah Daughter of Benja Linnel & Deborah 30 Sept 1792
Russil Son of Benjamin Linnel & Deborah 19 Decemr 1794
Heman Son of Benja Linnel & Deborah 13 July 1797
Prissia Daughter of Benja Linnel & Deborah 5 Novem 1799
Cuca* Daughter of Benja Linnel & Deborah 19 Fbruay 1802
Rebecca Daughter of Benja Linnel & Deborah 5 October 1804
Thankful Cole Linnell Daughter of Benjamin Linnel and Deborah his wife 24 June 1807
Catherine Linnel Daughter of Benjamin Linnel & Deborah his wife born 14 August 1809
Meriah Daughter of Benjamin Linnell and Deborah his wife was born June 30th 1813
[p. 74]
Eastham Births
Anna Daughter of Philip Young & Anna 4 September 1772

*?Sukey.—Editor.

Jenet Daughter of Ebenezer Young & Elizabeth 19 Oct 1755
Jediah Son of Ebenezer Young & Elizabeth 25 Oct 1757
Abigail Daughter of Ebenezer Young & Elizabeth 29 Oct 1759
Joseph Son of Ebenezer Young & Elisabeth 6 June 1765
Ebenezer Son of Ebenezer Young & Elizabeth 6 Sept 1767
Elizabeth Daughter of Ebenezer Young & Elizabeth 5 May 1770
Rebecca Daughter of Ebenezer Young & Elizabeth 24 July 1772
Easther Daughter of Ebenezer Young & Elizabeth 4 Sept 1774
Abigail Daughter of Nehemiah Young & Abigail 29 Decr 1772
Jonathan Son of Nehemiah Young & Abigail 3 Novr 1774
Linda Daughter of Nehemiah Young & Abigail 18 Sept 1776
Lucy Daughter of Nehemiah Young & Abigail 22 Novr 1777
Zeanous Son of Ebenezer Young & Elisabeth 18 Sept 1777
Molley Daughter of Jedediah Young & Phebe 1 August 1784
Abigail Daughter of Jedediah Young & Phebe 26 May 1786
Zenas Son of Jedediah Young and Phebe 29 April 1788
Phebe Daughter of Jedediah Young and Phebe 5 May 1790
Rebecca Daughter of Jedediah Young & Phebe 11 August 1791
Jedediah Son of Jedediah Young and Phebe 30 Septr 1793
Betsy Daughter of Moses Young and Rachel 6 August 1788
Phebe Daughter of Moses Young and Rachel 19 Novr 1792
Dorcas Daughter of Jedediah Young & Phebe 24 March 1795
Joanna Daughter of Moses Young & Rachel 26 July 1797
Moses Young Son of Moses young born 27 Octobr 1804
Ebenzar Son of Jedediah Young and Phebe his wife Was Born 27 April 1797
Joshua Son of Moses Young & Rachel his wife was 24 october 1781
Rachel Young Daughter of Josiah Young & Rachel Born 21 July 1799
Icy Daughter of Jedediah Young and Phebe his wife Was Born 23 Janary 1799
Lewis Son of Edmund Young and Mary his wife Was born 7 January 1773
Josiah Son of Jedediah young & Phebe his wife Was born 26 October 1801
Elkanah Young Son of Elkanah Young & Mary 16 Decemr 1775
Josiah Son of Jedidiah Young & Phebe his wife 19 Febury 1804
Dorcas Daughter of Jedediah Young & Phebe his Wife 14 May 1807
[p. 75]
Eastham Births
Daniel Son of Daniel Hammilton & Hannah 16 May 1769
Theodorus Son of Daniel Hammilton & Hannah 4 Oct 1772
Richard Son of Daniel Hammilton & Hannah 22 Oct 1774
Joseph Uriah & Hanah 2 Sons & a Daughter of Daniel Hamilton & Hanah 3 at a birth 12 June 1778
Abner Son of Sylvanus Higgins and Abigail 25 July 1766
Abigail Daughter of Sylvanus Higgins and Abigail 18 April 1768
Mercy Higgins Daughter of Sylvanus Higgins & Abigail 18 March 1770
Ruth Higgins Daughter of Silvanus Higgins & Abigail 18 Febr 1772

Thatcher Son of Edmund Snow & Mary His Wife was Born 2 October 1793

Susannah Daughter of Edmund Snow & Mary His wife was Born 7 Novemr 1795

Isaiah Son of Prince Snow & Reliance his wife was born 7 June 1786

Tamzin Daughter of Aaron Snow & Abigail his wife born 16 June 1808

Sirvila Daughter of Isaac Snow & Hannah his wife Born 26 August 1807

Thankful Daughter of Isaac Snow & Hannah 1 May 1787

Isaac Son of Isaac Snow and Hannah 6 Augt 1789

Ruth Daughter of Isaac Snow and Hannah 26 Janur 1792

Thomas Son of Aaron Snow and Abigail 7 April 1788

Abner Son of Aaron Snow and Abigail 1 August 1791

Hannah Daughter of Isaac Snow & Hannah his wife was born 27 Sept 1794

Dorcas Daughter of Isaac Snow & Hannah his wife was born 29 June 1797

Jonathan Son of Isaac Snow & Hannah his wife was born 13 August 1799

Russel Son of Isaac Snow & Hannah his wife was born 1 August 1802

Elisha son of Isaac Snow & Hannah his wife was born Oct 1st 1804

Aaron Son of Aaron snow & abigail his wife was born 10 March 1793

Phebe Daughter of Aaron Snow & abigail his wife was born 3 october 1796

Abigail Daughter of Aaron Snow & Abigail his wife was born 29 August 1798

Silvanus Son of Aaron Snow & abigail his wife was born 17 Sepr 1800

Elnathan Son of Aaron Snow & abigail his wife was born 2 July 1806

[p. 77]   Eastham Births

Thomas Hopkins Son of Joshua Hopkins & Ruth 10 octobar 1774

Rachel hopkins Daughter of Joshua Hopkins and Ruth 6 Septembr 1776

Phebe hopkins Daughter of Joshua hopkin and Ruth 19 Septembr 1779

John hopkins Son of Joshua Joshua hopkins and Ruth 13 July 1782

Mercy hopkins Daughter of Joshua hopkins and Ruth 10 July 1784

Joshua hopkins Son of Joshua hopkins and Ruth 3 January 1787

Giles Hopkins Son of Joshua Hopkins & Ruth 25 February 1791

Asa Son of Asa Higgins and Lucia his wife 19 Octr 1792

Knowles Son of Asa Higgins and Lucia 11 Novr 1794

Simeon Son of Asa Higgins and Lucia 24 July 1796

Lucy daughter of Asa Higgins and Lucy 6 April 1798

George Washington Son of Asa Higgins and Lucy his wife was born 29 June 1800

Joseph Higgins Son of Sylvanus Higgins & Abigail 18 march 1774

Tamsin Daughter of Sylvanus Higgins & Abigail 7 Febr 1776

Sylvanus Higgins Son of Sylvanus Higgins & Abigail 9 April 1778

John Hopkins Son of John and Prisilla Hopkins 15 March 1777

Lydia Hopkins Daughter of John & Prissilla Hopkins 17 Aril 1779

Samuel Hickman Son of James Experance Hickman 4 July 1776

Marcy Hickman Daughter of James and Experance 28 Decbr 1777

John Hickman Son of James and Experance 24 Novbr 1779

Thankful Hopkins Daughter of John Hopkins & Azuba 26 January 1778

Sarah dafter of Hezekiaa and Anna Higgins born at Eastham 10 November 1775

Saloma Dafter of Silvanus and Abigail Higgins born 18 March 1779

Silvanus Son of Silvanus and Abigail Higgins born 19 Sept 1783

Mary Daughter of James & Experance Hickman was Born 26 June 1786

Asa son of Elkanah Hopkins and Temperance 21 October 1786

Freeman son of Elkanah Hopkins and Temparence 24 Novembr 1787

Bangs son of Elkanah Hopkins and Temperence 7 April 1789

Elisha Son of Elkanah Hopkins and Temperence 14 January 1791

Elkanah Son of Elkanah Hopkins and Temperance 17 May 1792

Tempe Daughter of Elkanah Hopkins and Temperance 13 Sept 1794

Elisabeth Daughter of Elkanah Hopkins & Temperance 14 April 1796

Isaac Son of Elkanah Hopkins and Temperance 25 Decemr 1798

Davis Son of Elkanah Hopkins and Temperance 25 March 1801

Leonard Son of Elkanah Hopkins & Temperance 19 January 1803

[p. 76] Henan Son of Daived and Mary Snow was born 29 Sept 1766

Lusey Dafter of Daived and Mary Snow was born 5 Decm 1767

Daived Son of Daived and Mary Snow was born 19 Decm 1770

Mary Dafter of Daived and Mary Snow was born 5 Novr 1771

Josiah Son of Daived and mary Snow was Born 11 Octob 1773

Tamson Dafter of Daived and Mary Snow was Born 19 June 1775

Lydia Daughter of David Snow Born 25 Novmr 1803

Johnson Son of Ryal and Betty Snow was Born 24 July 1784

Nancy Dill Born in Eastham D Snows wife Daughter 2 June 1799

Ryal Son of Ryal and Betty Snow was Born 18 June 1786

Lucy Sparrow Daughter of Richard Sparrow & Elizabeth his Wife was born 27 June 1783

Richard Sparrow Son of Richard Sparrow & Elisebeth 31 august 1785

Joshua Knowles Sparrow Son of Richard Sparrow and Elisebeth 21 august 1787

Jesse Sparrow Son of Richard Sparrow & Elisibeth 13 octobr 1790

David Sears Son of David Sears & Martha 25 Decemr 1777

Edmond Snow Son of Edmond Snow and mary 19 Sept 1785

Joel Snow Son of Edmond Snow and mary 17 march 1788

Jesse Son of Edmund Snow and Mary His Wife was Born 15 June 1791

Horten Son of Asa Higgins and Lucy his wife was born 23 august 1806

Selina daughter of Seth Higgins & Martha 14 June 1773

Rebeckah daughter of Seth Higgins & Martha 21 Decemʳ 1774

Seth Son of Seth Higgins & Martha 28 August 1776

Thankfull Daughter of Seth Higgins & Martha 28 Decemʳ 1779

Martha Daughter of Seth Higgins & Martha 31 Decemʳ 1781

Elisabeth Daughter of Seth Higgins & Martha 14 Januaʳ 1785

Elisha Son of Seth Higgins & Martha 14 Novemʳ 1787

Mary Daughter of Seth Higgins & Martha 2 April 1790

Abisha Son of Seth Higgins & Martha 8 August 1793

William Son of Theophilus Hopkins & Tabatha 2 Fbruary 1766

[p. 78]   Eastham Berths

Isaac Knowles Son of abiatha Knowles and Hannah his Wife 22 may 1790

Seth Kenwrick Son of Jonathan Kenwrick & Hannah 17 August 177;

Rebecca Daughter of Simeon Kingman & Rebecca his wife was born in Bridgwater 24 March 1780

Freeman Son of Simeon Kingman and Rebecca his wife was born at Bridgwater 4 Septʳ 1781

Polly Daughter of Simeon Kingman and Rebecca his wife was born at Plymouth 14 August 1783

Patty Daughter of Simeon Kingman and Rebecca his wife was born at Bridgwater 1st Janʳʸ 1786

Matthew Son of Simeon Kingman and Rebecca his wife was born at Eastham 22 July 1789

Rebecca Daughter of Simeon Kingman and Rebecca his wife born at Eastham 11 Octʳ 1791

[p. 79] Joel Doane Son of Uriah Doane & Lydia his wife was born at Eastham December the 8th AD. 1785

Ebenezer Doane Son of Uriah & Lydia his wife was born at Eastham August the 3d AD 1787

Ruth Doane Daughter of Uriah & Lydia his wife was born at Eastham August the 31st AD 1789

Cynthia Doane Daughter of Uriah & Lydia his wife was born at Eastham Septʳ the 6th 1791

Elkanah Doane Son of Uriah and Lydia his wife was born at Eastham May the AD 1793

Beriah Son of Timothy Doane & Jedida was born Novʳ 25th 1782

Abigail daughter of Timothy Doane & Jedida was born March 5th 1784

Hitta daughter of Timothy Doane & Jedida was born Novʳ 15: 1785;

Lewis Son of Timothy Doane and Jedida was born Septʳ 24: 1787

Timothy Son of Timothy Doane and Jedida was born June 2nd 1789;

John Son of Timothy Doane and Jedida was born May 28th 1791

Sally daughter of Timothy Doane and Jedida was born Octʳ 9th 1794

Betty daughter of Timothy Doane & Jedida was born Novʳ 6th 1796

Born in the town of Orleans

Nancy daughter of Timothy Doane & Jedida was born Febr 19: 1799

Isaac Son of Timothy Doane & Jedidah was born June 4th 1804

[p. 80] Ichabod Higgins and Elisabeth Young both of Eastham were married by the Revd Mr Bascom Novbr 4th 1784 Recorded Elijah Knowles Town Clerk

Polly Higgins daughter of Ichabod and Elisabeth Higgins was born in Eastham August 27th 1785

Solomon Higgins Son of Ichabod and Elisabeth Higgins was born in Eastham April 25th 1788

Betsey Higgins daughter of Ichabod and Elisabeth Higgins was born in Eastham July 27th 1789

Lucy Higgins daughter of Ichabod and Elisabeth was born in Eastham December 25th 1790

Samuel Smith Son of Joseph Smith 3d and Mary Smith was born in Eastham August 2d 1766

Joseph Smith son of Joseph and Mary Smith was born in Eastham April 13th 1768

Josiah Smith son of Joseph 3d and Mary Smith was born in Eastham May 27th 1770

Abraham Smith son of Joseph Smith the 3d and Mary Smith was born in Eastham october 17th 1772

Polly Smith daughter of Joseph 3d and Mary Smith was born in Eastham March 16th 1774

[p. 81] Bangs Knowles Son of Simon* and Priscilla Knowles was born in Eastham March 9th 1789

Simeon Knowles Jr Son of Simeon Knowles and Priscilla was born in Eastham June 20th 1791

Chapman Seabury Son of Dct Joseph Seabury & Rebecca his Wife was born March 4th 1799

Deborah Seabury daughter of Doct Joseph and Rebecca Seabery was born in Harwich December 7th AD 1782

Benjamin Seabery Son of Joseph and Rebecca Seabery was in Eastham May 20th 1784

Joseph Seabery Junʳ Son of Joseph and Rebecca Seabery was born in Eastham March 4th 1786

Isaac Seabery Son of Joseph and Rebecca Seabery was born in Eastham March 8th 1788

John Seabery Son of Joseph and Rebecca Seabery was born in Eastham February 4th 1790

Nathan Seabury Son of Joseph and Rebecca Seabery was born in Eastham June 18th 1791

Tempa Seabury Daughter of Joseph and Rebecca Seabury was born in Eastham January the 20th 1793

George Son of Joseph Seabury and Rebecca his wife was born January the 4th 1795

*An error for "Simeon". "Simeon Knowels & prisilah Doane" married 1 January, 1788. "Marriages 1764-1844", p. 16.—*Editor*.

Salla Daughter of Joseph Seabury & Rebecca his wife was born December the 24th 1796

[p. 82] Nathaniel Lewis Cole Son of Jesse Cole and Tabitha was born in Eastham September 30th 1792

Sintha Daughter of Uriah Mayo & Bethiah his Wife was born November 4th 1792

Thomas Son of Uriah Mayo & Bethiah his wife was born April 7th 1794

Marcy Daughter of Uriah Mayo & Bethiah his wife was born February 22th 1797

Bethiah Daughter of Uriah Mayo & Bethiah his wife was born July 1th 1798

Joseph Son of Uriah Mayo & Bethiah his wife was born March 25th 1801

Elisha Son of Uriah Mayo & Bethiah his wife was born Novr 12th 1803

Benjamin Dill Son of Benjamin and Huldah Dill was born in Eastham Septembr 22d 1790

Phebe Dill daughter of Benjamin and Huldah Dill born in Eastham June 30th 1792

William Son of William Jackson & Mary his wife was born in Febrey Eastham in the year 1788

[p. 83] Joseph Hall and Abigail Young both of Eastham were Married by the Revr Mr Bascom May the 17th 1792

Joseph Hall Son of Joseph Hall and Abigail his wife was born at Eastham March 28th 1793

Edward Jarvis and Sarah Freeman both of Eastham were Married by the Revr Mr Bascom February the 15th 1780

Thankful Daughter of Edward Jarvis and Sarah his wife was born at Eastham September the 29 . 1782

Timothy Son of Edward Jarvis and Sarah his wife was born at Eastham June 9th 1784

John Son of Edward Jarvis and Sarah his wife was born in Eastham Sept the 12th 1786

Anna Daughter of Edward Jarvis and Sarah his wife was born at Eastham February the 4th 1788

Nabby Daughter of Edward Jarvis and Sarah his wife was born at Eastham October the 17th 1791

Sarah Daughter of Edward Jarvis & Sarah his wife was born July 24th 1793

Phebe Daughter of Edward Jarvis & Sarah his wife was born June 10th 1796

Polly Daughter of Edward Jarvis & Sarah his wife was born April the 22th 1799

Silvia Daughter of Edward Jarvis & Sarah his Wife was born in Orleans June 29th 1801

[p. 84] Nathaniel Paine and Azuba Higgins both of Eastham were Married by the Revr Mr Bascom Nov. 18th 1790

John Martin & Rachel Cohoon both of Eastham were Married by the Revr Mr Bascom Febr the 10th 1791

Abner H Son of Seth Sparrow and Mercy his wife was born in Orleans June the 16th AD. 1799

Seth Son of Seth Sparrow and Mercy his wife was born in Orleans July 29th 1801

Knowles son of Seth Sparrow and Mercy his wife was born in Orleans July 23th 1803

Olive Daughter of Seth Sparrow & Mercy his Wife was born in Orleans October 9th 1806

Joseph Son of Seth Sparrow & Mercy his wife was born July 9th 1809

Olive Daughter of Seth Sparrow & Marcy his wife was born Febry 2th 1812

[p. 85] Moses Higgins Jur & Hannah Rogers both of Eastham were Marred by the Revr Mr Bascom Sept 29th 1791

Polly Daughter of Moses Higgins & Hannah his wife was born February August the 23rd 1793

Jabez Son of Moses Higgins & Hannah his wife was born February the 28th 1796

Moses Son of Moses Higgins & Hannah his wife was born in Orleans December the 14th 1797

Benjamin Son of Moses Higgins & Hannah his wife was born in orleans March 26: 1800

Charlotte Daughter of Moses Higgins & Hannah his wife was born in Orleans August 4th 1802

Hannah Daughter of Moses Higgins & Hannah his wife was born Novm 4th 1804

Marcy Daughter of Moses Higgins & Hannah his wife was born Decmr 17 1806

Almira Daughter of Moses Higgins & Hannah his wife was born Sepr 3th 1808

Nathan Sparrow Son of Moses Higgins & Hannah his wife was born January 26—1812

Barnabas Smith & Hannah Knowles both of Eastham were Married by the Revr Mr Bascom Novr 15th 1791

Jesse Smith and Abigail Knowles were married by the Revr Mr Bascom Jesse Son of Jesse Smith and Abigail his wife was born Orleans November the Seventh 1797

Sarah Sparrow and Susannah Snow Daughters of Moses Higgins and Hannah his wife was born April 16th 1814

Charlotte Daughter of Moses Higgins and Hannah his wife was born august 23rd 1817

(To be continued)

EASTHAM AND ORLEANS, MASS., VITAL RECORDS

(Continued from page 89)

[p. 86] Prince Rogers & Mary Sparrow both of Eastham were Married by the Revr Mr Bascom April the 3d 1792

Sears Son of Joshua Rogers Jur and Debby his wife was born August 30: 1796

Freeman Son of Joshua Rogers & Debby was born in Orleans Oct 13: 1798

Blossom son of Joshua Rogers & Debby his wife was born Sept 18:: 1800

Polly Y. daughter of Joshua Rogers & Debby was born Aug 17th 1802

Joshua son of Joshua Rogers & Debby was born June 6th 1804

Isaiah Y. son of Joshua Rogers & Debby was born Aug 25th 1810

Deborah daughter of Joshua Rogers & Debby was born April 2d 181:;

Marshall son of Joshua Rogers & Debby was born Jany 27 1815

Benjamin Hurd and Phebe Gould both of Eastham were Married by the Revr Mr Bascom Octr the 4th 1792

Solomon Son of Benjamin Hurd and Phebe his wife was born Decmr 21th 1793

Johanna Daughter of Benjamin Hurd & Phebe his wife was born June 28th 1797

Gould Son of Benjamin Hurd & Phebe his wife was born may 28:: 1799

Phebe Daughter of Benjamin Hurd & Phebe his wife was born Octour 17th 1802

Joseph & Benjamin Sons of Benja Hurd & Phebe his wife was born Janu 22th 1801

Phebe Hurd Daughter of Benjamin Hurd & Phebe his wife was born October 14th 1804

Benjamin Hurd Son of Benjamin Hurd and Phebe his wife was born Sepr 27th 1806

Rutha gould Daughter of Benjamin Hurd & Phebe his wife was born Februy 20th 1809

Joseph Hurd Son of Benjamin Hurd and Phebe his wife was born December 22 1810

Eunice Daughter of Benjamin Hurd and Phebe his wife was born March 6th 1804

[p. 87] Michael Shearman & Lydia Higgins were married by Mr Bascom

Samuel Son of Michael Shearman & Lydia his wife was born March the 12th 1789

Richard Son of Michael Shearman and Lydia his wife was born June the 24th 1791

Marcy daughter of Michael Shearman and Lydia his wife was born February the 24 1795

Jonathan Son of Micah Sherman & Lydia his wife was born March 29th 1798

Debby Daughter of Micah Sherman & Lydia his wife was born Decmr august 29: 1802

Micah Son of Micah Sherman & Lydia his wife was born Decmr 29: 1804

Sally Daughter of Benjamin Hatch and Priscilla his wife born Nov 2nd 1818

Sukey Daughter of Benjamin Hatch and Priscilla born Feb 11th 1821

[p. 88] Zenas Rogers and Sally Mayo were married by the Revrd Mr Bascom December the 18th 1794

Charlotte Daughter of Zenas Rogers & Sally his wife was born in Orleans August the 20th 1797

Seth Son of Zenas Rogers & Sally his wife was born in Orleans July the 31: AD 1799

Zoar Son of Zenaus Rogers and Sally his wife was born January 10th 1801

Arozina Daughter of Israel Rogers & Eunice his Wife was born Novemr 7th 1804

Susannah Daughter of Israel Rogers & Eunice his wife was born Novemr 17th 1806

Israel Rogers son of Israel Rogers & Eunice his wife was born in orleans November 20th 1809

Stephen Snow son of Israel Rogers & Eunice his wife was born August 29th 1812

Eunice Snow Daughter of Israel Rogers and Eunice his wife was born July 28th 1814

Prince son of Israel Rogers and Eunice his wife born October 25 1816

Franklin son of Israel Rogers and Eunice his wife born January 24 1819

George Gould son of Israel Rogers & Eunice his wife born November 30 1823

Viana Daughter of Israel Rogers & Eunice his wife born June 28 1825

[p. 89] Elisabeth Daughter of James Rogers Jur & Lydia his wife was born in Orleans January the 4 1798

Viana Daughter of James Rogers Jur & Lydia his wife was born Novemr 3th 1800

Lydia Daughter of James Rogers Jur & Lydia his Wife was born in Orleans Febuary 21th 1803

Ruth Daughter of James Rogers Jur & Lydia his Wife was born January 17th 1805

Davis Son of James Rogers Jr & Lydia his wife born March 15th 1807

Ruth Daughter of James Rogers & Lydia his wife born August 12th 1810

Azahel Son of James Rogers & Lydia his wife born July 18th 1812

Hannah Daughter of James Rogers and Lydia his wife was born April 21 1815

Lucy Twining Daughter of James Rogers and Lydia his wife was born March 11 1816

James Son of James Rogers and Lydia his wife born March 12 1818

[p. 90] Betsy Daughter of Richard Rogers & Roxsana his Wife was Born May 8th 1784 in Eastham

Roxsana Daughter of Richard Rogers & Roxsana his Wife was Born December 26: 1786 in Eastham

Patty Daughter of Richard Rogers & Roxsana his Wife was Born June 6th 1790 in Eastham

Nancy Daughter of Richard Rogers & Roxsana his Wife was Born September 23th 1792 in Eastham

Alvah Rogers Son of Richard Rogers & Roxsana his wife was Born august 25th 1799 in orleans

Isaiah Cole Son of Nathan Cole and Anna his wife was born July 1st 1801

[p. 91] Jesse Cole was born Febr 11th 1755

Bethiah his Wife was born September 21 1752

Bethiah Daughter of Jesse Cole & Bethiah his Wife was born May 30th 1773

Joseph Son of Jesse Cole & Bethiah his wife was born March 13th 1776

Sarah Daughter of Jesse Cole & Bethiah his Wife was born April 16th 1778

Jesse Son of Jesse Cole & Bethiah his Wife was born April 25th 1781

Elisha Son of Jesse Cole & Bethiah his Wife was born June 4th 1784

Elizabeth Daughter of Jesse Cole & Bethiah his wife was born March 20th 1787

Benjamin Son of Jesse Cole & Bethiah his Wife was born Febr 21th 1792

Warner Eldredge son of Zachariah Small and Maribe his wife was born June 9th 1819

[p. 92] Barshua Daughter of Stephen Cole & Bethiah his wife was Born October 5th 1797

Jedidah Daughter of Stephen Cole & Bethiah his Wife was Born December 25th 1798

Timothy Son of Stephen Cole & Bethiah his Wife was Born August 6th 1800

Daniel Cole Son of Stephen Cole & Bethiah his wife was born Sep 5th 1804

Mary Daughter of Stephen Cole & Bethiah his wife was born August 4th 1806

Eunice Nickerson Daughter of Stephen Cole & Bethiah his wife was born June 28th 1809

Edwin Son of Taylor Smith and Betsy his wife was born October 9th 1816

Taylor Son of Taylor Smith and Betsy his wife was born October 1st 1818

[p. 93] Olive Daughter of Moses Snow & Huldah his Wife was Born Feby 20. 1790

Patty Daughter of Moses Snow & Huldah his Wife was Born November 19th 1792

Levina Daughter of Moses Snow & Huldah his Wife was Born March 2th 1795

Mary Daughter of Moses Snow & Huldah his Wife was Born November 14th 1796

Moses Son of Moses Snow & Huldah his Wife was Born August 12th 1798

Simeon Son of Moses Snow & Huldah his Wife was Born October 1st 1800

Francis Son of Moses Snow & Huldah his wife was born Sepr 3th 1803

Sparrow Son of Moses Snow & Huldah his Wife was born Novr 13th 1805

Emery Son of Moses Snow & Huldah his wife was born October 10th 1808

Giles Son of Moses Snow & Huldah his wife was born June 29th 1810

Loren Son of Moses Snow & Huldah his wife was born May 23th 1813

[p. 94] Jonathan Son of Stephen Snow & Martha his Wife was born in Eastham June 24th 1779

Rachel Daughter of Stephen Snow & Martha his Wife was Born in Eastham March 21th 1781

Eunice Daughter of Stephen Snow & Martha his wife was born Eastham January 28th 1783

Lettice Daughter of Stephen Snow & Martha his wife was born in Eastham Febr 23th 1785

Stephen Son of Stephen Snow & Martha his wife was born in Eastham January 1th 1787

Dean Smith Son of Stephen Snow & Martha his wife was born in Eastham November 5th 1788

Luther Son of Stephen Snow & Martha his wife was born in Eastham August 23th 1790

Marcy Daughter of Stephen Snow & Martha his wife was born in Eastham May 11th 1792

Priscilla and Anne Daughter of Stephen Snow & Martha his wife was born in Eastham May 7th 1795

David Son of Stephen Snow & Martha his wife was born in Orleans Janur 19th 1797

EASTHAM AND ORLEANS, MASS., VITAL RECORDS

(Continued from page 136)

[No. 6, p. 97] Thomas Son of Thomas Hopkins & Hannah his Wife was Born March 12th 1798

Ruth Daughter of Thomas Hopkins & Hannah his wife was born Sepr 24th 1802

Eunice Daughter of Thomas Hopkins & Hannah his wife was born Decmbr 24th 1806

Solomon Son of Thomas Hopkins & Hannah his wife was born Decmr 30 1807

Catherine Daughter of Jonathan Freeman & Eunice his wife was born July 31th 1805

Meris Son of Jonathan Freeman & Eunice his wife was born April 29th 1807

Eunice Daughter of Jonathan Freeman & Eunice his wife was born March 9th 1812

Polly King Daughter of Jonathan Freeman & Eunice his wife was born October 20th 1813

[p. 98] Joseph Son of Elnathan Snow Jr & Sarah his Wife was Born October 24th 1795

Benjamin Son of Elnathan Snow Jr & Sarah his Wife was Born August 16th 1798

Sally Daughter of Elnathan Snow Jr & Sarah his wife was born July 2d 1804

Jesse Cole Snow Son of Elnathan Snow Jr & Sarah his wife was born August 25th 1806

Ezra son of Elnathan Snow & Sarah his wife was born July 12th 1808

Joseph son of Elnathan Snow & Sarah his wife was born March 17th 1815

[p. 99] Olive Daughter of Samuel Linnell & Lydia his Wife was born Novemr 27th 1788

Edward Smith Son of Samuel Linnell & Lydia his wife was born July 2th 1791

Fanny Daughter of Samuel Linnell & Lydia his wife was born Janr 23th 1794

Edward Smith Son of Samuel Linnell & Lydia his wife was born Decemr 17th 1796

Keziah Daughter of Samuel Linnell & Lydia his wife was born April 7th 1799

Marcy Daughter of Samuel Linnell & Lydia his wife was born June 23th 1802

Hariot Daughter of Samuel Linnell & Lydia his wife was born Januy 28 1808

[p. 95] Richard Son of Zaccheus Higgins & Hannah his Wife Was Born November 16th 1786

Charles Son of Zaccheus Higgins & Hannah his Wife was born July 29th 1789

Polly Twining Daughter of Zaccheus Higgins & Hannah his wife was Born December 24th 1792

Carmy Son of Zaccheus Higgins & Hannah his Wife was Born april 9th 1793

Barnabas Son of Zaccheus Higgins & Hannah his wife was Born December 27th 1797

Zera Son of Zaccheus Higgins and Hannah his wife was born Sept 15 1801

[p. 96] Phebe Daughter of Aquillia Higgins & Tamzin his Wife was born November 1th 1797

Tamzin Daughter of Aquillia Higgins & Tamzin his wife was born October 29th 1799

Tamsa Daughter of Aquillia Higgins & Tamzin his wife was born February 3d 1801

Aquilla Son of Aquilla Higgins & Tamzin his wife was born october 15 1803

Ruby & Thirse Twins Daughters of Aquilla Higgins Tamzin his wife born Octor 3th 1806

Zedekiah son of Aquilla Higgins & Tamzin his wife born August 11th 1808

Haskel son of Aquillia Higgins & Tamzin his wife born June 31th 1810

Philana Daughter of Aquilla Higgins & Tamzin his wife born august 1811.

Olive Daughter of James Higgins & his wife was born February 21th 1804

Jonathan Son of James Higgins & Jerusha his wife was born May 2d 1806

James son of James Higgins & Jerusha his wif was born Octor 20th 1808

Ebenezer Son of James & Jerusha his wife was born January 1st 1811

Jerusha Daughter of James Higgins & Jerusha his wife was born March 29th 1813

Zebina Son of James Higgins & Jerusha his wife was born March 19th 1815

Israel Linnell son of James Higgins & Jerusha his wife was born Jul 10th 1817

Solomon Son of James Higgins and Jerusha his wife born Feb 4 1820

Wilson Son of James Higgins and Jerusha his wife born 'May 2nd 1822

(To be continued)

*So recorded.—Editor.

Marcy Frances Rogers Daughter of Jonathan Rogers Jr and Lucy his wife was born August 27th 1809

Samuel Rogers son of Jonathan Rogers Jr & Lucy his wife was born June 29th 1813

Dorcas Higgins Daughter of Jonathan Rogers Jun and Lucy his wife was born January 19th 1815

Lucy Snow Daughter of Jonathan Rogers Jun and Lucy his wife was born April 19th 1817

Jonathan Varnum Son of Jonathan Rogers Jur and Lucy his wife was born Sept 12th 1820

Julian Daughter of Jonathan Rogers Jur and Lucy his wife was born January 18th 1822

Sparrow Mayo Son of Jonathan Rogers Jun and Lucy his wife was born November 12th 1823

Julia Ann daughter of Jonathan Rogers Jr and Lucy his wife was born Nov 4th 1828

George W. son of Jonathan Rogers Jr and Lucy his wife was born April 11th 1830

[p. 100] Mary Daughter of Thomas Freeman & Phebe his Wife Was born Janry 27th 1799

Edward Son of Thomas Freeman & Phebe his wife was born April 10th 1800

Thomas Son of Thomas Freeman & Phebe his wife was born March 11th 1802

Eunice Daughter of Thomas Freeman & Phebe his wife was born April 13th 1803

Dorcas Daughter of Thomas Freeman & Phebe his wife born June 21th 1805

Thomas son of Thomas Freemen & Phebe his wife born July 8th 1806

Sullivan son of Thomas Freeman & Phebe his wife born March 22th 1809

Francis son of Thomas Freeman & Phebe his wife born Decemr 31th 1811

Lucy Freeman daughter of Thomas Dockrill and Mary Freeman was born Oct 17th 1825

Abner Freeman son of Jonathan Linnell & Bathsheba his wife was Born July 6th 1808

Jonathan Son of Jonathan Linnell & Bathsheba his wife born Sepr 1th 1811

John Son of Jonathan Linnell & Bathsheba his wife born March 19th 1814

Charlotte Daughter of Jonathan Linnell & Bathsheba his wife born Dec 23rd 1816

Sally Daughter of Jonathan Linnell & Bathsheba his wife born august 30th 1822

Tamzen Daughter of Jonathan Linnell & Bathsheba his wife born June 9th 1827

[p. 101] Zenas Son of Hezekiah Rogers & Mary his Wife was born June 7th 1774

Sarah Daughter of Hezekiah Rogers & Mary his wife was born April 6th 1776

Hezekiah Son of Hezekiah Rogers & Mary his wife was born June 23th 1778

Asa Son of Hezekiah Rogers & Mary his wife was born Febuy 4th 1780

Uriah Son of Hezekiah Rogers & Ruth his wife was born Februy 1th 1783

Yates Son of Hezekiah Rogers & Ruth his wife was born Octor 19th 1784

Eleazar Son of Hezekiah Rogers & Ruth his wife was born Sepr 4th 1786

Mary Daughter of Hezekiah Rogers & Ruth his wife was born July 12th 1788

Ruth Daughter of Hezekiah Rogers & Ruth his wife was born August 6th 1790

Abner Son of Hezekiah Rogers & Ruth his wife was born Septr 6th 1792

Hezekiah Son of Hezekiah Rogers & Ruth his wife was born August 16th 1794

Levi Son of Hezekiah Rogers & Ruth his wife was born December 8th 1797

Betty Daughter of Hezekiah Rogers & Ruth his wife was born Febry 4th 1800

Foster Son of Mary Rogers was born March 10th 1808

[p. 102] Rebecca Daughter of Joshua Gould & Molly his Wife was Born August 7th 1772

Josiah Son of Joshua Gould & Molly his wife was Born Sepr 23: 1774

Joshua Son of Joshua Gould & Molly his wife was Born Sepr 3th 1776

Jonathan Son of Joshua Gould & Molly his Wife was born May 18th 1779

Nathaniel Son of Joshua Gould & Molly his wife was born Feby 16th 1782

Thomas Son of Joshua Gould & Molly his Wife was born Nom 26th 1784

Molly Daughter of Joshua Gould & Molly his Wife was born Sepr 23th 1787

Benjamin Son of Joshua Gould & Molly his Wife was born June 7th 1790

Phebe Sparrow Daughter of Thomas L Mayo & Louisa his wife born Jany 4th 1828

Eliza Thomas Daughter of Thomas L Mayo & Louisa his wife born Janary 17th 1830

Albert Williams son of Thomas L Mayo & Louisa his wife born Nov 5th 1831

Azariah Doane son of Joshua Doane & Thankful his Wife was born Septemr 23th 1811

Isaac Snow son of Joshua Doane & Thankful his Wife was born Septemr 21th 1813

Joshua Son of Joshua Doane and Thankfull his wife was born oct 15th 1815

Thankful Daughter of Joshua Doane and Thankfu[l] his wife was born May 2nd 1820

Dorcas Snow Daughter of Joshua Doane and Thankful his wife born June 11th 1822

George H. son of Joshua Doane & Thankful his wife born July 28th 1825

Seth son of Joshua Doane & Thankful his wife was born April 2d 1830

[p. 106] Jonathan Kenwrick Jur & Betty Rogers were Married Novmr 13th 1783

Samuel K Son of Jonathan Kenwrick Jr & Betsy his wife was born Nomr 10/1784

Warren Anson Son of Jonathan Kenwrick Jr & Betsy his wife was born Octor 12th 1786

Betsey Daughter of Jonathan Kenwrick Jr & Betsey his wife was born May 29th 1788

Warren A Son of Jonathan Kenwrick J & Betsy his wife was born July 24 . 1790

Mercy Daughter of Jonathan Kenwrick Jr & Betsey his wife was born August 12th 1792

Esther Daughter of Jonathan Kenwrick Jr & Betsey his wife was born Apl 18th 1794

Jonathan 3d Son of Jonathan Kenwrick Jr & Betsey his wife was born Janr 29th 1796

Elizabeth Daughter of Jona. Kenwrick Jr & Betsey his wife was born Februr 18 : 1798

Alfred Son of Jonathan Kenwrick Jr & Betsey his Wife was born May 30 1800

Seth Son of Jonathan Kenwrick Jr & Betsey his wife was born July 16 . 1803

Fredrick Son of Jonathan Kendrick Jr & Betsey his wife born oct Octor 14th 1805

Carline Daughter of Jonathan Kendrick & Betty his wife born oct 30th 1809

[p. 107] Simeon Pepper & Mary Snow were Married October 2th 1794

Daniel Son of Simeon Pepper & Mary his wife Was Born Septemr 11th 1795

Polly Daughter of Simeon Pepper & Mary his wife was Born October 3th 1797

Nabby Daughter of Simeon Pepper & Mary his wife was Born August 9th 1800

Betsey C. daughter of Thomas L Mayo & Louisa his wife born Nov 15 1833

Rebecah A. daughter of Thomas L. Mayo & Louisa his wife was born March 3d 1839

Mercy E. daughter of Thomas L. Mayo & Louisa his wife was born Feb 18 . 1842

Jonathan M. son of Thomas L. Mayo & Louisa his wife was born Oct. 16th 1836

[p. 103] Timothy Bascom and Rebecca Gould were Married by the Revd Mr Jonathan Bascom November 19th 1795

Nabby Daughter of Timothy Bascom & Rebecca his Wife was born In Orleans March 15th 1800

Timothy Son of Timothy Bascom & Rebecca his Wife was born In Orleans October 9th 1802

Clement Son of Timothy Bascom & Rebecca his Wife was born In Orleans July 7th 1805

Timothy Son of Timothy Bascom & Rebecca his Wife was born in Orleans December 27th 1806

Tempy Daughter of Timothy Bascom & Rebecca his Wife was born February 28th 1809

William Son of Timothy Bascom & Rebecca his Wife was born August 18th 1811

[p. 104] Precilla Freeman Daughter of Aaron Higgins & abigail His Wife was born October 16th 1775

Betsy Daughter of Aaron Higgins & Abigail his wife was born august 24th 1777

Abigail Stevens Daughter of Aaron Higgins & Abigail his wife Was born August 17th 1783

Anna Parker Daughter of Aaron Higgins & Abigail His Wife Was Born March 28th 1785

Reuben Son of Aaron Higgins & Abigail his Wife was born April 23th 1788

Aaron Son of Aaron Higgins & Abigail His Wife Was born Augus: 24th 1790

David son of David Mayo and Polly his wife born October 21 1823

Thomas Sparrow Son of Richard Sparrow and Phebe his Wife Was born November 4th 1798

[p. 105] Lewis Young and Jerusha Higgins were Married by the Reverend Mr Bascom August 16th 1795

Lewis Son of Lewis Young & Jerusha his Wife was born August 4th 1797

Jerusha Daughter of Lewis Young & Jerusha his Wife was born October 14th 1799

Voltaire young Son of Lewis Young & Jerusha his Wife was born Sepr 25th 1801

Josiah Young Son of Lewis Young & Jerusha his Wife was born June 2th 1803

Sally pepper Daughter of Simeon Pepper & Mary his Wife was born in Orleans May 26th 1803

Sally Daughter of Simeon Pepper & Mary his wife was born January 22th 1807

Simeon Pepper Son of Simeon Pepper & Mary his wife was born Janu 6 . 1811

Nathaniel son of Dean S Nickerson and Phebe his wife born December 23 1825

Dean Bangs son of Dean S Nickerson & Phebe his wife born December 8 1827

Solomon Hurd son of Dean S Nickerson & Phebe his wife born December 15 1829

Azubah S. daughter of Dean S Nickerson & Phebe his wife born May 17 1832

Mercy S. daughter of Dean S Nickerson & Phebe his wife born May 17 1832

Phebe daughter of Dean S. Nickerson & Phebe his wife born February 29 1834

Ruth G. daughter of Dean S Nickerson & Phebe his born February 24 1840

Windsor son of Dean S. Nickerson & Phebe his wife was born June 9th 1842

[p. 108] Jonathan Bascom Jr & Sally Harding were Married by the Revd Jonathan Bascom September 6th 1800

Franklin Son of Jonathan Bascom Jr & Sally his Wife was born March 22th 1801

Betsy Daughter of Jonathan Bascom Jr & Sally his wife born May 7th 1803

Sally Daughter of Jonathan Bascom & Sally his wife born April 15th 1805

Jonathan Son of Jonathan Bascom & Sally his wife born Novemr 25th 1806

Catherine Harding Daughter of Jona Bascom & Sally his wife born april 12th 1808

Polly Daughter of Jonathan & Sally Bascom born March 11th 1810

Willard Son of Jonathan & Sally Bascom born Novemr 6th 1811

Andrew Jackson Son of Jonathan Bascom and Sally his wife born Febuary 3rd 1815

Tempy Daughter of Jonathan Bascom and Sally his wife was born May 10th 1816

[p. 109] Joshua Knowles Son of John Knowles & Thankfull His wife Was born Sepr 29th 1775

Joanna Daughter of John Knowles & Thankfull his wife was born Novem 3th 1779

John Knowles son of John Knowles & Thankfull his wife was born Janr 18th 1780

Rebecca Daughter of John Knowles & Thankfull his wife was born May 27th 1782

Lydia Daughter of John Knowles & Thankfull his wife was born Dcmr 9th 1785

Thankfull Daughter of John Knowles & Thankfull his wife was born March 10th 1787

Tempe Daughter of John Knowles & Thankfull his wife was born Nomr 26th 1789

Elisha Son of John Knowles & Thankfull his wife was born Nomr 25th 1791

Rachel Daughter of John Knowles & Thankfull his wife was born July 30 : 1794

Lydia Daughter of John Knowles & Thankfull his wife was born Dcmr 9th 1797

Uriah Son of Hezekiah Rogers Jur and Thankfull his wife was born January 19th 1819

Sally Crowell Daughter of Hezekiah Rogers Jur and Thankfull his wife was born October 19th 1821

Alexander Chase Son of Hezekiah Rogers Jun and Thankfull his wife was born January 7th 1825

Emily daughter of Hezekiah Rogers Jr & Thankful his wife was born Aug 14th 1839

[p. 110] Tabatha Daughter of Barnabas Twining Jr & Rebecca his wife was born Septr 24th 1796

John Son of Barnabas Twining Jr & Rebecca his wife was born Sepr 26 1798

Ebenezar Son of Barnabas Twining J & Rebecca his wife was born April 4th 1801

James & Joel Sons of Barnabas Twining Jr & Rebecca his wife was born July 11th 1804

Eunice Daughter of James Snow & Eunice his wife born Sept 11th 1828

James son of James Snow & Eunice his wife born April 10th 1830

Eliza Paine daughter of James Snow & Eunice his wife was Born Nov 17th 1833

Mary Frances daughter of James Snow & Eunice his wife was Born Oct. 12th 1835

Henry son of James Snow & Eunice his wife was born April 26th 1840

Freeman son of James Snow & Eunice his wife was born September 16th 1843

[p. 111] James Son of David Eldridge and Sarah his wife was born July 26th 1801

David Son of David Eldridge and Sarah his wife was born June 4th 1803

Elisha Linnel Son of Joseph Freeman & Phebe his wife was born August 31th 1811

Abigail Daughter of Joseph Freeman & Phebe his wife was born August 25th 1813

[p. 112] John Myrick & Thankful Linnell were Married July 11th 1780 in Eastham By the Rvd Jonathan Bascom

Prissa Myrick Daughter of John Myrick & Thankful his wife was born May 20th 1782

Lucy Daughter of John Myrick & Thankful his wife was born June 3th 1784

Samuel Myrick Son of John Myrick & Thankful his wife was born March 9th 1786

Phebe Daughter of John Myrick & Thankful his Wife was born March 30th 1788

Thankful Daughter of John Myrick & Thankful his Wife was born Oct 4th 1790

John Myrick & Hannah Knowles Were Married Novmr 17th 1793 in Eastham by the Revd Jonathan Bascom

Thankfull Daughter of John Myrick & Hannah his Wife was born Decmr 1th 1795

Hannah Daughter of John Myrick & Hannah his Wife was born March 21th 1798

Lucy Daughter of John Myrick & Hannah his wife was born Novr 5d 1800

John Son of John Myrick & Hannah his wife was born in orleans July 31 : 1802

Abigail Daughter of John Myrick & Hannah his wife was born January 2th 1806

Eliza Daughter of John Myrick & Hannah his wife was born Septum 13th 1808

[p. 113] John Freeman Son of Josiah Freeman & Phebe his wife was born Decmr 8d 1790

Phebe Freeman Daughter of Josiah Freeman & Phebe his wife was born octor 11d 1792

Josiah Son of Josiah Freeman & Phebe his wife was born Sepr 5th 1794

Nathaniel Son of Josiah Freeman & Phebe his Wife was born octor 10th 1796

Tamzin Daughter of Josiah Freeman & Phebe his Wife was born Jany 1th 1798

Hannah Daughter of Josiah Freeman & Phebe his wife was born august 4th 1801

Josiah Son of Josiah Freeman & Phebe his wife was Born June 6th 1804

David Crowell Son of Freeman H Rogers and Margary his wife was born November 28th 1823

Adeline Daughter of Freeman H Rogers and Margary his wife was born Nov 10th 1825

Margaret Ann daughter of Freeman H. Rogers and Margary his wife was born Feb 9th 1828

Thankful daughter of Freeman H. Rogers and Margary his wife was born Oct 8th 1829

Freeman H. son of Freeman H. Rogers & Margary his wife was born Oct 9th 1832

Esther Y. daughter of Freeman H. Rogers & Margary his wife was born Sept 12th . 1838

Zemira B. Son of Freeman H. Rogers and Margary his wife was born Sept 23d 1840

Benjamin C. son of Freeman H. Rogers & Margary his wife born April 2nd 1843

[p. 114] Hatsel Higgins Son of Hatsel Higgins was born Sepr 28th 1794 & Marcy his wife

Joshua Son of Hatsel Higgins & Marcy his Wife Was born January 25th 1795

Sparrow Son of Hatsel Higgins & Marcy his wife was born Octor 1th 1799

Leonard Son of Hatsel Higgins & Marcy his wife was born Novm 30th 1801

[p. 115] Esther Daughter of John Sparrow & Rosanna his wife was born august 29th 1794

Thomas Son of John Sparrow & Rosanna his wife was born Octr 4th 1796

John Sparrow Son of John Sparrow & Rosanna his wife was born Novm 2th 1798

Zede Son of John Sparrow & Rosanna his wife was born Sepr 24th 1800

Marcy Daughter of John Sparrow & Rosanna his wife born Jan . 9th 1802

Dean Smith Son of John Sparrow & Rosanna his wife was born Novmr 18th 1804

Rosanna Daughter of John Sparrow & Rosanna his wife was born Decmr 10th 1806

William Son of John Sparrow & Rosanna his wife was born Decm 31th 1808

Rosanna Daughter of John Sparrow & Rosanna his wife was born Septmbr 3th 1812

Joseph son of John Sparrow & Rosanna his wife born Feb 11 1815

Sineon son of John Sparrow Jr & Jerusha his wife born Dec 23: 1824

John son of John Sparrow Jr & Jerusha his wife born august 22 1822

Marcy Smith Daughter of John Sparrow Jr and Jerusha his wife was born Sept 7th 1828

[p. 116] Molly Daughter of Seth Sparrow & Mary his wife Was born July 12th 1795

Elizabeth Daughter of Seth Sparrow & Mary his wife was born June 12th 1797

Kezia Daughter of Seth Sparrow & Mary his wife was born april 23th 1802

Nabby Daughter of Seth & Mary born August 15: 1804

Vickery Son of Seth Sparrow & Mary his wife was born Octobr 23th 1807

Columba Son of Seth Sparrow & Mary his wife was born octobr 9th 1811

Susan M Daughter of John Jarvis & Thankful his wife born April 4th 1814

Timothy son of John Jarvis & Thankful his wife born May 6 1812

Simeon Mayo son of John Jarvis & Thankful his wife born April 16 1816

Lucinda Daughter of John Jarvis & Thankful his wife born Oct 16 1818

John King son of John Jarvis & Thankful his wife born October 23 1820

Permela Mayo Daughter of John Jarvis & Thankful his wife born Dec 9th 1823

Patia Daughter of John Jarvis & Thankfull his wife born Sept 12 1825

Sarah ann Daughter of John Jarvis & Thankful born July 19 1827

(To be continued)

INDEX

This is NOT an all-name index. References in the text to religious and civil officials, as such, have been omitted. Names may appear more than once on the same page.

ATKENS, Elisabath	71	ATKINS, Martha	52	ATWOOD, Abigail	135
ATKENS, Elisabath	115	ATKINS, Martha	91	ATWOOD, Abigail	171
ATKENS, Elisabath	129	ATKINS, Martha	144	ATWOOD, Abigaile	52
ATKENS, Hanah	115	ATKINS, Nathaniel	47	ATWOOD, Abigaile	64
ATKENS, Hannah	124	ATKINS, Nathaniel	48	ATWOOD, Abigel	109
ATKENS, Janina	115	ATKINS, Nathanll.	48	ATWOOD, Abigel	114
ATKENS, James	53	ATKINS, Paul	45	ATWOOD, Abigial	117
ATKENS, James	131	ATKINS, Paul	150	ATWOOD, Anne	15
ATKENS, Joseph	113	ATKINS, Samuel	34	ATWOOD, Anne	104
ATKENS, Joseph	115	ATKINS, Samuell	34	ATWOOD, Anne	149
ATKENS, Joseph	135	ATKINS, Sarah	124	ATWOOD, Apphia	54
ATKENS, Juriah	115	ATKINS, Sarah	151	ATWOOD, Asenath	112
ATKENS, Martha	84	ATKINS, Thankfl	115	ATWOOD, Azubah	165
ATKENS, Martha	115	ATKINS, Thomas	103	ATWOOD, Banges	36
ATKENS, Martha	130	ATKINS, Thomas	106	ATWOOD, Bangs	100
ATKENS, Mary	56	ATKINS, Thomas	149	ATWOOD, Bangs	106
ATKENS, Mary	115	ATKINS, Uriah	45	ATWOOD, Bangs	165
ATKENS, Mary	133	ATKINS, Winefred	48	ATWOOD, Barnabas	72
ATKENS, Phebe	75	ATKINS, Winnefred	48	ATWOOD, Barnabas	112
ATKENS, Phebe	115	ATKINS, Winnie	47	ATWOOD, Barnabas	167
ATKENS, Phebee	134	ATKINS, Winnie	48	ATWOOD, Beniamen	15
ATKENS, Sarah	115	ATTKINS, Bethiah	48	ATWOOD, Benimin	57
ATKENS, Thankful	73	ATTWOOD, Christopher	84	ATWOOD, Benjamin	113
ATKENS, Thankful	115	ATTWOOD, David	172	ATWOOD, Bethia	36
ATKENS, Thankfull	115	ATTWOOD, Eldad	15	ATWOOD, Bethiah	76
ATKINS, Anne	45	ATTWOOD, Gideon	84	ATWOOD, Bethiah	94
ATKINS, Anne	52	ATTWOOD, Hannah	84	ATWOOD, Bethiah	145
ATKINS, Anne	142	ATTWOOD, Joseph	84	ATWOOD, Bethya	36
ATKINS, Bethya	30	ATTWOOD, Joseph	172	ATWOOD, Christopher	36
ATKINS, Bethyah	48	ATTWOOD, Machiel	47	ATWOOD, Cristopher	111
ATKINS, Desire	34	ATTWOOD, Marie	15	ATWOOD, Daniel	86
ATKINS, Elisabeth	48	ATTWOOD, Nehemiah	172	ATWOOD, Daniel	113
ATKINS, Elisabeth	61	ATTWOOD, Sabery	172	ATWOOD, Daniel	162
ATKINS, Elisabeth	141	ATTWOOD, Samuel	84	ATWOOD, David	64
ATKINS, Elizabeth	24	ATTWOOD, Samuel	128	ATWOOD, David	70
ATKINS, Hannah	45	ATTWOOD, Sebray	172	ATWOOD, David	117
ATKINS, Hannah	111	ATTWOOD, Stephen	46	ATWOOD, David	171
ATKINS, Hannah	151	ATTWOOD, Susannah	84	ATWOOD, Debora	79
ATKINS, Henry	24	ATTWOOD, Tamzy	172	ATWOOD, Deborah	15
ATKINS, Henry	34	ATTWOOD, Thankful	84	ATWOOD, Deborah	57
ATKINS, Henry	47	ATWOD, Abagal	73	ATWOOD, Deborah	66
ATKINS, Isaac	34	ATWOD, Bangs	117	ATWOOD, Deborah	90
ATKINS, Isaiah	48	ATWOD, Jesse	152	ATWOOD, Deborah	120
ATKINS, James	45	ATWOD, Joshua	152	ATWOOD, Deborah	133
ATKINS, John	34	ATWOD, Mary	73	ATWOOD, Debro	86
ATKINS, John	45	ATWOD, Mary	136	ATWOOD, Debro	109
ATKINS, Joseph	34	ATWOD, Richard	136	ATWOOD, Debro	143
ATKINS, Joseph	45	ATWOD, Ruth	135	ATWOOD, Deliveranc	72
ATKINS, Joseph	52	ATWOD, Sarah	136	ATWOOD, Easter	139
ATKINS, Joseph	115	ATWOD, Thankful	152	ATWOOD, Ebenezer	15
ATKINS, Joseph	140	ATWOD, Thankfull	111	ATWOOD, Ebenezer	80
ATKINS, Joshua	48	ATWOOD, Abagel	73	ATWOOD, Ebenezer	113
ATKINS, Martha	45	ATWOOD, Abigail	117	ATWOOD, Ebenezer	140

ATWOOD, Ebenezor	80	ATWOOD, Jamimah	57	ATWOOD, Rebaca	72
ATWOOD, Ebenezor	101	ATWOOD, Jesse	59	ATWOOD, Richard	72
ATWOOD, Ebnezar	113	ATWOOD, Joanah	72	ATWOOD, Richard	106
ATWOOD, Ebnezar	135	ATWOOD, Joanah	97	ATWOOD, Richard	111
ATWOOD, Elazer	123	ATWOOD, Joanah	130	ATWOOD, Ruben	100
ATWOOD, Eldad	15	ATWOOD, Joanna	145	ATWOOD, Ruth	80
ATWOOD, Eldad	57	ATWOOD, John	15	ATWOOD, Ruth	111
ATWOOD, Eldad	113	ATWOOD, John	36	ATWOOD, Ruth	113
ATWOOD, Eldad	137	ATWOOD, John	67	ATWOOD, Samuel	64
ATWOOD, Eldad	141	ATWOOD, John	73	ATWOOD, Samuel	70
ATWOOD, Eleazor	146	ATWOOD, John	132	ATWOOD, Samuel	139
ATWOOD, Elezar	72	ATWOOD, John	137	ATWOOD, Sarah	15
ATWOOD, Elezer	72	ATWOOD, John	138	ATWOOD, Sarah	57
ATWOOD, Elezer	160	ATWOOD, John	168	ATWOOD, Sarah	76
ATWOOD, Eliezer	7	ATWOOD, Jonathan	100	ATWOOD, Sarah	81
ATWOOD, Eliezer	36	ATWOOD, Joseph	36	ATWOOD, Sarah	140
ATWOOD, Elisabeth	66	ATWOOD, Joseph	86	ATWOOD, Simeon	67
ATWOOD, Elisabeth	137	ATWOOD, Joseph	150	ATWOOD, Simeon	76
ATWOOD, Elisha	36	ATWOOD, Joshua	36	ATWOOD, Stephen	64
ATWOOD, Elisha	117	ATWOOD, Joshua	72	ATWOOD, Stephen	72
ATWOOD, Elisha	134	ATWOOD, Luse	72	ATWOOD, Stephen	90
ATWOOD, Enoch	165	ATWOOD, Lydia	57	ATWOOD, Stephen	143
ATWOOD, Ephraim	67	ATWOOD, Marcy	59	ATWOOD, Steven	24
ATWOOD, Ephraim	76	ATWOOD, Marcy	72	ATWOOD, Susana	86
ATWOOD, Ephraim	130	ATWOOD, Marget	57	ATWOOD, Thanckfull	128
ATWOOD, Esther	64	ATWOOD, Martha	82	ATWOOD, Thankful	59
ATWOOD, Eunis	100	ATWOOD, Martha	135	ATWOOD, Thankful	128
ATWOOD, Experience	86	ATWOOD, Martha	168	ATWOOD, Thankfull	67
ATWOOD, Freeman	117	ATWOOD, Mary	36	ATWOOD, Thankfull	81
ATWOOD, Gedion	117	ATWOOD, Mary	67	ATWOOD, Thankfull	95
ATWOOD, Hannah	15	ATWOOD, Mary	72	ATWOOD, Thankfull	141
ATWOOD, Hannah	18	ATWOOD, Mary	111	ATWOOD, Thankfull	145
ATWOOD, Hannah	36	ATWOOD, Mary	137	ATWOOD, Thomas	74
ATWOOD, Hannah	70	ATWOOD, Mary	147	ATWOOD, Thomas	100
ATWOOD, Hannah	86	ATWOOD, Mary	165	ATWOOD, Thomas	139
ATWOOD, Hannah	95	ATWOOD, Medad	64	ATWOOD, Timothy	67
ATWOOD, Hannah	145	ATWOOD, Mehetable	59	ATWOOD, Timothy	129
ATWOOD, Hannah	146	ATWOOD, Mercy	59	ATWOOD, William	67
ATWOOD, Hephzibah	113	ATWOOD, Mercy	64	ATWOOD, William	109
ATWOOD, Hipsiba	80	ATWOOD, Mercy	125	ATWOOD, William	150
ATWOOD, Isaac	137	ATWOOD, Mercy	156	AVERY, Job	150
ATWOOD, Israel	86	ATWOOD, Nathan	64	AVERY, John	96
ATWOOD, Israel	131	ATWOOD, Nathan	113	AVRY, Job	99
ATWOOD, Israel	140	ATWOOD, Nathanael	36		
ATWOOD, Isrel	86	ATWOOD, Nathaniel	72	— B —	
ATWOOD, James	59	ATWOOD, Nathaniel	100		
ATWOOD, James	72	ATWOOD, Nathaniel	106	BACER, Simeon	77
ATWOOD, James	86	ATWOOD, Nathaniel	123	BACON, Aphia	86
ATWOOD, James	105	ATWOOD, Nathaniel	125	BACON, Isaac	57
ATWOOD, James	112	ATWOOD, Nathaniel	146	BACON, Isaac	141
ATWOOD, James	128	ATWOOD, Phebe	64	BACON, Mary	70
ATWOOD, James	135	ATWOOD, Priscilah	171	BACON, Nathan	70
ATWOOD, James	149	ATWOOD, Rachal	113	BACON, Nathan	86

BACON, Nathanael	70	BAKER, Thankfull	65	BASCOM, Polly	188
BACON, Nathaniel	86	BAKER, Thomas	173	BASCOM, Rebecca	187
BACON, Nathaniel	111	BAKER, Vicery	173	BASCOM, Sally	188
BACON, Nathanll.	152	BAKER, William	28	BASCOM, Temperance	161
BACON, Ruth	70	BAKON, Keziah	96	BASCOM, Tempy	161
BACON, Sarah	70	BAKOR, Anthony	152	BASCOM, Tempy	187
BACON, Sarah	141	BANGES, Hannah	28	BASCOM, Tempy	188
BACON, Simion	134	BANGES, Hannah	40	BASCOM, Timothy	161
BACON, Thomas	70	BANGES, John	30	BASCOM, Timothy	187
BACON, Thomas	86	BANGES, Jonathan	11	BASCOM, Willard	188
BACON, Thomas	138	BANGES, Jonathan	12	BASCOM, William	161
BACONS, Ruth	130	BANGES, Jonathan	138	BASCOM, William	187
BACOR, Deborah	63	BANGES, Jonnathan	12	BASET, Elisabeth	128
BACOR, Hanah	113	BANGES, Joshua	24	BASET, Samuel	131
BACOR, Hanah	135	BANGES, Lidiah	32	BASSET, Deborah	125
BACOR, Isaac	99	BANGES, Lidya	36	BASSET, Desire	166
BACOR, Isaac	130	BANGES, Lydia	12	BASSET, Mary	42
BACOR, Moses	63	BANGES, Mercie	12	BASSET, Nehemiah	127
BACOR, Samuel	63	BANGES, Samuel	12	BASSET, Nehemiah	162
BACOR, Thankful	128	BANGES, Sarah	12	BASSET, Samuel	100
BADISHALL, William	137	BANGES, Thamoson	12	BASSETT, Deborah	154
BAKER, Abigail	173	BANGS, Apphiah	16	BASSETT, Hannah	8
BAKER, Abijah	173	BANGS, Bethiah	150	BATE, Mary	164
BAKER, Anthony	111	BANGS, Edward	11	BATEE, Mary	92
BAKER, Bennoni	173	BANGS, Edward	89	BATEE, Samuel	92
BAKER, Benoni	173	BANGS, Edward	102	BATY, Elisabeth	172
BAKER, Dean	173	BANGS, Edward	143	BATY, Elizabeth	172
BAKER, Deborah	63	BANGS, Elizabeth	12	BATY, Gideon	161
BAKER, Dinah	139	BANGS, Hannah	11	BATY, Gideon	172
BAKER, Dorcas	173	BANGS, James	129	BATY, Nathaniel	172
BAKER, Ebenezer	53	BANGS, Jonathan	11	BATY, Prince	172
BAKER, Ebenezer	63	BANGS, Jonathan	12	BATY, Rachal	161
BAKER, Elsa	173	BANGS, Jonnathan	11	BATY, Rachel	172
BAKER, Henry	173	BANGS, Joshua	13	BATY, Rebecca	172
BAKER, Isaac	43	BANGS, Mary	11	BATY, Sally	161
BAKER, Isaac	63	BANGS, Mercy	15	BATY, Sally	172
BAKER, Joseph	43	BANGS, Rebeca	17	BATY, Samuel	170
BAKER, Joshua	173	BANGS, Rebeckah	12	BATY, Thomas	172
BAKER, Mary	173	BANGS, Ruth	123	BAXTER, Jane	144
BAKER, Mercy Sparrow	173	OASCOM, Abigail	161	BEACON, Hannah	145
BAKER, Obadiah	173	BASCOM, Andrew Jackson	188	BEACON, Jonathan	70
BAKER, Phebe	173	BASCOM, Betsy	188	BEACON, Mary	70
BAKER, Richard	43	BASCOM, Betty	161	BEACON, Nathan	70
BAKER, Samuel	43	BASCOM, Catherine Harding	188	BEACON, Thomas	70
BAKER, Samuel	63	BASCOM, Charles	161	BEAKER, Isaac	149
BAKER, Samuel	78	BASCOM, Clement	187	BEAKER, Isaack	104
BAKER, Samuel	140	BASCOM, Franklin	188	BEAKER, Mary	109
BAKER, Samuell	12	BASCOM, Jona.	161	BEAKER, Mary	147
BAKER, Sarah	43	BASCOM, Jona.	188	BEAKER, Mary	149
BAKER, Sarah	63	BASCOM, Jonathan	161	BEAKER, Rebecka	101
BAKER, Sarah	125	BASCOM, Jonathan	188	BEAKER, Richard	146
BAKER, Simeon	43	BASCOM, Nabby	187	BEAKER, Serah	100
BAKER, Thankful	63	BASCOM, Phebe	161	BEAKER, Serah	147

BEAN, Benjamin	78	BILLS, Nathaneel	7	BROWN, David	109
BEAN, Benjamin	140	BILLS, Tho.	7	BROWN, David	112
BEE, Jane	126	BILLS, Thomas	7	BROWN, David	135
BEE, John	88	BINNY, John	9	BROWN, David	151
BEE, John	93	BISHOP, Damaris	38	BROWN, David Walker	63
BEE, John	144	BIXBE, Joseph	76	BROWN, Debora	69
BEE, Marcy	93	BIXBE, Moses	76	BROWN, Debora	70
BEE, Martha	93	BIXBE, Phebe	76	BROWN, Deborah	18
BEE, Martha	124	BIXBE, Sarah	81	BROWN, Deborah	96
BEE, Martha	159	BIXBE, Sarah	140	BROWN, Deborah	132
BEE, Rebaca	93	BIXBEE, Elizabeth	76	BROWN, Deborah	138
BEE, Rebaca	131	BIXBEE, John	76	BROWN, Ebenezor	96
BEE, Thomas	120	BIXBEE, Joseph	76	BROWN, Ebenezor	108
BEE, Thomas	133	BIXBEE, Moses	76	BROWN, Elisabath	89
BEEL, Sarah	152	BIXBEE, Phebee	76	BROWN, Elisabeth	56
BEEN, Benjamin	78	BOGUE, Joseph	101	BROWN, Elisabeth	75
BEEN, Mehitable	78	BOGUE, Joseph	147	BROWN, Elisabeth	89
BEEN, Sarah	78	BOGUE, Josh	146	BROWN, Elisabeth	141
BEREY, John	135	BOGUE, Lidea	109	BROWN, Elizabeth	86
BERRIE, Patience	12	BOORMAN, Thankfull	46	BROWN, Elizabeth	108
BERRY, Desire	7	BOREMAN, Thomas	142	BROWN, Elizabeth	149
BERRY, Desire	84	BOWN, Lidea	150	BROWN, Elizabeth	151
BERRY, Desire	141	BREEAD, Ann	116	BROWN, Elkanah	89
BERRY, Elisabeth	42	BREEAD, Nathaniel	116	BROWN, Elkanah	133
BERRY, Rebecka	98	BREED, Abigail	116	BROWN, Elkeny	120
BERRY, Rebecka	146	BREED, Ann	116	BROWN, Expearnce	129
BETEE, Gideon	92	BREED, Delivearnc	116	BROWN, Experince	81
BETEE, Nathaniel	92	BREED, John	116	BROWN, George	8
BETEE, Samuel	92	BREED, Josiah	116	BROWN, George	117
BETEE, Samuel	144	BREED, Nathanael	134	BROWN, George	149
BETEE, Thomas	92	BREED, Nathaniel	116	BROWN, George	152
BICKFOORD, Elisha	111	BROWN, -----	84	BROWN, Gorge	117
BICKFORD, Elisha	135	BROWN, Abigael	61	BROWN, Hannah	50
BICKFORD, Hannah	156	BROWN, Abigail	36	BROWN, Hannah	81
BICKFORD, Jemima	156	BROWN, Abigail	87	BROWN, Hannah	86
BIGFORD, Debora	26	BROWN, Abigail	128	BROWN, Hannah	97
BIGFORD, Elisha	133	BROWN, Abigail	142	BROWN, Hannah	108
BIGFORD, Hannah	26	BROWN, Abigaile	84	BROWN, Hannah	140
BIGFORD, Hannah	125	BROWN, Alce	117	BROWN, Hannah	145
BIGFORD, Jemima	125	BROWN, Ales	117	BROWN, Hephzibah	117
BIGFORD, Jeremiah	26	BROWN, Alice	117	BROWN, Isaac	129
BIGFORD, Jeremiah	149	BROWN, Anna	89	BROWN, James	8
BIGFORD, Mary	22	BROWN, Anne	104	BROWN, James	18
BIGFORD, Mary	37	BROWN, Anne	147	BROWN, James	89
BIGFUT, Elisha	65	BROWN, Bathsua	86	BROWN, James	97
BIGSBEE, Moses	140	BROWN, Beniamin	8	BROWN, James	123
BIGSBEE, Prissilla	138	BROWN, Beniamin	152	BROWN, James	130
BILLS, Anna	7	BROWN, Benjamin	136	BROWN, James	132
BILLS, Elizabeth	7	BROWN, Bethia	34	BROWN, James	145
BILLS, Gershom	7	BROWN, Bethiah	54	BROWN, Jane	8
BILLS, Joanna	7	BROWN, Bethiah	75	BROWN, Jane	18
BILLS, Mehitabel	7	BROWN, Damorus	108	BROWN, Jane	89
BILLS, Mercy	7	BROWN, David	50	BROWN, Jane	92

BROWN, Jane	144	BROWN, Mather	54	BROWN, Theoder	117
BROWN, Jemimah	75	BROWN, Mehetabel	36	BROWN, Thomas	18
BROWN, Jerusha	97	BROWN, Mehitabel	52	BROWN, Thomas	123
BROWN, Jesse	8	BROWN, Mehitable	86	BROWN, Thomas	143
BROWN, Jesse	86	BROWN, Mehitable	95	BROWN, Thomas	151
BROWN, Jesse	102	BROWN, Mehitable	145	BROWN, Thomas	156
BROWN, Jesse	142	BROWN, Mercy	19	BROWN, William	44
BROWN, John	50	BROWN, Mercy	72	BROWN, William	55
BROWN, John	89	BROWN, Mercy	89	BROWN, Zebulon	50
BROWN, John	99	BROWN, Nathanel	122	BROWN, Zebulon	84
BROWN, John	130	BROWN, Nathaniel	108	BROWN, Zebulon	140
BROWN, John	144	BROWN, Patience	147	BROWN, Zilpah	8
BROWN, Jonathan	96	BROWN, Phebee	117	BROWN, Zilpah	90
BROWN, Joseph	8	BROWN, Prisillah	117	BROWN, Zilpha	117
BROWN, Joseph	97	BROWN, Rebecca	8	BROWN, Zilpha	143
BROWN, Joseph	146	BROWN, Rebecca	72	BROWNE, Bethiah	19
BROWN, Joshua	72	BROWN, Rebecka	73	BROWNE, Joseph	19
BROWN, Joshua	73	BROWN, Rebecka	108	BROWNE, Martha	19
BROWN, Joshua	99	BROWN, Rebecka	147	BROWNE, Nathanel	128
BROWN, Joshua	139	BROWN, Ruth	8	BROWNE, Samuel	19
BROWN, Joshua	152	BROWN, Ruth	36	BULLARD, -----	142
BROWN, Knowles	72	BROWN, Ruth	55	BULLARD, Banjamin	103
BROWN, Liddiah	18	BROWN, Ruth	86	BULLARD, Benjamin	147
BROWN, Liddiah	44	BROWN, Ruth	136	BULLARD, Hannah	88
BROWN, Lidea	75	BROWN, Ruth	141	BURG, Martha	107
BROWN, Lidea	96	BROWN, Samuel	75	BURGAS, Sarah	55
BROWN, Lidea	109	BROWN, Samuel	96	BURGAS, Sarah	130
BROWN, Lidea	151	BROWN, Samuel	117	BURGE, Hannah	140
BROWN, Lidia	69	BROWN, Samuel	137	BURGE, Joseph	53
BROWN, Lidia	75	BROWN, Samuel	149	BURGE, Joseph	139
BROWN, Lidia	139	BROWN, Samuel	171	BURGE, Thankfull	141
BROWN, Marcy	111	BROWN, Samuell	36	BURGES, Hannah	123
BROWN, Marcy	143	BROWN, Samuell	54	BURGES, Hannah	154
BROWN, Marcy	152	BROWN, Samuell	160	BURGES, Martha	150
BROWN, Martha	18	BROWN, Sarah	50	BURGES, Mathias	99
BROWN, Martha	54	BROWN, Sarah	61	BURGES, Matthias	147
BROWN, Martha	73	BROWN, Sarah	89	BURGES, Mercy	136
BROWN, Martha	75	BROWN, Sarah	99	BURGES, Remembrance	146
BROWN, Martha	131	BROWN, Sarah	126	BURGES, Ruth	124
BROWN, Martha	133	BROWN, Sarah	131		
BROWN, Martha	147	BROWN, Silvenus	161	— C —	
BROWN, Martha	162	BROWN, Survia	99		
BROWN, Mary	40	BROWN, Susanah	97	CAHOON, Hannah	136
BROWN, Mary	50	BROWN, Susannah	44	CAHOON, James	129
BROWN, Mary	72	BROWN, Susannah	137	CAHOON, Mary	111
BROWN, Mary	75	BROWN, Thankful	128	CAHOON, Moses	149
BROWN, Mary	86	BROWN, Thankful	171	CAHOONE, Elisabeth	136
BROWN, Mary	90	BROWN, Thankfull	63	CAHOONE, Mary	151
BROWN, Mary	117	BROWN, Thankfull	73	CAHOONE, Moses	109
BROWN, Mary	127	BROWN, Thankfull	80	CAHOONE, Serah	147
BROWN, Mary	133	BROWN, Thankfull	87	CARR, Rosanna	170
BROWN, Mary	142	BROWN, Thankfull	126	CARTER, Hannah	30
BROWN, Mary	156	BROWN, Thankfull	140	CASH, Ann	80

Name	Page	Name	Page	Name	Page
CASH, Ann	134	COB, Joshua	75	COLE, Apphia	163
CASH, Samuell	31	COB, Mary	65	COLE, Apphiah	152
CASH, Stephen	104	COB, Mary	75	COLE, Apphya	34
CAVELER, Abagail	89	COB, Mercy	31	COLE, Apphya	67
CAVENDER, Abigial	123	COB, Nathan	65	COLE, Asa	112
CEHOON, Sarah	58	COB, Phebee	75	COLE, Asa	174
CHADWELL, Benjamin	145	COB, Richard	136	COLE, Aubah	161
CHANLE, Rebeckah	152	COB, Thankfull	26	COLE, Azuba	89
CHANLY, Rebecca	136	COB, Thomas	56	COLE, Azubah	165
CHASE, Bethiah	79	COB, Thomas	137	COLE, Barnabas	78
CHASE, Bethiah	129	COBB, Bethia	150	COLE, Barnabas	108
CHASE, Desire	12	COBB, Elisha	150	COLE, Barshua	184
CHASE, Ebenezar	173	COBB, Elkenah	155	COLE, Beniamine	110
CHASE, Mary	176	COBB, Elkenah	159	COLE, Benimin	54
CHASE, Nathan	173	COBB, Freeman	155	COLE, Benimin	110
CHASE, Sarah Linnell	176	COBB, Hannah	155	COLE, Benimine	110
CHEVER, Martha	168	COBB, Isaac	155	COLE, Benjamin	109
CHEVER, Samuel	173	COBB, Jerusha	159	COLE, Benjamin	151
CHEVER, Thanful	173	COBB, Mary	75	COLE, Benjamin	184
CHEVER, Thankfull	173	COBB, Scotto	159	COLE, Bethiah	121
CHILDS, Hannah	46	COFFIN, John Geyer	173	COLE, Bethiah	184
CHIPMAN, Mary	136	COFFIN, Mary	173	COLE, Bette	162
CHIPMAN, Tabatha	171	COFFIN, Obadiah	173	COLE, Betty	161
CHIPMAN, William	71	COHONE, Sarah	128	COLE, Betty	162
CHIPMAN, William	133	COHOON, Elisabeth	136	COLE, Charity	38
CHOHOON, Lydia	83	COHOON, Hanah	152	COLE, Clooe	160
CHRISP, Mary	44	COHOON, James	71	COLE, Daniall	124
CIPMAN, Marcy	71	COHOON, James	138	COLE, Daniel	19
CIPMAN, Martha	71	COHOON, Rachel	182	COLE, Daniel	25
CIPMAN, Marther	71	COHUNE, Lida	134	COLE, Daniel	90
CIPMAN, Mary	71	COKE, Beniamin	22	COLE, Daniel	91
CIPMAN, William	71	COKE, Mercy	22	COLE, Daniel	97
CLARK, John	93	COLE, Abial	173	COLE, Daniel	123
CLARK, John	144	COLE, Abiall	75	COLE, Daniel	125
CLARK, Lance Lot	147	COLE, Abiel	38	COLE, Daniel	141
CLARK, Lot	87	COLE, Abiel	168	COLE, Daniel	143
CLARK, Lot	141	COLE, Abiel	173	COLE, Daniel	155
CLARK, Seth	57	COLE, Abigail	67	COLE, Daniel	184
CLARK, Seth	141	COLE, Abigail	138	COLE, Daniell	17
CLOYES, Easter	54	COLE, Abigail	168	COLE, Danyel	25
CLOYES, Easter	131	COLE, Abigal	112	COLE, David	48
COALE, Benimine	110	COLE, Abigel	69	COLE, David	79
COALE, Daniel	91	COLE, Abner	38	COLE, David	112
COALE, Darkes	114	COLE, Andru	109	COLE, David	130
COALE, Desier	110	COLE, Anna	162	COLE, David	140
COALE, John	112	COLE, Anna	173	COLE, David	161
COALE, Martha	91	COLE, Anna	184	COLE, David	162
COALE, Theoapulus	112	COLE, Anne	61	COLE, Desier	54
COB, Bethiah	65	COLE, Anne	102	COLE, Desier	110
COB, Elisabeth	31	COLE, Apphia	34	COLE, Dorathy	90
COB, Elisha	75	COLE, Apphia	67	COLE, Dorcas	53
COB, Elisha	140	COLE, Apphia	102	COLE, Dorcas	127
COB, Eunis	75	COLE, Apphia	111	COLE, Dorcas	162

COLE, Dorces	121	COLE, Hannah	43	COLE, Jease	132
COLE, Doritha	34	COLE, Hannah	46	COLE, Jedidah	184
COLE, Dorkas	147	COLE, Hannah	48	COLE, Jeruase	113
COLE, Dorkes	54	COLE, Hannah	79	COLE, Jerusa	135
COLE, Dorkis	99	COLE, Hannah	89	COLE, Jerusha	38
COLE, Dorkis	102	COLE, Hannah	94	COLE, Jerusha	79
COLE, Dorkis	151	COLE, Hannah	102	COLE, Jerusha	91
COLE, Dorothy	143	COLE, Hannah	112	COLE, Jerusha	104
COLE, Drusila	129	COLE, Hannah	119	COLE, Jerusha	149
COLE, Drusilla	81	COLE, Hannah	122	COLE, Jesse	53
COLE, Ebenezer	91	COLE, Hannah	123	COLE, Jesse	67
COLE, Ebenezer	162	COLE, Hannah	125	COLE, Jesse	121
COLE, Ebenezor	91	COLE, Hannah	132	COLE, Jesse	167
COLE, Ebenezor	144	COLE, Hannah	137	COLE, Jesse	182
COLE, Edward	173	COLE, Hannah	144	COLE, Jesse	184
COLE, Elener	143	COLE, Hannah	155	COLE, Job	25
COLE, Elezabeth	78	COLE, Hannah	156	COLE, Joel	174
COLE, Eliner	19	COLE, Hannah	173	COLE, John	17
COLE, Elisabath	102	COLE, Hannah	174	COLE, John	19
COLE, Elisabath	112	COLE, Hazael	38	COLE, John	47
COLE, Elisabath	131	COLE, Heman	91	COLE, John	81
COLE, Elisabeth	53	COLE, Heman	173	COLE, John	92
COLE, Elisabeth	67	COLE, Henery	166	COLE, John	112
COLE, Elisabeth	75	COLE, Henry	75	COLE, John	134
COLE, Elisabeth	91	COLE, Hephzebah	19	COLE, John	140
COLE, Elisabeth	139	COLE, Hephzibah	8	COLE, John	144
COLE, Elisabeth	161	COLE, Hephzibah	17	COLE, John	167
COLE, Elisha	48	COLE, Hitty	168	COLE, John	174
COLE, Elisha	61	COLE, Hope	53	COLE, Jonathan	47
COLE, Elisha	104	COLE, Hubbert	19	COLE, Jonathan	53
COLE, Elisha	184	COLE, Isaac	34	COLE, Jonathan	112
COLE, Elizabeth	67	COLE, Isaac	102	COLE, Jonathan	123
COLE, Elizabeth	91	COLE, Isaac	147	COLE, Jonathan	149
COLE, Elizabeth	94	COLE, Isaiah	173	COLE, Jonathan	160
COLE, Elizabeth	147	COLE, Isaiah	184	COLE, Jonathan	168
COLE, Elizabeth	184	COLE, Israel	18	COLE, Jonathan	173
COLE, Elkeny	112	COLE, Israel	19	COLE, Jonethen	112
COLE, Ellanor	173	COLE, Israel	110	COLE, Jonothen	112
COLE, Epheriam	173	COLE, Israel	146	COLE, Joseph	19
COLE, Eunice	61	COLE, Israell	17	COLE, Joseph	31
COLE, Eunice Nickerson	184	COLE, James	17	COLE, Joseph	47
COLE, Eunis	101	COLE, James	25	COLE, Joseph	54
COLE, Garsham	89	COLE, James	46	COLE, Joseph	75
COLE, Gersham	89	COLE, James	47	COLE, Joseph	104
COLE, Gershom	31	COLE, James	81	COLE, Joseph	136
COLE, Gershom	142	COLE, James	94	COLE, Joseph	146
COLE, Halet	110	COLE, James	104	COLE, Joseph	147
COLE, Hanah	99	COLE, James	140	COLE, Joseph	184
COLE, Hanah	108	COLE, James	160	COLE, Joshua	47
COLE, Hanah	128	COLE, Jane	48	COLE, Joshua	61
COLE, Hanah	130	COLE, Jane	67	COLE, Joshua	78
COLE, Hannah	18	COLE, Jane	139	COLE, Joshua	91
COLE, Hannah	19	COLE, Jease	121	COLE, Joshua	94

COLE, Joshua	119	COLE, Mary	163	COLE, Rhode	160
COLE, Joshua	132	COLE, Mary	184	COLE, Robert	38
COLE, Joshua	145	COLE, Matha	91	COLE, Ruben	75
COLE, Joshua	173	COLE, May	19	COLE, Ruben	156
COLE, Joshua	174	COLE, Mehitable	110	COLE, Rufus	117
COLE, Josiah	160	COLE, Mercy	8	COLE, Rufus	134
COLE, Kezia	89	COLE, Mercy	53	COLE, Ruth	16
COLE, Kezia	104	COLE, Mercy	54	COLE, Ruth	17
COLE, Keziah	162	COLE, Mercy	81	COLE, Ruth	19
COLE, Keziah	164	COLE, Mercy	84	COLE, Ruth	25
COLE, Lettis	173	COLE, Mercy	95	COLE, Ruth	31
COLE, Liddiah	38	COLE, Mercy	97	COLE, Ruth	46
COLE, Lidea	94	COLE, Mercy	141	COLE, Ruth	53
COLE, Lidia	38	COLE, Mercy	167	COLE, Ruth	56
COLE, Lidy	174	COLE, Mercy	173	COLE, Ruth	78
COLE, Lois	81	COLE, Moses	47	COLE, Ruth	92
COLE, Lydia	38	COLE, Moses	89	COLE, Ruth	94
COLE, Marcus	94	COLE, Nathan	47	COLE, Ruth	121
COLE, Marcy	81	COLE, Nathan	78	COLE, Ruth	137
COLE, Marcy	121	COLE, Nathan	94	COLE, Ruth	144
COLE, Marcy	146	COLE, Nathan	167	COLE, Ruth	145
COLE, Margaret	122	COLE, Nathan	173	COLE, Sally	168
COLE, Marget	129	COLE, Nathan	174	COLE, Salvenas	78
COLE, Margret	102	COLE, Nathan	184	COLE, Salvenas	108
COLE, Markis	91	COLE, Nathanael	53	COLE, Salvenas	109
COLE, Markus	91	COLE, Nathanael	108	COLE, Samuel	102
COLE, Martha	62	COLE, Nathaniel	113	COLE, Samuel	147
COLE, Martha	67	COLE, Nathaniel	135	COLE, Sarah	19
COLE, Martha	91	COLE, Nathaniel Lewis	182	COLE, Sarah	19
COLE, Martha	102	COLE, Patience	31	COLE, Sarah	31
COLE, Martha	112	COLE, Patience	81	COLE, Sarah	56
COLE, Martha	152	COLE, Patience	89	COLE, Sarah	75
COLE, Martha	167	COLE, Patience	94	COLE, Sarah	78
COLE, Marther	112	COLE, Patience	141	COLE, Sarah	83
COLE, Marther	113	COLE, Phebe	47	COLE, Sarah	94
COLE, Mary	29	COLE, Phebe	125	COLE, Sarah	97
COLE, Mary	46	COLE, Phebe	155	COLE, Sarah	123
COLE, Mary	47	COLE, Phebe	173	COLE, Sarah	134
COLE, Mary	53	COLE, Phebee	104	COLE, Sarah	137
COLE, Mary	54	COLE, Phillip	110	COLE, Sarah	145
COLE, Mary	75	COLE, Prisillah	109	COLE, Sarah	154
COLE, Mary	81	COLE, Rachel	78	COLE, Sarah	167
COLE, Mary	89	COLE, Rebaca	104	COLE, Sarah	168
COLE, Mary	97	COLE, Rebaca	110	COLE, Sarah	173
COLE, Mary	98	COLE, Rebecca	25	COLE, Sarah	174
COLE, Mary	104	COLE, Rebecka	81	COLE, Sarah	184
COLE, Mary	121	COLE, Reliance	31	COLE, Sary	78
COLE, Mary	125	COLE, Reliance	89	COLE, Silvenis	108
COLE, Mary	131	COLE, Relience	89	COLE, Silvenis	150
COLE, Mary	140	COLE, Remick	38	COLE, Silvenos	108
COLE, Mary	146	COLE, Reuben	125	COLE, Sollomon	81
COLE, Mary	155	COLE, Reuben	174	COLE, Sollomon	108
COLE, Mary	162	COLE, Rhoda	160	COLE, Stephen	42

COLE, Stephen	76	COLINGS, Jonathan	121	COLLING, Joseph	30
COLE, Stephen	101	COLINGS, Jonathan	132	COLLING, Joseph	53
COLE, Stephen	140	COLINGS, Michel	131	COLLING, Lidia	142
COLE, Stephen	147	COLLENS, Abiel	52	COLLING, Martha	30
COLE, Stephen	184	COLLENS, Benjamin	18	COLLING, Matthew	142
COLE, Susana	97	COLLENS, Benjamin	146	COLLING, Ruth	25
COLE, Susana	102	COLLENS, Dorathy	52	COLLING, Samuell	30
COLE, Susanah	112	COLLENS, Elizabeth	52	COLLING, Solomon	30
COLE, Susanah	123	COLLENS, Hannah	18	COMBES, Thankfull	126
COLE, Susanah	146	COLLENS, James	18	COMBS, Samuel	133
COLE, Susanah	174	COLLENS, Jane	18	COMBS, Sarah	56
COLE, Susanna	34	COLLENS, Jane	31	COMBS, Thankfull	156
COLE, Susanna	173	COLLENS, John	9	COMES, Israel	145
COLE, Susanna	174	COLLENS, Jonathan	18	CONANT, Mary	131
COLE, Susannah	164	COLLENS, Jonathan	34	CONANT, Sarah	25
COLE, Susannah	171	COLLENS, Jonathan	136	CONANT, Sarah	32
COLE, Susannah	174	COLLENS, Joseph	9	CONNANT, Hannah	119
COLE, Suzanah	112	COLLENS, Joseph	18	COOCK, Caleb	171
COLE, Tabitha	182	COLLENS, Joseph	49	COOCK, Calib	171
COLE, Thankful	104	COLLENS, Lidia	18	COOCK, Jane	171
COLE, Thankful	168	COLLENS, Lois	49	COOCK, Lydea	171
COLE, Thankfull	47	COLLENS, Pasheler	147	COOCK, Ruth Smith	171
COLE, Thankfull	97	COLLENS, Prence	97	COOCK, Susannah	171
COLE, Thankfull	106	COLLENS, Prence	145	COOK, Abigail	77
COLE, Thankfull	149	COLLENS, Pricilla	89	COOK, Abigail	87
COLE, Theofulos	167	COLLENS, Prince	52	COOK, Abigel	146
COLE, Theophilas	81	COLLENS, Prince	97	OOOK, An	17
COLE, Thomas	38	COLLENS, Priscilla	143	COOK, Apphia	87
COLE, Thomas	110	COLLENS, Rebecca	49	COOK, Apphiah	77
COLE, Timothy	19	COLLENS, Rebecka	90	COOK, Barnabas	136
COLE, Timothy	34	COLLENS, Rebecka	97	COOK, Barnabas	152
COLE, Timothy	67	COLLENS, Rebecka	143	COOK, Barnabas	170
COLE, Timothy	68	COLLENS, Sarah	90	COOK, Bethah	87
COLE, Timothy	102	COLLENS, Sarah	143	COOK, Bethiah	28
COLE, Timothy	138	COLLENS, Saraie	9	COOK, Bethiah	77
COLE, Timothy	139	COLLINGS, Dennis	65	COOK, Betty	136
COLE, Timothy	184	COLLINGS, Dorathy	159	COOK, Betty	152
COLE, Tymothy	17	COLLINGS, Dorothy	123	COOK, Calab	86
COLE, Unice	81	COLLINGS, Fraces	65	COOK, Calab	171
COLE, Unis	110	COLLINGS, Joseph	123	COOK, Caleb	50
COLE, Unis	147	COLLINGS, Michael	65	COOK, Caleb	86
COLE, Vashti	134	COLLINGS, Michael	66	COOK, Caleb	171
COLE, Vashty	79	COLLINGS, Rebecca	65	COOK, David	171
COLE, Vashty	83	COLLINGS, Rebecca	66	COOK, Deborah	40
COLE, William	25	COLLING, David	31	COOK, Deborah	125
COLE, William	48	COLLING, Elezebeth	167	COOK, Deborah	159
COLE, William	79	COLLING, Hannah	30	COOK, Deborah	160
COLE, William	109	COLLING, Hannah	31	COOK, Dinah	99
COLE, William	131	COLLING, Hannah	48	COOK, Dorcas	160
COLE, William	150	COLLING, John	30	COOK, Dorcas	171
COLENS, Joseph	124	COLLING, John	31	COOK, Ebenezer	98
COLES, Danel	52	COLLING, Jonathan	54	COOK, Ebenezer	146
COLES, Martha	52	COLLING, Joseph	25	COOK, Ebenezor	98

COOK, Elijah	89	COOK, Phebe	161	COOKE, Deborah	34
COOK, Elisha	77	COOK, Phebe	170	COOKE, Deborah	50
COOK, Elisha	87	COOK, Rachel	161	COOKE, Deliverance	39
COOK, Elizabeth	89	COOK, Rebacca	77	COOKE, Desire	34
COOK, Ephraim	95	COOK, Rebacca	87	COOKE, Ebenezer	22
COOK, Ephraim	96	COOK, Rebacce	77	COOKE, Elisabeth	39
COOK, Ephraim	99	COOK, Rebecca	77	COOKE, Elisabeth	50
COOK, Ephraim	146	COOK, Rebecka	99	COOKE, Elisabeth	56
COOK, Eprain	99	COOK, Rebecka	150	COOKE, Elisabeth	141
COOK, Esenath	99	COOK, Richard	77	COOKE, Elizabeth	40
COOK, Gideon	99	COOK, Richard	87	COOKE, Elizebeth	42
COOK, Gideon	160	COOK, Richard	149	COOKE, Ephraim	22
COOK, Hannah	77	COOK, Ruben	96	COOKE, Hanah	74
COOK, Hannah	87	COOK, Ruben	99	COOKE, Hannah	50
COOK, Hannah	89	COOK, Ruth	98	COOKE, Hannah	63
COOK, Hannah	160	COOK, Samuel	120	COOKE, Hannah	138
COOK, Hannah	171	COOK, Samuel	160	COOKE, John	34
COOK, Isaiah	91	COOK, Samuel	171	COOKE, Joseph	22
COOK, Isayah	91	COOK, Samuell	86	COOKE, Joshua	22
COOK, Jacob	90	COOK, Samuell	160	COOKE, Joshua	40
COOK, Jacob	143	COOK, Sarah	77	COOKE, Joshua	131
COOK, James	91	COOK, Sarah	87	COOKE, Josia	34
COOK, Jane	171	COOK, Sarah	99	COOKE, Josiah	22
COOK, Joanna	77	COOK, Sarah	161	COOKE, Josiah	24
COOK, Joanna	87	COOK, Sarah	171	COOKE, Josiah	40
COOK, Joanna	162	COOK, Sarah	173	COOKE, Marcy	129
COOK, John	160	COOK, Shubal	99	COOKE, Martha	22
COOK, John	161	COOK, Shubal	109	COOKE, Mary	34
COOK, Joseph	160	COOK, Simeon	147	COOKE, Mercy	22
COOK, Joseph	173	COOK, Susanah	86	COOKE, Mercy	22
COOK, Joshua	89	COOK, Thankfull	99	COOKE, Moses	22
COOK, Joshua	90	COOK, Thankfull	100	COOKE, Nathanael	22
COOK, Joshua	91	COOK, Thankfull	146	COOKE, Nathaniel	109
COOK, Joshua	111	COOK, Thomas	99	COOKE, Pacienc	22
COOK, Joshua	136	COOK, Thomas	138	CCOKE, Patience	22
COOK, Joshua	143	COOK, Thomas	171	COOKE, Richard	22
COOK, Josiah	40	COOK, William	77	COOKE, Richard	40
COOK, Josiah	89	COOK, Zenas	87	COOKE, Richard	50
COOK, Josiah	143	COOK, Zenas	91	COOKE, Ruhama	22
COOK, Lidia	173	COOK, Zilpha	170	COOKE, Samuel	133
COOK, Lydia	77	COOKE, Abigail	39	COOKE, Sarah	50
COOK, Lydia	86	COOKE, Abigaile	50	COOKE, Sarah	130
COOK, Lydia	87	COOKE, Anna	29	COOKE, Shuball	22
COOK, Lydia	124	COOKE, Anne	50	COOKE, Simeon	22
COOK, Marcy	91	COOKE, Beniamin	22	COOKE, Thankfull	50
COOK, Marcy	170	COOKE, Benjamin	40	COOKE, Thomas	50
COOK, Nathan	77	COOKE, Caleb	39	COOKE, Thomas	69
COOK, Nathan	87	COOKE, Caleb	40	COOKS, Samuell	160
COOK, Nathan	171	COOKE, Caleb	74	COOKSON, John	89
COOK, Nathaniel	109	COOKE, Caleb	81	COOKSON, John	109
COOK, Nathaniel	149	COOKE, Caleb	86	COOKSON, John	123
COOK, Phebe	77	COOKE, Caleb	140	COOKSON, John	149
COOK, Phebe	87	COOKE, Caleb	142	COOLE, Daniell	25

COOLE, Mary	25	COVELL, Hannah	77	CROKER, William	116
COOLEY, Bridget	38	COVELL, Hannah	155	CROOEL, David	128
COOMBS, Content	111	COVELL, Hester	151	CROSBE, -----	12
COOMBS, Samuel	73	COVELL, Joannah	100	CROSBE, John	12
COOMBS, Sarah	132	COVELL, Marcy	89	CROSBE, Joseph	12
COOMES, Solomon	65	COVELL, Nathanael	139	CROSBE, Sarah	12
COOMS, Content	65	COVELL, Nathaniel	73	CROSBE, Simon	12
COOMS, Samuel	65	COVELL, Nathniel	76	CROSBE, Thomas	12
COOMS, Sarah	65	COVELL, Phebee	89	CROSBEY, Abiel	155
COOMS, Solloman	65	COVELL, Ruben	73	CROSBIE, Samuel	53
COOMS, Solomon	140	COVELL, Ruben	76	CROSBIE, Samuel	56
CORSBARY, Mary	135	COVELL, Ruben	77	CROSBIE, Samuel	137
CORTENGEL, Elisabath	121	COVELL, William	102	CROSBRY, Abiel	126
CORTENGILS, Elizath	132	COVELL, William	145	CROSBRY, Hanah	125
COUEL, Amay	89	COVELL, Willm.	100	CROSBY, Abiah	122
COUEL, Daniel	89	COVIL, David	102	CROSBY, Abiah	128
COUEL, Ephram	89	COVIL, Elisabeth	102	CROSBY, Abiel	168
COUEL, Ephram	90	COVIL, William	102	CROSBY, Anne	12
COUEL, Hannah	66	COWET, Jedidah	103	CROSBY, Daniel	94
COUEL, Marcy	90	CRISP, George	8	CROSBY, Daniel	144
COUEL, Mary	66	CRISP, Mercie	8	CROSBY, Deborah	168
COUEL, Mary	89	CRISP, Mercy	41	CROSBY, Ebenezer	12
COUEL, Mary	90	CRISPE, George	8	CROSBY, Eliezer	12
COUEL, Mercy	90	CRISPE, George	24	CROSBY, Elizabeth	18
COUEL, Phebe	65	CRISPE, Mary	8	CROSBY, Heman	161
COUEL, Sarah	77	CRISPE, Mary	24	CROSBY, Increase	12
COUEL, Solomon	89	CROCKER, Anna	170	CROSBY, Joseph	19
COUELL, Esther	111	CROCKER, Apphia	61	CROSBY, Joseph	168
COUELL, Hannah	127	CROCKER, Apphiah	170	CROSBY, Joshua	168
COUMS, Content	136	CROCKER, Job	61	CROSBY, Mercy	12
COVEL, Ephraim	89	CROCKER, Job	136	CROSBY, Moses	152
COVEL, Hannah	130	CROCKER, Jobe	61	CROSBY, Nathaniel	91
COVEL, Joanna	56	CROCKER, Joseph	106	CROSBY, Nathaniel	144
COVEL, Joanna	133	CROCKER, Joseph	149	CROSBY, Rebecca	168
COVEL, Joseph	8	CROCKER, Josiah	106	CROSBY, Samuel	18
COVEL, Mary	133	CROCKER, Licua	163	CROSBY, Simon	18
COVEL, Nathaniel	49	CROCKER, Lucia	106	CROSBY, Thankful	168
COVEL, Phebe	132	CROCKER, Lucia	163	CROSBY, Thankfull	158
COVEL, Philip	132	CROCKER, Lydia	173	CROSBY, Thankfull	168
COVEL, Ruben	76	CROCKER, Marcy	61	CROSBY, Theophilas	19
COVEL, Ruben	132	CROCKER, Mary	61	CROSBY, Thomas	12
COVEL, Sarah	132	CROCKER, Mercy	61	CROSBY, William	12
COVEL, William	56	CROCKER, Mercy	169	CROWELL, Abigail	58
COVEL, William	97	CROCKER, Relianc	61	CROWELL, Abigel	145
COVEL, William	147	CROCKER, Reliance	106	CROWELL, Alice	58
COVEL, Zeruiah	119	CROCKER, Temperence	173	CROWELL, David	81
COVEL, Zerviah	89	CROCKER, William	133	CROWELL, Hannah	145
COVEL, Zeviah	132	CROCKER, William	173	CROWELL, Jabez	58
COVELL, Ami	89	CROEL, Elisabath	134	CROWELL, John	58
COVELL, Ephraim	89	CROKER, Job	61	CROWELL, John	62
COVELL, Ephraim	143	CROKER, Marcy	61	CROWELL, John	63
COVELL, Hannah	73	CROKER, Mary	61	CROWELL, John	138
COVELL, Hannah	76	CROKER, Nathaniel	61	CRSBY, Abiah	128

CUFFE, Joseph	80	DILL, Benjamin	182	DOANE, Abigel	77
CUPY, Martha	100	DILL, Huldah	182	DOANE, Abigel	95
CURTIS, Prissila	149	DILL, James	107	DOANE, Abigel	99
CURTIS, Prissilla	76	DILL, James	125	DOANE, Abigel	144
CURTIS, Prissilla	139	DILL, James	159	DOANE, Abigel	146
CUSEN, Moses	89	DILL, Lydia	157	DOANE, Alce	83
CUSENS, Daniel	109	DILL, Nancy	180	DOANE, Ann	33
CUSENS, Daniel	134	DILL, Phebe	182	DOANE, Ann	40
CUSENS, Daniel	150	DILL, Samuel	125	DOANE, Ann	86
CUSENS, Experience	151	DILL, Samuell	157	DOANE, Anna	99
CUSHING, Mary	69	DILL, Samuell	159	DOANE, Anne	49
CUSHING, Mary	131	DILL, Thomas	95	DOANE, Anne	80
CUTLER, John	73	DILL, Thomas	107	DOANE, Anne	140
CUTLER, John	139	DILL, Thomas	129	DOANE, Anne	147
CUTLER, Sarah	73	DILL, Thomas	145	DOANE, Anne	159
		DILLINGHAM, Rebecca	142	DOANE, Anne	162
— D —		DIMMOCK, Silence	139	DOANE, Apphiah	21
		DIMOCK, Timothy	49	DOANE, Azariah	100
DAVIS, Hitty	174	DMES, Sarah	112	DOANE, Azariah	174
DAVIS, Jacob	92	DOAN, Abigail	49	DOANE, Azariah	187
DAVIS, Jacob	145	DOAN, David	30	DOANE, Beniamen	128
DAVIS, Job Crocker	174	DOAN, Dinah	38	DOANE, Benjamen	48
DAVIS, John	103	DOAN, Doritha	30	DOANE, Benjamin	157
DAVIS, John	169	DOAN, Elisabeth	48	DOANE, Beriah	174
DAVIS, John	174	DOAN, Elisha	151	DOANE, Beriah	181
DAVIS, Mercy	174	DOAN, Hannah	30	DOANE, Bersilla	119
DAVIS, Nathaniel	174	DOAN, Hannah	49	DOANE, Bethiah	159
DAVIS, Robert	174	DOAN, Israel	45	DOANE, Bettee	83
DAVIS, Ruth Crocker	174	DOAN, John	40	DOANE, Betty	161
DAVIS, Sarah	25	DOAN, Jonathan	30	DOANE, Betty	181
DAVIS, Sarah	108	DOAN, Joseph	7	DOANE, Bety	151
DAVIS, Serah	151	DOAN, Martha	38	DOANE, Bety	174
DEAN, Epheram	124	DOAN, Mary	7	DOANE, Biell	145
DEAN, Ephraim	64	DOAN, Patience	22	DOANE, Constant	9
DEAN, Jonas	93	DOAN, Patience	48	DOANE, Cynthia	181
DEAN, Jonas	129	DOAN, Phebe	158	DOANE, Daniel	7
DEAN, Thomas	120	DOAN, Prenc	45	DOANE, Daniel	45
DEAN, Thomas	133	DOAN, Prenc	140	DOANE, Daniel	92
DEAN, William	125	DOAN, Ruth	45	DOANE, Daniel	99
DEAN, William	159	DOAN, Samuel	38	DOANE, Daniel	145
DEANE, James	124	DOAN, Sarah	38	DOANE, Daniel	161
DEANES, Sarah	112	DOAN, Silvenus	158	DOANE, Darcas	99
DEANES, Sarah	134	DOAN, Solomon	38	DOANE, Darkes	114
DENNES, John	130	DOAN, Thomas	48	DOANE, David	30
DENNIS, William	57	DOAND, Zilliah	134	DOANE, David	86
DENNIS, William	137	DOANE, Abiel	97	DOANE, David	147
DEXTER, Thomas	163	DOANE, Abigail	75	DOANE, David	151
DICK, Elisabath	134	DOANE, Abigail	91	DOANE, David	159
DIER, Lidya	152	DOANE, Abigail	132	DOANE, Debora	57
DILEE, Mary	145	DOANE, Abigail	181	DOANE, Debro	57
DILEE, Samuel	143	DOANE, Abigaile	45	DOANE, Debro	77
DILL, Aron	107	DOANE, Abigaile	48	DOANE, Debro	99
DILL, Benjamin	157	DOANE, Abigal	174	DOANE, Desire	7

DOANE, Desire	84	DOANE, Ezekiah	21	DOANE, Jerusha	140
DOANE, Desire	154	DOANE, Ezekiel	86	DOANE, Jerusha	149
DOANE, Dinah	69	DOANE, George H.	187	DOANE, Jesse	72
DOANE, Dinah	138	DOANE, Hanah	62	DOANE, Joel	99
DOANE, Dorcas	38	DOANE, Hanah	72	DOANE, Joel	174
DOANE, Dorcas	71	DOANE, Hannah	7	DOANE, Joel	181
DOANE, Dorcas	99	DOANE, Hannah	22	DOANE, John	22
DOANE, Dorcas	139	DOANE, Hannah	30	DOANE, John	30
DOANE, Dorcas	174	DOANE, Hannah	38	DOANE, John	40
DOANE, Dorcas Snow	187	DOANE, Hannah	70	DOANE, John	86
DOANE, Doritha	30	DOANE, Hannah	71	DOANE, John	96
DOANE, Dorkis	58	DOANE, Hannah	77	DOANE, John	123
DOANE, Dorkis	83	DOANE, Hannah	109	DOANE, John	142
DOANE, Dorthey	72	DOANE, Hannah	130	DOANE, John	144
DOANE, Ebenezer	21	DOANE, Hannah	138	DOANE, John	171
DOANE, Ebenezer	181	DOANE, Hannah	139	DOANE, John	174
DOANE, Edmond	45	DOANE, Hannah	140	DOANE, John	181
DOANE, Edward	159	DOANE, Hannah	151	DOANE, Jonathan	72
DOANE, Eleazor	93	DOANE, Hannah	159	DOANE, Jonathan	139
DOANE, Eleazor	144	DOANE, Heman	100	DOANE, Josep	7
DOANE, Elezebath	158	DOANE, Heman	174	DOANE, Joseph	7
DOANE, Elijah	98	DOANE, Hezekiah	38	DOANE, Joseph	8
DOANE, Elijah	146	DOANE, Hezekiah	151	DOANE, Joseph	57
DOANE, Elijah	159	DOANE, Heziciah	134	DOANE, Joseph	58
DOANE, Elisabath	62	DOANE, Hitta	181	DOANE, Joseph	77
DOANE, Elisabath	72	DOANE, Hope	62	DOANE, Joseph	83
DOANE, Elisabath	131	DOANE, Hulda	49	DOANE, Joseph	84
DOANE, Elisabeth	7	DOANE, Huldah	57	DOANE, Joseph	92
DOANE, Elisabeth	158	DOANE, Huldah	141	DOANE, Joseph	100
DOANE, Elisebath	158	DOANE, Isaac	49	DOANE, Joseph	103
DOANE, Elisha	7	DOANE, Isaac	83	DOANE, Joseph	140
DOANE, Elisha	62	DOANE, Isaac	99	DOANE, Joseph	141
DOANE, Elisha	72	DOANE, Isaac	139	DOANE, Joseph	164
DOANE, Elisha	96	DOANE, Isaac	145	DOANE, Joshua	7
DOANE, Elisha	96	DOANE, Isaac	164	DOANE, Joshua	53
DOANE, Elisha	109	DOANE, Isaac	181	DOANE, Joshua	83
DOANE, Elisha	137	DOANE, Isaac Snow	187	DOANE, Joshua	100
DOANE, Elisha	145	DOANE, Isaace	40	DOANE, Joshua	102
DOANE, Elisha	151	DOANE, Isaiah	49	DOANE, Joshua	103
DOANE, Elisha	158	DOANE, Isaiah	62	DOANE, Joshua	158
DOANE, Eliza	174	DOANE, Isaiah	168	DOANE, Joshua	170
DOANE, Elizabeth	77	DOANE, Israel	45	DOANE, Joshua	174
DOANE, Elkanah	86	DOANE, Israel	53	DOANE, Joshua	187
DOANE, Elkanah	113	DOANE, James	72	DOANE, Ketura	146
DOANE, Elkanah	181	DOANE, James	128	DOANE, Kezia	126
DOANE, Elnathan	45	DOANE, James	158	DOANE, Keziah	30
DOANE, Elnathan	99	DOANE, Jane	96	DOANE, Keziah	57
DOANE, Elnathan	147	DOANE, Jease	131	DOANE, Keziah	96
DOANE, Enock	146	DOANE, Jedida	181	DOANE, Keziah	100
DOANE, Ephraim	21	DOANE, Jedidah	174	DOANE, Keziah	141
DOANE, Ephraim	38	DOANE, Jedidah	181	DOANE, Keziah	145
DOANE, Eunice	100	DOANE, Jerusha	49	DOANE, Keziah	155
DOANE, Eunice	161	DOANE, Jerusha	79	DOANE, Keziah	174

DOANE, Lewis	181	DOANE, Nathaniel	92	DOANE, Ruth	181
DOANE, Lidea	58	DOANE, Nathaniel	159	DOANE, Sally	181
DOANE, Lidea	68	DOANE, Nehemiah	21	DOANE, Samuel	38
DOANE, Lidea	90	DOANE, Nehemiah	38	DOANE, Samuel	40
DOANE, Lidea	144	DOANE, Nehemiah	83	DOANE, Samuel	68
DOANE, Lidia	159	DOANE, Nehemiah	159	DOANE, Samuel	99
DOANE, Lidya	7	DOANE, Noah	83	DOANE, Samuel	114
DOANE, Lot	159	DOANE, Noah	131	DOANE, Samuel	138
DOANE, Lucy	171	DOANE, Noah	159	DOANE, Samuel	151
DOANE, Lydia	159	DOANE, Patience	21	DOANE, Samuel Dill	159
DOANE, Lydia	181	DOANE, Patience	48	DOANE, Samuell	38
DOANE, Marcy	91	DOANE, Phebe	7	DOANE, Samuell	171
DOANE, Marcy	96	DOANE, Phebe	77	DOANE, Sarah	7
DOANE, Marcy	114	DOANE, Phebe	140	DOANE, Sarah	54
DOANE, Marcy	144	DOANE, Phebe	158	DOANE, Sarah	66
DOANE, Marcy	159	DOANE, Phebe	171	DOANE, Sarah	96
DOANE, Marcy	161	DOANE, Phebee	77	DOANE, Sarah	107
DOANE, Margared	49	DOANE, Polly	174	DOANE, Sarah	123
DOANE, Margeret	49	DOANE, Prence	77	DOANE, Sarah	132
DOANE, Margret	97	DOANE, Prince	77	DOANE, Sarah	138
DOANE, Margret	145	DOANE, Priscilla	68	DOANE, Sarah	150
DOANE, Martha	38	DOANE, Priscilla	159	DOANE, Sarah	170
DOANE, Martha	68	DOANE, Prisilah	181	DOANE, Sarah	174
DOANE, Martha	72	DOANE, Prissilla	159	DOANE, Serah	83
DOANE, Martha	90	DOANE, Rachel	83	DOANE, Seth	72
DOANE, Martha	114	DOANE, Rachel	86	DOANE, Seth	100
DOANE, Martha	143	DOANE, Rachel	121	DOANE, Seth	158
DOANE, Martha	162	DOANE, Rachel	129	DOANE, Seth	161
DOANE, Mary	7	DOANE, Rachel	132	DOANE, Seth	174
DOANE, Mary	38	DOANE, Rachel	146	DOANE, Seth	187
DOANE, Mary	42	DOANE, Rebecca	7	DOANE, Silvanus	72
DOANE, Mary	77	DOANE, Rebecca	23	DOANE, Silvenis	96
DOANE, Mary	86	DOANE, Rebecca	66	DOANE, Silvenus	123
DOANE, Mary	90	DOANE, Rebecca	139	DOANE, Silvenus	158
DOANE, Mary	92	DOANE, Rebecka	40	DOANE, Simeon	38
DOANE, Mary	100	DOANE, Rebecka	96	DOANE, Simeon	90
DOANE, Mary	102	DOANE, Ruben	48	DOANE, Simeon	98
DOANE, Mary	129	DOANE, Ruben	144	DOANE, Simeon	99
DOANE, Mary	143	DOANE, Ruben	161	DOANE, Simeon	174
DOANE, Mary	159	DOANE, Ruhama	21	DOANE, Simion	143
DOANE, Mary	170	DOANE, Ruhama	140	DOANE, Sollomon	83
DOANE, Mehetabel	22	DOANE, Ruhamah	81	DOANE, Solomon	22
DOANE, Mehetable	159	DOANE, Ruth	15	DOANE, Solomon	83
DOANE, Mercy	96	DOANE, Ruth	45	DOANE, Solomon	129
DOANE, Mercy	167	DOANE, Ruth	77	DOANE, Solomon	140
DOANE, Mhetable	174	DOANE, Ruth	92	DOANE, Solomon	170
DOANE, Molly	174	DOANE, Ruth	98	DOANE, Susannah	164
DOANE, Nancy	181	DOANE, Ruth	99	DOANE, Tamsan	164
DOANE, Nathan	30	DOANE, Ruth	119	DOANE, Tamsen	174
DOANE, Nathan	72	DOANE, Ruth	133	DOANE, Tamson	100
DOANE, Nathan	161	DOANE, Ruth	157	DOANE, Tamson	102
DOANE, Nathaniel	57	DOANE, Ruth	170	DOANE, Thankful	127
DOANE, Nathaniel	77	DOANE, Ruth	174	DOANE, Thankful	187

DOANE, Thankfull	62	ELDRED, Nathanael	32	FFREEMAN, Alice	25
DOANE, Thankfull	68	ELDRED, William	25	FFREEMAN, Anne	21
DOANE, Thankfull	187	ELDREDGE, Daniel	156	FFREEMAN, Apphiah	23
DOANE, Thomas	21	ELDREGE, Barnabas	98	FFREEMAN, Barnabas	24
DOANE, Thomas	48	ELDREGE, Barnabas	146	FFREEMAN, Barnabas	25
DOANE, Thomas	165	ELDREGE, Dorcas	103	FFREEMAN, Barnabas	42
DOANE, Timothy	68	ELDREGE, Jesse	97	FFREEMAN, Basbua	24
DOANE, Timothy	92	ELDREGE, Jesse	145	FFREEMAN, Bathshebe	13
DOANE, Timothy	129	ELDREGE, Mary	103	FFREEMAN, Bathshua	24
DOANE, Timothy	158	ELDREGE, Mulford	146	FFREEMAN, Bathshuah	24
DOANE, Timothy	174	ELDRIDG, Daniel	61	FFREEMAN, Benjamine	8
DOANE, Timothy	181	ELDRIDG, Daniel	141	FFREEMAN, Constant	23
DOANE, Tymothi	174	ELDRIDG, Debora	78	FFREEMAN, Constant	45
DOANE, Uriah	157	ELDRIDG, Debora	140	FFREEMAN, David	24
DOANE, Uriah	181	ELDRIDG, Dorcas	64	FFREEMAN, David	84
DOANE, William	157	ELDRIDG, Elisabeth	138	FFREEMAN, Ebenezer	21
DOANE, Zenos	159	ELDRIDG, Elisha	64	FFREEMAN, Edmond	77
DOCKRILL, Thomas	186	ELDRIDG, Jesse	64	FFREEMAN, Edmond	86
DOLE, Daniel	8	ELDRIDG, Martha	71	FFREEMAN, Edmound	42
DONE, Bethier	112	ELDRIDG, Mary	64	FFREEMAN, Eleazor	80
DONE, Edman	112	ELDRIDG, Sarah	140	FFREEMAN, Eliezer	41
DONE, Edmand	135	ELDRIDGE, Daniel	126	FFREEMAN, Eliezer	80
DONE, Elcany	135	ELDRIDGE, David	188	FFREEMAN, Elisabath	93
DONE, Enock	112	ELDRIDGE, James	188	FFREEMAN, Elisabeth	24
DONE, Hanah	112	ELDRIDGE, Martha	139	FFREEMAN, Elisabeth	45
DONNHAM, Beniah	33	ELDRIDGE, Sarah	188	FFREEMAN, Elisabeth	56
DONNHAM, Edman	33	ELDRIG, Daniel	61	FFREEMAN, Elisabeth	66
DOYLEY, Samuel	90	ELDRIG, Daniel	76	FFREEMAN, Elisha	24
DUNHAM, Beniamin	34	ELDRIG, Daniel	134	FFREEMAN, Elizabeth	23
DUNHAM, Bennaiah	33	ELDRIG, Elisabeth	61	FFREEMAN, Elizebeth	24
DUNHAM, Bennaiah	34	ELDRIG, Elisabeth Elisasebeth	61	FFREEMAN, Enoch	24
DUNHAM, Elizabeth	34	ELDRIGD, Mary	41	FFREEMAN, Eunice	45
DUNHAM, Hannah	34	ELKENS, Margeret	30	FFREEMAN, Eunis	63
DUNHAM, John	33	ELLIS, John	28	FFREEMAN, Gideon	63
DUNKIN, John	96	EMMES, Hannah	174	FFREEMAN, Hannah	25
DUNKIN, John	145	EMMES, Joshua	174	FFREEMAN, Hannah	42
DYER, Ebenezer	66	EVERY, John	145	FFREEMAN, Hannah	45
DYER, Ebenezer	138			FFREEMAN, Hannah	58
DYER, Ebenezer	161	— F —		FFREEMAN, Hannah	66
DYER, Fulk	71			FFREEMAN, Hannah	97
DYER, Fullk	129	FFISH, Bartholomew	53	FFREEMAN, Hatsuld	42
DYER, Jonathan	137	FFREEM, Rebecca	80	FFREEMAN, James	24
DYER, Jonathan	146	FFREEMA, Mary	25	FFREEMAN, James	25
DYER, Sollomon	151	FFREEMA, Samuel	25	FFREEMAN, Jane	45
DYER, William	13	FFREEMAMAN, Edmond	77	FFREEMAN, Jennet	21
		FFREEMAMAN, Prince	42	FFREEMAN, John	8
— E —		FFREEMAN, Abigael	41	FFREEMAN, John	24
		FFREEMAN, Abigail	21	FFREEMAN, John	41
EASTERBROOKE, Abigaile	45	FFREEMAN, Abigail	26	FFREEMAN, John	63
EATEN, Abel	126	FFREEMAN, Abigail	63	FFREEMAN, Jonathan	42
EATEN, Ebed	100	FFREEMAN, Abigaile	24	FFREEMAN, Jonathan	77
EATEN, Ebit	147	FFREEMAN, Abigel	25	FFREEMAN, Joseph	42
ELDRED, Elisabeth	10	FFREEMAN, Abigel	94	FFREEMAN, Joseph	63

FFREEMAN, Joshua	42	FFREEMAN, Samuell	24	FREEMAN, Alice	149
FFREEMAN, Joshua	63	FFREEMAN, Sarah	8	FREEMAN, Ann	74
FFREEMAN, Kezia	42	FFREEMAN, Sarah	29	FREEMAN, Ann	134
FFREEMAN, Liddiah	41	FFREEMAN, Seth	80	FREEMAN, Appiah	150
FFREEMAN, Lidiah	32	FFREEMAN, Simeon	24	FREEMAN, Barnabas	107
FFREEMAN, Loes	77	FFREEMAN, Susana	66	FREEMAN, Barnabas	145
FFREEMAN, Marcy	8	FFREEMAN, Susanah	42	FREEMAN, Barnabus	166
FFREEMAN, Marcy	25	FFREEMAN, Susanna	32	FREEMAN, Barshaba	62
FFREEMAN, Martha	66	FFREEMAN, Tamsen	63	FREEMAN, Barshaba	130
FFREEMAN, Mary	24	FFREEMAN, Thankfull	21	FREEMAN, Bethiah	65
FFREEMAN, Mary	25	FFREEMAN, Thankfull	58	FREEMAN, Bethiah	166
FFREEMAN, Mary	41	FFREEMAN, Thomas	13	FREEMAN, Betty	65
FFREEMAN, Mary	42	FFREEMAN, Thomas	28	FREEMAN, Betty	114
FFREEMAN, Mary	53	FFREEMAN, Thomas	42	FREEMAN, Bety	65
FFREEMAN, Mary	63	FFREEMAN, Thomison	63	FREEMAN, Catherine	185
FFREEMAN, Mary	66	FFREEMAN, William	32	FREEMAN, Constant	45
FFREEMAN, Mary	80	FFREMAN, Apphia	19	FREEMAN, Daniel	103
FFREEMAN, Mary	93	FFREMAN, Apthiah	24	FREEMAN, Daniel	149
FFREEMAN, Mary	100	FFRY, John	95	FREEMAN, David	141
FFREEMAN, Mercy	25	FINNIE, Mehetabell	137	FREEMAN, Dorcas	174
FFREEMAN, Mercy	42	FINNY, Abigaile	140	FREEMAN, Dorcas	186
FFREEMAN, Mercy	45	FISH, Lidya	137	FREEMAN, Dorothy	174
FFREEMAN, Mercy	56	FISH, Phebee	146	FREEMAN, Ebenezer	21
FFREEMAN, Mercy	63	FISH, Rhoda	152	FREEMAN, Edman	118
FFREEMAN, Moses	42	FISH, Roulan	90	FREEMAN, Edmond	140
FFREEMAN, Nathanael	66	FISH, Rouland	143	FREEMAN, Edmond	142
FFREEMAN, Nathaneel	41	FORD, Adam	123	FREEMAN, Edward	186
FFREEMAN, Nathanel	41	FORD, Peleg	105	FREEMAN, Elezebeth	174
FFREEMAN, Nathaniel	8	FORD, Pelegg	149	FREEMAN, Elies	149
FFREEMAN, Nathaniel	24	FORGE, Pelegg	149	FREEMAN, Eliezer	140
FFREEMAN, Nathaniel	41	FORSTOR, Mehitable	126	FREEMAN, Eliezer	168
FFREEMAN, Nathanll.	41	FOSTER, Isaac	125	FREEMAN, Elisabeth	150
FFREEMAN, Nathanll.	66	FOSTER, Isaac	155	FREEMAN, Elisha	77
FFREEMAN, Patience	21	FOSTER, John	163	FREEMAN, Elisha	140
FFREEMAN, Phebee	87	FOSTER, Mehitable	126	FREEMAN, Elisha	174
FFREEMAN, Prence	42	FRASOUR, John	130	FREEMAN, Elisha Linnel	188
FFREEMAN, Prince	42	FRASUR, Anna	86	FREEMAN, Elizabeth	107
FFREEMAN, Priscilla	9	FRASUR, Daniel	86	FREEMAN, Elizabeth	109
FFREEMAN, Prissila	24	FRASUR, John	86	FREEMAN, Elizabeth	144
FFREEMAN, Prissilla	25	FREEMAN, Abigail	21	FREEMAN, Eunice	125
FFREEMAN, Rachel	87	FREEMAN, Abigail	54	FREEMAN, Eunice	155
FFREEMAN, Rebecca	8	FREEMAN, Abigail	73	FREEMAN, Eunice	185
FFREEMAN, Rebecca	25	FREEMAN, Abigail	117	FREEMAN, Eunice	186
FFREEMAN, Rebecca	80	FREEMAN, Abigail	131	FREEMAN, Francis	186
FFREEMAN, Rebecka	80	FREEMAN, Abigail	134	FREEMAN, Gedion	136
FFREEMAN, Rebeka	80	FREEMAN, Abigail	174	FREEMAN, Gidan	112
FFREEMAN, Robert	45	FREEMAN, Abigail	188	FREEMAN, Gidean	114
FFREEMAN, Ruth	66	FREEMAN, Abigaile	21	FREEMAN, Hanah	112
FFREEMAN, Ruth	84	FREEMAN, Abigel	117	FREEMAN, Hanah	114
FFREEMAN, Saml.	24	FREEMAN, Abigel	145	FREEMAN, Hanna	163
FFREEMAN, Samuel	23	FREEMAN, Abigil	132	FREEMAN, Hannah	42
FFREEMAN, Samuel	24	FREEMAN, Abner	118	FREEMAN, Hannah	63
FFREEMAN, Samuel	25	FREEMAN, Abthya	23	FREEMAN, Hannah	114

FREEMAN, Hannah	118	FREEMAN, Mary	114	FREEMAN, Sullivan	186
FREEMAN, Hannah	136	FREEMAN, Mary	131	FREEMAN, Tamzin	189
FREEMAN, Hannah	137	FREEMAN, Mary	151	FREEMAN, Thankful	118
FREEMAN, Hannah	146	FREEMAN, Mary	166	FREEMAN, Thankfull	102
FREEMAN, Hannah	162	FREEMAN, Mary	174	FREEMAN, Thankfull	137
FREEMAN, Hannah	174	FREEMAN, Mary	186	FREEMAN, Thankfull	147
FREEMAN, Hannah	189	FREEMAN, Mercy	103	FREEMAN, Thomas	90
FREEMAN, Hatsel	42	FREEMAN, Mercy	137	FREEMAN, Thomas	143
FREEMAN, Hatsel	174	FREEMAN, Mercy	149	FREEMAN, Thomas	174
FREEMAN, Hezekiah	174	FREEMAN, Meris	185	FREEMAN, Thomas	186
FREEMAN, Isaac	84	FREEMAN, Nathan	65	FREEMAN, William	146
FREEMAN, Isaac	130	FREEMAN, Nathanael	138	FREEMAN, William	174
FREEMAN, Isaac	174	FREEMAN, Nathanael	139	FROST, Katharine	19
FREEMAN, James	166	FREEMAN, Nathaniel	41	FRY, John	144
FREEMAN, James	174	FREEMAN, Nathaniel	65		
FREEMAN, Jane	45	FREEMAN, Nathaniel	107	— G —	
FREEMAN, John	65	FREEMAN, Nathaniel	113		
FREEMAN, John	118	FREEMAN, Nathaniel	147	GAILS, Scarlot	152
FREEMAN, John	125	FREEMAN, Nathaniel	174	GEORGE, Martha	142
FREEMAN, John	138	FREEMAN, Nathaniel	189	GEORGE, Moses	150
FREEMAN, John	150	FREEMAN, Pheba	113	GILL, Tabathe	171
FREEMAN, John	160	FREEMAN, Phebe	121	GILLS, Abiga	117
FREEMAN, John	174	FREEMAN, Phebe	129	GILLS, Abijah	117
FREEMAN, John	189	FREEMAN, Phebe	141	GILLS, John	117
FREEMAN, Jonathan	118	FREEMAN, Phebe	174	GILLS, John	161
FREEMAN, Jonathan	133	FREEMAN, Phebe	186	GILLS, Lidia	161
FREEMAN, Jonathan	185	FREEMAN, Phebe	188	GILLS, Mary	69
FREEMAN, Joseph	113	FREEMAN, Phebe	189	GILLS, Scarlet	69
FREEMAN, Joseph	114	FREEMAN, Phebee	80	GILLS, Scarlet	117
FREEMAN, Joseph	135	FREEMAN, Polly King	185	GILLS, Scarlet	131
FREEMAN, Joseph	174	FREEMAN, Prince	42	GILLS, Tabatha	117
FREEMAN, Joseph	188	FREEMAN, Prince	164	GILLS, Tabathy	117
FREEMAN, Josiah	174	FREEMAN, Prissilla	123	GILLS, Tabethy	69
FREEMAN, Josiah	189	FREEMAN, Rachel	142	GILLS, William	161
FREEMAN, Keziah	163	FREEMAN, Rebaca	114	GODFRAIE, Georg	12
FREEMAN, Liddiah	41	FREEMAN, Rebakah	118	GODFRAIE, Hannah	12
FREEMAN, Lidia	77	FREEMAN, Rebecka	150	GODFRAIE, Mary	12
FREEMAN, Lidia	140	FREEMAN, Ruth	107	GODFRAIE, Moses	12
FREEMAN, Loes	114	FREEMAN, Ruth	110	GODFRAIE, Richard	12
FREEMAN, Loes	118	FREEMAN, Ruth	141	GODFRAIE, Ruth	12
FREEMAN, Lois	135	FREEMAN, Ruth	150	GODFRAIE, Samuel	12
FREEMAN, Lucy	186	FREEMAN, Ruth	151	GODFRAY, George	12
FREEMAN, Lydia	174	FREEMAN, Ruth	174	GODFRAY, Jonnathan	12
FREEMAN, Marah	163	FREEMAN, Samuel	25	GODFREE, Elisabeth	77
FREEMAN, Marcy	65	FREEMAN, Samuel	62	GODFREE, Elisabeth	140
FREEMAN, Marcy	112	FREEMAN, Samuell	23	GODFREE, Thomas	66
FREEMAN, Marcy	114	FREEMAN, Samuell	166	GODFREY, Hannah	89
FREEMAN, Marget	62	FREEMAN, Sammuell	23	GODFREY, Hannah	143
FREEMAN, Martha	164	FREEMAN, Sarah	114	GODFREY, Jonathan	18
FREEMAN, Mary	25	FREEMAN, Sarah	118	GODFREY, Lidea	151
FREEMAN, Mary	41	FREEMAN, Sarah	133	GODFREY, Mary	7
FREEMAN, Mary	42	FREEMAN, Sarah	182	GODFREY, Richard	32
FREEMAN, Mary	59	FREEMAN, Solomon	154	GODFRIE, Elizabeth	12

GODFRIE, Georg	12	GRAYHAM, William	147	HALL, Abigail	182
GODFRY, Thomas	133	GREAN, Benimin	119	HALL, Abigel	150
GOLD, Thomas	44	GREEN, Benjamin	54	HALL, Edward	56
GOOLD, Hanna	163	GREEN, Benjamin	141	HALL, Edward	137
GORGE, Joseph	54	GREEN, Desire	96	HALL, Joseph	142
GORGE, Joseph	131	GREEN, Desire	149	HALL, Joseph	182
GOULD, Abigail	174	GREEN, Mary	96	HALL, Josph	87
GOULD, Aphia	174	GREEN, Warren	96	HALLS, Jonathan	100
GOULD, Aphiah	163	GREEN, Warren	145	HALLET, Suzanah	129
GOULD, Benjamin	186	GREW, Abigail	69	HALLETT, John	52
GOULD, Elisabath	83	GREW, Abigel	70	HAMBELTON, Elisabath	117
GOULD, Elizabeth	147	GREW, Daniel	69	HAMBELTON, Elisabath	134
GOULD, Grace	169	GREW, James	69	HAMBELTON, Joseph	122
GOULD, Hannah	174	GREW, Jonathan	69	HAMBLEN, Anne	147
GOULD, James	174	GREW, Jonathan	70	HAMBLEN, Beniamine	152
GOULD, John	163	GREW, Jonathan	138	HAMBLEN, Benimin	136
GOULD, John	174	GREW, Susanah	69	HAMBLEN, Cornelius	152
GOULD, Jonathan	186	GRIFFETH, Abraham	84	HAMBLETON, John	91
GOULD, Joseph	174	GRIFFETH, Lazarus	144	HAMBLETON, Joseph	91
GOULD, Joshua	186	GRIFFETH, Lazerus	90	HAMBLETON, Joseph	144
GOULD, Josiah	186	GRIFFETH, Lidea	90	HAMBLETON, Matha	91
GOULD, Mary	150	GRIFFETH, Mary	90	HAMBLETON, Thomas	54
GOULD, Mary	155	GRIFFETH, Phebee	84	HAMBLIN, Beniamine	136
GOULD, Molly	186	GRIFFETH, Stephen	84	HAMBLIN, Cornelus	111
GOULD, Nathaniel	109	GRIFFITH, Stephen	84	HAMBLIN, Prisscillah	49
GOULD, Nathaniel	150	GRIFFITH, Stephen	141	HAMILTON, Benjamin	154
GOULD, Nathaniel	186	GRIFFUT, John	129	HAMILTON, Content	154
GOULD, Paine	155	GRIGG, Pacock	140	HAMILTON, Daniel	12
GOULD, Phebe	155	GRIGG, Pecock	80	HAMILTON, Daniel	123
GOULD, Phebe	174	GROAS, Elisabeth	128	HAMILTON, Daniel	154
GOULD, Phebe	183	GROAS, Jabez	127	HAMILTON, Daniel	179
GOULD, Priscilla	117	GROSE, Elles	128	HAMILTON, Hanah	179
GOULD, Priscilla	133	GROSE, Hinks	131	HAMILTON, Hannah	154
GOULD, Rebecca	174	GROSE, Jane	97	HAMILTON, Joseph	179
GOULD, Rebecca	186	GROSS, Abigail	74	HAMILTON, Mary	139
GOULD, Rebecca	187	GROSS, Abigaile	54	HAMILTON, Paul	154
GOULD, Ruth	155	GROSS, Alice	53	HAMILTON, Sarah	141
GOULD, Sarah	163	GROSS, Elis	103	HAMILTON, Uriah	179
GOULD, Thomas	125	GROSS, Elizabeth	80	HAMLEN, Ann	103
GOULD, Thomas	155	GROSS, Elizabeth	102	HAMLEN, Joshua	105
GOULD, Thomas	174	GROSS, Elizabeth	146	HAMLEN, Joshua	149
GOULD, Thomas	186	GROSS, Hinks	102	HAMLEN, Lidea	151
GRAHAM, William	103	GROSS, Hinks	103	HAMLIN, Beniamin	54
GRAY, Bennonie	42	GROSS, Hinks	145	HAMLIN, Eliezer	72
GRAY, Edward	42	GROSS, Jane	145	HAMLIN, Elijah	71
GRAY, Mehetabell	137	GROSS, Sarah	99	HAMLIN, Elisabeth	71
GRAY, Sarah	137	GROSS, Serah	146	HAMLIN, Elisha	71
GRAY, Thankfull	137	GROSS, Thomas	67	HAMLIN, Elisha	139
GRAY, Thomas	87	GROSS, Thomas	139	HAMLIN, Mary	82
GRAY, Thomas	142			HAMLIN, Mary	140
GRAYHAM, Betsey	174	— H —		HAMLIN, Sarah	72
GRAYHAM, Eliza	174			HAMMILTON, Daniel	46
GRAYHAM, John	174	HALL, Abigail	109	HAMMILTON, Daniel	179

HAMMILTON, Grace	46	HARDING, Elisabeth	54	HARDING, John	129
HAMMILTON, Hannah	179	HARDING, Elisabeth	84	HARDING, John	143
HAMMILTON, Mary	46	HARDING, Elisabeth	162	HARDING, John	146
HAMMILTON, Richard	179	HARDING, Elisabeth	174	HARDING, John	147
HAMMILTON, Theodorus	179	HARDING, Elizabeth	90	HARDING, John	174
HAMMILTON, Thomas	46	HARDING, Elizabeth	97	HARDING, Jonathan	111
HARDIN, Content	70	HARDING, Elizabeth	143	HARDING, Jonathan	135
HARDIN, Joseph	65	HARDING, Elizabeth	145	HARDING, Joseph	10
HARDIN, Samuel	70	HARDING, Elizabeth	149	HARDING, Joseph	28
HARDING, Abagil	114	HARDING, Eunas	79	HARDING, Joseph	45
HARDING, Abia	58	HARDING, Eunas	106	HARDING, Joseph	79
HARDING, Abiah	16	HARDING, Eunes	106	HARDING, Joseph	104
HARDING, Abiah	28	HARDING, Expearenc	114	HARDING, Joseph	106
HARDING, Abiah	58	HARDING, Expearnc	114	HARDING, Joseph	149
HARDING, Abiah	128	HARDING, Ezekel	109	HARDING, Joshua	21
HARDING, Abiah	133	HARDING, Ezekiel	58	HARDING, Joshua	28
HARDING, Ann	100	HARDING, Ezekiel	111	HARDING, Joshua	31
HARDING, Apphiah	117	HARDING, Ezekiel	151	HARDING, Joshua	84
HARDING, Arcelas	84	HARDING, Gideon	31	HARDING, Joshua	91
HARDING, Archelaus	174	HARDING, Gideon	174	HARDING, Joshua	106
HARDING, Archelaus	175	HARDING, Grace	129	HARDING, Joshua	163
HARDING, Archilaus	168	HARDING, Hanah	84	HARDING, Joshua	174
HARDING, Azubah	174	HARDING, Hanah	106	HARDING, Joshuah	31
HARDING, Barnabas	53	HARDING, Hannah	8	HARDING, Josiah	21
HARDING, Barnabas	70	HARDING, Hannah	21	HARDING, Josiah	28
HARDING, Barnabas	90	HARDING, Hannah	45	HARDING, Josiah	58
HARDING, Barnabas	111	HARDING, Hannah	53	HARDING, Josiah	71
HARDING, Barnabas	135	HARDING, Hannah	116	HARDING, Josiah	107
HARDING, Bethia	21	HARDING, Hannah	123	HARDING, Josiah	114
HARDING, Bethiah	130	HARDING, Hannah	146	HARDING, Josiah	174
HARDING, Bethya	21	HARDING, Hannah	156	HARDING, Lettis	117
HARDING, Carnelas	64	HARDING, Hannah	174	HARDING, Lucia	65
HARDING, Carnelas	65	HARDING, Isaac	58	HARDING, Lusia	70
HARDING, Chloe	71	HARDING, Isaac	105	HARDING, Margaret	116
HARDING, Content	70	HARDING, Isaac	107	HARDING, Margaret	117
HARDING, Content	167	HARDING, Isaac	114	HARDING, Martha	19
HARDING, Corneles	149	HARDING, Isaac	147	HARDING, Martha	21
HARDING, Cornelius	8	HARDING, James	8	HARDING, Martha	28
HARDING, David	58	HARDING, James	84	HARDING, Martha	45
HARDING, David	61	HARDING, James	91	HARDING, Martha	71
HARDING, David	131	HARDING, James	174	HARDING, Martha	149
HARDING, Ebenezer	21	HARDING, Jase	106	HARDING, Mary	8
HARDING, Ebenezer	84	HARDING, Jesse	21	HARDING, Mary	21
HARDING, Ebenezer	116	HARDING, John	10	HARDING, Mary	28
HARDING, Ebenezer	119	HARDING, John	28	HARDING, Mary	75
HARDING, Ebenezer	174	HARDING, John	79	HARDING, Mary	84
HARDING, Ebenezor	151	HARDING, John	84	HARDING, Mary	87
HARDING, Ebnezar	84	HARDING, John	91	HARDING, Mary	92
HARDING, Elisabath	70	HARDING, John	97	HARDING, Mary	109
HARDING, Elisabath	84	HARDING, John	100	HARDING, Mary	110
HARDING, Elisabeth	8	HARDING, John	116	HARDING, Mary	132
HARDING, Elisabeth	10	HARDING, John	117	HARDING, Mary	140
HARDING, Elisabeth	21	HARDING, John	122	HARDING, Mary	141

HARDING, Mary	144	HARDING, Seth	31	HAWS, Jeremiah	145
HARDING, Mary	152	HARDING, Seth	54	HAWS, Sarah	151
HARDING, Matha	71	HARDING, Seth	65	HAWSE, Phebe	136
HARDING, Maziah	8	HARDING, Seth	136	HAWSE, Thankfull	140
HARDING, Maziah	28	HARDING, Seth	152	HEARD, Elisabath	112
HARDING, Mercy	174	HARDING, Simon	79	HEARD, Elisabath	135
HARDING, Mercy	175	HARDING, Solomon	79	HEARD, Grace	9
HARDING, Nathan	8	HARDING, Susana	129	HEARD, John	9
HARDING, Nathan	65	HARDING, Susannah	44	HEDG, Elisabeth	49
HARDING, Nathan	147	HARDING, Thankful	70	HEDG, Elisha	49
HARDING, Nathanael	80	HARDING, Thankful	100	HEDG, Grace	49
HARDING, Nathanael	140	HARDING, Thankfull	48	HEDG, Grace	54
HARDING, Nathaniel	48	HARDING, Thankfull	126	HEDG, Jabez	49
HARDING, Nathaniel	84	HARDING, Thankfull	160	HEDG, Lamuel	49
HARDING, Nathaniel	164	HARDING, Theodore	70	HEDG, Lamuell	49
HARDING, Nathaniel	174	HARDING, Thehoder	130	HEDG, Mary	49
HARDING, Nathannel	28	HARDING, Theoder	54	HEDG, Mary	50
HARDING, Nehemiah	89	HARDING, Theoder	71	HEDG, Samell	49
HARDING, Nehemiah	143	HARDING, Theoder	91	HEDG, Samuel	49
HARDING, Nicholas	10	HARDING, Theodore	31	HEDG, Samuell	49
HARDING, Nickolus	100	HARDING, Theodore	141	HEDG, Samuell	50
HARDING, Phebe	8	HARDING, Thomas	8	HEDG, Samull	49
HARDING, Phebe	64	HARDING, Thomas	119	HEDG, Thankfull	49
HARDING, Pheby	109	HARDING, Thomas	134	HEDG, Thankfull	50
HARDING, Presila	65	HARDING, Thomas	174	HEDGE, Grace	49
HARDING, Priseler	64	HARDING, Timothy	90	HEDGE, Grace	50
HARDING, Prisila	65	HARDING, Zephaniah	10	HEDGE, Samuel	49
HARDING, Prisila	114	HARDING, Zepheniah	100	HEDGE, Samuel	50
HARDING, Prisile	65	HARRIS, Martha	139	HEMBELTON, Joseph	128
HARDING, Rachal	113	HARRIS, Mercy	73	HICKERMAN, Abiagail	159
HARDING, Rachel	135	HATCH, Benjamin	183	HICKERMAN, Abigail	125
HARDING, Rebaca	70	HATCH, Gamaleil	123	HICKERMAN, Bathsheba	128
HARDING, Rebaca	111	HATCH, Joseph	61	HICKERMAN, Mary	126
HARDING, Rebaca	114	HATCH, Joseph	128	HICKMAN, Experance	180
HARDING, Rebacca	172	HATCH, Mariam	135	HICKMAN, James	147
HARDING, Rebecca	58	HATCH, Moses	28	HICKMAN, James	180
HARDING, Rebecca	135	HATCH, Naler	84	HICKMAN, John	180
HARDING, Rebecca	136	HATCH, Naler	130	HICKMAN, Marcy	180
HARDING, Rebeckah	58	HATCH, Phebe	152	HICKMAN, Mary	160
HARDING, Sally	188	HATCH, Priscilla	183	HICKMAN, Mary	180
HARDING, Samuel	28	HATCH, Sally	183	HICKMAN, Samuel	180
HARDING, Samuel	70	HATCH, Solomon	132	HIGENS, Abigaiel	83
HARDING, Samuel	106	HATCH, Sukey	183	HIGENS, Abisha	175
HARDING, Samuell	10	HAUGH, Anne	139	HIGENS, Benjamin	29
HARDING, Samuell	162	HAUGH, Margeret	56	HIGENS, Benjamin	36
HARDING, Sarah	31	HAUGH, Margeret	139	HIGENS, Benjamine	36
HARDING, Sarah	54	HAUS, Phebe	152	HIGENS, Eleezer	48
HARDING, Sarah	71	HAUSE, Susanah	131	HIGENS, Elizebeth	48
HARDING, Sarah	91	HAUSE, Suzanah	100	HIGENS, Ichabod	22
HARDING, Sarah	102	HAWES, Edmund	161	HIGENS, Isace	36
HARDING, Sarah	119	HAWES, Jeremiah	97	HIGENS, James	110
HARDING, Sarah	174	HAWES, Lidea	109	HIGENS, Jediah	48
HARDING, Serah	91	HAWS, Bethia	149	HIGENS, Jemima	45

HIGENS, John	36	HIGGENS, Ebnezar	131	HIGGENS, Jease	83
HIGENS, Jonathan	29	HIGGENS, Edmond	82	HIGGENS, Jennet	131
HIGENS, Jonathan	30	HIGGENS, Eliakim	37	HIGGENS, Jennett	66
HIGENS, Joseph	22	HIGGENS, Eliakim	130	HIGGENS, Jesse	86
HIGENS, Joshua	48	HIGGENS, Elisabath	98	HIGGENS, Jesse	129
HIGENS, Liddia	22	HIGGENS, Elisabath	119	HIGGENS, Joanah	111
HIGENS, Mary	175	HIGGENS, Elisabath	129	HIGGENS, Joanna	76
HIGENS, Meletiah	22	HIGGENS, Elisabath	134	HIGGENS, Joanna	111
HIGENS, Richard	48	HIGGENS, Elisabeth	98	HIGGENS, Joannah	111
HIGENS, Sarah	48	HIGGENS, Elisabeth	122	HIGGENS, John	22
HIGENS, Thankfull	22	HIGGENS, Elisha	152	HIGGENS, John	36
HIGENS, Theophilas	48	HIGGENS, Elizabeth	22	HIGGENS, John	115
HIGENS, Thomas	83	HIGGENS, Elizabeth	98	HIGGENS, John	136
HIGGEN, Relians	80	HIGGENS, Elkeny	81	HIGGENS, John	152
HIGGEN, Solomon	80	HIGGENS, Elkeny	128	HIGGENS, Jonathan	22
HIGGENS, Abigaiel	83	HIGGENS, Elliot	175	HIGGENS, Jonathan	56
HIGGENS, Abigail	83	HIGGENS, Enoch	98	HIGGENS, Jonathan	107
HIGGENS, Abigail	130	HIGGENS, Enock	56	HIGGENS, Jonathan	132
HIGGENS, Abigail	175	HIGGENS, Enock	112	HIGGENS, Jonnathan	22
HIGGENS, Abigal	175	HIGGENS, Enock	133	HIGGENS, Joseph	55
HIGGENS, Abigial	175	HIGGENS, Enock	134	HIGGENS, Joseph	124
HIGGENS, Abijah	80	HIGGENS, Eunus	131	HIGGENS, Joseph	130
HIGGENS, Abisha	107	HIGGENS, Expearenc	112	HIGGENS, Joshua	36
HIGGENS, Ann	130	HIGGENS, Experanc	135	HIGGENS, Josiah	76
HIGGENS, Apphiah	71	HIGGENS, Freeman	71	HIGGENS, Lamuel	131
HIGGENS, Apphiah	111	HIGGENS, Freeman	78	HIGGENS, Lidia	36
HIGGENS, Apphiah	167	HIGGENS, Freeman	113	HIGGENS, Lidia	37
HIGGENS, Aron	111	HIGGENS, Freeman	129	HIGGENS, Lot	82
HIGGENS, Asenath	112	HIGGENS, Freeman	152	HIGGENS, Lydia	82
HIGGENS, Asenath	135	HIGGENS, Gideon	123	HIGGENS, Lydia	164
HIGGENS, Azubah	98	HIGGENS, Gidien	124	HIGGENS, Lydia	167
HIGGENS, Beniamin	36	HIGGENS, Hanah	107	HIGGENS, Marcy	82
HIGGENS, Beniamin	82	HIGGENS, Hanah	119	HIGGENS, Marcy	129
HIGGENS, Beniamine	36	HIGGENS, Hanah	134	HIGGENS, Marsy	115
HIGGENS, Benimin	81	HIGGENS, Hanna	82	HIGGENS, Martha	71
HIGGENS, Benimin	82	HIGGENS, Hannah	82	HIGGENS, Martha	84
HIGGENS, Benimine	135	HIGGENS, Hannah	110	HIGGENS, Martha	107
HIGGENS, Benjamin	36	HIGGENS, Hannah	150	HIGGENS, Martha	110
HIGGENS, Benjamine	36	HIGGENS, Hannah	164	HIGGENS, Mary	22
HIGGENS, Beriah	22	HIGGENS, Hezaaciah	110	HIGGENS, Mary	36
HIGGENS, Beriah	175	HIGGENS, Hiram	175	HIGGENS, Mary	121
HIGGENS, Bethiah	80	HIGGENS, Ichabid	118	HIGGENS, Mary	129
HIGGENS, Bryer	130	HIGGENS, Ichabod	22	HIGGENS, Mary	130
HIGGENS, Daniel	98	HIGGENS, Ichabod	36	HIGGENS, Mary	132
HIGGENS, David	164	HIGGENS, Ichabod	134	HIGGENS, Mary	133
HIGGENS, David	167	HIGGENS, Isaac	114	HIGGENS, Miriam	175
HIGGENS, Dean	80	HIGGENS, Isaac	175	HIGGENS, Moses	98
HIGGENS, Dorcas	134	HIGGENS, Isaiah	136	HIGGENS, Nathan	175
HIGGENS, Dorces	117	HIGGENS, Isiah	111	HIGGENS, Nathaniel	22
HIGGENS, Eanock	112	HIGGENS, Isiaiah	111	HIGGENS, Nathaniel	112
HIGGENS, Ebnezar	69	HIGGENS, Jadiah	37	HIGGENS, Oliver	167
HIGGENS, Ebnezar	84	HIGGENS, James	22	HIGGENS, Pheaby	135
HIGGENS, Ebnezar	107	HIGGENS, Jams	110	HIGGENS, Phebe	98

Name	Page	Name	Page	Name	Page
HIGGENS, Phebe	113	HIGGENS, Tabytha	119	HIGGINS, Alice	140
HIGGENS, Philip	111	HIGGENS, Thankfull	83	HIGGINS, Almira	182
HIGGENS, Philip	136	HIGGENS, Thankfull	84	HIGGINS, Ann	107
HIGGENS, Philip	152	HIGGENS, Thankfull	115	HIGGINS, Ann	108
HIGGENS, Polly	175	HIGGENS, Thankfull	130	HIGGINS, Anna	65
HIGGENS, Prissilla	167	HIGGENS, Theophilus	76	HIGGINS, Anna	83
HIGGENS, Rachel	133	HIGGENS, Thomas	37	HIGGINS, Anna	85
HIGGENS, Rachel	175	HIGGENS, Thomas	83	HIGGINS, Anna	180
HIGGENS, Rebaca	81	HIGGENS, Thomas	115	HIGGINS, Anna Parker	187
HIGGENS, Rebaca	114	HIGGENS, Thomas	133	HIGGINS, Apphia	90
HIGGENS, Rebecca	22	HIGGENS, Timothy	71	HIGGINS, Apphia	143
HIGGENS, Rebeckah	36	HIGGENS, William	54	HIGGINS, Apphya	31
HIGGENS, Rebekah	80	HIGGENS, William	131	HIGGINS, Aquilla	185
HIGGENS, Rebekah	175	HIGGENS, Zacchaus	135	HIGGINS, Aquillia	185
HIGGENS, Relianc	114	HIGGENS, Zaccheus	80	HIGGINS, Aron	107
HIGGENS, Rhoda	112	HIGGENS, Zera	37	HIGGINS, Asa	180
HIGGENS, Richard	36	HIGGENS, Zuriah	175	HIGGINS, Asa	181
HIGGENS, Richard	37	HIGGINS, -----	162	HIGGINS, Asenath	67
HIGGENS, Richard	164	HIGGINS, Aaron	171	HIGGINS, Asenath	160
HIGGENS, Ruben	164	HIGGINS, Aaron	187	HIGGINS, Azuba	182
HIGGENS, Ruth	152	HIGGINS, Abiel	69	HIGGINS, Azube	162
HIGGENS, Samuel	36	HIGGINS, Abigail	53	HIGGINS, Barnabas	73
HIGGENS, Samuel	128	HIGGINS, Abigail	67	HIGGINS, Barnabas	151
HIGGENS, Samuel	131	HIGGINS, Abigail	85	HIGGINS, Barnabas	185
HIGGENS, Sarah	22	HIGGINS, Abigail	92	HIGGINS, Barshaba	85
HIGGENS, Sarah	81	HIGGINS, Abigail	94	HIGGINS, Basheba	85
HIGGENS, Sarah	82	HIGGINS, Abigail	98	HIGGINS, Bathiah	80
HIGGENS, Sarah	83	HIGGINS, Abigail	109	HIGGINS, Bathsheba	85
HIGGENS, Sarah	98	HIGGINS, Abigail	123	HIGGINS, Bathsheba	164
HIGGENS, Sarah	110	HIGGINS, Abigail	160	HIGGINS, Bathshebe	85
HIGGENS, Sarah	112	HIGGINS, Abigail	179	HIGGINS, Benaiah	108
HIGGENS, Sarah	122	HIGGINS, Abigail	180	HIGGINS, Beniamen	29
HIGGENS, Sarah	128	HIGGINS, Abigail	187	HIGGINS, Beniamin	29
HIGGENS, Sarah	129	HIGGINS, Abigail Stevens	187	HIGGINS, Beniamin	62
HIGGENS, Sarah	136	HIGGINS, Abigaile	48	HIGGINS, Beniamin	82
HIGGENS, Sarah	152	HIGGINS, Abigaile	67	HIGGINS, Beniamine	50
HIGGENS, Sary	82	HIGGINS, Abigal	154	HIGGINS, Benimin	81
HIGGENS, Seth	79	HIGGINS, Abigal	160	HIGGINS, Benjam	81
HIGGENS, Seth	107	HIGGINS, Abigel	67	HIGGINS, Benjamin	29
HIGGENS, Seth	175	HIGGINS, Abigel	69	HIGGINS, Benjamin	62
HIGGENS, Simeon	152	HIGGINS, Abigel	83	HIGGINS, Benjamin	81
HIGGENS, Solomon	79	HIGGINS, Abigel	145	HIGGINS, Benjamin	83
HIGGENS, Solomon	80	HIGGINS, Abigel	150	HIGGINS, Benjamin	104
HIGGENS, Solomon	83	HIGGINS, Abigial	94	HIGGINS, Benjamin	108
HIGGENS, Solomon	124	HIGGINS, Abigiel	94	HIGGINS, Benjamin	140
HIGGENS, Solomon	129	HIGGINS, Abisha	181	HIGGINS, Benjamin	141
HIGGENS, Solomon	175	HIGGINS, Abner	179	HIGGINS, Benjamin	149
HIGGENS, Sparrow	164	HIGGINS, Abraham	68	HIGGINS, Benjamin	160
HIGGENS, Susanah	70	HIGGINS, Abraham	94	HIGGINS, Benjamin	182
HIGGENS, Susannah	84	HIGGINS, Absulom	55	HIGGINS, Beriah	31
HIGGENS, Susannah	130	HIGGINS, Adah	163	HIGGINS, Beriah	85
HIGGENS, Syrenus	175	HIGGINS, Alice	31	HIGGINS, Beriah	143
HIGGENS, Tabith	175	HIGGINS, Alice	83	HIGGINS, Bethiah	79

HIGGINS, Bethiah	175	HIGGINS, Elisabeth	29	HIGGINS, Expearnc	154
HIGGINS, Betsey	181	HIGGINS, Elisabeth	66	HIGGINS, Experience	29
HIGGINS, Betsy	187	HIGGINS, Elisabeth	67	HIGGINS, Experience	62
HIGGINS, Briah	85	HIGGINS, Elisabeth	68	HIGGINS, Experience	63
HIGGINS, Carmy	185	HIGGINS, Elisabeth	76	HIGGINS, Experience	67
HIGGINS, Charles	185	HIGGINS, Elisabeth	85	HIGGINS, Experience	138
HIGGINS, Charlotte	182	HIGGINS, Elisabeth	98	HIGGINS, Experience	145
HIGGINS, Cornelis	151	HIGGINS, Elisabeth	175	HIGGINS, Freeman	62
HIGGINS, Cornelius	67	HIGGINS, Elisabeth	181	HIGGINS, Freeman	78
HIGGINS, Daniel	66	HIGGINS, Elisebeth	31	HIGGINS, Freeman	85
HIGGINS, Daniel	85	HIGGINS, Elisebeth	85	HIGGINS, George Washington	180
HIGGINS, Daniel	109	HIGGINS, Elisebeth	167	HIGGINS, Gideon	97
HIGGINS, Daniel	151	HIGGINS, Elisha	31	HIGGINS, Hannah	43
HIGGINS, Darcos	174	HIGGINS, Elisha	69	HIGGINS, Hannah	50
HIGGINS, David	48	HIGGINS, Elisha	73	HIGGINS, Hannah	53
HIGGINS, David	65	HIGGINS, Elisha	78	HIGGINS, Hannah	62
HIGGINS, David	68	HIGGINS, Elisha	95	HIGGINS, Hannah	81
HIGGINS, David	83	HIGGINS, Elisha	138	HIGGINS, Hannah	82
HIGGINS, David	98	HIGGINS, Elisha	145	HIGGINS, Hannah	93
HIGGINS, David	107	HIGGINS, Elisha	149	HIGGINS, Hannah	103
HIGGINS, David	141	HIGGINS, Elisha	150	HIGGINS, Hannah	104
HIGGINS, David	164	HIGGINS, Elisha	175	HIGGINS, Hannah	119
HIGGINS, Dorathy	83	HIGGINS, Elisha	181	HIGGINS, Hannah	144
HIGGINS, Easther	63	HIGGINS, Elizabeth	66	HIGGINS, Hannah	149
HIGGINS, Easther	96	HIGGINS, Elizabeth	91	HIGGINS, Hannah	154
HIGGINS, Easther	107	HIGGINS, Elizabeth	97	HIGGINS, Hannah	155
HIGGINS, Easther	125	HIGGINS, Elizabeth	107	HIGGINS, Hannah	163
HIGGINS, Easther	174	HIGGINS, Elizabeth	144	HIGGINS, Hannah	175
HIGGINS, Ebenezer	22	HIGGINS, Elizabeth	146	HIGGINS, Hannah	182
HIGGINS, Ebenezer	62	HIGGINS, Elizabeth	160	HIGGINS, Hannah	185
HIGGINS, Ebenezer	67	HIGGINS, Elkanah	162	HIGGINS, Hannah Mayo	175
HIGGINS, Ebenezer	68	HIGGINS, Elkenah	50	HIGGINS, Haskel	185
HIGGINS, Ebenezer	107	HIGGINS, Elkenah	58	HIGGINS, Hatsel	189
HIGGINS, Ebenezer	138	HIGGINS, Elkenah	67	HIGGINS, Hatsuld	155
HIGGINS, Ebenezer	162	HIGGINS, Elkenah	83	HIGGINS, Heman	162
HIGGINS, Ebenezer	167	HIGGINS, Elkenah	141	HIGGINS, Henery	79
HIGGINS, Ebenezer	185	HIGGINS, Elkenah	-175	HIGGINS, Henery	80
HIGGINS, Ebenezor	67	HIGGINS, Elknah	160	HIGGINS, Hester	145
HIGGINS, Ebenezor	107	HIGGINS, Elnathan	97	HIGGINS, Hezekiaa	180
HIGGINS, Ebenezor	150	HIGGINS, Elnathan	127	HIGGINS, Horten	181
HIGGINS, Ebnezer	162	HIGGINS, Elnathan	156	HIGGINS, Icabord	67
HIGGINS, Edmond	154	HIGGINS, Enoch	98	HIGGINS, Icchabod	22
HIGGINS, Edmund	125	HIGGINS, Enock	66	HIGGINS, Ichabod	43
HIGGINS, Edmund	174	HIGGINS, Enock	98	HIGGINS, Ichabod	181
HIGGINS, Edmund	175	HIGGINS, Epheram	94	HIGGINS, Ichabud	53
HIGGINS, Edward	69	HIGGINS, Epherim	85	HIGGINS, Ichabud	91
HIGGINS, Elezebath	154	HIGGINS, Ephraim	67	HIGGINS, Ichabud	93
HIGGINS, Elezebeth	154	HIGGINS, Esther	48	HIGGINS, Ichabud	108
HIGGINS, Eliakim	62	HIGGINS, Esther	154	HIGGINS, Ichabud	144
HIGGINS, Eliakim	85	HIGGINS, Esther	174	HIGGINS, Isaac	50
HIGGINS, Eliakim	175	HIGGINS, Esther	175	HIGGINS, Isaac	62
HIGGINS, Eliazer	76	HIGGINS, Eunis	92	HIGGINS, Isaac	94
HIGGINS, Elisabath	85	HIGGINS, Eunis	94	HIGGINS, Isaac	135

HIGGINS, Isaac	145	HIGGINS, Jonathan	146	HIGGINS, Marcy	83
HIGGINS, Isaah	111	HIGGINS, Jonathan	175	HIGGINS, Marcy	85
HIGGINS, Isaiah	65	HIGGINS, Jonathan	185	HIGGINS, Marcy	156
HIGGINS, Isaiah	67	HIGGINS, Joseph	7	HIGGINS, Marcy	182
HIGGINS, Isaiah	107	HIGGINS, Joseph	55	HIGGINS, Marcy	189
HIGGINS, Isaiah	108	HIGGINS, Joseph	59	HIGGINS, Martha	31
HIGGINS, Israel	43	HIGGINS, Joseph	67	HIGGINS, Martha	62
HIGGINS, Israel	55	HIGGINS, Joseph	69	HIGGINS, Martha	72
HIGGINS, Israel	56	HIGGINS, Joseph	73	HIGGINS, Martha	78
HIGGINS, Israel	141	HIGGINS, Joseph	85	HIGGINS, Martha	79
HIGGINS, Israel	164	HIGGINS, Joseph	94	HIGGINS, Martha	107
HIGGINS, Israel Linnell	185	HIGGINS, Joseph	137	HIGGINS, Martha	139
HIGGINS, Jabez	156	HIGGINS, Joseph	180	HIGGINS, Martha	152
HIGGINS, Jabez	182	HIGGINS, Joshua	62	HIGGINS, Martha	162
HIGGINS, Jacob	94	HIGGINS, Joshua	63	HIGGINS, Martha	163
HIGGINS, James	81	HIGGINS, Joshua	125	HIGGINS, Martha	175
HIGGINS, James	140	HIGGINS, Joshua	138	HIGGINS, Martha	181
HIGGINS, James	149	HIGGINS, Joshua	147	HIGGINS, Marther	79
HIGGINS, James	150	HIGGINS, Joshua	155	HIGGINS, Marther	162
HIGGINS, James	163	HIGGINS, Joshua	160	HIGGINS, Mary	25
HIGGINS, James	185	HIGGINS, Joshua	189	HIGGINS, Mary	66
HIGGINS, Jane	31	HIGGINS, Josiah	76	HIGGINS, Mary	69
HIGGINS, Jane	69	HIGGINS, Josiah	163	HIGGINS, Mary	76
HIGGINS, Jane	73	HIGGINS, Josiah	174	HIGGINS, Mary	79
HIGGINS, Jane	85	HIGGINS, Kezia	174	HIGGINS, Mary	85
HIGGINS, Jane	91	HIGGINS, Keziah	163	HIGGINS, Mary	94
HIGGINS, Jathro	131	HIGGINS, Knowles	175	HIGGINS, Mary	169
HIGGINS, Jedediah	83	HIGGINS, Knowles	180	HIGGINS, Mary	175
HIGGINS, Jedediah	141	HIGGINS, Lamuel	83	HIGGINS, Mary	181
HIGGINS, Jedida	160	HIGGINS, Leonard	189	HIGGINS, Mehetabel	62
HIGGINS, Jedidiah	87	HIGGINS, Levi	76	HIGGINS, Mehetiable	174
HIGGINS, Jemima	85	HIGGINS, Levi	164	HIGGINS, Mehetible	62
HIGGINS, Jennet	76	HIGGINS, Levie	63	HIGGINS, Mehitabel	62
HIGGINS, Jerusha	175	HIGGINS, Liddiah	50	HIGGINS, Mehitabell	62
HIGGINS, Jerusha	185	HIGGINS, Lidea	56	HIGGINS, Mehitable	62
HIGGINS, Jerusha	187	HIGGINS, Lidea	149	HIGGINS, Mehittabel	62
HIGGINS, Jesse	55	HIGGINS, Lidia	50	HIGGINS, Melatia	108
HIGGINS, Jesse	97	HIGGINS, Lois	62	HIGGINS, Melatiah	22
HIGGINS, Joanah	76	HIGGINS, Lot	85	HIGGINS, Mercy	50
HIGGINS, Joanna	76	HIGGINS, Luce	94	HIGGINS, Mercy	137
HIGGINS, Joanna	85	HIGGINS, Lucia	180	HIGGINS, Mercy	138
HIGGINS, Joanna	111	HIGGINS, Lucy	67	HIGGINS, Mercy	167
HIGGINS, John	16	HIGGINS, Lucy	162	HIGGINS, Mercy	175
HIGGINS, John	53	HIGGINS, Lucy	180	HIGGINS, Mercy	179
HIGGINS, John	58	HIGGINS, Lucy	181	HIGGINS, Moses	48
HIGGINS, John	79	HIGGINS, Lydia	85	HIGGINS, Moses	97
HIGGINS, John	85	HIGGINS, Lydia	125	HIGGINS, Moses	107
HIGGINS, John	175	HIGGINS, Lydia	159	HIGGINS, Moses	146
HIGGINS, Jonathan	31	HIGGINS, Lydia	160	HIGGINS, Moses	156
HIGGINS, Jonathan	62	HIGGINS, Lydia	175	HIGGINS, Moses	182
HIGGINS, Jonathan	75	HIGGINS, Lydia	183	HIGGINS, Naomi	163
HIGGINS, Jonathan	83	HIGGINS, Marcy	55	HIGGINS, Nathan	66
HIGGINS, Jonathan	139	HIGGINS, Marcy	78	HIGGINS, Nathan	76

HIGGINS, Nathan	79	HIGGINS, Rebeccah	175	HIGGINS, Sarah	75
HIGGINS, Nathan	127	HIGGINS, Rebecka	89	HIGGINS, Sarah	76
HIGGINS, Nathan	156	HIGGINS, Rebecka	143	HIGGINS, Sarah	81
HIGGINS, Nathan	175	HIGGINS, Rebecka	146	HIGGINS, Sarah	85
HIGGINS, Nathan Sparrow	182	HIGGINS, Rebeckah	181	HIGGINS, Sarah	92
HIGGINS, Nathanael	66	HIGGINS, Rebeka	98	HIGGINS, Sarah	93
HIGGINS, Nathanael	137	HIGGINS, Reliance	29	HIGGINS, Sarah	98
HIGGINS, Nathanael	142	HIGGINS, Reuben	187	HIGGINS, Sarah	137
HIGGINS, Nathaniel	66	HIGGINS, Richard	48	HIGGINS, Sarah	139
HIGGINS, Nathaniel	88	HIGGINS, Richard	65	HIGGINS, Sarah	144
HIGGINS, Nehemah	164	HIGGINS, Richard	76	HIGGINS, Sarah	160
HIGGINS, Nehemiah	83	HIGGINS, Richard	91	HIGGINS, Sarah	170
HIGGINS, Obadiah	79	HIGGINS, Richard	107	HIGGINS, Sarah	175
HIGGINS, Olive	185	HIGGINS, Richard	138	HIGGINS, Sarah	180
HIGGINS, Paul	29	HIGGINS, Richard	175	HIGGINS, Sarah Sparrow	182
HIGGINS, Paule	147	HIGGINS, Richard	185	HIGGINS, Selina	181
HIGGINS, Peggy	174	HIGGINS, Robert	53	HIGGINS, Serah	150
HIGGINS, Phebe	75	HIGGINS, Roburt	154	HIGGINS, Seth	76
HIGGINS, Phebe	85	HIGGINS, Ruben	48	HIGGINS, Seth	91
HIGGINS, Phebe	185	HIGGINS, Ruben	85	HIGGINS, Seth	175
HIGGINS, Phebee	81	HIGGINS, Ruby	185	HIGGINS, Seth	181
HIGGINS, Phebee	105	HIGGINS, Ruth	7	HIGGINS, Shaw	167
HIGGINS, Phebee	107	HIGGINS, Ruth	53	HIGGINS, Silvanus	62
HIGGINS, Phebee	149	HIGGINS, Ruth	55	HIGGINS, Silvanus	180
HIGGINS, Phebee	150	HIGGINS, Ruth	56	HIGGINS, Silvenus	56
HIGGINS, Philana	185	HIGGINS, Ruth	62	HIGGINS, Simeon	58
HIGGINS, Philip	83	HIGGINS, Ruth	63	HIGGINS, Simeon	79
HIGGINS, Philip	167	HIGGINS, Ruth	73	HIGGINS, Simeon	163
HIGGINS, Phillip	73	HIGGINS, Ruth	79	HIGGINS, Simeon	175
HIGGINS, Polly	181	HIGGINS, Ruth	95	HIGGINS, Simeon	180
HIGGINS, Polly	182	HIGGINS, Ruth	146	HIGGINS, Simon	163
HIGGINS, Polly Twining	185	HIGGINS, Ruth	154	HIGGINS, Solomon	62
HIGGINS, Precilla Freeman	187	HIGGINS, Ruth	161	HIGGINS, Solomon	66
HIGGINS, Prince	62	HIGGINS, Ruth	179	HIGGINS, Solomon	79
HIGGINS, Prince	163	HIGGINS, Ruth	180	HIGGINS, Solomon	80
HIGGINS, Prince	174	HIGGINS, Saloma	43	HIGGINS, Solomon	181
HIGGINS, Priscilla	29	HIGGINS, Saml.	43	HIGGINS, Solomon	185
HIGGINS, Priscilla	78	HIGGINS, Samuel	56	HIGGINS, Sparrow	189
HIGGINS, Prisila	155	HIGGINS, Samuel	58	HIGGINS, Susanna	62
HIGGINS, Prissila	63	HIGGINS, Samuel	62	HIGGINS, Susanna	160
HIGGINS, Prissilla	139	HIGGINS, Samuel	85	HIGGINS, Susannah Snow	182
HIGGINS, Rachel	63	HIGGINS, Samuel	137	HIGGINS, Sylvanus	179
HIGGINS, Rachel	85	HIGGINS, Samuel	149	HIGGINS, Sylvanus	180
HIGGINS, Rachel	175	HIGGINS, Samuell	43	HIGGINS, Tabythy	133
HIGGINS, Rebacca	160	HIGGINS, Samuell	79	HIGGINS, Tamesin	67
HIGGINS, Rebeca	168	HIGGINS, Sarah	29	HIGGINS, Tamsa	185
HIGGINS, Rebecca	50	HIGGINS, Sarah	48	HIGGINS, Tamsin	180
HIGGINS, Rebecca	53	HIGGINS, Sarah	50	HIGGINS, Tamzin	185
HIGGINS, Rebecca	75	HIGGINS, Sarah	53	HIGGINS, Thankful	162
HIGGINS, Rebecca	79	HIGGINS, Sarah	55	HIGGINS, Thankfull	9
HIGGINS, Rebecca	123	HIGGINS, Sarah	62	HIGGINS, Thankfull	29
HIGGINS, Rebecca	140	HIGGINS, Sarah	66	HIGGINS, Thankfull	54
HIGGINS, Rebecca	175	HIGGINS, Sarah	69	HIGGINS, Thankfull	58

HIGGINS, Thankfull	78	HIGINSE, Mary	17	HOLBROOKS, Hanah	115
HIGGINS, Thankfull	79	HIGINSE, Richard	17	HOLBROOKS, Jeruse Done	97
HIGGINS, Thankfull	92	HILLER, Elizebeth	96	HOLBROOKS, Jesse	115
HIGGINS, Thankfull	107	HILLER, Jonathan	96	HOLBROOKS, Jonathan	115
HIGGINS, Thankfull	149	HILLER, Jonathan	131	HOLBROOKS, Luse	115
HIGGINS, Thankfull	181	HILLER, Mary	96	HOLBROOKS, Margret	97
HIGGINS, Theoder	79	HILLER, Sarah	96	HOLBROOKS, Sarah	76
HIGGINS, Theoder	92	HILLER, Tobias-Paine	96	HOLBROOKS, Sarah	79
HIGGINS, Theoder	144	HINCKLEY, Shuball	32	HOLBROOKS, Thomas	97
HIGGINS, Theodor	43	HINCKLY, Hanah	121	HOLBROOKS, Thomas	145
HIGGINS, Theophilas	76	HINCKLY, Seth	141	HOLBRUCKS, Marget	124
HIGGINS, Theophilus	75	HINKELY, Cyprian	127	HOLEBROKS, Naiman	131
HIGGINS, Theophilus	76	HINKELY, Expearance	129	HOLEBROOK, Abiezor	103
HIGGINS, Theophilus	139	HINKELY, Expearenc	86	HOLEBROOK, Elisha	109
HIGGINS, Thirse	185	HINKELY, Hannah	128	HOLEBROOKS, Elisabath	115
HIGGINS, Thomas	29	HINKELY, Thomas	77	HOLKER. Thomas	138
HIGGINS, Thomas	66	HINKELY, Thomas	132	HOLKER. Thomas	150
HIGGINS, Thomas	76	HINKELY, Zephaniah	127	HOMER, Bethiah	135
HIGGINS, Thomas	83	HINKLEY, Thankfull	86	HOMER, John	112
HIGGINS, Thomas	85	HINKLY, Thankful	136	HOHIWELL, Richard	140
HIGGINS, Thomas	140	HINKLY, Thankfull	129	HOPKENS, Giles	135
HIGGINS, Thomas	141	HIX, Joanna	13	HOPKENS, Hanah	130
HIGGINS, Thomas	175	HOLBROCKS, Marget	129	HOPKENS, Isaac	105
HIGGINS, Tully	175	HOLBROK, Lusha	135	HOPKENS, Isaac	106
HIGGINS, Unice	76	HOLBROKS, Abial	97	HOPKENS, Isaac	119
HIGGINS, Warrin	175	HOLBROKS, Abiezer	115	HOPKENS, Isaac	134
HIGGINS, William	58	HOLBROKS, Ezekel	79	HOPKENS, John	130
HIGGINS, William	63	HOLBROKS, Ezekiel	134	HOPKENS, Joseph	105
HIGGINS, William	123	HOLBROKS, Hanah	115	HOPKENS, Joshua	113
HIGGINS, William	154	HOLBROKS, Isaac Doane	97	HOPKENS, Marcy	135
HIGGINS, Wilson	185	HOLBROKS, Isaiah	97	HOPKENS, Mary	130
HIGGINS, Zacceus	62	HOLBROKS, John	97	HOPKENS, Rachel	152
HIGGINS, Zaccheus	48	HOLBROKS, Lusa	152	HOPKENS, Rebaca	132
HIGGINS, Zaccheus	175	HOLBROKS, Martha	79	HOPKENS, Samuel	115
HIGGINS, Zaccheus	185	HOLBROKS, Sarah	134	HOPKENS, Samuel	133
HIGGINS, Zacheas	100	HOLBROKS, Thomas	97	HOPKENS, Thankful	105
HIGGINS, Zacheus	48	HOLBROOK, Elisha	150	HOPKIN, Isaac	105
HIGGINS, Zacheus	62	HOLBROOK, Ezekiel	79	HOPKIN, Thankful	105
HIGGINS, Zacheus	147	HOLBROOK, Isaac Doane	171	HOPKINS, Abiel	127
HIGGINS, Zacheus	175	HOLBROOK, Isaiah	171	HOPKINS, Abiel	155
HIGGINS, Zebina	185	HOLBROOK, Lucia	111	HOPKINS, Abigael	29
HIGGINS, Zedekiah	78	HOLBROOK, Marcy	79	HOPKINS, Abigaell	20
HIGGINS, Zedekiah	185	HOLBROOK, Margaret	66	HOPKINS, Abigail	33
HIGGINS, Zenas	155	HOLBROOK, Martha	79	HOPKINS, Abigail	166
HIGGINS, Zera	185	HOLBROOK, Martha	103	HOPKINS, Abigaile	16
HIGGINS, Zoheth	67	HOLBROOK, Samuel	79	HOPKINS, Abigaile	59
HIGGNS, Mary	156	HOLBROOK, Thomas	123	HOPKINS, Affier	127
HIGINS, Bathsheba	53	HOLBROOK, Thomas	156	HOPKINS, Anna	175
HIGINS, Samuel	62	HOLBROOKE, Martha	147	HOPKINS, Asa	180
HIGINS, Sarah	108	HOLBROOKS, Abiezer	115	HOPKINS, Azuba	180
HIGINSE, Beniamin	17	HOLBROOKS, Abigel	149	HOPKINS, Bangs	180
HIGINSE, Elyakim	17	HOLBROOKS, Abizer	115	HOPKINS, Benjamin	30
HIGINSE, Jonathan	17	HOLBROOKS, Ezekel	79	HOPKINS, Caleb	33

HOPKINS, Curtis	166	HOPKINS, Joshuhua	76	HOPKINS, Steven	30
HOPKINS, Davis	180	HOPKINS, Judah	30	HOPKINS, Steven	33
HOPKINS, Deborah	33	HOPKINS, Judah	33	HOPKINS, Steven	38
HOPKINS, Deborah	40	HOPKINS, Leida	167	HOPKINS, Steven	48
HOPKINS, Elisabath	175	HOPKINS, Leonard	180	HOPKINS, Susanna	169
HOPKINS, Elisabeth	180	HOPKINS, Liddiah	29	HOPKINS, Tabatha	181
HOPKINS, Elisha	29	HOPKINS, Lide	149	HOPKINS, Tabathy	161
HOPKINS, Elisha	65	HOPKINS, Lidea	104	HOPKINS, Tamsan	164
HOPKINS, Elisha	166	HOPKINS, Lydia	164	HOPKINS, Temparence	180
HOPKINS, Elisha	180	HOPKINS, Lydia	166	HOPKINS, Tempe	180
HOPKINS, Elizabeth	30	HOPKINS, Lydia	180	HOPKINS, Temperence	180
HOPKINS, Elizabeth	33	HOPKINS, Marcy	166	HOPKINS, Thankful	106
HOPKINS, Elkanah	166	HOPKINS, Mary	25	HOPKINS, Thankful	164
HOPKINS, Elkanah	180	HOPKINS, Mary	29	HOPKINS, Thankful	169
HOPKINS, Eunice	185	HOPKINS, Mary	30	HOPKINS, Thankful	180
HOPKINS, Experience	65	HOPKINS, Mary	33	HOPKINS, Thankfull	140
HOPKINS, Freeman	180	HOPKINS, Mary	38	HOPKINS, Theodoar	174
HOPKINS, Giles	33	HOPKINS, Mary	53	HOPKINS, Theophilus	181
HOPKINS, Giles	169	HOPKINS, Mary	98	HOPKINS, Thomas	180
HOPKINS, Giles	180	HOPKINS, Mary	164	HOPKINS, Thomas	185
HOPKINS, Hannah	29	HOPKINS, Mary	166	HOPKINS, William	33
HOPKINS, Hannah	70	HOPKINS, Mary	168	HOPKINS, William	181
HOPKINS, Hannah	76	HOPKINS, Mary	169	HOPKNS, Joseph	169
HOPKINS, Hannah	174	HOPKINS, Mercy	128	HOPKNS, Mary	169
HOPKINS, Hannah	185	HOPKINS, Mercy	180	HORD, Deborah	9
HOPKINS, Isaac	90	HOPKINS, Nathanel	30	HORD, Jacob	9
HOPKINS, Isaac	105	HOPKINS, Phebe	29	HORD, John	9
HOPKINS, Isaac	123	HOPKINS, Phebe	76	HORF, Sarah	144
HOPKINS, Isaac	149	HOPKINS, Phebe	140	HORTEN, Abigaiel	69
HOPKINS, Isaac	180	HOPKINS, Phebe	180	HORTEN, Abigail	120
HOPKINS, Isack	175	HOPKINS, Pricillia	76	HORTEN, Abigail	133
HOPKINS, James	175	HOPKINS, Priscilla	127	HORTEN, Anne	84
HOPKINS, John	29	HOPKINS, Priscilla	156	HORTEN, Cushing	69
HOPKINS, John	33	HOPKINS, Prisilla	180	HORTEN, Elesebath	167
HOPKINS, John	65	HOPKINS, Prissilla	76	HORTEN, Elesebeth	167
HOPKINS, John	154	HOPKINS, Prissilla	169	HORTEN, Elnathan	167
HOPKINS, John	166	HOPKINS, Prissilla	-180	HORTEN, Eunice	84
HOPKINS, John	180	HOPKINS, Rachel	180	HORTEN, Eunice	171
HOPKINS, Jonathan	105	HOPKINS, Rebacah	166	HORTEN, Eunice	172
HOPKINS, Jonathan	164	HOPKINS, Rebecah	169	HORTEN, Hanah	84
HOPKINS, Jonnathan	38	HOPKINS, Rebecah	166	HORTEN, James	172
HOPKINS, Joseph	30	HOPKINS, Rebecca	139	HORTEN, John	167
HOPKINS, Joseph	169	HOPKINS, Rebekah	166	HORTEN, Lurane	69
HOPKINS, Joshua	25	HOPKINS, Ruth	30	HORTEN, Mary	69
HOPKINS, Joshua	29	HOPKINS, Ruth	33	HORTEN, Nathel	84
HOPKINS, Joshua	33	HOPKINS, Ruth	180	HORTEN, Nathaniel	84
HOPKINS, Joshua	76	HOPKINS, Ruth	185	HORTEN, Nathaniel	172
HOPKINS, Joshua	98	HOPKINS, Sally	169	HORTEN, Nathaniel Brown	172
HOPKINS, Joshua	139	HOPKINS, Samuell	30	HORTEN, Nathanil	84
HOPKINS, Joshua	152	HOPKINS, Seth	136	HORTEN, Nathni	172
HOPKINS, Joshua	166	HOPKINS, Smith	169	HORTEN, Obediah	84
HOPKINS, Joshua	180	HOPKINS, Solomon	185	HORTEN, Samuel	69
HOPKINS, Joshuah	29	HOPKINS, Steaven	30	HORTEN, Samuel	131

HORTEN, Samuel	167			KENNY, Mary	168
HORTEN, Samuell	167	**— J —**		KENNY, Polly	168
HORTEN, Samuell	171			KENNY, Sarah	168
HORTEN, Susanna	69	JACKSON, Hannah	155	KENT, William	132
HORTEN, Suzanah	112	JACKSON, Isra	152	KENWRECK, Samuell	154
HORTING, Elisabeth	84	JACKSON, Jabez	155	KENWRICK, Alfred	187
HORTING, Elnathan	84	JACKSON, Joseph	155	KENWRICK, Betsey	187
HORTING, Eunuce	84	JACKSON, Mary	182	KENWRICK, Betsy	187
HORTING, Jabez	84	JACKSON, William	182	KENWRICK, Elizabeth	187
HORTING, James	84	JAPHET, Elis	146	KENWRICK, Esther	187
HORTING, Nathanael	84	JARVIS, Ann	56	KENWRICK, Hannah	175
HORTING, Nathanel	84	JARVIS, Anna	182	KENWRICK, Hannah	181
HORTING, Natheal	84	JARVIS, Edward	182	KENWRICK, Jona	187
HORTING, Unis	84	JARVIS, Edward Tayler	56	KENWRICK, Jonathan	175
HORTING, William	84	JARVIS, John	56	KENWRICK, Jonathan	181
HORTON, Abigel	18	JARVIS, John	182	KENWRICK, Jonathan	187
HORTON, Doritha	30	JARVIS, John	190	KENWRICK, Lucy	175
HORTON, Elizabeth	18	JARVIS, John King	190	KENWRICK, Mercy	187
HORTON, Hannah	18	JARVIS, Lucinda	190	KENWRICK, Samuel K.	187
HORTON, Hannah	97	JARVIS, Nabby	182	KENWRICK, Samuell	123
HORTON, Hannah	145	JARVIS, Patia	190	KENWRICK, Seth	181
HORTON, James	18	JARVIS, Permela Mayo	190	KENWRICK, Seth	187
HORTON, John	18	JARVIS, Phebe	182	KENWRICK, Thomas	145
HORTON, Nathaniel	18	JARVIS, Polly	182	KENWRICK, Warren A.	187
HORTON, Nathaniel	150	JARVIS, Sarah	182	KENWRICK, Warren Anson	187
HORTON, Samuell	18	JARVIS, Sarah Ann	190	KING, Abigail	66
HORTON, Susanah	18	JARVIS, Silvia	182	KING, Elisabeth	66
HORTON, Suseannah	149	JARVIS, Susan M.	190	KING, Elizabeth	151
HORTTON, Hope	50	JARVIS, Thankful	182	KING, Isaac	134
HOWES, Sarah	38	JARVIS, Thankful	190	KING, John	100
HOWSE, Thomas	31	JARVIS, Timothy	182	KING, Samuel	66
HUBBARD, Sarah	19	JARVIS, Timothy	190	KING, Samuel	126
HULKER, Debora	70	JENNEY, Cornelias	111	KING, Samuel	138
HULKER, Thomas	69	JERVIS, Timathy	119	KING, Samuell	160
HULKER, Thomas	70	JERVIS, Timothy	132	KING, Stephen	52
HUNT, Hester	72	JO, Marcy	151	KING, Stephen	85
HUNTER, Elisha	81	JO, Marcy	152	KING, Stephen	105
HUNTER, Elisha	140	JO, Sam	146	KING, Stephen	149
HURD, Benja	183	JOB, Bette	88	KING, Zephenia	85
HURD, Benjamin	183	JOB, Betty	142	KINGMAN, Freeman	181
HURD, Ebenezer	136	JOB, Elisabeth	147	KINGMAN, Matthew	181
HURD, Eunice	183	JOB, Elizabeth	100	KINGMAN, Patty	181
HURD, Gould	183			KINGMAN, Polly	181
HURD, Jacob	53	**— K —**		KINGMAN, Rebecca	181
HURD, Johanna	183			KINGMAN, Simeon	181
HURD, Joseph	183	KENDRICK, Anson	163	KINNEY, Jesse	168
HURD, Joshua	136	KENDRICK, Betsey	187	KINNEY, John	168
HURD, Joshua	152	KENDRICK, Betty	187	KINNEY, Mary	168
HURD, Mary	98	KENDRICK, Carline	187	KINNEY, Nathan	151
HURD, Mary	146	KENDRICK, Fredrick	187	KINNY, Allen	168
HURD, Phebe	183	KENDRICK, Jonathan	187	KINNY, Heman	168
HURD, Rutha Gould	183	KENNY, Heman	168	KINNY, Jesse	168
HURD, Solomon	183	KENNY, Jesse	168	KINNY, Mary	168

KINNY, May	168	KNOWLES, Benj.	156	KNOWLES, Henery	172
KINNY, Nathan	168	KNOWLES, Benjamin	156	KNOWLES, Henrey	121
KINNY, Sarah	168	KNOWLES, Benjamin	175	KNOWLES, Henry	113
KINNY, Thankfull	168	KNOWLES, Benjin	127	KNOWLES, Henry	121
KNOLES, Elisabeth	75	KNOWLES, Benjin	156	KNOWLES, Henry	172
KNOWELS, Abigil	174	KNOWLES, Bethia	34	KNOWLES, Isaac	181
KNOWELS, Freeman	174	KNOWLES, Bethiah	99	KNOWLES, James	25
KNOWELS, Joshua	57	KNOWLES, Bethiah	118	KNOWLES, James	40
KNOWELS, Olive	174	KNOWLES, Bethiah	175	KNOWLES, James	80
KNOWELS, Rebaca	174	KNOWLES, Cloe	175	KNOWLES, James	114
KNOWELS, Reback	174	KNOWLES, Cornelius	25	KNOWLES, James	135
KNOWELS, Rebeca	174	KNOWLES, Cornelius	73	KNOWLES, James	140
KNOWELS, Rebecca	174	KNOWLES, Cornelius	139	KNOWLES, Jane	133
KNOWELS, Sarah	57	KNOWLES, David	175	KNOWLES, Jease	120
KNOWELS, Tempe	174	KNOWLES, Eadward	16	KNOWLES, Jerusha	34
KNOWELS, Willaam	174	KNOWLES, Edward	46	KNOWLES, Jerusha	175
KNOWLE, Martha	163	KNOWLES, Edward	97	KNOWLES, Jesse	40
KNOWLES, -----	158	KNOWLES, Edward	156	KNOWLES, Jesse	57
KNOWLES, Abiatha	175	KNOWLES, Edward	158	KNOWLES, Jesse	120
KNOWLES, Abiatha	181	KNOWLES, Edward	159	KNOWLES, Joanna	175
KNOWLES, Abiathar	175	KNOWLES, Edward	163	KNOWLES, Joanna	188
KNOWLES, Abigail	114	KNOWLES, Edwrd	97	KNOWLES, John	16
KNOWLES, Abigail	163	KNOWLES, Elijah	97	KNOWLES, John	25
KNOWLES, Abigail	167	KNOWLES, Elijah	172	KNOWLES, John	40
KNOWLES, Abigail	172	KNOWLES, Elisabeth	46	KNOWLES, John	99
KNOWLES, Abigail	175	KNOWLES, Elisabeth	70	KNOWLES, John	120
KNOWLES, Abigail	182	KNOWLES, Elisabeth	139	KNOWLES, John	138
KNOWLES, Abigel	75	KNOWLES, Elisabeth	172	KNOWLES, John	167
KNOWLES, Abigial	159	KNOWLES, Elisabeth	175	KNOWLES, John	175
KNOWLES, Abigial	170	KNOWLES, Elisha	188	KNOWLES, John	188
KNOWLES, Abithar	175	KNOWLES, Elkenah	160	KNOWLES, Joseph	128
KNOWLES, Abner	175	KNOWLES, Enos	34	KNOWLES, Joshua	57
KNOWLES, Alice	156	KNOWLES, Exparance	171	KNOWLES, Joshua	120
KNOWLES, Alice	160	KNOWLES, Exxa	175	KNOWLES, Joshua	132
KNOWLES, Amasa	175	KNOWLES, Ezubah	158	KNOWLES, Joshua	175
KNOWLES, Amos	25	KNOWLES, Frances	113	KNOWLES, Joshua	188
KNOWLES, Amos	142	KNOWLES, Freeman	156	KNOWLES, Joshuah	40
KNOWLES, Amos	163	KNOWLES, Freman	175	KNOWLES, Josiah	57
KNOWLES, Amos	175	KNOWLES, George Brown	163	KNOWLES, Josiah	123
KNOWLES, Ann	46	KNOWLES, Hanah	131	KNOWLES, Josiah	160
KNOWLES, Ann	97	KNOWLES, Hannah	46	KNOWLES, Lucretia	114
KNOWLES, Ann	116	KNOWLES, Hannah	120	KNOWLES, Lucy	172
KNOWLES, Ann	134	KNOWLES, Hannah	158	KNOWLES, Lydda	156
KNOWLES, Ann	172	KNOWLES, Hannah	159	KNOWLES, Lydia	116
KNOWLES, Anne	46	KNOWLES, Hannah	175	KNOWLES, Lydia	133
KNOWLES, Anne	65	KNOWLES, Hannah	175	KNOWLES, Lydia	175
KNOWLES, Anne	80	KNOWLES, Hannah	181	KNOWLES, Lydia	188
KNOWLES, Anne	141	KNOWLES, Hannah	182	KNOWLES, Marcy	120
KNOWLES, Azuba	34	KNOWLES, Hannah	189	KNOWLES, Marcy	170
KNOWLES, Azubah	113	KNOWLES, Harding	172	KNOWLES, Marcy	171
KNOWLES, Azubah	121	KNOWLES, Henery	113	KNOWLES, Margerey	175
KNOWLES, Bangs	181	KNOWLES, Henery	121	KNOWLES, Marth	142
KNOWLES, Barberie	43	KNOWLES, Henery	135	KNOWLES, Mary	21

Name	Page	Name	Page	Name	Page
KNOWLES, Mary	40	KNOWLES, Ruth	128	KNOWLS, Abigel	75
KNOWLES, Mary	80	KNOWLES, Ruth	136	KNOWLS, Abigial	159
KNOWLES, Mary	85	KNOWLES, Ruth	175	KNOWLS, Alice	156
KNOWLES, Mary	99	KNOWLES, Sally	175	KNOWLS, Amos	100
KNOWLES, Mary	113	KNOWLES, Saml.	175	KNOWLS, Amos	163
KNOWLES, Mary	121	KNOWLES, Samuel	25	KNOWLS, Ann	75
KNOWLES, Mary	135	KNOWLES, Samuel	99	KNOWLS, Ann	97
KNOWLES, Mary	141	KNOWLES, Samuel	175	KNOWLS, Ann	145
KNOWLES, Mary	156	KNOWLES, Samuell	34	KNOWLS, Azubah	98
KNOWLES, Mary	163	KNOWLES, Samuell	159	KNOWLS, Azubah	107
KNOWLES, Mary	170	KNOWLES, Sarah	46	KNOWLS, Bathiah	166
KNOWLES, Mary	175	KNOWLES, Sarah	57	KNOWLS, Benjamen	156
KNOWLES, Mehetable	120	KNOWLES, Sarah	97	KNOWLS, Benjamin	97
KNOWLES, Mercy	25	KNOWLES, Sarah	120	KNOWLS, Benjamin	156
KNOWLES, Mercy	33	KNOWLES, Sarah	121	KNOWLS, Bethia	92
KNOWLES, Mercy	46	KNOWLES, Sarah	128	KNOWLS, Bethiah	99
KNOWLES, Mercy	79	KNOWLES, Sarah	132	KNOWLS, Bethiah	134
KNOWLES, Mercy	140	KNOWLES, Seth	34	KNOWLS, Bety	75
KNOWLES, Nathanael	34	KNOWLES, Seth	40	KNOWLS, David	94
KNOWLES, Nathanel	25	KNOWLES, Seth	72	KNOWLS, David	99
KNOWLES, Nathaniel	80	KNOWLES, Seth	80	KNOWLS, Edward	46
KNOWLES, Nathaniel	113	KNOWLES, Seth	99	KNOWLS, Edward	97
KNOWLES, Nathaniel	175	KNOWLES, Seth	139	KNOWLS, Edward	145
KNOWLES, Nathaniel Atwood	171	KNOWLES, Seth	175	KNOWLS, Edward	156
KNOWLES, Obed	156	KNOWLES, Simeon	57	KNOWLS, Elizabeth	145
KNOWLES, Paul	40	KNOWLES, Simeon	181	KNOWLS, Enos	92
KNOWLES, Paul	114	KNOWLES, Simeoun	128	KNOWLS, Enos	145
KNOWLES, Phebe	159	KNOWLES, Simon	181	KNOWLS, Freeman	80
KNOWLES, Phebe	171	KNOWLES, Siruiah	114	KNOWLS, Freeman	136
KNOWLES, Phebe	172	KNOWLES, Susanah	57	KNOWLS, Freeman	168
KNOWLES, Phebee	113	KNOWLES, Susanah	123	KNOWLS, Gorg	156
KNOWLES, Priscilla	181	KNOWLES, Susannah	167	KNOWLS, Hannah	97
KNOWLES, Rachal	161	KNOWLES, Tamparnce	99	KNOWLS, Hannah	99
KNOWLES, Rachel	188	KNOWLES, Tempe	188	KNOWLS, Hatsel	107
KNOWLES, Rebaca	117	KNOWLES, Temperence	161	KNOWLS, Henry	75
KNOWLES, Rebaca	129	KNOWLES, Thankfull	158	KNOWLS, Hetsell	163
KNOWLES, Rebacah	99	KNOWLES, Thankfull	175	KNOWLS, Isaac	100
KNOWLES, Rebacca	160	KNOWLES, Thankfull	188	KNOWLS, James	107
KNOWLES, Rebacca	171	KNOWLES, Thomas	46	KNOWLS, James	150
KNOWLES, Rebacca	172	KNOWLES, Thomas	75	KNOWLS, James	163
KNOWLES, Rebeca	172	KNOWLES, Thomas	113	KNOWLS, James	164
KNOWLES, Rebecah	16	KNOWLES, Thomas	139	KNOWLS, Jerusha	103
KNOWLES, Rebecca	57	KNOWLES, Thomas	158	KNOWLS, John	136
KNOWLES, Rebecca	188	KNOWLES, Thomas	175	KNOWLS, John	152
KNOWLES, Rebeckah	25	KNOWLES, Thomisen	114	KNOWLS, John	167
KNOWLES, Rebeckah	175	KNOWLES, Treat	170	KNOWLS, Joseph	99
KNOWLES, Rebekah	160	KNOWLES, Willard	99	KNOWLS, Joshua	137
KNOWLES, Richard	25	KNOWLES, Willard	125	KNOWLS, Joshua	150
KNOWLES, Robert	167	KNOWLES, Willard	170	KNOWLS, Lidea	100
KNOWLES, Ruth	9	KNOWLES, Willard	171	KNOWLS, Lydia	163
KNOWLES, Ruth	25	KNOWLES, William	99	KNOWLS, Marcy	172
KNOWLES, Ruth	80	KNOWLES, William	175	KNOWLS, Mary	57
KNOWLES, Ruth	122	KNOWLS, Abigal	163	KNOWLS, Mary	152

KNOWLS, Mary	156	LENT, Rebkah	111	LINEL, Jonathan	133
KNOWLS, Mercy	103	LEWEN, Joseph	92	LINEL, Jonathan	136
KNOWLS, Mercy	136	LEWES, Abigal	124	LINEL, Jonathan	152
KNOWLS, Nathaniel	103	LEWES, Abigel	94	LINEL, Mary	65
KNOWLS, Nathaniel	109	LEWES, Isaih	94	LINEL, Rebeca	98
KNOWLS, Nathaniel	149	LEWES, Mary	105	LINEL, Rebecka	98
KNOWLS, Nathaniel	151	LEWES, Mary	149	LINEL, Rebecka	108
KNOWLS, Phebe	163	LEWES, Moses	171	LINEL, Ruth	65
KNOWLS, Prince	61	LEWES, Sarah	109	LINEL, Sarah	77
KNOWLS, Rachel	100	LEWES, Sarah	149	LINEL, Sarah	122
KNOWLS, Rebecca	136	LEWES, Solomon	98	LINEL, Sarah	129
KNOWLS, Rebecca	152	LEWES, Winslow	94	LINEL, Serah	71
KNOWLS, Rebecka	100	LEWIS, Apphia	15	LINEL, Thankful	118
KNOWLS, Rebecka	150	LEWIS, Apphia	141	LINEL, Thankful	133
KNOWLS, Richard	100	LEWIS, Beniamin	15	LINEL, Thankfull	109
KNOWLS, Richard	163	LEWIS, Elizabeth	175	LINEL, Thankfull	151
KNOWLS, Ruth	80	LEWIS, Elizebeth	165	LINEL, Thomas	65
KNOWLS, Ruth	96	LEWIS, John	175	LINEL, Thomas	71
KNOWLS, Ruth	100	LEWIS, Jone	15	LINEL, THomas	122
KNOWLS, Ruth	145	LEWIS, Joseph	155	LINEL, Thomas	129
KNOWLS, Samuel	61	LEWIS, Nathanael	15	LINEL, Uriah	65
KNOWLS, Samuel	97	LEWIS, Phebe	152	LINEL, Zeruiah	65
KNOWLS, Samuel	107	LEWIS, Rebecca	15	LINELL, Benjamin	116
KNOWLS, Samuel	146	LEWIS, Sarah	15	LINELL, Benjamin	166
KNOWLS, Samuell	159	LEWIS, Sarah	167	LINELL, Disier	165
KNOWLS, Samuell	162	LEWIS, Solomon	152	LINELL, Edmond	166
KNOWLS, Sarah	92	LEWIS, Solomon	162	LINELL, Elezebath	165
KNOWLS, Sarah	97	LEWIS, Solomon	175	LINELL, Elice	165
KNOWLS, Sarah	151	LEWIS, Tabitha	140	LINELL, Elknah	166
KNOWLS, Seth	80	LEWIS, Thomas	15	LINELL, Enoch	165
KNOWLS, Seth	110	LINCKELOO, James	53	LINELL, Hannah	165
KNOWLS, Seth	136	LINCOLNE, James	147	LINELL, Hannah	168
KNOWLS, Seth	151	LINCOLNE, Lidea	147	LINELL, John	165
KNOWLS, Solomon	163	LINEL, Abigel	71	LINELL, Jonathan	65
KNOWLS, Thomas	75	LINEL, Anna	122	LINELL, Jonathan	116
KNOWLS, Thomas	97	LINEL, Elisabeth	122	LINELL, Jonathan	117
KNOWLS, Willard	94	LINEL, Elisha	71	LINELL, Joseph	166
KNOWLS, Willard	99	LINEL, Elisha	98	LINELL, Joshua	166
KNOWLS, Willard	145	LINEL, Elisha	108	LINELL, Lettice	65
KNOWLS, Zuba	146	LINEL, Elisha	110	LINELL, Marah	166
KNOWLSE, Barbara	17	LINEL, Elisha	122	LINELL, Marcy	65
KNOWLSE, Mehittabell	17	LINEL, Elisha	146	LINELL, Martha	165
KNOWLSE, Richard	17	LINEL, Elisha	152	LINELL, Mary	165
KWLS, Abigial	159	LINEL, Elizabeth	71	LINELL, Mary	166
		LINEL, Elkanah	133	LINELL, Mehetable	165
— L —		LINEL, Expearns	65	LINELL, Priscilla	116
		LINEL, Hannah	71	LINELL, Priscilla	117
LAMKIN, Thomas	71	LINEL, Hannah	98	LINELL, Priscinlla	116
LAMKIN, Thomas	138	LINEL, Heman	71	LINELL, Rachal	65
LARRANCE, Isaac	107	LINEL, Heman	122	LINELL, Rachel	65
LARRANCE, Isaac	150	LINEL, Jonathan	65	LINELL, Rebeca	166
LECRAFT, Hannah	25	LINEL, Jonathan	71	LINELL, Rebekah	165
LENNETT, Bethya	34	LINEL, Jonathan	117	LINELL, Samuel	65

LINELL, Samuell	165	LINNEL, Jonathan	175	LINNELL, Jonathan	116
LINIL, Jonathan	123	LINNEL, Jonathan	186	LINNELL, Jonathan	118
LINKELOO, James	53	LINNEL, Joshua	175	LINNELL, Jonathan	140
LINKELOO, Lidea	53	LINNEL, Joshua	176	LINNELL, Jonathan	175
LINKERNU, Lidia	161	LINNEL, Mary	176	LINNELL, Jonathan	186
LINKERNUE, James	53	LINNEL, Mercy	176	LINNELL, Joseph	176
LINKERNUE, James	71	LINNEL, Phebe	175	LINNELL, Josiah	117
LINKERNUE, Joseph	71	LINNEL, Polly	175	LINNELL, Josiah	175
LINKERNUE, Josiah	71	LINNEL, Precilla	175	LINNELL, Keziah	185
LINKERNUE, Lydia	53	LINNEL, Prissia	179	LINNELL, Lydia	185
LINKERNUE, Lydia	71	LINNEL, Rebecca	52	LINNELL, Marcy	185
LINKERNUE, Rebaca	71	LINNEL, Rebecca	176	LINNELL, Meriah	179
LINKERNUE, Ruth	71	LINNEL, Rebecca	179	LINNELL, Molly	118
LINKERNUE, Suzanah	71	LINNEL, Russil	179	LINNELL, Olive	185
LINKHORNEW, Ann	155	LINNEL, Sally	175	LINNELL, Priscilla	116
LINKHORNEW, James	53	LINNEL, Sally	176	LINNELL, Priscilla	118
LINKHORNEW, James	155	LINNEL, Sarah	122	LINNELL, Sally	186
LINKHORNEW, Joseph	155	LINNEL, Sarah	175	LINNELL, Samuel	185
LINNE, Heman	175	LINNEL, Sarah	176	LINNELL, Sarah	176
LINNE, Sarah	175	LINNEL, Stephen	122	LINNELL, Solomon	116
LINNEL, Abigail	40	LINNEL, Stephen	175	LINNELL, Solomon	175
LINNEL, Abigal	122	LINNEL, Sukey	179	LINNELL, Tamsen	186
LINNEL, Abner Freeman	186	LINNEL, Thankful	175	LINNELL, Thankful	189
LINNEL, Anna	175	LINNEL, Thankful	176	LINNELL, Thankful Cole	179
LINNEL, Bathsheba	186	LINNEL, Thankfull	175	LINNELL, Thankfull	85
LINNEL, Benja.	179	LINNEL, Thankfull	176	LINNELL, Thankfull	118
LINNEL, Benjamin	175	LINNEL, Thomas	40	LINNELL, Thankfull	176
LINNEL, Benjamin	179	LINNEL, Thomas	122	LINNELL, Thomas	85
LINNEL, Catherine	179	LINNEL, Thomas	179	LINNELL, Thomas	117
LINNEL, Cuca	179	LINNEL, Uriah	175	LINNELL, Thomas	140
LINNEL, David	40	LINNEL, Uriah	176	LINNELL, Uriah	176
LINNEL, Deborah	179	LINNEL, Zeruiah	175	LINNELL, Washington	176
LINNEL, Easther	175	LINNELL, Abigail	138	LINNL, Sarah	176
LINNEL, Edmond	176	LINNELL, Abigaile	66	LONG, William	147
LINNEL, Eles	176	LINNELL, Abigal	162	LOTHROP, Bershuah	21
LINNEL, Eliasha	175	LINNELL, Ales	175	LUEN, Joseph	144
LINNEL, Elisabeth	40	LINNELL, Bathsheba	186	LUES, Abigel	94
LINNEL, Elisabeth	128	LINNELL, Benjamin	179	LUES, Archeles	146
LINNEL, Elisha	40	LINNELL, Charlotte	186	LUES, Archelus	98
LINNEL, Elisha	165	LINNELL, Deborah	179	LUES, Hanna	94
LINNEL, Elisha	175	LINNELL, Edward Smith	185	LUES, Isaiah	94
LINNEL, Elizebeth	40	LINNELL, Elijah	176	LUES, John	98
LINNEL, Elizebth	40	LINNELL, Elkenah	85	LUES, John	130
LINNEL, Hannah	40	LINNELL, Ellice	175	LUES, Nathaniel	75
LINNEL, Haskel	176	LINNELL, Faba	118	LUES, Nathaniel	132
LINNEL, Heman	175	LINNELL, Fanny	185	LUES, Solomon	128
LINNEL, Heman	179	LINNELL, Goold	116	LUES, Susannah	146
LINNEL, Isaac	175	LINNELL, Hannah	54	LUES, Suseana	98
LINNEL, Isaac Young	176	LINNELL, Hariot	185	LUIS, -----	61
LINNEL, Israel	175	LINNELL, Hitta	175	LUIS, Apphya	57
LINNEL, James	175	LINNELL, John	175	LUIS, Charles	61
LINNEL, James	176	LINNELL, John	186	LUIS, Debora	80
LINNEL, Jonathan	40	LINNELL, Jonathan	85	LUIS, Ebenezer	80

Name	Page	Name	Page	Name	Page
LUIS, George	15	MAY, Mary	41	MAYO, Benjamin	167
LUIS, George	54	MAY, Nathanael	139	MAYO, Benjamin	176
LUIS, George	137	MAY, Nathaniel	41	MAYO, Benjamine	176
LUIS, Judith	80	MAY, Pricila	41	MAYO, Bethiah	182
LUIS, Rebecca	57	MAY, Rebecca	135	MAYO, Betsey C.	187
LUIS, Rebecca	137	MAY, Serah	150	MAYO, Bettee	92
LUIS, Sarah	69	MAYO, -----	28	MAYO, Betty	125
LUIS, Sarah	138	MAYO, -----	43	MAYO, Carline	176
LUIS, Solomon	136	MAYO, ----h	28	MAYO, Constant	61
LUIS, Thomas	52	MAYO, Abigail	15	MAYO, Constant	154
LUIS, Thomas	61	MAYO, Abigail	54	MAYO, Constianc	124
LUIS, Thomas	80	MAYO, Abigail	67	MAYO, Content	65
LUIS, Thomas	139	MAYO, Abigail	119	MAYO, Content	140
LUIS, William	55	MAYO, Abigail	131	MAYO, Daniel	103
LUIS, William	138	MAYO, Abigail	167	MAYO, Daniel	147
LUMBARD, Caleb	26	MAYO, Abigaile	15	MAYO, Danyell	25
LUMBARD, John	83	MAYO, Abigel	92	MAYO, David	187
LUMBARD, Rebaca	133	MAYO, Abijah	92	MAYO, Debora	92
LUMBART, Jediah	83	MAYO, Abijah	158	MAYO, Dilly	171
LUMBART, Jediah	134	MAYO, Abner	176	MAYO, Easse	92
LUMBART, Jediah	152	MAYO, Albert Williams	186	MAYO, Easter	76
LUMBART, Jedidiah	136	MAYO, Alic	131	MAYO, Ebenezer	13
LUMBART, John	134	MAYO, Alice	61	MAYO, Ebenezer	28
LUMBART, Rebaca	128	MAYO, Alice	62	MAYO, Ebenezer	124
LUMBERD, Jedediah	109	MAYO, Alice	138	MAYO, Ebenezer	154
LUMBERT, Benjamin	151	MAYO, Alis	13	MAYO, Ebenezor	150
LUMBERT, Jedediah	150	MAYO, Ann	41	MAYO, Eebnezer	167
		MAYO, Ann	111	MAYO, Elekiel	92
— M —		MAYO, Anna	66	MAYO, Eles	77
		MAYO, Anna	133	MAYO, Elesebeth	167
MAAKER, David David	132	MAYO, Anna	176	MAYO, Eliakim	49
MAGNER, William	128	MAYO, Annah	109	MAYO, Elisabath	131
MAKER, Hanah	76	MAYO, Anne	54	MAYO, Elisabeth	13
MAKER, Hanah	132	MAYO, Apphia	54	MAYO, Elisabeth	15
MAKER, Hannah	73	MAYO, Asa	28	MAYO, Elisabeth	48
MAKER, James	8	MAYO, Asa	66	MAYO, Elisabeth	49
MAKER, Jane	147	MAYO, Asa	92	MAYO, Elisabeth	61
MAKER, Joshua	119	MAYO, Asa	127	MAYO, Elisabeth	139
MAKER, Joshua	132	MAYO, Asa	130	MAYO, Elisabeth	143
MAKER, Joshue	127	MAYO, Asa	155	MAYO, Elisha	13
MAKER, Liddiah	49	MAYO, Asaph	176	MAYO, Elisha	25
MAKER, Mary	109	MAYO, Barbara	43	MAYO, Elisha	54
MAKER, Mary	151	MAYO, Barbary	43	MAYO, Elisha	72
MARK, John	111	MAYO, Bashua	144	MAYO, Elisha	171
MARTEN, Alexander	152	MAYO, Bathsheba	28	MAYO, Elisha	182
MARTEN, Elanor	167	MAYO, Bathsheba	48	MAYO, Eliza Thomas	186
MARTIN, Alexander	111	MAYO, Bathshebe	13	MAYO, Elizabeth	44
MARTIN, Bryan	167	MAYO, Bathsuah	13	MAYO, Elizabeth	81
MARTIN, Elisebeth	167	MAYO, Beniamin	152	MAYO, Elizabeth	91
MARTIN, John	167	MAYO, Benimine	114	MAYO, Elizabeth	103
MARTIN, John	182	MAYO, Benjamen	167	MAYO, Elizabeth	149
MAY, Ebenezor	61	MAYO, Benjamin	52	MAYO, Elizebeth	13
MAY, Gidion	77	MAYO, Benjamin	81	MAYO, Elizebeth	97

MAYO, Ellis	76	MAYO, James	146	MAYO, Lidia	10
MAYO, Ese	144	MAYO, James	162	MAYO, Lidia	71
MAYO, Esse	92	MAYO, Jemina	113	MAYO, Louisa	186
MAYO, Esther	123	MAYO, Jemimah	81	MAYO, Louisa	187
MAYO, Esther	154	MAYO, Jemimah	135	MAYO, Lydia	43
MAYO, Eunic	176	MAYO, Jeremiah	81	MAYO, Lydia	158
MAYO, Eunis	86	MAYO, Jeremiah	140	MAYO, Lydia	159
MAYO, Eunis	128	MAYO, Jerusha	61	MAYO, Marcy	76
MAYO, Euns	176	MAYO, Jerusha	127	MAYO, Marcy	123
MAYO, Expearanc	92	MAYO, Joanna	13	MAYO, Marcy	124
MAYO, Expearinc	92	MAYO, Joanna	111	MAYO, Marcy	146
MAYO, Experence	167	MAYO, Joanna	136	MAYO, Marcy	176
MAYO, Experience	28	MAYO, Johannah	152	MAYO, Marcy	182
MAYO, Experience	92	MAYO, John	12	MAYO, Martha	70
MAYO, Gerusha	156	MAYO, John	25	MAYO, Martha	79
MAYO, Gideon	77	MAYO, John	32	MAYO, Martha	130
MAYO, Gideon	129	MAYO, John	67	MAYO, Martha	134
MAYO, Gidion	77	MAYO, John	92	MAYO, Martha	138
MAYO, Hanah	72	MAYO, John	124	MAYO, Mary	11
MAYO, Hannah	13	MAYO, John	135	MAYO, Mary	37
MAYO, Hannah	16	MAYO, John	144	MAYO, Mary	40
MAYO, Hannah	33	MAYO, John	158	MAYO, Mary	41
MAYO, Hannah	49	MAYO, John	159	MAYO, Mary	43
MAYO, Hannah	53	MAYO, Jonathan	61	MAYO, Mary	52
MAYO, Hannah	54	MAYO, Jonathan	138	MAYO, Mary	61
MAYO, Hannah	61	MAYO, Jonathan	176	MAYO, Mary	65
MAYO, Hannah	72	MAYO, Jonathan M.	187	MAYO, Mary	71
MAYO, Hannah	93	MAYO, Jonathen	167	MAYO, Mary	72
MAYO, Hannah	97	MAYO, Joseph	54	MAYO, Mary	119
MAYO, Hannah	119	MAYO, Joseph	81	MAYO, Mary	122
MAYO, Hannah	144	MAYO, Joseph	119	MAYO, Mary	127
MAYO, Hannah	155	MAYO, Joseph	134	MAYO, Mary	128
MAYO, Hannah	160	MAYO, Joseph	161	MAYO, Mary	133
MAYO, Hannah	176	MAYO, Joseph	164	MAYO, Mary	142
MAYO, Heman	167	MAYO, Joseph	176	MAYO, Mary	143
MAYO, Heman	176	MAYO, Joseph	182	MAYO, Mary	171
MAYO, Henry	12	MAYO, Joshiah	158	MAYO, Mary	176
MAYO, Henry	162	MAYO, Joshua	49	MAYO, Mehetabel	77
MAYO, Hulda	114	MAYO, Joshua	81	MAYO, Mehetabell	67
MAYO, Irael	76	MAYO, Joshua	97	MAYO, Mehitabel	140
MAYO, Isaac	28	MAYO, Joshua	126	MAYO, Mehitabell	67
MAYO, Isaac	96	MAYO, Joshua	129	MAYO, Mehitabell	78
MAYO, Isaac	144	MAYO, Joshua	167	MAYO, Mehitable	41
MAYO, Isaac	155	MAYO, Joshue	126	MAYO, Mehitable	67
MAYO, Isaac	176	MAYO, Josiah	167	MAYO, Mercie	43
MAYO, Isaiah	176	MAYO, Josiah	176	MAYO, Mercy	18
MAYO, Israel	43	MAYO, Judah	43	MAYO, Mercy	49
MAYO, Israel	76	MAYO, Judah	71	MAYO, Mercy	76
MAYO, Israel	139	MAYO, Judah	139	MAYO, Mercy	81
MAYO, James	12	MAYO, Lamuel	171	MAYO, Mercy	99
MAYO, James	25	MAYO, Lemuel	92	MAYO, Mercy	125
MAYO, James	54	MAYO, Lemuel	127	MAYO, Mercy	136
MAYO, James	97	MAYO, Lidea	92	MAYO, Mercy	140

MAYO, Mercy	152	MAYO, Rebecka	147	MAYO, Sarah	161
MAYO, Mercy	154	MAYO, Rebecka	149	MAYO, Sarah	164
MAYO, Mercy	156	MAYO, Rebekah	167	MAYO, Sarah	165
MAYO, Mercy	176	MAYO, Richard	43	MAYO, Sarah	167
MAYO, Mercy E.	187	MAYO, Richard	86	MAYO, Sarah	176
MAYO, Molly	171	MAYO, Richard	87	MAYO, Sary	167
MAYO, Nathanael	13	MAYO, Richard	141	MAYO, Sears	176
MAYO, Nathanael	15	MAYO, Robert	13	MAYO, Serah	86
MAYO, Nathanael	67	MAYO, Robert	41	MAYO, Seth	176
MAYO, Nathanel	13	MAYO, Robert	70	MAYO, Simeon	92
MAYO, Nathanell	13	MAYO, Robert	139	MAYO, Simeon	161
MAYO, Nathaniel	13	MAYO, Robert	176	MAYO, Simeon	176
MAYO, Nathaniel	25	MAYO, Ruth	15	MAYO, Simeon	190
MAYO, Nathaniel	40	MAYO, Ruth	43	MAYO, Sintha	182
MAYO, Nathaniel	41	MAYO, Ruth	59	MAYO, Sparrow	176
MAYO, Nathaniel	67	MAYO, Ruth	61	MAYO, Susanah	176
MAYO, Nathaniel	95	MAYO, Ruth	67	MAYO, Susanna	92
MAYO, Nathaniel	97	MAYO, Ruth	76	MAYO, Susanna	176
MAYO, Nathaniel	145	MAYO, Ruth	81	MAYO, Susannah	158
MAYO, Nathaniel	146	MAYO, Ruth	86	MAYO, Tabatha	171
MAYO, Nathanll.	15	MAYO, Ruth	102	MAYO, Tabitha	92
MAYO, Nathanyell	24	MAYO, Ruth	109	MAYO, Tabitha	171
MAYO, Patience	96	MAYO, Ruth	111	MAYO, Thakful	61
MAYO, Phebe	74	MAYO, Ruth	114	MAYO, Thankfull	48
MAYO, Phebe	97	MAYO, Ruth	135	MAYO, Thankfull	58
MAYO, Phebe	122	MAYO, Ruth	138	MAYO, Thankfull	61
MAYO, Phebe	123	MAYO, Ruth	151	MAYO, Thankfull	77
MAYO, Phebe	129	MAYO, Ruth	152	MAYO, Thankfull	107
MAYO, Phebe	139	MAYO, Sally	183	MAYO, Thankfull	137
MAYO, Phebe	161	MAYO, Sammual	167	MAYO, Thankfull	140
MAYO, Phebe Sparrow	186	MAYO, Samuel	52	MAYO, Theopeulus	113
MAYO, Phebee	41	MAYO, Samuel	95	MAYO, Theophilas	43
MAYO, Phebee	76	MAYO, Samuel	119	MAYO, Theophilas	144
MAYO, Polly	176	MAYO, Samuel	134	MAYO, Theophilas	149
MAYO, Polly	187	MAYO, Samuel	141	MAYO, Theophilos	167
MAYO, Prissilla	76	MAYO, Samuel	146	MAYO, Theophilus	28
MAYO, Rebaca	113	MAYO, Samuel	176	MAYO, Theophilus	52
MAYO, Rebaca	114	MAYO, Samuell	9	MAYO, Theophilus	61
MAYO, Rebcca	28	MAYO, Samuell	25	MAYO, Theophilus	107
MAYO, Rebecah A.	187	MAYO, Samuell	126	MAYO, Theophilus	119
MAYO, Rebecca	28	MAYO, Samuell	156	MAYO, Theophilus	130
MAYO, Rebecca	40	MAYO, Sarah	12	MAYO, Theophilus	167
MAYO, Rebecca	52	MAYO, Sarah	37	MAYO, Theophilus	176
MAYO, Rebecca	54	MAYO, Sarah	46	MAYO, Theoplius	176
MAYO, Rebecca	61	MAYO, Sarah	49	MAYO, Theopulas	130
MAYO, Rebecca	76	MAYO, Sarah	77	MAYO, Theopulas	133
MAYO, Rebecca	86	MAYO, Sarah	81	MAYO, Thephilas	107
MAYO, Rebecca	119	MAYO, Sarah	92	MAYO, Tho:	43
MAYO, Rebecca	140	MAYO, Sarah	114	MAYO, Thomas	25
MAYO, Rebecka	61	MAYO, Sarah	123	MAYO, Thomas	43
MAYO, Rebecka	86	MAYO, Sarah	130	MAYO, Thomas	48
MAYO, Rebecka	91	MAYO, Sarah	140	MAYO, Thomas	49
MAYO, Rebecka	144	MAYO, Sarah	156	MAYO, Thomas	52

MAYO, Thomas	76	MERICK, William	21
MAYO, Thomas	81	MERIFIELD, Simeon	98
MAYO, Thomas	111	MERIFIELD, Simeon	146
MAYO, Thomas	122	MERIGHN, John	132
MAYO, Thomas	129	MERIGN, John	74
MAYO, Thomas	130	MERREK, Mary	30
MAYO, Thomas	139	MERRICK, Betty	54
MAYO, Thomas	151	MERRICK, Elisabeth	38
MAYO, Thomas	176	MERRICK, Elisabeth	54
MAYO, Thomas	182	MERRICK, Elisabeth	55
MAYO, Thomas L.	186	MERRICK, Elizabeth	28
MAYO, Thomas L.	187	MERRICK, Hannah	66
MAYO, Thomisen	161	MERRICK, Hannah	138
MAYO, Tryphene	167	MERRICK, Isaac	77
MAYO, Uriah	176	MERRICK, Isaac	140
MAYO, Uriah	182	MERRICK, Joseph	18
MAYO, William	25	MERRICK, Joseph	28
MAYO, William	41	MERRICK, Joseph	38
MAYO, William	72	MERRICK, Joseph	55
MAYO, William	139	MERRICK, Joshua	10
MEEKER, David	65	MERRICK, Mary	55
MELVEL, Abigail	42	MERRICK, Mary	56
MELVEL, David	42	MERRICK, Mary	57
MELVEL, Elisabeth	42	MERRICK, Mary	137
MELVEL, Mary	42	MERRICK, Phebe	82
MELVEL, Thomas	42	MERRICK, Phebe	84
MELVIL, David	42	MERRICK, Phebe	140
MELVIL, Mary	42	MERRICK, Phebe	141
MELVILE, David	22	MERRICK, Rebecca	38
MELVILE, Mary	22	MERRICK, Ruben	55
MELVILE, Mary	42	MERRICK, Sarah	8
MERECK, Isacca	31	MERRICK, William	20
MERECK, William	31	MERRICK, William	54
MEREEN, Daniel	94	MERRICKE, Beniamin	31
MEREEN, Hannah	94	MERRICKE, Joseph	31
MEREEN, John	94	MERRICKE, William	31
MEREEN, Rebacca	94	MEYRICK, Bettee	103
MEREEN, Ruth	94	MEYRICK, Elesabeth	110
MERICK, Abigel	92	MEYRICK, Elizabeth	92
MERICK, Elisabeth	55	MEYRICK, Elizabeth	96
MERICK, John	17	MEYRICK, Elizabeth	97
MERICK, Joseph	28	MEYRICK, Elizabeth	151
MERICK, Joseph	55	MEYRICK, Elizebeth	28
MERICK, Mary	17	MEYRICK, Isaac	28
MERICK, Mary	28	MEYRICK, Isaac	77
MERICK, Rebecca	17	MEYRICK, Joseph	28
MERICK, Rebecca	20	MEYRICK, Joseph	92
MERICK, Ruth	17	MEYRICK, Joseph	100
MERICK, Sara	17	MEYRICK, Joseph	151
MERICK, Steeven	17	MEYRICK, Mary	146
MERICK, Steven	15	MEYRICK, Nathan	100
MERICK, William	17	MEYRICK, Nathanll.	92
MERICK, William	20	MEYRICK, Phebee	77

MEYRICK, Rebecka	152
MEYRICK, Ruben	92
MEYRICK, Ruben	97
MEYRICK, Ruben	145
MEYRICK, William	28
MEYRICK, William	54
MEYRICK, William	96
MEYRICK, William	145
MEYRICK, William	149
MIRICK, Mary	114
MIRICK, Mary	135
MIRRICK, Elisabeth	7
MITCHEL, James	103
MITCHELL, William	53
MOGER, Lidea	109
MOGER, Lidea	150
MOLFORD, John	45
MOLFORD, Mary	42
MORES, John	58
MORES, John	160
MORES, Phebe	58
MORES, Susanna	160
MORES, Susannah	58
MORES, Treat	58
MORES, Treat	160
MORS, Elipelet	130
MORSE, Elifelet	70
MOSES, Lidea	101
MOSES, Lidea	147
MOTT, Ebenezor	90
MOTT, John	93
MOTT, John	144
MULFFORD, Anne	56
MULFFORD, Anne	137
MULFFORD, Elisabeth	140
MULFFORD, Jemima	42
MULFFORD, Jemima	73
MULFFORD, John	73
MULFFORD, John	139
MULFFORD, Mary	42
MULFFORD, Mercy	73
MULFFORD, Thomas	42
MULFORD, Anna	9
MULFORD, Anna	42
MULFORD, Dorcas	42
MULFORD, Elisabeth	42
MULFORD, Hannah	9
MULFORD, Hannah	42
MULFORD, Jemima	128
MULFORD, John	9
MULFORD, John	114
MULFORD, John	135
MULFORD, John	176

MULFORD, Marcy	73	MYRICK, Lucy	164	NEWCOMB, Thomas	42
MULFORD, Marcy	136	MYRICK, Lucy	189	NEWCOME, Debora	138
MULFORD, Marcy	144	MYRICK, Lydia	115	NEWCOME, Deborah	36
MULFORD, Mary	42	MYRICK, Marcy	115	NEWCOME, Joannah	42
MULFORD, Mary	114	MYRICK, Marcy	159	NEWCOME, Rebecca	36
MULFORD, Mercy	93	MYRICK, Mary	95	NEWCOME, Simon	30
MULFORD, Mercy	152	MYRICK, Mercy	126	NICHERSON, Mary	18
MULFORD, Patience	9	MYRICK, Nathaniel	168	NICHERSON, Mercy	13
MULFORD, Patience	48	MYRICK, Phebe	70	NICHERSON, Nicholas	13
MULFORD, Ruth	176	MYRICK, Phebe	189	NICHERSON, William	13
MULFORD, Thomas	9	MYRICK, Prissa	189	NICKASON, David	91
MULFORD, Thomas	42	MYRICK, Rachal	121	NICKASON, David	143
MULFORD, Thomas	136	MYRICK, Rachel	121	NICKASON, Elkenah	107
MULFORD, Thomas	143	MYRICK, Rebekah	164	NICKASON, Elkenah	150
MUTE, Ebenezor	143	MYRICK, Ruben	97	NICKASON, Jeremiah	145
MYRIC, Bettee	89	MYRICK, Ruth	164	NICKASON, Jesse	99
MYRICK, Abigail	189	MYRICK, Samuel	189	NICKASON, Jesse	100
MYRICK, Abigel	97	MYRICK, Samuell	70	NICKASON, Jesse	146
MYRICK, Barbary	160	MYRICK, Sarah	168	NICKASON, Martha	88
MYRICK, Barbry	115	MYRICK, Seth	151	NICKASON, Rachel	100
MYRICK, Betty	162	MYRICK, Thankful	189	NICKASON, Rebecka	147
MYRICK, Dorcas	164	MYRICK, Thankfull	189	NICKASON, Ruben	151
MYRICK, Elezabeth	162	MYRICK, William	70	NICKASON, Serah	147
MYRICK, Elisabath	131	MYRICK, William	121	NICKASON, Thomas	107
MYRICK, Elisabath	132	MYRICK, William	130	NICKASON, Thomas	150
MYRICK, Elisabeth	67	MYRICK, William	164	NICKERSON, Abigail	125
MYRICK, Elisabeth	70	MYRICK, William	176	NICKERSON, Azubah S.	188
MYRICK, Elisabeth	71	MYRIK, Elisabath	69	NICKERSON, Bethiah	85
MYRICK, Elisabeth	125	MYRIK, Josiah	132	NICKERSON, Bethiah	131
MYRICK, Elisabeth	128			NICKERSON, Dean Bangs	188
MYRICK, Eliza	189	— N —		NICKERSON, Dean S.	188
MYRICK, Elizabeth	151			NICKERSON, Deborah	123
MYRICK, Elizabeth	160	NED, Beck	150	NICKERSON, Deborah	125
MYRICK, Esther	168	NED, David	94	NICKERSON, Deborah	154
MYRICK, Fear	115	NED, David	145	NICKERSON, Eldad	111
MYRICK, Fear	161	NED, Jeremiah	89	NICKERSON, Eli	122
MYRICK, Gideon	164	NED, Moses	150	NICKERSON, Elifalet	130
MYRICK, Gideon	176	NETAS, Joseph	142	NICKERSON, Elifelet	66
MYRICK, Hannah	85	NETIS, Joseph	88	NICKERSON, Elisabath	74
MYRICK, Hannah	151	NEWCOM, Elisabeth	137	NICKERSON, Eunice	86
MYRICK, Hannah	164	NEWCOMB, Abigail	171	NICKERSON, Expearenc	128
MYRICK, Hannah	176	NEWCOMB, David	80	NICKERSON, Hannah	85
MYRICK, Hannah	189	NEWCOMB, David	128	NICKERSON, Hannah	86
MYRICK, Heman	121	NEWCOMB, Ebenezer	81	NICKERSON, Hannah	122
MYRICK, Isaac	167	NEWCOMB, Ebenezor	102	NICKERSON, Hannah	162
MYRICK, John	70	NEWCOMB, Edward	42	NICKERSON, Hatsall	85
MYRICK, John	189	NEWCOMB, Elizebeth	42	NICKERSON, Hatsall	86
MYRICK, Joseph	70	NEWCOMB, Eunice	104	NICKERSON, Heman	85
MYRICK, Joseph	115	NEWCOMB, Joseph	103	NICKERSON, Jesse	170
MYRICK, Joseph	121	NEWCOMB, Simon	42	NICKERSON, John	25
MYRICK, Joshua	121	NEWCOMB, Simon	111	NICKERSON, Jonathan	122
MYRICK, Josiah	121	NEWCOMB, Susannah	136	NICKERSON, Judeth	49
MYRICK, Leydia	130	NEWCOMB, Tamson	123	NICKERSON, Mary	25

PAINE, Elisebeth	152	PAINE, Joshua	167	PAINE, Phebe	76
PAINE, Elisha	23	PAINE, Joshua	176	PAINE, Phebe	88
PAINE, Elizabeth	21	PAINE, Josiah	37	PAINE, Phebe	100
PAINE, Elkenah	12	PAINE, Josiah	85	PAINE, Phebe	121
PAINE, Elkenah	62	PAINE, Josiah	121	PAINE, Phebe	122
PAINE, Elkenah	138	PAINE, Josiah	160	PAINE, Phebe	135
pAINE, Enoch	122	PAINE, Lide	87	PAINE, Phebe	139
PAINE, Experience	92	PAINE, Lidia	13	PAINE, Phebe	155
PAINE, Febe	114	PAINE, Lidia	143	PAINE, Phebe	169
PAINE, Hannah	9	PAINE, Lois	14	PAINE, Phebe	170
PAINE, Hannah	12	PAINE, Lois	77	PAINE, Phebee	12
PAINE, Hannah	13	PAINE, Lois	140	PAINE, Phebee	91
PAINE, Hannah	14	PAINE, Marcy	91	PAINE, Philip	14
PAINE, Hannah	33	PAINE, Marcy	92	PAINE, Phillip	14
PAINE, Hannah	62	PAINE, Marcy	98	PAINE, Prisilla	13
PAINE, Hannah	70	PAINE, Marcy	146	PAINE, Prissilla	80
PAINE, Hannah	82	PAINE, Marcy	155	PAINE, Prissilla	140
PAINE, Hannah	100	PAINE, Marcy	176	PAINE, Rachal	160
PAINE, Hugh	12	PAINE, Marie	18	PAINE, Rebacca	160
PAINE, Isaac	21	PAINE, Mary	21	PAINE, Rebecca	23
PAINE, Isaac	88	PAINE, Mary	23	PAINE, Rebecca	37
PAINE, Isaac	125	PAINE, Mary	24	PAINE, Rebecka	98
PAINE, Isaac	155	PAINE, Mary	37	PAINE, Rebecka	146
PAINE, James	62	PAINE, Mary	96	PAINE, Recka	146
PAINE, James	121	PAINE, Mary	131	PAINE, Relience	168
PAINE, Jedida	85	PAINE, Mary	139	PAINE, Richard	33
PAINE, John	37	PAINE, Mary	145	PAINE, Richard	82
PAINE, John	62	PAINE, Mary	147	PAINE, Richard	100
PAINE, John	75	PAINE, Mercy	21	PAINE, Richard	126
PAINE, John	98	PAINE, Mercy	22	PAINE, Richard	140
PAINE, John	109	PAINE, Mercy	37	PAINE, Richard	160
PAINE, John	116	PAINE, Mercy	92	PAINE, Richard	170
PAINE, John	138	PAINE, Mercy	176	PAINE, Ruth	57
PAINE, John	151	PAINE, Moses	13	PAINE, Ruth	85
PAINE, Jonathan	12	PAINE, Myrick	169	PAINE, Ruth	98
PAINE, Jonathan	37	PAINE, Nathanael	21	PAINE, Ruth	129
PAINE, Jonathan	91	PAINE, Nathanael	37	PAINE, Samuel	21
PAINE, Jonathan	92	PAINE, Nathanael	70	PAINE, Samuel	88
PAINE, Jonathan	144	PAINE, Nathanal	122	PAINE, Samuel	149
PAINE, Joseph	32	PAINE, Nathanel	21	PAINE, Samuel	150
PAINE, Joseph	33	PAINE, Nathaniel	37	PAINE, Samuel	176
PAINE, Joseph	100	PAINE, Nathaniel	98	PAINE, Samuell	21
PAINE, Joseph	125	PAINE, Nathaniel	116	PAINE, Sarah	37
PAINE, Joseph	159	PAINE, Nathaniel	129	PAINE, Sarah	57
PAINE, Joseph	169	PAINE, Nathaniel	133	PAINE, Sarah	85
PAINE, Joseph	170	PAINE, Nathaniel	182	PAINE, Sarah	108
PAINE, Joshua	13	PAINE, Nicholas	13	PAINE, Sarah	110
PAINE, Joshua	21	PAINE, Nicholas	14	PAINE, Sarah	116
PAINE, Joshua	65	PAINE, Patienc	21	PAINE, Sarah	137
PAINE, Joshua	88	PAINE, Patience	21	PAINE, Sarah	151
PAINE, Joshua	138	PAINE, Patience	33	PAINE, Sarah	165
PAINE, Joshua	142	PAINE, Patiene	21	PAINE, Sarah	171
PAINE, Joshua	155	PAINE, Phebe	13	PAINE, Sarah	176

PAINE, Seath	165	PEIRCE, Hannah	105	PEPPER, Hannah	163
PAINE, Seth	21	PEIRCE, Isaac	34	PEPPER, Isaac	19
PAINE, Seth	88	PEIRCE, Isace	111	PEPPER, Isaac	56
PAINE, Seth	122	PEIRCE, Johua	86	PEPPER, Isaac	91
PAINE, Seth	165	PEIRCE, Joseph	136	PEPPER, Isaac	155
PAINE, Seth	171	PEIRCE, Silas	101	PEPPER, Isaace	19
PAINE, Solomon	23	PEIRSE, Elesabath	53	PEPPER, Joseph	19
PAINE, Susanna	176	PENE, Isaac	96	PEPPER, Joseph	79
PAINE, Thankful	116	PENEY, Isaac	131	PEPPER, Joseph	140
PAINE, Thankfull	13	PENFIELD, Benjamin	162	PEPPER, Joseph	166
PAINE, Thankfull	26	PEPER, Benjamin	163	PEPPER, Knowles	155
PAINE, Thankfull	65	PEPER, Benjamin	176	PEPPER, Lydia	79
PAINE, Thankfull	78	PEPER, Benjamine	163	PEPPER, Lydia	129
PAINE, Thankfull	129	PEPER, Freeman	163	PEPPER, Marcy	91
PAINE, Thankfull	138	PEPER, Hannah	163	PEPPER, Marcy	162
PAINE, Thankfull	140	PEPER, Hannah	176	PEPPER, Marcy	166
PAINE, Thankfull	160	PEPER, Haskel	163	PEPPER, Mary	19
PAINE, Theophilas	98	PEPER, Isaace	19	PEPPER, Mary	91
PAINE, Theophilas	145	PEPER, Rebaca	74	PEPPER, Mary	187
PAINE, Tho.	12	PEPER, Salla	163	PEPPER, Mary	188
PAINE, Thomas	12	PEPER, Sarah	163	PEPPER, Mercy	32
PAINE, Thomas	13	PEPER, Simeon	176	PEPPER, Molle	155
PAINE, Thomas	26	PEPER, Simon	163	PEPPER, Nabby	187
PAINE, Thomas	53	PEPP, Isaace	19	PEPPER, Phebe	76
PAINE, Thomas	62	PEPPER, Abial	155	PEPPER, Phebe	155
PAINE, Thomas	100	PEPPER, Abial	156	PEPPER, Phebe	156
PAINE, Thomas	121	PEPPER, Abiel	155	PEPPER, Phebe	176
PAINE, Thomas	122	PEPPER, Abigal	162	PEPPER, Phebee	76
PAINE, Thomas	128	PEPPER, Abigel	76	PEPPER, Polly	187
PAINE, Thomas	129	PEPPER, Abigil	163	PEPPER, Rebaca	132
PAINE, Thomas	155	PEPPER, Anne	156	PEPPER, Rebacca	79
PAINE, Thomas	157	PEPPER, Apphia	19	PEPPER, Rebecca	79
PAINE, Thomas	170	PEPPER, Apphia	34	PEPPER, Rebecka	79
PAINE, Timothy Doane	176	PEPPER, Apphia	76	PEPPER, Rebeckah	79
PAINE, Uriah	170	PEPPER, Apphia	136	PEPPER, Rebekah	79
PAINE, Wiliam	110	PEPPER, Apphia	152	PEPPER, Robart	91
PAINE, William	37	PEPPER, Apphiah	19	PEPPER, Robert	19
PAINE, William	85	PEPPER, Apphiah	155	PEPPER, Robert	91
PAINE, William	100	PEPPER, Benjamin	76	PEPPER, Robert	93
PAINE, William	108	PEPPER, Benjamin	162	PEPPER, Robert	144
PAINE, William	141	PEPPER, Benjamin	163	PEPPER, Robort	155
PAINE, William	151	PEPPER, Daniel	79	PEPPER, Ruth	79
PAINE, William	165	PEPPER, Daniel	187	PEPPER, Ruth	132
PALMER, Anne	55	PEPPER, Elisabath	128	PEPPER, Sally	188
PANE, John	131	PEPPER, Elisabeth	57	PEPPER, Samuell	79
PARKER, Eunice	176	PEPPER, Elisabeth	79	PEPPER, Sarah	79
PARKER, John	176	PEPPER, Elisabeth	137	PEPPER, Simeon	187
PARKER, Nathaniel	171	PEPPER, Elisha	156	PEPPER, Simeon	188
PARKER, Seth Doane	176	PEPPER, Elisha	176	PEPPER, Sollomon	76
PAYNE, Mary	96	PEPPER, Elizebeth	19	PEPPER, Soloman	176
PAYNE, Sarah	102	PEPPER, Hanna	162	PEPPER, Solomon	19
PEARS, Samuel	114	PEPPER, Hannah	79	PEPPER, Solomon	76
PEINE, Hanna	164	PEPPER, Hannah	124	PEPPER, Solomon	127

PEPPER, Solomon	139	
PEPPER, Solomon	155	
PEPPER, Solomon	156	
PEPPER, Solomon	171	
PEPPER, Tamson	163	
PEPPER, Thomas Knowles	176	
PEPR, Hannah	163	
PERCE, Hannah	149	
PERCE, John	125	
PERCE, Joseph	136	
PERCE, Samuell	123	
PERS, Joshua	132	
PERS, Samuel	135	
PETTE, Rebecca	40	
PHINNEY, Samuel	54	
PIERCE, Joshua	142	
PIERCE, Samuale	57	
PIKE, Ann	132	
PIKE, Elisha	96	
PIKE, Elisha	132	
PIKE, Martha	46	
PIKE, Patience	31	
PIRCE, Isaac	151	
PIRCE, Silas	147	
PIRSE, Elisabath	130	
PIRSS, Lemuel	129	
POLLE, Mary	130	
POMPMORE, Joshua	74	
PORENTON, Bial	146	
PRATT, Ephraim	145	
PRENCE, Jane	29	
PRENCE, Thomas	29	

— Q —

QUANSET, Darkas	74

— R —

RALPH, David	103
RALPH, Elezar	131
RALPH, Jemima	146
RALPH, Joshua	151
RAMECK, Cristian	58
RAMECK, Hannah	58
RAMICK, Cristian	58
RAMICK, Hannah	58
RAY, Jemima	146
REMICH, Abraham	40
REMICH, Christian	40
REMICH, Elizebeth	40
REMICH, Marcy	40
REMICK, Christan	119
REMICK, Christan	123
REMICK, Christan	133
REMICK, Christarn	58
REMICK, Christian	58
REMICK, Christian	137
REMICK, Christran	58
REMICK, Cristan	119
REMICK, Daniel	58
REMICK, Elisabeth	38
REMICK, Elisabeth	58
REMICK, Elisabeth	73
REMICK, Elisabeth	139
REMICK, Elkenah	119
REMICK, Freeman	119
REMICK, Hanah	119
REMICK, Hannah	58
REMICK, Hannah	151
REMICK, Isaac	58
REMICK, Joseph	58
REMICK, Joseph	177
REMICK, Martha	72
REMICK, Martha	139
REMICK, Mercy	58
REMICK, Mercy	59
REMICK, Mercy	137
REMICK, Mercy	149
REMICK, Sarah	58
REMICK, Sarah	119
REMICK, Sarah	125
REMICK, Sarah	177
RICH, Abagill	103
RICH, Abigail	126
RICH, Abigail	156
RICH, Amos	77
RICH, Ann	14
RICH, Ann	135
RICH, Anna	14
RICH, Anne	14
RICH, Bethiah	77
RICH, Bethiah	131
RICH, Cornelius	152
RICH, David	33
RICH, David	97
RICH, David	126
RICH, David	145
RICH, Elisabath	128
RICH, Elisabeth	77
RICH, Elisabeth	97
RICH, Elisha	103
RICH, Hannah	97
RICH, Hannah	124
RICH, Hope	80
RICH, Hope	109
RICH, Hope	151
RICH, Huldah	14
RICH, Isaac	103
RICH, James	33
RICH, John	33
RICH, John	50
RICH, John	51
RICH, John	80
RICH, John	83
RICH, John	139
RICH, John	140
RICH, Joseph	14
RICH, Joseph	33
RICH, Joseph	72
RICH, Joshua	51
RICH, Joshua	113
RICH, Joshua	135
RICH, Josiah	125
RICH, Josiah	156
RICH, Lamuel	97
RICH, Lamuel	145
RICH, Lidia	87
RICH, Lydia	127
RICH, Marcy	77
RICH, Marcy	143
RICH, Marry	51
RICH, Martha	125
RICH, Marther	103
RICH, Mary	50
RICH, Mary	51
RICH, Mary	77
RICH, Mary	103
RICH, Mary	134
RICH, Mary	138
RICH, Matha	156
RICH, Mather	103
RICH, Mercy	33
RICH, Mercy	139
RICH, Moses	51
RICH, Moses	124
RICH, Moses	128
RICH, Namiah	87
RICH, Obadia	14
RICH, Peeter	77
RICH, Priscilla	14
RICH, Prissila	14
RICH, Rebecca	72
RICH, Rebecca	139
RICH, Rebeckah	14
RICH, Reuben	136
RICH, Richard	14
RICH, Richard	71
RICH, Richard	128

RICH, Richard	138	ROBINS, Joseph	54	ROGERS, Deborah	183
RICH, Robart	86	ROBINS, Samuell	12	ROGERS, Dorcas Higgins	186
RICH, Robart	87	ROBINS, Thankfull	54	ROGERS, Ebenezer	63
RICH, Robart	130	ROBINS, Thankfull	68	ROGERS, Ebenezer	138
RICH, Roben	51	ROBINS, Thankfull	138	ROGERS, Ebenezer	163
RICH, Robert	51	RODGERS, Elizabeth	22	ROGERS, Eleazer	186
RICH, Robert	142	RODGERS, Joseph	114	ROGERS, Elezar	114
RICH, Ruben	51	RODGERS, Thomas	22	ROGERS, Eliazer	22
RICH, Ruben	87	ROGARS, Judah	74	ROGERS, Eliazer	41
RICH, Ruben	103	ROGER, Elisabeth	139	ROGERS, Eliezer	29
RICH, Ruben	147	ROGERS, -----	165	ROGERS, Eliezer	152
RICH, Ruth	103	ROGERS, Abegal	168	ROGERS, Elisabeth	41
RICH, Ruth	109	ROGERS, Abiail	178	ROGERS, Elisabeth	57
RICH, Ruth	151	ROGERS, Abiather	168	ROGERS, Elisabeth	61
RICH, Samuel	33	ROGERS, Abigael	19	ROGERS, Elisabeth	177
RICH, Sarah	14	ROGERS, Abigail	50	ROGERS, Elisabeth	183
RICH, Sarah	33	ROGERS, Abigail	168	ROGERS, Elisebath	122
RICH, Sarah	43	ROGERS, Abigail	178	ROGERS, Elisebeth	123
RICH, Sarah	71	ROGERS, Abigaile	49	ROGERS, Elisha	122
RICH, Sarah	90	ROGERS, Abigel	114	ROGERS, Elisha	123
RICH, Sarah	138	ROGERS, Abigel	135	ROGERS, Elishabeth	122
RICH, Sarah	143	ROGERS, Abner	186	ROGERS, Elizabeth	22
RICH, Silvanus	14	ROGERS, Adeline	189	ROGERS, Elizabeth	41
RICH, Thankful	103	ROGERS, Adnah	178	ROGERS, Elizebeth	30
RICH, Thankfull	33	ROGERS, Alexander Chase	188	ROGERS, Elkanah	136
RICH, Thankfull	51	ROGERS, Allen	178	ROGERS, Elkenah	41
RICH, Thankfull	77	ROGERS, Alvah	184	ROGERS, Elkenah	99
RICH, Thankfull	97	ROGERS, Alven	178	ROGERS, Elkenah	143
RICH, Thankfull	111	ROGERS, Anna	178	ROGERS, Elkenh	99
RICH, Thankfull	146	ROGERS, Arozina	183	ROGERS, Elknah	99
RICH, Thankfull	152	ROGERS, Asa	186	ROGERS, Emily	188
RICH, Thomas	33	ROGERS, Azahel	184	ROGERS, Enoch	176
RICH, Thomas	77	ROGERS, Benjamin	178	ROGERS, Esther Y.	189
RICH, Thomas	140	ROGERS, Benjamin	184	ROGERS, Eunice	183
RICH, Zaccheus	14	ROGERS, Benjamin C.	189	ROGERS, Eunice Snow	183
RIDER, Debro	79	ROGERS, Bethiah	176	ROGERS, Febe	50
RIDER, Exsperience	128	ROGERS, Betsy	184	ROGERS, Foster	186
RIDER, Marcy	79	ROGERS, Betty	186	ROGERS, Franklin	183
RIDER, Marcy	123	ROGERS, Betty	187	ROGERS, Freeman	183
RIDER, Mercy	139	ROGERS, Blossom	183	ROGERS, Freeman M.	189
RIDER, Seth	79	ROGERS, Charlotte	183	ROGERS, George Gould	183
RIDER, Seth	98	ROGERS, Chrisp	89	ROGERS, George W.	186
RIDER, Seth	145	ROGERS, Crisp	41	ROGERS, Hanah	52
RIDER, Simeon	123	ROGERS, Crisp	141	ROGERS, Hanah	89
RIDER, Thankfull	98	ROGERS, Crisp	176	ROGERS, Hanah	131
RIDER, Thankfull	146	ROGERS, Daniel	178	ROGERS, Hannah	19
RIDLEY. -----	12	ROGERS, David	165	ROGERS, Hannah	22
RIDLEY. Ann	46	ROGERS, David Crowell	189	ROGERS, Hannah	41
RIDLEY. Elizebeth	48	ROGERS, Davis	183	ROGERS, Hannah	89
RIDLY. Deborah	129	ROGERS, Debby	183	ROGERS, Hannah	107
ROBENS, Melatia	147	ROGERS, Deborah	154	ROGERS, Hannah	150
ROBINS, James	9	ROGERS, Deborah	176	ROGERS, Hannah	163
ROBINS, James	54	ROGERS, Deborah	178	ROGERS, Hannah	170

ROGERS, Hannah	177	ROGERS, Joshua	163	ROGERS, Mercy	98
ROGERS, Hannah	178	ROGERS, Joshua	183	ROGERS, Mercy	99
ROGERS, Hannah	182	ROGERS, Josiah	99	ROGERS, Mercy	177
ROGERS, Hannah	184	ROGERS, Josiah	168	ROGERS, Nabby	178
ROGERS, Henery	123	ROGERS, Josiah	177	ROGERS, Nancy	184
ROGERS, Henery	125	ROGERS, Josiah	178	ROGERS, Nathanael	57
ROGERS, Henery	154	ROGERS, Judah	41	ROGERS, Nathanael	61
ROGERS, Henry	178	ROGERS, Judah	81	ROGERS, Nathanael	139
ROGERS, Hezekiah	186	ROGERS, Judah	106	ROGERS, Nathaniel	52
ROGERS, Hezekiah	188	ROGERS, Judah	109	ROGERS, Nathaniel	61
ROGERS, Isaac	49	ROGERS, Judah	141	ROGERS, Nathaniel	99
ROGERS, Isaac	90	ROGERS, Judah	149	ROGERS, Nehemiah	61
ROGERS, Isaac	98	ROGERS, Judah	151	ROGERS, Patience	144
ROGERS, Isaac	178	ROGERS, Judah	178	ROGERS, Patty	184
ROGERS, Isaiah Y.	183	ROGERS, Julia Ann	186	ROGERS, Polly Y.	183
ROGERS, Israel	163	ROGERS, Julian	186	ROGERS, Prence	159
ROGERS, Israel	183	ROGERS, Ledia	154	ROGERS, Prince	89
ROGERS, Jabiz	61	ROGERS, Levi	186	ROGERS, Prince	163
ROGERS, James	18	ROGERS, Lidea	89	ROGERS, Prince	178
ROGERS, James	19	ROGERS, Lucy	163	ROGERS, Prince	183
ROGERS, James	24	ROGERS, Lucy	186	ROGERS, Prinse	163
ROGERS, James	49	ROGERS, Lucy Snow	184	ROGERS, Prudence	47
ROGERS, James	52	ROGERS, Lucy Twining	178	ROGERS, Rebeca	177
ROGERS, James	89	ROGERS, Lurana	168	ROGERS, Rebecca	98
ROGERS, James	122	ROGERS, Luther	183	ROGERS, Rebecca	178
ROGERS, James	123	ROGERS, Lydia	184	ROGERS, Rebecka	90
ROGERS, James	143	ROGERS, Lydia	99	ROGERS, Rebecka	98
ROGERS, James	154	ROGERS, Marcy	168	ROGERS, Rebekah	163
ROGERS, James	177	ROGERS, Marcy	178	ROGERS, Rebekah	177
ROGERS, James	183	ROGERS, Marcy	186	ROGERS, Reuben	168
ROGERS, James	184	ROGERS, Marcy Frances	189	ROGERS, Richard	136
ROGERS, Jams	89	ROGERS, Margaret Ann	189	ROGERS, Richard	152
ROGERS, Jeans	123	ROGERS, Margary	183	ROGERS, Richard	184
ROGERS, John	41	ROGERS, Marshall	41	ROGERS, Roxsana	184
ROGERS, John	41	ROGERS, Martha	90	ROGERS, Ruth	61
ROGERS, John	49	ROGERS, Martha	143	ROGERS, Ruth	98
ROGERS, Jonathan	52	ROGERS, Martha	18	ROGERS, Ruth	122
ROGERS, Jonathan	56	ROGERS, Mary	19	ROGERS, Ruth	183
ROGERS, Jonathan	89	ROGERS, Mary	49	ROGERS, Ruth	184
ROGERS, Jonathan	141	ROGERS, Mary	89	ROGERS, Ruth	186
ROGERS, Jonathan	177	ROGERS, Mary	92	ROGERS, Salley	177
ROGERS, Jonathan	178	ROGERS, Mary	98	ROGERS, Sally	183
ROGERS, Jonathan	186	ROGERS, Mary	142	ROGERS, Sally Crowell	188
ROGERS, Jonathan Varnum	186	ROGERS, Mary	145	ROGERS, Samuel	18
ROGERS, Joseph	22	ROGERS, Mary	176	ROGERS, Samuel	41
ROGERS, Joseph	24	ROGERS, Mary	186	ROGERS, Samuel	89
ROGERS, Joseph	41	ROGERS, Mary	99	ROGERS, Samuel	178
ROGERS, Joseph	89	ROGERS, Matha	41	ROGERS, Samuel	186
ROGERS, Joseph	102	ROGERS, Mehitabel	67	ROGERS, Samuell	125
ROGERS, Joseph	135	ROGERS, Mehitabell	139	ROGERS, Samuell	154
ROGERS, Joseph	178	ROGERS, Mehitabell	61	ROGERS, Sarah	50
ROGERS, Joseph Lothrop	178	ROGERS, Mehitable	41	ROGERS, Sarah	52
ROGERS, Joshua	99	ROGERS, Mercy		ROGERS, Sarah	57

ROGERS, Sarah	61	ROGERS, Uriah	188	SEARS, Azubah	98
ROGERS, Sarah	89	ROGERS, Viana	183	SEARS, Azube	163
ROGERS, Sarah	178	ROGERS, William	168	SEARS, Bethiah	98
ROGERS, Sarah	186	ROGERS, Yates	186	SEARS, David	98
ROGERS, Sears	183	ROGERS, Zackeus	151	SEARS, David	180
ROGERS, Selvenus	163	ROGERS, Zemira B.	189	SEARS, Hannah	36
ROGERS, Serah	98	ROGERS, Zenas	168	SEARS, Hannah	132
ROGERS, Seth	168	ROGERS, Zenas	183	SEARS, Josiah	98
ROGERS, Seth	183	ROGERS, Zenas	186	SEARS, Josiah	128
ROGERS, Silence	61	ROGERS, Zenaus	183	SEARS, Martha	70
ROGERS, Silvanas	89	ROGERS, Zoar	183	SEARS, Martha	130
ROGERS, Silvenis	89	ROGGARS, Joseph	124	SEARS, Martha	180
ROGERS, Silvenus	159	ROGGERS, Elizabeth	38	SEARS, Mercy	168
ROGERS, Solomon	98	ROGGERS, James	122	SEARS, Samuel	98
ROGERS, Sparrow Mayo	186	ROGGERS, John	41	SEARS, Silas	36
ROGERS, Stephen	98	ROGGERS, Joseph	38	SEERS, Daniel	99
ROGERS, Stephen	177	ROGGERS, Nathanel	41	SEERS, Daniel	146
ROGERS, Stephen Snow	183	ROGGERS, Nathaniel	22	SEERS, Debro	150
ROGERS, Sullivan	178	ROGGERS, Reliance	157	SEERS, Hannah	102
ROGERS, Susanah	163	ROGGERS, Sarah	38	SEERS, Hannah	147
ROGERS, Susanah	178	ROGGERS, Thomas	22	SEERS, Hope	139
ROGERS, Susanna	21	ROGRS, James	128	SEERS, Jerusha	98
ROGERS, Susanna	37	RYDER, Exsperenc	123	SEERS, John	9
ROGERS, Susanna	49	RYDER, Garsham	53	SEERS, Joshua	91
ROGERS, Susanna	89	RYDER, Gasham	130	SEERS, Joshua	144
ROGERS, Susanna	106	RYDER, Lydia	80	SEERS, Josiah	98
ROGERS, Susanna	149	RYDER, Lydia	134	SEERS, Josiah	146
ROGERS, Susanna	159			SEERS, Marcy	98
ROGERS, Susanna	163	**— S —**		SEERS, Paul	142
ROGERS, Susanna	178			SEERS, Serah	150
ROGERS, Susannah	49	SAVAGE, Ebenezer	42	SEERS, Thankfull	83
ROGERS, Susannah	106	SAVAGE, Susannah	41	SEERS, Thankfull	140
ROGERS, Susannah	163	SAVIDG, Thomas	143	SEERS, Thomison	138
ROGERS, Susannah	183	SAVIG, Thomas	90	SEGER, Shadreck	82
ROGERS, Susanannah	49	SAWYER, Sarah	150	SEGER, Shadreck	140
ROGERS, Tempe	178	SCIFFE, Mary	138	SELEW, Asa	58
ROGERS, Temperance	61	SCUDER, Mehitabel	22	SELEW, Ebenezer	58
ROGERS, Thankful	134	SEABERY, Benjamin	181	SELEW, John	58
ROGERS, Thankful	188	SEABERY, Isaac	181	SELEW, Marcy	58
ROGERS, Thankful	189	SEABERY, John	181	SELEW, Mercy	58
ROGERS, Thankfull	188	SEABERY, Joseph	181	SELEW, Philip	58
ROGERS, Thomas	22	SEABERY, Rebeca	181	SESACKS, Gorge	133
ROGERS, Thomas	49	SEABERY, Rebecca	181	SESAKS, Gorge	133
ROGERS, Thomas	50	SEABURY, Chapman	181	SESOCKS, Gorge	72
ROGERS, Thomas	90	SEABURY, Deborah	181	SEVERENCE, Ebenezer	12
ROGERS, Thomas	98	SEABURY, George	181	SEVERENCE, Martha	28
ROGERS, Thomas	125	SEABURY, Joseph	181	SEVERENCE, Peter	75
ROGERS, Thomas	143	SEABURY, Joseph	38/88	SEVERENCE, Peter	139
ROGERS, Thomas	146	SEABURY, Nathan	181	SHAW, Constant	9
ROGERS, Thomas	177	SEABURY, Rebecca	181	SHAW, Constant	107
ROGERS, Thomas	178	SEABURY, Rebecca	182	SHAW, Elkanan	9
ROGERS, Timothy	178	SEABURY, Salla	182	SHAW, Elkenah	83
ROGERS, Uriah	186	SEABURY, Tempa	181	SHAW, Georg	9

SHAW, George	9	SMALLEY, Hannah	45	SMITH, Bethia	50
SHAW, George	83	SMALLEY, Rebecca	45	SMITH, Bethia	143
SHAW, George	92	SMALLY, Benjamin	45	SMITH, Bethya	42
SHAW, George	139	SMALLY, Edward	123	SMITH, Bethya	44
SHAW, Hannah	9	SMALLY, Joseph	145	SMITH, Bethya	54
SHAW, Hannah	12	SMALLY, Prissila	104	SMITH, Bethyah	44
SHAW, Hannah	72	SMALLY, Rebecca	45	SMITH, Betsy	184
SHAW, Hannah	139	SMALY, Hannah	30	SMITH, Betty	52
SHAW, James	83	SMITH, -----	39	SMITH, Betty	128
SHAW, John	9	SMITH, -----	69	SMITH, Betty	154
SHAW, John	83	SMITH, --ean	115	SMITH, Betty	171
SHAW, John	92	SMITH, Abigael	31	SMITH, Bety	178
SHAW, John	142	SMITH, Abigaell	15	SMITH, Cloe	178
SHAW, John Holder	123	SMITH, Abigail	54	SMITH, Content	31
SHAW, John Holder	154	SMITH, Abigail	74	SMITH, Daniel	31
SHAW, Jonathan	9	SMITH, Abigail	109	SMITH, Danll.	31
SHAW, Jonathan	90	SMITH, Abigail	159	SMITH, David	15
SHAW, Jonathan	143	SMITH, Abigail	182	SMITH, David	75
SHAW, Lydia	8	SMITH, Abigaile	26	SMITH, David	117
SHAW, Marcy	83	SMITH, Abigaile	33	SMITH, David	137
SHAW, Martha	92	SMITH, Abigel	33	SMITH, David	161
SHAW, Mary	83	SMITH, Abigel	55	SMITH, David	171
SHAW, Mercy	83	SMITH, Abigel	97	SMITH, Davis	176
SHAW, Rebeca	9	SMITH, Abigel	109	SMITH, Dean	176
SHAW, Rebecca	37	SMITH, Abigel	145	SMITH, Dean	178
SHAW, Willm.	163	SMITH, Abigle	26	SMITH, Deborough	17
SHEARMAN, Lydia	183	SMITH, Abraham	181	SMITH, Desire	109
SHEARMAN, Marcy	183	SMITH, Ann	99	SMITH, Desire	151
SHEARMAN, Michael	183	SMITH, Ann	159	SMITH, Dorcas	71
SHEARMAN, Richard	183	SMITH, Anne	71	SMITH, Ebenezer	42
SHEARMAN, Samuel	183	SMITH, Anner	176	SMITH, Ebenezer	65
SHERMAN, Debby	183	SMITH, Asa	178	SMITH, Ebenezer	119
SHERMAN, Jonathan	183	SMITH, Barnabas	57	SMITH, Edward	99
SHERMAN, Lydia	183	SMITH, Barnabas	65	SMITH, Edward	123
SHERMAN, Micah	183	SMITH, Barnabas	99	SMITH, Edward	160
SIHON, Saml.	146	SMITH, Barnabas	132	SMITH, Edward	169
SIMON, Easter	89	SMITH, Barnabas	182	SMITH, Edward	178
SION, Sam	97	SMITH, Bashaba	178	SMITH, Edwin	184
Siprus	100	SMITH, Basheba	150	SMITH, Eleazer	124
SKUDER, Hannah	13	SMITH, Bathsheba	109	SMITH, Elezabath	115
SMALE, Edward	8	SMITH, Bathshua	26	SMITH, Elezear	115
SMALE, Elisabeth	26	SMITH, Bathshua	104	SMITH, Elezer	159
SMALE, Joseph	97	SMITH, Beniamine	152	SMITH, Elisabath	99
SMALE, Joseph	137	SMITH, Benjamin	19	SMITH, Elisabath	109
SMALE, Mary	30	SMITH, Benjamin	111	SMITH, Elisabeth	24
SMALEY, Joseph	52	SMITH, Benjamin	159	SMITH, Elisabeth	69
SMALL, Maribe	184	SMITH, Benjamin	161	SMITH, Elisabeth	70
SMALL, Warner Eldredge	184	SMITH, Bennet	28	SMITH, Elisabeth	160
SMALL, Zachariah	184	SMITH, Bennitt	41	SMITH, Elisabeth	178
SMALLEY, Benimin	80	SMITH, Beriah	41	SMITH, Elisebeth	70
SMALLEY, Benimin	134	SMITH, Beriah	42	SMITH, Elisebeth	166
SMALLEY, Benjamin	45	SMITH, Beriah	145	SMITH, Elisha	66
SMALLEY, Edward	156	SMITH, Beriah	145	SMITH, Elisha	67

SMITH, Elisha	70	SMITH, Huldah	104	SMITH, John	149
SMITH, Elisha	119	SMITH, Isaac	16	SMITH, John	155
SMITH, Elisha	131	SMITH, Isaac	37	SMITH, John	178
SMITH, Elizabeth	13	SMITH, Isaac	59	SMITH, Jonathan	16
SMITH, Elizabeth	97	SMITH, Isaac	70	SMITH, Jonathan	33
SMITH, Elizabeth	145	SMITH, Isaac	99	SMITH, Jonathan	38
SMITH, Elizabeth	178	SMITH, Isaac	100	SMITH, Jonathan	65
SMITH, Elkanah	125	SMITH, Isaac	147	SMITH, Jonathan	138
SMITH, Elkenah	154	SMITH, Isaac	151	SMITH, Jonathan	139
SMITH, Elkeny	117	SMITH, Isaac	178	SMITH, Jonathan	147
SMITH, Enoch	37	SMITH, Isaiah	119	SMITH, Joseph	22
SMITH, Ephraim	171	SMITH, James	19	SMITH, Joseph	23
SMITH, Ester	166	SMITH, James	21	SMITH, Joseph	26
SMITH, Eunice	67	SMITH, James	31	SMITH, Joseph	38
SMITH, Eunice	70	SMITH, James	44	SMITH, Joseph	39
SMITH, Eunice	128	SMITH, James	120	SMITH, Joseph	53
SMITH, Eunice	136	SMITH, Jane	115	SMITH, Joseph	70
SMITH, Eunice	159	SMITH, Jaremiah	117	SMITH, Joseph	104
SMITH, Eunis	75	SMITH, Jean	115	SMITH, Joseph	122
SMITH, Expearanc	133	SMITH, Jedida	164	SMITH, Joseph	128
SMITH, Expearnc	120	SMITH, Jedida	176	SMITH, Joseph	139
SMITH, Experience	71	SMITH, Jedidah	108	SMITH, Joseph	147
SMITH, Ezekiel	154	SMITH, Jennet	66	SMITH, Joseph	178
SMITH, Ezeriah	159	SMITH, Jennet	67	SMITH, Joseph	181
SMITH, Ezra	38	SMITH, Jennett	66	SMITH, Joshua	19
SMITH, George	109	SMITH, Jeremiah	15	SMITH, Joshua	70
SMITH, Giddeon	150	SMITH, Jeremiah	33	SMITH, Joshua	150
SMITH, Gideon	59	SMITH, Jeremiah	41	SMITH, Joshua	159
SMITH, Gideon	109	SMITH, Jeremiah	109	SMITH, Joshua	171
SMITH, Gidien	108	SMITH, Jerimiah	147	SMITH, Josiah	66
SMITH, Grace	19	SMITH, Jerusa	75	SMITH, Josiah	181
SMITH, Grace	26	SMITH, Jerusha	59	SMITH, Judith	139
SMITH, Grace	38	SMITH, Jesse	16	SMITH, Kezia	171
SMITH, Grace	39	SMITH, Jesse	65	SMITH, Knowles	178
SMITH, Grace	115	SMITH, Jesse	75	SMITH, Lamuel	104
SMITH, Grace	135	SMITH, Jesse	109	SMITH, Lamuell	159
SMITH, Grace	178	SMITH, Jesse	139	SMITH, Ledda	154
SMITH, Grase	114	SMITH, Jesse	159	SMITH, Lemuell	126
SMITH, Hanah	15	SMITH, Jesse	182	SMITH, Levi	19
SMITH, Hanah	109	SMITH, Joel	159	SMITH, Levi	120
SMITH, Hanah	115	SMITH, John	13	SMITH, Levi	159
SMITH, Hannah	15	SMITH, John	23	SMITH, Levie	115
SMITH, Hannah	19	SMITH, John	24	SMITH, Levie	147
SMITH, Hannah	23	SMITH, John	39	SMITH, Liddiah	50
SMITH, Hannah	123	SMITH, John	41	SMITH, Lidea	107
SMITH, Hannah	160	SMITH, John	42	SMITH, Lidea	150
SMITH, Heman	52	SMITH, John	44	SMITH, Lidia	23
SMITH, Heman	117	SMITH, John	52	SMITH, Lidia	171
SMITH, Heman	154	SMITH, John	56	SMITH, Lidya	70
SMITH, Heman	168	SMITH, John	127	SMITH, Loes	108
SMITH, Henry	120	SMITH, John	128	SMITH, Lucy	178
SMITH, Hiphzibah	50	SMITH, John	141	SMITH, Lydia	74
SMITH, Hulda	178	SMITH, John	146	SMITH, Lydia	117

SMITH, Lydia	124	SMITH, Nathanael	74	SMITH, Reliance	145
SMITH, Lydia	132	SMITH, Nathanel	31	SMITH, Reth	57
SMITH, Lydia	178	SMITH, Nathaniel	55	SMITH, Richard	109
SMITH, Lydiah	117	SMITH, Nathaniel	94	SMITH, Richard	110
SMITH, Marcy	23	SMITH, Nathaniel	144	SMITH, Richard	176
SMITH, Marcy	42	SMITH, Nathaniel	151	SMITH, Ruben	104
SMITH, Marcy	117	SMITH, Nathaniel	154	SMITH, Ruben	167
SMITH, Marcy	159	SMITH, Nehemiah	109	SMITH, Ruth	52
SMITH, Martha	26	SMITH, Nehemiah	176	SMITH, Ruth	57
SMITH, Martha	57	SMITH, Oliver	176	SMITH, Ruth	59
SMITH, Martha	103	SMITH, Phebe	37	SMITH, Ruth	75
SMITH, Martha	147	SMITH, Phebe	52	SMITH, Ruth	109
SMITH, Martha	159	SMITH, Phebe	59	SMITH, Ruth	115
SMITH, Mary	15	SMITH, Phebe	70	SMITH, Ruth	119
SMITH, Mary	16	SMITH, Phebe	120	SMITH, Ruth	120
SMITH, Mary	26	SMITH, Phebe	161	SMITH, Ruth	128
SMITH, Mary	28	SMITH, Phebe	171	SMITH, Ruth	178
SMITH, Mary	31	SMITH, Phebe	178	SMITH, Samuel	21
SMITH, Mary	37	SMITH, Phebee	52	SMITH, Samuel	22
SMITH, Mary	38	SMITH, Phebee	130	SMITH, Samuel	26
SMITH, Mary	39	SMITH, Phebee	149	SMITH, Samuel	38
SMITH, Mary	41	SMITH, Phenies	119	SMITH, Samuel	39
SMITH, Mary	42	SMITH, Phenies	133	SMITH, Samuel	44
SMITH, Mary	54	SMITH, Philip	117	SMITH, Samuel	65
SMITH, Mary	59	SMITH, Philip	161	SMITH, Samuel	71
SMITH, Mary	74	SMITH, Phinehas	119	SMITH, Samuel	99
SMITH, Mary	99	SMITH, Phinehas	120	SMITH, Samuel	102
SMITH, Mary	104	SMITH, Phinias	19	SMITH, Samuel	104
SMITH, Mary	114	SMITH, Polly	176	SMITH, Samuel	130
SMITH, Mary	119	SMITH, Polly	181	SMITH, Samuel	137
SMITH, Mary	135	SMITH, Prince	178	SMITH, Samuel	146
SMITH, Mary	143	SMITH, Prisila	75	SMITH, Samuel	147
SMITH, Mary	147	SMITH, Prissilla	115	SMITH, Samuel	178
SMITH, Mary	149	SMITH, Rachal	171	SMITH, Samuel	181
SMITH, Mary	150	SMITH, Rachel	123	SMITH, Samuel King	178
SMITH, Mary	151	SMITH, Ralph	15	SMITH, Samuell	39
SMITH, Mary	181	SMITH, Ralph	37	SMITH, Samuell	41
SMITH, Mehitabel	42	SMITH, Ralph	38	SMITH, Sarah	13
SMITH, Mercy	8	SMITH, Raph	17	SMITH, Sarah	23
SMITH, Mercy	15	SMITH, Rebacca	154	SMITH, Sarah	24
SMITH, Mercy	150	SMITH, Rebeca	99	SMITH, Sarah	26
SMITH, Mercy	172	SMITH, Rebeca	168	SMITH, Sarah	31
SMITH, Mercy	178	SMITH, Rebeca Smith	168	SMITH, Sarah	65
SMITH, Moses	66	SMITH, Rebecca	15	SMITH, Sarah	70
SMITH, Moses	70	SMITH, Rebecca	24	SMITH, Sarah	73
SMITH, Moses	136	SMITH, Rebecca	28	SMITH, Sarah	75
SMITH, Moses	152	SMITH, Rebecka	96	SMITH, Sarah	104
SMITH, Nabby	176	SMITH, Rebecka	99	SMITH, Sarah	119
SMITH, Nathan	59	SMITH, Rebecka	104	SMITH, Sarah	125
SMITH, Nathan	70	SMITH, Rebeckah	39	SMITH, Sarah	134
SMITH, Nathan	131	SMITH, Rebekah	50	SMITH, Sarah	139
SMITH, Nathanael	33	SMITH, Rebekah	123	SMITH, Sarah	159
SMITH, Nathanael	54	SMITH, Reliance	98	SMITH, Sarrah	23

Name	Page	Name	Page	Name	Page
SMITH, Seth	23	SMITH, Zoah	147	SNOW, Benjamin	185
SMITH, Seth	65	SMITH, Zoath	26	SNOW, Benjamine	10
SMITH, Seth	99	SMITH, Zoeth	59	SNOW, Bethiah	37
SMITH, Seth	128	SMITH, Zoheth	102	SNOW, Bethiah	56
SMITH, Seth	141	SMITH, Zoheth	109	SNOW, Bethiah	121
SMITH, Silvenos	52	SMITH, Zoheth	111	SNOW, Bethshua	37
SMITH, Silvenus	162	SMITH, Zoheth	123	SNOW, Bethyah	44
SMITH, Silvenus	178	SMITH, Zoheth	152	SNOW, Betty	90
SMITH, Simeon	33	SNO, Anna	17	SNOW, Betty	93
SMITH, Simeon	81	SNO, Mark	17	SNOW, Betty	123
SMITH, Simeon	109	SNO, Marke	17	SNOW, Betty	180
SMITH, Simeon	110	SNO, Sara	17	SNOW, Charls Lee	178
SMITH, Simeon	128	SNO, Silvenus	94	SNOW, Collier	94
SMITH, Simeon	176	SNOW, -----	66	SNOW, Constant	24
SMITH, Simneon	146	SNOW, Aaron	50	SNOW, D.	180
SMITH, Simon	109	SNOW, Aaron	165	SNOW, Daived	180
SMITH, Sollomon	104	SNOW, Aaron	180	SNOW, Daved	122
SMITH, Sollomon	149	SNOW, Abagil	93	SNOW, David	49
SMITH, Solomon	19	SNOW, Abiathar	164	SNOW, David	122
SMITH, Solomon	104	SNOW, Abigaell	30	SNOW, David	136
SMITH, Stephen	86	SNOW, Abigail	91	SNOW, David	152
SMITH, Stephen	104	SNOW, Abigail	125	SNOW, David	163
SMITH, Susana	26	SNOW, Abigail	155	SNOW, David	180
SMITH, Susanah	111	SNOW, Abigail	165	SNOW, David	184
SMITH, Susanna	41	SNOW, Abigail	180	SNOW, Dean Smith	184
SMITH, Susannah	41	SNOW, Abigel	91	SNOW, Doan	170
SMITH, Suzanah	135	SNOW, Abigel	95	SNOW, Doan	178
SMITH, Tamzon	59	SNOW, Abigel	103	SNOW, Doane	90
SMITH, Taylor	184	SNOW, Abner	83	SNOW, Doane	178
SMITH, Temperance	178	SNOW, Abner	150	SNOW, Dorcas	180
SMITH, Thakfull	65	SNOW, Abner	180	SNOW, Ebenezer	50
SMITH, Thankful	57	SNOW, Abnor	147	SNOW, Ebenezer	66
SMITH, Tnankful	65	SNOW, Ann	123	SNOW, Ebenezer	95
SMITH, Thankfull	65	SNOW, Anna	15	SNOW, Ebenezor	107
SMITH, Thankfull	105	SNOW, Anna	29	SNOW, Ebenezor	150
SMITH, Thankfull	149	SNOW, Anne	48	SNOW, Edman	114
SMITH, Thomas	13	SNOW, Anne	165	SNOW, Edmond	180
SMITH, Thomas	15	SNOW, Anne	184	SNOW, Edmund	180
SMITH, Thomas	16	SNOW, Aphiah	178	SNOW, Edward	13
SMITH, Thomas	37	SNOW, Apphia	178	SNOW, Edward	17
SMITH, Thomas	109	SNOW, Aron	99	SNOW, Edward	29
SMITH, Thomas	151	SNOW, Aron	146	SNOW, Edward	73
SMITH, Timothy	171	SNOW, Bathsheba	107	SNOW, Edward	79
SMITH, William	41	SNOW, Bathsheba	150	SNOW, Edward	94
SMITH, William	50	SNOW, Bathshua	66	SNOW, Edward	121
SMITH, William	65	SNOW, Beniamin	53	SNOW, Edward	131
SMITH, Williams	23	SNOW, Beniamin	124	SNOW, Edward	162
SMITH, Williams	64	SNOW, Beniamin	139	SNOW, Edwardard	66
SMITH, Williams	71	SNOW, Beniamine	46	SNOW, Elesabath	90
SMITH, Williams	139	SNOW, Benjamin	46	SNOW, Elesibeth	109
SMITH, Williams	141	SNOW, Benjamin	53	SNOW, Elezabeth	73
SMITH, Zerviah	178	SNOW, Benjamin	71	SNOW, Eliabeth	66
SMITH, Zoah	26	SNOW, Benjamin	104	SNOW, Elisabath	29

SNOW, Elisabath	93	SNOW, Giles	184	SNOW, James	10
SNOW, Elisabath	121	SNOW, Grace	13	SNOW, James	59
SNOW, Elisabeth	29	SNOW, Grace	17	SNOW, James	90
SNOW, Elisabeth	46	SNOW, Grace	49	SNOW, James	150
SNOW, Elisabeth	48	SNOW, Hanah	59	SNOW, James	161
SNOW, Elisabeth	62	SNOW, Hanah	81	SNOW, James	164
SNOW, Elisabeth	66	SNOW, Hanah	94	SNOW, James	188
SNOW, Elisabeth	69	SNOW, Hannah	29	SNOW, James Knowles	178
SNOW, Elisabeth	75	SNOW, Hannah	30	SNOW, Jane	10
SNOW, Elisabeth	109	SNOW, Hannah	37	SNOW, Jane	30
SNOW, Elisabeth	121	SNOW, Hannah	48	SNOW, Jane	53
SNOW, Elisabeth	138	SNOW, Hannah	59	SNOW, Jane	59
SNOW, Elisabeth	139	SNOW, Hannah	62	SNOW, Jane	93
SNOW, Elisabeth	171	SNOW, Hannah	65	SNOW, Jane	144
SNOW, Elisebeth	168	SNOW, Hannah	66	SNOW, Jane	147
SNOW, Elisha	30	SNOW, Hannah	72	SNOW, Jease	80
SNOW, Elisha	50	SNOW, Hannah	83	SNOW, Jease	114
SNOW, Elisha	95	SNOW, Hannah	84	SNOW, Jedida	164
SNOW, Elisha	146	SNOW, Hannah	94	SNOW, Jedidah	164
SNOW, Elisha	180	SNOW, Hannah	109	SNOW, Jesse	49
SNOW, Eliza Paine	188	SNOW, Hannah	113	SNOW, Jesse	80
SNOW, Elizabeth	22	SNOW, Hannah	135	SNOW, Jesse	114
SNOW, Elizabeth	29	SNOW, Hannah	139	SNOW, Jesse	135
SNOW, Elizabeth	36	SNOW, Hannah	161	SNOW, Jesse	180
SNOW, Elizabeth	66	SNOW, Hannah	180	SNOW, Jesse Cole	185
SNOW, Elizabeth	151	SNOW, Harding	121	SNOW, Joel	180
SNOW, Elkens	91	SNOW, Heman	98	SNOW, John	30
SNOW, Elkens	147	SNOW, Heman	121	SNOW, John	48
SNOW, Elkins	30	SNOW, Heman	164	SNOW, John	49
SNOW, Elkins	91	SNOW, Heman	180	SNOW, John	65
SNOW, Elnarthan	166	SNOW, Henry	50	SNOW, John	121
SNOW, Elnathan	67	SNOW, Henry	98	SNOW, John	138
SNOW, Elnathan	91	SNOW, Henry	146	SNOW, John	152
SNOW, Elnathan	130	SNOW, Henry	188	SNOW, John	157
SNOW, Elnathan	165	SNOW, Hope	50	SNOW, John	160
SNOW, Elnathan	166	SNOW, Hope	66	SNOW, Johnson	180
SNOW, Elnathan	180	SNOW, Hope	103	SNOW, Jonathan	8
SNOW, Elnathan	185	SNOW, Huldah	184	SNOW, Jonathan	49
SNOW, Emery	184	SNOW, Isaac	59	SNOW, Jonathan	58
SNOW, Ephriem	80	SNOW, Isaac	165	SNOW, Jonathan	59
SNOW, Eunas	56	SNOW, Isaac	180	SNOW, Jonathan	122
SNOW, Eunice	122	SNOW, Isaac Freeman	178	SNOW, Jonathan	137
SNOW, Eunice	161	SNOW, Isaace	30	SNOW, Jonathan	180
SNOW, Eunice	170	SNOW, Isaiah	180	SNOW, Jonathan	184
SNOW, Eunice	184	SNOW, Jabez	13	SNOW, Joseph	10
SNOW, Eunice	188	SNOW, Jabez	17	SNOW, Joseph	23
SNOW, Eunis	150	SNOW, Jabez	29	SNOW, Joseph	79
SNOW, Experience	59	SNOW, Jabez	62	SNOW, Joseph	81
SNOW, Ezra	185	SNOW, Jabez	66	SNOW, Joseph	83
SNOW, Francis	184	SNOW, Jabez	131	SNOW, Joseph	93
SNOW, Freeman	80	SNOW, Jabez	138	SNOW, Joseph	106
SNOW, Freeman	188	SNOW, Jabiz	13	SNOW, Joseph	121
SNOW, Gideon Smith	164	SNOW, Jabiz	66	SNOW, Joseph	140

SNOW, Joseph	149	SNOW, Martha	104	SNOW, Nathanel	109
SNOW, Joseph	185	SNOW, Martha	152	SNOW, Nathaniel	50
SNOW, Joseph Crocker	178	SNOW, Martha	184	SNOW, Nathaniel	79
SNOW, Joshua	29	SNOW, Marther	73	SNOW, Nathaniel	90
SNOW, Joshua	48	SNOW, Mary	10	SNOW, Nathaniel	95
SNOW, Joshua	66	SNOW, Mary	13	SNOW, Nathaniel	121
SNOW, Joshua	129	SNOW, Mary	29	SNOW, Nathaniel	143
SNOW, Josiah	10	SNOW, Mary	30	SNOW, Nathaniel	152
SNOW, Josiah	62	SNOW, Mary	53	SNOW, Nathaniel	164
SNOW, Josiah	69	SNOW, Mary	56	SNOW, Nathanil	121
SNOW, Josiah	138	SNOW, Mary	57	SNOW, Nathanll.	110
SNOW, Josiah	180	SNOW, Mary	69	SNOW, Nicholas	8
SNOW, Keziah	104	SNOW, Mary	90	SNOW, Nicholas	24
SNOW, Lettice	184	SNOW, Mary	93	SNOW, Nicholas	29
SNOW, Levina	184	SNOW, Mary	94	SNOW, Olive	184
SNOW, Lidea	93	SNOW, Mary	121	SNOW, Osborn	95
SNOW, Lidea	144	SNOW, Mary	122	SNOW, Paine	80
SNOW, Lidea	147	SNOW, Mary	125	SNOW, Patty	184
SNOW, Lidia	10	SNOW, Mary	131	SNOW, Phebe	49
SNOW, Lidia	53	SNOW, Mary	144	SNOW, Phebe	88
SNOW, Lidia	59	SNOW, Mary	159	SNOW, Phebe	90
SNOW, Lidia	90	SNOW, Mary	164	SNOW, Phebe	142
SNOW, Lidiah	30	SNOW, Mary	180	SNOW, Phebe	161
SNOW, Loes	114	SNOW, Mary	184	SNOW, Phebe	165
SNOW, Lois	80	SNOW, Mary	187	SNOW, Phebe	166
SNOW, Loren	184	SNOW, Mary Frances	188	SNOW, Phebe	167
SNOW, Lowes	80	SNOW, Mecaiah	107	SNOW, Phebe	180
SNOW, Lucy	178	SNOW, Mecaiah	150	SNOW, Phebee	146
SNOW, Lusey	180	SNOW, Mehitable	94	SNOW, Pheby	30
SNOW, Luther	184	SNOW, Mercy	30	SNOW, Pheby	93
SNOW, Lydia	30	SNOW, Mercy	49	SNOW, Pheby	122
SNOW, Lydia	80	SNOW, Mercy	79	SNOW, Pheby	166
SNOW, Lydia	81	SNOW, Mercy	99	SNOW, Prence	29
SNOW, Lydia	127	SNOW, Mercy	103	SNOW, Prence	109
SNOW, Lydia	130	SNOW, Mercy	125	SNOW, Preselah	122
SNOW, Lydia	155	SNOW, Mercy	150	SNOW, Presilah	122
SNOW, Lydia	180	SNOW, Mercy	166	SNOW, Princ	178
SNOW, Marcy	56	SNOW, Micaga	109	SNOW, Prince	168
SNOW, Marcy	79	SNOW, Micaiaah	80	SNOW, Prince	180
SNOW, Marcy	93	SNOW, Micaiah	49	SNOW, Priscilla	121
SNOW, Marcy	119	SNOW, Micaijah	109	SNOW, Priscilla	122
SNOW, Marcy	122	SNOW, Micajah	37	SNOW, Priscilla	184
SNOW, Marcy	134	SNOW, Micajah	49	SNOW, Prisellah	122
SNOW, Marcy	146	SNOW, Moses	98	SNOW, Prisilla	122
SNOW, Marcy	170	SNOW, Moses	122	SNOW, Prissilla	91
SNOW, Marcy	184	SNOW, Moses	184	SNOW, Rachal	94
SNOW, Margeret	29	SNOW, Mycaga	109	SNOW, Rachel	184
SNOW, Margeret	30	SNOW, Nabby	164	SNOW, Rebecca	53
SNOW, Margeret	57	SNOW, Nathan	104	SNOW, Rebecca	90
SNOW, Margeret	141	SNOW, Nathan	130	SNOW, Rebecca	126
SNOW, Margret	91	SNOW, Nathanael	83	SNOW, Rebecka	90
SNOW, Mark	29	SNOW, Nathanael	84	SNOW, Rebecka	143
SNOW, Marke	29	SNOW, Nathanael	138	SNOW, Rebeckah	10

SNOW, Rebeckah	30	SNOW, Sarah	152	SNOW, Susanna	91
SNOW, Reliance	178	SNOW, Sarah	157	SNOW, Susannah	104
SNOW, Reliance	180	SNOW, Sarah	164	SNOW, Susannah	139
SNOW, Rhode	160	SNOW, Sarah	185	SNOW, Susannah	163
SNOW, Robart	56	SNOW, Sarie	10	SNOW, Susannah	180
SNOW, Robert	30	SNOW, Serah	146	SNOW, Suseanna	91
SNOW, Robert	56	SNOW, Seth	59	SNOW, Suseanna	149
SNOW, Robert	150	SNOW, Sil	94	SNOW, Suzanah	80
SNOW, Robert	171	SNOW, Silas	126	SNOW, Suzanah	121
SNOW, Ruben	90	SNOW, Silvanus	29	SNOW, Suzannah	132
SNOW, Ruben	121	SNOW, Silvanus	94	SNOW, Tabathy	94
SNOW, Ruben	132	SNOW, Silvanus	125	SNOW, Tabitha	29
SNOW, Russel	180	SNOW, Silvanus	180	SNOW, Tabitha	92
SNOW, Ruth	8	SNOW, Silveni	94	SNOW, Tabitha	144
SNOW, Ruth	10	SNOW, Silvenis	94	SNOW, Tamson	80
SNOW, Ruth	19	SNOW, Silvenis	144	SNOW, Tamson	180
SNOW, Ruth	30	SNOW, Silvenus	93	SNOW, Tamzin	180
SNOW, Ruth	49	SNOW, Silvenus	159	SNOW, Thankful	80
SNOW, Ruth	59	SNOW, Simeon	184	SNOW, Thankful	164
SNOW, Ruth	91	SNOW, Simon	178	SNOW, Thankful	180
SNOW, Ruth	104	SNOW, Sirvila	180	SNOW, Thankfull	23
SNOW, Ruth	111	SNOW, Soloman	80	SNOW, Thankfull	46
SNOW, Ruth	131	SNOW, Soloman	81	SNOW, Thankfull	50
SNOW, Ruth	152	SNOW, Solomon	80	SNOW, Thankfull	53
SNOW, Ruth	164	SNOW, Solomon	83	SNOW, Thankfull	59
SNOW, Ruth	180	SNOW, Solomon	134	SNOW, Thankfull	73
SNOW, Ryail	121	SNOW, Sparro	93	SNOW, Thankfull	79
SNOW, Ryal	180	SNOW, Sparrow	93	SNOW, Thankfull	81
SNOW, Sally	185	SNOW, Sparrow	178	SNOW, Thankfull	106
SNOW, Salvenas	94	SNOW, Sparrow	184	SNOW, Thankfull	139
SNOW, Salvenas	119	SNOW, Steaven	37	SNOW, Thankfull	149
SNOW, Salvenas	134	SNOW, Stephen	22	SNOW, Thankfull	164
SNOW, Samuel	50	SNOW, Stephen	29	SNOW, Thatcher	180
SNOW, Samuel	66	SNOW, Stephen	30	SNOW, Thomas	13
SNOW, Samuel	90	SNOW, Stephen	37	SNOW, Thomas	29
SNOW, Samuel	93	SNOW, Stephen	49	SNOW, Thomas	36
SNOW, Samuel	103	SNOW, Stephen	90	SNOW, Thomas	50
SNOW, Samuel	124	SNOW, Stephen	98	SNOW, Thomas	53
SNOW, Samuel	144	SNOW, Stephen	122	SNOW, Thomas	90
SNOW, Samuell	29	SNOW, Stephen	143	SNOW, Thomas	91
SNOW, Samuell	164	SNOW, Stephen	146	SNOW, Thomas	94
SNOW, Sarah	12	SNOW, Stephen	171	SNOW, Thomas	126
SNOW, Sarah	13	SNOW, Stephen	184	SNOW, Thomas	143
SNOW, Sarah	17	SNOW, Stephen	154	SNOW, Thomas	144
SNOW, Sarah	26	SNOW, Stephn	10	SNOW, Thomas	165
SNOW, Sarah	29	SNOW, Steven	21	SNOW, Thomas	180
SNOW, Sarah	46	SNOW, Steven	37	SNOW, Treat	93
SNOW, Sarah	81	SNOW, Steven	178	SNOW, Treat	103
SNOW, Sarah	84	SNOW, Sulliven	59	SNOW, Unice	66
SNOW, Sarah	94	SNOW, Susanah	91	SNOW, William	59
SNOW, Sarah	114	SNOW, Susanah	50	SNOW, William	171
SNOW, Sarah	123	SNOW, Susanna	53	SNOW, Zedekiah	178
SNOW, Sarah	134	SNOW, Susanna	75	SNOW, Zerviah	59

SONOW, Mary	121	SPARROW, Hannah	77	SPARROW, Kezia	189
SONOW, Nathaniel	121	SPARROW, Hannah	78	SPARROW, Knowles	182
SOUTHERNE, Mercy	23	SPARROW, Hannah	89	SPARROW, Lidea	77
SOW, Anna	29	SPARROW, Hannah	117	SPARROW, Lucy	180
SPARO, John	17	SPARROW, Hannah	123	SPARROW, Lydia	134
SPARO, Jonathan	17	SPARROW, Hannah	125	SPARROW, Lydia	172
SPAROW, Marcy	182	SPARROW, Hannah	143	SPARROW, Marcy	172
SPARROW, Olive	182	SPARROW, Hannah	154	SPARROW, Marcy	189
SPARROW, Richard	24	SPARROW, Hannah	155	SPARROW, Marcy Smith	189
SPARROW, Seth	182	SPARROW, Hannah Snow	172	SPARRGW, Mary	31
SPARROW, -----	127	SPARROW, Hannah Sparrow	31	SPARROW, Mary	77
SPARROW, Abigaile	9	SPARROW, Harry	172	SPARROW, Mary	100
SPARROW, Abigel	77	SPARROW, Isaac	71	SPARROW, Mary	102
SPARROW, Abigel	152	SPARROW, Isaac	72	SPARROW, Mary	133
SPARROW, Abner H.	182	SPARROW, Isaac	117	SPARROW, Mary	147
SPARROW, Anna	56	SPARROW, Isaac	130	SPARROW, Mary	178
SPARROW, Anna	57	SPARROW, Isaac	136	SPARROW, Mary	183
SPARROW, Anne	56	SPARROW, Isaac	152	SPARROW, Mary	189
SPARROW, Anne	178	SPARROW, Isaac	178	SPARROW, Mary	190
SPARROW, Apphia	56	SPARROW, Isack	112	SPARROW, Mercy	31
SPARROW, Apphia	57	SPARROW, Jabes	102	SPARROW, Mercy	53
SPARROW, Apphiah	24	SPARROW, Jabez	102	SPARROW, Mercy	54
SPARROW, Benjamin	71	SPARROW, Jabez	112	SPARROW, Mercy	72
SPARROW, Columba	190	SPARROW, Jabiz	102	SPARROW, Mercy	78
SPARROW, Dean Smith	189	SPARROW, James	57	SPARROW, Mercy	117
SPARROW, Dorcas	71	SPARROW, James Linnel	172	SPARROW, Mercy	156
SPARROW, Dorcas	162	SPARROW, Jerusha	189	SPARROW, Mercy	172
SPARROW, Dorkis	71	SPARROW, Jesse	180	SPARROW, Mercy	182
SPARROW, Dorkis	107	SPARROW, John	24	SPARROW, Molly	162
SPARROW, Dorkis	150	SPARROW, John	56	SPARROW, Molly	189
SPARROW, Elezebith	178	SPARROW, John	96	SPARROW, Nabby	189
SPARROW, Elezibeth	178	SPARROW, John	104	SPARROW, Nathanael	56
SPARROW, Elisabath	112	SPARROW, John	149	SPARROW, Olive	182
SPARROW, Elisabeth	31	SPARROW, John	178	SPARROW, Patience	32
SPARROW, Elisabeth	56	SPARROW, John	189	SPARROW, Phebe	130
SPARROW, Elisabeth	67	SPARROW, Jonathan	54	SPARROW, Phebe	187
SPARROW, Elisabeth	138	SPARROW, Jonathan	71	SPARROW, Phebee	71
SPARROW, Elisabeth	178	SPARROW, Jonathan	112	SPARROW, Pheebe	67
SPARROW, Elisebeth	117	SPARROW, Jonathan	135	SPARROW, Priscilla	136
SPARROW, Elisebeth	180	SPARROW, Jonathan	138	SPARROW, Priscilla	152
SPARROW, Elisebith	178	SPARROW, Joseph	77	SPARROW, Prissilla	31
SPARROW, Elisibeth	180	SPARROW, Joseph	78	SPARROW, Rebaca	113
SPARROW, Elizabeth	24	SPARROW, Joseph	140	SPARROW, Rebaca	117
SPARROW, Elizabeth	96	SPARROW, Joseph	162	SPARROW, Rebaca	152
SPARROW, Elizabeth	145	SPARROW, Joseph	182	SPARROW, Rebackah	42
SPARROW, Elizabeth	161	SPARROW, Joseph	189	SPARROW, Rebeca	117
SPARROW, Elizabeth	180	SPARROW, Joshua	56	SPARROW, Rebecca	31
SPARROW, Elizabeth	189	SPARROW, Joshua	71	SPARROW, Rebecca	49
SPARROW, Elizebith	178	SPARROW, Joshua	112	SPARROW, Rebecca	65
SPARROW, Elzebeth	178	SPARROW, Joshua Knowles	180	SPARROW, Rebecca	72
SPARROW, Ester	178	SPARROW, Josiah	117	SPARROW, Rebecca	117
SPARROW, Esther	189	SPARROW, Josiah	172	SPARROW, Rebecca	136
SPARROW, Hannah	72	SPARROW, Kezia	162	SPARROW, Rebecca	138

SPARROW, Rebecca	141	SPARROW, Thomas	189	SWEAT, Benjamin	156
SPARROW, Rebecca	178	SPARROW, Tohomas	102	SWEAT, Elisabeth	55
SPARROW, Rebeck	87	SPARROW, Vickery	190	SWEAT, Elisabeth	138
SPARROW, Rebecka	78	SPARROW, Vicry	162	SWEAT, Hanah	54
SPARROW, Rebecka	86	SPARROW, William	189	SWEAT, John	55
SPARROW, Rebeckah	24	SPARROW, Zede	189	SWEAT, Joseph	53
SPARROW, Rebeckah	152	SPARROW, Zerviah	172	SWEAT, Mary	52
SPARROW, Rebekah	117	STARR, Jonathan	133	SWEAT, Mary	141
SPARROW, Rebekah	178	STEBBENS, Benoni	129	SWEAT, Noah	54
SPARROW, Richard	31	STEPHENS, Abigel	146	SWEAT, Sarah	53
SPARROW, Richard	54	STEPHENS, Hanah	131	SWEAT, Sarah	54
SPARROW, Richard	56	STEPHENS, Jerusha	146	SWEAT, Shabner	123
SPARROW, Richard	72	STEPHENS, Rebaca	131	SWEAT, Shabner	159
SPARROW, Richard	117	STEPHENS, Rebeca	96	SWEAT, Solomon	156
SPARROW, Richard	123	STEPHENS, Richard	81	SWEAT, Zibe	55
SPARROW, Richard	139	STEPHENS, Richard	140	SWEEAT, Solomon	125
SPARROW, Richard	178	STETSON, James	95	SWEET, Benjamin	125
SPARROW, Richard	180	STEVENS, Richard	13	SWEET, John	96
SPARROW, Richard	187	STEWARD, Ebenezer	53	SWEET, Joseph	134
SPARROW, Rosanna	189	STONE, Mary	145	SWEET, Mary	86
SPARROW, Samuel	172	STROUT, Debora	70	SWEET, Mehetable	127
SPARROW, Sarah	31	STROUT, Deborah	139	SWEET, Sarah	129
SPARROW, Sarah	77	STROUT, George	38	SWET, Experience	105
SPARROW, Sarah	86	STROUT, Hannah	13	SWET, Hannah	90
SPARROW, Sarah	92	STROUT, Joanna	36	SWET, Hannah	143
SPARROW, Sarah	102	STROUT, Mary	12	SWET, John	55
SPARROW, Sarah	117	STROUT, Sarrah	15	SWET, John	132
SPARROW, Sarah	142	STUBBS, James	58	SWET, Joseph	55
SPARROW, Sarah	145	STUBBS, Luke	71	SWET, Joseph	74
SPARROW, Sarah	172	STUBBS, Luke	139	SWET, Mary	55
SPARROW, Seth	162	STUBS, James	128	SWET, Mary	130
SPARROW, Seth	178	STUBS, Rebeckah	124	SWET, Sarah	123
SPARROW, Seth	182	STUBS, Rebekah	123	SWET, Sarah	124
SPARROW, Seth	189	STUBS, Samuel	135	SWET, Sollomon	100
SPARROW, Seth	190	STUBS, Susannah	81	SWET, Sollomon	147
SPARROW, Simeon	189	STUBS, Suzanah	128	SWET, Ziba	55
SPARROW, Sollomon	71	STUDLEY, Hannah	140	SWETE, Sarah	122
SPARROW, Soln	162	STURGES, Thomas	110		
SPARROW, Solomon	162	STURGES, Thomas	151	**— T —**	
SPARROW, Solon	162	STUTS, Thomas	123		
SPARROW, Stephen	56	STUTSON, James	145	TACTHER, Sarah	147
SPARROW, Stephen	57	STUTSON, Robert	127	TAILER, Ann	132
SPARROW, Stephen	112	STUTT, Thomas	128	TAILER, Mary	146
SPARROW, Stephen	136	SUTTON, Alce	38	TAILLER, John	150
SPARROW, Stephen	137	SUTTON, Marah	38	TAILLER, Mary	98
SPARROW, Stephen	152	SUTTON, Thomas	38	TALER, Ann	119
SPARROW, Steven	24	SUTTON, William	38	TALER, Isaac	117
SPARROW, Tabitha	178	SWEAT, Anna	55	TALER, Isaac	134
SPARROW, Thankfull	104	SWEAT, Barnabas	55	TALER, John	70
SPARROW, Thomas	56	SWEAT, Beninin	53	TALER, John	130
SPARROW, Thomas	166	SWEAT, Beninin	54	TALOR, Abigael	170
SPARROW, Thomas	178	SWEAT, Benjamin	53	TATCHER, Rebecka	147
SPARROW, Thomas	187	SWEAT, Benjamin	140	TAYLER, Anna	178

TAYLER, John	178	THACHER, Jane	99	TREAT, Elisabeth	136
TAYLER, Lyda	178	THATCHER, Elizabeth	104	TREAT, Elizabeth	44
TAYLER-JARVIS, Edward	56	THATCHER, Jane	150	TREAT, Elizabeth	58
TAYLLER, John	107	THATCHER, Rebecka	147	TREAT, Elizebeth	45
TAYLOR, Abigail	59	THATCHER, Sarah	147	TREAT, Eunice	45
TAYLOR, Abigail	179	THATCHER, Serah	104	TREAT, Experience	58
TAYLOR, Abigaile	59	THATCHER, Thomas	71	TREAT, Experience	147
TAYLOR, Abigal	165	THATCHER, Thomas	104	TREAT, Hannah	58
TAYLOR, Almena	179	THATCHER, Thomas	138	TREAT, Hannah	103
TAYLOR, Amasa	179	Thomas	147	TREAT, Jane	44
TAYLOR, Anna	178	THOMAS, Anne	75	TREAT, Jane	45
TAYLOR, Anna	179	THOMAS, Barshaba	124	TREAT, Jemima	151
TAYLOR, Anne	59	THOMAS, Ebenezer	75	TREAT, Jemimah	111
TAYLOR, Banges	179	THOMAS, Evan	75	TREAT, John	45
TAYLOR, Benja.	179	THOMAS, Prince	75	TREAT, John	56
TAYLOR, Benjamin	165	THOMAS, Roger	75	TREAT, John	58
TAYLOR, Benjamin	179	THOMAS, Roger	139	TREAT, Joseph	45
TAYLOR, David	165	THOMAS, Susana	75	TREAT, Joshua	45
TAYLOR, David	179	THOMAS, Susanna	75	TREAT, Joshua	138
TAYLOR, Davis	178	THOMAS, Suseana	75	TREAT, Marcy	134
TAYLOR, Edward	59	TILSSON, Elizabeth	33	TREAT, Martha	58
TAYLOR, Edward	165	TILTON, Marcy	95	TREAT, Mary	44
TAYLOR, Edward	179	TILTON, Marcy	145	TREAT, Mary	50
TAYLOR, Eunice	165	TOBIAS, Thomas	100	TREAT, Mary	113
TAYLOR, Eunice	179	TOBY, Hestar	133	TREAT, Mary	135
TAYLOR, Hannah	179	TOBY, Hester	133	TREAT, Mercy	58
TAYLOR, Isaac	178	TOBY, Will	108	TREAT, Nathaniel	45
TAYLOR, James	179	TOBY, Will	151	TREAT, Phebee	58
TAYLOR, John	16	TOM, Marcy	80	TREAT, Rachel	58
TAYLOR, John	59	TOMLIN, -----	12	TREAT, Rachel	136
TAYLOR, John	165	TOMLIN, Easter	139	TREAT, Robert	44
TAYLOR, John	178	TOMLIN, Joanna	138	TREAT, Robert	45
TAYLOR, John	179	TOTMAN, Stephen	100	TREAT, Saml.	45
TAYLOR, Jonathan	179	TOTMAN, Stephen	145	TREAT, Samuel	44
TAYLOR, Jonathn	165	TOTMON, Stephen	96	TREAT, Samuel	45
TAYLOR, Joseph	179	TOUR, Anna	147	TREAT, Samuell	13
TAYLOR, Joshua	179	TOUR, Elizabeth	149	TREAT, Samuell	45
TAYLOR, Lidya	165	TOWER, Anna	147	TREAT, Samull	45
TAYLOR, Mary	8	TOWER, Cornelas	144	TREAT, Sarah	50
TAYLOR, Mary	59	TOWER, Cornelis	93	TREAT, Sarai	44
TAYLOR, Mary	165	TOWER, Elizabeth	149	TREAT, Serah	58
TAYLOR, Mehitable	179	TOWER, John	105	TREATE, Sarah	123
TAYLOR, Phebe	165	TOWER, Mary	105	TREET, Anna	115
TAYLOR, Phebe	179	TOWER, Mercy	105	TREET, Marcy	83
TAYLOR, Polly	179	TRASE, Apphiah	24	TREET, Marcy	131
TAYLOR, Rebekah	165	TREASEY, Susannah	49	TREET, Martha	71
TAYLOR, Richard	179	TREAT, Abigail	44	TREET, Martha	133
TAYLOR, Ruth	179	TREAT, Abigaile	13	TREET, Mary	75
TAYLOR, Sally	179	TREAT, Abigaile	45	TROWBRIDGE, Catup	167
TAYLOR, Simeon	179	TREAT, Abigel	58	TWINEING, William	24
TAYLOR, Susannah	165	TREAT, Abigel	135	TWININ, Hannah	103
TAYLOR, Waters	179	TREAT, Abigil	111	TWINING, Abegal	167
TAYLOR, Zobeth	179	TREAT, Anna	133	TWINING, Abigail	114

TWINING, Abigail	119	TWINING, Martha	167	UNQUIT, Eleazeser	146
TWINING, Abigail	167	TWINING, Mercy	14		
TWINING, Abigal	135	TWINING, Mercy	16	**— V —**	
TWINING, Abigel	57	TWINING, Mercy	83		
TWINING, Alice	178	TWINING, Mercy	119	VICKERIE, Elisabeth	34
TWINING, Ann	24	TWINING, Mercy	141	VICKERS, Elisabath	120
TWINING, Anna	162	TWINING, Molla	167	VICKERY, David	94
TWINING, Anna	178	TWINING, Nathan	119	VICKERY, David	138
TWINING, Apphia	57	TWINING, Nathanel	14	VICKERY, Dorcas	138
TWINING, Barnabas	16	TWINING, Prince	90	VICKERY, Elisabath	133
TWINING, Barnabas	90	TWINING, Prince	170	VICKERY, Elizabeth	94
TWINING, Barnabas	119	TWINING, Rebecca	188	VICKERY, Hudson	94
TWINING, Barnabas	125	TWINING, Ruth	16	VICKERY, Hudson	156
TWINING, Barnabas	141	TWINING, Ruth	57	VICKERY, Joanna	13
TWINING, Barnabas	143	TWINING, Ruth	138	VICKERY, Martha	94
TWINING, Barnabas	167	TWINING, Ruth	170	VICKERY, Sarah	76
TWINING, Barnabas	188	TWINING, Stephen	90	VICKERY, Sarah	140
TWINING, Barnabus	167	TWINING, Stephen	162	VICKRY, David	94
TWINING, Cloe	170	TWINING, Stephen	178	VICKRY, Hudson	123
TWINING, David	167	TWINING, Steven	14	VICKRY, Martha	94
TWINING, Ebenezar	188	TWINING, Suzanna	17	VICORY, Dorkis	166
TWINING, Elezer	170	TWINING, Tabatha	119		
TWINING, Eliazer	14	TWINING, Tabatha	188	**— W —**	
TWINING, Eliezer	57	TWINING, Tabitha	119		
TWINING, Elijah	57	TWINING, Tamsen	167	WAKER, Elisabeth	86
TWINING, Elijah	170	TWINING, Thankful	170	WAKER, John	20
TWINING, Elisabeth	55	TWINING, Thankfull	16	WAKER, Mehitabel	20
TWINING, Elisabeth	119	TWINING, Thankfull	61	WALK, Andru	54
TWINING, Elizabeth	16	TWINING, Thankfull	138	WALKER, Aaron	157
TWINING, Elizabeth	41	TWINING, Thos.	178	WALKER, Andrew	54
TWINING, Hanna	164	TWINING, Thomas	57	WALKER, Andrew	56
TWINING, Hannah	16	TWINING, Thomas	61	WALKER, Andrew	127
TWINING, Hannah	90	TWINING, Thomas	131	WALKER, Andrew	132
TWINING, Hannah	143	TWINING, Thomas	162	WALKER, Andru	54
TWINING, Hannah	167	TWINING, William	16	WALKER, Anna	54
TWINING, Hannah	170	TWINING, William	17	WALKER, Anne	56
TWINING, James	188	TWINING, William	24	WALKER, Benjamin	157
TWINING, Joanna	7	TWINING, William	57	WALKER, David	56
TWINING, Joanna	17	TWINING, William	96	WALKER, David	63
TWINING, Joel	188	TWINING, William	141	WALKER, David	121
TWINING, John	14	TWINING, William	162	WALKER, David	128
TWINING, John	90	TWINING, William	170	WALKER, Debora	64
TWINING, John	119	TWINING, William	178	WALKER, Debora	141
TWINING, John	188	TWINING, Zachariah	149	WALKER, Dorcas	54
TWINING, Jonathan	90	TWINING, Zachariah	151	WALKER, Dorces	54
TWINING, Jonathan	119	TWINNING, Hannah	170	WALKER, Elazer	157
TWINING, Jonathan	133	TWINNING, Lucy	170	WALKER, Eleazer	157
TWINING, Jonathan	167	TWINNING, Prince	170	WALKER, Eleazor	56
TWINING, Jonathan	170	TWINNING, Steven	14	WALKER, Elezer	123
TWINING, Joseph	170	TWWINING, Ruth	62	WALKER, Elezer	157
TWINING, Lidy	170			WALKER, Elisabeth	45
TWINING, Lidya	119	**— U —**		WALKER, Elisabeth	46
TWINING, Lois	170			WALKER, Elisabeth	59

WALKER, Elisabeth	142	WALKER, Phebe	159	WARD, Gorge	119
WALKER, Elizabeth	26	WALKER, Preselah	121	WARD, John	103
WALKER, Elizebeth	45	WALKER, Prissilla	56	WARD, Joseph	59
WALKER, Hanah	70	WALKER, Prissilla	150	WARD, Joseph	103
WALKER, Hanah	121	WALKER, Rachel	157	WARD, Lydia	119
WALKER, Hannah	56	WALKER, Rebaca	112	WARD, Mary	59
WALKER, Hannah	121	WALKER, Rebacca	112	WARD, Mary	103
WALKER, Hanner	121	WALKER, Rebecca	112	WARD, Prissilla	59
WALKER, Jabesh	26	WALKER, Rejoyce	45	WARD, Rebecca	59
WALKER, Jabez	45	WALKER, Rejoyce	92	WEBAR, Jonathan	135
WALKER, Jabez	46	WALKER, Rejoyce	144	WEBB, Beniamin	138
WALKER, Jabez	136	WALKER, Richard	45	WEBB, Benjamin	74
WALKER, Jabiz	45	WALKER, Richard	59	WEBB, Mary	74
WALKER, Jeremiah	45	WALKER, Richard	138	WEBB, Mehitabel	74
WALKER, Jeremiah	139	WALKER, Samuel	112	WEBB, Mehtabel	74
WALKER, Jerusha	157	WALKER, Samuel	150	WEBB, Thomas	74
WALKER, Joanna	59	WALKER, Samuell	20	WEBBER, Jonathan	113
WALKER, John	17	WALKER, Samuell	112	WEBBER, Richard	15
WALKER, John	19	WALKER, Sarah	20	WEBER, Elizabeth	102
WALKER, John	20	WALKER, Sarah	26	WEBER, Elizabeth	147
WALKER, John	26	WALKER, Sarah	54	WEKENET, Mary	146
WALKER, John	54	WALKER, Sarah	88	WETHEREL, Mercy	93
WALKER, John	70	WALKER, Sarah	112	WETHREL, Hanah	72
WALKER, John	112	WALKER, Sarah	120	WETHREL, John	72
WALKER, John	151	WALKER, Sarah	133	WETHREL, Mary	72
WALKER, Joshua	20	WALKER, Sarah	142	WETHREL, William	72
WALKER, Joshua	54	WALKER, Sarah	157	WETHREL, William	133
WALKER, Liddia	112	WALKER, Susanah	157	WHITE, Immanuel	62
WALKER, Lidia	86	WALKER, Susanna	54	WHITNEE, John	107
WALKER, Lidia	142	WALKER, Susanna	56	WHITNEE, Josiah	107
WALKER, Lucy	157	WALKER, Susanna	136	WHITNEE, Seth	107
WALKER, Mahetable	119	WALKER, Susanna	147	WHITNEY, John	103
WALKER, Marcy	54	WALKER, Susannah	112	WHORF, Sarah	144
WALKER, Marcy	112	WALKER, Susannah	167	WIKNOT, Mery	97
WALKER, Marcy	144	WALKER, Willam	121	WILCOT, Elisabeth	136
WALKER, Mary	45	WALKER, William	17	WILCUT, Elisabeth	59
WALKER, Mary	135	WALKER, William	26	WILCUT, John	109
WALKER, Matthew	59	WALKER, William	56	WILE, Bethuel	129
WALKER, Mehetable	112	WALKER, William	63	WILE, Joshua	100
WALKER, Mehetable	134	WALKER, William	108	WILE, Joshua	131
WALKER, Mehittabell	138	WALKER, William	121	WILE, Moses	54
WALKER, Mercy	20	WALKER, William	128	WILE, Moses	131
WALKER, Mercy	46	WALKER, William	157	WILE, Ruth	132
WALKER, Mercy	94	WALKER, Zibiah	119	WILE, Sarah	115
WALKER, Mercy	136	WARD, Barzillah	103	WILE, Sarah	133
WALKER, Mercy	152	WARD, Daniel	103	WILE, Thankfull	129
WALKER, Nathanael	56	WARD, David	59	WILEY, Bethuel	86
WALKER, Nathanael	59	WARD, Elisabeth	103	WILEY, Mary	111
WALKER, Nathanael	135	WARD, Elisha	103	WILEY, Mary	136
WALKER, Nathaniel	54	WARD, Ezekiel	59	WILEY, Thankfull	71
WALKER, Peter	54	WARD, Georg	36	WILIE, Moses	139
WALKER, Phebe	70	WARD, George	59	WILLCUT, Elisabeth	152
WALKER, Phebe	121	WARD, George	119	WILLCUT, John	151

WILLEY, Levi	123	WORD, William	103
WILLIAMS, Hannah	13	WORMELY, John	83
WILLIAMS, Mathew	135		
WILLIAMS, Mathu	114		
WILLIAMS, Mehitabell	138		
WILLIAMS, Simeon	170		
WILLIAMS, William	146		
WILLIAMSON, Bulah	145		
WILLIAMSON, George	44		
WILLIAMSON, Hiphziba	140		
WILLIAMSON, Hiphzibah	80		
WILLIAMSON, Thankfull	67		
WILLIAMSON, Thankfull	138		
WILLY, Levi	124		
WING, John	85		
WING, John	141		
WINSLOW, Thomas	150		
WITHEREL, Elizabeth	146		
WITHEREL, Jemima	85		
WITHEREL, Jemima	143		
WITHEREL, Rachell	95		
WITHEREL, Rachell	144		
WITHERELL, Mercy	144		
WITHERIL, Grace	65		
WITHERIL, John	65		
WITHERIL, Lusana	65		
WITHERIL, Mercy	65		
WITHERIL, Theophilus	65		
WITHERIL, William	65		
WITHREL, Mary	72		
WITHREL, Theophilus	72		
WITHREL, William	72		
WIXAM, Barnabas	41		
WIXAM, Elizabeth	13		
WIXAM, Joshua	41		
WIXAM, Lidia	41		
WIXAM, Prence	41		
WIXAM, Robert	41		
WIXAM, Sarah	41		
WIXOM, Jemima	17		
WIXOM, Robert	17		
WOMLEY, John	129		
WOOD, Hephziba	138		
WOOD, Margaret	49		
WORD, Barzillah	119		
WORD, Benjamin	119		
WORD, Berzillah	119		
WORD, Georg	119		
WORD, George	119		
WORD, Gorge	134		
WORD, Joseph	113		
WORD, Joseph	119		
WORD, Joseph	135		

— Y —

YATES, Debro	145
YATES, Exprience	144
YATES, Hannah	107
YATES, Mary	36
YATES, Reliance	143
YATS, Hanna	162
YATS, Joh	17
YATS, John	17
YEATS, John	50
YEATS, Marcy	44
YEATS, Mary	141
YONG, John	38
YOUND, Ebnezar	71
YOUND, Isaac	170
YOUND, Pricilla	170
YOUND, Sarah	170
YOUNG, Abigael	33
YOUNG, Abigail	38
YOUNG, Abigail	126
YOUNG, Abigail	156
YOUNG, Abigail	170
YOUNG, Abigail	179
YOUNG, Abigail	182
YOUNG, Abigaile	21
YOUNG, Abigaile	56
YOUNG, Abigal	170
YOUNG, Abigel	57
YOUNG, Abigiel	126
YOUNG, Ann	33
YOUNG, Ann	74
YOUNG, Anna	165
YOUNG, Anna	179
YOUNG, Anne	33
YOUNG, Anne	56
YOUNG, Anne	91
YOUNG, Anne	165
YOUNG, Apphiah	170
YOUNG, Azuba	165
YOUNG, Azube	162
YOUNG, Barnabas	66
YOUNG, Barnabas	74
YOUNG, Barnabas	132
YOUNG, Barnabas	133
YOUNG, Bathsheba	164
YOUNG, Beniamin	46
YOUNG, Beniamin	136
YOUNG, Benjamin	46
YOUNG, Bethiah	69

YOUNG, Betsy	179
YOUNG, Constant	154
YOUNG, Daniel	46
YOUNG, Daniel	87
YOUNG, Daniel	143
YOUNG, David	33
YOUNG, David	38
YOUNG, David	74
YOUNG, David	90
YOUNG, David	132
YOUNG, David	143
YOUNG, Dorcas	33
YOUNG, Dorcas	179
YOUNG, Dorkis	102
YOUNG, Dorkis	147
YOUNG, Easther	33
YOUNG, Easther	179
YOUNG, Ebenezer	69
YOUNG, Ebenezer	179
YOUNG, Ebenzar	179
YOUNG, Ebnezar	71
YOUNG, Ebnezar	132
YOUNG, Edmond	69
YOUNG, Edmund	179
YOUNG, Eleaner	111
YOUNG, Eleazor	90
YOUNG, Elesibeth	91
YOUNG, Elezer	74
YOUNG, Eliezer	69
YOUNG, Elisabath	122
YOUNG, Elisabeth	8
YOUNG, Elisabeth	57
YOUNG, Elisabeth	58
YOUNG, Elisabeth	69
YOUNG, Elisabeth	122
YOUNG, Elisabeth	123
YOUNG, Elisabeth	143
YOUNG, Elisabeth	179
YOUNG, Elisabeth	181
YOUNG, Elisebath	74
YOUNG, Elisebeth	58
YOUNG, Elisebeth	167
YOUNG, Elish	8
YOUNG, Elisha	7
YOUNG, Elisha	8
YOUNG, Elisha	69
YOUNG, Elisha	143
YOUNG, Elizabeth	91
pOUNG, Elizabeth	166
YOUNG, Elizabeth	179
YOUNG, Elizebeth	48
YOUNG, Elizebeth	154
YOUNG, Elkanah	168

YOUNG, Elkanah	179	YOUNG, John	33	YOUNG, Marcy	90
YOUNG, Elkenah	37	YOUNG, John	38	YOUNG, Marcy	122
YOUNG, Elkenah	99	YOUNG, John	46	YOUNG, Marcy	143
YOUNG, Elkenah	146	YOUNG, John	82	YOUNG, Marcy	156
YOUNG, Eunes	91	YOUNG, John	104	YOUNG, Martha	29
YOUNG, Ezra	90	YOUNG, John	139	YOUNG, Martha	37
YOUNG, Ezra	124	YOUNG, John	140	YOUNG, Martha	48
YOUNG, Ezra	154	YOUNG, John	149	YOUNG, Martha	64
YOUNG, Frances	170	YOUNG, John	152	YOUNG, Martha	112
YOUNG, Hanah	87	YOUNG, John	166	YOUNG, Martha	124
YOUNG, Hannah	26	YOUNG, Jonathan	36	YOUNG, Marther	134
YOUNG, Hannah	33	YOUNG, Jonathan	111	YOUNG, Mary	18
YOUNG, Hannah	80	YOUNG, Jonathan	135	YOUNG, Mary	37
YOUNG, Hannah	90	YOUNG, Jonathan	154	YOUNG, Mary	38
YOUNG, Hannah	140	YOUNG, Jonathan	170	YOUNG, Mary	102
YOUNG, Heman	69	YOUNG, Jonathan	179	YOUNG, Mary	111
YOUNG, Henery	126	YOUNG, Jonathan Freeman	165	YOUNG, Mary	123
YOUNG, Henry	33	YOUNG, Joseph	25	YOUNG, Mary	151
YOUNG, Henry	48	YOUNG, Joseph	38	YOUNG, Mary	165
YOUNG, Henry	91	YOUNG, Joseph	95	YOUNG, Mary	179
YOUNG, Henry	143	YOUNG, Joseph	97	YOUNG, Mercy	13
YOUNG, Henry	144	YOUNG, Joseph	127	YOUNG, Mercy	74
YOUNG, Henry	156	YOUNG, Joseph	179	YOUNG, Mercy	78
YOUNG, Hery	91	YOUNG, Joshua	37	YOUNG, Mercy	105
YOUNG, Hester	144	YOUNG, Joshua	69	YOUNG, Mercy	149
YOUNG, Hesther	91	YOUNG, Joshua	81	YOUNG, Mery	146
YOUNG, Hope	53	YOUNG, Joshua	129	YOUNG, Micajah Snow	165
YOUNG, Icy	179	YOUNG, Joshua	179	YOUNG, Molley	179
YOUNG, Isaac	78	YOUNG, Josiah	91	YOUNG, Moses	48
YOUNG, Isaac	82	YOUNG, Josiah	179	YOUNG, Moses	74
YOUNG, Isaac	127	YOUNG, Josiah	187	YOUNG, Moses	87
YOUNG, Isaac	135	YOUNG, Judah	109	YOUNG, Moses	140
YOUNG, Isaac	156	YOUNG, Judah	151	YOUNG, Moses	179
YOUNG, Isaac	170	YOUNG, Kezia	170	YOUNG, Nathan	37
YOUNG, Israel	19	YOUNG, Keziah	155	YOUNG, Nathan	56
YOUNG, Israel	146	YOUNG, Lewis	179	YOUNG, Nathan	57
YOUNG, James	25	YOUNG, Lewis	187	YOUNG, Nathan	137
YOUNG, James	123	YOUNG, Lidea	87	YOUNG, Nathan	147
YOUNG, James	154	YOUNG, Lidea	151	YOUNG, Nathanael	74
YOUNG, Jams	69	YOUNG, Lidia	13	YOUNG, Nathanael	78
YOUNG, Jane	34	YOUNG, Lidia	38	YOUNG, Nathanel	165
YOUNG, Jane	74	YOUNG, Lidya	136	YOUNG, Nathanyell	38
YOUNG, Jane	111	YOUNG, Linda	170	YOUNG, Nehemiah	90
YOUNG, Jane	152	YOUNG, Linda	179	YOUNG, Nehemiah	126
YOUNG, Jedediah	179	YOUNG, Loes	109	YOUNG, Nehemiah	155
YOUNG, Jediah	179	YOUNG, Lois	33	YOUNG, Nehemiah	170
YOUNG, Jenet	179	YOUNG, Lois	151	YOUNG, Nehemiah	179
YOUNG, Jennet	13	YOUNG, Lucy	170	YOUNG, Phebe	100
YOUNG, Jerusha	187	YOUNG, Lucy	179	YOUNG, Phebe	131
YOUNG, Joanna	75	YOUNG, Lydia	74	YOUNG, Phebe	170
YOUNG, Joanna	139	YOUNG, Lydia	136	YOUNG, Phebe	179
YOUNG, Joanna	179	YOUNG, Marcy	49	YOUNG, Phebee	97
YOUNG, Joannah	13	YOUNG, Marcy	78	YOUNG, Phebee	145

YOUNG, Philip	114	YOUNG, Ruth	36	YOUNG, Voltaire	187
YOUNG, Philip	162	YOUNG, Ruth	54	YOUNG, Watson	69
YOUNG, Philip	165	YOUNG, Ruth	131	YOUNG, Watson	166
YOUNG, Philip	179	YOUNG, Ruth	138	YOUNG, Zabulon	135
YOUNG, Phillip	162	YOUNG, Ruth	152	YOUNG, Zeanous	179
YOUNG, Phillip	165	YOUNG, Ruth	162	YOUNG, Zebbulon	129
YOUNG, Priscilla	156	YOUNG, Samuel	57	YOUNG, Zebelon	122
YOUNG, Prisscilla	33	YOUNG, Samuell	74	YOUNG, Zebulon	78
YOUNG, Prissilla	52	YOUNG, Sarah	46	YOUNG, Zebulon	114
YOUNG, Prissilla	137	YOUNG, Sarah	48	YOUNG, Zebulon	122
YOUNG, Rachel	179	YOUNG, Sarah	74	YOUNG, Zebulon	151
YOUNG, Rebaca	156	YOUNG, Sarah	90	YOUNG, Zenas	179
YOUNG, Rebecc	74	YOUNG, Sarah	91	YOUNG, Zibatha	132
YOUNG, Rebecca	8	YOUNG, Sarah	94	YOUNG, Zibiah	96
YOUNG, Rebecca	16	YOUNG, Sarah	143	YOUNG, Zilah	74
YOUNG, Rebecca	37	YOUNG, Sarah	170	YOUNGE, Abigael	14
YOUNG, Rebecca	58	YOUNG, Seth	37	YOUNGE, Abigael	24
YOUNG, Rebecca	74	YOUNG, Seth	91	YOUNGE, Anna	33
YOUNG, Rebecca	80	YOUNG, Silvenus	58	YOUNGE, David	33
YOUNG, Rebecca	140	YOUNG, Simeon	58	YOUNGE, Henerie	38
YOUNG, Rebecca	179	YOUNG, Snow	165	YOUNGE, Isaace	26
YOUNG, Rebecka	100	YOUNG, Sollomon	91	YOUNGE, James	26
YOUNG, Rebecka	146	YOUNG, Solomon	128	YOUNGE, John	24
YOUNG, Rebecka	147	YOUNG, Stephen	54	YOUNGE, John	38
YOUNG, Rebeckah	101	YOUNG, Stephen	131	YOUNGE, Joseph	26
YOUNG, Reliance	48	YOUNG, Thankful	78	YOUNGE, Mary	31
YOUNG, Reliance	62	YOUNG, Thankful	116	YOUNGE, Mary	104
YOUNG, Reliance	138	YOUNG, Thankful	133	YOUNGE, Rebecka	33
YOUNG, Robart	56	YOUNG, Thankful	156	YOUNGE, Robert	38
YOUNG, Robart	57	YOUNG, Thankful	165	YOUNGE, Samuel	26
YOUNG, Robart	58	YOUNG, Thankfull	46		
YOUNG, Robart	133	YOUNG, Thankfull	78		
YOUNG, Robert	13	YOUNG, Thankfull	111	— Z —	
YOUNG, Robert	57	YOUNG, Thankfull	139		
YOUNG, Robert	137	YOUNG, Thankfull	152	ZOATH, Maier	69
		YOUNG, Thomas	48		

www.ingramcontent.com/pod-product-compliance
Lightning Source LLC
Chambersburg PA
CBHW081432270326
41932CB00019B/3178